Economic Reforms in Ghana

T0342486

Economic Reforms in Ghana

The Miracle and the Mirage

Edited by
ERNEST ARYEETEY
JANE HARRIGAN
& MACHIKO NISSANKE

JAMES CURREY
OXFORD

WOELI PUBLISHING SERVICES
ACCRA

AFRICA WORLD PRESS
TRENTON, NJ

James Currey, an imprint of Boydell & Brewer Ltd
PO Box 9, Woodbridge, Suffolk IP12 3DF, UK
and of Boydell & Brewer Inc.
668 Mount Hope Ave, Rochester, NY 14604, USA
www.jamescurrey.com
www.boydellandbrewer.com

Woeli Publishing Services
P. O. Box NT 601, Accra New Town
Ghana

Africa World Press
P. O. Box 1892
Trenton, NJ 08607
USA

A CIP catalogue record for this book is available
from the British Library

ISBN 978–0–85255–163–9 (James Currey Hardback)
ISBN 978–0–85255–164–6 (James Currey Paperback)
ISBN 978–9964–978–66–2 (Ghana edition)

Typeset in 9/10.5 Times by Woeli Publishing Services

This publication is printed on acid-free paper

Contents

Acknowledgements

This book is the outcome of a collaborative effort among economists at the Institute of Statistical, Social and Economic Research (ISSER) and the Economics Departments at the University of Ghana, the School of Oriental and African Studies (SOAS), the University of Manchester and the University of Warwick. The collaboration among these institutions resulted from an academic link programme supported by the British Council and funded by the erstwhile Overseas Development Administration (ODA) (now the Department for International Development (DfID)). The generous assistance that the link in economics provided, allowed British and Ghanaian economists to interact closely for a period of three years to produce this volume. We really appreciate the assistance, including that from British Council staff in Accra.

While the link support facilitated travel and contact among researchers, it was left to the Danish Embassy in Accra to fund the production costs of this volume. Through a very generous grant from the embassy, and the moral support of the ambassador Mrs Birgit Storgaard Madsen, the authors' conference mentioned earlier was convened to carry out a peer review of the various chapters. It proved to be a very effective way of introducing the intellectual rigour required of academic publications. Without the Danish support it is unlikely that we would have been able to produce this volume within the time that we set ourselves. That support also facilitated the very useful participation of Finn Tarp from the University of Copenhagen in the project as well as considerable support from Anita Alban of WHO.

We have received tremendous support from a number of people who were not directly linked to the participating institutions. Tony Killick from ODI agreed to contribute a chapter that helped us to link up the current exercise with a similar exercise in the 1960s. William F. Steel from the World Bank also supported the endeavour with many years of experience on the Ghanaian economy. Debbie Wetzel agreed to write a chapter at short notice, as did Lionel Demery, both from the World Bank. Stephen Younger, Matthew Powell and Markus Goldstein also allowed themselves to be persuaded to contribute to various chapters, and we greatly appreciate their kind gesture. In similar fashion, Kweku Appiah and S. George Laryea-Adjei from the National Development Planning Commission brought a fresh insight to our discussions of poverty. We appreciate the contributions that each of these persons made in getting the volume this far.

Ernest Aryeetey
Jane Harrigan
Machiko Nissanke

List of Contributors

Appiah, Kweku is Deputy Director, Social Policy Division, National Development Planning Commission, Ghana.

Aryeetey, Ernest is Associate Professor , Institute of Statistical, Social and Economic Research, University of Ghana, Legon.

Asante, Yaw is Senior Lecturer, Department of Economics, University of Ghana, Legon.

Boateng, Kwabia is Senior Lecturer, Department of Economics, University of Ghana, Legon.

Bortei-Doku Aryeetey, Ellen is Senior Research Fellow, Institute of Statistical, Social and Economic Research, University of Ghana, Legon.

Brownbridge, Martin is at UNCTAD, Geneva.

Demery, Lionel is Principal Economist at the World Bank, Washington, DC.

Dordunoo, Cletus is Director, Policy Analysis and Strategic Studies Division, Ghana Institute of Management and Public Administration, Accra.

Fine, Ben is Professor, Department of Economics, School of Oriental and African Studies. University of London.

Gockel, Augustine is Lecturer, Department of Economics, University of Ghana, Legon.

Goldstein, Markus is a Ph.D student at University of California, Berkeley and Research Associate, Institute of Statistical, Social and Economic Research, University of Ghana, Legon.

Gyimah-Boadi, E. is Director, Governance Unit, Institute of Economic Affairs, Accra.

Harrigan, Jane is Senior Lecturer, School of Economic Studies, University of Manchester.

Harrington, Richard is Senior Lecturer, School of Economic Studies, University of Manchester.

Jeffries, Richard is Senior Lecturer, School of Oriental and African Studies, University of London.

Killick, Tony is Senior Research Fellow, Overseas Development Institute, London.

Laryea-Adjei, S. George is Planning Officer, National Development Planning Commision, Ghana.

Nissanke, Machiko is Senior Lecturer, Department of Economics, School of Oriental and African Studies, University of London.

Nixson, Frederick is Professor, School of Economic Studies, University of Manchester.

Nyanteng, Victor is Senior Research Fellow, Institute of Statistical, Social and Economic Research, University of Ghana, Legon.

Oduro, Abena is Lecturer, Department of Economics, University of Ghana, Legon.

Powell, Matthew is DfID Adviser, Ghana Statistical Service, Accra.

Round, Jeffery is Reader, Department of Economics, University of Warwick.

Seini, A. Wayo is Senior Research Fellow, Institute of Statistical, Social and Economic Research, University of Ghana, Legon.

Steel, William F. is Private Sector Adviser, Africa Technical Department, the World Bank, Washington, DC.

Tarp, Finn is Associate Professor, Department of Economics, University of Copenhagen.

Tsikata, G. K. is Lecturer, Department of Economics, University of Ghana, Legon.

Wetzel, Deborah is Economist at the Office of the Senior Vice President, the World Bank, Washington, DC.

Younger, Stephen is Associate Professor, Department of Economics, Cornell University, Ithaca, NY.

Introduction

Since independence in 1957, Ghana has tried a number of approaches to achieving acceptable rates of growth and development. It began with a push for rapid industrialization in the 1960s, using a variety of control measures and state intervention. In the 1970s, the interventions continued but with little indication as to what the ultimate development goals were. Starting from the mid-1980s, a comprehensive reform programme was launched on the basis of a liberalized policy regime. On account of significant initial growth and respectable macroeconomic stability in the short term, Ghana came to be seen as a 'front-runner in adjustment' world-wide. This growth and stability was not sustained beyond the short term. While the reform programme has not been repudiated, at the time this book project was conceived in 1995 there was a growing feeling of uncertainty among Ghanaian policy-makers about the wisdom of continuing to reform when results of past efforts had not been sustained. Many Ghanaians could not attach credibility to reforms that had not been consistent in their outcomes. A major question for both policy-makers and the population was 'Do we continue to pursue a package of reform measures in the face of unsustained outcomes?' or 'Do we go back to *ad hoc* policies of doing what seems feasible at any given time?' Unfortunately, the economic conditions have not changed and those questions remain relevant. This book is intended to help answer them and also show how to conceive of structural change and development.

In putting together the present volume, we have been aware of the existence of a number of partial reviews of the performance of the Ghanaian economy for the period 1983–91, aimed at assessing the impact of structural adjustment policies in different areas of the economy. These partial reviews have often been carried out either by foreign independent consultants or staff of donor agencies that supported the reform programme. Until now, there had been no comprehensive review of the Ghanaian economy that involved independent Ghanaian academics working with equally independent outside academics.

This book is designed to provide a more objective, systematic and comprehensive view of developments in the Ghanaian economy. It brings together a critical mass of independent analyses of changes (or the lack of them) that have taken place in the Ghanaian economy since the mid-1960s, when the last serious comprehensive evaluation of policy and structural changes was carried out (Birmingham, Neustadt and Omaboe 1967). The nearly 30-year span of the review permits a comparison of pre-adjustment economic structures and performance with developments since reforms were begun. It allows a clear insight into what the initial conditions for reforms were, providing significant information and analyses of policies and outcomes. Independent assessments of the processes of reform and structures, as well as performance in specific areas and sectors allow the introduction of a historical perspective into Ghana's current experiences.

A major conclusion we draw from the various reviews and analyses carried out here is that both the interventionist and liberal economic policies applied at different times, though always

1

motivated by a desire to achieve broader growth and development outcomes, failed to achieve sustained growth and development beyond the short term. Ghana saw good growth performance (averaging 5%) and relatively stable macroeconomic conditions between 1985 and 1991, as it had done previously in 1969–71. What the two periods had in common was fiscal prudence. The structure of the economy did not change under both controlled and liberalized regimes.

A substantial part of Ghana's policy development has been influenced from outside. Indeed the country has never been lacking in policy advice informed by relevant international trends and intellectual developments. At an authors' conference held in Accra in April 1997 to discuss the various chapters of this book, many of the participants agreed that the lack of success could be explained by either 'right policies applied within the wrong institutional arrangements' or 'the wrong sequencing of otherwise appropriate policy instruments'. In a few instances, the policies were judged to be inappropriate for the environment. Explanations for the policy difficulties abound. They range from unstable political environments, which are actually also derived from the economic difficulties, to capacity problems in the public sector, the private sector and civil society. This book uses the various explanations for particular anomalies, as presented in the chapters, to draw up a framework for addressing the question of why growth has remained unsustained in its concluding chapter.

Summary of Chapters
The volume is presented in seven parts, each dealing with a number of topical issues. These are

Part One	—	Macroeconomics, Structure and Growth;
Part Two	—	Fiscal, Saving and Investment Profiles;
Part Three	—	External Sector Performance
Part Four	—	Developments in Factor Markets;
Part Five	—	Sectoral Performance;
Part Six	—	Socio-Economic Development, and finally,
Part Seven	—	The Way Forward.

Part One begins with an introductory chapter by Aryeetey and Harrigan. This chapter sets the broad tone for the discussion that follows. It provides an overview of macroeconomic and sectoral policies since 1970, and analyses the performance of the economy under the two regimes. It shows quite clearly that despite the introduction of comprehensive reforms from 1983 onwards covering the fiscal, monetary and exchange-rate regimes as well as the various productive sectors, the growth performance could not be maintained beyond the late 1980s. For some sectors, including agriculture and manufacturing, growth following the reforms was unable to restore them to production levels of the early 1970s.

In view of the importance of the political environment to policy development and policy implementation, the second chapter by Gyimah-Boadi and Jeffries offers coherent explanations of the various socio-political forces that have influenced economic policy-making. They do not accept in its entirety the Batesian suggestion of 'urban bias' in policy, and provide useful and interesting discussions of other factors including ideology and leadership style and how these are perceived by the general public in explaining the acceptance or otherwise of economic policy.

In Chapter 3, Killick introduces the reader not acquainted with Ghana's economic history to the details of its structure over a thirty-four year period. He suggests that very little structural change has taken place in that long period and that the economy remains basically fragile. Killick's arguments are fleshed out by Powell and Round in Chapter 4 with a detailed analysis using a Social Accounting Matrix to obtain a snapshot of the structure of the economy for 1993. Their study shows that 'Ghana is still heavily dependent on exports of a few primary products, notably timber, cocoa and minerals'. There is a considerable lack of inter-industry linkages more than thirty years after a major push towards industrialization was made.

In Part Two, the discussion of fiscal policies by Dordunoo (Chapter 5) provides information on the trends in government revenues and expenditures over a twenty-five year period. Essentially, it portrays the decline and collapse in the 1970s and 1980s and their revival in the latter part of the 1980s. Interestingly the structure of the revenues and expenditures shows little change in the entire period. Chapter 6 by Wetzel provides some insight into the broad uses of public expenditures, evaluating them in terms of composition and effectiveness in meeting government's objectives. She concludes that public expenditures, while often well-meant and allocated to sectors and areas that are important for the state's developmental objective, have usually been ineffective. Chapter 7 by Brownbridge, Gockel and Harrington discusses saving and investment. They attribute poor saving and investment performance to the absence of adequate incentives in the midst of a very risky environment, while policy interventions are sometimes inappropriate.

Part Three includes chapters on 'Exchange rate policies and the balance of payments' by Harrigan and Oduro; 'The external trade sector' by Oduro, and 'External finance, foreign aid and debt' by Harrigan and Younger. In Chapter 8, Harrigan and Oduro demonstrate that both the control and liberal regimes that were in place in the period under study had little impact on the stabilization of the real exchange rate, even though the exchange rate was a major determinant of macroeconomic performance. Oduro shows in Chapter 9 that, while it is important that trade policy is compatible with other macroeconomic and growth objectives, this is not enough. 'The creation of an environment conducive to the expansion the tradeable goods sector is critical.' Thus physical infrastructure, for example, is as important as a good trade policy. In Chapter 10, Harrigan and Younger confirm the fact that the impact of aid on growth in Ghana is not quite firmly established, even though there are a number of ways in which aid inflows have facilitated the achievement of a number of social and economic objectives, particularly in the 1980s. Aid definitely made it possible for the government after 1983 to spend more on health and education.

The discussion of factor markets in Part Four embraces the financial sector and the labour market. Aryeetey, Nissanke and Steel suggest that Ghana applied both interventionist and liberal policies at different times in the financial sector. These policies were expected to have a positive influence on the performance of the financial market in terms of deepening it and assisting in the provision of various financial services to the real sector. The outcomes under the two policy regimes do not suggest any significant differences, a fact which they attribute to structural and institutional constraints. The difficulty in analyzing labour market developments in Ghana is quite well underscored in the paper by Boateng and Fine. The absence of reliable labour data makes it impossible to test various theoretical positions on how labour markets would respond to liberalized wage regimes. Thus, despite the wide-ranging reforms that took place in Ghana from 1983, there is little evidence of growth in formal employment. Most of the growth in employment has been in the informal sector under fragmented market conditions, characterized by low wages.

The assessment of sectoral performance in Part Five covers the industrial sector and the agricultural sectors. Writing on the industrial sector, Asante, Nixson and Tsikata, show how erratic and inconsistent the responses have been to various policy regimes. There have seldom been consistent outcomes, despite the fact that various sub-sectors of manufacturing have experience good growth over the years. The reforms saw capacity utilization improve for a number of sub-sectors, but this was often less than the earlier levels of the mid-1970s. To a larger extent, difficult responses from manufacturing were the outcome of restrained investment following reforms in a difficult environment. While manufacturing has faced considerable problems, the mining sector has not experienced the same problems. Its performance after the reforms was remarkable, particularly for gold. The major explanation was the rapid and sustained growth in investment, partly arranged by the state, with international mining and financial conglomerates. In Chapter 14, Nyanteng and Seini discuss the problems of the agricultural sector and suggest that the biggest constraint has been the fluctuation in weather conditions. Of course, policies cannot have an impact on this, but they can be expected to influence labour and land productivity by attracting the appropriate investments. This has not taken place for several decades, despite growing rhetoric about the importance of agriculture. The result is that the performance of the agricultural sector has been one of the least satisfactory among Ghana's economic sectors.

The discussion of socio-economic developments in Part Six embraces a discussion of social policy, poverty trends, and then the gender dimensions of economic performance. In Chapter 15, the discussion of 'the evolution of social policy' by Aryeetey and Goldstein suggests that Ghana has never been able to articulate a social policy for its development. It has pursued various forms of rural development which have tended to emphasize economic services as against social services. This is generally due to the fact that the main social problem is perceived to be poverty, which is considered to be largely a rural phenomenon that has to be countered with improved economic services in rural areas. Instead of developing a rational social policy, it is assumed that the rural development could serve as a *de facto* social policy, an approach that ensured that targeting for various social programmes became impossible. The enormity of the poverty crisis is confirmed in Chapter 16 by Appiah, Demery and Laryea-Adjei agree that poverty remains a major problem even after a decade of economic reforms. They illustrate various dimensions of poverty and use survey data to suggest that the strains of poverty experienced before the mid-1980s were dampened by some of the cushioning effects of the inflows that accompanied the reforms. This was not enough, however, to make a convincing case about the impact of reforms on poverty. In Chapter 17 on gender, Bortei-Doku Aryeetey shows how women have made a direct, but often unacknowledged contribution in the agricultural and informal sectors, particularly regarding food security. Despite this contribution, she argues that women continue to be disadvantaged by lack of access to productive assets, education and training, time-saving technology and child care. Because most of the new incentives under the adjustment programme were focused on areas where women were not competitive, namely export crop production, the extractive industries and capital-intensive industry, they have tended to by-pass women's economic interests.

To wrap up the discussions, and looking ahead in Part Seven, Aryeetey and Tarp in Chapter 18 take a look at the essential elements of the reform approach of structural adjustment and its experience in Ghana in the light of prevailing theoretical expectations and explain why the reforms have not yielded the desired outcomes over a longer period, i.e. structural change and medium-term growth. In their view, the reforms suffered from the lack of a long-term vision that will guide the initial growth into sustainable economic activities. The absence of a conducive institutional environment, that encourages debate and confidence in the economic system, is considered to be a problem. 'The economic and social environment is yet to be modified with a view to promoting the accumulation of factors of production, their efficient use and the introduction of better technologies.' They insist that 'muddling through' along the lines of 'orthodoxy' as Ghana is currently doing will not be enough.

We need to note that the analyses in the various chapters have been constrained to a very large extent by the wide variation in data sources, each with its own degree of inaccuracies. In particular, the data on sectoral performance and on labour markets were badly affected. But the data discrepancies have not been allowed to affect too adversely the quality of analyses carried out as these have been objectively informed by other experiences. We have tried to synchronize the data employed in the various chapters, and there therefore remain only a few discrepancies that cannot simply be ironed out by changing sources as in the discussions on labour and industry. These variations only serve to confirm the need for proper data collection and dissemination by the national authorities.

Reference

Birmingham, W. Neustadt, I. and Omaboe, E. N. (eds) 1967 *The Study of Contemporary Ghana, Vol. 2: Some Aspects of Social Structure*. London: Allen and Unwin.

Macroeconomics, Structure & Growth

1

Macroeconomic & Sectoral Developments Since 1970

ERNEST ARYEETEY
& JANE HARRIGAN

1. Introduction

Ghana has often been characterized as the beacon on the African continent (World Bank, 1993). It was the first African country to gain independence from colonial rule in March 1957, and under the eloquent leadership of its first President, Kwame Nkrumah, it provided inspiration and critical material support to a range of African nationalist movements across the continent. Imperialism and neo-colonialism were forcefully repudiated, and Pan-African socialist ideas captured the centre-stage in development thinking. Despite its role as the 'black star' of Africa (ODI, 1996), Ghana also pursued at various times economic policies that with hindsight have proved to be self-destructive (Toye, 1991).

These different development policies have, to a large extent, been related to the then pre-vailing development orthodoxies. While the approaches employed in putting economic development concepts into practice have often been undermined by incompatible socio-political tendencies, the economic policies articulated have usually been fashioned to achieve internationally acceptable growth and development objectives in vogue at the time, through the use of fairly standard economic policy tools.

Thus, if the policy outcomes often left much to be desired, they were not always the result of 'wrong' policy choices. By this we mean that many of the broad policy goals and choices could be argued to have been acceptable under the prevailing socio-political conditions. What can be argued to have contributed significantly to poor policy outcomes has been the fact that, since independence, not much effort has been made to place the implementation of those economic policies within the appropriate socio-political framework. Thus, economic management and policy implementation have been quite unsatisfactory for significant parts of the country's economic history.

Indeed, the fairly standard development objectives and approaches that have been set have often been supported by well-known development concepts. Following the attainment of independence, Ghana, like many other African countries, was guided by the declaration of the first Development Decade (1960–70) by the UN. World-wide there was a great deal of optimism about the rate of change which could take place in developing countries. Many African leaders believed that Africa could achieve in a few decades what Europe had taken centuries to achieve. This led to the adoption of growth-oriented development approaches and strategies, relying on the remarkable demonstration effect of advanced modern growth-oriented technologies. Rapid

Thanks are due to Martin Brownbridge for comments on an earlier draft of this chapter.

industrialization, with either the state or foreign private investors providing the capital required, was perceived to be the key to development. Within that first Development Decade, African governments aimed at growth rates that ranged between 4% and 7% per annum, at a time when their actual performance usually showed rates far less than 4%. In that period, following such eminent economists as Arthur Lewis, Nicholas Kaldor and others, economic policy's main conceptual requirement was to establish the determinants of growth as the first step in the process of determining how to make the economy grow faster.

The fascination with growth through industrialization would explain why, under Ghana's Seven-Year Development Plan (1963/64–1969/70), as much as 20% of the total investment budget was devoted to the development of industry and trade. That this fascination could not be linked to any one political group is demonstrated by the fact that, under the Stabilization Plan (1967–9) following President Nkrumah's overthrow in 1966, this proportion rose to 56.8% and then fell marginally to 54.8% under the One-Year Plan (1970/71). The importance African governments attached to industrial development throughout the 1960s was made clear by their public investment policies. In those days, only a very few African countries did not appreciate rapid industrialization, especially if they could find a willing financier. This is well documented in the study by Damachi and his colleagues (1976). Differences were to be discerned only in who owned the investment capital, the state versus the private sector.

By the beginning of the 1970s, the development strategies of many developing countries, particularly in Africa and Latin America, had come up for critical appraisal. The results of the first development efforts indicated a number of problems and aroused concerns among both academics and policy-makers. It had become clear that, even though African governments had aimed at raising living standards for their entire populations by increasing incomes in both rural and urban areas, and among different economic groups, the patterns of development that had emerged had tended to concentrate development in a few economic sectors as well as in a few cities. Thus, almost every African country had its share of dichotomous development, with wide and growing disparities in income and access to basic social and economic services, leading to growing political unrest.

Since the earlier growth and development outcomes did not suggest significant 'trickle-down' in many countries, including Ghana, the logical next step in the 1970s appeared to be to attack the problem of growing poverty more directly. This led to a number of development concepts which had as their central theme 'planning to meet basic needs' (Stewart, 1985). According to Streeten (1972), this approach was developed for three main reasons, namely, that the assumed justifications for the earlier emphasis on the economic growth decade had proved unfounded. These assumptions were:

(i) that economic growth would trickle down automatically through rising demand for labour, greater productivity, higher wages, lower prices, etc.;
(ii) that governments were democratic and concerned about the fate of the poor and would use progressive taxation and social services to spread benefits downwards;
(iii) that accumulation of capital, infrastructure and productive capacity was essential to improve the lot of the poor later on.

Streeten (1979) suggested that each of these assumptions turned out to be wrong or 'at least not universally true'. It therefore became necessary to adopt an approach which called for direct redistribution. Among the international development institutions the approach was to support large integrated development projects. Welfare economics was apparently being given a new orientation from the sociological literature. The concepts placed a lot of emphasis on achieving a development that ensured provision of the basic needs of the majority of the population (Streeten, 1979).

In Ghana, as with the earlier push for rapid growth, the interest in focusing on basic needs cut across political barriers. It was at the heart of the rural development programmes of the

Busia Government, and also influenced the military takeover in 1972 in view of its concern with high inflation and the introduction of such programmes as 'Operation Feed Yourself' and 'Operation Feed Your Nation'. In terms of economic policies, the need not to make life unbearable for the disadvantaged was at the core of policies that might well be described as *dirigiste*. At the same time, however, macroeconomic policy was characterized by lax management with the pursuit of expansionary fiscal and monetary policies. Misplaced as they turned out to be, the policies of intervention in the functioning of markets were certainly influenced, even if only partially, by what was then current development thinking.

By the beginning of 1983, inappropriate macroeconomic and institutional development policies, combined with various external shocks, had led to a severe deterioration in economic performance. Large fiscal deficits, financed primarily by borrowing from the domestic banking system, had given rise to high rates of inflation and an overvalued currency. Government intervention in the economy, as well as massive expansion of the public sector through the establishment of a large number of state enterprises, had destroyed any incentives for private capital accumulation. The distorted exchange rate discouraged exports, thus leading to a sharp fall in export earnings. A severe shortage of foreign exchange and imported goods led to a deterioration of services and decline in capital investment. There was a decline in real growth and real per capita income, thereby inducing a large proportion of the educated labour force to leave the country.

The worsening situation forced the radical PNDC government to embark on comprehensive economic reforms in 1983. The Economic Recovery Programme (ERP) that was put in place with support from the IMF, the World Bank and other multilateral and bilateral donors, was made up of a comprehensive set of policies to reform the fiscal, monetary and trade sectors (see Chapter 18 for details). After the initial bout of stabilization measures, the adjustment phase was begun in 1987 with the medium-term objective of laying the foundation for sustained output growth and the attainment of a viable external payments position. Targets were set for economic growth at around 5–5.5% per annum, an increase in the level of investment from about 10% of GDP in 1986 to 23% in 1989, an increase in national savings from 7% of GDP to 15% by 1989, and improvement of the management of resources within the public sector. In accordance with known norms for structural adjustment programmes, a rationale for the ERP was to increase the capacity of the economy to adjust to both external and internal shocks and to generate sustainable growth and development. Emphasis was placed on a flexible exchange rate policy and the gradual liberalization of the exchange and trade system in order to improve the allocation of resources and the external payments position.

In this chapter we discuss in broad terms the contents of the various economic policies Ghanaian governments have followed since 1970, drawing attention to factors that have influenced them and providing only broad views on what their outcomes have been. Later chapters address more specific issues of policy and outcome in some detail. Ghana's macroeconomic and sectoral policies in the period fall broadly into two distinct and sharply contrasting periods: 1972–83 and 1983 to the present. This distinction will form the basis of most of the comparisons made in this book.

In the next two sections, we assess macroeconomic policies and outcomes in the two periods. The trade and payments regimes are examined, along with the associated balance of payments performance. Fiscal policy and performance are analysed, including government revenues and expenditures, the magnitude of the public sector deficit and the manner of its financing. Finally, monetary policies and their effect on savings and investment behaviour are assessed. Macroeconomic outcomes under the ERP are then evaluated using two methodologies: the before versus after method, whereby key macroeconomic indicators in the 1972–83 period are compared with those in the 1983–96 period, and the plan versus outcome method, where the actual outcomes achieved for key macroeconomic variables are contrasted with the targeted outcomes established jointly by the government, the World Bank and the IMF.

In sections 4 and 5, we move from the macro to the meso level and highlight salient policies in the two periods in the major sectors of the Ghanaian economy, namely, agriculture, industry and services. Particular attention is given to the impact of macro policy on sectoral perform-ance. The general nature of structural transformation since the early 1970s is also highlighted. One important question this raises is why the Ghanaian economy appears to have by-passed the Lewis stage of structural transformation (Lewis, 1954), under which a dominant agricultural sector is replaced by a dominant industrial sector, and instead has moved from agricultural dominance to dominance of the services sector.

2.   Macroeconomic Management and Outcomes 1970–83

During much of the 1970-83 period it is somewhat misleading to refer to 'macroeconomic management' as there was very little that could be so described. This was particularly true of the Acheampong military regime of 1972–8 when what happened to the budget and to mon-etary variables was the result of decisions taken on political rather than economic grounds by a regime that showed no understanding of their macroeconomic consequences. As argued in Bates's theories on African political economy (Bates, 1981), the Acheampong regime, lacking legiti-macy, used economic instruments to buy the support of urban interest groups such as organized labour, students and senior bureaucrats, thus leading to decisions that were politically rational for regime survival but economically irrational (see Chapter 2).

The Trade and Payments Regime and Performance

Since independence Ghana's trade and payments regime has passed through several cycles of controls and liberalization.[1] With the exception of 1978–80, when there was an abortive at-tempt at liberalization, the period 1972–82 can be characterized as a quantity-controlled re-gime. Apart from the 139% devaluation in 1978, the exchange rate was held constant whilst import quantities were strictly controlled through Bank of Ghana foreign-exchange allocations. The controls generated a trade surplus throughout most of the period (Table 1.1), but this was achieved at a low-level equilibrium with import and export volumes declining throughout. Between 1970 and 1981 the exports/GDP ratio fell from 20.7 to 3.6, whilst the import ratio fell from 18.5 to 3.6 (Armah, 1993). A growing service account deficit, however, meant that the current account balance and the overall balance were in surplus in only 4 of the 11 years. These surpluses were predominantly due to the trade surplus rather than capital inflows (Jebuni *et al.*, 1994a).[2]

High rates of inflation averaging 40% during the 1970s meant that the exchange rate be-came increasingly overvalued, such that by 1982 overvaluation was estimated at 816% (Werlin, 1994). This misaligned exchange rate eroded the competitiveness of exports, whilst limitations on imported inputs and consumer goods also inhibited export production and production more generally, causing extremely low capacity utilization. At the same time suppressed producer prices led to declining cocoa production and extensive smuggling. Despite the overvaluation and the fact that the Marshall-Lerner elasticity conditions appear to hold for Ghana (Ghartey, 1987), devaluation was used only once in an attempt to boost foreign-exchange earnings so as to enable a relaxation of the stranglehold on imports.

The main cause of the inflation and overvaluation was credit creation, largely to fund a growing fiscal sector deficit (Franco, 1979). During the period domestic credit grew at an average compound rate of 22% per annum which deviated considerably from the optimal rate necessary to achieve balance of payments equilibrium (*Ibid.*, Table 1.4). Mansfield (1980)

---

[1] Following Bhagwati's taxonomy (Bhagwati, 1978) a controlled regime is one which uses quantitative import restrictions to manage the balance of payments in the face of a fixed exchange rate, whilst a liberal-ized regime uses a flexible exchange rate and a rationalized tariff structure.

[2] The military government of Acheampong which came to power in 1972 repudiated some debts, making access to international capital difficult particularly in the first half of the 1970s.

Table 1.1 Key Macroeconomic Indicators 1970–83

	1970	1971	1972	1973	1974	1975	1976	1977	1978	1979	1980	1981	1982	1983
GDP (current cedis million)	2259	2501	2815	3502	4666	5283	6526	11163	20986	28231	42853	72626	864551	184038
Real GDP growth	6.78%	5.56%	-2.50%	15.3%	3.39%	-12.87%	-3.52%	2.29%	8.48%	-7.82%	6.25%	-3.50%	-6.92%	-4.56%
Balance of payments (US$ m)														
trade accounts	52	-34	161	213	-29	150	89	29	113	263	195	-243	18.3	-61
current account	-68	-146	108	127	-172	17	-74	-80	-46	122	29	-421	-109	-174
overall balance	NA	NA	NA	109	-142	106	137	-9	-46	36	-30	-289	-10	-173
Narrow fiscal deficit														
million cedi[a]	-31	-58	-122	-248	-190	-422	-592	-1212	-1678	-1875	-3041	-4606	-4364	-4514
as % GDP	-1.4	-2.3	-4.3	-7.1	-4.1	-8.0	-9.1	-10.9	-8.0	-6.6	-7.1	-6.4	-5.1	-2.5
Money supply growth rate broad money M_2	22.2%	27.3%	33.1%	12.2%	33.9%	22.4%	25.7%	37.3%	54.4%	25.6%	47.7%	40.3%	38.9%	12.4%
Inflation CPI	3.5%	5.1	20.3%	1.68%	24.3%	41.2%	41.2%	121.2%	73.2%	54.4%	50.1%	116.5%	19.2%	128.7%
Exchange rate Cedi; US$	1.020	1.030	1.330	1.149	1.149	1.149	1.149	1.149	2.750	2.750	2.750	2.750	2.750	30.00
Gross fixed capital formation as % GDP	12.0%	12.4%	8.78	7.6%	11.9%	11.6%	9.8%	9.4%	6.5%	6.7%	6.1%	4.7%	3.5%	3.8%

Note: [a] Narrow fiscal deficit excluding expenditure financed by foreign loans and grants.
Source: IMF, *Balance of Payments Yearbook*; World Bank, 1987b; ISSER, 1993.

likewise relates the reduction of exports and GDP to the government's weak tax and revenue base causing deficit financing which fuelled inflation.

Fiscal Policy Performance

Throughout the 1973-83 period the government ran a deficit fiscal policy, with the growth rate of expenditures outpacing the growth rate of revenues. As a percentage of GDP the deficit peaked in 1977 at 10.9% and then steadily declined (Table 1.1).

Its persistence is partly explained by the weak revenue base. The country has a low marginal propensity to tax, even by sub-Saharan African standards, owing to the large share of services and agriculture in GDP, both of which are difficult to tax (Dordunoo 1994). This problem was exacerbated by the government's policy stance. The poor price incentives offered to cocoa farmers caused cocoa exports to decline from 413,000 tons in 1970 to 179,000 tons in 1982, thus eroding tax revenues, whilst the import-substituting industrialization strategy created an industrial structure which was highly dependent on government subventions. The tight stranglehold on imported inputs resulting from the trade and payments regime caused real GDP to decline and led to massive capacity under-utilization which further narrowed the tax base. The 33% decline in import volumes between 1970 and 1982 also reduced the tax revenue from trade.

The erosion of the tax base, because of dwindling domestic production, exports and imports, forced cutbacks in real government expenditure on non-wage essential services, maintenance and investment. Between 1970 and 1982 development expenditures as a percentage of GDP fell from 3.5% to 1.1%, whilst recurrent expenditures fell from 15.8% to 10.2%. This contributed to the collapse in economic and social infrastructure and further eroded output and the revenue base. Civil service wage differentials also declined, contributing to a major brain drain.

Between 1973 and 1983 the public sector deficit was predominantly financed by domestic borrowing, mostly from the Bank of Ghana, ie. printing of money with little recourse to external sources of funding. The Acheampong government's repudiation of external debts meant that during the period up to 1983 the government could raise little external finance to support its deficit. Between 1970 and 1983 domestic credit to the central government increased dramatically from 0.89% to 9.23% of GDP, whilst growth in the money supply averaged 31% per annum (Table 1.1).

Monetary Policy

The period 1972–82 has been characterized as an era of distinct monetary indiscipline (Sowa, 1994), with rapid growth in the money supply. With the decline in Ghana's external creditworthiness the extension of domestic bank credit to both the private and the public sector was the main source of monetary growth. Over the period the government expropriated an increasing share of domestic credit rising from 64% in 1973 to 90.6% in 1983.

Credit allocations from the commercial banks to different economic activities and sectors were nominally controlled by the Bank of Ghana, using end-of-year ceilings. However, in practice these controls had little impact on actual credit allocation (see Chapter 11). The targets were often missed by a wide margin and many of the loans that ostensibly went to priority sectors such as agriculture were diverted to other uses. The main influence on credit allocation during this period was informal pressure on bank managers from the government, politicians and the military to lend to particular borrowers. Large rents accrued to those who could secure credit, and with lax audit procedures the domestic banks become involved in corruption (Toye, 1991: 154).

Using a monetary approach to the balance of payments, Franco (1979) has argued that the excessive increases in domestic credit were the principal cause of the balance-of-payments deficit in the first half of the 1970s. However, as Teal and Giwa (1985) correctly point out in their critique of Franco, under a quantity-controlled trade regime the main impact of money growth will be on inflation rather than the balance of payments. Excess demand caused by money growth forced up the price of non-tradeables and import substitutes which, due to quantity controls on imports, essentially became non-tradeables. This argument is echoed by Sowa and Kwakye (1991) and Sowa (1994), who show that the rapid growth in money supply contributed to inflation which peaked at 121.2% in 1977 and averaged 51% per annum between 1970 and 1983 (Table 1.1). Excessive money creation did, nevertheless, have an eventual negative effect on the balance of payments since rapid domestic inflation, under a quantity-controlled fixed exchange-rate regime, led to exchange-rate overvaluation and declining export competitiveness. Another adverse effect of rapid inflation was an erosion of real wages leading to extensive export of human capital.[3]

In the face of inflationary pressures created by monetary policy the government's failure to adjust nominal interest rates adequately led to large negative real rates of interest which discouraged domestic savings. They declined from 12% of GDP in 1970 to less than 4% in 1982. Despite loose credit policies, macroeconomic mismanagement and the sharp deterioration in overall economic performance contributed to a fall in investment, both public and private, with Gross Fixed Capital Formation falling from 12% of GDP in 1970 to 3.5% in 1982 (Table 1.1).

In a vain attempt to control deficit-induced inflation the government instituted a large number of price controls which drove goods into parallel markets and contributed to rent-seeking behaviour and corruption (Toye, 1991: 154). Pricing controls also acted as a further disincentive to private sector investment.

Lax fiscal and monetary policy with deficit-driven monetary expansion contributing to inflation led to a vicious downward spiral of real exchange rate overvaluation, balance of payments problems, tightening import controls, declining output, tax base erosion, increased fiscal deficits and further monetary expansion. This adverse configuration of fiscal, monetary and trade and payments policies was a major explanatory factor in the catastrophic 30% decline in real per capita income during the 1970s which demoted Ghana from its status as a middle-income country to a low-income country.

The Macroeconomic Crisis of the Early 1980s

The period 1973–82 can be classified as nothing short of an unmitigated economic disaster. Real GDP per capita, real export earnings, cocoa exports, import volumes and domestic savings and investment all declined dramatically, whilst inflation averaged over 50% per annum. Large balance of payments deficits developed, particularly in the early 1980s, such that gross official foreign reserves were depleted, and external payments arrears accumulated, amounting to 90% of export earnings by the end of 1982. The economic and social infrastructure was near collapse, the majority of economic transactions took place in parallel markets, and there had been a massive haemorrhage of human capital. The economy was finally brought to its knees by a series of exogenous shocks, namely, the second oil price hike of 1979 and a combination of severe drought and forced repatriation of one million Ghanaian workers from Nigeria in 1983. It was in this condition of economic crisis that the government approached the Bretton Woods institutions requesting a stabilization and structural adjustment package which became known as the Economic Recovery Programme (ERP).

3. Macroeconomic Management and Outcomes under the ERP 1983–96

As indicated earlier, the ERP aimed to realign relative prices in favour of directly productive

---

[3] Real wage erosion was exacerbated for private sector employees by the contraction of the economy and by the collapse of the government's revenue base for public sector employees.

activities and exports, liberalize controls, rehabilitate the country's economic and social infra-structure, and encourage private sector savings and investment (World Bank, 1987a: 2). In addition, and as a prerequisite for success, there was an overarching aim of introducing sound macroeconomic management by restoring fiscal and monetary discipline and by liberalizing the trade and payments regime.

The Trade and Payments Regime and Performance

Liberalization of the trade and payments regime has been the centre-piece of the ERP. The purpose of liberalization has been to narrow the gap between the official and parallel exchange rate by means of devaluation and to provide foreign exchange to ease import strangulation with the aim of increasing output, particularly in the export sector. Policy targets have been three-fold: to achieve a viable balance of payments position in order to build up reserves equivalent to 3–4 months of imports; to clear the arrears so as to restore international creditworthiness; and to introduce current account convertibility.

Initially the move to a more realistic exchange rate took place through a series of devalua-tions. Between April 1983 and January 1986 the value of the cedi fell from ¢2.75 per $1 to ¢90 per $1. Administrative allocation of foreign exchange was replaced in 1986 by a system relying on a Bank of Ghana auction. This was superseded in 1992 by an interbank market. Initially the auction applied to 'second-tier' foreign-exchange transactions whilst the higher officially de-termined rate applied to imports of petroleum and essential drugs, cocoa exports and debt service. In February 1987 the exchange rate was unified with the auction market rate applied to all officially funded transactions. The auction helped to reduce the parallel market premium from 2,100% in the early 1980s to about 30% by 1987, thus eliminating much rent-seeking corruption caused by the previous distortion. The new exchange rate system led to a precipi-tous decline in the nominal value of the cedi from ¢30 to $1 in 1983 to ¢1900 to $1 in the second quarter of 1996. In recent years, however, due to high rates of inflation and large capital inflows to support the adjustment programme, the real value of the cedi has been appreciating. The Bank of Ghana, now that it has adequate reserves, occasionally intervenes in the foreign-exchange markets to support the value of the cedi or to smooth out seasonal fluctuations.[4]

To complement reform of the exchange system, access to the official foreign-exchange mar-ket auctions was gradually widened until there were practically no restrictions on imports into Ghana, with import licences being abolished in 1989. In addition to the removal of quantitative import restrictions, the tariff system was overhauled early in the adjustment programme to the extent that the tariff rate now often lies between 10% and 30%. On the export side, reforms were introduced in 1991 so that non-traditional exporters no longer had to surrender their foreign-exchange receipts to the Bank of Ghana, although the ruling still applied to gold and cocoa exports.

During the liberalization period, import volumes have increased continuously. This is partly due to trade liberalization releasing pent-up demand. But it is also due to positive income growth rates and large capital inflows. The decline in the anti-export bias of the trade and payments regime has led to increases in export volumes particularly in the traditional sectors of cocoa, gold and timber, although there has been little in the way of export diversification. Throughout the liberalization period, however, the trade balance has been in deficit in all years (Table 1.2), compared with trade surpluses in most years of the preceding control regime. Despite large increases in export volumes, declining terms of trade and a massive surge in externally funded imports required to increase industrial production have ensured a deficit. The current account has also been in deficit throughout the entire period 1983–95. Inflows of

---

[4] Toye (1991: 191) has argued that the series of step-wise devaluations separated by plateaux of stability cre-ated by the auctions suggested that the government was managing the weekly forex auction to the extent that the exchange regime was still not completely liberalized.

long- and short-term capital, particularly official transfers in support of the ERP, have, however, enabled the overall balance to register a surplus in most years, thus enabling substantially larger holdings of international reserves. The importance of foreign capital is shown by the fact that between 1982 and 1994 total external debt outstanding increased from 36.6% of GNP to 101.5%. Indeed, foreign transfers have been largely responsible for the ability to maintain the import liberalization programme and the foreign-exchange auction[5] in the face of declining international cocoa prices, as well as helping to support the public sector budget. However, as discussed below, these capital inflows have created problems in terms of monetary management and crowding-out of the private sector (Jebuni *et al.*, 1994a; Younger, 1992).

Fiscal Policy and Performance

The main fiscal objective of the ERP has been to reduce fiscal deficits in order to help control inflation and prevent crowding-out of the private sector. The instruments used were the introduction of cost recovery measures, reduction of subsidies, divestiture of state-owned enterprises, retrenchment of civil servants, improvements in the efficiency of tax collection, widening of the tax net and general fiscal and aggregate demand restraint. At the same time the government made efforts to rehabilitate the economic and social infrastructure with increasing outlays on essential services and maintenance, as well as the expansion of priority projects. To help with this prioritization process, a three-year Public Sector Investment Programme was introduced, which covered a core of 100 projects, with a focus on rehabilitation rather than on new projects. In 1987, an inner core of 29 projects was identified for protection in budget implementation.[6]

During the 1980s there was considerable success with fiscal policy. Increased revenue, which rose from 6% of GDP in 1983 to 15% in the second half of the decade, and foreign financing permitted central government expenditure to increase from 11% of GDP in 1984 to 19% in the later 1980s. Capital expenditure on infrastructure rose to 8% of GDP, and expenditure was initially restructured towards non-wage operations including increased shares for social services. By 1986 the government budget, narrowly defined to exclude externally funded projects, registered a surplus. This enabled the government to retire domestic debt, i.e. make net repayments to the domestic banks which enabled resources to be released to the private sector and helped dampen the growth of money supply and inflation. The broader budget remained in deficit, however, hovering around 5% of GDP in the second half of the 1980s (Table 1.2). The World Bank's general assessment of this period was that 'although fiscal policy is improving, there is still scope to do better' (World Bank, 1994: 41). In particular, the government still owns many production activities and transfers to public bodies continue to drain the budget.[7]

In the election year of 1992, when the Rawlings military regime made its transition to democracy, fiscal indiscipline re-emerged: civil service wages were increased by 80%, expanding the government wage bill by 38.7%; tax revenues fell, due in part to the poor 1991/92 cocoa harvest; election pressures pushed up rural development expenditures; and there was a shortfall in net foreign financing. As a result, a narrow deficit of 3.4% emerged in 1992 with a 2.5% deficit registered in 1993, whilst the broad deficit increased to over 10% of GDP. Although in

---

[5] In 1988 69% of finances for the forex auction came from foreign sources (Jebuni *et al.*, 1994a: 1169).

[6] There have been occasional World Bank and IMF clashes in Ghana over fiscal policy, with the Fund pushing for fiscal restraint and the Bank pushing supply-side policies such as reduction of the cocoa tax (which accounts for around 25% of tax revenue), higher civil service wages and salaries to improve public sector management and a higher PSIP than the Fund believed was feasible whilst preserving macroeconomic balance (Toye, 1991: 164).

[7] Sowa (1994) has calculated that during the 1980s the fiscal deficit was consistent with the growth, money supply, and inflation targets only in 1985 and 1989.

Table 1.2   Key Macroeconomic Indicators 1984-95

	1984	1985	1986	1987	1988	1989	1990	1991	1992	1993	1994**	1995**
GDP (current cedis million)	271	343	511	746	1051	1417	2032	2575	3009	3949	5186	
Real GDP growth %	8.6	5.1	5.2	4.8	5.6	5.1	3.3	5.3	3.9	5.0	3.8	
Balance of payments (US$ m.)												
trade accounts	33	-36	61	-125	-112	-195	-308	-321	-470	-664	-342	-257
current account	-39	-134	-43	-97	-66	-99	-229	-253	-378	-559	-254	-145
overall balance (= change in net international reserves)	36	141	-61	140	181	156	105	137	-123	53	172	257
Broad fiscal deficit billion cedis	-8.3	-14.0	-28.3	-37.8	-56.1	-75.0	-98.0	-103.5	-321.7	-427.1	-352.2	
as % GDP*	-3.1	-4.1	-5.5	-5.1	-5.3	-5.3	-4.8	-4.0	-10.7	-10.8	-6.8	
Narrow fiscal deficit as GDP	-1.5	-1.6	0.6	1.2	0.9	1.3	0.6	2.0	-3.4	-2.5		
Money supply growth rate broad money	25.1%	65.0%	66.5%	57.1%	43.0%	60.6%	22.6%	69.2%	52.0%	27.0%	46.0%	38%
Inflation CPI	39.7%	10.4%	24.6%	39.8%	31.4%	25.2%	37.2%	18.0%	10.1%	25.0%	24.9%	60.0%
Foreign debt outstanding: GDP	25.9	35.5	57.1	71.4	59.2	64.4	58.5	59.3	61.8	78.6	92.3	
Real interest rate	8.2	-2.4	-14.8	-12.5	-6.8	-10.7	14.1	18.9	6.1	3.3	1.0	
Exchange rate, annual average Cedi: US$	36.0	54.4	106.4	162.4	202.4	270.0	330.0	375.0	437.0	649.0	956.6	1,200
Gross fixed capital formation as % GDP	6.9	9.6	9.4	10.4	11.3	13.3	14.4	15.8	12.8	14.8	15.9	
Private investment as % GDP	4.4	5.4	2.1	2.5	3.3	5.5	7.6	8.1	4.3	4.9	4.4	
Gross domestic savings as % GDP	4.2	6.6	5.8	3.9	5.4	5.6	6.0	7.8	2.0	-1.0	4.4	

Note: *) Broad fiscal deficit includes expenditures financed from foreign loans and grants, which are excluded from the narrow budget.
Source: World Bank, 1995, Statistical Appendices.

1994 the government engineered a major fiscal turnaround,[8] fiscal pressures re-emerged in the run-up to the 1996 election (CEPA, 1996). It has been suggested by some analysts (*Ibid.*) that the official fiscal figures mask the true size of the government deficit.

The deficits of the 1990s have created several macroeconomic problems. Heavy government borrowing from the Bank of Ghana has led to accelerated growth of the money supply, with M_2 growing by 52% in 1992, 27% in 1993 and 46% in 1994 (Table 1.2). This has contributed to accelerating inflation which peaked at around 60% in 1995 (CEPA, 1996). In addition, the inability to control the fiscal deficit has resulted in increased crowding-out of the private sector which helps to explain the weak response of private investment to the ERP (Younger, 1992: 1539; Aryeetey, 1994: 1216; Islam and Wetzel, 1991). Between 1990 and 1993 the average return on Treasury bills was 34%, enabling the government to attract extensive resources from a banking sector which finds it easier to invest in low risk high yield government paper than to lend to the private sector.[9]

Monetary Policy and Performance

'Inflation has been the albatross of Ghana's Economic Recovery Programme . . . (it) appears to be the macro problem for which no antidote has been found' (Sowa, 1994: 1105). The same could be said of the growth of the money supply.

The policy prescriptions of the IMF's Polak model (Polak, 1957), namely, that tight credit should be used to reduce domestic absorption in order to cure a balance of payments deficit and reduce inflation, have been attempted throughout Ghana's ERP. In the 1980s, the credit squeeze was implemented through IMF credit ceilings, selective credit controls, high reserve ratios, and steadily increasing administered interest rates. Since 1987/8, the markets have been allowed to determine interest rates, and in 1992 the monetary system was liberalized with a move towards greater use of open market operations, primarily through the issue of Bank of Ghana and Treasury bills.

In addition to stabilization objectives, monetary policy under the ERP has aimed to improve resource allocation, with increased mobilization of domestic savings seen as a precondition for increased investment. Since 1988, when the World Bank introduced a financial sector adjustment loan, banking reforms have been implemented to improve financial intermediation.[10] The banking system has been progressively liberalized and a stock market established, while the policy of restoring a positive real interest rate was intended to accelerate the process of financial deepening (Aryeetey, 1994: 1216; Chapter 11 of this volume).

The results of monetary policy under the ERP have been extremely disappointing. Although gross domestic savings as a percentage of GDP rose somewhat in the late 1980s, by 1994 the rate was no higher than at the start of the reform period (Table 1.2). Gross fixed capital formation increased from 6.9% of GDP in 1984 to 15.9% in 1994 but this increase has been largely led by the public sector (Table 1.2) with a poor response from the private sector (apart from the mining sector). The money supply has continued to grow at an average annual rate of almost 50%, and inflation has remained in double digit figures, peaking at 60% in 1995. A crucial question is: why was money supply growth in the second half of the 1980s and the 1990s so rapid whilst at the same time government domestic borrowing was reduced in real terms and private sector borrowing remained very low? The answer lies in the monetization of foreign

---

[8] Towards the end of the year, further divestiture of holdings in Ashanti Goldfields Company were undertaken to raise $200 m. to finance the deficit.
[9] Of the ¢501 billion of Treasury bills and stocks issued by September 1993 the non-bank public held only ¢185.2 bn. Although the reserve requirement for commercial banks was to hold 52% in Bank of Ghana bills and Treasury bills and 5% in cash the actual ratios retained exceeded 70%.
[10] The Bank and the IMF have clashed in Ghana over the Fund's tight credit policy which the Bank believes has hampered supply response to improved incentives. The Fund's answer was that improved financial intermediation, rather than a relaxation on credit, was the correct solution and this view prevailed (Toye, 1991).

debt flows which contributed to a large proportion of the money supply growth (this is discussed in more detail at the end of this section).

Real interest rates have been negative during much of the ERP period because of high inflation (Table 1.2), while a rapidly growing money supply has created excess liquidity in the banking system. Yet private investment has been low. Tight credit policy in the form of high nominal lending rates and a reserve ratio which stood at 57% by the early 1990s have been used in an attempt to stem the growth of the money supply and inflation. This has contributed to the credit constraints on the private sector (Aryeetey, 1994; Younger, 1992; Sowa, 1994). Prior to the bank restructuring in 1990 the commercial banks also had little new money available for lending because existing loans were not being serviced. Throughout the period, what little bank lending went to the private business sector financed working capital rather than fixed investment.

Private investment has also been low, because of the perception of uncertainty in the political and economic environment. In an attempt to counteract inflation the monetary authorities have resorted to constant introductions of new Bank of Ghana rediscount rates and revision of reserve requirements, resulting in a variability of credit flow to the private sector and undermining its confidence in the banking system (Aryeetey, 1994; Jebuni *et al.*, 1994a).[11] High rates of domestic inflation and rapid exchange rate depreciation which increased the demand for working capital have discouraged private fixed investment, particularly with the re-emergence of macroeconomic instability in the 1990s when private investment fell back to 4.4% of GDP (Table 1.2).

During the second half of the 1980s the government's narrow fiscal accounts registered a surplus (Table 1.2) enabling it to retire some of its domestic debt, thus releasing some resources for the private sector. Indeed, private sector investment as a percentage of GDP increased from 2.1% in 1986 to 8.1% in 1991, although most of this rise was attributable to gold mining investment all of which was foreign-financed. Domestic bank lending to the private sector changed only marginally during this period. In contrast, the 1990s have witnessed a clear public sector crowding-out of private investors.[12] In particular, since 1991, large fiscal deficits financed by the issue of high yielding Treasury bills have attracted enormous resources from the banking sector (Aryeetey, 1994).[13] This has led many people to argue that private sector investment-led growth requires tighter fiscal policy together with looser monetary policy (Younger, 1992; CEPA, 1996).[14]

The sector particularly affected by low investment is the manufacturing sector. By 1990 it was utilizing only 37% of its capacity, partly due to shortage of working capital with manufacturing contributing only 9% to GDP over the 1984–91 period. In the light of macro instability, entrepreneurs have been drawn into the services sector, particularly the distributive trade, which has low sunk costs and shorter turnover periods. Liberalization of imports has also inhibited investment in manufacturing which now faces intense import competition, and this has discouraged bank lending to the sector. The inflow of private foreign investment has also been sluggish, with the exception of investment in the privatized mining sector.

The poor mobilization of domestic savings during the ERP can be partly explained by the persistence of negative real rates of interest over the 1984–90 period (Table 1.2). In the 1990s

---

[11] In 1979 and 1982 many investors lost their assets to the government, following arbitrary government decisions, and this memory continued for a long time to affect private sector confidence (Aryeetey, 1994; Jebuni *et al.*, 1994).

[12] Chhibber and Shafik (1990) have estimated the elasticity of private investment to real private credit to be 0.58.

[13] It has often been observed that the monetary authorities in Ghana are rather weak, making it difficult to maintain an independent monetary policy stance. Rather, monetary policy usually accommodates fiscal requirements.

[14] Younger (1992) has also argued that the government should attempt to raise revenue through more incentive-neutral taxes, i.e. income and value-added taxes which would constrain private sector expenditures in general rather than just limiting investment through tight credit.

rapid inflation and exchange rate depreciation have discouraged domestic savings and caused a lack of confidence in the banking system. More generally, the wide spread between deposit and lending rates of interest has discouraged both savings and investment and inhibited financial intermediation (Aryeetey, 1996).

Assessing the Macroeconomic Success of the ERP

There are three main ways of assessing the impact of any economic reform programme, namely, 'before versus after' analysis, 'plan versus actual outcome' analysis and 'with versus without' analysis (Mosley *et al.*, 1995: 181–7). Here the first two will be applied. In interpreting these results two important exogenous factors, one positive, the other negative, should be borne in mind: namely, the abnormally high level of external financial support for the ERP and the exceptionally unfavourable terms of trade during the ERP period.

In the 'before versus after' assessment we can compare average annual values for key macroeconomic variables in the period immediately prior to the ERP with those registered during the ERP. This is done in Table 1.3 which divides the ERP into two periods, 1984–90 and 1991–4. The assessment is generally favourable. In the 1984–90 period GDP growth staged a dramatic recovery,[15] the balance of payments went from deficit to surplus, a small fiscal surplus was registered, inflation fell, and gross fixed capital formation as a percentage of GDP doubled. The external trade and current account deteriorated, however, suggesting that the overall surplus was largely due to the inflow of loans and grants, whilst growth of the money supply accelerated. Performance in the 1991–4 period, although still an improvement on most counts over 1978-83, deteriorated somewhat compared with the first phase of the ERP, and this raises questions about the sustainability of the reform programme. GDP growth rates slowed, the trade and current account deficits grew larger with a corresponding decline in the overall balance of payments surplus, fiscal deficits re-emerged and money supply growth remained

Table 1.3   Before Versus After Analysis of Key Macroeconomic Indicators

	Annual Ave 1978–83	Annual Ave 1984–90	Annual Ave 1991–94
Real GDP growth	–1.34%	5.4%	4.5%
Balance of payments (US$ m.)			
trade account	47.5	–97.4	–449.2
current account	–99.8	–101.0	–361
overall balance	–102.0	98.3	59.7
Narrow fiscal deficit as % GDP	–5.95	0.21	–1.3
Broad money growth	36.6%	50.0%	46.4%
Inflation CPI	73.7%	29.8%	19.9%
Gross fixed capital formation as % GDP	5.2	10.8	14.8

Source: Tables 1.1 and 1.2.

---

[15] Toye (1991) has suggested that part of the reason for GDP recovery in the early stages of the ERP was a series of favourable exogenous shocks, namely, improvement in the weather after a period of drought and a 37% improvement in the terms of the trade with the recovery of cocoa prices.

high. Inflation and gross fixed capital formation both improved, however, although the inflation figure for 1995 peaked at 60%.

The plan versus actual outcome assessment is presented in Table 1.4. Using this analysis, the ERP appears less successful. The real GDP growth rate fell slightly below target, whilst inflation, domestic savings, gross fixed capital formation, private investment, broad money growth and the balance of payments trade account all missed their targets by a significant margin. Only in the case of the government budget deficit and the balance of payments current account and overall balance did actual outcomes surpass the target. This begs the question as to whether Ghana's donors expected too much of the ERP, thus setting unrealistic planned outcomes.

Table 1.4   Plan Versus Actual Outcome Analysis of Key Macroeconomic Indicators

	Annual Ave. 1984–91 Plan	Annual Ave. 1984–91 Actual	Deviation
Real GDP growth %	5.11	4.66	–0.45
Inflation	22.30	28.30	–6.00
Domestic savings as % GDP	1990 plan 15	1990 actual 6.0	–9.0
Gross fixed capital formation as % GDP	18	14.4	–3.6
Private Investment as % GDP	15	7.6	–7.4
Broad government deficit	Ave. 1987–9 plan –7.3	Ave. 1987–8 actual –5.2	+2.1
Broad money growth	20.2	55.9	–35.9
Balance of payments (US$ m.)			
trade balance	–135.7	–334.7	–199.0
current account	–342.6	–268.0	+74.6
overall balance	111.7	130.0	+18.3

Source: World Bank, 1987b; Sowa, 1994; Aryeetey, 1994.

The Monetarist versus Structuralist Debate on Ghana's Macro Policy

There has been a myriad of explanations put forward as to why inflation has persisted during the ERP. One debate centres around the role of rapid exchange rate depreciation and rising import prices. The conventional view is that this has been inflationary (Dordunoo, 1994). On the other hand, Toye (1991: 170 and Chhibber and Shafik, 1991) argue that since most important prices (except for petroleum) were already transacted at the parallel exchange rate, depreciation of the official exchange rate did not exert powerful inflationary pressures.[16] Other ERP reforms which are often claimed to have contributed to inflation include price decontrol and higher cocoa prices, the latter leading to demand-pull inflation.

Many analysts argue that the prime cause of persistent inflation has been the rapid growth of the money supply (Table 1.2) (Chhibber and Shafik, 1990; Younger, 1992; Aryeetey, 1994). An important question is: why was monetary growth so high during the ERP (it averaged 51%

per annum during 1986-94), and why, despite the reduction in government borrowing, was the private sector crowded out of credit markets?

Between 1985 and 1993 M2 was roughly constant at about 17% of GDP (Table 1.5). Credit to the public sector from the banking system fell by more than 10 percentage points of GDP between 1985 and 1991. Public sector net credit was actually negative in 1991. Despite this, private sector borrowing declined from 6.2% of GDP in 1985 to 4.3% in 1989 (subsequent figures are not strictly comparable because of the removal of non-performing loans from the banks' balance sheets, but it is clear that private sector borrowing remained very low thereafter).

The major source of monetary growth during the ERP was the domestic currency counterpart of Bank of Ghana (BoG) repayments of foreign-exchange loans contracted by the government and parastatals (many of which had been contracted before the ERP and were in arrears). This appears under the revaluation account in BoG monetary statistics. It has been the biggest contributor to M2 growth in every year during the period 1986–94 except 1991 and 1992 (when the rise in the BoG's net foreign assets (NFA) and public sector borrowing respectively made larger contributions) (Table 1.5).

The revaluation account is effectively a domestic currency loan by the BoG to the public sector, and represents a form of quasi-fiscal deficit. The domestic currency equivalent of these foreign-exchange loans was multiplied many fold by devaluation, with the consequence that the debtors had no possibility of being able to repay them out of their income. Hence the BoG made the repayments on their behalf during the early part of the ERP. By 1986 the revaluation account amounted to 26% of GDP and was more than 50% larger than the entire broad money supply. Had the government or other debtors reimbursed the BoG for some of the foreign-exchange repayments it made, M2 growth would obviously have been much lower, but the fiscal consequences would have been enormous.

The change of 18 percentage points of GDP in the Net Foreign Assets of the BoG which occurred after 1986 (Table 1.5) points to another cause of money supply growth, namely, inflows of capital. In the period since 1986 increased aid and loan inflows in support of the ERP created an excess supply of foreign exchange which was monetized (Younger, 1992; Sowa, 1994; Chhibber and Shafik, 1990). Between 1985 and 1991 annual disbursements of public and publicly guaranteed external debt increased from US$183 m. to US$440 m. (see Chapter 10). Tight credit policies to the private sector were used in an unsuccessful attempt to sterilize the capital inflows.

Capital inflow has created 'Dutch Disease' symptoms, namely demand-pull upward pressure on non-tradeables' prices, helping to explain persistent inflation and real exchange rate appreciation. Younger (1992) has argued that these inflows should be regarded as a permanent positive shock, and that in order to cure inflation the increased money supply should be diverted into increased imports. In order for this to take place he argues that the exchange rate should be allowed to appreciate (through nominal appreciation rather than through domestic inflation), and that nominal devaluation in Ghana has been excessive. The danger of such a strategy, however, is that it would undermine the competitiveness of exports and import substitutes, leading to declining production of tradeables and even greater aid dependence and vulnerability to fluctuations in capital inflows which may turn out not to be permanent. For this reason such a strategy has been resisted by the Bank of Ghana. BoG staff argue that the cedi's value should be allowed to reflect the underlying economic conditions and that the root causes of inflation, such as recent government deficits and quasi deficits, money supply growth, and structural constraints on the supply side of the economy, should be tackled instead.

---

[16] Chhibber and Shafik (1991) using regression analysis also argue that devaluation was actually anti-inflationary since it had a positive effect on the government budget, thus reducing the rate of monetisation and inflation. This argument is echoed in World Bank (1987b).

Table 1.5   Money Supply and its Components: Percentages of GDP 1985–96

	1985	1986	1987	1988	1989	1990	1991	1992	1993	1994	1995	1996
M2	16.2	16.7	17.4	18.0	16.9	13.9	12.7	17.3	16.8	18.6	17.5	19.4
Credit Public[a]	9.3	6.8	4.1	2.0	0.7	-1.0	-2.1	1.8	1.7	13.0	13.5	13.7
Credit Private	6.2	7.3	6.3	5.5	4.3	3.1	3.2	4.6	4.8	5.2	5.2	7.4
NFA-BoG	-12.5	-24.1	-179	-13.0	-9.5	-7.4	-3.7	-7.0	-6.0	0.7	2.4	5.6
Revaluation	12.2	26.0	23.9	21.4	19.5	16.3	14.1	12.8	14.7	6.0	2.9	4.0

Note: [a] Credit Public is all credit to the government and public enterprises except for cocoa financing.
NFA = net foreign assets: this only includes the BoG and not the NFA of the commercial banks.

Sources: Monetary data up to 1987 are from IMF, *Review of Monetary Management in Ghana*, 1989; data from 1988 are from BoG Monetary Survey Statistics in the *Annual and Quarterly Reports*. GDP is from IMF, *International Financial Statistics Yearbooks*.

In addition to foreign capital inflows, another major cause of rapid money supply growth has been the large fiscal deficits of the 1990s and parastatal borrowing[17] (Younger, 1992; Aryeetey, 1994; Sowa, 1994), which have been accommodated by the monetary authorities. This necessitated a tight credit squeeze on the private sector, thus crowding-out private sector investment. Foreign-financed inflows which generally go to the public sector have intensified this crowding-out effect.

The monetary impact of the revaluation account operations, the subsequent balance of payments surpluses, and the 1992 fiscal deficit, was large because the banking system was very shallow, with M2 amounting to only 17% of GDP. Even relatively small monetary injections of 2-3% of GDP could lead to substantial percentage rises in base money and in M2. This is one of the reasons why monetary control has proved so difficult: the BoG has very little room for manoeuvre. If the quasi fiscal deficits and BoP surpluses are regarded as having been largely unavoidable, the only means the BoG had to restrain M2 growth was restrictions on bank credit to the private sector. But as this was itself a relatively small component of M2 (only about 30% at the most), restricting it could have only a small impact on overall monetary growth.

In recent years there has been a growing structuralist critique of the above monetary explanations of inflation in Ghana (Sowa and Kwakye, 1991; Sowa, 1994; CEPA, 1996), which argues that real factors in the form of structural supply-side constraints are more pronounced in Ghana's inflationary spiral. Sowa's econometric regressions are used to suggest that, in both the short and the long run, inflation is influenced more by output volatility than by monetary factors with the elasticity of inflation with respect to output being almost unity. One significant output variable is food production, which has a weight of almost 50% in the CPI and which so far has not been addressed by policy.[18] The low growth rate and capacity utilization of the industrial sector, which is often attributed to structural constraints, is another supply-side factor sometimes put forward to explain inflation. However, this is unlikely to have more than a small impact on inflation because industrial output accounts for less than 10% of aggregate expenditure. In the light of the structuralist critique the following view is now emerging:

In conclusion we would like to emphasise that the underlying current policy framework is flawed for its over-reliance on aggregate demand management policies to the exclusion of supply enhancing policies. (CEPA, 1996: 14)

Thus, to keep inflation under control, more attention should be paid to policies which will enhance growth in real output. Any anti-inflationary policy that neglects the supply side is not likely to be successful. (Sowa, 1994: 1112)

This view that the ERP has relied too much on macro management, particularly tight credit policies, and that there is a need for a more sector-orientated supply-side strategy is being adopted by many of Ghana's major donors such as the European Union, UNDP and more gradually the World Bank (World Bank, 1995).[19] However, the structuralist critique might be able to explain short-term jumps in inflation (e.g. when there is a drought) but it is difficult to see how supply-side weaknesses can generate persistent high rates of inflation unless there are continued high rates of monetary growth. Given the rates of money supply growth that have occurred

---

[17] In 1992 and 1993 respectively the government ran a narrow budget deficit of 3.4% and 2.5% of GDP. In 1994 and 1995 quasi-fiscal problems emerged when the Cocoa Marketing Board borrowed heavily from overseas to finance the purchase of a large cocoa crop at increased producer prices. The Bank of Ghana had to sterilize the inflow of foreign exchange from buoyant cocoa and gold exports.
[18] Agricultural output grew at only 2% during 1987–91, less than the population growth rate. This has been attributed to structural constraints which were found to be more important than price and exchange-rate policies (World Bank, 1994: 147). The peak 60% inflation in 1995 coincided with a particularly poor food harvest.
[19] The UN's new Special Initiative for Africa has a strong sector-based focus.

in Ghana since the start of the ERP, it is hardly surprising that inflation has been high (only a large and continued fall in the velocity of circulation would have allowed these rates of money supply growth to be consistent with low inflation). A structuralist explanation is not needed: it would only be useful if it could show that money supply increases were somehow caused by inflation rather than the other way round. The argument that sectoral supply-side policies should be strengthened to boost output growth rates is valid, but unless there is effective demand management, inflation will not be reduced. Given the rates of growth of nominal demand in the economy, inflation would still be high even if the real growth rate were to double to 10% (which is not very plausible).

The alarming experience, whereby it took 10 years to stabilize Ghana's macroeconomy followed by an almost immediate collapse in macroeconomic management in 1992, has raised questions as to whether Ghana really is the adjustment paradigm of sub-Saharan Africa. Donors and government, after fourteen years of investment in adjustment, are understandably reluctant to acknowledge such a possibility. However, private sector investment remains at 4.4% of GDP, exactly the same rate as in 1984, and real GDP growth in 1994 fell to 3.8%, much of it driven by donor-funded public expenditure. The economy has become aid-dependent with the debt to GNP ratio now at 101.5%, inflation has remained in double figures throughout the ERP, the money supply continues to grow at an average annual rate of 50%, narrow fiscal deficits have re-emerged, the value of the cedi has experienced a precipitous decline and a balance of payments surplus is largely the result of capital inflows in the form of grants and loans. In this context, even if the structuralist explanation of inflation is rejected, it is still valid to ask whether concentrating on macro policy without adequately focusing on sectoral policies to overcome structural supply-side constraints has been the best option within the overall adjustment framework. Clearly, macro management, particularly control of the money supply, is essential, but this needs to be accompanied by strong efforts to boost food production, generate private sector investment, diversify the export base, and rejuvenate the industrial sector.

4.   Sectoral Policies and Outcomes 1970–83

Policy statements and other documents in the 1970s suggest that a two-pronged approach to development was to be applied, relying on a balanced development of the agricultural and industrial sectors. This balanced approach was to safeguard the principles of equitable growth and self-reliance that were supposed to be at the core of the government programme. One of the objectives of the Five-Year Development Plan of the Acheampong government was spelled out as:

> The promotion of national economic independence in terms of creation of effective links between sectors of the economy so that development becomes mutually reinforcing. Both agricultural and industrial sectors were expected to be the sources of growth, with backward and forward linkages developed between them.

A feature of economic policy in the period, however, became the divergence between policy statements and implementation. The inconsistency and instability of macroeconomic policy seen earlier rendered the implementation of sectoral policies and programmes difficult. There were problems in financing the local costs of some sectoral development projects because of the declining revenue base. The inadequate supply of necessary imported spare parts and raw materials due to the shortage of foreign exchange also slowed down project implementation on several fronts.

As a consequence, the first few years of the 1980s saw the beginnings of a transformation in the sectoral composition of GDP as the contribution of services to GDP began to increase and that of agriculture began to fall (Table 1.6). This was transformation in the midst of economic decline. The price and quantitative controls, policy inconsistencies and contradictions had created the conditions for a rapid decline in the directly productive activities. The productive sectors were relatively worse hit by the dangerous cocktail of policies, leaving the services sector, with its low demand for fixed capital and its rapid turn-over rate, as the least devastated.

Table 1.6   Sectoral Distribution of Real GDP Period Averages (%)

	1970–75	1976–82	1983–86	1987–90	1991–95
Agriculture	52	51	52	46	42
Industry	19	17	12	14	14
Services	29	32	36	40	44

Source: Calculated from Statistical Services, *Quarterly Digest of Statistics,* various issues, ISSER (1996).

Agricultural Development Policies and Outcomes

At the beginning of the 1970s, the agricultural sector was the dominant economic sector accounting for more than half of GDP and employing approximately 60% of the economically active population. Aside from playing a critical growth function, the sector was also an important source of foreign exchange and government revenue. In addition, the performance of agriculture, particularly food crop production, was crucial to controlling inflation since a significant source of domestic inflation was increases in local food prices.

But agricultural GDP registered negative growth rates between 1972 and 1975 (Table 1.7). Its share of real GDP also declined from 58% in 1972 to 49% in 1978. Although the mean growth rate in the subsequent period up to 1982 was positive, it masks the negative growth rates in the earlier part of that period. Agricultural production was not able to keep up with the growth of population. The declining significance of agriculture would have been acceptable only if it had been the result of general economic growth rather than economic decline. The general explanations provided for the poor performance of agriculture have been inappropriate macroeconomic policies, poor pricing policies, poor infrastructure, ineffective extension services and inappropriate technologies (see Chapter 14).

During the 1970s the principles of agricultural self-reliance and balanced development were reflected in the government ambition of providing cheap food, to be realized through, first, the 'Operation Feed Yourself' programme (OFY) and then through a number of integrated agricultural development programmes for all regions. The OFY programme's objectives were an increase in food production and the supply of raw materials to meet the demands of industry. Regional agricultural targets were set, and these were to be achieved through the provision of extension services and technical support to farmers and access to credit. The OFY programme has been observed to have suffered from poor planning, the tendency to concentrate resources on large commercial farmers and state farms, and infrastructural bottlenecks. Inadequate attention was paid to developing rural infrastructure (Chazan, 1983; Girdner *et al.,* 1980; and Marshall, 1976).

The OFY programme was not successful in achieving its production targets. The rise in local food prices persisted largely because the expansion in supply was insufficient to match the increases in effective demand. The sector suffered from a shortage in the supply of required inputs. This was because the appreciating real exchange rate and the anti-export bias in the trade regime discouraged exporting, thus reducing the capacity to import. Capital expenditures bore the brunt of attempts to restrain excessive government spending. Public sector investments in the rural areas, for example the feeder roads programme, could not be sustained and this undermined the success of the programme.

Table 1.7   Sectoral Growth Rates 1972–95 Period Averages (%)

	1972–75	1976–82	1983–86	1987–90	1991–95
Agriculture	–2.3	1.4	1.5	1.3	2.7
Industry	1.9	–7.3	5.6	7.0	4.3
Services	0.2	1.2	5.7	7.9	6.1

Source: Ibid.

As for the integrated agricultural development programmes, the best expression of how these were supposed to work is seen in the experiences of the Upper Region Agricultural Development Programme (URADEP). It was designed and initiated in 1975 as one of several package programmes for all the regions of Ghana in consultation with international development agencies. It had as its objective the development of the Upper Region through the provision of farm support services from specific service centres in order to increase agricultural production and farm incomes. URADEP was designed to achieve incremental rates of agricultural production which were to reach their peak in 1981 when the original programme investment period was intended to end. Thus the annual increase in the production of various crops and other agricultural produce by 1981 was targeted as follows:— 4,000 metric tonnes of millet; 12,000 mt of sorghum; 5,000 mt of maize; 30,000 mt of rice; 11,000 mt of groundnuts; 15,000 mt of yams; 7,000 mt of cowpeas; 18,000 mt of seed cotton; 6,000 mt of tomatoes; and 3,000 mt of meat. 'Thus if the programme targets are achieved family incomes from improved crop production could be increased by 32% per annum' (World Bank, 1975).

The production of most crops showed considerable variation throughout the programme's implementation period, and by 1981, less than half the crops had achieved the expected increases (Aryeetey, 1985). In the case of some crops, production by 1980 was substantially less than before the programme was initiated, thus compelling the World Bank review mission (Morris, 1980) to conclude that 'the return on the project is substantially less than forecast, and the project to date may have been barely successful in economic terms'. It is generally acknowledged that the integrated agricultural programmes that have been implemented in the Volta Region and also in the Northern Region have had little impact on the performance of the agricultural sector.

It was not only the food sector that showed poor performance. The cocoa sector suffered from the unfavourable macroeconomic policy stance. The production of cocoa, which reached its peak with an output of over 557,000 metric tonnes in 1965, declined to its lowest level in the 1983/84 season with an output of about 158,000 mt, about 63% less than the output in 1980/81. The exchange rate policy made it impossible for the government to pursue a realistic cocoa pricing policy. At the prevailing fixed exchange rate, an increase in nominal producer prices would have meant the government accepting a decline in cocoa revenues, which it was unwilling to accept because of its heavy dependence on this source of revenue. Farmers responded to the decline in real producer prices by not replanting or maintaining the tree stock. The quality of the tree stock was further eroded because of the inadequate supply of insecticides and spraying cans; even though they were heavily subsidized, the foreign-exchange constraint limited the quantities that could be imported for use in the cocoa industry.

Industrial Development Policies and Outcomes
There was a dramatic expansion in manufacturing capacity in the 1960s through the implementation of a state-led import-substituting industrialization (ISI) strategy. During a brief attempt at liberalization between 1966 and 1971 there was a slow-down in the establishment of state-

owned enterprises. However, with the adoption of the principle of self-reliance and the desire to capture the 'commanding heights of the economy', the state-led ISI strategy was revived in the 1970s. In addition to expansion in manufacturing production and capacity through ISI, policy statements also emphasized an expansion in manufactured exports. Export diversification was considered necessary if the foreign-exchange constraint on the economy was to be reduced. Ghana resembled most other developing countries in adopting an inward-oriented trade strategy. This was because of the export pessimism at the time regarding the ability of primary exports to generate the necessary foreign exchange required for rapid growth. However, unlike the East Asian tigers that were able to make the transition from an ISI strategy to an outward-oriented one, Ghana remained stuck at the ISI stage.

Severe sectoral policy conflicts existed, while there was a mismatch between policy objectives and implementation. An expansion in manufactured exports could occur within the context of an ISI strategy only if measures were introduced to counteract the anti-export bias inherent in that strategy. Unfortunately such a policy mix was not achieved in Ghana during the 1970s. The overvalued exchange rate discouraged exports and there was a failure in policy design to ensure that adequate foreign exchange was generated domestically to meet the needs of the highly import-dependent manufacturing sector. The export promotion package that was introduced initially to encourage manufactured exports suffered from severe bureaucratic related problems (see Chapter 13). Another problem was lack of a coherent industrial policy. In the Five-Year Development Plan for the period 1975/76–79/80 the policy objectives for the manufacturing sector were self-sufficiency in selected consumer goods industries, diversification of the industrial sector, encouragement of small-scale industries and promotion of manufactured exports. A wide range of industries were expected to be supported, namely, sugar, milk, beverages, edible oils, soap, textiles, footwear, metals, electrical, transport, salt, caustic soda, fertilizers and animal feeds. Production targets were set, but policy-makers did not identify the priority sectors. With this lack of a clearly articulated set of priorities, the sector fell prey to the vagaries of the macroeconomic policy stance, and expenditures were not focused.

The implementation of the ISI strategy was soon undermined by balance-of-payments and revenue considerations. Tariff rates were adjusted frequently in response to government revenue considerations and the face value of import licences was adjusted to meet the available foreign exchange (Jebuni *et al.*, 1994b). An assessment of the protectionist system in the early 1970s described it as being subject to random variation. It could not be explained by any *a priori* factors (Leith, 1974). The structure of incentives in place was not that intended by policy-makers but had evolved in response to their reactions to the changing balance-of-payments and government revenue situations. The result was uncertainty and instability in the policy framework that was not supportive of production and investment in the manufacturing sector.

The mining sector was badly affected by the failure to marry the foreign-exchange saving and foreign-exchange generating policy objectives effectively. The anti-export bias in the trade regime and the inadequate supply of foreign exchange made it impossible for mining companies to purchase the necessary machinery and spare parts.

Developments in the Services Sector

The services sector, which is usually referred to as the tertiary sector of the economy, has the unique role of stimulating economic growth by making product and factor markets function efficiently. Interestingly, throughout the period under examination, there were no specific economic policies for the development of the sector. Thus, the expansion of the services sector in the period 1970-82 may be explained by the shift in the structure of incentives in favour of the non-traded goods sector as the real exchange rate appreciated. Secondly, the price and quantitative controls and the highly uncertain and unpredictable policy environment discouraged activities in the productive sectors after 1975. Investments in these sectors tended to require more substantial sunk costs and to have longer gestation periods than some activities in the services sector, for example trading.

5.   Sectoral Policies and Outcomes under the ERP

Underlying the economic reforms since 1983 has been economic liberalism, i.e. the removal of price and quantitative restrictions that prevent the free interplay of market forces, and the privatization of all aspects of economic activity. This 'free marketism' has determined the context within which sectoral policies have been designed and the issues that have received attention. But, in addition to the broad benefits sectors were expected to derive from the freeing of the market, considerable investment has been made by the government in all the major sectors in order to improve their production directly, albeit with varying results.

Clearly the sectoral contribution to the growth of GDP has not been uniform since the reforms began. During the five-year period (1987–91), growth in the agricultural sector lagged behind the rest of the economy, as shown in Table 1.7. During 1987–90, agricultural GDP grew at only 1.3% per annum, which was not enough to offset the estimated rate of population growth of 2.6%. Indeed, it was the negative agricultural growth of 2% in 1990 that depressed the growth of the whole economy in that year. Industrial sector growth has been second to that of the services sector, with 7% average annual rate of growth during 1987–90. In 1989, however, the rate of growth of industrial gross domestic product fell to 2.6% which was well below the previous year's level of 7.2%. During 1987–90, the services sector grew every year by more than 6%, averaging an annual 8% for the period.

Agricultural Sector Developments

Agricultural sector policy since 1983 has been concerned largely with liberalizing product and input markets, privatizing the sector and removing state monopolies (see Chapter 14 for details). Price controls and subsidies no longer exist within the agricultural sector and, with the exception of the external marketing of cocoa, the marketing of agricultural products and inputs has been privatized. Although liberalization did not occur within the timeframe agreed between the government and the World Bank, most policy agreements have been implemented. The main exception is the continuing monopoly of the Cocoa Board in the external marketing of cocoa.

The correction of the macro-level distortions facilitated the removal of some sectoral price distortions. With the devaluation of the nominal exchange rate, nominal cocoa producer prices could be raised without jeopardizing government revenues. A concern in the early years of the reforms was the bias in the incentive structure against food crops. The price of food relative to cocoa prices experienced a dramatic drop between 1983 and 1987 (Loxley, 1991). Agricultural sector policy for a greater part of the period since 1983 focused on cocoa because of the overriding concern on the part of the World Bank with expanding export earnings, particularly traditional exports. This policy weakness is acknowledged in a statement by a World Bank division chief: 'We considered agriculture as cocoa for too long; this was a blind spot. . . . The nexus issues are now critical' (Armstrong, 1996: 80).

After the initial reforms, cocoa began recovering from its lowest production level recorded in the 1983/84 season, but the recovery has been slow. Even though cocoa continues to contribute a significant share of the country's export earnings, its future remains uncertain, given the volatility of international cocoa prices and the aggressive production strategies of other producers. For many Ghanaians, if Ghana is to compete effectively in a cocoa market characterized by uncertain foreign price prospects, it is important that the costs of production and marketing are reduced at the same time as a programme to process cocoa beans is pursued. Currently being debated is the issue of whether privatization of cocoa marketing, and the marketing of agricultural inputs such as fertilizer, will generate the level of efficiency required for survival in a highly competitive market.

The Medium Term Agricultural Development Strategy begun in 1991 was an attempt to address the weaknesses in agricultural policy. It has as its guiding principles the creation of an enabling environment for agricultural growth and the encouragement of private sector participation. The aim is to instill efficiency and competitiveness in the sector. There is the concern, however, that the removal of subsidies on inputs is at cross purposes with the objective of improving productivity and food security. Input use declined with the removal of the subsidies and only began to rise in 1994 when the price of some fertilizers fell.

The performance of the agricultural sector continues to be erratic because the sector is still subject to a myriad of problems and growth registered only an average of 2.7% over the period 1991–95 (Table 1.7). Getting prices right is not sufficient to ensure sustained growth if several non-price constraints hamper the ability to respond to the new liberalized environment. A number of problems need to be addressed that have not been adequately looked at because of the narrow focus of the strategy. In the assessment of agricultural policy in the World Bank's country assistance review, it was recognized that 'there remains a need for more in-depth analytical work to identify specific constraints to increase private investment in agriculture and to propose specific remedies' (Armstrong, 1996: 84).

Industrial Sector Developments

The ERP policy focus for the industrial sector has been on improvement in the incentive structure using the exchange rate and trade taxes, privatizing the state-owned enterprises (SOEs) and streamlining the regulatory framework. Trade liberalization has been an important instrument of industrial policy. The reduction in tariff rates and the removal of quantitative restrictions were expected to increase competitiveness and efficiency in the manufacturing sector. In recent years, the concern has been to ensure that import tariffs and domestic taxes do not place domestic industry at an undue disadvantage. At the same time privatization of the SOEs was seen as the prescription to stop the haemorrhaging of the state's resources to loss-making enterprises. It was also viewed by the World Bank as a means of improving the environment for private sector participation.

To improve the regulatory framework in which firms operate, the 1971 Manufacturing Industries Act, the 1974 Price Control Decree and the 1976 Control of Sale of Specific Goods Decree were repealed. A new Investment Code was enacted to encourage foreign direct private investment. Measures have also been introduced to streamline investment procedures.

However, policy towards the manufacturing sector has suffered from similar shortcomings to those of the agricultural sector. The emphasis has been on liberalization and not sufficiently on addressing the non-price variables that affect production and investment. Policy towards the industrial sector is suggestive of a naive belief that the performance of industry, particularly manufacturing, was determined solely by the distortions emanating from the exchange-rate policy and the trade regime. It was also believed that the protectionist trade regime had encouraged inefficiency and that once increased competition was introduced through trade liberalization the sector would become leaner and more efficient. However, years of protection and lack of competition as well as stagnation due to import strangulation had considerably weakened the production capacity of the manufacturing sector. The sector has been unable to compete effectively in the new liberalized environment because of obsolete machinery, outmoded production practices and inadequate management techniques. It needs to be re-invigorated, and getting prices right is not enough to do the trick (see Chapter 13).

The major difference between industrial policy before and after 1983 is the macroeconomic policy and trade regime within which economic agents in the sector operate. In both periods industrial policy suffered from a lack of sector specificity. Assistance to the manufacturing sector has been thematic rather than sector-specific. For example, there are programmes to assist small-scale enterprises and non-traditional exports irrespective of the sectors in which they are located.[20] A sector-specific approach to industrial policy can pay significant dividends if the sectors that are chosen do have the potential for growth. Given the limited resources, concentration of these resources on a winner is an advantage. The counter arguments are that i) if they would have grown anyway, then there is no need for special assistance; ii) the wrong sector may be chosen; and iii) assistance to some sectors whilst excluding others will introduce distortions. However, if there are non-price distortions and constraints holding back manufacturing production in general, special assistance to those industries that will generate positive rates of return would be beneficial. If a thematic approach to industrial policy is to be adopted rather than a sectoral one, it is necessary that the policy should address those major constraints that are known to impact on a wide range of industries. The weakness of the thematic approach adopted so far in Ghana is that this has not happened. Since 1994, some intervention has been adopted with the introduction of the Business Assistance Fund to assist distressed enterprises. The project is rather limited, however, and it is not certain that it will be able to address the problems of manufacturing at the sector-wide level.

The mining sector has benefited from the exchange rate policy and the inflow of loans to the sector to purchase much-needed equipment and spare parts. Legislation has provided a clear framework for mining investments and this has contributed to the inflow of foreign direct investment to the sector.

Services Sector Developmets

The services sector has thrived in the liberalized environment, registering strong positive growth rates (Table 1.7). Retail and wholesale activities in particular have responded quite dramatically to the dismantling of controls. Tourism activities have also expanded rapidly since 1983, encouraged particularly by the real depreciation of the currency and the increase in import capacity due to the inflow of loans and grants. There has been more policy interest in the tourism industry than in the past. This may be interpreted as a consequence of the outward-oriented strategy that has been adopted. Funding has been received from external donors to support projects in the sector. Institutional structures are being developed to facilitate expansion; for example, the establishment of a hotel and tourism training institute in 1991 and the creation of a Ministry of Tourism in 1993.

An expansion in financial services has also occurred within the framework of the financial sector reforms. Again these reforms are concerned with liberalization of the financial system through the removal of controls, the reduction of state participation in the sector and the encouragement of private sector participation. New institutions have been introduced with the aim of encouraging efficiency in the provision of financial services as well as providing new financial instruments to meet the needs of the productive sectors. Expansion has occurred within the telecommunications sector with the inflow of loans to rehabilitate the infrastructure and the withdrawal of the state monopoly in the provision of these services. Finally, government services, boosted by inflows of aid resources, have also expanded during the ERP.

Assessing Sectoral Developments since 1970

By 1995 the structure of production had changed with the services sector accounting for the largest contribution to real GDP (Table 1.6). This cannot, however, be taken to imply a fundamental change in the structure of the economy, as such structural change requires a wider set of transformations over a longer period (see Chapter 3). But the fact that the directly productive activities, i.e. agriculture and industry, have not been able to register similar growth rates is

---

[20] With the non-traditional exports sector a more sector-specific strategy had been adopted. Even here, however, the emphasis is more on providing marketing contacts than on tackling production-related problems.

remarkable. This has been largely because of the failure of sectoral policies to address the constraints to production and investment adequately. In the past five years the instability and uncertainty emanating from the macro policy stance has contributed to making it even more difficult for firms and farmers to deal with firm- and sector-level constraints.

Obviously, the prevailing structure of production may jeopardize growth in the long run if the services sector does not evolve into an export-oriented one. The tertiary sector is traditionally seen as providing services to the productive sectors to facilitate the smooth running of their operations. If these sectors do not expand as rapidly as the tertiary sector, and if most of the business of the tertiary sector depends on the performance of the productive sectors, future growth of the sector may be constrained, thus constraining overall economic growth. Tapping external markets, through the provision of banking, construction and recreation facilities to foreigners, may be the path to ensuring economic growth in the long run if agriculture and industry continue to lag behind. But they should not be allowed to do so.

6.   Conclusion

The severe setbacks that Ghana has suffered in the march towards sustained economic growth and development raise a number of fundamental questions about growth and development concepts, policies and management within defined socio-political settings. As noted earlier, the country has tried a number of policies founded on known development concepts. Those policies have failed to yield the same results that they have sometimes yielded elsewhere. We tend to take the view that, in the period since 1970, the fact that two seemingly different policy approaches have not led to growth beyond the short term suggests that there is a critical need to look beyond the contents of economic policy and to ensure that policy is placed within an appropriate socio-political framework and that the management and implementation of economic policy, including macroeconomic policy, are adequate.

The significance of the economic management issues is reflected in the growing concern among Ghanaians about the lack of effectiveness of current government initiatives and the slow growth of the economy. The fact that hardly any macroeconomic targets have been achieved in the past decade is definitely worrying. The difficulty in synchronizing monetary and fiscal policies between the Bank of Ghana and the Ministry of Finance, culminating in fiscal indiscipline, raises alarm bells. The certain knowledge that the budget is not taken seriously by institutions charged with its implementation is problematic. There is obviously a lack of coordination between the spending arms of government and those responsible for overseeing this, resulting in the deficits that lie at the bottom of macroeconomic instability. The result is increasing frustration and despondency among the population.

References

Armah, B. (1993) 'Trade Structures and Employment Growth in Ghana: A Historical Comparative Analysis 1960–89', *African Economic History* Vol. 21: 21–36.

Armstrong, R. P. (1996) *Ghana Country Assistance Review. A Study in Development Effectiveness,* A World Bank Operations Evaluation Study. Washington, DC: World Bank.

Aryeetey, E. (1985) 'Decentralizing Regional Planning in Ghana', *Dortmunder Beitraege zur Raumplanung,* Vol. 42, Dortmund.

Aryeetey, E. (1994) 'Private Investment Under Uncertainty in Ghana'; *World Development,* Vol. 22, No. 8.

Aryeetey, E. (1996) *The Formal Financial Sector in Ghana After the Reforms.* Working Paper No. 86. London: Overseas Development Institute.

Aryeetey, E., Asante, Y. and Kyei, A. (1992) 'Mobilising Domestic Savings for African Development and Diversification', International Development Centre, Queen Elizabeth House, Oxford University (Mimeo).

Bates, R. (1981) *Markets and States in Tropical Africa: The Political Bias of Agricultural Policies.* Berkeley, CA: University of California Press.

Bhagwati, J. (1978) *Foreign Trade Regimes and Economic Development: Anatomy and Consequences of Exchange Controls.* New York: Ballinger.

CEPA (1996) *Macroeconomic Review and Outlook.* Accra: Centre for Economic Policy Analysis.

Chazan, N. (1983) *An Anatomy of Ghanaian Politics: Managing Political Recession 1969–82.* Westview Special Studies on Africa. Boulder, CO: Westview Press.

Chhibber, A. and Shafik, N. (1990) *Exchange Reform, Parallel Markets, and Inflation in Africa: The Case of Ghana,* World Bank Working Papers, No. 427 (May).

Chhibber, A. and Shafik, N. (1991) 'The Inflationary Consequences of Devaluation with Parallel Markets: The Case of Ghana', in Chhibber A. and Fischer S. (eds.) *Economic Reform in Sub-Saharan Africa,* a World Bank Symposium. Washington, DC: World Bank.

Damachi, U.G., Routh, G. and Taha, A. E. A. (1976) *Development Paths in Africa and China.* London and Basingstoke: Macmillan.

Dordunoo, C. (1994) 'The Structure and Policy Implications of a Macroeconomic Model of Ghana', *World Development,* Vol. 22, No. 8.

Franco, G. (1979) 'Domestic Credit and Balance of Payments in Ghana', *Journal of Development Studies,* Vol. 15, No. 2.

Ghartey, E. (1987) 'Devaluation as a Balance of Payments Corrective Measure in Developing Countries: A Study Relating to Ghana', *Applied Economics,* Vol. 19.

Girdner, J., Oluronsola, V., Fronig, M. and Hansen, E (1980) 'Ghana's Agricultural Food Policy', *Food Policy,* February.

Islam, R. and Wetzel, D. (1991) *The Macroeconomics of Public Sector Deficits: A Case Study of Ghana.* Washington, DC: World Bank.

ISSER (1993) *The State of the Ghana Economy 1992,* Institute of Statistical, Social and Economic Research, University of Ghana, Legon.

ISSER (1994) *The State of the Ghana Economy 1993,* Institute of Statistical, Social and Economic Research, University of Ghana, Legon.

Jebuni, C. D., Oduro, A. D. and Tutu, K. A. (1994a) 'Trade and Payments Regime and the Balance of Payments in Ghana' *World Development,* Vol. 22, No. 8.

Jebuni, C. D., Oduro, A. D. and Tutu, K. A. (1994b) *Trade, Payments Liberalisation and Economic Performance in Ghana,* AERC Research Paper No. 27, Nairobi.

Leith, J. C. (1974) *Foreign Trade Regimes and Economic Development: Ghana,* NBER. New York and London: Columbia University Press.

Lewis, A. (1954) 'Economic Development with Unlimited Supplies of Labour', *The Manchester School,* Vol. 22.

Loxley, J. (1991) *Ghana: The Long Road to Recovery 1983–90.* Ottawa: The North-South Institute,

Mansfield, C. (1980) 'Tax Base Erosion and Inflation: The Case of Ghana', *Finance and Development,* Vol. 17, No. 3.

Marshall, J. (1976) 'The State of Ambivalence: Right and Left Options in Ghana', *Review of African Political Economy,* No. 5, Jan–April.

Morris, J. C. H., (1980) *Report of ODA/IBRD Joint Supervision Mission to URADEP, 29 Sept.–17 Oct. 1980.* Washinton, DC: World Bank, West Africa Department.

Mosley, P., Harrigan, J. and Toye, J. (1995) *Aid and Power: The World Bank and Policy Based Lending.* London: Routledge, Vol. 1.

ODI (1996) *Adjustment in Africa: Lessons from Ghana, Briefing Paper,* No. 3, July.

Polak, J. (1957) 'Monetary Analysis of Income Formation and Payments Problems', *IMF Staff Papers,* November.

Sowa, N. (1994) 'Fiscal Deficits, Output Growth and Inflation Targets in Ghana', *World Development*, Vol. 22, No. 8.

Sowa, N. and Kwakye, J. (1991) 'Inflationary Trends and Control in Ghana', *AERC Research Report*, Nairobi.

Stewart, F. (1985) *Planning to Meet Basic Needs*. London and Basingstoke: Macmillan.

Streeten, P. (1972), *The Frontiers of Development Studies*. New York: Halsted.

Streeten, P. (1979) 'From Growth to Basic Needs', *Basic Needs Strategy as a Planning Parameter.* Berlin: German Foundation for International Development.

Teal, F. and Giwa, Y. (1985) 'Domestic Credit and the Balance of Payments in Ghana: A Comment', *Journal of Development Studies*, Vol. 21, No. 4

Toye, J. (1991) 'Ghana', Chapter 14 in Mosley *et al.*

Werlin, H. (1994) 'Ghana and South Korea: Explaining Development Disparities', *Journal of Asian and African Studies,* Vol.29, No.3–4.

World Bank (1975) *Ghana: Appraisal Document of the Upper Regional Agricultural Development Programme*. Washington, DC: World Bank, West Africa Department.

World Bank (1987a) *Ghana: Policy Framework Paper*. Washington, DC: World Bank.

World Bank (1987b) *Ghana: Policies and Issues of Structural Adjustment*, Report No. 6635–GH. Washington, DC: World Bank.

World Bank (1993) *Ghana 2000 and Beyond: Setting the Stage for Accelerated Growth and Poverty Reduction*. Washington, DC: World Bank, Africa Regional Office, West Africa Department, February.

World Bank (1994) *Adjustment in Africa: Reforms, Results and the Road Ahead*. New York: Oxford University Press.

World Bank (1995) *World Development Report*. Oxford and New York: Oxford University Press.

Younger, S. (1992) 'Aid and Dutch Disease: Macroeconomic Management when Everybody Loves You', *World Development*, Vol. 20, No. 11.

2 The Political Economy of Reform

E. GYIMAH-BOADI
& RICHARD JEFFRIES

1. Introduction

Study of the politics of economic policy in African states has been dominated over the past 15 years by liberal political economy, and more especially the rational choice theory of Robert Bates (1981). Starting from the assumption that African government leaders are rational maximizers of their political interests, just as economic actors seek to maximize their economic interests, Bates argues that such leaders formulate economic policy primarily on the basis of political expediency. More specifically, since urban groups, such as bureaucrats, industrialists and workers, are better organized and hence have more political clout and influence than agricultural smallholders, African governments tend to intervene in markets, under the guise of industrial development, in order to transfer resources from the latter to the former ('urban bias'). For example, they tax export agriculture via state marketing boards in order to finance the expansion of government employment, maintain overvalued exchange rates in order to cheapen the cost of imports for industrialists and urban consumers, and seek administratively to lower food prices so as to benefit both urban workers and their employers. Such government intervention also generates rents for distribution as political patronage. These policies, Bates argues, not only disadvantage agricultural smallholders but, over the long term, are collectively deleterious. They nonetheless tend to be maintained in the interests of political survival. On this view, one might observe, ideological influences are relatively unimportant compared with short-term political and economic interests, and governments are presented as lacking any significant degree of autonomy and being quite tightly constrained by the local configuration of social forces.

It is proposed in this chapter to explore the utility of the Batesian approach in explaining the politics of economic policy and policy reform in Ghana from 1970 to 1996. In *Markets and States in Tropical Africa,* Bates several times referred to the policies of the Acheampong regime (1972–8) in Ghana as a classic case of urban bias. If this were really the case, however, at least two questions would obviously arise. First, how could policies designed to protect the economic interests of urban groups have resulted, by 1978, in severe impoverishment of the mass of the urban population, arguably indeed in hurting the urban population even more severely than most rural dwellers? Closely related to this, how could it be that policies adopted according to the logic of political rationality resulted in such a political débâcle, with mounting urban political opposition from 1975 to 1978, culminating in the execution by firing squad of Acheampong and seven fellow military officers by the AFRC in June 1979? Second, Bates' argument concluded by emphasizing the political obstacles to policy reform, and more especially to economic liberalization. Yet, a few years after the publication of Bates' book, Rawlings' PNDC regime was to start implementing measures of economic liberalization, and was subsequently to sustain them, without arousing the levels of urban political opposition predicted by Bates' theory. Is it then a basic weakness of 'urban bias' theory, as argued, for example, by Grindle and Thomas (1991), that it has difficulty in explaining policy change, more especially economic liberalization, in terms consistent with its own assumptions?

This chapter will explore the extent to which Bates' theory can be developed and modified, in terms consistent with its own assumptions, in order to meet such explanatory difficulties, and, alternatively, the extent to which it needs to be supplemented by other considerations - for example, the role of ideology — or even to be replaced by other explanatory models.

2.   The Acheampong Regime (1972–8)

The Acheampong regime's policies consisted essentially of a return, with some slight modifications, to the policies of the Nkrumah government after the brief and ineffectual liberal interregnum of the NLC and Busia regimes. It is first necessary, therefore, briefly to review these. The Nkrumah regime had embarked in 1961–6 on a highly ambitious 'dirigiste' strategy of import-substituting industrialization via the establishment of state-owned enterprises. This had been financed partly by milking the cocoa sector and partly by contracting large external loans. As Genoud argued many years ago, a major driving force behind this strategy lay in the ideological influence of a highly statist brand of economic nationalism on the CPP leadership (Genoud, 1969). In addition, it had the political advantage of providing 'jobs for the boys' and hence payoffs for the CPP's most active political constituency, the large numbers of educated and semi-educated emerging from Ghana's schools and universities and demanding employment (Jeffries, 1982). This latter consideration increasingly won out, in practice, over more strictly economic considerations. Owing partly to gross overmanning and chronic mismanagement, the new state-owned industries nearly all proved unprofitable and became a huge burden on public finances (Seidman, 1978). When cocoa production fell, from 572,000 tons in 1964/5 to slightly over 400,000 tons the following year, and was accompanied by a fall in world market prices, the Nkrumah government found itself with a chronic foreign-exchange problem and massive foreign debts. Rather than respond by devaluing the national currency, however, the government resorted to a system of comprehensive import controls. Although intended to give preference to essential capital or intermediate goods, this system was mismanaged by corrupt bureaucrats so as to facilitate the establishment of virtual monopolies in increasingly scarce imported consumer items. Hence the alarming increase in administrative corruption and the rate of inflation in 1964–6 — a pattern which, as we shall see, was to recur in even more extreme form in 1975–8.

Although the NLC military government which succeeded Nkrumah's in 1966 claimed to pursue a more open economic policy, its practical moves in the direction of liberalization were extremely limited. In effect, it simply attempted to improve the administration of import programming. The NLC was doubtless deterred from more radical measures by political considerations. The Nkrumah regime's policies had created large blocs of people — parastatal managers, parastatal employees organized in a relatively powerful trades union movement, urban inhabitants more generally — who had vested interests in maintaining the policy status quo and who subscribed to the nationalist ideology which rationalized this. Hence the public outcry that greeted the NLC's privatization of two state-owned corporations in 1967 (Killick, 1978: 313; Gyimah-Boadi, 1991).

The Busia regime (1969–72) was more determinedly committed to liberalization, partly on ideological grounds and partly because it saw the rural population, and more especially the cocoa farmers of the Ashanti and Brong-Ahafo Regions, as its main political constituency (Austin and Luckham, 1975). Accordingly it undertook the abolition of import controls. It was initially unprepared, however, to take adequate measures, such as tax increases, to contain the demand for imports to levels within the country's import capacity (i.e., to substitute market restraints on demand as an allocative device). This, together with a fall in the world market price for cocoa, resulted in the major balance of payments crisis of 1971. Then, however, the Busia regime did act decisively. The December 1971 devaluation, which would have increased the average landed cedi price of imports by about 90% was, in Killick's words:

> The most decisive break with the past of any action since the 1966 coup. Had it been adequately reinforced by measures at home [the National Development Levy and the cuts in civil servants' perks in the 1971 budget were steps in the right direction here] and had the 1972 coup not supervened, it would, on reasonable assumptions, have brought market forces into play to keep imports within the country's spending capacity, stimulated exports and permitted import and (eventually) exchange controls to be dismantled (Killick, 1978: 303).

Economically desirable as such measures might have been, however, they aroused widespread urban disapproval. The Busia regime had already lost the sympathy of much of the urban population through its summary dismissal of 568 civil servants, its high-handed treatment of the judiciary in the 'Sallah case' and its dissolution of the Trades Union Congress (Austin, 1975; Jeffries, 1978). It was scarcely the most diplomatic of moves, moreover, to announce the devaluation and other austerity measures a few days before Christmas. Colonel Ignatius Acheampong judged, correctly, that a coup d'etat would meet with little opposition in the politically crucial urban areas so long as the incoming regime reversed these measures.

This is not to say that the coup of 13 January 1972 was specifically motivated by opposition to these measures. There is evidence that Acheampong had been planning a coup since 1970, and that he and his fellow conspirators were motivated largely by a sense of grievance at their lack of promotion under the NLC and Busia regimes (Plave Bennett, 1975). The significance of the December 1971 austerity measures lay largely in the fact that Acheampong knew he could now appeal to a wider resentment in the officer corps over reductions in their amenities and allowances. Busia accurately described the coup, therefore, as 'an officers' amenities coup arising from their grievances at my efforts to save money' (*ibid.*). Acheampong and his fellow members of the National Redemption Council seem to have had little in the way of a common political or economic programme. They might well be said to have stumbled into an economic programme largely as a result of their need to rationalize the coup to the Ghanaian (more specifically urban) public. This does not mean, however, that ideological influences were unimportant. In the first place, this rationalization combined ideological elements with more direct appeals to material interests. In the second place, Acheampong himself, having quickly asserted his personal dominance within the junta, seems genuinely to have believed in a statist brand of economic nationalism:

> The political frame of reference which has guided . . . actions and . . . advice in the past two years must be cast into the rubbish heap of history. This means a departure from the laissez-faire so-called free market economy and the institution of effective planning in the allocation and utilization of resources (Plave Bennett, 1975).

We shall return to this point later.

The rationale for the Acheampong takeover in January 1972, then, was that the Busia government's devaluation amounted to a confession of economic failure. It was also presented as an unpatriotic surrender to external pressures. More prosaically, of course, the new NRC government's 44% revaluation of the Cedi staved off the most painful effects of the 1971 devaluation on Ghanaian consumers, and more especially the predominantly urban consumers of imported goods (Chazan, 1983: 162). This decision, or at least the way in which it was presented, was arguably one of most important decisions in Ghana's post-colonial economic history. It placed the Acheampong regime, and to a somewhat lesser extent successor regimes, under a political imperative not to devalue, whatever the economic consequences of failing to do so; for it fostered the 'myth' — still current in 1983 — that to devalue would be to commit political suicide. In turn, the refusal of the Acheampong regime and (with the exception of a minor devaluation under Akuffo in 1978) its successor to devalue until 1983, even as Ghana's balance of payments deteriorated severely after 1974 and even as the gap between official and parallel ('black-market') rates of exchange widened dramatically, was arguably the single most important cause of Ghana's economic catastrophe in the period 1975–83 (Jeffries, 1982).

It is clear, then, that the single most important economic policy of this period was heavily influenced by 'political rationality'. Pursuing Batesian analysis further, one might note that the new military regime faced an especially acute problem of 'legitimacy', given that it had ousted an elected civilian regime which had thus far displayed no intention of refusing to submit itself to popular judgement at the polls in two years' time. From the start, therefore, it was especially concerned to cultivate the support of various urban social groups by attending to their immediate grievances. To organized labour, Acheampong restored the legal privileges which made for a relatively strong trade union movement. To university students, he restored the grants which the previous administration had sought to replace by loans payable on graduation. To senior civil servants, he restored the housing allowances and other privileges which the previous administration had cancelled as part of its austerity measures (Hansen and Collins, 1980).

Throughout his tenure of office, Acheampong sought to maintain an especially close alliance with the trades union movement. The TUC leadership were regularly consulted and gained a number of benefits: the extension of the unions' right to bargain collectively to almost all parastatal employees; a large increase in public sector employment (which was unfortunately largely unproductive and a huge burden on the government's budget); and, in the face of growing shortages and distributional crises in 1975–8, a major role for the TUC and the national unions in distributing basic commodities to their members through a variety of co-operative arrangements. This no doubt helps explain why the unions refused to join in the growing public protests against the government in 1977–8 as the economy collapsed around it (Akwetey, 1994).

The main lines of economic policy in 1972–5 were presented by Acheampong as aiming at 'national self-reliance' — a kind of Nkrumahism without the 'socialist' content. In line with this, his government moved quickly not only to revalue the currency but to repudiate outright all foreign debts tainted with fraud or corruption; embarked on the policy of 'participation' by taking over majority shares in mining and other major industries hitherto owned exclusively by foreign companies; and promulgated the Investment Policy Decree by which the 'Commanding Heights of the Economy' were transferred into the hands of Ghanaians. Such policies, and the economic nationalism informing them, clearly appealed predominantly to the urban population.

To the extent that it concerned itself with agricultural development, the Acheampong regime focused on food production as exemplified in 'Operation Feed Yourself' and in the special encouragement given to expanding rice production in the North. Even here, the predominant concern was arguably to cheapen the cost of food for urban consumers, though in the event such programmes proved of little lasting benefit either to agricultural smallholders or to urban consumers. The strategy chosen to stimulate Northern rice production, for example, via heavily subsidized inputs rather than price incentives, tended to benefit relatively small numbers of politically well-connected large-scale farmers rather than the majority of smaller farmers. As many of these large-scale farmers, including several senior military officers, took to smuggling most of their rice into neighbouring territories for higher prices paid in (unlike the cedi)'a convertible currency, urban consumers failed to benefit from any increased supply to local markets (Antoine, 1984).

Cocoa producers and cocoa production suffered especially severely from the regime's pricing policies and its maintenance of an increasingly overvalued currency. After one increase in the producer price in 1974, the regime refused to raise it further despite generally high and rising world market prices for cocoa. In 1977–8 the real producer price was only 41% of its 1974–5 level, while the London spot price had approximately doubled (Austin, 1996). This was, in the long term, a form of economic sado-masochism since it induced a further decline in the amount of cocoa produced and sold through official channels, export taxes on which provided the bulk of government revenue. Official cocoa exports fell from an average of 430,000 metric tons in the 1969–72 period to 277,000 tons in 1977–8 (Mansfield, 1980). Although this almost certainly reflected a fall in cocoa production, it even more certainly involved a vast increase in the smuggling of cocoa into Côte d'Ivoire and Togo as the real exchange value of the cedi declined and the real value of the Ghanaian producer price plummeted commensurately. Nyanteng has shown that, during most of the 1970s, Ghana's nominal producer price was below that of its neighbours even at official rates of exchange; at parallel (or black-market) rates, the real producer price was generally four or five times higher in Togo and seven or eight times higher in the Côte d'Ivoire (Nyanteng, 1980: 24).[1]

It is easy to see, then, why this combination of policies should be classified by Bates as an extreme form of 'urban bias', and the above analysis has suggested that currying the support of urban groups was indeed an influence in their adoption. The problem, at the level of theory and logic, lies in jumping from this to the conclusion that such policies indicated the dominance of political over economic rationality, that they were adopted merely or primarily for reasons of political survival and expediency. It remains perfectly possible, and actually seems quite likely, that they were adopted also because they were believed, both by Acheampong and by a large section of the Ghanaian intelligentsia, to be economically rational. Acheampong's policies were certainly in line with the developmental notions of much of Ghana's intelligentsia at the time, and it seems likely that he genuinely believed they were the path to prosperity. It was easy, after all, to look back to the Nkrumah period and to see it as, overall, one of very considerable economic achievement. Moreover, it seems excessively reductionist to present this statist brand of economic nationalism as merely a rationalization of the short-term material interests of various urban groups. Acheampong's policies may well have been sadly misconceived, insufficiently appreciative of the importance of encouraging agricultural exports in order to finance this or any other developmental strategy, insufficiently concerned with ensuring the efficiency of state-owned enterprises and (partly reflecting a military 'commandist' mentality) excessively trusting of the power of government regulation, working against the grain of market forces, to deal with Ghana's economic problems. But, if they were nonetheless sincerely believed to be the way to a self-reliant form of national development, this is very different from saying that they were simply designed to provide short-term economic benefits to powerful urban groups, thereby cultivating political support. This point is important for understanding responses to the economic disaster of the later Acheampong period amongst Ghana's intelligentsia, and for appreciating fully the sources and nature of opposition to post-1983 liberalization. Ideological influences, in short, have mattered in the politics of economic policy in Ghana.

Whether such policies are explained in terms of 'urban bias' or rather, as suggested here, in terms of a misconceived, crudely nationalist development strategy, there is, of course, no real difficulty in explaining why they ended up impoverishing much of the urban population. The real wage levels of urban workers, for example, depended heavily on the level of government revenues, which was severely hit by the fall in the volume of cocoa sold through official channels. In this sense, the farmers wreaked their revenge on the state and its employees. In addition, in consequence of Acheampong's refusal to devalue the cedi, the government found itself in a position where it was levying taxes at the official rate of exchange and at official prices, whereas it was having to purchase many of its requirements at black-market rates — approximately ten

---

[1] In an unpublished IMF paper, U. Okonkwo has provided an estimate of the difference in real producer prices as of 1978 which is rather lower than Nyanteng's, probably owing to a different estimate of the black market exchange rate for the cedi; but the substantive point is clear enough.

times higher by 1978. As, at the same time, an increasing proportion of GDP shifted from productive (and relatively easily taxable) to distributive (and relatively non-taxable) activities, the state machinery itself was characterized by dramatic impoverishment. Mansfield (1980) estimates that the government's revenue-to-GDP ratio fell from 20.5% in 1970/71 to 15.5% in 1974/5 and then, precipitously, to 6.5% in 1977/8. It was inevitable, therefore, that the real wages of government employees should fall dramatically. Moreover, the government's inability to finance basic infrastructural maintenance meant that supplies of food from the interior decreased and prices shot up, fuelled by the government's inflationary monetary policies. One could, of course, elaborate almost endlessly on the ways in which excessively urban-biased policies proved, over time, self-defeating.

It is more important here to note that this was not how most urban Ghanaians appeared to perceive the problem. Most urban Ghanaians attributed their increasing immiseration to the phenomenon of 'kalabule' — embezzlement, corruption and 'cheating' by, for example, market traders as well as government officials (Ocquaye, 1980). Such corruption and embezzlement did, of course, increase phenomenally in the later years of the regime and greatly aggravated the growing gap between rich and poor as well as the deterioration of government finances (Jeffries, 1989: 75–98). Indeed, Gareth Austin (1996) has recently argued that what he terms 'trade-off arguments', such as 'urban bias' — according to which governments trade off their own interests against economic growth — cannot adequately explain economic decline of the kind which occurred in Ghana in 1975–83 as distinct from mere economic stagnation. Such economic decline can scarcely be politically rational, and must be explained in terms of a shift towards 'kleptocracy', which in turn results from the effect of political instability in shortening policymakers' time horizons. It deprives governments of the resources they need for patronage and also highlights the political impotence of the civilian population.

There is clearly something in this. More specifically, Austin is surely correct in arguing that the growing corruption of the later Acheampong years was not politically purposeful. It was not designed to maintain broad-based patronage structures, but rather to benefit small numbers of cronies. Nonetheless, Austin arguably underestimates the importance of misconceived economic policy itself in generating both economic decline and the growth of kleptocracy/*kalabule*. The distinction between economic stagnation and economic decline during this period is, after all, largely coterminous with the distinction between francophone and anglophone countries (with the notable exception, of course, of oil-rich Nigeria). This is because the anglophone states had their own currencies. Liberation from the requirement to maintain convertibility of the domestic currency also freed them to inflict more damage on their local economies. In Ghana more specifically, Acheampong was able consistently to refuse to devalue during this period, and at the same time to remedy revenue shortages simply by instructing the Central Bank to print more money, precisely because Ghana, unlike the members of the CFA franc zone, possessed an independent Central Bank and its own currency (Teal, 1986).

So far as growing kleptocracy/kalabule is concerned, Austin quite rightly argues that we need to explain this process. The increasing political insecurity of the regime — which he emphasizes — developed, however, with economic failure and therefore needs to be referred back to economic policy. Moreover, Austin arguably seeks to attribute too much to the nature of military rule as such and to Acheampong's 'self-interested' motivation. Massively corrupt as Acheampong and other government leaders eventually became, and indeed so engrossed in self-enrichment as to become diverted from careful calculations of political survival, the evidence does not suggest that they initially formulated economic policy with such venal intentions. Joe Appiah, admittedly a not entirely disinterested observer, described Acheampong, shortly after he came to power, thus: 'My first impression of him was favorable; a young, dynamic and religious soldier with a sense of mission' (Appiah, 1990: 336).[2] Richard Rathbone described the NRC of 1972–5 as 'a

---

[2] Appiah accepted the position of Ambassador Plenipotentiary in the Acheampong government.

boy-scoutish CPP in army uniforms', and the almost universal impression at the time was one of reasonable honesty and patriotic purposefulness (Rathbone, 1978: 30).

Why, then, did Acheampong and his colleagues in government become so corrupt? This was largely, one might argue, because of the way in which government policies and regulations, initially adopted for reasons of 'urban bias' and economic nationalism, structured incentives so as to encourage rent-seeking and thereby over time induced a process of political decay. There were, after all, enormous windfall profits to be made out of gaining access to import licences and to foreign exchange at official rates of exchange, then selling imported goods on parallel markets at rates of exchange five to ten times higher. Over time, government officials charged with allocating import licences and foreign exchange understandably started to demand a share of such profits, in the form of kickbacks, for themselves. Members of the junta, realizing what was happening, then attempted to monopolize such allocation as far as possible in their own hands. The theory of 'the increased political discount rate' is also relevant here (Levi, 1988: 32–3). This discount rate is an expression of how much present value future returns have for the government. As economic deterioration proceeded and government leaders began to feel increasingly politically insecure, the government's political discount rate mounted and government leaders focused increasingly on gaining immediate and tangible economic benefits, discounting longer-term economic and political benefits. Government turned into a get-rich-quick racket. Similar policies arguably had similar effects in quite a number of African states.

Such a model of the development of kleptocracy is in some ways quite closely aligned to Bates' 'urban bias' theory and might at first sight appear to be simply supplementary to it. Bates, after all, argues that certain types of policy tend over time to be collectively deleterious, ultimately hurting the urban groups they were initially intended to benefit. What is being argued here is, on one level, simply that, under certain circumstances, the same policies tend to be even more deleterious. The theoretical implications are, however, more far-reaching. Bates' theory is premised on the notion that governments behave in a consistently politically rational manner. What is being argued here is that this is clearly not always the case. Governments may shift away from considerations of political rationality to those of self-enrichment; and a Batesian theoretical framework cannot itself provide an adequate explanation of why or when this occurs.

Students and professionals led the opposition to Acheampong, demanding a return to civilian rule. A students' demonstration in May 1976 initiated a series of confrontations, including a notably effective professionals' strike in July 1977, courageously maintained and repeated in the face of quite brutal government repression (Chazan, 1983: 234–74). In September 1976, Acheampong first mooted the idea of a 'union government' (UNIGOV) which, he claimed, had suddenly come to him in a dream. He then had to be pressured, however, into taking each next step: to appoint the Koranteng-Addow Committee to formulate a more specific proposal in the light of civilian views; then to agree to a referendum on this proposal; then to name a date (I July 1979) for military withdrawal.

Through all this, and with the economy collapsing around him, Acheampong steadfastly maintained his belief that no-one could govern better and that, even more certainly, no-one else was going to get the chance. Deliberately vague as government presentations of 'UNIGOV' invariably were, the notion was commonly perceived as a thinly disguised attempt to limit (non-party) civilian representation to one element, along with the military and the police, in a tripartite structure and to ensure Acheampong's own 'election' as president. One might perhaps be forgiven for suggesting that his opponents were spurred on not only by their anger at his destruction of their country's economy, but also by the infuriating way in which he consistently insulted their intelligence. The whole show became increasingly farcical. Public meetings of the People's Movement for Freedom and Justice (PMFJ), formed by leading civilian political leaders to canvass for a 'No' vote in the referendum, were broken up by variously titled groups of pro-government activists, the financing of which must have accounted for a substantial part of that year's 135% increase in the money supply. At one stage, an American evangelist, Clare Prophet, was wheeled out to declare that 'UNIGOV' was clearly divinely inspired because its tripartite structure corresponded to the Trinity. The Electoral Commissioner was obliged to flee for his life on the night of the referendum when he tried to insist on the legal arrangements for the counting of votes. It was scarcely surprising, therefore, that opposition supporters refused to accept the declared results — supposedly producing a majority in favour of UNIGOV by 54 to 46%.

Thankfully this was to prove Acheampong's last real stand. Following a wave of protests and detentions, he was displaced on 5 July 1978 by a 'palace coup' led by Lt. General Fred Akuffo, who promised, more credibly than his predecessor, an early but orderly return to civilian rule. The student-professional alliance thus achieved a notable degree of success and certainly demonstrated that civilian attitudes remained a force of some consequence in Ghanaian politics.

3.   The Akuffo, AFRC and Limann Regimes (1978–81)

The brief Akuffo regime (Supreme Military Council 2, 5 July 1978 to 4 June 1979) had two public faces. On the one hand, it implemented a number of well-intentioned if unpopular economic measures (including a 60% devaluation of the cedi), released the political detainees, dismissed the most notoriously racketeering members of the previous regime (including Maj. Gen. E. Utuka, commander of the border guard, later to be executed by the Armed Forces Revolutionary Council), appointed a Constituent Assembly to formulate a new constitution and, from 1 January 1979, legalized the formation of political parties to contest general elections scheduled for June. On the other hand, it did nothing to bring these same racketeers to account (Chazan, 1983: 275–74). Although Akuffo had sought to justify his coup on the grounds that Acheampong had been running the government as a 'one-man show', the latter was merely stripped of his military rank and confined to his home village. None of his assets were to be confiscated by the state and no legal moves instituted against him. Increasingly, Akuffo's rationale was seen as a ruse on the part of the members of the Supreme Military Council 2 to exonerate themselves from a responsibility they shared. As the date of the elections approached, rumours spread to the effect that deals had been struck with the main political parties guaranteeing immunity from any legal proceedings after the handover of power.

The very imminence of the return to civilian rule brought to a head feelings of injustice and frustration which had been mounting within the military. The distribution of privilege had become as grossly unequal within the armed forces as in society at large. The ranks had suffered the hardships caused by the regime of pillage and, in addition, found themselves the butt of insults directed by civilians against the military as a whole. It was in this situation that Flt.-Lt. Jerry Rawlings was arrested for leading a mutiny on the night of 15 May. The state-owned press reported his trial at which the prosecuting attorney recounted Rawlings' motives with evident sympathy. On the morning of 4 June he was sprung from gaol in the course of what was less an organized coup than a general uprising of the ranks. Later in the day he was nominated by them as chairman of the Armed Forces Revolutionary Council (AFRC) (Okeke, 1982; Ocquaye, 1980).

Insofar as there was a shared conception of the aims of the coup, therefore, this was provided by Rawlings' supposed views as recounted at his trial:

> People were dying of starvation in the teeth of a few well-fed who even had a chance of growing fatter, and when the economy of this country was being dominated by foreigners, especially Arabs and Lebanese whom successive governments had failed to question about their nefarious activities. The first accused then started talking about widespread corruption in high places . . . [which] could be remedied only by going the Ethiopian way (Okeke, 1982: 130).

Rawlings appeared to prefer a non-violent spring-clean both within the military and in society at large. It was initially very uncertain, however, not only to worried observers but also to Rawlings himself, just how much direction over the purging process he would be able to exert.

Prior to his court-martial, he had been a virtually unknown air force pilot. As of 4 June, the whole command structure within the army had broken down. Rawlings' control of the spring-cleaning process was, then, at least until the end of June, highly uncertain. He did, nevertheless, manage to establish certain basic principles and general guidelines for the punishment of 'exploiters' which roughly reflected his own sense of what was just. In somewhat schematic fashion, this might be summarized as follows. He distinguished between the prime responsibility of a few government leaders, the opportunistic self-enrichment of a larger group of senior military and bureaucratic officials together with local and foreign businessmen, and the more or less unwilling participation of very many ordinary people in the *kalabule* system. A crucial turning-point here was his negotiation of an understanding with rank-and-file leaders that he would agree to the execution of eight senior military officers, including three former heads of state — Afrifa, Acheampong and Akuffo — only on condition that there were to be no further capital punishments. Equally crucial in consolidating civilian support was his early promise that the period of spring-cleaning would be quite brief, and that the elections for the return to civilian rule would proceed as scheduled (on 18 June) (Jeffries, 1989: 84–6).

Rawlings sought to channel the 'revolution' along socially constructive lines by speaking frequently on the theme of the need for moral reform, for greater honesty and integrity in government leaders, and for the masses to hold government to account by taking their civil rights and duties more seriously than in the past. Ghanaians, he said, had been 'hitting their heads on the ground like lizards' because they were cowards, closing their eyes to the evils perpetrated against them. Accordingly, he is sometimes criticized for the naivety of his 'moralizing' during the AFRC period, and for his failure to recognize or address the structural causes of kalabule and economic decline (for example, Hansen and Collins, 1980). There is an important element of truth here: the AFRC's equation of high commodity prices with 'exploitation' was very naive, and its attempts to produce immediate economic benefits for the man in the street simply back-fired. The forced sale of stocks of imported goods at controlled prices proved a once-for-all benefit as these stocks were not replenished. Similarly, the supply of foodstuffs from the rural areas virtually dried up at the height of the soldiers' attempt to enforce low controlled prices in the markets. On the other hand, the AFRC was in power far too briefly to be able to implement any distinctive macroeconomic policies.

In the remarkably free and fair elections of June 1979, the People's National Party (constructed on the remnants of the old Nkrumahist CPP organization) won a somewhat uninspiring victory (Jeffries, 1980; Chazan, 1983: 284–300). Rawlings handed over power to its victorious presidential candidate, Dr. Hilla Limann, in September, making it clear that the new government's readiness to uphold the principles of the AFRC revolution would be closely monitored. The most pressing task facing the new administration was clearly to rescue the economy from further collapse. Yet, confronted with the need for bold and radical decisions, the Limann government offered mostly incremental measures and apparent lethargy.

The main economic initiatives of the Limann government were twofold (Chazan, 1983: 311–20). First, it sought to improve government finances by introducing new taxes and reducing government expenditures, which hardly endeared it to a population which had already endured severe deprivation, and which seemed especially unjust when the parliamentarians proceeded, in September 1980, to raise their own salaries to 4,500 cedis a month (the minimum wage at the time was 4 cedis a day). Secondly, it sought to attract increased foreign investment and large allotments of foreign aid, neither of which was forthcoming, given the parlous state of the economy and the government's refusal to accede to IMF stabilization measures, including most importantly the demand for a substantial devaluation of the cedi.

Limann was admittedly in a very real political dilemma here, fearing that this would precipitate the fall of his regime. His government's control over the army was tenuous and left-wing groups, such as the June 4th Movement (backed by Rawlings), had started to mobilize from soon after the handover as though in readiness for an assault. The regime was also internally divided among three main factions: the socialist hardliners, the old guard of CPP patronage politicians and the new guard of younger parliamentarians calling for a more technocratic orientation. This obviously made agreement on decisive action difficult. Nonetheless, had Limann bitten the bullet and signed an IMF agreement at an early stage, fresh from his electoral victory, his government might well have survived any opposition to this measure. Certainly, without it, his economic policies, as outlined above, were doomed to make little impact on the scale of the economic crisis.

As it was, mass living standards continued to plummet. This became all the more intolerable when scandals broke revealing that some government and party leaders were engaged in self-enrichment through corruption and embezzlement. Finally, the Limann government's inept attempts first to buy off and then to disparage Jerry Rawlings, to use intelligence operatives to harass him and his close associates, even to denigrate the whole AFRC episode, simply backfired, lending a touch of martyrdom to his already heroic popular status. Notwithstanding Rawlings' statement in 1979 that he did not wish to be 'a time-bomb behind a civilian government', few were surprised, therefore, when he re-assumed power on 31 December 1981.

4. Rawlings-Provisional National Defence Council and National Democratic Congress (1982–96)

There were two distinct phases to the Rawlings-PNDC economic policies. The first dramatic but rather short-lived phase was a distributionist-cum-populist mobilization one — occurring from the beginning of the PNDC and ending in late 1983. This involved the imposition and tightening of controls on prices of imported consumer items and locally produced food, rent, and transport fares, energetically enforced by militant elements of the Worker's/People's Defence Committees — along the lines begun in the 4 June interregnum and continued in a modified form in the 'vigilante' system of the Limann administration. The goods of hapless traders accused by vigilantes of hoarding and overpricing were confiscated and sold off to the public at reduced prices. In somewhat extreme but certainly dramatic cases, traders' sheds and tables were destroyed and whole markets (tagged as 'dens of corruption' and symbols of the discredited commercial order) were razed to the ground (similar to the fate suffered by the Makola market in 1979). There was also an effort to institutionalize the new order of populist and ostensibly equitable distribution of consumer goods through the newly created people's and co-operative shops. And in actions subsequently backed by decrees, militant elements imposed rent reductions and ordered landlords to rent out unoccupied rooms (Rothchild and Gyimah-Boadi, 1989).

There was also an anti-corruption drive which included vetting of lifestyles and investigation into sources of individual income and wealth — through newly created extra-judicial bodies such as the Public Tribunals, Citizen's Vetting Committee and the National Investigations Committee. These bodies adopted a decidedly populist tone and delivered what an enthusiastic supporter described as 'simple, straightforward justice', meting out heavy and sometimes unusually cruel and/or humiliating penalties (such as public whipping and the carrying of human excreta) (*ibid.*).

In a mood similar to that of the early Acheampong/NRC government's unilateral cancellation of external debts, the Rawlings regime declared its intention to confront international capital/ imperialism and its perceived hold on the Ghanaian economy. In the period under review, leading spokesmen took every opportunity to denounce international capital and its representatives in Ghana as well as Western countries in general as malevolent 'imperialist forces'. Foreign companies were threatened with nationalization. However, very little came of this except the takeover of the Ghana Textile Company by its workers and the apparently successful renegotiation of the agreement between the government and Kaiser Aluminum over the latter's Ghana-based subsidiary — Volta Aluminum Company (VALCO) (Rothchild and Gyimah-Boadi, 1989).

A major component of this hyper-nationalist mood was the new rulers' determination to forge ahead with spontaneous and self-reliant national development, symbolized principally by a resolve against taking IMF and World Bank loans and against the devaluation of the cedi that this would almost certainly entail. In lieu of external help, much hope was placed on the possibility of economic renewal through labour mobilization and conscription. Students from the three universities and other institutions of higher learning left their campuses, turned themselves into task forces, and commandeered private bulk haulage vehicles to evacuate cocoa and other cash crops locked up in the hinterland. Students, People's Defence Committees, Workers' Defence Committees, and other popular organizations mobilized themselves, and forced private contractors and others to participate in the rehabilitation of roads and other broken-down public infrastructure. There was also talk of rounding up the idle youth, putting them through character remoulding programmes and directing them into agricultural activities (Rothchild and Gyimah-Boadi, 1989).

To combat inflation, mop up excess liquidity and, at the same time, punish those rightly or wrongly perceived as having exploited the common people, possibly in collaboration with imperialist and multinational interests, the government embarked on a confiscation of ¢50.00 notes — the largest denomination of the local currency at the time. Individual and company bank accounts deemed by the regime to be too high were also ordered to be frozen.

Some of the actions associated with programmes in the first phase of Rawlings — PNDC economic policies were certainly dramatic. In their worst manifestations, they imposed unspeakable cruelties and egregious indignities on many innocent Ghanaians. Among other perverse consequences, some cadres of the revolution used them as a pretext for settling personal scores. The emphasis on distribution and populist mobilization certainly reflected the emergence and ideological influence of a critical mass of left-wing intelligentsia. Thus the claim by Ahiakpor (1985) and others that the decade preceding the coup of 31 December 1981 had seen a significant increase in the number of Ghanaian intellectuals adhering to neo-Marxist dependency theories of development and underdevelopment is largely true. Radical intellectuals, based in the universities, notably the Law Faculty of the University of Ghana, and in the national student movement and the political organizations dominated by them or their students/henchmen, such as the June Fourth Movement, New Democratic Movement and Kwame Nkrumah Revolutionary Guards, had certainly been influential in the policies and programmes of the early PNDC period (Hansen, 1987; Folson, 1993; Ray, 1986). These individuals and the political organizations in which they prevailed were most probably also influential, if not dominant, in the organizations that came to symbolize early PNDC populism and became the chief implementers of its policies — the People's and Workers' Defence Committees (Hansen, 1987; Yeebo, 1985; Ray, 1986).

The pursuit of populist mobilization policies also reflected Rawlings' own personal convictions and inclinations as a 'Robin Hood moralist' (Jeffries, 1982, 1991; Ahiakpor, 1991). His statement 'So long as there is no justice, I would dare say "Let there be no peace"' was often quoted with relish by the revolutionaries and enthusiastically cited to justify some of the militant anti-market and confiscatory programmes mentioned above. Indeed, the short-term effect of the radical populist measures and the anti-corruption drive undertaken in the Rawlings-AFRC interregnum (such as the strict enforcement of official controls on prices, rents and fares, the sale of goods confiscated from traders) seemed to provide a concrete basis for hope that the Ghanaian political economy could be reformed along somewhat radical lines. It was also helpful to the cause of populism and of opposition to the political and economic status quo that there was considerable frustration with the PNP and its perceived incompetence and alleged corruption as captured in the writings on that period by Chazan (1983: 306–24) and Ninsin (1985: 93–110).

However, it is also important to note that, apart from the intensity and zeal of their implementation, the populist policies were not all that novel. They were broadly consistent with the ideologies of economic development (a mixture of economic nationalism, vague pan-Africanism and socialism) that had been in vogue since the days of Nkrumah and held with varying degrees of conviction and coherence among the Ghanaian intelligentsia, technocrats and middle classes. Such ideological currents had underlain the socialist reconstruction policies of Nkrumah in the early and mid-1960s (Genoud, 1969; Killick, 1978). They had also inspired the opposition to and eventual abandonment of neo-liberal reforms in the NLC era, impelled the Busia government to retreat from economic liberalism/laissez-faire and, most notably, inspired the anti-market policies of the Acheampong era — beginning with the unilateral repudiation of external debt (Frimpong-Ansah, 1991: 94-114; Huq, 1989). The resort to strict rationing of essential goods recalls the rationing of import licences introduced in the late Nkrumah period, 'the festivals of the oppressed' in the 4 June interregnum, and the 'vigilante' system under the Limann administration. The attack on traders in the early PNDC period was foreshadowed by the draconian decrees against smuggling, hoarding and overpricing enacted in the Acheampong period and enforced largely through regular courts (Magistrate Maximus Atta Fynn and his draconian sentences on persons convicted of 'selling above the control price'). The razing to the ground of markets had its precedent in the burning of Makola in 1979. Similarly, populist mobilization in the early PNDC era was reminiscent of "Operation Feed Yourself" and other schemes in which students were deployed as labour brigades to harvest sugarcane at Dahwenya. One may agree with Maxwell Owusu who argues that this recurrent pattern of militant and populist phenomena is a 'ritual of rebellion' deeply rooted in Ghanaian traditions of 'popular anti-colonial and anti-chief protests going back to the early period of colonial rule, including the Asafo uprisings of the interwar period in Ghana' (Owusu, 1996, 1989, 1986).

The second and more sustained phase of economic policy reforms began roughly from late 1983. It involved the liberalization of foreign exchange, which began in 1983 with a series of large, both disguised and open devaluations of the local currency, and proceeded to the decriminalization of foreign-exchange transactions (through the institution of privately operated forex bureaux from 1988). It also involved the removal of price controls, so that by 1991 only eight goods (imported rice, sugar, baby food, cement, textiles, drugs, matches and soap) were subject to price regulations; and, even then, this regulation was administered jointly by the statutory Prices and Incomes Board, traders and producers, using guidelines established by a tripartite committee of government, employers and trade unions. In addition, imports were liberalized through the abolition of the previous system of import licensing, replaced by import declaration; the tariff structure was significantly simplified; some tariff rates were reduced; and the level of protection was moderated. There was also a liberalization of exports, including schemes under which exporters of timber and the so-called non-traditional commodities/crafts were allowed to retain part of the foreign exchange earned by their exports, in addition to receiving tax concessions. The state made a marked retreat from some of the advanced positions it had taken in the economy through a privatization programme in which a number of state-provided services were subcontracted to private operators and most of the country's over 300 parastatals were earmarked for divestiture (Gyimah-Boadi, 1991). Finally, the government enacted relatively liberal investment and trading codes, aimed at attracting private investors.

It is important to note that commitment to neo-liberal economic policies has remained quite strong in the post-PNDC period, in an era of significant political liberalization in which constitutional and multi-party government has replaced quasi-military rule. The sale of half of the government's shares in Ashanti Goldfields Corporation in 1994 and the placement of high-profile SOEs on the privatization list, the restructuring of the investment promotion bureaucracy and the increase in the number of high-profile official tours abroad to drum up foreign investment, all underscore the continued desire to press ahead with neo-liberal reforms.

What were the reasons for the so-called 'U-turn' in PNDC economic policy, and how far are these reasons compatible with Bates' theory? One might well argue, in line with Bates, that persistence with urban-biased policies plus popular mobilization had clearly become politically irrational by 1983. Such policies were clearly failing to deal with the deep crisis in which the Ghanaian political economy had become mired. This failure, together with concrete problems and exigencies of the period — such as the severe drought and accompanying famine in 1982/ 3, the bush fires that destroyed export and food crops, and the repatriation of about one million Ghanaians from Nigeria in early 1983 — arguably threatened the very survival of the nascent PNDC regime. Such developments, moreover, produced what Callaghy has called 'the trough factor' (Callaghy, 1990). The very depth of the crisis concentrated government minds wonderfully and also induced a greater degree of popular readiness for a radical change in economic strategy.

More specifically, it became increasingly clear that economic recovery was impossible without large-scale foreign assistance. The PNDC had approached the Soviet bloc for help but had been advised to go to the IMF. In the end, it felt that it had no alternative but to do so, and to adopt the necessary liberalizing policies, if it was to survive. With regime, and arguably even national, survival at stake, it did not require the political ascendancy of a 'virtuous coalition' or a 'technocratic change team' to stumble into neo-liberal economic reforms. Bates' analysis admittedly focuses on the role of domestic interest groups in keeping regimes in power. It would be consistent with his general approach, however, to argue that external interests became major players in Ghanaian politics at this stage, as economic crisis and indebtedness increased the government's dependence on such interests.

It is questionable, however, whether such an explanation is really accurate or genuinely consistent with Bates' emphasis on short-term political rationality as the motive for government policies. Over the long term one might readily agree that economic liberalization in alliance with external interests offered the best hope for the regime's survival. In the short term, however, it entailed enormous political risks; and the regime did, after all, possess alternatives of a sort. Sad as the state of the economy undoubtedly was, it was arguably no worse than that of, for example, Sierra Leone, where the regime staggered on for several more years, refusing to implement economic reforms. Economies can always sink lower, and, where regimes are only concerned with immediate political survival, frequently do. Rawlings' decision to go to the IMF was clearly an act of pragmatism rather than of ideological conversion, but it was effectively taken in late 1982 (when Kwesi Botchwey initiated negotiations) rather than as a desperate response to the crisis of 1983, and seems to have been motivated by a genuine concern to engineer economic recovery. Insofar as political considerations were involved, these were most probably long-term rather than short-term. If the notion of political rationality is extended to cover long-term as well as short-term considerations, then it obviously becomes quite vacuous.

Predictably enough from a Batesian standpoint, the implementation of neo-liberal economic reforms presented massive political challenges for the PNDC government. The retreat from leftwing/populist economic policies created considerable disaffection among its popular class supporters. Rightly or wrongly, they felt that the change in the direction of economic policy (from populist and socialist mobilization) amounted to a 'betrayal of the principles of the 31 December revolution' (Ahiakpor, 1991). They became increasingly embittered over the PNDC's resort to 'negative' instrumentalities of demand management. They were particularly disappointed by the government's decision to devalue the local currency, and resentful of the efforts to control the wage bill through a programme of public sector job retrenchment and restraints on wages, withdrawal of subsidies on basic consumer goods (notably, petroleum products), and the introduction of user fees for state-provided services such as education, health, water and electricity. The student fraction of the populist front complained bitterly about inadequate stipends and mounted largely futile protests over the partial commercialization of their board and lodging facilities. The leaders of these groups were to denounce the economic reform programme as a 'betrayal of the revolution' (Rothchild and Gyimah-Boadi, 1986), and elements within the front were reported to have organized counter-coups in a bid to overturn the 'thermidorean' trend (Ray, 1986).

While the economic reform programme antagonized the PNDC's popular class supporters, it was not necessarily supported by, nor did it mollify, the other articulate classes in Ghanaian society, at least in the short run. Business people resented aspects of the neo-liberal reform measures such as the increased cost of foreign exchange and imported production inputs (associated with the devaluation of the currency), exposure to rigorous international competition following the liberalization of trade, and taxation in the name of mobilization of domestic revenue, which they perceived as extortionate. The managerial and professional fraction of this group tended to complain about the loss of state subsidies to which they had previously enjoyed privileged access, and the presence of numerous expatriate consultants on ERP assignments from the World Bank, the IMF, and the UN. These new grievances were added to the old ones arising from the populist outbursts of the early months of the Rawlings-PNDC 'revolution'. Elements from this camp also reportedly attempted to effect their own coup(s). The fact remains, however, that neither this group, with its seething resentment of Rawlings and his regime, nor the disaffected working class was able to topple the regime or even present any very effective organized opposition to the reforms. The long-held belief that economic liberalization would be politically ruinous in a country whose political configuration was dominated by urban interests proved to be vastly exaggerated.

This was largely, no doubt, because of the unusual degree of political skill and determination with which the Rawlings-PNDC regime managed the reform process. Allowing for a degree of oversimplification, the principal strategies employed can be summarized as follows: carefully calibrated and largely symbolic gestures to appease the populist, nationalist, and moralist supporters of the regime, as manifested in a radical foreign policy that emphasized solidarity with socialist countries (such as Romania, Cuba, Nicaragua, and East Germany up until the collapse of the Eastern bloc in 1989, and radical African countries such as Libya and Burkina Faso under Thomas Sankara); radical pan-Africanism which echoed the years of Nkrumah and the early Acheampong/NRC period; high-profile anti-corruption drives against the elites in an effort to sustain the impression that the regime was working hard to defend the interests of the common man; and regular claims to the virtues of 'probity and accountability' on the part of members of the regime. These were combined with limited measures to appease the middle class, such as opening up the membership of the defence committees to the elite and curbing their anti-establishment militancy. The regime also co-opted some members of the elite, for example, traditional rulers such as Nandom Na Polkuu Konkuu Pulku Chiri IV, Agogohene Nana (Lawyer) Akuoko Sarpong and Agona Nsabene Nana (Lawyer) Obuadum, and ex-politicians such as J. Y. Jantuah and J. A. Kuffour.

Complementing clever politics, symbolic gestures, appeasement, and co-optation were an assortment of authoritarian practices. These included quasi-corporatist arrangements involving pro-government and/or government-sponsored organizations such as the June 4th Movement, 31st December Women's Movement, Ghana Private Road Transport Union, and Mobisquads of the National Mobilization Programmes. Such organizations remained 'organs of the revolution' long after the 'revolution' had been abandoned. The crucial area of wage policy was managed by the Tripartite Committee of the Prices and Incomes Board, with representatives of the Ghana Employers' Association, the Trades Union Congress and the Ministry of Finance. The Trades Union Congress remained nominally independent but was subject to government pressure and to close surveillance by pro-PNDC activists so as to ensure the election of sympathetic senior officials. PNDC strategy also entailed extensive use of repressive measures such as detention without trial of government critics, and kangaroo tribunals which not infrequently meted out cruel and unusual punishment, including execution for political offences (Gyimah-Boadi, 1990; Ocquaye, 1993: 154–75; Boahen, 1989). Tight control of the media stifled expressions of criticism. The *Free Press* was closed down in 1983 and the *Catholic Standard* banned in late 1985 after ridiculing the government, leaving the *Pioneer* as the only newspaper that offered an alternative perspective on national affairs (Nugent, 1995).

Too much emphasis on such repressive measures would, however, be misleading. The PNDC regime, and more especially Rawlings himself, enjoyed a substantial reservoir of goodwill amongst the Ghanaian masses, in the urban even more than the rural areas at this stage. Relatively few ordinary people placed much faith in the nostrums of the socialist intellectuals, and to focus on the latter's disenchantment with the regime's turning to the IMF is to misrepresent popular attitudes more generally. Many ordinary people still saw Rawlings as 'our man' and were willing to trust in his doing his best for them. A great deal of the regime's surveillance was done for it by pro-Rawlings enthusiasts. This factor is arguably just as important as repression in explaining the relatively low level of overt resistance to the economic reforms.

By this combination of measures, then, the PNDC regime developed a relatively strong, authoritarian state. It would be a mistake to draw too close an analogy here with the strong states of the East Asian NICs. The Ghanaian state continued to lack the bureaucratic reliability, efficiency and capacity of such states. It did, however, serve to provide the Ministry of Finance with a high degree of insulation from domestic political pressures and to cow potential political opposition. This certainly furnishes a more accurate explanation of how the PNDC government was able to sustain implementation of neo-liberal reforms than the Bates thesis. Quite contrary to what a Batesian logic would lead one to expect, the reforms were not, for several years at least, backed by an effective coalition. Though it may be argued that the publication of a *Rural Manifesto* (Ministry of Rural Development and Co-operatives, 1984) provided an early hint of the pro-rural course the regime planned to chart, and sponsorship of the ill-fated Ghana Federation of Agricultural Co-operatives (Togbe Sasraku's GHAFACOOPS) represented a nascent attempt to give structure to the evolving alliance between the PNDC and the rural farmers, coalition building did not prove possible in the early phase of the neo-liberal reforms. The farmers proved difficult to organize politically, whilst, as noted above, there was very little in those reforms that appealed to the popular class or the left-wing intellectual supporters of the regime, and the middle class/elite remained aloof and mostly hostile. The prevailing politics of 'revolutionary populism' and authoritarianism had to suffice, at least until the late 1980s.

By the late 1980s, however, coalition building had become both possible and necessary. The economic reforms had survived long enough to have engendered a fairly large coterie of beneficiaries. There was also a clear need to legitimize a regime that appeared to have outlived its 'provisional' status and had to respond to the growing external and domestic pressure to democratize. Seen in this light, the local government reforms, decentralization and the establishment of district assemblies in 1987–9 represented the most serious effort at coalition building by the Rawlings/PNDC regime to date (Gyimah-Boadi, 1990; Ayee, 1993; Nugent, 1995). The reforms, officially presented as the first politico-administrative steps in the construction of a national edifice of 'true democracy' from the bottom up, provided an opportunity for the regime to penetrate the countryside and to tap the latent support it believed it had in those areas. The new (elected and appointed) assembly members, grateful to the PNDC for their elevation, the government-appointed District Secretaries and the local branches of the revolutionary organs (such as the Committees for the Defence of the Revolution whose District Organizing Assistants entered the assemblies as government appointees, the 31st December Women's Movement and the Mobisquads) had the potential to serve as the nucleus of a Rawlings-PNDC political machine in the rural areas.

The local government reforms were also used to build on the process of rapprochement begun in the mid-1980s when elements of the middle and upper strata of Ghanaian society became included in the regime. The Rawlings government cleverly used its power to appoint one-third of the members of the Assemblies to tap into the conventional national and local patron-client networks. Thus, government appointees to the assemblies included many traditional rulers (such as Baffour Osei Akoto, the chief linguist of the Asantehene and a stalwart of the anti-Nkrumah opposition in the 1950s), commercial farmers, traders, professionals, religious leaders, retired public servants, and even politicians from the banned political parties. The presence of establishment professionals and statesmen in the PNDC political hierarchy was also expanded at this time (with the inclusion of people like A. K. Yankey, General Secretary of the Trades Union Congress; K. B. Asante, ex-civil servant, politician in the Third Republic and, for a very brief period, a Secretary in the early PNDC days; A. A. Munufie, minister in the Busia-Progress Party government; and Osagyefo Nana (Dr.) Agyeman Badu, Paramount Chief of Dormaa on key national commissions and bodies). Thus, if the PNDC cobbled a coalition together in the latter years of its eleven-year rule, it was not all that different from the coalitions that backed other post-colonial Ghanaian regimes — although the presence of ex-populists and members of non-establishment societal organizations gave it a somewhat different flavour. The main difference lay, of course, in its appeal to rural dwellers and the PNDC government's attempt to capitalize, politically, on its redress of urban bias.

This might well help to explain Rawlings' agreement, after a period of initial resistance, to return to multi-party politics. International pressure was obviously a major factor, but Rawlings was the more prone to give in to this after the government's intelligence networks revealed extensive support for the regime in the countryside. Farmers might be difficult to organize as effective coalition partners in an authoritarian regime, but their votes could contribute a great deal to the democratic legitimization of a government. In both the 1992 and 1996 elections, Rawlings' victory resulted largely from the strength of his support in the rural areas, and this might in turn be attributed in large part to improved agricultural producer prices and to the focusing of development projects in rural rather than urban areas. Victory could also be taken to represent, in part, a reward for the fact that the two Rawlings regimes have moved Ghana closer to a 'developmental state' — at least in the managerial sense of a return to macroeconomic stability, enhancement of state revenue, augmentation of the manpower base of the state, and rehabilitation/expansion of infrastructure, especially the extension of the national electricity grid to the Brong Ahafo and Northern Regions (Gyimah-Boadi, 1995a; Jeffries, 1993).

Such a 'political economy' analysis of the election results needs, however, to be qualified quite heavily. The voting pattern in the two elections was hardly an unambiguous reflection of 'winners' and 'losers' of the neo-liberal economic reforms. The pro-Rawlings vote in the rural areas was relatively strong in both elections, but it was weak among such reform-beneficiaries as the cocoa farmers of the Ashanti Region (Jeffries and Thomas, 1993; Jeffries, 1996; Gyimah-Boadi, 1995b, 1997). Political opposition to Rawlings, moreover, appears to have turned on factors other than economic policies and the distribution of benefits therefrom. Many stalwarts of the domestic capitalist class, who were presumed beneficiaries of this capitalist restoration of the economy, including the so-called 'mobitel men', were active in the opposition camp (Hart and Gyimah-Boadi, 1997). Equally, Rawlings and the NDC performed quite strongly in the relatively poor constituencies of Accra, where many voters had been hit especially hard by structural adjustment. It is important to note also here that, notwithstanding the popularity of the 'kume preko' demonstrations against the introduction of VAT in 1995 and other episodic challenges to the reforms, a coherent anti-reform coalition (representing opposition to structural adjustment and neo-liberal economic policies) failed to emerge even in the urban areas. This no doubt had something to do with the process of ideological change which had occurred in Ghana, and indeed internationally, since the late 1980s.

5. Conclusion

Our discussion has sought to show that urban bias provides only a partial explanation of the policies of pre-1983 Ghanaian regimes (such as that of Acheampong). Batesian rational choice theory needs to be supplemented, first, by an acknowledgement of the impact of ideological factors and, secondly, by a model of the growth of 'kleptocracy', if it is to explain the quite extraordinary economic and political débâcle experienced in Ghana in the late 1970s and early 1980s. Moreover, such rational choice theory — more specifically the postulate of the need for a 'reform coalition' — provides very little explanation of Rawlings' sustained implementation of the liberalizing economic reforms, or of how he managed this process politically. Our analysis has suggested that this explanatory weakness derives from two simplistic assumptions in particular.

First, Bates' theory assumes that African governments possess very little autonomy, and that their economic policy-making is therefore tightly constrained by the dominant socio-political forces in their societies. Now this may sometimes be true, but it is not always true, and certainly not always equally true. New governments, for example, both military and civilian, are likely to experience a honeymoon period during which they enjoy a greater degree of autonomous policy-space than older regimes (Nelson, 1990). More especially, charismatic leaders of quasi-revolutionary regimes, such as Rawlings or Museveni, are likely to enjoy an unusual degree of insulation. The main constraint on their policy formulation is likely to come from the ideological preconceptions of left-wing, nationalist intellectuals amongst their supporters. Both Rawlings and Museveni proved sufficiently politically skilful, however, to be able to consolidate their personal dominance over and against this constraint. Skilled political leaders, as these examples illustrate, can engineer a greater degree of autonomy for their regimes. The Rawlings case also illustrates the point that tight control of the military and para-military forces can free regimes, for a time and relatively speaking at least, from dependence on the support of (urban or rural) civilian groups. Over the longer term, of course, an authoritarian strategy is likely to become decreasingly effective. But by the time (the late 1980s) that this was becoming the case in Ghana, the benefits of the policy reforms were sufficiently extensive, in the rural areas at least, to make feasible a switch to a strategy of 'democratic' legitimization.

The second over-simple assumption of Batesian 'rational choice' theory is that people's political behaviour is a simple and direct expression of their economic interests, especially their interests as members of particular socio-economic groups. If, for example, a government implements policies which hurt the economic interests of urban wage-earners, then, on this analysis, these wage-earners can be expected to oppose those policies and even confront the regime. There is, of course, some truth to this, but it is also a very limited and in some ways quite misleading truth. For it assumes that people do not operate with, for example, a concern with the wider development of their community or their nation, or with a sense of what is 'just'. There is an abundance of evidence, in fact, that the political behaviour of most Ghanaians (as of other people) is very significantly influenced and qualified by such concerns. More specifically, a decision to take part, at the risk of having one's head crushed, in an urban street protest is likely to be influenced very significantly by the level of anger felt at the perceived injustice of particular measures in relation to the conduct of government leaders. The 1977–8 protests against the Acheampong regime, for example, were clearly motivated by a very high level of such anger. One of the reasons why the PNDC regime was able to sustain the implementation of policy reforms which hurt the immediate interests of various urban groups lay arguably in the fact that the regime leaders were widely perceived to be at least relatively honest and 'trying to do their best' for Ghana.

The point here is not to propose an alternative political economy theory which better explains the reform process in Ghana and other African states. Bates' 'urban bias' theory arguably still provides the best analytical starting-point. The point is rather to acknowledge the limitations of any such political economy theory. It is bound to constitute a highly simplified model of political reality. There is no very good reason, therefore, to expect any such theory to be able to provide historically adequate explanations in particular cases. The range of political variables which are likely to play an important role in any particular case is too wide, and their dependence on essentially unpredictable, historically contingent factors, such as leaders' 'charisma', intelligence, motivation and political skilfulness, is too great. Adequate historical explanations must therefore be contextually specific, and theory-relevant rather than theory-dependent.

References

Ahiakpor, James (1985) 'The Success and Failure of Dependency Theory: the Experience of Ghana', *International Organization* Vol. 39, No. 3.

Ahiakpor, James (1991) 'Rawlings, Economic Policy Reform and the Poor: Consistency or Betrayal?', *Journal of Modern African Studies* Vol. 29, No. 4.

Akwetey, Emmanuel (1994) *Trade Unions and Democratization: A Comparative Study of Zambia and Ghana*, University of Stockholm, Stockholm Studies in Politics.

Antoine, Adrien (1984) 'The Politics of Rice Farming in Ghana, 1972–79'. PhD thesis, University of London.

Appiah, Joe (1990) *The Autobiography of an African Patriot*. New York: Praeger.

Austin, Dennis (1975) 'Introduction' in Austin and Luckham.

Austin, Dennis and Luckham, Robin (eds) (1975) *Politicians and Soldiers in Ghana, 1966–72*. London: Frank Cass.

Austin, Gareth (1996) 'National Poverty and the "Vampire State" in Ghana', *Journal of International Development* Vol. 8, No. 4.

Ayee, J. R. A. (1993) 'Decentralization and Local Government Under the PNDC' in E. Gyimah-Boadi, (ed.) *Ghana Under PNDC Rule*. Dakar: Codesria Book Series.

Bates, Robert (1981) *Markets and States in Tropical Africa: The Political Basis of Agricultural Policies*. Berkeley, CA: University of California Press.

Boahen, A. Adu (1989) *The Ghanaian Sphinx: Reflections on the Contemporary History of Ghana, 1972–1987*. Accra: Ghana Academy of Arts and Sciences.

Callaghy, Thomas (1990) 'Lost Between State and Market: The Politics of Economic Adjustment in Ghana, Zambia and Nigeria' in J. Nelson (ed.), *Economic Crisis and Policy Choice*. Princeton, NJ: Princeton University Press.

Chazan, Naomi (1983) *An Anatomy of Ghanaian Politics: Managing Political Recession, 1969–1982*. Boulder, CO: Westview Press.

Folson, Kweku (1993) 'Ideology, Revolution and Development — the Years of J. J. Rawlings' in E. Gyimah-Boadi (ed.) *Ghana Under PNDC Rule*. Dakar: Codesria Books.

Frimpong-Ansah, Jonathan (1991) *The Vampire State in Africa: the Political Economy of Decline in Ghana*. London: James Currey.

Genoud, Roger (1969) *Nationalism and Economic Development in Ghana*. New York: Praeger.

Grindle, Merilee and Thomas, John (1991) *Public Choices and Policy Change*. Baltimore, MD: Johns Hopkins University Press.

Gyimah-Boadi, E. (1990) 'Economic Recovery and Politics in the PNDC's Ghana', *Journal of Commonwealth and Comparative Politics* Vol. XXVIII, No. 3.

Gyimah-Boadi, E. (1991) 'State Enterprise Divestiture: Recent Ghanaian Experiences' in Donald Rothchild (ed.), *Ghana: The Political Economy of Recovery*. Boulder, CO: Lynne Rienner Publishers.

Gyimah-Boadi, E. (1995a) 'Explaining the Economic and Political Successes of Rawlings: The Strength and Limitations of Public Choice Theories' in J. Harriss, C. Lewis and J. Hunter (eds) *The New Institutional Economics and Third World Development*. London/New York: Routledge.

Gyimah-Boadi, E. (1995b) 'Adjustment, State Rehabilitation and Democratization' in T. Mkandawire and A. Olukoshi (eds) *Between Repression and Liberalization: the Politics of Structural Adjustment in Africa*. Dakar: Codesria.

Gyimah-Boadi, E. (1997) 'Ghana's Encouraging Elections: The Challenges Ahead', *Journal of Democracy* Vol. 8, No. 2.

Hansen, Emmanuel (1987) 'The State and Popular Struggles in Ghana, 1982–1986' in P. Anyang' Nyong'o (ed.) *Popular Struggles for Democracy in Africa*. London: Zed Books.

Hansen, Emmanuel and Collins, Paul (1980) 'The Army, the State and the Rawlings Revolution', *African Affairs* 79.

Hart, Elizabeth and Gyimah-Boadi, E. (1997) 'Business Associations and Ghana's Political Transition', paper presented at the conference on Business Associations and the State in Africa, at the American University, Washington, DC., 9 February, (mimeo).

Huq, M. M. (1989) *The Economy of Ghana: The First 25 Years since Independence*. London: Macmillan.

Jeffries, Richard (1978) *Class, Power and Ideology in Ghana: The Railwaymen of Sekondi*. Cambridge: Cambridge University Press.

Jeffries, Richard (1980) 'The Ghanaian Elections of 1979', *African Affairs* Vol. 79, No. 316.

Jeffries, Richard (1982) 'Rawlings and the Political Economy of Underdevelopment in Ghana', *African Affairs* Vol. 81, No. 324.

Jeffries, Richard (1989) 'Ghana: the Political Economy of Personal Rule' in D. B. Cruise O'Brien, J. Dunn and R. Rathbone (eds) *Contemporary West African States*. Cambridge: Cambridge University Press.

Jeffries, Richard (1991) 'Leadership Commitment and Political Opposition to Structural Adjustment in Ghana' in D. Rothchild (ed.) *Ghana: the Political Economy of Recovery*. Boulder CO: Lynne Rienner Publishers.

Jeffries, Richard (1993) 'The State, Structural Adjustment and Good Government in Africa', *Journal of Commonwealth and Comparative Politics* Vol. 31, No. 1.

Jeffries, Richard (1996) 'Ghana's PNDC Regime: A Provisional Assessment', *Africa* Vol. 66, No. 2.

Jeffries, Richard and Thomas, Clare (1993) 'The Ghanaian Elections of 1992', *African Affairs* Vol. 92, No. 368.

Killick, Tony (1978) *Development Economics in Action: A Study of Economic Policies in Ghana*. London: Heinemann.

Levi, M. (1988) *Of Rule and Revenue*. Berkeley, CA: University of California Press.

Mansfield, Charles Y. (1980) 'Tax-base Erosion and Inflation: the Case of Ghana' *Finance and Development*, September.

Ministry of Rural Development and Co-operatives (1984) *The Rural Manifesto (Policies, Plans and Strategies of the Ministry of Rural Development and Cooperatives to Effect Accelerated Rural Development in Ghana)*.

Nelson, Joan (1990) 'Conclusions' in J. Nelson (ed.) *Economic Crisis and Policy Choice: the Politics of Adjustment in the Third World*. Princeton, NJ: Princeton University Press.

Ninsin, Kwame (1985) *Political Struggles in Ghana, 1967–1981*. Accra: Tornado Publications.

Nugent, Paul (1995) *Big Men, Small Boys and Politics in Ghana: Power, Ideology and the Burden of History, 1982–1994*. Accra: Asempa Publishers.

Nyanteng, V. K. (1980) *The Declining Ghana Cocoa Industry: An Analysis of Some Fundamental Problems*. Legon: ISSER.

Okeke, Barbara (1982) *4 June: A Revolution Betrayed*. Enugu: Ikenga Publishers.

Ocquaye, Mike (1980) *Politics in Ghana, 1972–79*. Accra: Tornado Publications.

Ocquaye, Mike (1993) 'Law, Justice and Revolution' in E Gyimah-Boadi (ed.) *Ghana Under PNDC Rule*. Dakar: Codesria Book Series.

Owusu, Maxwell (1986) 'Custom and Coups: a Juridical Interpretation of Civil Order and Disorder in Ghana', *Journal of Modern African Studies* Vol. 24, No. 1.

Owusu, Maxwell (1989) 'Rebellion, Revolution, and Tradition: Reinterpreting Coups in Ghana', *Studies in Society and History* Vol. 31, No. 2.

Owusu, Maxwell (1996) 'Tradition and Transformation: Democracy and the Politics of Popular Power in Ghana', *Journal of Modern African Studies* Vol. 34, No. 2.

Plave Bennett,Valerie (1975) 'Epilogue: Malcontents in Uniform' in Austin and Luckham.

Rathbone, Richard (1978) 'Ghana' in J. Dunn (ed.) *West African States: Failure and Promise*. Cambridge: Cambridge University Press.

Ray, Donald (1986) *Ghana: Politics, Economics and Society*. Boulder, CO: Lynne Rienner.

Rothchild, Donald and Gyimah-Boadi, E. (1986) 'Ghana's Economic Decline and Development Strategies' in J. Ravenhill (ed.) *Africa in Economic Crisis*. London and New York: Macmillan.

Rothchild, Donald and Gyimah-Boadi, E. (1989) 'Populism in Ghana and Burkina Faso', *Current History* Vol. 38, No. 538.

Seidman, Ann (1978) *Ghana's Development Experience*. Nairobi: East African Publishing House.

Teal, Francis (1986) 'The Foreign Exchange Regime and Growth: a Comparison of Ghana and the Ivory Coast' *African Affairs* Vol. 85, No. 339.

Yeebo, Zaya (1985) 'Ghana: Defence Committees and the Class Struggle', *Review of African Political Economy* Vol. 32.

3 Fragile Still? The Structure of Ghana's Economy 1960–94

TONY KILLICK*

1. Starting Points

Why should we be interested in structure? One good reason is that there are intimate connections between processes of structural change and long-term economic growth. Although it is a literature which is currently out of fashion, the seminal historical and cross-section researches of Kuznets and Chenery established a number of generalizations about patterns of structural transformation during economic growth against which we can assess the Ghanaian record.[1] In the most summary terms, they found that progression of an economy from low- to middle-income status is associated with the following changes in economic structures, a pattern which will be referred to below as the 'modernization model':

- rising ratios of saving, investment and exports to GDP, and a declining excess of investment over saving;
- a rising share of government consumption in total expenditures;
- a proportionate shift in the composition of exports away from non-oil primary products towards manufactures, and an increasing diversification of exports;
- a decline in the share of agriculture in GDP and employment, and a rise in the shares of manufacturing and (to a lesser extent) services;
- within manufacturing, a proportionate shift away from relatively simple consumer goods (food, textiles, clothing) towards industries producing intermediate inputs (e.g. chemicals) and later towards the production of certain capital goods (machinery) and durable metal consumer goods;
- a strong relative growth in energy consumption;
- financial deepening: a relative growth of the financial sector and monetization of economic activities (Goldsmith, 1969, 1983);

* There is a personal element to this paper. I first went to Ghana in 1961, as an Assistant Lecturer at the University of Ghana, staying until 1965. During that time I was lucky enough to be asked to contribute to a *Study of Contemporary Ghana* (Birmingham, Neustadt and Omaboe, 1966, 1967), the first volume of which was largely about the structure of the economy. The volume for which this present chapter has been prepared is in some respects a sequel to that early study and therefore provides me with an opportunity to examine what has happened to the structure of the economy since I first studied it. I am grateful to Ranjita Rajan for help in the arduous task of preparing data for this paper. Mozammel Huq and Nii Sowa are among those to whom I am indebted for helpful comments on an earlier draft.
[1] The following generalizations are drawn largely from Kuznets (1964 and 1966) and from Syrquin and Chenery (1989).

- declining mortality and fertility rates; increasing urbanization;
- the development of institutions (North, 1990) and increasing productive utilization of modern technologies (although, being unquantifiable, these variables do not feature much in the statistical analyses of the authors cited earlier);
- a growth of formal sector activities relative to the informal sector.

These *associations* between income growth and structural change do not necessarily tell us anything about the direction of causality. However, present-day understanding of growth processes suggests that in a number of respects causality runs from structural change to growth. The rise in the *investment ratio* (and associated increases in saving) has been rehabilitated in growth theory because of its role in facilitating technological progress. More controversially, many still see *industrialization* as an important causative feature of the growth process, again because of a superior ability to produce training and technological externalities. The balance of the large empirical literature on the export-growth connection lies firmly in favour of those who see *export growth* as an important source of (non-export) economic growth. The balance of the evidence also favours viewing the development of the *financial sector* as a prime mover in economic growth, although this empirical literature is less well developed. And everyone nowadays agrees on the importance of education and other forms of *skill creation*.

Quite apart from these hypothesized sources of economic growth, a further reason for studying economic structures is evidence that structural flexibility, *per se,* is conducive to improved economic performance. Syrquin and Chenery (1986) found movements of resources from low- to high-productivity sectors to be a major source of total factor productivity growth, with reallocations in the same direction within sectors probably having a similar effect. More generally — and of growing importance in an increasingly integrated world economy — all economies constantly have to adapt to changing economic circumstances and opportunities, with those flexible enough to respond quickly being better able to take advantage of world trading opportunities and technological change than less adaptable economies, and to do so at a lower cost in terms of output and employment forgone.[2]

It is no secret that Ghana's economy has not grown much since the early 1960s. Indeed, it has slipped from being classified (by the World Bank) as a middle-income country to a low-income country. The question arises as to what, in that case, we might expect of the behaviour of the structural indicators just referred to. If the fit between structural change and economic growth were perfect, the prediction for a non-growing economy would be that the structure would also remain unchanged. However, no-one suggests that there is such a one-to-one relationship and it would be interesting to discover whether, despite economic stagnation, Ghana's economy has undergone the types of transformation associated with modernization, and which variables appear closely tied to growth and which do not.

We are additionally fortunate in having a rather rich literature on the economy of Ghana to draw upon — probably unique among the economies of Africa. In addition to the two Birmingham, Neustadt and Omaboe volumes already mentioned, there is a path-breaking study by Szereszewski (1965) on structural changes in the period 1891–1911, and my own later study of economic policies in Ghana also offers pertinent material (Killick, 1978). Huq's (1989) study provides a wealth of material on the 1970s through to the mid-1980s, while Rimmer (1992) provides an admirable account of economic policies and outcomes for 1950-90. Moreover, Ghana's second period of being fashionable, following the introduction of structural adjustment measures in 1983, has generated a large volume of additional recent writings.

Over and above the reasons already given for wanting to utilize these resources for a study of structural change, the earlier literature on Ghana throws up a number of generalizations or hypotheses against which to set the record of the last three decades. First, Szereszewski shows that,

---

[2] For a development of this thesis see Killick, 1995, especially Chapters 1 and 12.

whereas the economy underwent profound structural shifts during the period 1891–1911 (notably the introduction of cocoa and gold mining and the associated development of the railway), 'structural change lost its momentum after 1911, and after fifty years Ghana's economy retains a close affinity with 1911 Gold Coast' (Szereszewski , 1965:112). However, he noted a resumption of change in the early 1960s — a pattern of change which the present writer subsequently characterized as follows:

> In appearance . . . Ghana's economy was being modernized in conformity with the classical patterns of development. "Investment wirhout growth" does not adequately describe the paradox of the Ghanaian economy, for it was also a case of "modernization without growth". (Killick, 1978: 170)

Secondly, an influential *Report on Financial and Physical Problems of Development in the Gold Coast* commissioned by the colonial administration (Seers and Ross, 1952) was written around the following generalization about the structure of the economy: 'If we were forced to sum up the Gold Coast economy in one word, the word we would choose would be "Fragile".'[3] Seers and Ross were particularly concerned with what they saw as an inflationary bias imparted to the economy by supply bottlenecks (of which a shortage of harbour capacity, as well as the more fundamental difficulty of low supply elasticities in agriculture, was at that time a preoccupation) and we shall return to this characterization to see if it is still relevant nearly fifty years later. This topic is also taken up by Aryeetey and Harrigan in Chapter 1.

Lastly, we should bear in mind that adjustment policies, of the type pursued since 1983, are intended to induce certain changes in the composition of the economy, which is why it is called *structural* adjustment: a reallocation of resources in favour of the production of tradeables *vis-à-vis* non-tradeables; reallocations away from the state in favour of the private sector (although in Ghana it is unclear that this has been an objective of the successive Rawlings administrations post-1983); and reduced imbalances between investment and saving, and between exports and imports, resulting from an improved quality of macroeconomic management.

The following analysis is built round two tables. Table 3.1 presents international comparisons for 1960 and 1994 of selected structural indicators for Ghana, India, Thailand and Turkey. Three chief criteria were used in selecting the comparators: availability of data; an initial level of per capita income either less than, or (in the case of Turkey) not much above, Ghana's in 1960; and substantial but not extreme economic growth since 1960 (a test which led to the dropping of South Korea, which started the period with a per capita income substantially lower than Ghana's and finished it at a level twenty-five times as great).

Table 3.2 presents a much fuller set of structural and other indicators for Ghana alone, including data for 1980 as well as for 1960 and 1994. The earliest and latest of these years are the first and last for which reasonably complete data were available. The choice of 1980 needs more explanation. In principle, 1982 or 1983 might have better represented the nadir of the economy in that period but because of a drought and a large-scale repatriation of workers from Nigeria in 1982 it was an unrepresentatively extreme time of adversity. From that perspective, 1980 may provide a better representation.

Some heavy cautions are necessary. Our approach requires consistent, comparable data drawn from time series 34 years long. This has limited the range of indicators which we can draw upon. Even so, as will be indicated in the text, some of the results may better reflect the inadequacies of the statistics than the reality of the economy. It is particularly frustrating that we have been unable to utilize the results of the revisions of the national accounts which are currently in progress. Access to the new series might well have modified the story which unfolds below. Secondly, we are taking three one-year snapshots of the economy. A great deal happens between

---

[3] See Killick, 1966: 412–13, for a brief account of the Seers-Ross report.

our chosen years which goes unrevealed, and for individual series single-year entries may be abnormal. However, we have tried to safeguard against this, or to draw attention to any apparent aberrations. Moreover, the dangers of single-year observations are reduced by the long time-span involved: the general tendency is likely to dominate single-year movements around the trend line.

A further limitation is that we are in no position to demonstrate causality from structural to welfare variables in Ghana and must merely have recourse to the general understanding of the wellsprings of economic growth summarized earlier. Similarly, it is outside the self-imposed remit of this chapter to go far in analyzing the *causes* of the features revealed. What is provided here is an overview. Subsequent chapters take readers more deeply into the underlying forces that have been at work.

2.   International Comparisons, 1960 and 1994

It is easily forgotten that at the time of independence Ghana was regarded as one of the better placed of what we now call the developing countries — and not with that fatal qualification, 'by the standards of Africa'. In terms of average incomes, absence of a balance of payments constraint, a sound budgetary situation and a well-functioning public administration, Ghana compared well with many other of the nations starting out on the road of economic modernization and development. Thus, Omaboe, from the perspective of the early 1960s, wrote of '. . . the special qualities which Ghana possesses within the underdeveloped group of countries' and was able to state that 'Ghana now enjoys levels of social and welfare services which are in advance of those of most underdeveloped countries and in some urban centres are not far behind those of some developed countries' (Omaboe, 1966: 23, 28).

The statistics in Table 3.1 show the extent of the country's relative decline since that time. Comparisons with Thailand offer the most dramatic illustrations: a country which (to the extent that such figures have meaning) started in 1960 with an average income just half the Ghana figure but which by 1994 had raised that average five-fold while Ghana's had diminished, so that by the end the Thai figure was three times as great as that of Ghana. Comparisons with the other two countries in the table also show Ghana's decline, albeit less dramatically. Starting with a per capita income level a little higher than that of Ghana, Turkey ended the period with an average more than 3½-times as high. India, starting from a level only a third of Ghana's, ended the period with only a narrow remaining gap, having expanded its average income by 75% while that of Ghana slipped back.

Bearing in mind the generalizations set out earlier about the nature of the structural transformation which accompanies economic growth, most of the other indicators in Table 3.1 are also to Ghana's disadvantage:

*   *Industrialization,* and a parallel relative decline in the share of agriculture, has progressed much further in the three comparator countries, although they all started with a more substantial manufacturing base than did Ghana (items 4 and 5). The contrast in the pace of industrialization is reinforced by the data on energy use (item 12).

While it is true that in proportionate terms the figures in item 5 show Ghana to have achieved the fastest rate of industrialization, with a four-fold increase in the share of manufacturing, this was from a tiny base and examination of the data shows that all of this relative growth occurred in the first half of the 1960s, followed by stagnation thereafter. However, we should bear in mind that each of the comparator countries started with a much larger domestic market than Ghana — a particular advantage when it comes to industrial development — as is crudely indicated by the following figures of total GDP in 1960 (in current US$ million): Ghana 1,521; India, 34,365; Thailand, 3,032; and Turkey, 7,727.

Table 3.1   International Comparisons of Structural Indicators, 1960 and 1994

		GHANA		INDIA		THAILAND		TURKEY	
Indicator		1960	1994	1960	1994	1960	1994	1960	1994
1.	Real per capita GDP								
	(a) US $	227	188	79	137	114	581	281	694
	(b) 1960=100	100	83	100	174	100	508	100	247
2.	Total population (1960=100)	100	248	100	214	100	218	100	221
3.	Total fertility rate	7.3	5.3	5.7	3.3	6.4	2.0	6.3	3.2
4.	Agriculture/GDP (%)	41	46	50	30	40	10	41	16
5.	Manufacturing/GDP (%)	2	8	14	18	13	29	13	20
6.	Gross domestic investment/GDP (%)	24	16	17	23	16	40	16	22
7.	Gross domestic saving/GDP (%)	17	4	14	21	17	35	13	23
8.	Exports/GDP (%)	28	23	5	12	17	39	3	21
9.	Money supply (M$_2$)/GDP (%)	18	17	26	58	23	101	21	64
10.	Adult illiteracy (%)	84	36	72	48	32	6	62	18
11.	Secondary school enrolment (%)	5	38	20	44	13	97	14	60
12.	Per capita energy use	47	91	50	243	27	770	113	995
13.	Fertilizer consumption (100 gms per ha of arable land)	n.a.	38	n.a.	720	n.a.	544	n.a.	702

Sources: As in Table 3.3

At the same time, the statistics of fertilizer use suggest that agricultural modernization in each of the three comparators had left Ghana far behind (item 13), although this is admittedly an imperfect indicator.

- ·*Saving and investment* were by 1994 far higher in the comparator countries (items 6 and 7). But despite maintaining higher investment rates their resource gaps (as a percentage of GDP) were far smaller: India, –2%; Thailand, –5%; Turkey +1%, against Ghana's –12%.
- All three comparator countries had achieved far greater success with the growth of *exports* (item 8). The expanding economies had each substantially raised the share of exports in total GDP, while in stagnant Ghana the share had declined a little - a result consistent with a view which sees export performance as a key determinant of economic growth.
- *Financial deepening,* proxied by the growth of M$_2$ money supply relative to GDP (item 9), had gone much further in the comparator countries.

Happily, not all the comparisons show Ghana in a poor light. The two *educational* indicators, illiteracy and secondary school enrolment (items 10 and 11), reveal the country's achievements as not far out of line with the others, a remarkable result, given the often appalling state of the economy and public finances when these improvements were being won.

The *demographic* indicators (items 2 and 3) are interesting. Ghana's population grew the most but not by a large margin, with all four populations more than doubling in the period. The contrast between the broadly similar population growth and widely differing income growth suggests that population growth is not a prime influence on economic performance. Note, though, that Ghana started and finished with higher fertility rates than the others. Only higher death rates prevented its demographic explosion far outstripping the others - not a satisfactory solution.

Of these various comparisons, two stand out as especially noteworthy. First, the contrast in export performance could hardly be starker. Compare the following (constant-price) growth rates of per capita exports for 1960-94. As can be seen, when compounded over the 34-year time span, the cumulative effect of such differences in growth is huge:

Table 3.2

	growth rate (% p.a.)	growth rate compounded over 34 years (%)
Ghana	−0.9	−26
India	4.9	+510
Thailand	7.4	+1130
Turkey	8.7	+1710

Sources: As in Table 3.3

Secondly, the contrasts in saving and investment performance are equally stark, and appallingly to Ghana's disadvantage. As will be argued later, a 16% investment ratio in 1994 was inadequate to sustain satisfactory future growth and modernization. But it is the saving figure which stands out. As of 1994, Ghana was getting the worst of both worlds: an inadequate level of investment was nevertheless generating a high and probably unviable level of dependence on inflows of finance (mostly aid) from the rest of the world. More on this later.

Lastly, the data in Table 3.1 seem to dispose of a 'poverty trap' explanation of Ghana's failure to develop, i.e. that it was unable to do so because it started poor. We have pointed out that, in fact, the economy was relatively prosperous at the beginning of the 1960s. Two of the three comparator countries started with much lower average incomes and yet both achieved substantial growth and development, Thailand spectacularly so. By the same token, then, Ghana's particularly poor savings record cannot be attributed to initial poverty (although present-day poverty is indeed a factor).

3.   Ghana's Economic Structure, 1960, 1980, 1994

Further light is thrown on various aspects of the results just described as we turn now to consider the more detailed structural indicators presented in Table 3.3, which also includes figures for 1980. The following paragraphs will briefly highlight the results obtained, while Section 4 asks how these should be interpreted and what policy inferences might be drawn.

Welfare outcomes

First, the figures in item A4 confirm the decline in *per capita income* already reported and appear to suggest that this has been continuous throughout, so that the period of structural adjustment appears to be associated with further income reductions. This is misleading, however. Per capita income reached its lowest point in 1983, following the drought and the general trauma of the early 1980s, when the index value of income (1960=100) fell to 69. There was then a 20% improvement between 1983 and 1994, a growth rate per capita of about 2% p.a. On the other hand, that incomes should still not have recovered even to their 1960 level (to the extent that such long time series on incomes have meaning) places the achievements of the post-1982 period in a sobering context. Similar — but more extreme — trends are revealed by the data on the real value of average formal-sector earnings in item F3, showing a catastrophic fall in 1960-80 and a substantial recovery since, but one leaving the 1994 figure far below its 1960 starting point.

Table 3.3 Selected Indicators of the Structure of the Ghanaian Economy, 1960, 1980, 1994[a]

	1960	1980	1994
A. DEMOGRAPHIC & WELFARE INDICATORS			
A1. Population size (mn)	6.7	10.7	16.6
A2. Population growth rate (% p.a.)	3.1[c]	2.4	3.1
A3. Total GDP in constant prices (1960=100)[d]	100	153	218
A4. Per capita GDP in constant prices (1960=100)[d]	100	89	83
A5. Total fertility rate (births per woman)	7.3[c]	6.5	5.3
A6. Expectation of life at birth (years)	45.5[c]	51.6	56.4
A7. Infant mortality rate (per 1000 live births)	143	98	79
B. RESOURCE USES			
B1. Private consumption (% GDP)	73	84	84
B2. Public consumption (% GDP)	10	11	12
B3. Gross domestic investment (% GDP)	24	6	16
B4. Gross domestic saving (% GDP)	17	5	4
B5. Resource balance (B3 minus B2)	–7	–1	–12
B6. Exports of goods and non-factor services (% GDP)	28	7	23
B7. Imports of goods and non-factor services (% GDP)	30	6	32
B8. External debt (% GNP)	3.6[e]	31.6[f]	101.5[f]
B9. Debt servicing as % exports[f]	n.a.	13.1	24.6
C. FISCAL & MONETARY			
C1. Government current revenues (% GDP)[n]	15.1	7.1	18.5
C2. Government current expenditures (% GDP)[n]	13.6	11.6	18.7
C3. Money supply (M_2) as % GDP	18	19	17
C4. Persons per commercial bank branch (000s)	51[b]	60[g]	57[i]
C5. Shares of total outstanding commercial bank credit (%)			
Public sector	54	67	77[j]
Private sector	46	33	23[j]
D. INDUSTRIALIZATION & PRODUCTIVITY			
D1. Shares in GDP (%):			
Agriculture	41	58	46
Manufacturing	2	8	8
Services	n.a.	30	39
D2. Structure of manufacturing value-added (% of total)			
Food, beverages, tobacco	38	37	36
Textiles & clothing	0.00	11	5
Machinery and transport equipment	10	2	2
Chemicals	4	5	10
Other	49	46	47
D3. Per capita energy use (kg of oil equivalent)	47	121	91

Table 3.3 cont'd.

E.	COMPOSITION OF TRADE			
E1.	Primary products as % of total exports	90	80[g]	77
E2.	Share of top three exports in total (%)	83[b]	91[g]	84[h]
E3.	Composition of imports by end-use (%)			
	Consumer goods	50[b]	17[g]	n.a.
	Intermediate goods	24[b]	30[g]	n.a.
	Capital goods	22[b]	27[g]	n.a.
	Fuel	5[b]	27[g]	n.a.
E4.	Net barter terms of trade (1987=100)[d]	102	156	64

F.	LABOUR AND HUMAN DEVELOPMENT			
F1.	Sectoral shares in total employment (%)			
	Agriculture	64	53	52
	Industry	14	20	19
	Services	22	27	29
F2.	Total recorded (formal sector) employment (000s)			
	Private sector	149	46	n.a.
	Public sector	184	291	n.a.
	Total	333	337	n.a.
F3.	Index of real average monthly formal sector earnings	100	21	38[l]
F4.	Adult illiteracy	84[c,m]	n.a.	36
F4.	Adult illiteracy	84[c,m]	n.a.	36
F5.	Primary school enrolment rate (%)	38	69	88
F6.	Secondary school enrolment rate (%)	5	36	39
F7.	Urbanization: % of population living in towns	23	31	36

Notes:
[a] Most entries refer to the indicated year but some are for adjacent or nearby years. Any large variations are noted separately.
[b] *Source:* Birmingham *et al.*, Vol.1 (1966).
[c] *Source:* Birmingham *et al.*, Vol.2 (1967).
[d] Construction of these time series involved 'chaining' together more than one series with differing base years.
[e] *Source:* Killick and Szereszewski, 1969: 104.
[f] *Source:* World Bank *World Debt Tables* (various issues)
[g] *Source:* Huq, 1989.
[h] *Source:* CEPA, 1996.
[i] *Source:* Bank of Ghana.
[j] *Source:* ISSER, 1996.
[k] *Source:* GSS, *Quarterly Digest of Statistics* (various issues), cited by Fine and Boateng (this volume), rebased to 1960.
[l] '1994' figure is for 1991 (latest available).
[m] This records the proportion of adults who had never attended school. It therefore understates illiteracy.
[n] *Source:* Wetzel, 1995, Tables 3.2 and 3.4. The revenue figures exclude grants.

Sources: Unless stated otherwise, data are drawn from the World Bank database, as published in its annual *World Tables* (various issues) and *World Development Report*, augmented by data from IMF *International Financial Statistics* (yearbooks, various issues). Such sources have been preferred over Ghanaian and academic publications to minimize the problems of breaks in series and in concept definition.

It is interesting to juxtapose the per capita income results with the numbers for the *terms of trade* in item E4, for the country's troubles are sometimes blamed on unfavourable movements in world prices. What the detailed data show is that the terms of trade actually improved quite substantially during the period of most rapid economic decline (although there were large fluctuations in both directions and a collapse in the early 1980s), whereas the economic gains of the later period have been won in the face of an adverse movement in relative trade prices, particularly in the early 1990s. The period of the direst economic decline, the Acheampong years 1972–8, were actually marked by rather strong terms of trade, particularly in 1976–8. Movements in the relative prices of imports and exports therefore do not emerge as having much predictive value for the wider performance of the economy.

Given the hunger for jobs and the enormous impact which access to formal sector work can make on poverty, directly and indirectly through the despatch of remittances to the rural poor, it seems appropriate, if unconventional, to consider trends in *formal sector employment* under the heading of welfare indicators. The data set out in item F2 are unfortunately limited to 1960 and 1980. Between these years total recorded employment remained essentially unchanged (despite a 60% growth in population over the period). During this time there was a huge drop in private sector employment. Expansion in the public sector was sufficient to offset this decline but this was unsustainable. Adjustment measures since 1983 have brought many job losses in the public sector but, in a reversal of fortunes, it appears that this time the private informal sector has to some extent come to the rescue, with an expansion here tending to offset the decline of the public sector as employer of last resort. Private formal sector employment growth has, however, been disappointing (see chapter 12). If it is one of the marks of a successfully developing economy that it throws up an expanding number of formal sector jobs (and if the reality corresponds to the data), then Ghana's failure is even more complete than as indicated by per capita income trends, particularly bearing in mind that the working-age population has more than doubled over this period.

Welfare indicators are not uniformly adverse, however. *Mortality* (and probably morbidity) rates have improved, as shown in items A6 and A7. If the estimates are accurate, the life expectation at birth of the average Ghanaian increased by almost a quarter between 1960 and 1994, while infant mortality nearly halved. Such trends would be inconsistent with any drastic increase in poverty among large swathes of the population, as would the continuing rapid *growth of the population* (item A2), expanding as rapidly today as it was in 1960 (but on the basis of lower levels of both mortality and fertility). And at any other time in world history the fact that Ghana's population today is 2½ times as large as it was in 1960 (item A1) would have been regarded as a phenomenon outside the range of previous human experience.

Resource Uses

We return now to the *saving-investment* story (items B1–5). The table shows that, having increased in 1960–80, the share of private consumption in GDP remained unchanged at the high level of 84% in 1980-94. At the same time, the share of public consumption inched up, so that by 1994 total consumption absorbed almost the whole (96%) of GDP, leaving saving at negligible levels. (Bear in mind the historical observation that savings rates are supposed to increase over time in a developing country, as Table 3.1 showed them to have done in the three comparator countries.) At the same time, the investment level, having fallen to a mere 6% of GDP by 1980, had recovered substantially by the later year, due almost entirely to a rise in public sector investment, leaving a *resource gap* to be filled by capital inflows, equal to 12% of GDP. Chapter 7 by Brownbridge *et al.* examines the saving-investment record in detail and confirms the broad picture emerging above.

Trends in *imports and exports* are scarcely less dramatic or discouraging (items B6 and B7). Note first the extraordinary collapse of (recorded) exports, relative to GDP, in 1960-80, related, of course, to the increasingly extreme levels of overvaluation of the currency during these years. With aid and other sources of foreign capital drying up in this period, the consequence was that

imports too had to be curtailed, falling even more drastically than exports, with serious consequences for the performance of the economy, as well as for human well-being.

Since 1980 (actually, since 1983) there has been a scarcely less dramatic recovery of exports,
to 23% of GDP in 1994, although leaving the ratio still a little below the 1960 figure. But look
at what happened to the import ratio in the same 14 years: up over five-fold. This is the flip side
of the consumptionist bias of the economy revealed, negatively, by the low savings figure, possible chiefly because of the resumption of large-scale aid inflows (see Chapter 10 by Harrigan
and Younger for evidence of the large increase in aid inflows between 1983 and 1989).

The figures on the *public finances* (items C1 and C2) broadly mirror the trends portrayed
above: a collapse in government revenues (relative to GDP) in 1960–80 tracked by a much
smaller decline in government spending, leading to the emergence of the government as a major
dis-saver in the economy (a situation resulting in large, monetised budget deficits and a conse-
quential rapid inflation). This was followed by a substantial improvement in the revenue ratio in
1980–94, again tracked by a smaller expenditure shift in the same direction. The restoration of
the government's revenue base is surely one of the more impressive achievements of the post-
1983 policies, but the continuing failure of the government even to cover its everyday expenditures with current revenues (excluding grant income) is a major source of weakness, contributing to the disastrous saving record mentioned earlier.

Moreover, the true extent of the fiscal improvement is in dispute and there are serious doubts
about the accuracy of the budgetary data. There appears to be a discrepancy between fiscal
statistics showing the budget as balanced and banking sector figures showing that the public
sector remains heavily dependent on borrowings from the banking system. This is shown by the
data on public-private shares in the distribution of *bank credit* (item C5). In fact, the state's share
has risen significantly since 1980, inevitably raising interest rates and tending to crowd out the
credit requirements of private borrowers. This does not sit well with an adjustment strategy
supposedly based on the growth of the private sector.

One other aspect of the pattern of resource uses should be noticed, a direct consequence of
the financing gaps, namely, the growth in the country's *external indebtedness* (items B8 and
B9).[4] In consequence Ghana's debt-servicing payments relative to exports have risen substantially, notwithstanding the growth of exports, the denominator, since the mid-1980s. Once again,
doubts are raised about the longer-term viability of a recovery path with such a strong
consumptionist bias.

Modernization

Table 3.3 contains a number of indicators of the extent of modernization. We noted earlier the
absence of *industrialization* of output after the mid-1960s, and this is borne out in item D1,
which shows an unchanged share of manufacturing between 1980 and 1994. A similar picture is
revealed in the sectoral composition of total (i.e. formal and informal) employment (item F1),
with some rise during the first period and no significant change since then. The relative stagnation of manufacturing no doubt contributes powerfully to the finding in Chapter 4 by Powell and
Round that even as late as 1993 there was a marked lack of inter-industry linkages between the
various sectors of the economy, for it is the manufacturing sector, above all, which creates and
feeds upon such linkages. Conversely, however, the data do not support the idea that import
liberalization has led to any significant de-industrialization in recent years, with manufacturing
holding an unchanged share of GDP (items D1 and F1) and industry holding an unchanged share
of total employment.

What about trends *within* manufacturing? Have these perhaps conformed more closely to the
modernization model? Summary statistics are set out in item D2, with more detailed information

---

[4] The low debt figure for 1960 is a little misleading, in that there was a rapid growth in indebtedness in
1960-5, with the debt-service ratio reaching 18.5% by the final year (Rimmer, 1992: 82).

provided in Chapter 13 by Asante *et al.* Overall and perhaps unsurprisingly, the picture is a rather stagnant one, with the food, beverages and tobacco, and 'other' (chiefly wood products) categories dominant throughout. Textiles and clothing have risen and fallen, while chemicals have risen and risen, both as the modernization model would predict, but machinery and transport equipment have almost slipped off the screen.

The bald figures in Table 3.3 (item D1) on the share of services in GDP evidently hide a complex story, but unfortunately examination of more detailed data indicates that there is insufficient consistency over time in the measurement of the services sector to be able to write with any confidence about long-term trends within that broad 'sector'. It seems, though, that services have been the most dynamic broad sector of activity (CEPA, 1997: 23–4) in the 1990s, and it is probable that these years saw a relative decline in government services, and perhaps of traditional services, and particularly rapid growth in transport and wholesale and retail trade. This is consistent with the view in this chapter of the strong consumptionist bias in the post-1983 revival, and with a relative absence of the type of restructuring in favour of tradeables discussed later.

Item E3, recording the end-use *composition of imports,* casts further light (although equivalent data are unfortunately unavailable for a recent year). As can be seen, there were major changes in the 1960–80 period, with a large fall in the share of consumer goods, increases in producer goods and a large rise in fuel imports, consequent on the two oil shocks of the 1970s. This pattern of change is, of course, consistent with the import-substituting nature of the industrialization which occurred in the 1960s, although we should remember that by 1980 industry was starved of needed imported inputs and equipment, and was therefore operating at only a fraction of rated capacity.

Certainly, there is little sign of a significant breakthrough of Ghanaian manufactures into world export markets (Baah-Nuakoh *et al.,* 1996), itself indicative of low levels of industrial efficiency by international standards. Items E1 and E2 provide indicators of trends in the *composition of exports.* In judging these figures we should remember that the modernization model predicts a decline in the share of non-oil primary products in total exports and reduced reliance on one or a small number of products. The data show that this has not occurred.

There has actually been more movement on exports than the figures convey, however, for they do not reflect the establishment in the 1960s of the VALCO aluminium smelter as a significant foreign-exchange earner (its earnings are not included in the official export statistics, but in 1980 these contributed the equivalent of 12% of total export earnings — Huq, 1989: 203). Also, *within* the primary product category there has been a rapid growth during the last decade in exports of gold, earnings from which more than tripled between 1990 and 1995, finally pushing King Cocoa off his throne. However, it should be borne in mind that in terms of net retained foreign exchange a dollar's worth of gold earnings is by no means equivalent to a dollar's worth of cocoa, with a substantial part of gold earnings leaking back out of the economy to pay for imported inputs, equipment and profit remittances. Overall, it is fair to say that there is as yet little sign of a decisive modernization and diversification of Ghana's export structure, certainly much less than developing countries in other parts of the world have achieved.

Another aspect of modernization strongly associated with economic growth is *financial deepening,* for which we have two indicators (items C3 and C4), both providing negative results. By common consent, there was a retreat from monetization during the 1970s and into the early 1980s, resulting from rapid inflation and the penal effects of 'currency reforms' as discussed in Chapters 7 and 11. The M_2/GDP ratio also records a decline between 1980 and 1994 but this is misleading, there having been a gradual but fairly steady rise from the low point of 1983 (11.3%) to the 1994 level of 18.6% (see ISSER, 1996: 36). A broadly similar picture emerges from the figures on the density of bank branch coverage (item C4). Financial deepening has yet to occur, although since 1990 there has been an encouraging growth in the number of commercial banks operating in the country.

It would be highly desirable to include some definitive indicators of the extent of *technologi-*

cal progress over these years, given the accelerating pace of change in the rest of the world. Unfortunately, we can offer only unsatisfactory scraps of information. First, there are data on per capita *energy use* (item D3) (in kg of oil equivalents). In low-income countries, utilization of modern productive technologies is likely to be associated with increased energy use, but the trend in Ghana is shown to have been not very buoyant (although the fall recorded for the later period is probably misleading, with the 1980 figure inflated by the extremely high levels of fuel subsidy then in force). In this regard, we have already commented on the large contrasts with other countries, as recorded in Table 3.1 (item 12). We have also drawn attention to the enormous differences between Ghana's use of fertilizers (an indicator of the modernization of agriculture) and those of the comparator countries in Table 3.1 (item 13). If this is at all an adequate indicator, it suggests that Ghana's agriculture operates in a different technological world from that of the other three countries, although these figures partly reflect the difference between extensive and intensive modes of cultivation. The impression of continuing backwardness is, however, supported by the conclusion reached by Nyanteng and Seini in Chapter 14:

> Labour productivity in Ghana['s agriculture] is equally very low and this can be attributed to the very simple traditional tools used in farm production . . . Due to the undulating terrain, particularly in the forest zone, the predominantly small farm sizes and some economic factors, the use of modern farm equipment . . . is not widespread . . .

A survey conducted by Lall and Wignaraja has provided information on the technological characteristics of manufacturing. This concluded that 13 out of 32 firms surveyed could be classified as 'technologically competent' but added a crucial rider (1996: 14):

> It has to be emphasised that inclusion in this list *does not mean that these firms are technologically capable by world standards*. On the contrary, the evidence suggests that the level of technological mastery by Ghanaian firms of the technologies they use is relatively poor. There is little or no process or product development by even the best sample firms that can be regarded as "innovative".

They conclude later (p.29) that, 'The most striking feature of the findings on Ghana *is how low overall levels of skill and competence in manufacturing industry are*' (emphasis in the original in both cases).

By welcome contrast, evidence of movement in desired directions is provided by the data on *literacy and school enrolment* (items F4–6). Major improvements have been achieved since the abysmal days of colonial neglect, improvements all the more creditable given the difficult economic conditions during much of this period. Note, however, that most of the improvement in enrolment rates occurred during 1960-80, with only small improvements since then.

Unfortunately, while enrolment rates have risen, it appears that the quality of education provided has deteriorated. Thus, a World Bank study reported the results of tests given to sixth grade primary school pupils 'which indicated in two successive years of tests that only some 2 per cent of students were able to answer more than 60 per cent of relatively simple mathematics and English questions correctly' (Armstrong, 1996: 87, who goes on to catalogue a substantial list of other indicators of failing quality).

Finally, we should note that urbanization has proceeded throughout the whole period, notwithstanding the absence of growth or industrialization and the stagnation of recorded formal sector employment (item F7).

4. Comments on the Results

How should we characterize the evidence just presented? First, we can return to the modernization model summarized at the beginning of the chapter. We have found few systematic signs of modernization in Ghana: in per capita income terms, the economy has not grown, nor has it experienced the structural changes associated with growth. A number of variables seem quite independent of economic performance: namely population growth, urbanization and other de-mographic variables, and the educational indicators already discussed (drawing attention to the fact that human skill formation is powerless alone to generate economic progress). We also note later the failure of certain structural variables to move in line with the modest recovery in eco-nomic growth post-1983, most notably saving. In other respects the absence of modernization has gone along with the poor growth record: the cessation of industrialization; the structure of exports; and the absence of financial deepening.

Turning from the model to the Ghanaian case, we earlier quoted Szereszewski's (1965) ob-servation that structural change lost its momentum in Ghana between 1911 and the middle of the century but that change had been resumed in the 1960s, as well as the present writer's descrip-tion of that resumption as 'modernization without growth'. Looking back from the perspective of the late twentieth century, how do these things appear now?

It is clear from the details of the discussion, if not from the snapshots provided in the tables, that Szereszewski was right to notice a resumption of change in the early 1960s. There were four notable aspects of this: (i) a rather rapid industrialization, albeit from a tiny base, so that the share of manufacturing in GDP rose from a mere 0.8% in 1955 to 2.3% in 1961 and 9.7% in 1965; (ii) an accompanying rapid growth in the capital stock; (iii) large improvements in educa-tional provisions, as already noted; but (iv) a deterioration in macroeconomic balances, generat-ing a large negative resource deficit (which grew from –3% of GDP in 1960 to –9% in 1965 — Killick, 1978: 88), the first symptoms of currency overvaluation and of a serious foreign-ex-change constraint, deteriorating public finances and the re-emergence of substantial inflation.

Moreover, although there was industrialization it was achieved behind an undiscriminating protection that paid little heed to efficiency and competitiveness — a legacy which, as we have seen, is still reflected in the lacklustre performance of the industrial sector and its limited ability to compete internationally. Relatively high investment levels drove up the capital stock, it is true, but in inefficient, low-productivity directions.[5] It is, in fact, superficial to associate the 1960s expansion of manufacturing with the model of modernization. As I noted at the time, many of the manufacturing firms were tiny, with fewer than six employees, and technologically very simple (Killick, 1978: 277). There was a dualistic industrial sector, with few points of contact between the many small concerns and the few large 'modern' ones.

In short and always excepting the educational improvements, the resumption of structural change in the Nkrumah period was only a superficial modernization. It was also unsustainable, quickly collapsing in the mid-1960s. Those who are nowadays inclined to hark back nostalgi-cally to those years should be reminded that this was a period, certainly of ambition but also of gross economic mismanagement. It was then that economic deterioration was set in motion.

Since the mid-1960s, as we have seen, there has been little decisive structural change and in some respects a deterioration. The resource balance has remained highly adverse, with growing external indebtedness; industrial modernization has halted; there has been only limited progress with the modernization and diversification of exports; there has been no financial deepening; so far as can be judged, the rate of technological progress has been far slower than in other parts of the world. Ghana today retains many of the attributes of what in 1960 was called an underdevel-oped economy.

This account also implicitly draws attention to some of the limitations of policy achievements since 1983. We have noted some positive features: large recoveries in the investment and export ratios, and in tax revenues. But at the same time we have noted the slow-down (perhaps reversal, once quality is taken into account) in educational improvements. Furthermore, there are ques-tions about the sustainability of a pattern of recovery in which total consumption continues to

---

[5] See Leith, 1975, for a detailed study of the protectionism of the Nkrumah period.

absorb almost the whole of GDP, in which there is a heavy reliance on development assistance, which, however, is an increasingly unreliable source of capital,[6] in which the proportionate rise in imports has been far greater than that of exports (Table 3.2, items B6 and B7), and in which the public sector continues to claim the lion's share of total domestic credit, contributing to the absence of financial deepening.

Structural adjustment, we should remember, seeks to induce certain shifts in the pattern of the economy: reallocations in favour of tradeables and the private sector, and reduced macro imbalances. Does the 1980–94 evidence suggest that post-1983 policies have been successful in these respects?[7]

We have already discussed the macro balances to some extent. There were obviously major improvements in macroeconomic management after 1982, of which the grasping of the exchange-rate nettle was the most decisive action. Budgetary deficits were reduced and the import constraint greatly relaxed. Moreover, these improvements were secured while public (but not private) sector investment was revived, and despite a serious worsening in the terms of trade in 1988–91. Against this, there was a well-publicized deterioration in the macro balances, particularly in the fiscal situation, in 1992–3 and, although there has since been an improvement, there remain doubts about the soundness of fiscal management (CEPA, 1997: 4–7). There has been substantial inflation, both causing and in turn being aggravated by the further depreciation of the cedi.

At the risk of excessive repetition, the unsustainability of the present saving-investment situation cannot be overemphasized. A saving ratio of just 4% provides no basis for any sustained recovery, however liberal external donors may be. Compare that figure with the average saving ratio of 26% for the other three countries in Table 3.1. This situation should be viewed against a history over most of the last three decades when the country has not been renewing its capital stock. In Killick (1978: 68) it was estimated that, as at 1968–9, maintenance of the existing capital stock alone required a gross investment ratio of around 13% of GDP. In reality, the records show that during 1970–94 gross investment fell below that level in 17 of the 25 years, and in only two of those years did it rise above 15%. Of course, the volume of investment required to renew the capital stock will have diminished in the 1970s and beyond, as capital was being consumed, but even since the later 1980s it seems probable that the capital stock has been rebuilt only slowly. For modernization and structural adaptation higher investment levels would be needed — and yet even today's levels are resulting in unsustainable resource gaps. The urgency of acting on the savings front simply cannot be exaggerated. It is here worth recalling one of Szereszewski's historical findings: that by 1911, poor and underdeveloped though it was, the economy was generating domestic saving estimated at nearly a fifth of GDP (although much of this was in the form of capitalised labour, to create the cocoa industry).[8]

What about the desired relative shift since 1983 from non-tradeables to tradeables? Unfortunately, these concepts are not easily translated into national accounts data. Ultimately, almost everything is tradeable: tradeability is a matter of degree. However, the figures in Table 3.2 do provide some pointers.

On the one hand, the recovery in the export ratio (item B6) is an important change in the desired direction, with quite a rapid (c. 10% p.a.) growth in export volumes in 1983–94 (CEPA, 1996: 69). Notable is the increase in gold exports. On the other hand, the even larger increase in imports (item B7) is almost certainly not what was desired, because of its implications for the domestic production of import substitutes (increasing the production of tradeables includes ex-

---

[6] Total OECD aid to developing countries has been declining since the early 1990s and Chapter 10 by Harrigan and Younger shows a rather steeply declining trend in Ghana's aid receipts since 1989.

[7] See Rimmer, 1992, chapters 7 and 8, for comparisons of policies in 1972–82 and 1983–90.

[8] See Szereszewski, 1965, Appendix C. His national accounts estimates for 1911 imply a gross domestic saving ratio of 17.6%.

panding import substitutes as well as exports). Moreover, the figures on the sectoral composition of GDP (item D1) also show a trend quite contrary to a desire to boost tradeables, with manufacturing stagnant, agriculture declining and the share of (mainly non-tradeable) services rising.

What about the shift of resources from the public to the private sector which is a goal of most adjustment programmes? Again, our evidence does not suggest much progress. About the only trend with the 'right sign' is the decline of the public sector in total formal sector employment. In all other respects the data in Table 3.2 point to a relative growth in the state sector rather than its opposite. Public sector consumption has risen a little as a proportion of GDP (item B2); government revenues have risen sharply as a share of GDP (item C1) (although an increase from the level to which they had sunk at the beginning of the 1980s was certainly desirable); the share of the state sector in bank credit has also gone up (item C5). Not recorded in the table is an additional fact, that almost all the revival in investment has come from the public sector, with private investment remaining obstinately low in all but a handful of years (see Chapter 1 by Aryeetey and Harrigan, Table 1.2). Overall, then, while there was some macroeconomic stabilization in the 1980s and desirable improvements in investment, exports and tax revenues, there have been few signs of decisive structural shifts of the type normally desired in structural adjustment programmes.

Finally, we can return to Seers and Ross's characterization of the Ghanaian economy as 'fragile'. Would this still be a reasonable description? Of course, the specifics have changed since colonial times but has the generally unresponsive nature of the economy? A persuasive case can be made out that it has not.

First, we can recall the rather muted response of the economy to the measures introduced since 1983. If we take 1985 as the first year of 'normal' response,[9] per capita income grew at about 2.5% p.a. in 1985–90, slowing to under 1.5% p.a. in 1990–5. A growth in average incomes by about a fifth in ten years is not to be disparaged, given the impoverishment that had gone before, but it is not dramatic. Given the depths to which the economy had sunk by the early 1980s, a more elastic rebound might have been hoped for.

The weakness, already noted, of the 'structural' aspects of structural adjustment can also be cited: the relatively unchanging nature of the economy and the near-absence of the types of resource reallocation looked for in adjustment programmes, although the rather rapid growth in export volumes is an encouraging exception to the general story. The too-low levels of saving and investment and the apparent absence of financial deepening suggest a still limited flexibility in the economy, as also, we suspect, do the still very limited technological capabilities in agriculture, industry and elsewhere in the economy.

If by fragile we mean inflexible, then the economy is still fragile. Yet during the economic development which occurred in earlier times and in the way in which they coped with the adversities of the more recent past, Ghanaians have demonstrated time and again their resilience and their responsiveness to incentives, positive and negative. If the economy is nonetheless fragile, the answer must lie with the constraints which prevent this human responsiveness from being translated into a flexible economy. Precisely this issue of constraints is taken up by the late Frimpong-Ansah (1996) in a provocative analysis for the Danquah Memorial Lectures, pointing an accusatory finger at the deadening hand of a parasitic state. Aryeetey and Tarp in the concluding chapter of this book also argue that the state has failed to develop an appropriate institutional structure to reduce transactions and information costs which inhibit private sector development.

Additional factors suggest themselves, however. One is the still severe shortage of modern skills and of high-quality training for their acquisition, which contributes to the country's limited ability to take advantage of modern technological know-how. It must also be doubted whether

---

[9] Total GDP actually declined in real terms in 1981, 1982 and 1983 — a response to the drought as well as to economic mis-management — and then jumped by nearly 9% in 1984, partly because of a resumption of more normal weather. Thereafter, annual GDP growth settled down at around 4.5% in most years.

much progress could be achieved on the basis of anything like the present financial system, which is apparently still marked by a strong resistance to the adoption of competitive modes of operation. Finally, while the continuing domination and ambiguity of the state certainly aggravate the problem, it should not be taken for granted that, were the state to withdraw, a sufficient supply of modern entrepreneurial talent would be forthcoming for a dynamic private sector to drive forward the modernization of the economy at a satisfactory pace — an issue also related to the problem of low saving and investment which has already been given a sufficient airing above.

References

Armstrong, Robert P. (1996) *Ghana Country Assistance Review: A Study in Developmental Effectiveness.* Washington, DC: World Bank Operations Evaluation Department.

Baah-Nuakoh, A., Jebuni, C. D., Oduro A. D. and Asante, Y. (1996) *Exporting Manufactures from Ghana: Is Adjustment Enough?* London, Overseas Development Institute and University of Ghana.

Birmingham, W., Neustadt, I. and Omaboe, E. N. (eds) (1966) *A Study of Contemporary Ghana. Vol. 1: The Economy of Ghana.* London: Allen and Unwin.

Birmingham, W., Neustadt, I. and Omaboe, E. N. (eds) (1967) *A Study of Contemporary Ghana. Vol. 2: Some Aspects of Social Structure.* London: Allen and Unwin.

Centre for Policy Analysis (CEPA) (1996) *Macroeconomic Review and Outlook, 1996.* Accra: CEPA.

Centre for Policy Analysis (CEPA) (1997) *Macroeconomic Review and Outlook, 1997.* Accra: CEPA.

Frimpong-Ansah, Jonathan H. (1996) *Flexibility and Responsiveness in the Ghana Economy* (the 29th J.B. Danquah Memorial Lectures). Accra: Ghana Academy of Arts and Sciences.

Gockel, Augustine F. (1996) *The Formal Social Security System in Ghana.* Accra: Friedrich Ebert Foundation.

Goldsmith, Raymond W. (1969) *Financial Structure and Development.* New Haven, CT and London: Yale University Press.

Goldsmith, Raymond W. (1983) *The Financial Development of India, Japan and the United States.* New Haven, CT and London: Yale University Press.

Huq, M. M. (1989) *The Economy of Ghana: The First 25 Years Since Independence.* London: Macmillan.

Institute of Statistical Social and Economic Research (ISSER) (1996), *The State of the Ghanaian Economy in 1995.* Legon: University of Ghana.

Killick, Tony (1966) 'The Possibilities of Economic Control' in Birmingham *et al.*, Vol. 1.

Killick, Tony (1978) *Development Economics in Action: A Study of Economic Policies in Ghana.* London: Heinemann Educational Books.

Killick, Tony (ed.) (1995) *The Flexible Economy: Causes and Consequences of the Adaptability of National Economies.* London: Routledge.

Killick, T and Szereszewski, R. (1969) 'The Economy of Ghana' in P. Robson and D. A. Lury (eds), *The Economies of Africa.* London: Allen and Unwin.

Kuznets, Simon (1964) *Economic Growth and Structure.* London: Heinemann.

Kuznets, Simon (1966) *Modern Economic Growth: Rate, Structure and Spread.* New Haven, CT: Yale University Press.

Lall, Sanjaya and Wignaraja, Ganeshan (1996) *Skills and Capabilities: Ghana's Industrial Competitiveness.* Oxford: Centro Studi Luca d'Agliano and Queen Elizabeth House. Development Studies Working Paper No. 92, March.

Leith, J. Clark (1975) *Foreign Trade Regimes and Economic Development: Ghana.* New York: National Bureau of Economic Research, Columbia University Press.

North, Douglass C. (1990) *Institutions, Institutional Change, and Economic Performance.* Cambridge: Cambridge University Press.

Omaboe, E. N. (1966) 'An Introductory Survey' in Birmingham *et al.*, Vol. 1.

Rimmer, Douglas (1992) *Staying Poor: Ghana's Political Economy, 1950–1990.* Oxford: Pergamon Press.

Seers, Dudley and Ross, C. R. (1952) *Report on Financial and Physical Problems of Development in the Gold Coast.* Accra: Government Printer, July.

Syrquin, Moshe and Chenery, Hollis (1989), 'Three Decades of Industrialisation', *World Bank Economic Review* Vol. 3, No. 2, May.

Szereszewski, R. (1965) *Structural Changes in the Economy of Ghana, 1891–1911.* London: Weidenfeld and Nicolson.

Wetzel, Deborah L. (1995) 'The Macroeconomics of Fiscal Deficits in Ghana, 1960–94'. D.Phil., Oxford University.

4

Structure & Linkage in the Economy of Ghana: A SAM Approach

MATTHEW POWELL
& JEFFERY ROUND*

1. Introduction

The purpose of this chapter is to examine some structural features of the Ghana economy using a recently compiled social accounting matrix for Ghana for the year 1993. A social accounting matrix (SAM) is a particular representation of the national accounts of an economy designed to establish 'who gets what' from the domestic product and to record how different economic agents interact either through market transactions or via identifiable transfers. A common misconception is that a SAM is the same as an input-output table. However, as we shall see, a SAM is intended to show much more detailed information about social and economic institutions in an economy, even though input-output transactions do usually constitute an important part of the whole picture.

Social accounting matrices have been compiled for many economies in sub-Saharan Africa and in a wide variety of other regions of the world (Pyatt and Round, 1985). The earliest SAMs were constructed in the early 1970s when distributional issues began to assume more prominence in development policy (Pyatt and Round, 1977). Indeed, SAMs have already been constructed for Ghana (for example, Dordunoo, 1996) but the SAM presented and discussed here is the first to be assembled by the Ghana Statistical Service and hence is fully consistent with a set of national accounts. It therefore offers the first real opportunity to examine the economy-wide structure in detail. By 'structure' is meant more than simply the structure of production: it applies to institutions and the interactions between a variety of economic agents in Ghana and with the rest of the world. The overriding aim is to chart salient features of the economy portrayed by the 1993 Ghana SAM. However, it should be noted that there are two other important reasons for compiling a SAM. First, it has often proved to be a good way of synthesizing data from different sources where these data may be of uneven quality — an important reason, given the difficulties frequently faced in national accounts estimation. Secondly, as a representation of integrated macro and meso-level data the SAM has proved to be a useful data framework for a wide range of economy-wide models, including fixed-price multiplier, computable general equilibrium, programming and other multisectoral models (Robinson, 1989). Neither the compilational

*This chapter is based on work undertaken by a team of statisticians in the Ghana Statistical Service which included P. Debra, D. Amable, D. Abuabassah, E. Asuo-Afram and R. Tonhie published in Ghana Statistical Service (1997). Special gratitude is due to these collaborators and to Mr Addomah-Gyabbaah (Deputy Government Statistician) for his advice and support. Helpful comments by Finn Tarp on an earlier version are gratefully acknowledged. However, the authors are solely responsible for the views expressed here.

nor modelling directions will be pursued in any depth here, athough there will be some examination of the multipliers implied by the SAM structure in a later section.

The SAM represents a 'snapshot' of the Ghana economy in 1993 and is not intended to shed light on 'dynamics' or the development process. Clearly there is no technical reason why this exercise might not be repeated for other years or after suitable intervals of time. But to compile a SAM even for one year is a major effort in terms of time, expertise and other valuable resources. Nevertheless even one SAM can be instructive and useful in a variety of contexts because the structure of the Ghana economy is unlikely to change dramatically in the short or medium term even though it is not fixed or a static entity. However, there is still an issue as to the choice of year for compilation: there is unlikely to be a 'typical' year as year-to-year events can so easily affect the overall picture. Here the choice was 1993 primarily because it was the most recent year for which most of the required data were available. Hence the reasons are largely statistical rather than economic. But, as noted by Aryeetey and Harrigan in Chapter 1, savings were reckoned to be abnormally low and there was an unusually high balance of payments deficit, and this has to be borne in mind when using the SAM for structural analysis.

Details of the compilation procedures underlying the Ghana SAM are complex.[1] However, it is important to note that many data sources were used to compile the Ghana SAM. These included industrial surveys, the Ghana Living Standards Survey (GLSS) 1991–92, government accounts, balance of payments statistics, agricultural surveys, Bank of Ghana data, etc. It is also important to note that the coverage of 'production activity' includes small-scale household sector activity, which in turn comprises much of the activity usually referred to as the 'informal sector'[2] as well as imputations of non-market production especially in agriculture and in rural areas generally. Obviously the resulting estimates are not necessarily of uniform reliability, although they are considered the best that can be obtained given the data sources and procedures currently available. The SAM compilation forms part of a major re-estimation of the national accounts for Ghana which has started with the 1993 data. The ensuing estimates reported in this chapter are therefore expected to be at variance with corresponding estimates for 1993 reported in other chapters.

The chapter is organized in three sections. Section 2 presents a simple overview of the SAM framework introducing the aggregated results of the revised national accounts for Ghana in 1993. Section 3 extends this discussion by considering some structural characteristics of the economy based on a more detailed version of the SAM. Finally, in section 4 we examine some features of interdependence in Ghana by deriving and commenting on some accounting multipliers that correspond to the 1993 SAM.

2.   The SAM Framework

Although there is no single, representative framework for a SAM there are some basic rules to which all SAMs should conform. First, it must be square: thus the accounts recording transactions and transfers in the economy are represented both as rows (showing receipts, or 'resources') and as columns (showing payments, or 'uses'). Secondly, it is a single-entry system which means that each transaction is recorded only once — as a payment from one account and as a receipt by another. Thirdly, it is comprehensive, in the sense that it records the full circular flow of income within a complete set of macroeconomic accounts. Fourthly, to qualify as a *social* accounting matrix it should include some disaggregation of institutional sectors, ideally including a further disaggregation of the household sector, and a mapping of income to different categories of factors of production. Clearly many SAMs extend well beyond these minimum requirements and

---

[1] Full details are provided in the main report and other source material (Ghana Statistical Service, 1997).
[2] The informal sector has been defined in alternative ways and is subject to wide interpretation. Here it is confined essentially to unincorporated business activity reported by respondent households in the GLSS, although this is bound to exclude most illegal and irregular activity which is largely unreported. The measurement of informal sector activity in Ghana is considered in Ghana Statistical Service (1996a).

record a variety of additional interrelationships including, for example, detailed capital and financial transfers between institutional sectors (flow of funds) and even links with demographic and environmental accounts.

To illustrate these general features we introduce a simplified and highly aggregated version of the Ghana SAM in Table 4.1.[3] The matrix consists of five blocks of rows and columns and the numerical entries are expressed in billions of cedis (at current prices). Each block consists of disaggregated sets of accounts but these will not be referred to in any detail in this section. The first row and column represents the production account and shows the supply and use of commodities, as conventionally represented in an input-output table. Total intermediate consumption of the products of each activity is shown in cell (1,1). The rest of the production account row shows the expenditure on products by final users (final consumption expenditure, fixed capital formation and change in stocks, and exports). The production account column shows imports and the generation of valued added (inclusive of net taxes on products), which is the Ghana gross domestic product valued at market prices (3846.0). The account balances as it shows the uses and resources of products available in Ghana from domestic supply and imports. The second account records the generation and distribution of different kinds of factor income. In the second row the domestic product appears as a receipt from the production account (cell (2,1) and net factor income from abroad is a receipt from the rest of the world account (cell (2,5). The total factor income received is 'national income' (3866.6) which is shown as a payment to the current account of institutional sectors in the second column (cell (3,2)) because it represents the income received in return for factor services provided. Institutional sectors also receive net current transfer income from abroad (263.2) shown in cell (3,5). There are also property incomes and current transfer payments between institutions (cell (3,3)) which in total amount to 616.2 but which net out to zero at the aggregate level. The balancing item on the current account for institutions is gross domestic savings (487.1) which enters as a payment to the combined capital accounts (cell (4,3)). Domestic savings are augmented by capital transfers from abroad (493.6) in cell (4,5) to give the total resources to finance gross fixed capital formation and the change in stocks (834.4) in cell (1,4) and net lending abroad (146.3) in cell (5,4). The final row and column show the balance of transactions with the rest of the world. This completes the aggregate picture of the 1993 national accounts for Ghana in matrix format.

Table 4.1   Outline SAM in Schematic Form: Ghana 1993 (billions of cedis)

SAM accounts	Code	(1)	(2)	(3)	(4)	(5)	TOTAL
Production Activities	(1)	Intermediate consumption 2073.4		Final consumption expenditure 3626.5	Fixed capital formation + Δ stocks 834.4	Exports 693.3	7212.7
Factor accounts	(2)	Domestic product 3846.0				Net employee compensation from RoW -5.5	3840.5
Institutions' current accounts	(3)		National income 3840.5	Property income and current transfers 616.2		Net current transfers from RoW 263.2	4720.2
Capital accumulation accounts	(4)			Savings 487.1	Capital transfers 33.9	Net capital transfers from RoW 493.6	1014.6
Rest of the world accounts	(5)	Imports 1298.3			Net lending abroad 146.3		1444.6
TOTAL		7239.6	3840.5	4720.2	1014.6	1444.6	

[3] Blocks of accounts in the full schema (Ghana Statistical Service, 1997) have been aggregated and condensed to simplify exposition.

The overall structure of Table 4.1 is simple and quite appealing from the point of view of ascertaining how the macroeconomic accounts fit together in aggregate. Diagonal entries are shaded to signify cells where transactions take place between sub-accounts but which net out to zero in aggregate. Key aggregates are shown in 'boxed' cells. The individual cells show the main transactions and the circular flow of income in a quite graphic way, in particular to show how income moves through and within the system from one account to the next. None of the estimates in Table 4.1 makes any allowance for the consumption of fixed capital (depreciation). However, this would not affect the overall balance, it would merely affect the size and representation of particular aggregates (GDP, fixed capital formation and savings).

Four features of the relative magnitudes of the aggregates are particularly noteworthy. First, we note the high trade dependence of the economy: imports are 33.8% of GDP (market prices), while exports are 18%. The composition of exports and imports will be noted in section 3. Secondly, (aggregate) gross domestic savings are seen to amount to 12.7% of national income. At first sight this estimate for domestic savings might be a matter of some debate, but the accounts clearly show that any changes to it would have immediate consequences for other estimates if accounting balance is to be maintained. Thirdly, despite low domestic savings, capital formation is relatively high (21.7% of GDP) as most of the finance for domestic investment comes from abroad: net capital transfers from abroad are almost as large as domestic savings.[4] Fourthly, as a natural counterpart of the investment-savings gap the current external balance in 1993 (net lending abroad less net capital transfers from abroad) was substantial, amounting to a deficit of 347.3, or 9% of GDP. These are important insights about the aggregate picture of the economy of Ghana and it provides the background for more detailed insights in subsequent sections.

3. Structural Characteristics of the Ghana Economy in 1993

Ghana SAM with institutional sectors

Disaggregations of the SAM portrayed in Table 4.1 can, in principle, take a variety of forms. Clearly, it is tempting to try to achieve a fine and detailed set of sub-classifications throughout. But in Ghana, as in most economies, it is not possible from the data available to achieve more than a limited disaggregation and compromises in the choice of classifications have to be made so as to achieve acceptable levels of reliability in the reported estimates. For example, household surveys are designed to yield statistically sound estimates up to a given level of disaggregation and if classifications are adopted beyond this level of disaggregation then the results may not be reliable.

A version of the full SAM[5] is shown as Table 4.2. It shows blocks of accounts together with some limited disaggregation of each block. Initially the production accounts (labelled 'activities') are split into just three sectors: agriculture, industry and services, although further details of the production structure are shown and discussed later in this section. The 'factor' accounts include nine accounts covering three broad categories: employee compensation, operating surplus and mixed income. The 'distribution and use of income' and 'capital' accounts are subdivided by broad institutional sector following standard international guidelines. The sectors comprise households, corporate enterprises (financial and non-financial), government and non-profit institutions serving households ('NPISH', which include private schools, clinics, etc.) while households are further disaggregated into urban and rural household categories. Finally, we show two accounts for the 'rest of the world' to distinguish external transactions on current and capital account.

---

[4] The high aid dependency implied here is underlined and referred to in Aryeetey and Harrigan (chapter 1) and Harrigan and Younger (Chapter 10).
[5] A mini version of the full SAM is included as Table A.1 in an appendix to this paper.

Table 4.2   SAM for Ghana 1993 (billions of cedis)

Column account groups:
- 1 ACTIVITIES: (1) Agriculture, (2) Industry, (3) Services
- 2 FACTORS: (4) Comp of Employees Skilled Male, (5) Comp of Employees Unskilled Male, (6) Comp of Employees Skilled Female, (7) Comp of Employees Unskilled Female, (8) Mixed Income (Gross) Skilled Male, (9) Mixed Income (Gross) Unskilled Male, (10) Mixed Income (Gross) Skilled Female, (11) Mixed Income (Gross) Unskilled Female, (12) Operating Surplus (Gross), (13) Indirect Taxes on production
- 3 INSTITUTIONS, DISTRIBUTION AND USE: (14) Households - Rural, (15) Households - Urban, (16) Non Financial Corporations, (17) Financial Corporations, (18) Government, (19) Non Profit Institutions Serving Households
- 4 INSTITUTIONS CAPITAL: (20) Households - Rural, (21) Households - Urban, (22) Non Financial Corporations, (23) Financial Corporations, (24) Government, (25) Non Profit Institutions Serving Households
- FINT & FIXED CAPL: (26) Financial Assets, (27) Fixed Capital Formation, (28) Increases in Stocks
- 5 ROW: (29) Current, (30) Capital

Row	1	2	3	4	5	6	7	8	9	10	11	12	13	14	15	16	17	18	19	20	21	22	23	24	25	26	27	28	29	30
1 Agriculture	219.7	131.2	300.7											685.3	950.8													-162.9	224.3	
1 Industry	103.7	557.0	441.5											318.9	476.9												866.4	76.1	481.4	
1 Services	172.8	146.8	236.8											218.1	306.7			568.2	85.7								54.8	0.0	7.6	
2 Skilled Male	44.8	63.6	162.1																											
2 Unskilled Male	135.8	102.7	74.6																											
2 Skilled Female	5.3	10.7	68.5																											
2 Unskilled Female	17.0	13.0	75.2																											
2 Mixed Inc. Skilled Male	235.2	111.7	69.7																											
2 Mixed Inc. Unskilled Male	726.9	175.1	26.7																											
2 Mixed Inc. Skilled Female	4.0	13.7	178.4																											
2 Mixed Inc. Unskilled Female	212.7	91.3	170.8																											
2 Operating Surplus (Gross)	20.5	353.0																												
2 Indirect Taxes on production	1.4	6.4	2.5																											
3 Households - Rural				141.0	191.7	26.9	42.3	187.7	263.5	21.7	257.5			15.1	0.1	7.8	2.4	10.9											24.9	
3 Households - Urban				224.3	208.9	63.8	56.2	234.4	708.1	22.7	225.0			0.5	19.1	9.8	2.9	13.5											31.0	
3 Non Financial Corporations												386.8		5.4	6.7	17.7	16.3	0.1	-40.5											
3 Financial Corporations												55.7		52.1	64.7	2.2	20.3	2.1	0.2										10.1	
3 Government	56.3	358.0	1.4									94.3	10.4			24.8	130.5	99.6	38.3	1.8	0.2								147.6	
3 Non Profit Institutions Serving Households												7.5			85.7					0.9	3.5								47.7	
4 Households - Rural														-103.5												97.6				
4 Households - Urban															-13.0											13.2				
4 Non Financial Corporations																285.5							7.1	1.0		256.0				
4 Financial Corporations																	89.2					1.5		17.9		166.0				
4 Government																		221.0								391.7				
4 Non Profit Institutions Serving Households																			7.8							0.9				
Financial Assets																						-87.7	-2.0	-0.4	3.2					
Fixed Capital Formation																				-8.9	-3.8	69.5	255.2	260.8	5.4					
Increases in Stocks																				1.5	3.2	66.6	22.6	327.4	0.0					
5 Current	52.1	1010.1	196.0											1.6	2.0											146.3			347.3	
5 Capital																														
TOTAL (31)	2048.3	3164.3	2005.1	365.2	400.6	90.6	98.5	422.1	971.7	44.4	482.4	544.3	10.4	1193.5	1819.9	347.8	229.1	1039.8	93.5	-3.7	4.6	548.4	275.8	612.8	8.7	1071.8	921.3	-86.8	1301.9	493.6

Source: Ghana Statistical Service, 1997, and Table A.1 (Discrepancies are due to rounding).

In the factor accounts we distinguish between categories of employees by gender and skill (defined according to the level of education attained). Operating surplus and mixed income are distinguished on the basis of the type of enterprise. Operating surplus is identified as a return to the capital employed in corporate or quasi-corporate enterprises. By contrast, mixed income arises in unincorporated enterprises which are almost entirely household sector enterprises and represent 'informal' activity in the broadest sense of the term. The informal sector can be seen to generate a significant part of the domestic product of Ghana and some features of this are set out in section 3. Here we note that as it is difficult to distinguish the returns to labour and the returns to capital in the case of an own account worker or employer in a small household sector enterprise, hence this income is classified as mixed income. However, it is also classified according to the gender and skill level of the entrepreneur. In the household accounts we only report a distinction between urban and rural households. Although more detailed disaggregations are possible, estimates (especially of household savings) become much less reliable.

Some features of the 1993 SAM shown in Table 4.2 can now be highlighted. Again, it should be noted that all figures are in billions of cedis (at current prices). First, we consider the payment of income by production activities to factors: cell (2,1). We note that 37.9% of gross domestic product (i.e. 1460.0) is generated in the agricultural sector (defined here to include forestry and fishing); 34.3% in industry (including mining, manufacturing and construction); and the remaining 27.7% in services (including public administration and trade services).[6] These estimates include imputed incomes of many non-market activities which arise from household-based agricultural and informal sector activities. It is clear that the patterns of factor income generation across each of the three production sectors differ markedly and in accordance with expectations. For example, the majority of value added in 'agriculture' is classified as mixed income (80.7% of the total value added in that sector), most of which is attributed to male, unskilled farmers and entrepreneurs, although we know that the generation of this income involves unpaid family helpers, mainly women and children. Only 13.9% of income generated in this sector is employee compensation, and 9.3% is accounted for by male, unskilled labour. The pattern of factor income generated in the service sector is quite different. The largest share (50.8%) is employee compensation, with 37.4% being attributed to male employment, although this is the sector which generates most reported female employee compensation. Mixed income is also sizeable, generating 32.8% of the sector's value added. In the industry sector 26.8% of value added comes from operating surplus in corporate (and quasi-corporate) enterprises. But again, mixed income is significant, generating 29.7% of industry value added. Most of the net indirect taxes arise from taxes on industrial products. Overall, by far the largest contributing factor to total gross domestic product is mixed income, accounting for 50% of the total. Almost two-thirds of this emanates from the agricultural sector. It not only shows the significance of small-scale agriculture but also of small-scale industry and service activity generally. As noted later, most of this is associated with the household sector — and much of this is 'informal'.

Next we consider the payment of factor income to institutional sectors (cell 3,2), and then the composition of total income across these sectors after including the receipt of property income and current income transfers. We see from Table 4.2 that the patterns of factor income received by urban and rural households are broadly similar, the only significant difference being in the receipt of mixed income from unskilled male-and female-headed farms and businesses. Most male-headed business income is received by urban households (67.6%) whereas just over a half of the female-headed income in this category is received by rural households (53.0%). Urban households received 45.3% of the domestic product (1743.2) as direct remuneration in the form

---

[6] Note the pronounced differences between the sectoral percentages, based on the revised national accounts for Ghana, and those reported in Killick (chapter 3). The methodology has been substantially revised: it takes account of new data sources (such as the Ghana Living Standards Survey) and adopts a new methodology recommended by the inter-agency SNA(1993).

of employee compensation or mixed income, and rural households received 29.4% (1132.3). Most operating surplus is attributable to non-financial corporations (i.e. 386.8), while 426.1 is a revenue by government in the form of net indirect taxes (taxes on products, less subsidies, plus fees and licences).

Adjacent to the factor income receipts in row 3 are the intersectoral payments of property income and current transfers between institutions (cell 3,3). Of the overall total of 616.2 the government is by far the most important sector in the redistributive process, receiving a total of 371.8 (mainly in the form of direct taxes) and making payments of 250.8, including 99.6 within the government sector itself. Both urban and rural households are reported as small net providers of such income (44.8 and 36.7 respectively), non-financial companies make net payments and financial companies are net recipients. The Bank of Ghana is classified as a part of the financial corporations sector and the latter item includes debt write-offs. Urban and rural households are also shown as receiving net transfers from abroad of 29.0 and 23.3 respectively, while the government also received 147.6 in transfers from abroad. Although these intersectoral transactions do not appear large relative to the factor income generated, they are an important component and represent most of what we know about the redistributive process. However, estimates are notoriously difficult to derive and the results must therefore be treated with a good deal of caution. It is highly likely, for example, that households report only a small fraction of income transfers, either as receipts or payments, and the true figures for both are likely to be somewhat higher.

Column 3 (the distribution and use of income accounts) shows current account outlays by institutional sectors. Cell 1,3 shows the expenditures of institutions on products. These are current expenditures by the household and government sectors on both domestically produced and imported products. Cell 3,3, property income and current transfers between institutional sectors, have already been referred to. However, the next account shows the implied sectoral composition of domestic savings. In Table 4.1 gross domestic savings in Ghana in 1993 were reported to be 487.1 in aggregate, and now cell 4,3 of Table 4.2 shows the sectoral contributions to this total. It is clear from the breakdown that the household sector as a whole is estimated to dissave by -116.5, with urban and rural households contributing -103.5 and -13.0 respectively. These amount to 8.7 % and 0.7 % of total income in each household sector respectively. All other institutions contribute positively to domestic savings. The general government sector budget surplus is 221.0, and the NPISH sector shows a trading surplus of 7.8, but the largest contribution to domestic savings comes from non-financial companies (285.5). It is perhaps important to further emphasize the significance of these findings in the context of the SAM and our comments in section 2. It is tempting to argue that the implied dissaving by households is due to shortfalls in reported income of one form or another. But such shortfalls would be matched by expenditures (or outlays) somewhere else in the system, such are the constraints inherent in the SAM, so the results must have some degree of credibility.

The capital accounts show the sectoral balances between the receipt of capital finance and investments in real and financial assets. This again summarizes more detailed estimates provided elsewhere (Ghana Statistical Service, 1997 and Table A1 in the appendix) on the integrated flow of funds accounts. Estimates of real investment in the form of gross fixed capital formation in 1993 amounted to 921.2 (including 55.0 formally attributable to trade margins on these goods), and the change in stocks was 86.8, these figures by activity (product) of origin shown in the row of the activity accounts. The allocation of this investment across institutional sectors is shown in rows 27 and 28 of block 4 of the appendix SAM, this constituting part of the uses of capital financial resources by institutional sectors. Thus, most fixed capital formation (566.6) takes place in the non-financial corporations sector, 327.4 in the government sector, and a relatively small amount in the remaining institutional sectors. Similarly, row 28 records the sectoral allocation of change in stocks. The acquisition of financial assets by institutional sectors (which may be negative) is shown similarly in row 26 of the same block. Each of these acquisitions of real and financial assets corresponds to outlays in the columns of capital accounts of institutions, matching receipts of capital resources in the rows, of which savings form part and the increase in financial liabilities (column 26) also constitutes a substantial part. In cell 4,4 we see the estimated (direct) intersectoral capital transfers, but these are estimated to be small relative to transfers via the flow of funds.

Supply and use table

In the discussion so far the production accounts have been set out in a fairly aggregative form. However, more detailed information is now shown on the production and pattern of trade in goods and services. This information is set out in Table 4.3 which comprises four main panels of data and which constitutes the input-output accounts for Ghana. It shows the supply and use of ten categories of products according to fourteen categories of production activities, further subdivided according to the institutional sector in which the production activity takes place. The four numbered panels refer to the supply of products by activities (panel 1), the intermediate use of products by activities (panel 2), the value added generated in activities (panel 3), and the final use of products (panel 4). The product accounts are shown as the columns of panels 1 and 2 (supply and intermediate use) and in panel 3 (final use). The production activity (by sector) accounts are shown along the rows of panels 1, 2 and 3.

The table can be read as follows. Each cell of panel 1 shows the total supply of a product by an activity at basic prices (i.e. these are the amounts receivable by the producer, net of margins and net taxes on products). The total supply of each product, including imports, valued inclusive of margins and net product taxes, is obtained from the column totals of panel 1. These totals are not shown but match exactly the total use of products shown below panel 4. Panels 2, 3 and 4 are transposed versions of conventional input-output accounts. Thus, intermediate consumption and final uses of each product (panels 2 and 4) are shown down the columns rather than along the rows. Intermediate use is distinguished by activity and final use by final consumption (and by sector), gross capital formation and exports. They show, for example, that manufacturing industry (based in the household sector) used 130.0 of agriculture, forestry and fishing products, and that households consumed 1799.2 for final use. Similarly, value added by activity is shown in the rows of panel 3, with sub-categories of value added in the columns. For example, manufacturing industry (again based in the household sector) generated value added in the form of 13.5 as compensation of employees, 137.1 as mixed income, 9.5 as allowances for capital consumption and 5.2 as indirect taxes on production. The total output of activities (row sums of panel 1) match the total inputs (row sums of panels 2 and 3), as shown.

What features of the structure of production in Ghana can be ascertained from Table 4.3? The contributions to 1993 gross domestic product by each activity can be obtained from the row totals (not shown) of panel 3. According to this classification the activity which contributed the most to GDP is agriculture and livestock (29.3%), the vast majority of which, as expected, is generated in the household sector and comprises imputed and cash income. The cocoa sector contributed only 2.1% to GDP.[7] It is interesting to note that 30.1% of value added is generated in farms classified as part of the household sector. The forestry and logging and the fishing activities contributed at least as much to GDP as cocoa. Of the remaining activities those which contributed the most to GDP were manufacturing (10.6%) and construction (8.4%). The export figures confirm that Ghana is still heavily dominated by exports of primary goods. Besides 'agricultural, forestry and fishing' products (i.e. cocoa, timber, etc.) which collectively amounted to 32.4% of total exports, the largest category of export products was 'ores and minerals' (44.5%). Metal (5.5%) and non-metallic products (15.9%) were small contributors in value by comparison.

The patterns of aggregate household consumption, gross capital formation and stock-build-

---

[7] One of the results of the revised national accounts is to suggest that the value added in cocoa has been over-recorded in the past.

Table 4.3   Supply and Use Table: Ghana 1993 (billions of cedis)

1. SUPPLY

2. INTERMEDIATE USE

3. VALUE ADDED

4. FINAL USE

Final Consumption	Households	1,799.2	52.6	487.7	228.5	63.5	46.4	1.2	90.4	822	111.0
	Government									15.8	552.4
	Non Profit Inst Serving Households										85.7
Gross Fixed Capital Form.	Non Govt.				5.0	277.0	311.9				
Stock building	Govt Services				6.9	263.8	56.7				
Exports og Goods and Services		-164.9	12.4	185.3	3.3	110.5	38.2				7.3

TOTAL USE

	2,244.1	534.9	898.9	696.0	844.3	432.4	1.6	384.0	423.4	758.0

Key   hh=households
       nfc=non financial corporations
       fc=financial corporations
       gg=general government
       npish= non profit institutions serving households

Source Ghana Statistical Service (1997)

ing implied by panel 4 (final use) of Table 4.3 contain few surprises. The vast majority of household final consumption (actual and imputed) is on 'agricultural' products (60.7%), and most fixed capital formation uses 'metal products and machinery' (46.6%) and 'construction' (52.5%). What is much harder to ascertain from Table 4.3 is the nature and degree of interdependence between production activities in Ghana. This is because the intermediate consumption of products by activities (i.e. raw material purchases) is recorded as a combined purchase of domestically produced and imported products, so care has to be taken in interpreting the table of results in this respect. An analysis of interdependence is carried out in section 4.

Sectoral profiles and informal sector activity
The information on activity by institutional sector shown in Table 4.3 provides sufficient detail for an analysis of the sectoral contributions to GDP. The 1993 estimates are summarised in Table 4.4, which shows the generation of value added both by broad activity grouping and according to the institutional sector in which the production originates.

The value added generated in the household sector arises from production activity in farms and other agricultural units, and unincorporated businesses, operated by employers or workers on own account, which generate income through marketed or non-marketed output. Table 4.4 shows that 2112.5 billions of cedis (62% of total value added) is generated in the household sector. As noted earlier, most of this household sector production activity is 'informal sector' activity,[8] covering farm as well as non-farm production, and market and non-market activity, the latter largely being an imputed valuation. A large proportion of the total income generated in the household sector is derived from agricultural activity, amounting to 1315.4 (or 62.3%), of which the majority is in agriculture and livestock (981.8) and fishing (206.1). Indeed, the household sector contributes the vast majority of the value added in 'agriculture' (94%), whereas it contributes 411.3 (or 42.8%) of 'manufacturing' and 385.8 (or 36.2%) of 'services'. Overall these figures confirm the importance of the informal sector in Ghana and its significant contribution to Ghana GDP.

4.   Interdependence in the Ghanaian Economy

Analytical background
One immediate use of the SAM is to examine linkages in the economy and to try to identify the most important structural features that emerge. Clearly a SAM is only a snapshot of one period's transactions and the pattern of transactions may not be immutable. Therefore care has to be taken in drawing inferences on the basis of just one SAM. However, parts of the SAM structure are unlikely to change dramatically over the short or medium term especially insofar as they capture technological features or reflect intrinsic social or behavioural characteristics of the economy. Therefore, bearing this caveat in mind, we shall now examine the nature of interdependence in the Ghanaian economy and, in particular, the relationships between production structure, income generation and distribution as portrayed by the 1993 SAM. The analysis in this section is based on a method developed by Pyatt and Round (1985) which, in turn, is based on a simple fixed coefficient model, although it should be emphasized that the aim here is not to construct a formal model of the economy *per se*. As we stated at the outset, it is simply to examine features and some possible implications of the existing economic structure of Ghana.

The starting point is to observe the overall framework of the SAM and to distinguish between sets of endogenous and exogenous accounts. This distinction is central to the analytical frame-

---

[8] This excludes certain 'formal' sector activities in the household sector such as doctors, lawyers and other regulated and quasi-corporate activity. Results reported in Ghana Statistical Service (1996a and b) suggest that approximately 95% of household activity may be classified as 'informal'.

work that now follows. In the simplest of terms, endogenous accounts are those from which outlays can reasonably be assumed to be determined (endogenously), given the total income (or output) levels of those accounts. Correspondingly, exogenous accounts are those where outlays are considered to be determined outside the system and are therefore 'given' for present purposes. The analytical framework then relies on a simple fixed-price multiplier model, better thought of as a set of 'accounting multipliers', where we simply rely on the structure of the SAM and average (or marginal) propensities derived from it to determine the endogenous outlays. These patterns of endogenous outlays are defined by a matrix of propensities *A*, the cells of which show the receipt of account *i* (row *i*) per unit of outlay of account *j* (column *j*).

Table 4.4 Sectoral Contributions to Ghana GDP 1993 (billions of cedis)

	HH	NFC	FC	GG	NPISH	TOTAL
Cocoa	51.2	20.9				72.1
Agriculture & Livestock	981.8	22.0				1,003.8
Forestry and Logging	76.4	31.2				107.7
Fishing	206.1	14.1				220.2
Sub-total	*1,315.4*	*88.3*				*1,403.7*
Mining and Quarrying	16.9	194.5				211.4
Manufacturing	165.3	198.0				363.3
Electricity and Water		99.6				99.6
Construction	229.1	44.3		13.4		286.8
Sub-total	*411.3*	*536.4*		*13.4*		*961.1*
Wholesale, Retail, Hotels & Restaurants	218.8	5.9				224.7
Transport Storage & Communication	83.9	82.1				166.0
Finance, Real Estate & Business Services	18.4		128.3	11.7		158.4
Public Administration				168.2		168.2
Education and Health		4.2		223.3	2.5	230.0
Other Community, Social, Personal & Service	64.6	2.0		18.1	33.5	118.1
Sub-total	*385.8*	*94.2*	*128.3*	*421.2*	*36.0*	*1,065.4*
Total	2,112.5	718.9	128.3	434.6	36.0	3,430.3
Net Indirect Tax on Products						415.7
TOTAL GDP						3,846.0

Key: HH   households
   NFC   non financial corporations
   FC   financial corporations
   GG   general government
   NPISH non profit institutions serving households

Referring back to Tables 4.1 and 4.2, five blocks of accounts are distinguished in the overall structure: activities, factors, institutions (distribution and use), institutions (capital), and rest of the world. In line with previous applications of the method (Pyatt and Round, 1985), the government, capital and rest of the world accounts are treated as exogenous accounts. The endogenous accounts (and hence the matrix A) can therefore be represented in terms of three blocks of accounts: activities, factors and institutions' 'distribution and use' accounts (but excluding government). Thus it is as though we consider the effects of exogenous injections of income (resources) into the endogenous accounts arising from a change in exports, investment or government expenditure[9] by tracing the multiplier repercussions of these injections through and around the system.

Against this background, the total incomes (and hence outlays) of the endogenous accounts y can be expressed in terms of exogenous income injections x and endogenous incomes Ay. In turn this defines a multiplier matrix M based on the matrix of propensities A as follows:

$$y = Ay + x$$
$$= (I - A)^{-1} x = Mx \qquad (1)$$

where M is a multiplier matrix. Equation (1) simply shows the overall effect on endogenous account totals necessary to maintain the same overall structure of endogenous transactions (A) as in the original SAM, given a set of exogenous injections x. It is similar to an input-output model except that A is an extended matrix of propensities embracing all endogenous transactions and not just interindustry transactions between activities.

The Pyatt-Round method builds on this simple structure and shows that (1) can be expressed as

$$y = M_{a3}M_{a2}M_{a1}x \qquad (2)$$

where the decomposition into M_{a1}, M_{a2} and M_{a3} represents separate components of interdependence in the endogenous part of the system. In particular, we distinguish the multiplier effects within, across and between the blocks of accounts for production activities, factors of production, and institutional sectors (households and enterprises), as follows. M_{a1} captures the 'within block' multipliers, which comprise the input-output multipliers together with a similar set of multipliers showing the effect if the pattern of transfers between institutional sectors is maintained. M_{a2} shows the multiplier effects which might arise from an income injection into the accounts of one block on the accounts of a different block. For example, it could show the effect of an income injection into activities (e.g. construction) on household income, excluding input-output and other 'within block' multipliers. We shall call these 'across block' effects. Finally, M_{a3} shows the 'between block' effects of an injection into one block on the accounts of that same block, resulting from the linkages around the system but excluding the effects within blocks which are already included in M_{a1}. The M_{a3} multipliers are particularly interesting because they isolate a measure of the 'global' interdependence between sectors, factors and institutions in the system.

A more convenient version of the multiplier decomposition is to express it in 'Stone-additive' form (Pyatt and Round, 1985), using the identity:

$$M_{a3}M_{a2}M_{a1} \equiv I + (M_{a1} - I) + (M_{a2} - I)M_{a1} + (M_{a3} - I) M_{a2}M_{a1}$$

---

[9] These injections could be negative (e.g. retrenchment of government expenditure) but we shall consider them to be positive for simplicity and ease of comparison.

where the right-hand side components may be expressed as I, M_1, M_2 and M_3. Hence we may write

$$y = [I + M_1 + M_2 + M_3]x \tag{3}$$

where M_1, M_2 and M_3 are now the 'additive' multiplier effects with broadly similar interpretations to the corresponding multiplicative effects.

Multipliers for the Ghana SAM

The analytical approach outlined above can be used to examine the economy-wide effects of a unit injection into particular endogenous accounts of the system as depicted by the structure of the Ghana SAM for 1993.[10] The experiments are limited to a selection of endogenous accounts and in particular those which might reasonably be subject to direct changes of income either from the rest of the world (e.g. exports), government (e.g. government expenditure), or from the capital account (e.g. fixed capital formation), although, in principle, any of the endogenous accounts of the system could be considered. In order to simplify exposition the exogenous impacts are standardized to represent an injection of 100 units (representing multiples of cedis). All impacts will be described in terms of an 'increase', although in multiplier terms the impacts would be negative if an exogenous decrease in sectoral income is postulated. Table 4.5 summarizes the effects of a separate injection of income into four activity accounts, broadly representative of postulated changes in exports, capital formation and government expenditure. Obviously it must be emphasized that the multiplier analysis is only indicative of linkage and income transmission, and for this reason some of the results are aggregated in the table to avoid a misleading interpretation or are otherwise qualified below.

Consider first an injection of 100 units into cocoa arising, say, from an additional 100 units of exports in value terms. In the first panel of Table 4.5 we see the possible effects (under the strict assumptions of the fixed-price multiplier model) on selected accounts and hence of different facets of economic activity. In particular we have highlighted the effects on factors and households alongside the overall effects on production activity. The first column of the decomposition (I) shows the initial impact, in this case 100 in cocoa. As this is the only initial impact it also constitutes the total initial impact on production activities. The 'within block' multiplier (M_1) captures the input-output multipliers, and it can be seen that only 62 additional units of output would be generated indirectly through inter-industry linkages. Therefore the interdependence between groups of activities (i.e. the input-output linkage) is quite weak. The next column shows the M_2 effects, which in this case are the effects of increased cocoa production on factor and household income taking account of the production linkages only. The results suggest that unskilled/male workers and mixed income are the biggest direct recipients of factor incomes (by 21 and 31 units respectively) and that urban and rural households directly benefit by an extra 68 units in total.[11] Finally the column M_3 shows the additional 'between block' multiplier effects arising from the linkages between parts of the system after accounting for the initial injections of income and the multiplier effects through I, M_1 and M_2. Here we see that unskilled/male workers receive a further 13 units, although this is proportionately less than is received by other factors in M_2; and mixed income picks up a further 83 units, almost three times the direct income generated to this factor by the initial expansion of cocoa in M_2.

---

[10] Some slight modifications were introduced to the calculation of matrix A. In the Ghana SAM urban households dissave. Here it is assumed that urban households neither save nor dissave out of a marginal unit of income.

[11] Note that distributional effects of urban and rural houholds are distinguished in Table 4.5 as they are in the SAM. However, this illustrates that the simple averaging assumption employed in the multiplier analysis can be misleading. In this case it is likely that rural households would benefit substantially more than urban households from the factor income generated.

Table 4.5   Selected Multiplier Effects Derived from the Ghana SAM (Injections of 100 units of income)

Account in which injection originates	Account affected by injection	1	M_1	M_2	M_3	M
Cocoa	Employees: skilled/male			10	9	18
	Employees: unskilled/male			21	13	34
	Employees: skilled/female			1	1	3
	Employees: unskilled/female			4	2	6
	Mixed Income			31	83	115
	Operating Surplus			8	12	20
	Urban Households			40	67	107
	Rural Households			28	43	71
	Cocoa	100	0		7	108
	Total Activity Impact	100	62		244	406
Mining	Employees: skilled/male			9	6	15
	Employees: unskilled/male			17	8	25
	Employees: skilled/female			0	1	1
	Employees: unskilled/female			1	2	3
	Mixed Income			9	50	58
	Operating Surplus			32	7	40
	Urban Households			22	41	63
	Rural Households			17	26	43
	Mining	100	3		4	107
	Total Activity Impact	100	36		148	284
Construction	Employees: skilled/male			4	9	14
	Employees: unskilled/male			5	13	18
	Employees: skilled/female			0	2	2
	Employees: unskilled/female			0	2	3
	Mixed income			59	85	144
	Operating Surplus			12	12	24
	Urban Households			45	69	114
	Rural Households			25	44	70
	Construction	100	0		8	108
	Total Activity Impact	100	48		251	399
Education and Health	Employees: skilled/male			33	11	44
	Employees: unskilled/male			15	15	30
	Employees: skilled/female			19	2	21
	Employees: unskilled/female			13	3	15
	Mixed Income			1	101	102
	Operating Surplus			13	15	28
	Urban Households			50	81	132
	Rural Households			32	52	84
	Education and Health	100	0		9	109
	Total Activity Impact	100	14		296	410

The increase in factor income translates into further income to institutional sectors of which urban and rural households receive 67 and 43 units respectively. The M_3 multipliers also show activity effects. The total multiplier effect here is 244 which is substantially greater than the input-output multipliers (M_1) although the multiplier for cocoa, unsurprisingly, is still very small amounting to only 7 units.

So what do these M_3 multipliers actually show? They are sometimes substantially greater than and certainly quite different from either the initial effects or those captured by M_1 and M_2. The M_3 multipliers indicate the degree of connectedness arising from the (endogenous) income transmission *between* blocks of accounts. Thus, for example, the extra factor income generated in M_2 is paid to households, then spent on the output of domestic activity, generating further factor income, and after similar subsequent cycles around the system it ultimately leads to an extra 83 units of mixed income, 25 units of employee compensation (combined), and so on. The same interpretation is true of the M_3 multipliers for household and other institution income, and of activity output.

The total multiplier effect of the initial injection into cocoa (i.e. the total of all four components) is shown in the final column. But it is the breakdown by component that is the most significant finding. It indicates that the impact of a boost in the output of cocoa through system-wide (i.e. between block) linkage is much greater than that which arises from the direct effects and input-output linkages alone, and we shall see that this finding is repeated in the results of income injections into other sectors.

The second panel shows similar computations associated with an expansion of the output of mining by 100 units. Again, the input-output effects (M_1) are small (36 units in total). The direct effects on factor and household income (M_2) of the initial injection into mining, combined with the input-output linkages, are much smaller than was the case with cocoa, except for the generation of operating surplus (capital income) where the additional income is 32. Urban and rural households benefit by only an extra 22 and 17 respectively so the combined household income multiplier arising from the production linkages is 39 as opposed to 67 in the case of cocoa. Finally we note that the M_3 'between block' effects, are also smaller. This is not at all surprising when we note that, although the initial impacts in the cocoa and mining sectors are the same (100 units), the injection into mining results in smaller M_1 and M_2 effects, hence the stimulus to M_3 is bound to be smaller. Nevertheless, the *pattern* of the M_3 urban-rural household income effects is similar to that for cocoa in spite of the lower level of income generated.

While the first two panels consider two sectors that are closely identified with exports, the third panel looks at the multiplier effects of a 100 unit increase in the output of construction, which is more closely identified with an increase in fixed investment. The input-output effects (M_1) are again small (48 units). The direct effects on factor and household income (M_2) are now much greater with regard to mixed income and very low in terms of employee compensation, and are relatively more heavily oriented towards income generation in urban households as compared with either of the export activity experiments, even though the combined household income multiplier is roughly comparable with that of the injection into cocoa. Note that the M_2 multipliers show the direct and indirect effects, in input-output terms, of the initial impacts, on factor and household incomes. Again, the M_3 multipliers are not too dissimilar to those for cocoa, either in terms of levels or the patterns of impact.

The final panel considers an injection of 100 units of income into the health and education activity: that is, it is as if there is an increase in provision which is tantamount to an increase in the output of this sector. Obviously, in the context of policies of reform and adjustment it might be more appropriate to consider a retrenchment in health and education provision. In other words, to posit the question: what do the implied SAM linkages tell us about the likely effects of a 100 unit *decrease* in expenditure on health and education? But to maintain a consistent approach we choose here to consider an *increase* in provision. The input-output linkages (M_1) are very small indeed for this sector (14 units). As might be expected, the direct effects on factor income (M_2)

have more impact on skilled employees and little impact on mixed income, reflecting the formal nature of the employment generated. Correspondingly the M_3 multipliers show some sizeable indirect impacts: the levels of factor income generated are higher than the other three sectoral expansions considered above and hence the urban and rural household income multipliers, 81 and 52 respectively, are also relatively large. These results suggest that the indirect effects of changes in the output of the health and education sector are large overall, the income effects (in terms of levels) possibly being at least as large as comparable exogenous increases in the output of cocoa.

Some interesting general results emerge f.om the decompositions in Table 4.5. First, in terms of input-output linkages it seems that production activities in Ghana are not very interdependent. Other results (not shown here) indicate that only by stimulating manufacturing and trade services are more inter-industry linkage effects generated than for the activities considered here. Secondly, the effects of injections into activities on factor income and ultimately household income captured by M_2 appear to differ markedly in terms of both levels and composition, but are nevertheless in line with expectations. Thirdly, while the system-wide linkages (i.e. 'between block' linkages as depicted by M_3) certainly differ in 'levels', the 'patterns' of income effects seem broadly similar regardless of which account the injection originates. Moreover, these system-wide linkages are substantial relative to the size of M_1 and M_2, confirming the potential importance of these linkages as portrayed by the SAM.

The multiplier decomposition analysis is not conclusive evidence of what might happen as a result of unitary injections of income: it is, at best, simply an indication of what is implied by the 1993 SAM structure and hence of the relative size and composition of the linkages in the system as a whole. As emphasized at the outset, the analytical framework is based on simplifying assumptions some limitations of which will be readily apparent. The relationships are linear, the analysis is static, the sharp distinction between exogenous and endogenous parts of the system may be questionable, and no distinction is made between quantity and price effects of the resultant changes (Stone, 1985). Nevertheless, and notwithstanding these important caveats, some broader implications of the results can be ascertained. It seems that, on the basis of comparable (unitary) injections, cocoa has a larger impact on the economy than mining, especially in terms of the overall multiplier effect on household income. On the same basis, a stimulus to construction activity has a comparable effect to that of cocoa on activity generally and on household income in particular. But most important of all is the observation we now make of the economy-wide effects of health and education expenditures. The benefits of such expenditures are often viewed solely in terms of the welfare effects and in particular the social investment in knowledge, skills and well-being of the population. However, this analysis adds a further dimension by indicating that such expenditures also have important and possibly more immediate multiplier effects on the output of activity and on the incomes of factors and households. These effects are substantial, and seem to be at least as great as the multipliers associated with cocoa and mining. Put another way, a reduction in these social expenditures may have (negative) multiplier effects on activity levels and income, and this needs to be borne in mind in the design and implementation of policies of adjustment and reform.

5. Conclusion

The SAM for 1993 provides one of the first real opportunities to examine the structure of the economy in Ghana in any detail. Even at an aggregate level the internal consistency checks on the national accounts reveal some striking features about the economy. Ghana is still heavily dependent on exports of a few primary products, notably timber, cocoa and minerals. Despite the low level of domestic savings, investment, largely financed by inflows from overseas, is quite high. This imbalance between savings and investment is reflected in a substantial current external account deficit. Apart from the large export activities the other major features of the economy are the government sector and, above all, the household-based agricultural activities which provide most of the food consumed by the population. The economy is extremely open, with large imports of manufactures.

On the basis of estimates at a more detailed sectoral level it seems that there are marked disparities in the savings positions of the household sector, corporate enterprises and the government: in 1993 the household sector actually dissaved overall. Of course, these results may be peculiar to 1993 and therefore may not be indicative of the past or the future. The earlier series of the national accounts suggest that this may indeed be the case, and that domestic savings were relatively low in 1993.

An examination of the more detailed structure of the Ghanaian economy reveals a marked lack of 'inter-industry' linkages: important linkages do exist, however, in terms of the wider circulation of income referred to here as 'system-wide' linkages. A cursory examination of the effects of a change in the output of selected activities shows quite different effects on the size and composition of income generation, especially when the system-wide linkages in the economy are taken into account. A more detailed investigation will have to await further analysis of the SAM. Nevertheless the analysis here has shown the potential differences in the economic impacts of mining and agriculture, and some quite revealing results of the economic effects of public expenditures on health and education, which may have an important bearing on any analysis of the effects of economic reform.

References

Ghana Statistical Service (1996a) *Measuring Informal Sector Activity in Ghana*. Accra, July.

Ghana Statistical Service (1996b) *Measuring Household Income and Expenditure in the Third Round of the Ghana Living Standards Survey (1991/92): A Methodological Guide*. Accra, May.

Ghana Statistical Service (1997) *A Social Accounting Matrix for Ghana 1993*. Accra.

Dordunoo, C (1996) 'An Analysis of Exchange Rate and Trade Policy using a Computable General Equilibrium Model of Ghana'. Paper presented to an AERC workshop, Nairobi, May.

Pyatt, G. and Round, J. I. (1977) 'Social Accounting Matrices for Development Planning', *Review of Income and Wealth*. Series 23, No 4.

Pyatt, G. and Round, J. I. (1985) *Social Accounting Matrices: A Basis for Planning*. Washington, DC: World Bank.

Robinson, S. (1989) 'Multisectoral Models', Chapter 18 in H. Chenery and T. N. Srinivasan (eds) *Handbook of Development Economics*. Vol. 2. Amsterdam: North-Holland, Elsevier Science Publishers.

SNA (1993) *System of National Accounts*. Commission of the European Communities, International Monetary Fund, Organization for Economic Co-operation and Development, United Nations, World Bank, Brussels/Luxembourg, New York, Paris, Washington DC, respectively.

Stone, J. R. N. (1985) 'The Disaggregation of the Household Sector in the National Accounts'. Chapter 8 in Pyatt and Round.

Mini SAM for Ghana 1993

Account	#	1	2	3	4	5	6	7	8	9	10	11	12	13	14	15	16	17	18	19	20	21	22	23	24	25	26	27	28
		PRODUCTS										**ACTIVITIES**														**INCOME GENERATION**			
Agriculture Forestry & Fisheries Products	1											6.8	235.3	0.5											1.0				
Ores, Minerals, Electricity, Gas & Water	2															142.9									43.6				
Food Beverages, Textile, Apparel & Leather	3											13.0	17.0	9.8	53.2	37.5	49.8	8.9	68.3	16.0	159.6	8.4	15.1	5.4					
Other Non Metal Transportable Goods	4												2.6	14.1		1.1	5.3	6.1	37.6		12.2	3.4							
Metal Products and Machinery	5											5.2				29.3		3.2			0.6	7.2							
Construction Work	6											1.1									0.4								
Trade Services	7	196.3	6.7	64.4	94.8	75.4	-437.6																						
Transport Storage & Communication Services	8								227.5			24.4	58.8	8.3	2.9	1.3	13.2		15.5	130.0	2.1	13.9	13.9	3.5	15.4				
Business Services	9											3.8	17.8	10.7	10.2	15.2	22.1	0.5	9.8	10.3	38.6	88.2	88.2	18.6	37.2				
Community Social and Personal Services	10																				0.7								
AGRICULTURE Cocoa	11	126.9																											
Agriculture & Livestock Act	12	1331.2																											
Forestry and Logging	13	151.2																											
Fishery	14	286.4																											
INDUSTRY Mining and Quarrying	15	306.5		4.2																									
Manufacturing	16	5.6	0.3	529.7	326.4	53.2																							
Electricity and Water	17	142.0	142.0																										
Construction	18						432.4																						
SERVICES Wholesale, Retail Hotels & Restaurants	19							437.8																					
Transport Storage & Communication	20																												
Financial Intermediation, Real Estate & Business Services	21																												
Public Administration & Extra Territorial org/Bodies	22								384.0	285.4																			
Education and Health	23									257.6																			
Other Community Social Personal & Servants	24		0.4							215.1																			
Generation of Income (GDP) Compensation of Employees	25		55.5									39.1	115.2	16.5	32.2	90.9	62.0	31.5	25.5	12.7	77.7	83.6	117.9	200.5	49.6	954.9	1920.6		
Mixed Income (Gross)	26											27.7	893.8	72.1	185.2	16.9	146.6	228.4	228.4	60.6	60.6	18.0	50.3	30.2	60.6		386.8	94.3	7.5
Operating Surplus (Gross)	27											5.3	-5.2	17.6	2.8	103.6	149.6	31.7	210.8	0.0	26.2	56.8	50.3	30.2	7.4			10.4	
Indirect Taxes on production	28												1.4	1.4		5.2	5.2	1.2	1.2	1.2	1.5			-0.7	0.5				
PRIMARY DISTRIBUTION OF INCOME Households	29																												
Non Financial Corporations	30																												
Financial Corporations	31		114.7																										
Government	32			167.0	77.0																								
Non Profit Institutions Serving Households	33								1.4																				
SECONDARY DISTRIBUTION OF INCOME Households	34																												
Non Financial Corporations	35																												
Financial Corporations	36																												
Government	37																												
Non Profit Institutions Serving Households	38																												
USE OF INCOME Households	39																												
Non Financial Corporations	40																												
Financial Corporations	41																												
Government	42																												
Non Profit Institutions Serving Households	43																												
CAPITAL ACCOUNTS Households	44																												
Non Financial Corporations	45																												
Financial Corporations	46																												
Government	47																												
Non Profit Institutions Serving Households	48																												
CAPITAL FORMATION (Non Financial Assets) Fixed Capital	49																												
Increases in Stocks	50																												
Change in Financial Assets Monetary Gold and SDRs	51																												
Currency & Demand Deposits	52																												
Other Deposits	53																												
Short Term Loans	54																												
Long Term Loans	55																												
Government Stock	56																												
Other Shares & Securities	57																												
Insurance Technical Reserves	58																												
Trade Credit	59																												
Other	60																												
REST OF THE WORLD Current	61		90.9	79.0	185.8	107.8	638.7																						
Capital	62								195.9																				

N.B All Figures Are Shown in Billions of Current Cedis

	1 DISTRIBUTION OF INCOME				2 DISTRIBUTION OF INCOME						USES OF INCOME					CAPITAL ACCOUNT					GFCF		FINANCIAL ACCOUNT										ROW	
	29	30	31	32	33	34	35	36	37	38	39	40	41	42	43	44	45	46	47	48	49	50	51	52	53	54	55	56	57	58	59	60	61	62
1											1799.2											-143.0											224.9	3.3
2											52.6											12.4											309.0	28.5
3											487.7											185.3											3.3	
4											228.5										11.8	-159.4											110.5	
5											63.5										540.8	44.0											38.2	
6											46.4										368.6													
7											1.2																							
8											90.4																							
9											82.2			15.8																				
10											111.0			552.4	85.7																		7.3	
29	2.4																																	
30		16.5	-16.4																														10.1	
31			38.1	126.6																													-15.6	
32			66.7																															
33					7.5																													
34	396.6	142.1		444.9		33.1	17.6	4.2	24.4																								55.9	
35						12.1	1.2	0.1	0.1	-40.5																								
36							2.2	-17.8		2.1																							163.3	
37						116.7	24.8	63.8	99.6	0.2			1.1																				47.7	
38	2875.5					2845.1				38.3																								
39						311.8					-116.5	311.8																						
40							90.4																											
41								789.2					89.2																					
42														221.0																				
43									93.5						7.8																			
44																6.3		7.1	0.0				110.8											
45																2.5		17.9	3.2					65.4										
46																	22.6																	
47																566.6	-3.3	327.4																
48																-61.6	-2.0	-0.4	3.6															
50																-8.3	133.7	39.9															3.3	
51																9.7	40.3	15.5																
52																-59.9	-105.4	118.0																
53																39.3	134.5	63.8							38.1							97.9	
54																5.4	47.0	20.6							38.1							261.4	
55																2.2										124.8						3.3	35.8
56																										41.5	238.0					28.5	
57																86.8	8.3										109.0						
58																												2.2			66.6
59																		0.9											91.3	1.8		
60																		2.0											61.4	0.2		
61																										17.4			3.1	-16.4		
62	3.6																						3.6		87.3	30.3			25.1		347.3	

II Fiscal, Saving & Investment Policies

5 Fiscal Trends

1970–95

CLETUS K. DORDUNOO

1. Introduction

The Government of Ghana, like those of many developing countries that adopted socialist ideologies in the 1950s and the 1960s, resorted to heavy government expenditures out of line with the revenues mobilized, resulting in heavy fiscal deficits in the 1970s and the early 1980s. The negative budget balances were essentially financed through the banking system. The government's failure to keep expenditures in line with revenues mobilized forced Ghana to take on a heavy domestic debt. This practice has been partially justified by the popular Keynesian proposition which advocates borrowing to finance expenditures to stimulate private investment. The response from the monetarists would be the counter-argument that such borrowing stimulates inflationary pressures. They urge restraint on government spending and central bank policies to restrict money supply expansion in order to stabilize the macroeconomy (Seidman, 1986: 105–92). The trends will show that the public sector shrank steadily in size from the mid-1960s until 1983 before beginning to grow again thereafter. The initial expansion was slow and restrained, until 1992. In terms of structure, however, the discussion here will show little change in public finances.

The chapter is structured as follows. It first addresses the pre-1983 fiscal crisis and post-1983 fiscal policy reforms in section 2. Section 3 traces the trends and structure of government revenue, followed by the analysis and description of government expenditure in section 4. Section 5 focuses on the dilemma of public finance and sources of financing the deficits as well as the pattern of budget balance, and the impact of deficit financing on inflation, interest rates, exchange rates in general, and the domestic debt in particular. There are some concluding remarks in section 6.

2. The Pre-1983 Fiscal Crisis and Post-1983 Fiscal Policy Reforms

The Pre-1983 Fiscal Crisis

The budget showed deficits for all years in the period 1970–83. The budget deficit as a proportion of the GDP was –4.34% in 1971, and deteriorated to over –13% of GDP in 1976 and 1977. Thereafter, it declined steadily to about –3% of GDP in 1983. Indeed, by 1977 the budget deficit (in 1975 prices) exceeded ¢750 million in absolute terms, which was more than 50% of the total expenditure in relative terms. The main causes of the budget deficits include trade shocks and a fall in international transactions, decline in economic activity, inadequacies and errors in domestic policy, and serious misalignment of the real exchange rate which was accompanied by the emergence of parallel markets in the 1970s and early 1980s, all of which adversely affected government revenues as well as the over-stretched public sector activity.

The worsening terms of trade (ToT) for Ghana's exports relative to imports have been a major cause of the severe external debt situation. The terms of trade index which was 100 (1975 prices) declined over the years to an all-time low of 33.9 in 1985. (In the first half of the 1990s, it recovered moderately and averaged 58.) The adverse movements in the ToT meant that, even though the volume of exports measured by the quantity index has been about three times the per unit volume of imports, the current account balance has been in deficit. This resulted in huge borrowing from external sources to finance the deficit. The main burden on the public sector accounts is captured by huge interest payments and amortization. The foreign interest payments as a proportion of recurrent expenditure averaged about 8% over the 1970–83 period, whilst interest and amortization payments rose from a low of about 15% in the 1970s to over 20% of recurrent expenditure in the early 1980s.

The most dramatic effect of the deterioration in both the terms of trade and the value of international transactions prior to 1983 is exhibited by the rapid decline in taxes on international transactions relative to taxes on domestic goods and services. In 1970, taxes on domestic goods were about 5% of GDP and those on internationally traded goods almost 12%. But they declined steadily to 2.4% and 0.9% respectively by 1982. The degree of openness of the economy since September 1983 contributed to the recovery of taxes on international trade, and the devaluation of the cedi from ¢2.75 per dollar (for the period 1978–82) to an average of ¢30 per dollar (in 1983) increased the foreign-exchange tax receipts in cedi terms (Dordunoo, 1994).

The average propensity to tax (APT) was 0.14 for the period 1970–95 as captured by the total tax revenue-GDP ratio. The decline in real GDP between 1970 and 1983 meant a fall in the level of real tax revenue. In addition, the decline in economic activity was accompanied by a reduction in the tax-GDP ratio, due to many factors including the closure of some industrial and business enterprises. Between 1970 and 1983 the APT fell by over 16 percentage points from 22.14% to a low of 5.6%, while the level of real income also declined from ¢5,349 m. (1975 prices) to ¢4,747 m. (1975 prices) indicating a fall of 11% in taxable income. All these led to a reduction in overall government revenue and therefore an increase in the deficit.

The impact on the deficit of domestic policy inadequacies and errors and the attendant over-stretched public sector activities works through both the revenue and the expenditure sides of the account. The major policy inadequacies and errors could be located in the government's erroneous belief that excessive increases in money supply can be mopped up through high Treasury bill rates via open market operations over a long period of time. Instead of adopting a prudent monetary policy to stabilize the economy, the government resorted to inflationary taxation and the capturing of huge seigniorage to achieve its high expenditure target. Thus inflationary taxation and seigniorage as a proportion of GDP averaged about 3% and 1.2% respectively over the period 1984–89 (Sowa, 1996) and were even higher in earlier periods. The high nominal interest rate consequent on the high inflation rate increased the interest payments burden on the public sector account. Indirectly, the increase in the rate of interest had persistently increased the overall cost of production, partially resulting in the closure of many industrial enterprises which were a vital taxable base of the economy. Many firms had closed down their businesses in order to engage in what in local parlance is termed 'kalabule'. In fact, by 1983, a large part of employed labour was in trade and 'kalabule' or 'profiteering' business in the informal sector which was difficult to tax. In addition to fixed nominal exchange rates, prices and foreign-exchange allocation were subjected to a complex set of restrictions and controls. Indeed, prices of over 700 goods were rigidly fixed in the formal sector, resulting in long queues, empty shelves in the shops, and underground speculative activities which were difficult to tax.

The exchange-rate policy errors, i.e. the policy of adopting a fixed nominal exchange rate over a long period of time (with the attendant emergence of parallel markets), in the 1970s and early 1980s led to an overvaluation of the cedi and appreciation of the real exchange rate. The exchange rate misalignment impacted negatively on growth, external competitiveness and the balance of payments. The exchange rate overvaluation captured by the difference between the official and the parallel exchange rate not only reduces production for exports (such as cocoa and non-traditional exports) but also reduces the government's ability to earn revenue. In addition activities in the parallel market are not taxed; therefore, as the size of the informal sub-market increases, the ability of the government to increase tax revenue is reduced (for details refer to Dordunoo, 1996a; Dordunoo and Njinkeu,1995; Dordunoo 1995c; Youngblood *et al.,* 1992).

Expansionary fiscal policies were reflected in ever growing public expenditure, with the revenue lagging behind over a long stretch of time up to 1983. The major driving force behind the excessive expenditure was the ever increasing recurrent account, especially for wages and salaries. This is because the government was the largest formal sector employer. Over the same period revenues lagged behind expenditures because of the reduction in economic activity, among other factors, which in turn led to a drastic contraction in the tax base. This, in addition to problems of tax administration, induced a faster decline in the level of real revenues.

The period 1970–83 was characterized by erratic behaviour and a rapid decline in both government revenue and expenditure in real terms of about 10% per annum, even though in nominal terms both revenue and expenditure had been increasing since 1973 by an average of over 35% per annum. The trend of the inflation rate captured by the GDP price (PGDP) deflator (index) clearly underscores the sharp dichotomy between the trends captured by the real and nominal fiscal performance. The PGDP inflation rate accelerated to over 92% per annum in 1978 and decelerated slightly thereafter, only to rise to a high of about 140% per annum by 1983. The reduction in real expenditure fell heavily on development expenditure which decreased from 22.3% of GDP in 1970 to as low as 9% of GDP in 1983. This in turn reduced the level of economic activity and the rate of investment, especially on physical infrastructure, health and education.

Total revenue as a proportion of GDP clearly indicates the latter years of the crisis period, particularly 1981–3, as the nadir of Ghana's ability to raise revenues. The revenue-GDP ratio which was over 22.14% in 1970 fell drastically to about 6% per annum in the 1981–3 period. The expenditure-GDP ratio which also was as high as 29.81% in 1976 also fell to as low as 8.25% by 1983, and the budget deficit stood at 2.25% of GDP.

Despite the fact that deficits have generally been high, the trend of total expenditure is strongly (but not rigidly) influenced by the revenues or resources mobilized by the government. Hence, for the periods when real resource mobilization had been on the down-trend, real expenditure has also been on the downward trend. Thus, even though the highest deficit recorded over the 1970–95 period was in 1976 (when the deficit-GDP ratio was -13.34%) the lowest ebbs of expenditure-GDP and revenue-GDP ratios were recorded in 1983. This period coincided with the period when the level of real GDP was also at its lowest point. Indeed, by 1983 fiscal development had reached crisis point, thereby necessitating fiscal policy reform which was part and parcel of the overall package of the economic recovery programme (ERP) which the government began in September 1983.

The Post-1983 Fiscal Policy Reforms

The causes of Ghana's economic crisis in the early 1980s were many and varied. But it must be noted that the severe bush fires due to prolonged drought and the accompanying famine, as well as the return of about a million Ghanaians expelled from Nigeria in 1983 were major features of the period before economic policy reforms were resorted to. In 1983 the economic recovery programme (ERP) was put in place to stabilize the economy and set it on a growth path. After achieving a fair degree of stabilization, a structural adjustment programme (SAP) was implemented from 1986 to bring about sustained growth and development of the economy.

Various policy instruments were adopted under the ERP and SAP to streamline the performance of the economy. The major instruments used (not always successfully) to address fiscal imbalance were government-revenue augmenting through improvement in tax collection and government-expenditure reducing through retrenchment of workers on the government payroll. The policy package for monetary and financial management consisted of selective credit controls, retirement of government debts to the banks, financial sector restructuring and establishment of the stock exchange. At the centre of Ghana's SAP were trade and exchange rate policies which tended to free the exchange rate from the excessive controls that characterized policies prior to ERP.

The major objectives of the ERP and later the SAPs were: to restore the capacity of the government to mobilize national resources in order to reduce the overall deficits on the public sector accounts; to reduce the rate of inflation, promote economic growth, and achieve export recovery, through a realignment of the incentive structure towards productive economic activities; and the rehabilitation of the physical and social infrastructure. Indeed, it was in 1984, barely three months after the ERP had begun, that foreign grants substantially became an integral component of the overall budgetary account. It was no surprise therefore that from 1984 the role of external grants was fully incorporated into government finance. We shall return to this issue when we address the composition of both government revenue and expenditure.

There are many reasons for the poor performance of revenue mobilization, relating to the erosion of the tax base. The serious erosion of the tax base was due to many factors, namely, (i) persistent over-valuation of the cedi as addressed in the previous section; (ii) large divergence between official prices (the base on which taxes are assessed) and market prices (at which actual transactions take place); (iii) overall reduction in official economic activity; (iv) increase in informal and parallel or black market activities which were not taxed; (v) heavy subsidy on many transactions especially in the state-owned enterprises (SOEs); (vi) a fall in the earnings from cocoa and therefore in the duties on cocoa; and (vii) a decline in world prices, particularly of cocoa, especially from 1976 to 1978.

The major reasons behind the over-runs of expenditure above revenue were also varied. The factors identified as responsible for the relatively high-level expenditures include the following: (i) over-staffing in the public enterprises and therefore ever-rising remuneration; (ii) wastage in the public sector, especially heavy losses of the SOEs; (iii) wastage and indiscipline in the accounting for items comprising transport, travel, fuel, maintenance, stationery, school feeding, etc.; and (iv) lack of accountability including corruption on the part of public officers and government bureaucrats which was partly the consequence of low salaries for civil and public servants. This last led to the establishment of two anti-fraud agencies, namely, the Serious Fraud Office and the Commission for Human Rights and Administrative Justice in the early 1990s.

Critical review of the fiscal crisis led to the fiscal policy reform process. To recapitulate, the primary fiscal objective of the ERP and the SAPs embarked upon by the Government of Ghana assisted by the International Monetary Fund (IMF) and the World Bank was to reduce the government budget deficit through two policy measures in the following areas:

(a) increase in the efforts of tax and non-tax revenue mobilization through (i) adjustment of the exchange rate to realistic levels, (ii) broadening the export base of the economy, and (iii) decontrolling prices of goods and services; and
(b) selective reduction in some items of government expenditure and elimination of waste through (i) privatization of inefficient SOEs, (ii) introduction of strict expenditure monitoring and control to reduce the pervasive financial indiscipline in the system, and (iii) redeployment and/or retrenchment of excess labour in the civil cum public administration system.

In the above context, therefore, the development of an effective tax collection mechanism and the widening of the tax net were seen as ways of achieving high revenue targets. On the expenditure front, reduction of government activity in business, avoidance of waste as well as the 'right' sizing of the public administration system (PAS) were an integral part of policy measures to achieve fiscal objectives during the policy reform process.

The government's various national budget statements reflect the major fiscal policy guidelines for the fiscal years since April 1983. An annotated summary of the main fiscal policies for the period 1983–95 is provided in Appendix 1, covering, first, revenue mobilization and tax measures, and, second, expenditure allocation and control policies.

3.   Government Revenue: Trends and Structure

Tax Versus Non-Tax Revenue

The major revenue mobilization policies, comprising tax, tariff rates and fees and related general macroeconomic policies, explain the general trends and structure exhibited by tax and non-tax revenue as well as the composition of the tax structure, namely, direct versus indirect tax revenues. These are analysed in this sub-section. First nominal revenues are deflated by the general GDP price deflator (PGDP) to obtain real revenues; secondly, revenue items all computed as proportions of real GDP and also as proportions of total revenue in order to analyze the structural shift. The data used are given in Tables 5.A1 and 5.A2 at the end of the chapter.

1970–83. For the period 1970–83, tax and non-tax revenues (including grants) showed a consistent downward trend both in real terms and as a proportion of real GDP. The total real revenue was ¢1,184.52 m. in 1970 but declined steadily to as low as ¢264.15 m. in 1983 (see Figure 5.1 for details). The downward trend was exhibited strongly by taxes on both income and property, and international transactions, but to a lesser extent by taxes on domestic goods and services.

Figure 5.1: Trends in Government Revenue 1970–95
(in 1975 million cedis)

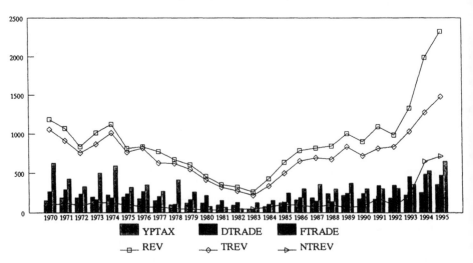

Notes: YPTAX = Property & Income Tax; DTRADE = Tax on Domestic Trade;
FTRADE = Tax on Foreign Trade; REV = Total Revenue; NTREV = Non–tax Revenue.

Taxes on income and property which stood at 2.8% of GDP in 1970 declined to barely 0.9% in 1983; taxes on domestic goods and services fell from 5% in 1970 to less than 1% in 1983, while those on international transactions fell from about 12% to 0.9% in 1982 only to recover to about 2.7% in 1983. The underlying factors were the general decline and instability in GDP growth, the dwindling tax base and a fall in the rate of property acquisition. Following the unilateral declaration of a moratorium/repudiation of foreign debt in 1972 by the Acheampong administration, Ghana was shunned by the donor and international community. This led to a fall in foreign grants as a component of total revenue from ¢4.7 m. in 1973 to nil or close to zero between 1974 and 1979 (Dordunoo, 1990).

As a proportion of GDP, total revenue (including grants) fell steadily from 22.14% in 1970 to 5.24% in 1983. The major contributory factor was the drastic decline in tax revenue from 19.81% in 1970 to 4.58% in 1983, reflecting the fall in the taxable base and rampant tax evasion and/or avoidance especially in the period 1979–83.

1984–95. The Economic Recovery Programme and the related fiscal discipline led to the reversal of the downward trend in government revenues. The period 1984–95 witnessed rapid growth in government revenue from a low of ¢431.63 m. in 1984 to ¢2,321.22 m. in 1995 in real terms. In percentage terms, revenue increased from 8.37% of GDP in 1984 to over 27% in 1995.

Government revenue also underwent some structural changes over the 1970–95 period. Compared with the 1970–83 period, there was a shift in revenue generation from tax to non-tax sources. In the 1970s, about 90% of revenue came from taxes, reaching the peak of 93.28% in 1979. However, in the 1980s and 1990s, the proportion fell to 74.36% by 1991 and further to 63.8% in 1995. The shift in composition has resulted in an increase in the non-tax component from a low of 7.97% in 1970 to as high as 32.72% and 30.95% respectively in 1994 and 1995.

The relative decline in tax revenue was counterbalanced by inflows from non-tax revenue categories, particularly grants, income and fees as well as, at a later stage (since 1992), receipts from divestiture and Non-Performing Assets Recovery Trust (NPART) activities. While the growth in grants slowed down over the period 1992–94, the boost in revenue collection came from income and fees as well as divestiture receipts and positive inflows from NPART. Thus in 1994, for example, divestiture and NPART receipts totalled some ¢395 billion (in current prices) or 31% of total revenue. The only worry about this development is that divestiture and NPART receipts are capital receipts and should not be treated as recurrent sources of revenue, especially as they may dry up as soon as the divestiture programme comes to an end.

During the period 1989–92, the growth rate of real revenues fell. In addition to the crucial shifts in the revenue collection pattern, this led to the need to introduce policy measures to streamline and manage the implementation of revenue collection effectively. The climax of these policy measures was meant to be the introduction of the value-added-tax (VAT) system. However, because of a variety of difficulties, particularly poor policy formulation relating to the timing of the VAT, the threshold (and therefore the tax base) and the tax rate, as well as poor implementation, the VAT had to be withdrawn a few weeks after its introduction in 1995.

Direct Versus Indirect Taxation

In principle, taxes generally fall into two major categories. The first, direct taxes, are imposed directly on incomes earned by individuals, groups of individuals or companies. The second, indirect taxes, fall primarily on the sale of goods and are either absorbed by the seller or passed on to the buyer or shared between the two. Direct tax revenue comprises tax on employees (PAYE), the self-employed, companies and others. Put together, this cluster relates to taxes on personal, corporate, property income and profit taxes. The second cluster comprises domestic indirect tax consisting of excise duty, sales tax and petroleum excise, as well as international indirect tax which consisting of import taxes and export duties, as well as cocoa duties, among others.

1970–83. The trend of property and income taxes and indirect taxes was generally the same as the overall tax pattern. They were fairly high in 1970 but declined steadily to 1983, even though there were variations in the structure. For the period 1970–83, direct taxes on property, income and profits averaged about 20% of total revenue. Indeed in 1970 only 12.77% of total revenue emanated from direct taxes. This showed an increase to 28.6% in 1982 but thereafter declined to 16.89% in 1983. The generally low proportion of direct tax revenue in overall government revenue was compensated by the huge proportion of indirect tax revenue. In 1970, both domestic and international indirect taxes made up 75.37% of total revenue. With the relative increase in direct taxes in 1975, the composition of indirect taxes declined slightly to 68.38%. By 1983, indirect tax revenue amounted to 65.46% of total tax revenue.

Despite the relative decline, it is important to note that the Ghana Government, like many African governments, relies much more heavily on indirect than direct taxes. The main reasons are that indirect taxes are generally easier to collect and tend to capture most people, especially non-wage or casual workers. Hence, indirect taxes provide a broader tax net since they reach a larger number of people who are not wage earners. In Ghana, these constitute about 70% of the population. Secondly, the government believed, and still does believe, that it can use indirect taxes to influence the pattern of consumption. Thus, as reflected in the tax polices, high taxes were placed on luxuries, and such commodities as cigarettes, alcohol, etc., considered injurious to health, in order to reduce or discourage consumption or (in cases where they had become habits and had low elasticities) to increase government revenues.

1984–95. Since 1984 the general trend of direct and indirect taxes has been in an upward direction as can be seen in Figure 5.1. In 1984 direct taxes made up 17.73% of overall government revenue. They increased to an all-time high of 28.15% in 1988 and thereafter declined steadily to 15.41% in 1995. The obvious shift in the pattern is the relative reduction in indirect taxes from 60.81% to a little less than 50% in 1995.

It is vital to point out that the thrust of direct taxes has been to reduce the excessive progressivity of personal income taxes through the reform of exemptions and tax brackets. Corporate taxes have witnessed a curtailment of rates and a reduction in sectoral differential rates. Corporate taxes were lowered in 1988 from 55% to 45% for businesses in manufacturing, farming, and exporting, and from 55% to 50% in 1989 for the remaining firms, other than those in banking, insurance, commercial activities, and printing. Further tax reductions occurred in 1991 when the budget provided for a 35% corporate tax rate applicable to agriculture, manufacturing, real estate, construction and services and extended to all enterprises in the manufacturing sector capital allowances provided under the Investment Code (Ministry of Finance, 1991 Budget Statement, and Kapur *et al.*, 1991). A salient outcome of the various reforms of the tax system has been the changing composition of tax revenues. As at 1992, the share of corporate tax in total revenue had fallen to 8.2% from the 1984 figure of 10.1%. This was attributable to a reduction in the tax rate as an incentive for the expansion of corporate activity, falling profitability rates, and a narrowing of the corporate tax base (Tsikata and Amuzu, 1993).

In the sphere of trade tax policy, Ghana's import tariff structure has been described as moderate by developing country standards, with most tariffs in the 20–25% range (World Bank, 1989b). Alongside exchange rate reform, there was a dismantling of the huge tariff block that characterized the pre-adjustment epoch. Price distortions arising from tariffs and protectionist measures were removed, with maximum tariffs of over 50% in the pre-ERP era reduced to less than 25%. The import licensing scheme together with the import programming and monitoring committee (which was in charge of import licensing) were abolished in January 1989. In this regard, and quoting from World Bank (1992: 12):

> . . . it should be noted that unlike many other countries Ghana did not go through the transitional trade liberalisation phase of converting its quantitative restrictions into equivalent tariffs before gradually lowering the latter. Instead it dismantled its vast system of quantitative restrictions and import licensing at the same time as it proceeded to reduce the level and range of its tariffs and then restructure the rates within the same time. The transition must have been too abrupt for some industries.

By way of summary, the concessionary tariff which ranged between 10% and 25% from 1983 to 1988 was removed in 1989; tariffs on basic raw materials were reduced from 25% to 10% in 1989, while tariffs on 'other' raw materials which were in the neighbourhood of 30% were reduced to 15% in 1987 and to 10% by 1990. For capital goods, import tariffs fell from 30% between 1983 and 1985 to 15% in 1988 and 1989 and then to 10% in 1990 (GATT, 1991).

As far as sales taxes are concerned, there was an integration of the *ad hoc* excise duties on a wide range of mass consumption manufactures with a broadened sales tax. In 1989, there was a phasing out of protection remaining in the form of sales tax and excise tax, and by 1992, the special import tax, which covered a wide range of sensitive industries, had been reduced gradually from 40% to 10% across the board. However, critics have argued that the reforms have been too abrupt and damaging to local businesses, as pointed out above. Yet, this criticism, as observed by Leechor (1994) among other researchers, does not take cognizance of the limited extent to which tariffs have been curtailed under a policy that has been phased in over five to seven years. But, when viewed against 37 years of a draconian protection policy, a period of 10 or more years may be required to phase in the liberalization process. We are inclined therefore in this study to identify ourselves with the findings of the World Bank study quoted above.

It is also crucial to note an exceptional development in the area of indirect taxes. Each year the petroleum tax rate has witnessed tremendous increases. In the 1995 budget statement, for instance, the ex-pump price of premium gasoline went up by 25.6% for the 1995 fiscal year alone. These increments made petroleum excise the largest contributor to total revenue, rising from about 5% in 1987 to 21% of total revenue in 1993. (see Table 5.1).

Table 5.1   Petroleum Excise as a Share of Total Revenue

Year	1987	1988	1989	1990	1991
Petroleum Tax	4.9%	7.4%	7.0%	20.4%	20.4%
Year	1992	1993	1994	1995	1996
Petroleum Tax	19.2%	21.0%	19.5%	19.7%	18.3%

Source: Various Budget Statements (Calculated by the author).

4. Government Expenditure: Trends and Structure

Recurrent Expenditure

Public sector outlays may theoretically be divided into four categories, namely, consumption by government, investment by government, transfers to the private sector and interest payment on the public debt (domestic and foreign). But in operational terms there are nine categories as outlined earlier. In terms of analyzing the trends and structure of government expenditure these are usually regrouped into two major components, namely, recurrent and capital expenditure. This sub-section analyses recurrent expenditure, followed by a sub-section addressing capital expenditure in a more general framework focusing on the recurrent versus development expenditure dichotomy.

1970–83. For the period 1970–83 government expenditure in general exceeded revenue, even though its overall trend in real terms had been on the decline by over 10% per annum. Thus in absolute terms, while expenditure as a whole was ¢1,163.2 m. (in 1975 constant prices), it fell to as low as ¢391.42 m. in 1983. The same trend was exhibited by recurrent expenditure, which in real terms was ¢904.17 m. in 1970 but declined steadily to ¢345.66 m. in 1983 in absolute terms as illustrated in Figure 5.2. However, as a proportion of total government expenditure, recurrent outlays which were 77.73% in 1970 rose to 90.77% in 1982, but declined slightly to 88.31% in 1983.

Figure 5.2: Trends in Government Expenditure 1970–95
(in 1975 million cedis)

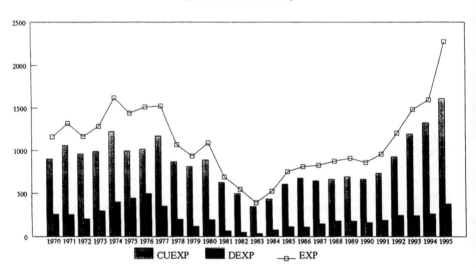

Notes: CUEXP = Current Expenditure; DEXP = Development Expenditure;
EXP = Total Expenditure.

Over this period the major component responsible for the above trends was personal emoluments (including wages and salaries). Over 50% of recurrent expenditure went on this item, due mainly to the over-staffed public administration system (PAS). Thus other recurrent expenditure items have generally been comparatively low, ranging between 20 and 40%. Interest payments, especially on domestic debt, were less than 3% of recurrent expenditure, whilst for the whole period special outlays were virtually nil.

It is important to point out that much of the payments captured under the personal emoluments item were for the civil service only and therefore exclude organizations receiving subventions. The outlay on subventions was the second largest component of recurrent expenditure, at over 10%.

1984–95. We noted earlier that the over-staffed PAS and the SOEs overburdened the government recurrent (and development) expenditures. Since the government was the largest formal sector employer, the recurrent expenditure driven mainly by the huge wage bill took a disproportionate share of total expenditures. In addition, the non-performance of SOEs resulted in huge transfers from government to support them. To correct the deplorable state of the government accounts, some key fiscal policy measures were put in place during the era of economic reform, namely, (i) cost recovery measures such as in health care and education, (ii) reduction of over-staffed positions in the public sector, resulting in a redeployment or retrenchment exercise since 1987, with the aim of raising salaries in the civil and public service in general, (iii) improved monitoring of expenditure and (iv) adequate appropriations for operating and maintenance outlays, particularly in the identified priority areas of agriculture, health and education.

Since 1987, with the redeployment of about 12,000 employees per annum up to 1991 as well as the above policy measures, coupled with the introduction of a 'cash and carry' system in government hospitals, recurrent expenditure fell from 88.31% of total expenditure in 1983 to 70.72% by 1995. A welcome development, however, between 1987 and 1991 was the reduction in personal emoluments as a proportion of recurrent expenditure to an average of 42% from the over 50% of the pre-reform period. However, even though average real salaries have risen moderately, the resurgence in the hiring of civil servants since 1992 (supposedly more qualified and more experienced) has denied civil servants their expected real salary increase.

Government real recurrent expenditure in absolute terms exhibited a steady upward trend from ¢523.98 m. in 1984 to ¢1,607.87 m. by 1995. Thus as a proportion of the real GDP, the rise was from 8.39% in 1984 to 18.74% in 1995. While this increase did not necessarily give cause for concern, the structure of recurrent expenditure did, especially after 1991. In 1987 interest payments as a proportion of GDP were about 1.42%; by 1995 they rose to 4.93%. As a proportion of recurrent expenditure, interest payment on domestic debt was less than 3% in 1990; this had risen to as high as 19.1% in 1995. In 1990, interest payments on domestic and external debt as a proportion of recurrent expenditure were 16.7% (2.9% on domestic and 13.8% on foreign debt). This rose steadily over the years to 27% (19.1% on domestic and 7.9% on external debt) in 1995, as illustrated in Table 5.2. Clearly, domestic debt has taken over from foreign debt as the major source of debt servicing from public sector accounts, due to the government's heavy domestic borrowing as well as the high rate of interest on the debt instruments.

Table 5.2   Interest Payments on Debt (¢'million or %)

Items	1990	1991	1993	1994	1995	1996 Budget Estimate
Domestic Interest	5,776	29,627	91,988	166,449	232,948	434,500
Foreign Interest	27,318	13,201	43,916	63,697	95,756	144,800
Total Interest Payments	33,094	42,828	135,904	230,146	328,704	579,300
Total Recurrent Expenditure	198,193	263,714	596,558	838,962	1,220,309	1,804,936
Domestic Interest Payment % of Recurrent Expenditure	2.91%	11.23%	15.42%	19.84%	19.09%	24.07%
Foreign Interest Payment % of Recurrent Expenditure	13.79	5.01%	7.36%	7.59%	7.85%	8.02%
Total Interest Payment % of Recurrent Expenditure	16.70%	16.24%	22.78%	27.43%	26.95%	32.09%

Source: Budget Statement, various issues (Calculated by the author).

From the foregoing it is clear that, apart from personal emoluments, interest payments have become the next largest single item on the recurrent expenditure account. Thus, with the former at about 38% and interest payments taking about 28.38%, the two items appropriated over 66% of recurrent expenditure. This has led to a serious burden not only on the recurrent but on the whole government expenditure account. As we shall note later, this has strong implications for the amount of money allocated for development expenditure.

For now it is important to note that the accelerated growth in interest payments, on domestic debt in particular and to a lesser extent on foreign debt (in absolute terms), led to interest payments overtaking total development expenditure. Thus development expenditure (in current prices), which was ¢18,552 m. in 1987 as against interest payments of ¢10,587 m. in the same year, had increased by 1995 to only ¢208,317 m. as against interest payments of ¢325,285 m. (Dordunoo, 1995b and 1996b). Hence, there is a need for the government to undertake a careful appraisal of its recurrent expenditure pattern and take the necessary policy steps to address the current structure of the recurrent account.

Government Capital Expenditure vis-à-vis Total Outlay

The pattern of capital expenditure in general, and development expenditure in particular, as well as the structure of the total public outlay are of crucial concern to the fiscal authorities. For the two separate sub-periods 1970–83 and 1984–95 respectively, the concern has been mainly in two directions. The first is the ever increasing interest payments as a proportion of recurrent expenditure; the second is the crowding-out effect of recurrent expenditure on both the government's development expenditure and the private sector's access to credit.

1970–83 Real development expenditure for the 1970–78 period was the highest in Ghana's recent economic history. The peak of real development expenditures came in 1974–6. In relative terms, real development expenditure exceeded 20% of real GDP over the three years.

However, owing to the general decline in economic activity and the corresponding slowdown in government outlay, real development expenditure declined steadily between 1977 and 1983 to an all-time low of 7.28% of real GDP in 1983. The period 1978–83 was characterized by negative growth rates in real GDP and real investment. Much of the economic and social infrastructure was in disrepair, with the roads featuring yawning pot-holes. In addition almost all the utilities, such as water and electricity, were in disrepair, while the ports were virtually unusable.

1984–95 As part of the overall attempts at rehabilitating the country's physical and social infrastructure, two major priorities were put in place under the ERP, namely, (i) improved allocation of operations and maintenance expenditure, and (ii) improved planning and implementation of public investment programmes (PIP) to increase the returns on these expenditures.

Real development expenditure, which was 8.39% of real GDP in 1984, increased steadily to 18.74% in 1995. In absolute terms, real development expenditure, which was ¢432.75 m. in 1984, rose to ¢1,607.87 m. in 1995. To enhance the appropriate allocation of funds for the rehabilitation of the physical, economic and social infrastructure, a three-year rolling PIP has been put in place since 1986. It should be noted, however, that this is not the first time the concept of the PIP has been applied in Ghana. It dates back to the 1950s, 1960s and the 1970s. The application of the concept in 1986 is similar to, if not the same as, that applied in the Third 5-Year Development Plan for the period 1975–80 prepared by the Ministry of Finance and Economic Planning.

The PIP in 1993 covered 97% of total government development outlay financed from the budget and project grants. Out of the PIP total, about 60% was allocated for the rehabilitation of roads, highways, ports, etc., and 30% to directly productive, mainly agricultural services and for rehabilitating the cocoa and mining sectors. Social sector development accounted for about 10%, with an emphasis on health and educational facilities. As pointed out earlier, interest payments exceeded total development expenditure by 1992. Apart from this dramatic shift in the structure of the public sector accounts, external loans, grants and other financial support had become a significant proportion of the total government expenditure in general and of development expenditure in particular, exhibiting a high degree of dependence on donor assistance.

The contribution of grants, loans and other aid inflows to the total budget and the capital budget, is presented in Tables 5.3 and 5.4 respectively. Total donor assistance as a proportion of total budget expenditure ranges between 43.6% and 81.4%. Apart from 1993 when donor assistance was over 80% of total expenditure, the proportion is below 63% for the remaining years. The donor contribution to capital expenditure is above 70% for all years, ranging between 71.4% and 88.5%.

By all standards the heavy dependence of the total budget expenditure on official inflows (excluding on-lent facilities to the private sector) as well as the heavy reliance on donor sources for capital expenditure underscores the importance of the donor community in the budgetary process. It is important to note that donors have also been financing recurrent expenditure indirectly through account switching in the implementation of the budget as well as through primary balance of payments support and counterpart/matching funds.

Table 5.3   Aid Flows and Budget Expenditure (US$ million or %)

Items	1990	1991	1992	1993	1994	1995
Grants	85.26	183.46	200.90	209.70	41.27	112.60
Loans	419.60	304.44	388.81	619.74	482.60	529.60
Total Donor Assistance	504.86	487.90	589.71	919.44	523.87	642.20
Total Budget Expenditure	808.94	956.26	1,021.22	1,129.22	1,201.56	1,235.07
Donor Assistance of as % of Total Expenditure	62.4%	51.0%	57.7%	81.4%	43.6%	52.0%
Exchange Rate (¢ : $1)	326.30	367.70	500.20	750.90	956.73	1,146.40

Source: Computed by the author from Budget Statements, BoP Accounts and Schedule of Aid Flows (Commitment and Disbursements; Government of Ghana (1993) (Dordunoo, 1995c).

Table 5.4   Contribution of Donor Assistance to Development Budget (¢ million or %)

Items	1990	1991	1992	1993	1994	1995
Development Expenditure	48,300	60,785	98,449	119,254	165,605	208,317
Development Expenditure	100%	100%	100%	100%	100%	100%
Domestic Funding	11.5%	14.6%	28.2%	22.1%	28.6%	27.6%
Donor Funding (%)	88.5%	85.4%	71.8%	77.9%	71.4%	72.4%

Source: Computed by the author from Summary of Donor Funding by Sector of major projects. (Errors may come from exchange-rate changes and timing of aid flows to PIP projects). Main source of data from Various Budget Statements, Consultative Group Documents, and Budget Summary (Broad based) (Dordunoo, 1995c).

The effect of heavy reliance on external inflows, captured by the rising debt-GDP ratio and the debt-export ratio, shows that both the solvency and the liquidity ratios have been critical for Ghana and indeed qualify it as a severely indebted low income country (SILIC). A much more disastrous effect of donor support is its distortionary impact on domestic resource mobilization and the denial of the budget's useful function as both a political tool and an economic instrument for resource mobilization cum allocation and conflict resolution.

The overall structure and trends in government expenditure are captured in Figure 5.2. As may be deduced, recurrent expenditure has been increasing at a much more rapid rate than development expenditure.[1]

---

[1]   Even though the development expenditure captured is not the whole capital outlay, the expenditures on net lending, the special efficiency fund and allocation for the NAM conference in 1991 are only minute proportions of the overall capital account.

5.   Pattern of Budget Balance, its Financing and Impact on Domestic Debt

The Budget Deficit Dilemma and Financing Sources

It is important to state that it is not always the case that when a government runs a deficit budget it will automatically add to its debts. In actual practice a government which incurs a deficit can finance it through any one or more of the following four broad means, namely, (i) running down its cash reserves, (ii) selling some of its assets like properties, shares in companies, and even enterprises, etc., (iii) printing more currency and using it (which in turn will increase money supply), and (iv) borrowing (from central and/or commercial banks or from the general public internally or externally) and spending it. The Government of Ghana over the years utilized more or less all of these means. Each method used in financing the deficit has its own merits and demerits; however, none of them can be self-sustaining over a long period of time. The Government of Ghana ran down all its cash reserves and could not use them as a major source of finance. The proceeds of divestiture (of state enterprises) were also not a source of finance until 1991/92 when this became a fairly large but irregular source of finance averaging about 2.22% of GDP (or 5.2% of total expenditure) for the period 1992–95. This leaves printing of money and borrowing from the banking and private sectors as the regular sources of financing the deficit. The case of printing money and its accompanying seigniorage averaged about 3% of GDP (as analysed earlier). The major source of finance of the deficit in Ghana has been borrowing from both the banking and the private sector which for the study period averaged about 5% of GDP for the worst years (i.e., the years prior to 1983 and after 1991).

It is vital to point out, therefore, that the changes in the public domestic debt are a reflection of the extent to which the government borrows to finance its deficit. It is important to note, however, that this source of finance is also not sustainable, since there is the possibility of running into a debt trap.

Ghana has been caught in a serious public finance dilemma as a result of the continuous use of loans to finance the deficit. The country has had to increase expenditure on health, education, and social welfare. At the same time there has been the need to increase the pace of infrastructural development. And yet the ability to raise tax revenues was impaired by low tax effort, poor productivity and an inefficient tax system at least prior to 1983. In the face of rising expenditure vis-à-vis low revenues, Ghana has had to borrow heavily from both domestic and foreign sources, resulting in the rapid accumulation of both domestic and external debts. The rapid expansion of total debts in general and domestic debt in particular coupled with high interest rates have resulted in an increase in interest payments, especially in the pre-ERP periods and from 1991 to 1995. Thus even as the country needs more funds to undertake development projects, greater and greater proportions of total expenditure have tilted towards wages and salaries (over 35%) and interest payments (over 20%). By 1992 interest payments had exceeded development expenditure which averaged less than 18% of total government outlay.

While the government runs deficits in order to achieve a rapid rate of development, it ends up creating a huge domestic debt which in turn swallows the greater part of the very funds needed for development and, therefore, enhances the chances of further deficits. The high deficit crowds out the private sector, propels a high rate of inflation and interest rates which jointly increase the macroeconomic instability and the already high cost of production by the private sector which is supposed to be the engine of growth. In the next sub-section we highlight the pattern of budget balance, followed by a discussion of the structure of deficit financing and the holdings and composition (or structure) of domestic debt.

Pattern of Budget Balance and Structure of Deficit Financing

Budget Balance. The budget balance refers to the total central government revenue and grants minus total expenditure. Since 1960 in only 6 years (1970, 1989, 1990, 1991, 1994 and 1995) was the budget in surplus. However, when the divestiture receipts (which are capital earnings) are excluded, it was only in two years (1970 and 1989) that the budget recorded a surplus (see Figure 5.3).

The trend reveals widening deficits from a modest surplus in 1970 to –13.24% of real GDP (or –46.56% of total expenditure) in 1977. However, since then there was a steady reduction in the size of the deficit up to 1979. In 1980, it increased to –10.36% of real GDP (or –57.52% of total expenditure) but thereafter showed a steady reduction up to 1988. In 1989, the budget balance turned positive; the surplus was maintained up to 1991, due to an improvement in revenue mobilization, an increase in receipts from both divestiture and NPART activities, and a relative reduction in expenditure. Following an uncontrolled expenditure in 1992, mainly because of the democratization process characterized by both presidential and parliamentary elections, deficits reared their ugly heads again, averaging over –2% of GDP for 1992 and 1993, followed by a moderate surplus for 1994 and 1995.

Figure 5.3: Trends in Government Budget Balance 1970–95
(in 1975 million cedis)

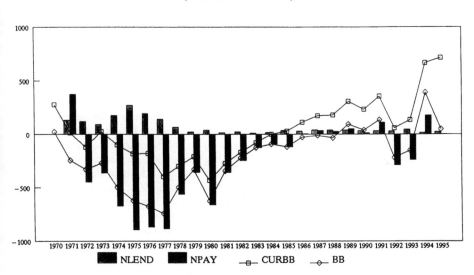

Notes: NLEND = Net Lending; NPAY = Net Payments; CURRBB = Current Budget Balance; BB = Budget Balance.

Excluding actual capital flows and transfers yields a current budget balance as illustrated in Figure 5.3. The trend for the current balance generally follows the same pattern as the total balance except that deficits on the current account occurred for only 1972 and 1974–83, but thereafter the accounts remained positive since 1984 even though they became very unstable between 1992 and 1995.

Deficit Financing. The path traced by deficit financing is a mirror image of the budget deficits and indicates the main sources of funds for this purpose. The main sources of financing have been domestic loans, of which the largest component was from the Bank of Ghana (BoG). This was followed by net external loans, which have been quite small (see Figure 5.4 for the trend of sources for government budget deficit financing).

**Figure 5.4: Trends in Government Budget Financing 1970–95
(in 1975 million cedis)**

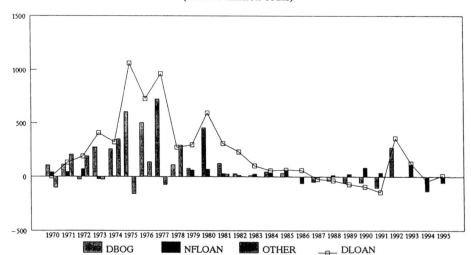

Notes: DBOG = Loans from Bank of Ghana; NFLOAN = Net Foreign Loans;
OTHER = Other Loans; DLOAN = Total Domestic Loans.

From the perspective of sources, the main financial flows to the public sector (including non-financial SOEs and COCOBOD) were flows from the monetary authority, the domestic banks, and the private sector. For the earlier periods particularly between 1971 and 1981 as well as in 1992, borrowing from the monetary authority (or BoG) formed the greatest part of financing the fiscal deficits; this averaged over 2% of GDP directly augmenting the money supply. There is enough empirical evidence to infer that money financing of the deficits in the 1970–77 period was generally very inflationary (see, example, Islam and Wetzel, 1994; Dordunoo, 1996a).

By way of summary, the main effects of deficit financing (and/or monetary accommodation) are the following: (i) persistent inflation and macroeconomic instability, (ii) rapid exchange-rate depreciation, (iii) high interest rates and widening of the spread between lending and deposit rates, (iv) crowding-out of the private sector, and (v) expansion in domestic debt. Thus the inability of the various governments to adopt realistic fiscal discipline in the 1970s in order to balance or run a surplus on the budget triggered a lot of negative developments, including expanding the domestic debt from an already high level. We now turn to the domestic debt.

Domestic Debt Holdings and Composition
After expanding in the first part of the 1970s, the general trend of real domestic debt exhibited a fairly steady path with a slow downward movement between 1977 and 1991 when it reached an all-time low of ¢134.99 m. in real terms. As a proportion of real GDP, the real debt fell from over 35.33% in 1976 to 1.87% in 1991. It was, therefore, disturbing to see the real domestic debt on the rise again from 4.08% of real GDP in 1992 to as high as 11.09% in 1995 indicating the loss of fiscal discipline that Ghana had enjoyed in the 1985–91 period under the SAPs (Dordunoo, 1996b).

It is important to point out that, even though real expenditure was increasing, a narrow surplus was achieved between 1985 and 1991, enabling the government to retire some of its debts and release resources for the private sector. It should also be emphasized that the surpluses of 1994, showing a dramatic reversal of the 1992 deficit, were only possible because of transitory divestiture receipts. This raises a worrisome concern as to whether the surplus would be sustained in the near future.

Domestic Debt Holdings. Between 1970 and 1973 the major holder of domestic debt was the SSNIT which held more than 50% of the debt. Since 1974, however, the BoG became the largest holder of the domestic debt. The path traversed by BoG holdings between 1975 and 1986 was virtually the same as the total debt, with the former ranging between 75% of total domestic debt in 1977 and a little under 50% in 1988. Between 1989 and 1992, the holdings of BoG and SSNIT were almost the same.

However, by 1993 there was a structural shift in which BoG holdings increased again to the pre-1983 levels, commanding more than 63% of the total domestic debt. It is instructive to note that both commercial and secondary banks held a fair proportion of the domestic debt. Thus the BoG and the commercial cum secondary banks constituted the largest holders of domestic debt indicating the extent to which money financing has been heavily accommodative (see Figure 5.5 for details).

Figure 5.5: Domestic Debt by Holdings
(in 1975 million cedis)

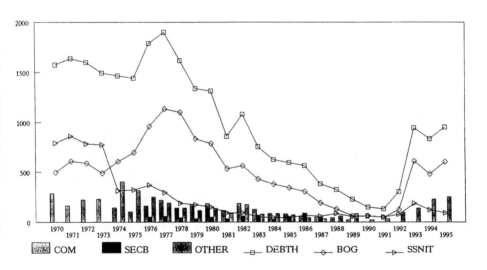

Notes: COM = Commercial Banks; SECB = Secondary Banks; OTHER = Other;
DEBTH = Total Debt Holdings; BOG = Bank of Ghana;
SSNIT = Social Security and National Insurance Trust.

Domestic Debt Composition. In terms of structure, the largest proportion of domestic debt has been, and still is, tilted toward long-term debt. Apart from 1974 and 1992 when short-term debt was larger than long-term debt, the remaining 24 years of the 26-year observation sample were characterized by larger ratios of long-term debt of over 70% on average, as illustrated in Figure 5.6. More than 90% of the long-term debt comprised stocks and bonds.

Figure 5.6: Domestic Debt by Composition
(in 1975 million cedis)

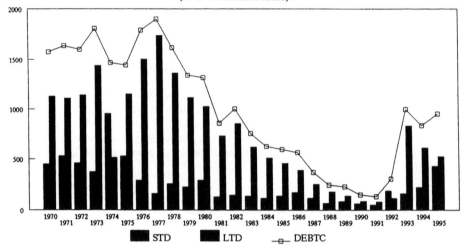

Notes: STD = Short−term Debt; LTD = Long−term Debt; DEBTC = Debt Composition.

6.   Conclusions

In this chapter we outlined trends in Ghana's fiscal sector and put forward explanations for the circumstances that led to the economic decline, the fiscal crises of the pre-1983 period and the post-1983 fiscal policy reforms. We also reviewed the relevant concepts and the accounting identities adopted in the preparation of the public sector accounts.

The major conclusions include the following: the fiscal crisis of the pre-1983 period and its re-emergence since 1992 were primarily driven by expenditure overruns rather than inability to meet revenue targets. Some of the major factors underlying expenditure overruns include over-stretched public sector activities, the overstaffed public administration system, and waste of resources in the public sector, especially in the state-owned enterprises.

Even though revenue targets have often been exceeded, it has been inferred that the revenue-GDP ratio was generally lower than was desirable in the pre-ERP period. The factors responsible for the low revenue-GDP ratio include trade shocks, serious misalignment of the real exchange rate, and the draconian regulation of prices.

Of a total sample period of 26 years in only 6 years was the budget in surplus. When divestiture receipts are excluded, however, it was only in two years (1970 and 1989) that the budget recorded a surplus. The worst periods of deficits were 1971–85, 1992 and 1996. The period 1986–91 witnessed dramatic improvements in fiscal policy. Indeed, the government was able to retire some of its debt and release resources for the private sector. Thus the domestic debt-GDP ratio, which was over 35% in 1976, fell to less than 10% a decade later and thereafter declined further reaching an all-time low of 1.9% in 1991. However, thereafter, the debt-GDP ratio resumed its upward trend, reaching over 11% in 1995 following the renewed deficit since 1992. The 1993–95 surplus was due to the transitory inflow of divestiture receipts and therefore raises the question of whether the surplus is sustainable.

The driving force behind the recent fiscal deficits of the 1990s and, therefore, the increases in the domestic debt, is the government's loss of control over fiscal discipline and policy management, resulting in high inflation, rapid depreciation of the cedi, and erosion of confidence in the economy. In order to achieve a favourable environment, the government should re-engineer fiscal discipline to reinstate the macroeconomic stability of the post-1983 and the pre-1992 eras.

References

Dordunoo, C.K. (1996a) 'The Impacts of Exchange Rate Changes on Growth and Inflation in Sub-Saharan Africa', Paper presented at the 1996 Fall, Meeting of Project LINK of UN Group of Experts on World Economy, September 30–Oct 4, Universite de Lausanne, Switzerland.

Dordunoo, C. K. (1996b) 'Ghana Economic Forecasts (1996–2000): Vision 2020 and an Alternative Scenario', *Ghana Economic Outlook* Vol. 1, No. 2, September, a publication of the Policy Analysis and Strategic Studies Division (PASSD), GIMPA, Greenhill, Achimota.

Dordunoo, C.K. (1995a) 'Exchange Rate Reforms in Sub-Saharan Africa: Some Lessons for Policy Management', Paper presented at the 1995 World Congress of the International Economic Association (IEA), Tunis, 17–22, December.

Dordunoo, C.K. (1995b) 'The Impact of Interest Rate Policy Reform on Private Sector Savings and Investment in Ghana (1970–93)', *Journal of Management Studies,* Vol. 12, December, pp. 46–72.

Dordunoo, C.K. (1995c) 'The National Budgetary Process in Ghana: Towards an Improved Financial Management', Paper presented at the AERC Budgetary Process Project Seminar/Workshop in Johannesburg, 2–9 December.

Dordunoo, C.K. (1994) *The Foreign Exchange Market and the Dutch Auction System in Ghana,* AERC Research Paper 24. Nairobi: African Economic Research Consortium.

Dordunoo, C.K. (1990) 'Ghana's Foreign Debt and Policy Recommendations (A Multiple Discriminant Analysis)', *Nigerian Financial Review* Vol. 3 No. 2, Info-data Publication, Lagos, June.

Dordunoo, C.K., Odubogun, K., Ssemogerere, G. and Kasekende, L. (1997) *A Comparative Study of Foreign Exchange Policy Management in Ghana, Nigeria and Uganda,* AERC Special Paper 27, Nairobi: African Economic Research Consortium (AERC).

Dordunoo, C.K. and Njinken, D. (1995) 'Foreign Exchange Regimes and Macroeconomic Performance in Sub-Saharan Africa'. Paper presented at the Plenary Session of the December 1995 AERC Workshop, 2–9 December, Johannesburg.

Ghana Statistical Service, *Quarterly Economic Digest of Statistics,* Various Issues, Accra.

General Agreement on Tariffs and Trade (GATT) (1991) *Trade Policy Review Mechanism: Ghana.* Geneva: GATT.

Islam, R. and Wetzel, D. (1994) 'Ghana: Adjustment, Reform, and Growth', Chapter 7 in W. Easterly, C.A. Rodriguez, and K. Schmidt-Hebbel (eds), *Public Sector Deficits and Macroeconomic Performance.* Washington, DC: World Bank.

Kapur, I., Hadjimichael, M. T., Hilbers, P., Schiff, J. and Szymczak, P. (1991) *Ghana: Adjustment and Growth, 1983–91,* IMF Occasional Paper No 84. Washington, DC: IMF, September.

Leechor, C. (1994) 'Ghana: Frontrunner in Adjustment', Chapter 4 in I. Hussain, and R. Faruqee (eds) *Adjustment in Africa: Lessons from Country Case Studies.* Washington, DC: World Bank.

Ministry of Finance/Government of Ghana, *The Budget Statement and Economic Policy of the Government of Ghana.* Various Issues, Accra.

Ministry of Finance/Government of Ghana, *Consultative Group Document,* Paris/World Bank. Various Issues, Accra.

Ministry of Finance/Government of Ghana (1977) *Five Year Development Plan 1975/76–1979/80,* Parts I, II and III Accra.

Seidman, A. (1986) *Money, Banking and Public Finance in Africa.* London and Atlantic Heights, NJ: Zed Books.

Sowa, N. K. (1996) *Policy Consistency and Inflation in Ghana.* AERC Research Paper 43. Nairobi: African Economic Research Consortium.

Tsikata, G. K. and Amuzu, G.K. (1993) 'Fiscal Development Policies and Options' in V. K. Nyanteng (ed.), *Policies and Options for Ghanaian Economic Development.* Institute of Statistical, Social and Economic Research, University of Ghana, Legon.

World Bank (1989a) *Ghana: Structural Adjustment for Growth.* Country Economic Memorandum. Washington, DC: World Bank.

World Bank (1989b) *Trends in Developing Economies 1989.* Washington DC: World Bank.

World Bank (1992) *Ghana: 2000 and Beyond: Setting the Stage for Accelerated Growth and Poverty Reduction.* Washington, DC: World Bank.

World Bank (1994) *World Development Report 1994.* Washington, DC: World Bank.

Youngblood, C.E., Dordunoo, C.K., Larrain, F.B., Younger, S.D. and Grennes, T.J. (1992) *Ghana: Macroeconomic Environment for Export Promotion.* Prepared for USAID Mission to Ghana by Sigma One Corporation, Research Triangle Park, NC.

Appendix 1. Annotated Summary of Fiscal Policies (1983–95)

Revenue Mobilization Policies

1983 April   Tariff schedules are simplified to rates of 0, 25, and 30%.
                  New taxes are introduced on wealth (property and non-commercial vehicles) and taxes on rental income increased.
                  Government begins an ongoing effort to improve tax collection.

1984 June   Personal income tax rates are lowered, and taxes on cigarettes and beer raised.

1985 April   Significant revenue initiative is launched including increased taxes on beer, cigarettes, airport and casino services, gasoline and special unnumbered licences for imports. Many government fees are also increased.

1987 February   Corporate tax rate on manufacturing concerns reduced from 55% to 45%.
                  Reduction of effective income tax rates, particularly at the higher levels.
                  The 10% special sales tax on goods imported under SUL is abolished.
                  Import sales taxes now imposed on such goods as milk, rice and prepared fish from other countries.
                  Special tax on cigarettes, beer, alcoholic and non-alcoholic beverages.
                  Excise duties imposed on all locally produced goods except petroleum products. Tobacco, alcoholic and non-alcoholic beverages merged into sales taxes.
                  The 10% sales tax on the domestic consumption of electricity is abolished.
                  Abolition of import duty and purchase tax on all commercial vehicles.
                  Reduction of duty rates on basic rate materials and capital goods.

1988 January   Reintroduction of sales tax clearance certificate to enforce timely payment of sales tax and excise duties collected by manufacturers on behalf of government.
                  Abolition of the requirement for importers to obtain a licence to allow them access to foreign exchange.
                  Increase in the price of petroleum products by a range of 20 to 30%.
                  Abolition of Special SUL tax.

1989 January   Tax rates lowered further to raise the 'take-home' pay of workers.
                  The dividend-withholding tax of 30% converted to a final tax of 30%.
                  A second rate of 50% introduced for all corporate bodies except companies operating in banking, insurance, commerce and printing sectors which will continue to pay corporate tax at 55%.
                  The basic tax rate reduced from 25% to 22.5%. Beer, cigarettes, alcoholic and non-alcoholic beverages will now attract the standard sales tax of 22.5% instead of 7.5% and lower excise duty rates.
                  The 20% tax on SUL imports abolished.
                  Personal taxes: increase in standard personal exemption and top marginal rate shifted to a higher income level.

1990 January   Introduction of super sales tax on luxury goods, ranging from 50% to 500%.
                  The payment of excise duty will continue to be restricted to the production of alcoholic and non-alcoholic beverages and tobacco. To enable firms in these sectors to retain enough funds for reinvestment and expansion of plant

capacity, it was decided to reduce excise duty rates by 5%.

Goods which already attract special taxes will continue to attract them in addition to the special import duty and sales tax, except for the textile factories tax which has been reduced from 40% to 10%.

Personal Income Tax: The government kept the same bracket and personal exemption structure as in 1989.

Company Income Tax: The rate for the construction sector was lowered from 50% to 45%. The rate for all other sectors was lowered from 55% to 50%.

Capital Gains Tax: The initial allowance was increased and the rate structure altered. The previous treatment of capital allowances, i.e., the calculation of the capital gains tax, was discontinued.

Gift Tax: The rate brackets were increased.

Sales Tax: No change in basic rates or structure except for a variance in sales tax on cars according to engine capacity from 10% to 35%.

Vehicle Tax: Flat rate of 10% on petrol-driven cars over 1,600 cc and diesel cars over 1,800 cc.

Excise Taxes: All excise taxes reduced by 5% points. Collection mechanism tightened.

Import Duties: The 15% rate on semi-processed intermediate goods was eliminated by collapsing it into the 10% rate. Import duties on cars range from 5% to 20%, depending on engine capacity.

Special Tax: The 40% rate on textile imports reduced to 10%.

1991 January	The minimum tax exemption level raised from ¢126,000. Income above ¢3 million per annum will now be taxed at 25%, and 55% for those above 1.2 million in 1990.

Other reliefs instituted include marriage, old age, children's education, and relief in respect of social security, provident funds, life insurance, and other pensions contributions.

Corporate Tax: The rate applicable to agriculture, manufacturing, real estate, construction and services lowered to 35%.

The withholding tax on dividends reduced to 15%.

For the export sector corporate tax rebates were raised to a range from 60% to 75% for agriculture (from 30% to 40%) and manufacturing (from 25% to 30%) depending on the proportion of output exported. The customs duty drawback rate was increased to 100%.

All interest income on deposits, debentures, bonds, Treasury bills annuities, or similar assets, with the exception of interest earned by individuals, will be taxed.

Indirect Taxes: Tax rate on goods currently enjoying concessional rates was lowered to 7.5% and goods with standard rates are taxed at 17.5%.

The super sales tax was reduced to the new range of 10% to 100%.

1992 January	Corporate tax rate for commerce, printing and publishing reduced from 50% to the standard rate of 35%.

Corporate tax rate on financial institutions reduced from 50% to 45%.

Withholding tax on dividends reduced from 15% to 10%.

Personal income tax threshold raised from ¢126,000 to ¢150,000.

Top marginal tax bracket raised from 25% to 35% and applicable to salaries over ¢14 million as against ¢3 million in 1991.

	Special tax of 10% introduced as a protective measure for domestic industry. Import duties and sales taxes on some building materials have been abolished.
1992 June	Establishment of Parliamentary Committee of Finance.
1993 January	Increase in petroleum tax leading to increase in ex-pump prices of petroleum products. Premium from ¢222 to ¢355 per litre, kerosine from ¢156 to ¢250 and liquified petroleum gas (LPG) from ¢100 to ¢120 per kilo. Reduction in corporate income tax from 45% to 40%. Home Finance and other companies engaged in provision of homes to be exempt from taxation. Contract for design and implementation of VAT signed.
1994 January	Increases between 30% and 40% tax rates imposed on the first 4 income bands. 100% increase in the tax rate from ¢100/day to ¢200/day on owners of commercial vehicles. Sales tax on imported goods reduced to two standard rates — 15% for concessionary/standard goods and 35% for luxury goods. Building materials removed from zero-rated list to a concessionary rate of 10%. 16 imported commodities to attract the same tax level as the domestically-produced counterparts. Debt Collection Unit established in Ministry of Finance.
1994 December	VAT Bill passed into law to become operational in March 1995.
1995 January	Introduction of personal tax relief of 51.4% Simplification of import duty rates from 0%, 15% and 35% to 0% and 17.5% for various categories of imports. Discretionary tax exemptions require parliamentary approval.
1995 March	Sales tax converted into value-added tax (VAT) at a flat rate 15.5% from 15%.
1995 June	Tax revolt led to withdrawal of VAT and reintroduction of sales tax at 15%.

Expenditure Policies

1983 April   Minimum wage raised from 12 to 25 cedis per day.

1984 March   Public sector wages and salaries increased by 40%.

1985 January   Civil service wages and salaries doubled.

1986 January   Minimum wage increased from 70 to 90 cedis per day.
Wages and salaries of civil servants adjusted for inflation and to widen the ratio of top to bottom pay scale from 2:1.

1987   Redeployment and/or retrenchment policies.
Public expenditure policies to focus on increased provisions for operation and maintenance of existing investment, and cost recovery for public services.
Commercial orientation to be given to SOEs through mergers, divestiture and liquidations, etc.

1988   Divestiture Implementation Committee set up as part of the privatization/divestiture of SOEs.

1989 January   Release of ¢80 m. to the National Board for Small-Scale Industries for use as a revolving fund for the procurement of scarce but essential raw materials for the sector.

1989 February   Government finalized the Small and Medium Enterprises Project which provides the sector with adequate funding facilities in excess of ¢8 billion.
A provision of ¢5 billion made in the budget for the rehabilitation and expansion of facilities of some companies.

1992 July   Introduction of pay and grading system as part of Civil Service Reform Programme.

1993 January   Introduction of a nine-digit expenditure code on cheques issued by Treasury Officers to facilitate classification of expenditure items for ease of reconciliation with the monetary/Treasury accounts at the Bank of Ghana.
Creation of District Assembly Common Fund (DACF); 5% of national revenue to be consigned to the DACF.
Nationwide/rural electrification to increase to 43% from 33% in 1992 (12% in 1989).

1994 January   Business Assistance Fund (BAF) established with initial amount of ¢10 billion; ¢250 m. Private Enterprise Foundation (PEF); ¢100 m. to Council for Indigenous Business Association (CIBA); ¢34 billion to the District Assemblies Common Fund (DACF).

Introduction of Expenditure Tracking and Control System in three Ministries Departments and Agencies (MDAs) to monitor and control expenditure.

1995 January   Extension of EXTRACON to 26 MDAs requiring submission of returns by the first week of ensuing month.
Continuation of divestiture of SOEs. SOEs with government guaranteed foreign debts assume full responsibilities.

Appendix 2. Some Basic Concepts and Identities

In order to put the study in a proper perspective, there are some important conceptual issues to be reviewed. Firstly, it should be noted that the 'public sector accounts' in this study, includes only the accounts of the central government and excludes the unrelated accounts of the local government or the District Assemblies but includes the transfers into the District Assembly Common Fund (DACF).

Secondly, it is vital to point out that development expenditure, which is a component of capital expenditure, may or may not include capital expenditure financed through external project loans or foreign assistance tied to projects. Consequently, the development expenditure may at times refer only to direct government expenditure on development projects or the local counter-part funding of foreign assisted projects. In this respect, therefore, we have a corresponding concept of 'narrow' or 'broad' coverage. Where the foreign assistance tied to projects is included we have broad coverage definition. Otherwise, the definition is said to be narrow. In the case where the overall budget balance is a broad coverage, it must be noted that the development expenditure includes foreign financed projects of the central government (World Bank, 1989a). Unless otherwise stated our concept of the budget balance is the broad coverage.

Additionally, it is crucial to remember that the term special efficiency fund includes provision for retrenchment programme (which commenced in 1987) including (re-)training. It should also be noted that net lending (and net payments) which are at times included as a component of capital expenditure, in this study, are included as components of the budget balance items in keeping with the public sector accounts as presented by the Ghana Statistical Service.

It is also important to present an outline of the basic relationships and the accounting identities covering budget balance, revenue, expenditure, deficit financing, as well as the holdings and composition of the domestic debt which may guide our analysis. The summary of fiscal performance is captured by budget balance which is the difference between the total revenue (including grants) and expenditure (as in Equation E1 presented below). It is referred to as fiscal surplus (if it is positive) or deficit (if it is negative) or fiscal balance (if it is equal to zero) throughout this paper.

As regards the revenue (in Equation E2), there are three major components, namely, tax revenue which comprises taxes on income and property, taxes on domestic goods and services or excise tax, and taxes on international transactions, non-tax revenue (such as fees, sale of goods, rents, royalties, etc.), as well as foreign grants. As in Equation E3, there are two components of tax revenue, namely, direct and indirect taxes. The indirect tax (in Equation E4) comprises excise duties on domestically traded goods and taxes on international transactions.

The government expenditure may be classified into two categories, namely, recurrent expenditure (comprising wages and salaries, debt servicing, transportation and fuel, etc.), and capital expenditure (consisting of development expenditure, net lending and special efficiency funds) as in Equation E5. In Equation E6, recurrent expenditure comprises 6 basic elements, namely, personal, travelling and transport, etc., subvented organisation's expenses, retirement benefits, interest payments, and special outlays. Equation E7 decomposes capital expenditure into three categories: development expenditure, net lending, and special efficiency fund. There are three elements in the development expenditure captured in Equation E8, viz., construction works, plants, equipment, furniture and vehicles (or item 8), and other capital expenditure.

Budget financing sources include Bank of Ghana (BoG), other domestic loans, and net foreign loans in Equation E9. Equation E10 specifies the holdings of domestic debt by 5 main institutions, namely, BoG, Commercial Banks, Secondary Banks, SSNIT and others. Debt composition in Equation 10 has two components: short-term and long-term debts. Equation E11 states the components of short-term debt as: ways and means advances, treasury bills and government current account borrowing. In Equation E12, we decompose long-term debts into compulsory stocks, stocks and bonds, and other funds owed to Cocobod, railways, ports, compensatory saving, etc.

In symbols we may specify the above relationships in the following identities:

Budget Balance:
E1. BB   =   REV – EXP ^{3}/£ 0
Government Revenue:
E2. REV   =   NTREV + TREV+ GRANTS
E3. TREV   =   DTREV + ITREV
E4. ITREV   =   DTRADE + FTRADE
Government Expenditure:
E5. EXP   =   CUEXP + KAEXP
E6. CUEXP   =   PEMO + TGEMRO + SUBS + RBEN + INTP + SOUTL
E7. KAEXP   =   DEXP + NLEND + SEFFIF
E8. DEXP   =   CONST + PEFV + OTHERK
Budget Deficit Finance:
E9. BDF   =   DBOG + DLOAN + NFLOAN
Domestic Debt Holdings and Composition:
E10. DEBTH   =   BOG + COMB + SECB + SSNIT + OTHERH
E10. DEBTC   =   STD + LTD
E11. STD   =   WAMA + TBILLS + GCA
E12. LTD   =   COMS + SAB + OTHERC

Where   BB   =   Budget balance
   REV   =   Total government revenue
   EXP   =   Government expenditure
   NTREV   =   Non-tax revenue
   TREV   =   Tax revenue
   GRANTS   =   Foreign grants
   DTREV   =   YPTAX = Direct tax revenue or income
   and property tax
   ITREV   =   Indirect tax revenue
   CUEXP   =   Current or recurrent expenditure
   KAEXP   =   Capital expenditure
   DEXP   =   Development expenditure
   SEFFIF   =   Special efficiency fund
   YPTAX   =   Income and property tax
   DTRADE   =   Domestic goods and services tax
   PEMO   =   Personal emolument (comprising wages and salaries, etc)
   TGEMRO   =   Travelling and transport; general expenditure; mainte-
                        nance, repairs and renewals; and other current expenses
                        including student feeding
   SUBS   =   Subventions (expenditure on subvented organisations)
   RBEN   =   Retirement benefits
   INTP   =   Interest payments
   SOUTL   =   Special outlays
   NLEND   =   Net lending
   CONST   =   Construction works
   PEFV   =   Plant, equipment, furniture and vehicles
   OTHERK   =   Other capital expenditure
   FTRADE   =   International transactions tax
   BDF   =   Budget deficit financing
   DBOG   =   Bank of Ghana component of domestic loans

cont. p.114

SUMMARY OF CENTRAL GOVERNMENT FINANCES
(Millions of Cedis in 1975 Prices)

	1970	1971	1972	1973	1974	1975	1976	1977	1978	1979	1980	1981	1982
TOTAL REVENUE & GRANT	1184.52	1073.15	836.44	1013.09	1122.22	814.80	834.85	775.82	674.27	605.31	481.80	353.25	325.03
Tax Revenue	1059.76	912.69	756.58	869.68	1014.43	765.40	820.63	631.10	624.74	549.38	418.56	318.69	274.76
Taxes on Income & Property	151.29	188.31	189.62	197.38	223.24	198.10	175.03	150.21	99.56	120.78	119.66	96.66	92.95
Taxes on Domestic Goods & Se	265.06	290.35	233.83	164.39	185.60	237.80	268.65	203.24	108.79	165.22	218.02	153.69	128.69
Taxes on International Transact	627.64	427.63	328.85	501.16	594.02	319.30	352.55	270.74	414.02	260.76	79.01	68.40	48.84
Nontax Revenue	94.41	119.05	90.11	134.88	115.74	104.40	74.04	71.13	49.53	40.69	36.93	30.78	47.05
Grants	7.89	7.89	0.85	8.16	0.14	0.00	0.00	0.50	0.00	0.00	6.34	3.78	3.22
TOTAL EXPENDITURE	1163.25	1317.40	1164.01	1281.82	1619.61	1438.60	1511.21	1521.10	1070.69	934.43	1087.11	683.34	547.33
Recurrent	904.17	1061.56	959.01	987.92	1220.67	997.40	1016.18	1170.57	872.00	815.48	891.36	625.89	496.80
Development	259.08	255.84	205.00	293.89	398.94	441.20	495.04	350.53	198.69	118.96	195.75	67.45	50.53
Special Efficiency Fund													
CURRENT ACCOUNT DEFIC	260.36	11.58	-122.57	25.00	-98.45	-182.60	-181.33	-394.74	-299.87	-210.17	-429.56	-272.64	-171.77
TOTAL BUDGET DEFICIT/S	21.27	-244.26	-327.57	-268.60	-497.39	-623.80	-876.36	-745.28	-496.59	-329.13	-825.31	-340.08	-222.30
Net Lendings	—	130.38	118.73	90.79	175.28	272.70	193.91	138.97	64.59	23.00	37.55	12.64	23.14
Net Payments	—	374.64	-446.30	-359.69	-672.66	-896.50	-870.27	-884.25	-563.16	-352.13	-662.86	-352.72	-245.44
FINANCING													
Internal Loans	1.67	129.40	188.34	407.94	320.30	1059.70	730.75	959.91	273.20	294.12	595.02	306.38	230.04
of which BOG	104.45	110.67	-25.84	269.94	255.60	605.20	502.18	724.51	109.62	76.05	454.33	121.70	26.83
External Loans (Net)	38.00	41.16	70.25	-23.78	3.49	-0.70	3.86	-2.92	-2.01	58.01	67.84	26.32	13.31
Other Receipts	-102.77	204.08	187.70	-24.48	348.88	-162.50	134.95	-72.74	291.97	0.00	0.00	25.29	2.09
Total Net Receipts	-63.10	374.64	446.30	359.69	672.66	896.50	870.27	884.25	563.16	352.13	662.86	352.72	245.44

	1983	1984	1985	1986	1987	1988	1989	1990	1991	1992	1993	1994	1995
TOTAL REVENUE & GRANT	284.15	431.63	636.89	789.80	819.88	848.46	1003.93	901.83	1095.03	987.20	1329.98	1987.87	2321.22
Tax Revenue	217.55	339.92	503.07	655.58	694.56	678.27	838.37	722.73	814.30	837.56	1033.13	1275.29	1480.66
Taxes on Income & Property	44.62	76.52	121.72	163.16	187.39	236.30	218.28	174.37	188.30	181.94	221.04	254.83	357.70
Taxes on Domestic Goods & St	45.31	106.57	132.29	190.28	146.61	141.12	246.51	245.26	344.74	348.17	456.32	487.61	472.87
Taxes on International Transact	127.62	156.83	249.06	302.13	360.56	298.84	373.59	303.11	301.26	307.46	355.77	532.85	650.31
Nontax Revenue	45.13	74.29	106.23	91.09	76.97	98.82	65.67	85.25	179.10	91.35	224.91	650.35	718.35
Grants	1.47	17.42	25.60	43.13	48.36	69.37	99.89	93.85	101.63	58.29	71.92	62.23	121.99
TOTAL EXPENDITURE	391.42	523.98	756.65	817.61	832.91	881.86	910.44	863.49	859.39	1205.42	1480.95	1598.29	2273.46
Recurrent	345.56	432.75	607.66	678.31	645.45	666.49	695.65	668.56	739.14	930.17	1194.09	1322.27	1607.87
Development	34.93	76.08	115.38	109.56	148.60	179.44	178.78	182.93	188.43	245.34	242.90	261.01	378.88
Special Efficiency Fund													
CURRENT ACCOUNT DEFIC	-81.51	-1.12	29.23	111.49	174.43	179.97	308.27	233.27	355.89	57.03	135.87	685.81	713.35
TOTAL BUDGET DEFICIT/S	-127.26	-92.35	-119.76	-27.81	-13.03	-35.40	83.48	38.34	135.64	-218.21	-150.99	391.58	47.76
Net Lendings	10.82	15.14	33.81	29.74	38.86	35.92	36.01	32.00	31.82	29.90	43.98	13.02	20.58
Net Payments	-127.27	-92.35	-119.76	3.33	32.51	23.48	48.45	11.43	109.52	-285.76	-237.07	176.08	0.00
FINANCING													
Internal Loans	102.25	57.73	64.11	59.26	-23.06	-37.02	-71.51	-94.37	-145.20	359.55	124.21	-42.15	7.63
of which BOG	11.74	44.92	32.91	-2.01	-47.06	-38.16	-55.93	-55.58	-102.37	268.85	0.00	0.00	0.00
External Loans (Net)	25.02	34.62	55.65	-62.60	-9.45	13.54	23.05	82.95	35.68	0.71	112.86	-133.91	-55.39
Other Receipts	0.00	0.00	0.00	0.00	0.00	0.00	0.00	0.00	0.00	0.00	0.00	0.00	0.00
Total Net Receipts	127.27	92.35	119.76	-3.33	-32.51	-23.48	-48.45	-11.43	-109.52	360.26	237.07	-176.08	-47.76

Source: Statistical Service, Quarterly Digest of Statistics, Various Issues

(a) DOMESTIC DEBT BY HOLDINGS (in 1975 million cedis)

	1970	1971	1972	1973	1974	1975	1976	1977	1978	1979	1980	1981	1982
Total Domestic Debt	1576.50	1635.85	1598.35	1493.77	1464.83	1441.30	1791.36	1899.36	1617.03	1339.47	1315.43	861.89	1062.01
Bank of Ghana	498.57	610.27	590.87	480.58	605.31	697.60	959.46	1136.84	1104.06	836.96	799.65	533.60	566.48
Commercial Banks	287.05	164.40	223.79	229.84	143.48	104.00	161.59	218.82	139.36	178.27	186.02	116.69	186.62
Secondary Banks	0.00	0.00	0.00	0.00	0.00	0.00	50.58	58.07	43.72	34.10	49.85	34.86	60.88
SSNIT	790.88	861.18	783.69	774.40	311.79	324.10	370.66	294.63	189.20	174.62	152.24	92.40	91.57
Others	0.00	0.00	0.00	0.00	404.24	315.60	249.07	190.99	140.69	115.52	137.66	84.32	176.46

	1983	1984	1985	1986	1987	1988	1989	1990	1991	1992	1993	1994	1995
Total Domestic Debt	756.14	627.36	596.70	565.18	383.73	326.18	228.32	151.72	134.99	306.21	948.80	837.05	951.73
Bank of Ghana	431.97	379.01	341.81	304.04	191.87	131.13	64.05	64.30	46.71	127.78	614.33	483.74	605.33
Commercial Banks	126.24	86.46	82.32	58.41	49.66	43.15	23.40	2.90	2.40	0.70	0.55	0.43	0.36
Secondary Banks	69.30	28.23	55.03	89.35	48.65	0.00	0.00	0.00	0.00	0.00	0.00	0.00	0.00
SSNIT	50.32	45.53	45.80	68.02	58.68	88.59	55.86	62.35	51.66	80.40	189.20	123.45	91.52
Others	78.31	88.13	71.75	45.37	34.87	63.30	85.00	22.18	34.22	97.33	142.72	229.44	254.51

(b). DOMESTIC DEBT BY COMPOSITION (in 1975 million cedis)

	1970	1971	1972	1973	1974	1975	1976	1977	1978	1979	1980	1981	1982
Short Term	448.62	529.18	458.05	372.36	552.38	527.65	289.55	162.67	256.15	225.25	290.73	130.71	148.54
Ways & Means Advances	35.85	103.52	69.26	72.56	132.61	72.55	38.84	0.00	52.30	54.01	92.88	47.98	37.98
Treasury Bills	412.77	425.66	388.79	299.80	0.00	161.35	250.70	162.67	113.60	164.56	156.42	82.73	110.57
Govt Current Account	0.00	0.00	0.00	0.00	819.77	293.95	0.00	0.00	90.25	6.68	41.43	0.00	0.00
Long Term	1127.88	1106.67	1140.31	1436.66	512.45	1150.30	1501.81	1736.69	1360.89	1114.22	1024.70	731.17	855.58
Compulsory Stocks	136.95	120.53	99.94	28.99	31.37	15.50	6.60	4.23	2.07	1.54	1.04	0.54	0.43
Stocks & Bonds	535.66	626.54	729.24	740.72	92.59	977.55	1467.32	1714.51	1349.51	1105.62	1018.71	728.06	852.97
Cocobod Loans	30.12	31.06	26.91	21.87	67.21	34.40	16.00	10.38	5.39	4.12	2.90	1.50	1.27
Railways & Ports Loans	20.32	20.95	18.15	14.76	11.85	8.50	6.60	4.28	2.22	1.70	1.20	0.62	0.53
Compensatory Savings	49.95	50.53	42.71	14.76	9.48	6.80	5.28	3.28	1.70	1.24	0.84	0.44	0.37
Others	354.69	257.07	223.36	615.56	299.94	107.55	0.00	0.00	0.00	0.00	0.00	0.00	0.00
Total Domestic Debt	1576.50	1635.85	1598.35	1809.02	1464.83	1441.30	1791.36	1899.36	1617.03	1339.47	1315.43	861.89	1004.12

	1983	1984	1985	1986	1987	1988	1989	1990	1991	1992	1993	1994	1995
Short Term	136.48	116.95	139.02	173.69	118.58	97.14	86.45	63.48	52.28	188.71	162.34	223.81	428.15
Ways & Means Advances	46.84	34.32	28.44	20.07	14.42	0.00	0.00	0.00	0.00	0.00	0.00	0.00	0.00
Treasury Bills	89.64	66.26	60.21	52.13	51.09	37.74	86.45	63.48	52.28	97.17	114.65	141.76	229.31
Govt Current Account	0.00	16.38	50.37	101.49	53.08	29.40	0.00	0.00	0.00	91.54	47.69	82.05	198.84
Long Term	619.66	510.40	457.69	391.49	253.02	179.45	139.87	88.24	82.71	117.50	832.15	613.25	523.58
Compulsory Stocks	0.14	0.09	0.06	0.06	0.04	0.03	0.00	0.00	0.00	0.00	0.00	0.00	0.00
Stocks & Bonds	587.83	489.04	440.38	379.98	244.79	173.17	135.01	84.74	79.80	117.41	832.08	613.19	523.53
Cocobod Loans	0.53	0.39	0.33	0.23	0.17	0.13	0.10	0.07	0.06	0.05	0.04	0.01	0.01
Railways & Ports Loans	0.22	0.16	0.14	0.10	0.05	0.05	0.04	0.03	0.02	0.02	0.02	0.03	0.03
Compensatory Savings	0.15	0.11	0.09	0.07	0.05	0.04	0.02	0.02	0.01	0.01	0.01	0.01	0.01
Others	30.78	20.61	16.67	11.05	7.93	6.03	4.70	3.39	2.81	0.00	0.00	0.00	0.00
Total Domestic Debt	756.14	627.36	596.71	565.18	371.61	246.59	226.32	151.72	134.99	306.21	994.49	837.05	951.73

Note: From 1985 onwards, stocks and bonds embody values for treasury bonds, bearer bonds, development bonds, long term government stocks, and government stocks.
Sources: Bank of Ghana, Quarterly Economic Bulletin, Various Issues; World Bank, Ghana Towards Structural Adjustment, 1985, 1991; Bank of Ghana's Annual Reports

DLOAN	=	Domestic Loans for financing the deficit
NFLOAN	=	Net foreign loans
DEBTH	=	Domestic debt by holdings
DEBTC	=	Domestic debt by composition
BOG	=	Bank of Ghana holdings of domestic debt
COMB	=	Commercial Banks holding of domestic debt
SECB	=	Secondary Banks holdings of domestic debt
SSNIT	=	Social Security and National Insurance Trust holdings domestic debt
OTHERH	=	Holdings of domestic debt by other institutions and agencies including the private sector.
STD	=	Short-term debt
LTD	=	Long-term debt
WAMA	=	Ways and means advances (short-term)
TBILLS	=	Treasury bills (short-term)
GCA	=	Government current account (short-term)
COMS	=	Compulsory stocks (long-term)
SAB	=	Stocks and bonds (long-term)
OTHERC	=	Long-term debt components owed to Cocobod, Railways and Ports, Compensatory saving and other miscellaneous agencies and institutions.

6 Promises & Pitfalls in Public Expenditure

DEBORAH WETZEL*

1. Introduction

Public expenditures are among a government's principal instruments of economic policy and are the foundation of the state's role in an economy. The effectiveness with which the state raises and spends resources also has an important impact on the fiscal deficit, the growth of inflation and structural aspects of the economy.

Chapters 1 and 5 discussed a number of issues concerning the overall fiscal balance and fiscal policy. This chapter, looks more closely at how public expenditures in Ghana have evolved over the years. In the Nkrumah years, state expenditure in industry and infrastructure were seen as the key to modernization and development. Yet the promise of these expenditures met the pitfalls of weak expenditure management systems, soft budget constraints and an incentive structure created by a heavily controlled economy. Four decades later, while the Economic Recovery Programme brought major changes in economic policy, many of the issues concerning the role of the state and the allocation of public expenditures still persist and are even compounded by the large inflows of external resources.

In what follows, we look first at trends in total expenditure and net lending and some of the factors behind these trends. We then turn to consideration of the economic and sectoral decomposition of these expenditures. Finally, we evaluate public expenditure in terms of both its composition and its effectiveness in meeting the government's objectives.

2. The Ups and Downs of Total Expenditure and Net Lending

Figure 6.1 shows the overall pattern of total expenditure and net lending as a share of GDP from 1957 to 1996.[1]

---

* The author works in the office of the Senior Vice President and Chief Economist, The World Bank. The views expressed in this chapter are solely those of the author and do not represent the official views of the World Bank.
[1] Data are for the central government only and come from the Central Bureau of Statistics, *Statistical Yearbook,* 1967–68 and the *Quarterly Digest of Statistics,* various years. Net lending refers to loans made by the government to state-owned enterprises and public institutions, which are frequently not repaid and are thus classified as 'above the line' expenditures. 'Broad' coverage from 1983 includes externally financed project grants and loans. Data on externally financed project grants and loans come from the World Bank as do data for 1995 and 1996. Note that this definition may still exclude current expenditures financed by quick disbursing loans. See Wetzel (1995) for further details.

Figure 6.1: Ghana's Total Expenditure and Net Lending 1957–1996

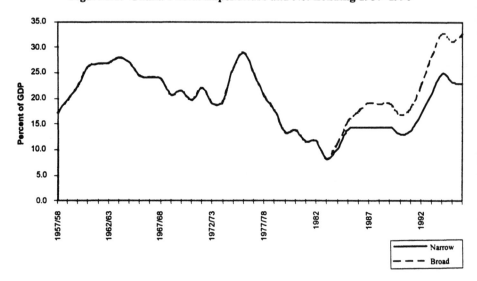

The solid line reflects what is referred to as the 'narrow coverage' of central government expenditures. Traditionally, Ghana's public expenditure accounts have excluded externally financed projects and programmes on the grounds that the government did not need to concern itself with their financing. Strictly speaking, therefore, comparisons across decades should be made based on the narrow definition. However, in the years since the ERP, significant external finance has supported a great deal of public expenditure and to exclude this leads to a substantial underestimation of government expenditure. We therefore also show the 'broad' definition of public expenditure, which includes these externally financed expenditures. There are no systematic data on externally financed expenditures on projects and programmes prior to 1983, so up to 1983 the broad and narrow measures are the same. One may hazard a guess that externally financed expenditures were negligible in the period from 1966 to 1983. From 1957 to 1966, externally financed expenditures were likely to be sizeable although there is little detailed information available.[2]

Figure 6.1 shows that central government expenditures and net lending have clearly demonstrated significant volatility over the years. In the transition to independence, Nkrumah had made far-reaching promises in order to mobilize political support. He held strong nationalist and socialist beliefs which shaped his approach to economic policies and development. He was strongly influenced by the development thinking of the time, which argued that a substantial increase in the ratio of investment to national income was the key to breaking out of poverty (see Killick, 1978: Chaps. 2 and 3). Substantial increases in public expenditure were therefore an important component of Nkrumah's economic policies. This expenditure was largely focused on infrastructure and social services and in later years on developing the 'commanding heights' of the economy (Frimpong-Ansah, 1991: 78). These expenditures helped to address the very high expectations that Nkrumah had engendered in terms of the government's provision of goods,

---

[2] While in the early 1960s government rhetoric was largely opposed to foreign borrowing, by 1964 it became clear that the government had borrowed extensively through the use of medium-term suppliers' credits. Although the magnitude is difficult to pin down, in 1964 the government estimated that such credits amounted to some 6% of GDP. Difficulty in meeting payments for these suppliers' credits led to debt-rescheduling negotiations in 1966, 1968 and 1970. See Wetzel, 1995: 115 and World Bank, 1975.

services and jobs. Figure 6.1 shows the substantial increase in expenditures from 1957 to 1964.

The National Liberation Council (NLC) (1966–9) and the Progress Party (PP) (1970–71) concentrated on efforts to restore internal and external macroeconomic balance with more emphasis on an outward orientation and less emphasis on the state. During this period public expenditures were brought back to about 20% of GDP. The coup in 1972 brought a return to heavy emphasis on state control and state expenditure, and public expenditures shot up dramatically, reaching just under 30% of GDP. With the collapse of the state that ensued public expenditure fell dramatically, falling to 8% of GDP in 1983.[3]

The decision to move towards an adjustment programme was a significant shift in the pronouncedly populist but somewhat piecemeal approach that had been pursued in the first two years of the PNDC government. Essentially, as both the economy and civil society fell apart, it became clear that the government had neither the economic policies nor the access to capital to address the situation. On top of it all, in 1982 and 1983, Ghana experienced a severe drought, which caused a substantial reduction in agricultural production; extensive bush fires, which caused damage throughout the countryside; and Nigeria's expulsion of approximately one million Ghanaians who had been working in the country illegally, amounting to the re-absorption of an additional 10% of the population.

The decision to undertake an adjustment programme was made and announced in the April 1983 budget. The ERP began a period of stabilization and adjustment under the auspices of a structural adjustment programme. As part of this programme, revenue collection improved and public expenditures increased to about 14% of GDP (narrow definition) — a level at which they stabilized in 1991. The foreign assistance supporting the programme allowed an increase in expenditures of an additional 3–4%. With the onset of elections in 1992, however, expenditures once again increased sharply. In 1994 the narrow measure peaked at 25% of GDP, while the broad measure peaked at 33% of GDP in 1996. Such shares of public expenditure are as high as independent Ghana has ever experienced and are high relative to other low- and even middle-income developing countries.[4]

What factors could be driving these rather dramatic changes in expenditure? Wetzel (1995) considers some of the determinants of overall expenditure for the period from 1957–94. On the economic side, while there was no evidence of a significant long-term relationship between expenditure and key macroeconomic variables, in the short term increases in expenditure were found to be most strongly influenced by changes in GDP, in the price level and in import volumes.[5]

Perhaps a more important determinant of expenditures in Ghana has been the political rationale. Theories of personal or predatory rule[6] shed some light on the phases of expansion in expenditure seen above. While Nkrumah had considerable legitimacy at independence, the expectations placed on the state were very high. In addition to serving his approach to development, massive expansion of the state allowed him to establish the new state's legitimacy and to reward his loyal supporters. As Nkrumah became more authoritarian and opposition mounted, there was a need to expend greater resources to maintain his legitimacy. Since reserves had been depleted and revenue from cocoa was falling, he was forced to turn to monetary finance. By 1965, the economic situation had deteriorated and opposition was so widespread that Nkrumah

---

[3] For greater detail on the underlying events and political economy of these periods see Frimpong- Ansah (1991) and Chazan (1983, 1988 and 1991).

[4] For example, in 1994 total central government expenditures as a share of GDP were 27.5% in Kenya, 18.2% in Zambia, 20.4% in Chile, 16.3% in Indonesia and 24.7% in Malaysia.

[5] Although clearly causality between these variables may run both ways.

[6] Systems of personal or predatory rule have been discussed in Brennan and Buchanan (1980), Bates (1981), Jackson and Rosberg (1982), Lal (1984), Sandbrook (1985), Levi (1988), Callaghy (1990) and Frimpong-Ansah (1991). Although the focal points of these writers vary, the basic elements of their approaches to personal rule are common. See Chapter 2 for a detailed discussion of these issues.

could no longer buy support and his regime fell.

The rapid increase in expenditures in the mid-1970s can be attributed to similar factors. The coup in 1972 brought down a democratically elected government and had little in the way of legitimacy. The return to policies of nationalism and rapid expansion of the state, and the increases in expenditure that went along with them, were used as in earlier days as a means of developing legitimacy and support. As the regime became increasingly unpopular, its time horizon shortened and there was an increased incentive to take as much out of the system as possible. At the same time, production was declining, so the resources required to feed the patronage system came to be in short supply, thus reinforcing the dwindling of support (Leith and Lofchie, 1993).

The third increase in expenditures began in 1983, but really took off after 1992 following almost ten years of fiscal stability. While this episode is markedly different from the previous two cycles of increasing expenditures, there is one key commonality. This concerns the establishment of legitimacy. Rawlings took power from a democratically elected government in 1981. For many years he maintained an authoritarian regime. Given the force of his personality, the depths to which the state had sunk in the pre-ERP period and his history of coercion, the new regime was able to survive without the support of the patronage system of previous periods. However, as time passed and the economic situation improved, his legitimacy was increasingly questioned (Rothchild, 1991). The elections of 1992 were thus intended to provide him with a democratic mandate. Uncertain of his support, however, expenditures increased; most notably, the civil service was provided with an 80% wage increase on the eve of the election. At the same time tax collection fell and the increases in expenditure were financed with an overdraft from the Bank of Ghana (World Bank, 1994).

Jeffries (1992) found that in a survey of urban attitudes towards the Economic Recovery Programme, whereas only 28% of those surveyed thought they were better-off than five years previously, 78% felt that the current government had done well. The most common reason given by respondents for such approval was the many improvements that could be seen in the country; the improved roads, the plentiful goods in the markets, the materializing development projects of one kind and another, testifying to the fact that the PNDC leaders were spending money properly and trying their best for the country. With these as the yardstick for approval it was no surprise that, in the run-up to the 1996 elections, expenditures continued to be substantially higher than in the pre-electoral period, although the government had recourse to a greater degree of external financing to support them.

Let us now turn to consider how these expenditures were allocated.

3.   Expenditures by Economic Classification

Table 6.1 presents the economic classification of total expenditures and net lending (broad definition) as a share of GDP for the five periods discussed above. When considering recent expenditure patterns in comparison with the pre-ERP periods, a few points stand out:

*   With the onset of the ERP, current expenditures dropped in the period from 1983 to 1991 and capital expenditures increased. Both current and capital expenditures increased sharply in the 1992-6 period, exceeding the shares of GDP in all previous periods.
*   After dropping in 1983–91, wages as a share of GDP have returned to their pre-ERP share.
*   The share of resources dedicated to goods and services, which includes operations and maintenance, has declined from the pre-ERP periods.
*   Interest payments have increased dramatically, reaching 4% of GDP in the 1992–6 period.

Figure 6.2 shows how the composition of these economic classifications as a share of total expenditure and net lending (broad coverage) has changed over time.

Expenditure composition in the first phase of the Economic Recovery Programme (1983–92)

Table 6.1   Central Government Expenditure and Net Leading by Economic Classification (Broad Coverage)

(in % of GDP)	1957–66	1967–71	1972–82	1983–91	1992–96
Current	13.7	15.9	13.7	10.1	16.4
Consumption	8.6	9.6	8.7	6.6	8.6
o/w Wages	na	5.5	5.0	3.9	5.8
o/w Goods and Services	na	4.1	3.8	2.7	2.8
Interest	0.7	1.7	1.9	1.5	4.0
Transfers	4.4	4.6	3.1	2.0	3.8
Capital Expenditures	7.0	3.7	3.3	5.1	11.8
Net Leading	2.8	1.2	1.6	0.5	0.4
Other[a]	0.5	0.7	0.2	0.2	0.8
Total Expenditure and Net Lending	25.1	21.6	18.8	16.2	29.4

Note: [a]Pre-1987 equals statistical discrepancy between reported components and reported total. Post-1987 equals special efficiency fund to cover redeployment costs.

Sources: Central Bureau of Statistics, *Statistical Yearbook,* 1967–68; *Quarterly Digest of Statistics,* and World Bank data.

seems to be reasonably similar to those in the preceding two periods. The bulk of expenditure is dedicated to consumption — 42% of total expenditures in 1983–92 compared with 46% in the 1976–71 and 1972–82 periods. With a reduction in the share allocated to transfers and net lending, the amount spent on capital expenditure also increased.

In contrast, the data for the 1992–6 period show a rather substantial change from the previous periods, with a dramatic increase in the share of resources allocated to capital expenditure and significant reductions in the share allocated to consumption. During this period net lending and transfers were reduced and interest payments as a share of total expenditure increased.

A key question when considering the impact of public expenditure on the economy is the share allocated to consumption versus that allocated to investment. Consumption may prompt higher levels of demand which support growth in the short term, but which may not be sustainable. Investment may, on the one hand, help promote economic growth if it is directed towards high return areas. On the other hand, if public investment is in low-return activities, or if it crowds out potential private sector activity, it may have a harmful impact on growth (see Chapter 18). We see from the above data that, as a share of total expenditure, consumption was larger than investment in all periods except for 1992–6.

Consumption consists of two principal categories: wages and expenditures on goods and services. While the reform programme was initially successful in bringing wages down from 5% to 3.9% of GDP, they increased again to 5.8% of GDP in the 1992–6 period.[7]Of greater concern is the steady drop in resources allocated to other goods and services. Incorporated in 'other goods and services' are the operations and maintenance costs necessary for maintaining and

---

[7] Civil service reform and the decompression of wages have been an important aspect of the reform programme that has yet to be fully implemented. A large civil service that is paid low wages is generally less effective than a small civil service that is paid at rates which are more competitive with the private sector. The government undertook a major civil service reform programme in the mid-1980s, including redundancies, but this has not been sustained. The 80% increase in civil service wages just prior to the 1992 elections was one catalyst of the macroeconomic difficulties the government has experienced since then.

Figure 6.2: Total Central Government Expenditure and Net Lending Classified by Economic Category
(as a share of total expenditure and net lending)

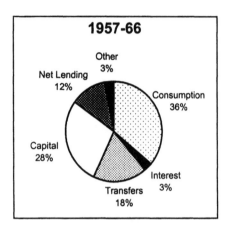

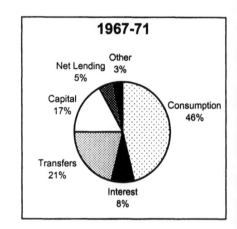

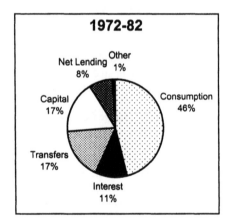

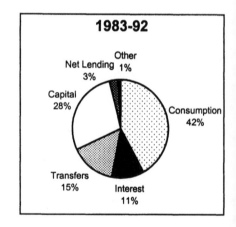

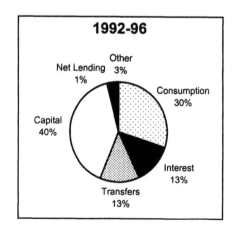

effectively using the existing capital stock. Each and every public expenditure review carried out by the World Bank or by the government itself has highlighted the need to allocate more resources to operations and maintenance in order to use the existing capital stock (textbooks for schools, drugs for hospitals, maintenance of roads) effectively. A bias clearly exists in favour of expenditure on new capital stock and rehabilitation as opposed to maintenance (see World Bank (1989, 1990, 1992) and Republic of Ghana (1995b, 1996, 1997b). This is despite the high rate of return that expenditures on operations and maintenance often provide.[8]

Another aspect that stands out in the data is the dramatic increase of expenditures devoted to interest payments. Expenditures on interest rose from 1.5% of GDP in the 1983–91 period to 4% of GDP in the 1992–6 period. In 1996, for the first time interest payments as a share of GDP exceeded domestically financed capital expenditures (5.2% and 4.9% of GDP respectively). The government has relied increasingly not only on foreign borrowing but on Treasury bills at high interest rates, to finance its expenditures (see Chapter 5). In recent years it has also increased its borrowing externally on non-concessional terms. The risk is that it will find itself on an explosive path, with increasing amounts of interest to be paid entailing increasing expenditure, which requires more borrowing to finance.

Finally, the data also show some interesting trends with respect to investment. Capital expenditure constituted 7% of GDP and 28% of total expenditures during the years 1957–66. As discussed above, this was the period of Nkrumah's state-led economic policy, when the state was viewed as having a key role in all aspects of the economy and particularly in providing a state-led investment push. In the subsequent two periods, capital expenditure fell to about 3% of GDP and 17% of total expenditures. Restoring and rehabilitating economic infrastructure was a key component of the ERP, so it is not too surprising to see a rebound in capital expenditure to 5% of GDP and 28% of total expenditures during 1983–91. It is surprising, however, to see that capital expenditure doubled, reaching 11.8% of GDP, during the 1992–6 period and as a share of total expenditures increased to 40%. Whether intentional or not, investment in Ghana has not only continued to be state-led, but is becoming increasingly more so. For the 1992–6 period, the national accounts estimate of gross domestic investment was 16.4% of GDP, implying that private sector investment had averaged about 4.6% of GDP — only a quarter of total investment.

An additional consideration is the degree to which these various expenditures have been financed by external resource flows. Data on the use of external resource flows by economic classification are not available. However, the difference between the broad and narrow expenditure definitions does give us an indication of the share of the capital expenditure that is externally financed. During the 1983–91 period, 3.5% of GDP or 69% of central government capital expenditures were financed by external project grants and loans. During the 1992–6 period, the ratio was the same; of the 11.8% of GDP allocated to capital expenditure, 70% was financed by external projects and loans. External resources have thus made a substantial contribution to Ghana's public investment.

4.   Expenditures by Sectoral Classification

Data on the sectoral classification of public expenditures are only available for the 'narrow' definition of public expenditures. These include recurrent expenditures and the development budget, but exclude expenditures financed by external projects and grants. (We consider below the information that is available on the sectoral composition of external loans and grants.) Table 6.2 considers three broad categories of sectoral expenditure: public services, economic services, and social services.

Public services consists of expenditures on such items as government administration, foreign affairs, justice and internal security. These items reflect the most basic functions of the state

---

[8] In India, specific road maintenance has been found to have a return of 113%. And in Indonesia, the return on maintenance in the irrigation sector is 117% in Java and 90% off Java (see Pradhan, 1996: 22).

Table 6.2　Central Government Expenditure by Sectoral Category (Narrow Coverage)

	1957–66	1967–71	1972–82	1983–91	1992–96
(as a share of GDP)					
Public Services[a]	**5.4**	**6.0**	**4.3**	**2.9**	**4.5**
Economic Services	**9.0**	**4.9**	**3.9**	**2.4**	**3.4**
Agriculture	2.0	1.4	1.6	0.6	0.3
Infrastructure	5.0	2.4	1.9	1.3	2.3
Roads	1.1	0.9	1.0	0.9	2.1
Transport, Storage and Communication	1.9	1.0	0.3	0.2	0.1
Power/Electricity	1.1	0.1	0.0	0.0	0.1
Water and Sanitation	0.9	0.7	0.6	0.2	0.1
Other Economic Services	2.0	1.1	0.4	0.5	0.8
Social Services	**6.1**	**6.9**	**6.4**	**5.2**	**6.0**
Education	3.7	4.2	3.6	3.0	4.4
Health	1.3	1.4	1.3	1.2	1.3
Other Social Expenditures	1.1	1.4	1.5	1.1	0.3
(as a share of total expenditures and net lending-narrow coverage)[b]					
Public Services	**22.3**	**28.1**	**22.9**	**23.0**	**20.7**
Economic Services	**37.4**	**22.5**	**20.9**	**18.7**	**15.8**
Agriculture	8.4	6.4	9.1	4.7	1.3
Infrastructure	20.8	11.0	9.6	10.3	10.8
Roads and Waterways	4.8	2.4	4.8	o.8	9.6
Transport, Storage and Communication	8.1	4.6	1.6	1.9	0.3
Power/Electricity	4.2	0.6	0.2	0.2	0.4
Water and Sanitation	3.6	3.4	3.0	1.4	0.5
Other Economic Services	8.2	5.1	2.3	3.7	3.6
Social Services	**25.2**	**32.2**	**33.8**	**39.9**	**28.1**
Education	15.3	19.6	19.1	22.9	20.3
Health	5.2	6.3	7.0	8.7	6.2
Other Social Expenditures	4.7	6.2	7.7	8.3	1.6

Notes: [a] *Quarterly Digest* data to 1987 are broken down into general administration, defence and justice and police. Data from 1987 are broken down as foreign affairs, interior and defence and other government.

    [b] Categories do not add up to 100 because 'unallocable expenditures', which include transfers to local government, interest payments on public debt, and others are not shown.

Sources: Central Bureau of Statistics, *Statistical Yearbook, 1967/68; Quarterly Digest of Statistics,* various years, and World Bank data.

in establishing and enforcing the 'rules of the game'. Expenditures on public services were highest during the 1967–71 period at 6% of GDP and 28% of all expenditures. During 1957–66, expenditures allocated to public services were 5.4% of GDP and 22.3% of total expenditure (narrow definition). Compared with earlier periods, expenditure on public services as a share of GDP has fallen, although they still constitute about a fifth of total expenditures.

The second broad category is economic services. These refer to a range of activities, some of which have a greater rationale for public intervention than others. Agriculture is one of the main categories under this heading. In general there is no inherent reason for the government to play a role in actual agricultural production. This can and is carried out by the private sector in economies throughout the world. There are, however, public-good arguments for the government to invest in research and development, in extension services to help disseminate public information, and in the prevention of crop diseases that may spread and in which the individual incentives for treatment are limited. In Ghana, the portion of expenditures allocated to agriculture has been small. This is at least in part because agriculture in Ghana has been dominated by cocoa and expenditures concerning the cocoa sector are carried out under the auspices of the COCOBOD, and are not incorporated into the central government budget (apart from the export tax received on cocoa, which has long been a significant component of revenue). The expenditures recorded under this category also include those for fisheries and forestry. The share of expenditure allocated to agriculture was at its highest during the 1957-66 period at 2% of GDP and 8.4% of total expenditure. Since then it has continually declined, reaching 0.3% of GDP and 1.3% of total expenditures (narrow coverage) in 1992–6 .

The second item included under economic services is infrastructure. Traditionally the provision of infrastructure has been perceived to be one of the principal functions of the state. Given the magnitude of infrastructure investment and its 'lumpy' nature, there seems little incentive for an individual to undertake such large investments. In addition, infrastructure has typically been considered a natural monopoly, with the necessary grids, pipes and tracks put in place by the government. Recently, there has been much discussion about the private provision of public infrastructure, but even where this is possible there is usually a strong role for the government. Table 6.2 shows that, during the Nkrumah years, spending on infrastructure was 5% of GDP and a fifth of total public expenditures and was spread fairly evenly across roads and waterways; transport, storage and communications; power and electricity; and water and sanitation. During the 1972–82 period, expenditure on infrastructure fell to an average of 1.9% of GDP and 9.6% of total expenditure. The rehabilitation of infrastructure was a key component of the ERP, but domestically financed infrastructure remained relatively low at 1.3% of GDP, and 10.3% of total expenditures(narrow coverage) went to infrastructure. This increased to 2.3% of GDP and almost 11% of total expenditures (narrow coverage) in 1992–6, the bulk of it going to the roads sector. As we shall see below, most of the expenditure on infrastructure was financed with external resources.

The third major category of expenditure is social services, including education, health and other social expenditures. As is typical in many African states, these social services have for many years been provided by the state at all levels. Because of the importance of basic education and health to a country's economic wherewithal and the quality of life of its citizens, their provision is considered an appropriate public service (see Chapter 15). At the secondary and tertiary levels of service delivery the debate still continues. While there are some public-good reasons for a government role at these higher levels, complete provision by the public sector is not usually called for. As a share of GDP, expenditure on social services remained fairly steady across the five periods under consideration. As a share of GDP, social expenditures declined with the onset of the ERP, but their share of total expenditure increased to just under 40%. And while expenditure on social services increased as a share of GDP in the 1992–6 period, it fell as a share of total expenditures. Across all time periods, within the social services, education has received the largest share of resources. A large portion of these expenditures reflects teachers' salaries.

To sum up, for recurrent and domestically financed capital expenditures (the narrow coverage), during the 1957–66 period the government placed priority on the provision of economic services, with social services a close second and public services a not too distant third. For the four subsequent periods, priorities shifted with the provision of social services receiving priority, then public services, and then economic infrastructure. An important consideration is that the salaries of teachers and health workers are included as part of the narrow budget definition and this may explain the magnitude of spending in this sector. We also need to take into account that the narrow definition excludes externally financed capital expenditure, and based on the discussion above we are probably missing out on a large portion (70%) of spending in sectors that are likely candidates for external assistance.

5. The Sectoral Composition of Externally Financed Expenditures

Given the importance of externally financed projects and programmes it is useful to consider the sectoral allocation of expenditures financed from abroad. Unfortunately data providing a sectoral decomposition of the disbursements of external loans and grants are only available beginning in 1987. In addition, these data are not a perfect complement to the narrow measure of expenditures above, so it is not possible to aggregate the two.[9] Nevertheless, it is enlightening to consider the sectoral allocation of these loans and grants and to compare it with the allocation of narrowly defined expenditures discussed above.

Table 6.3 shows that a different pattern emerges for the allocation of externally financed resources from that for domestically financed resources. The bulk of disbursements of external loans and grants is allocated to the economic services category. Some 8.7% of GDP and 92.1% of total disbursements fall under this category in the 1987-91 period and slightly less — 7.4% of GDP and 87.1% of total disbursements — in 1992-6. In the 1987–91 period, the remaining external resources are evenly split between public services and social services, whereas in the 1992–6 period, 10% of external disbursements went to social services and 3% to public services.

Within the economic services category, the largest portion of disbursements of external loans and grants went to 'other economic resources' — 58% in 1987–91 and 33% in 1991–6. It appears from the data that disbursements of adjustment loans have been classified in this category because they are economy-wide and cannot be attributed to a single sector.[10]

Infrastructure received the next largest portion of disbursements of external loans and grants — 2.5% of GDP and 27.7% of external disbursements in 1987–91 — and this was evenly spread across roads; transport, storage and communications; and power, with water and sanitation receiving a smaller share. In the 1992–6 period, the share of external resources dedicated to infrastructure increased further, reaching 3.7% of GDP and 43.2% of all external disbursements. Most of this increase went to roads.

In 1987–91 the amount of external disbursements directly allocated to social services was relatively low, with education receiving only 1.1% of total disbursements and health 2.5%. In the 1992–3 period the amount devoted to the social services as a share of GDP tripled, and as a share of total disbursements more than doubled.[11]

---

[9] The data available on the sectoral allocation of external loans and grants include all external loans and grants, not just those that fund capital expenditure, which are included in the broad deficit measure. Some of these external loans and grants may be to public agencies other than the government and therefore may not be included in the budgetary accounts. The total of external loans and grants is higher than the external financing included in the broad expenditure measure and there is no basis for knowing whether including the external loans and grants above and beyond capital financing would either be double counting or would include entities not covered by the budget.

[10] Similar ratios exist for data on the disbursement of World Bank credits. Just over half was for adjustment credits that could not be classified by sector. The remainder was for credits that could be identified by sector (see Armstrong, 1996: 26).

[11] Note that in social services and in agriculture the amount disbursed was only a third of the amount committed during the 1987–91 period. While this ratio has improved since then, it raises some important public expenditure management issues that will be discussed below.

Table 6.3   Sectoral Classification for Public Expenditures (Narow coverage) and for External Loans and Grant Disbursements, 1987–91 and 1992–96

	Total Public Expenditures and NL (Narrow Coverage)		Disbursements of External Loanss and Grants	
	1987–91	1992–96	1987–91	1992–96
(as a share of GDP)				
Public Services	**2.8**	**4.5**	**0.3**	**0.2**
Economic Services	**2.5**	**3.4**	**8.7**	**7.4**
Agriculture	0.5	0.3	0.6	0.9
Infrastructure	1.4	2.3	2.5	3.7
Roads	1.1	2.1	0.7	1.7
Transport, Storage and Communication	0.2	0.1	0.8	0.8
Power/Electricity	0.0	0.1	0.8	0.8
Water and Sanitation	0.1	0.1	0.2	0.4
Other Economic Services	0.5	0.8	5.6	2.8
Social Services	**6.2**	**6.0**	**0.4**	**0.9**
Education	3.4	4.4	0.1	0.5
Health	1.4	1.3	0.2	0.4
Other Social Expenditures	1.4	0.3	0.0	0.1
(as a share of total expenditures/share of external loan and grant disbursements) [a]				
Public Services	**19.8**	**20.7**	**3.8**	**3.0**
Economic Services	**18.0**	**15.8**	**92.1**	**87.1**
Agriculture	3.9	1.3	6.1	10.8
Infrastructure	10.3	10.8	27.7	43.2
Roads	7.8	9.6	7.7	19.3
Transport, Storage and Communication	1.2	0.3	8.7	9.9
Power/Electricity	0.2	0.4	8.9	9.6
Water and Sanitation	1.1	0.5	2.4	4.3
Other Economic Services	3.9	3.6	58.2	33.2
Social Services	**44.2**	**28.1**	**4.1**	**9.8**
Education	24.4	20.3	1.1	5.0
Health	9.9	6.2	2.5	4.2
Other Social Expenditures	9.9	1.6	0.5	0.6

Note: [a] Categories do not add up to 100 because 'unallocable expenditures', which include transfers to local govern ments, interest payments on public debt, and other, are not shown.

Sources: Central Bureau of Statistics, *Statistical Yearbook, 1967/68; Quarterly Digest of Statistics,* various years, and Republic of Ghana/World Bank (1997).

Table 6.3 indicates a certain complementarity between domestically financed expenditures and the sectoral allocations of disbursements of external loans and grants. If we exclude the 'other economic services' category, most disbursements went to infrastructure, and roads in particular, whereas domestically financed expenditure was focused more on social expenditures. This would seem a sensible strategy, given that infrastructure projects are typically capital-intensive, whereas social services typically have a high recurrent cost component. Information on the current/capital breakdown of expenditures financed through disbursements of external loans and grants is unfortunately not available, so there is no way of evaluating the above hypothesis with data. It would also be useful to know the ultimate use of quick-disbursing money, but information is also lacking here.

6.   Evaluating the Composition of Ghana's Public Expenditures

The above data indicate that public expenditures are playing an increasingly important role in the economy. As in the early days of independence it seems that the government is looking toward public expenditures to catalyze the country's economic growth in the absence of a strong private sector. Such a strategy has not been successful in the past and it is not clear that it will be now. To a certain degree this hinges on the productivity of public expenditures in meeting their stated objectives and whether the right mix of expenditures has been proposed.[12]

The budgeting and expenditure management process is the basis on which most allocations are made. In its recent public expenditure reviews, the Government of Ghana has identified important general issues in the public expenditure management system (Republic of Ghana, 1995b). The 1993 review identified the following key issues:

- lack of data on actual expenditures (as opposed to budgeted expenditures);
- problems with the budget planning and implementation cycle;
- a budgetary system that does not create incentives for effective budget management;
- ineffective management of personal emoluments (wages, benefits, etc),
- insufficient allocations to non-wage operations and maintenance expenditure.

The more recent 1994 review focused on development expenditure and identified a number of key issues also, especially in the implementation of the Public Investment Programme (PIP). These problems include:

- a proliferation of projects on a scale too small to be effectively assessed and monitored;
- difficulties in undertaking feasibility analysis on these projects. Only a quarter of new projects in the PIP have feasibility studies carried out (see Table 6.4).
- budget allocations are not based on a ranking of projects in order of priority;
- a long age-profile of projects with uncontrolled variation of on-going projects often undermining the productivity of projects;
- difficulty in delivering matching funds for foreign-financed projects.

The government recognizes that there are substantial weaknesses in the public expenditure management processes, and has put into place a programme addressing these issues. Despite the progress that has been made since the early 1980s, the overall budget planning and strategy still appear to be done in a rather piecemeal process, with budget allocations being determined based on increments from previous years and without any reference to overall policy objectives. Certain sectors have experienced substantial budget overruns; others have not received their full budget allocations. As more and more resources are channelled through the state budget, it is

---

[12] It also hinges on whether the amount of expenditure undertaken can be sustainably financed, but this issue is dealt with elsewhere in this volume.

Table 6.4   PIP Projects and Feasibility Studies

PIP (years)	No. of PIP sectors	No. of projects	No. of on-going projects	No. of new projects	No. of feasibility studies in new projects
1986–88	9	201	123	78	25
1988–90	12	314	253	61	20
1989–91	12	342	290	52	16
1990–92	14	387	347	40	15
1991–93	14	402	366	36	13
1992–94	14	417	380	37	13
1993–95	14	404	365	39	10
1994–96	16	411	369	42	10

Source: Republic of Ghana, 1995: 12.

increasingly important that these resources should be used to their most productive purposes — not least because the financing of ever-increasing expenditures is soaking up an increasing amount of the credit available in the economy and creating an incentive for the banking system to invest in government Treasury bills rather than private sector activities (see Chapter 11 on the financial sector). Given the problems that exist in the management of public expenditure, it is difficult to have confidence that expenditures, and especially the marginal ones, are reaching the activities in which they will have the highest rate of return.

With respect to evaluation of the economic composition of expenditures, countries often exhibit three biases: a bias towards new capital investments, the under-funding of non-wage operations and maintenance, and the over-staffing of a poorly paid civil service. All of these biases appear to be relevant in Ghana.

The mean capital expenditure of developing countries in 1985–90 was 4.9% of GDP. As we saw in Table 6.1, in the period 1983–91, Ghana's average capital expenditure was 5.1% of GDP. This more than doubled to 11.8% of GDP in 1992–6. The difficulties with the implementation of the public investment programme process discussed above, raise concerns about whether the magnitude of increased expenditures is being productively used. We shall consider in more detail below the productivity of investments in two of these sectors.

One of the problems cited in the public expenditure reviews is that a considerable number of older projects drag on through the use of variation orders and take a long period of time to be fully implemented and closed. At the same time, there is a fairly large number of new projects implemented in each PIP cycle, the bulk of which do not have feasibility studies. The number of new projects (many driven by the donor community), combined with the stock of on-going projects, implies that resources are spread very thin and this may hinder effective implementation of the overall capital expenditure programme. Certainly, for those capital expenditures that are foreign-financed, disbursements are often delayed because of delays in project implementation.

There is also clearly a preference for allocating expenditures to new projects as opposed to providing resources for operations and maintenance of existing projects. The mean for expenditure on other goods and services across all developing countries for 1985–90 is 4% of GDP. During 1987–91 the share allocated to this in Ghana was 2.7% of GDP. In 1992–6, when capital expenditures doubled, the share allocated to non-wage goods and services was 2.8% of GDP, roughly the same as in the previous period. Clearly the capital/recurrent expenditure balance is not appropriate and is likely to limit the productivity of current capital expenditures.[13]

As far as wages are concerned, the mean for developing countries for 1985–90 is 6.6% of GDP. At 3.9% of GDP in the 1987–91 period and at 5.8% of GDP, during 1991–6, Ghana's share allocated to wages is not excessive. What has arisen as a difficulty is that the large size of the civil service implies a relatively low wage rate, which is not competitive with the private sector and may make the civil service less productive than it might otherwise be.

A final issue in the evaluation of the economic composition of expenditures is the amount allocated to interest payments. On average the mean of interest payments for developing countries was 3.5% of GDP in the 1985–90 period. While Ghana's interest payments in 1983–91 were moderate, the increase to 4% of GDP in 1992–6 raises serious concerns about the sustainability of the current level of expenditure, especially for a low-income country.

Pradhan (1995) set out three broad criteria for evaluating the sectoral allocation of expenditure. The first is the *identification of the role of the public sector* versus the private sector. In the first instance, the proposed expenditure should be undertaken by the private sector if it is profitable at the prevailing market prices, unless there are compelling market failures that suggest that government intervention will lead to better outcomes. It is then necessary to determine whether the intervention should take the form of regulating the private sector, financing or subsidizing private sector provision, or financing and provision by the public sector itself. Secondly, if there is a legitimate role for public expenditures, then a *cost-benefit analysis* of alternative expenditure allocations needs to be undertaken to determine those that make the greatest contribution. Thirdly, some assessment of impact on the poor, through incidence analysis, is important if the government is trying to achieve poverty reduction objectives. To evaluate sectoral expenditure these criteria would need to be applied to sectoral allocations; however, only a limited analysis of *inter*sectoral allocations can take place without an analysis of *intra*sectoral allocations. While such detailed analysis is beyond the scope of this chapter, we draw together below some of the existing information on the effectiveness of sectoral expenditure in two key areas of government expenditure: roads and education.

As set out in the data above, the government has devoted a considerable amount of its resources to infrastructure. With changing technologies, views as to the appropriate role of the state regarding infrastructure are also changing. For example, in telecommunications, satellite and microwave systems are replacing long-distance wire networks and cellular systems are replacing local distribution networks. These changes remove the network-based monopoly and provide greater scope for competition.[14] Nevertheless, there is still an important role for the public provision of certain infrastructure, such as roads.

The roads sector in Ghana has three programmes, each managed by a separate agency: the Ghana Highway Authority (GHA), the Department of Urban Roads (DUR) and the Department of Feeder Roads (DFR), all of which are under the Ministry of Roads and Highways. In the 1993–6 period, total expenditures for the three programmes were allocated in the ratio of 62:22:17 (GHA:DUR:DFR). About 55% of this expenditure was financed through the Government of Ghana's Road Fund, and some 11% via non-concessional external debt.

In a recent Government of Ghana/World Bank Infrastructure Expenditure review, the Government of Ghana sets out the general principles by which it chooses road investments.[15] Generally a 15% rate of return is required on all projects, whatever the source of funding. The GHA gives

[13] Heller (1991) set out what are referred to as "r coefficients" or the ratio of net recurrent expenditure requirements to the total investment costs of a project for various sectors. For a period in the mid-1980s Ghana aimed to meet certain r coefficient levels tailored to Ghana, but these targets levels were not reached. See the various public expenditure reviews.

[14] See the 1994 *World Development Report* (World Bank, 1994) on Infrastructure for Development for greater detail on the changing role of the state in infrastructure.

[15] This section draws on Government of Ghana/World Bank, 1997.

priority to improving the main national road network, seeking a greater economic and social integration of the country. The DUR prioritizes filling the critical gaps and the alleviation of bottlenecks in the primary and secondary urban networks. The Department of Feeder Roads targets Districts with high agricultural potential. All agencies are said to prioritize road rehabilitation or upgrading (as opposed to new road construction). Regional development and equity are additional criteria used in selecting road investments, as is providing access to deprived areas. Finally, in a few cases, political factors are a determinant.

While road investments generally comply with the 15% EER criterion, those that are selected are not necessarily the projects with the highest return. There are serious concerns about the cost-effectiveness of road expenditures. The first is that routine periodic maintenance is the most cost-effective type of expenditure in the roads sector, but relatively expensive rehabilitation is favoured at the expense of maintenance. Secondly, the cost-effectiveness of contractor-promoted, export-credit financed and directly negotiated road contracts is a matter of concern. Recent costs comparisons have been made between competitive bid-based projects and negotiated contracts. Excluding finance charges, the negotiated cost per kilometre of construction was found to be six times higher for negotiated contracts than for competitively bid contracts. Thirdly, there is concern about the cost-effectiveness of design road standards, with recent projects seen as being over-designed (excessive width, high cost kerbs, etc.) Finally, large cost-overruns in recent years highlighted the numerous variations orders on contracts. These have typically enormously increased the costs of projects both in absolute terms and in costs per kilometre.

In terms of its impact on the poor, expenditure on roads has not met its objectives of regional development and equity. From 1993 to 1996 investment on roads centred on the Greater Accra Region. Most regions gained about 600-800 cedis per capita per year in investments in roads during this period. However, in Greater Accra, investments amounted to over 2000 cedis per capita. In four regions — Western, Central, Ashanti and Greater Accra — all communities reported having access to a motorable road. These regions absorbed 57% of road expenditure by the government in 1992–6. The remainder was shared between seven regions where such access was not universal. In the Eastern, Upper West, and Northern Regions, two-fifths of the communities did not have access to a motorable road, and yet these three regions received only 23% of the investment allocation. In sum, budget implementation does not appear to have met the objectives of regional development and equity and improving access. It is also likely that it was not as successful as had been hoped in removing bottlenecks in the moving of people and goods across all regions of the country. While it is not possible to provide a specific rate of return on the whole of the government's expenditures, it seems that they have not been as productive as was expected.

In education a variety of market failures are the basis for government intervention. The most commonly cited is the failure to produce the positive social externalities stemming from literacy and numeracy. Primary education is believed to lead to 'good citizenship' and to lessen crime. The role of education in lowering fertility and improving women's understanding of health and nutrition has also received much attention. Education is also believed to generate technological innovation and improved worker productivity that help to promote growth. Generally, lower levels of education are seen to yield greater externalities than higher education. The argument for greater government involvement at lower levels rests on this. In addition, capital market failures and imperfect information are also cited as rationales for government intervention in education. In most developing countries individuals are unable to borrow against their future life time income for education. Finally, a number of interventions have been based on the rationale that consumers and producers do not have full information (although implicit in this is that government planners have better information).

In its early days of independence Ghana had one of the region's most developed educational sectors.[16] By 1983 the sector had undergone massive decline. The proportion of expenditures

---

[16] This discussion draws on Armstrong, 1996: Chapter 4.

allocated to education fell to 1% in 1983 and 1984 and a mass exodus of trained teachers resulted in their being replaced by untrained teachers (44% of primary teachers and 33% of secondary teachers were untrained in 1985) with little in the way of instructional materials. In 1986 the government introduced a comprehensive education reform programme. Its goals were: to replace the previous English-style academic education with a more practically oriented curriculum, to reduce the number of years required to complete the primary and secondary cycles, to increase access to basic education for the rural masses and to improve quality, all in a financially sustainable manner.

In terms of inputs progress in the reforms has been substantial. Textbooks and teachers' manuals incorporating the new curriculum have been provided and distributed; many teachers have been provided with at least some in-service training for the new curriculum; the structural changes have been fully implemented, and cost-saving and cost-sharing measures have been put into place at all but the tertiary level (an important qualification). The outcomes have been varied. While the infrastructure has been expanded to reach many more people, there is evidence that the quality of education has suffered in the process. There is also little indication that the poor have benefited significantly from the expansion in facilities as the share on spending for them did not change. (Chapter 15 discusses in detail the outcomes of the social sector reforms.) (See also Demery *et al.*, 1995).

Conclusion

Issues of the role of the state in economic development have been a matter of debate for decades. The competing camps of 'minimal state role' vs. 'state planning' have to some degree come to a common ground in recent years. What is fundamental is to have an effective state; there is no point in the government playing a large role, if it can do nothing well. While there are certain key functions that the state must perform, the size of the state must be geared towards its capacity.

In Ghana since 1957, the government has vacillated between an all-encompassing state and a collapsed one. With the onset of the ERP, the government appeared to have reached an effective equilibrium concerning its role, capacity and financial sustainability. Since 1992, however, this equilibrium has been lost and, despite the pro-private sector rhetoric, the policies as far as public spending is concerned are those of a government pursuing state-led growth. Questions of the sustainability of the recent course of action arise when one considers the imbalance between capital and non-wage operations and maintenance expenditure. The magnitude of interest payments and the foreign-financed expenditures also raise questions of sustainability. And while, in principle, high levels of capital expenditure should promote growth, it is not at all clear that expenditure is being allocated to the highest-return areas of the economy or being used efficiently to remove existing bottlenecks and improve quality.

In terms of sectoral allocations, public expenditures do seem to be allocated to the areas where there is an important role for government. But again the question comes down to one of effectiveness. Roads are an important public good, but it seems that the government is not managing expenditure in this area particularly well. In terms of education, again, while there is an important role for government, addressing the issue of quality is as important as increasing expenditures. It appears that more could be done with less. Ghana has long had an inclination to believe in the promise of the state and its ability to catalyze growth. Although the government is attempting to come to grips with the pitfalls of weak public expenditure administration and limited capacity, it may wish to be more modest about what it can accomplish in terms of delivering effective public services, without undermining its other economic objectives.

References

Armstrong, Robert P. (1996) *Ghana Country Assistance Review: A Study in Development Effectiveness.* Washington, DC: World Bank, Operations Evaluation Department.

Bates, Robert (1981) *Markets and States in Tropical Africa.* Berkeley, CA: University of California Press.

Brennan, G. and Buchanan, J.M. (1980) *The Power to Tax: Analytical Foundations of A Fiscal Constitution.* Cambridge: Cambridge University Press.

Callaghy, Thomas (1990) 'Lost Between State and Market: The Politics of Economic Adjustment in Ghana, Zambia and Nigeria' in Joan Nelson (ed.) *Economic Crisis and Policy Choice: The Politics of Adjustment in the Third World.* Princeton, NJ: Princeton University Press.

Central Bureau of Statistics, Republic of Ghana (1962) *1961 Statistical Yearbook.* Accra.

Central Bureau of Statistics, Republic of Ghana (1968) *1967–68 Statistical Yearbook.* Accra.

Central Bureau of Statistics, Republic of Ghana (1981) *Economic Survey, 1977–80.* Accra.

Chazan, Naomi (1983) *An Anatomy of Ghanaian Politics: Managing Political Recession, 1969–1982.* Boulder, CO: Westview Press.

Chazan, Naomi (1988) 'Ghana: Problems of Governance and the Emerging Civil Society' in L. Diamond, J. Linz and S. Lipset (eds) *Democracy in Developing Countries.* Vol. II. Boulder, CO: Lynne Rienner.

Chazan, Naomi (1991) 'The Political Transformation of Ghana Under the PNDC' in Rothchild.

Demery, Lionel, Chao, Shiyan, Bernier, René and Mehra, Kalpana (1995) *The Incidence of Social Spending in Ghana.* PSP Discussion Paper No. 82. Washington, DC: World Bank, Poverty and Social Policy Department.

Frimpong-Ansah, Jonathan (1991) *The Vampire State in Africa: The Political Economy of Decline in Ghana.* London: James Currey.

Heller, P.(1991) 'Operations and Maintenance' in Chuke-Young and Richard Hemming, (eds) *Public Expenditure Handbook: A Guide to Policy Issues in Developing Countries.* Washington, DC: IMF, Government Expenditure Analysis Division, Fiscal Affairs Department.

Jackson, Robert and Rosberg, Carl (1982) *Personal Rule in Black Africa: Prince, Autocrat, Prophet, Tyrant.* Berkeley, CA: University of California Press.

Jeffries, Richard (1992) 'Urban Popular Attitudes Towards the Economic Recovery Programmeme and the PNDC Government in Ghana' *African Affairs,* 91, No. 363.

Killick, Tony (1978) *Development Economics in Action: A Study of Economic Policies in Ghana.* London: Heinemann, Educational Books.

Lal, Deepak (1984) *The Predatory State.* DRD Discussion Paper. Washington, DC: World Bank.

Leith , J. Clark and Lofchie, Michael F. (1993) 'The Political Economy of Structural Adjustment in Ghana', in R. Bates and A. Krueger (eds) *Political and Economic Interactions in Economic Policy Reform: Evidence from Eight Countries.* Oxford: Basil Blackwell.

Levi, Margaret (1988) *Of Rule and Revenue.* Berkeley, CA: University of California Press.

Pradhan, Sanjay (1996) *Evaluating Public Spending: A Framework for Public Expenditure Reviews.* World Bank Discussion Paper No. 323. Washington, DC: Work Bank.

Republic of Ghana (1995a) *Enhancing Welfare Through Improved Public Expenditure Management.* Report Prepared by the Government of Ghana for the 8th Meeting of the Consultative Group for Ghana.

Republic of Ghana (1995b) *Public Expenditure Review 1994: Effective Planning and Execution of the Development Budget.* Accra: Ministry of Finance.

Republic of Ghana (1996) *Public Expenditure Review 1995: Implementation of Previous Recommendations and the Way Forward.* Accra: Ministry of Finance.

Republic of Ghana/World Bank (1997a) 'Infrastructure Expenditure Review' (draft).

Republic of Ghana (1997b) *Public Expenditure Review 1996: Delivery of Economic Infrastructure.* Accra: Ministry of Finance.

Rothchild, Donald (ed.) (1991) *Ghana: The Political Economy of Recovery.* Boulder, CO: Lynne Rienner.

Sandbrook, Richard (1985) *The Politics of Africa's Economic Stagnation.* Cambridge: Cambridge University Press.

Wetzel, Deborah (1995) 'The Macroeconomics of Fiscal Deficits in Ghana: 1960–1994'. D.Phil thesis, Oxford University.

World Bank (1975) 'Fiscal and Balance of Payments Aspects of Ghana's Development'. Report No. 638a-GH. World Bank Internal Publication. 19 May.

World Bank (1989) 'Ghana: Public Expenditure Review, 1989–91'. Report No. 7673-GH. World Bank Internal Publication.

World Bank (1990) 'Ghana: Public Expenditure Review, 1990–92'. Report No. 8616-GH. World Bank Internal Document.

World Bank (1992) Ghana: Public Expenditure Review: 1992–94. World Bank Internal Document.

World Bank (1994) 'Ghana: Financial Sector Review: Bringing Savers and Investors Together'. Report No. 13423-GH. World Bank Internal Publication, 29 December.

7 Saving & Investment

MARTIN BROWNBRIDGE
AUGUSTINE FRITZ GOCKEL
& RICHARD HARRINGTON

1. Introduction

The weakness of capital investment has been a feature of the Ghanaian economy since the end of the state-led investment drive in the mid-1960s. During the 1970s and early 1980s economic policies were simultaneously unconducive to investment and discouraging to saving, especially saving in a useful financial form. The economy experienced a serious financial shallowing, and both public and private investment fell to low levels. Policy reforms and the growth of the economy in the 1980s brought about some modest recovery in public investment. Domestic saving remained depressed and a substantial saving-investment gap, financed by external capital inflows and aid, emerged as a result.

This chapter considers the experience of both investment and saving over the period from the early 1970s to the mid-1990s and considers some of the factors which have contributed to what has been a weak performance. Section 2 looks at investment in terms of the levels of both public and private investment and, where data are available, its sectoral composition, and analyzes the causal factors behind the main trends. Section 3 looks at saving and some of the policies which have affected the volume of saving as well as inhibiting the development of the financial system.

Before proceeding, two notes of caution are warranted. First, much of the data may be of poor quality. The investment data are unlikely to be very accurate. The methodologies used for estimating fixed investment, which are based on statistics of local production and imports of investment goods, are somewhat crude. They probably fail to fully capture investment in mining development, agriculture, land improvement and in some informal sector businesses. As these sectors have been expanding during the ERP, it is likely that the data underestimate actual investment levels[1]. Moreover, estimating the composition of investment between public and private sectors is problematic. There is little investment data for the state-owned enterprises (SOEs), and the government budget does not include a comprehensive estimate of all its fixed capital expenditures. Errors in estimating public investment will inevitably affect the accuracy of pri-

---

[1] There is a large discrepancy between the estimates of gross investment provided by the Ghana Statistical Service (GSS) in the *Quarterly Digest of Statistics,* on which the data in Table 7.1 are based, and the gross investment estimates presented in the Social Accounting Matrix in Chapter 4 of this volume. The GSS estimates gross investment in 1993 as ¢584 billion, whereas Powell and Round provide an estimate of ¢861 billion, almost 50% higher. If the actual investment level is closer to Powell and Round's estimate than that of the GSS, Ghana's investment performance has been, at least in 1993, much stronger than the official data suggest.

vate investment data because the latter are derived as a residual by deducting the former from total investment.

The poor quality of data applies equally to saving. There is insufficient information to permit robust estimates of aggregate saving adequate for a full analysis of saving in Ghana. Only total private saving and government saving could be derived. These estimates are derived from gross domestic saving (GDS), which is itself calculated as the residual after consumption (both private and public) has been deducted from GDP measured at market prices. Government saving is then deducted from GDS to produce total private saving. Government saving is itself the difference between government revenue and recurrent government expenditure. Beyond this, information is not available to enable the disaggregation of total private saving into personal saving and corporate saving. As is to be expected, the estimates of saving are subject to all the problems inherent in residual estimates.

It is therefore important to exercise caution in interpreting the observed trends in saving. Nevertheless, it must be noted that saving rates would remain low even if we could correct for underestimation. Saving in agriculture and the informal sector is probably the most underestimated. A further problem is that it is not possible to derive any sophisticated measures of the financial depth or shallowness of the economy and we rely on ratios of different measures of money to national income.

Secondly, explaining private investment and saving is problematic because many of the factors which influence actual decisions are the expectations, hopes and fears of business executives and of private persons and these are not readily observable. Hence, while it is possible to identify the main factors which had a potential effect on investment and saving decisions, it is harder to determine their relative importance.

2. Investment

Government Policies Prior to the ERP

The period between 1970 and 1983 was characterized by political instability, inconsistent economic policies and economic decline. It is difficult to delineate any coherent strategy towards investment in this period, but certain features do stand out.

First, government policy generally favoured the public sector over the private sector, especially in the allocation of scarce resources such as finance and foreign exchange. There was an expansion of the state-owned enterprise (SOE) sector (by 1980 there were around 280 SOEs), although public investment became increasingly constrained by shortages of resources. The government compulsorily acquired equity stakes in the large foreign companies in the mid-1970s, and nationalized some small manufacturers in 1979. From 1971 manufacturing investment required approval from the relevant government ministry.

Secondly, policy served to hold down, below market clearing levels, the real cost of capital through an overvalued exchange rate (which made imported capital goods cheaper) and interest rate controls (real lending rates were usually negative). There was as a consequence excess demand for foreign exchange and credit, with access to these resources rationed through administrative controls, such as the import licensing system.

Thirdly, public sector banks provided equity and loan finance for investment projects, although many of these projects were commercially unsuccessful and were to form a significant share of the banks' non-performing assets in the 1980s.

Fourthly, a range of fiscal incentives, including tax holidays, accelerated depreciation allowances and exemptions from customs duty on imported capital equipment, were offered to investors approved by the Capital Investments Board — later renamed the Ghana Investment Centre (GIC) — under a series of investment laws (Huq, 1989: 130).

Fifthly, there were large policy-induced distortions in rates of return to different sectors arising from the combination of price controls and subsidies, taxes, import controls, preferential interest rates. The export sectors were among the major losers, suffering from negative rates of protection as a result of import controls, a grossly overvalued exchange rate and, in the case of cocoa, high rates of taxation. Sixthly, government policy was not conducive to foreign investment. Foreign-exchange controls restricted profit repatriation and, as noted above, foreign companies were partially nationalized as part of an indigenization policy.

Trends in Public and Private Investment Both public and private investment were depressed during the 1970–83 period. Total investment averaged less than 10% of GDP, a level clearly far below that required to offset the depreciation of the existing capital stock, let alone expand it. By the early 1980s the consequences were evident in the deterioration of the infrastructure, obsolete and broken-down machinery in factories, and declining productive capacity in major export industries.

Private investment levels were not only low but exhibited a declining trend during this period; from an annual average of 7.9% of GDP in the first half of the 1970s to 4.1 % in the second half and 3% of GDP during 1980–83. Public investment levels averaged only 3.6% of GDP in the first half of the 1970s, a reflection of the stabilization and austerity measures pursued at the time, rose to 4.8% in the second half of the decade but then fell to 1.3% during 1980–83 as the government's revenue base collapsed (Table 7.1).

Table 7.1   Public, Private* and Total Investment: % of GDP 1970–94

Year	Public Investment	Private Investment	Total
1970–74	3.6	7.9	11.5
1975–79	4.8	4.1	8.9
1980–83	1.3	3.0	4.3
1984–87	5.5	3.6	9.1
1988–91	7.6	5.1	13.7
1992–94	10.0	4.5	14.5

Note: *) Private investment includes changes in stocks.
Sources: For 1970–85 Islam and Wetzel, 1994: 361, 364 and for 1986–94 World Bank, 1995: 78.

Although only limited data are available on the sectoral composition of investment in this period certain trends are evident. Little investment took place in the country's major export industries. In the cocoa industry, planting and replanting of trees averaged around 2000 hectares per annum during 1970–83, a negligible proportion of the total tree stock. Investment levels in the gold, diamond and bauxite mining industries were too low to prevent the real value of the capital stock falling sharply between 1970 and 1980. In the gold mining industry, which at that time was the country's second largest export earner after cocoa, fixed assets contracted by 37% in real terms in the 1970s. There was some investment in large-scale mechanized rice production in the North of the country, encouraged by government policies which included loans at preferential interest rates, subsidized machinery and fertilizer, tax incentives, protection from imports and price guarantees (Konings, 1986: 170–2). With the exception of the VALCO aluminium smelter, construction of which had begun in the 1960s, and which benefited from a variety of concessions and guarantees not available to other investors, there was a dearth of foreign investment.

Factors Affecting the Level of Investment There is no shortage of reasons to explain the low rates of public and private investment during the years 1970–83. Incentives to invest were depressed by both economic policies and the prolonged economic crisis, investors faced severe constraints in credit and foreign-exchange markets, and the risks of investment were greatly intensified by political instability and the often arbitrary application of administrative controls.

Incentives for firms to invest in the expansion or upgrading of capital stock were depressed for two reasons. First, the profitability of export production was undermined by overvalued exchange rates, the restrictive import regime, and, for the cocoa industry, excessive rates of taxation and marketing costs. Secondly, firms selling on the domestic market faced at best a stagnant demand for their output, due to the decline of domestic production and income. Although firms often enjoyed high effective rates of protection from imports, opportunities for expanding output through import substitution had probably been exhausted by the mid-1960s (Killick, 1978).

Exchange rate and interest rate policies held down the real cost of capital, but the efficacy of these policies to stimulate investment was negated because of severe shortages of real saving, bank credit and foreign exchange. These constraints were especially acute for the private sector, which was crowded out of credit and foreign-exchange markets by administrative controls, such as the minimum liquidity ratios imposed on banks and import licensing, which channelled scarce resources to the public sector.

The economy's supply of saving, foreign exchange and credit was reduced by the effects of adverse price incentives (not least the overvalued exchange rate and negative real deposit interest rates) and by the deterioration in the performance of the economy. Domestic saving was reasonably strong in the early 1970s, averaging 15.5% of GDP during 1970–74, but was on a declining trend thereafter (see section 3 below). Government saving was consistently negative after 1974, largely because of the collapse of tax revenues, most of the SOEs made either losses or at best modest profits, and voluntary private saving (as opposed to forced saving via seigniorage) was constrained by low incomes (Huq, 1989: 238–46). Given the country's lack of creditworthiness on international capital markets, the inflow of foreign saving was too low to compensate for the weak domestic saving effort.

The economy also experienced drastic financial shallowing with M2 falling from 26% of GDP in the mid-1970s to only 13% in the mid-1980s (see section 3 below). The contraction of the banking system, together with the large public sector borrowing requirement, severely restricted the supply of bank credit to the private sector. Furthermore, the structure of lending rates did not sufficiently discriminate between credits with different risks and maturities. Lending rates were practically the same for overdraft facilities and for more risky lending. In the case of the priority sectors, which were considered by the banks as the more risky sectors, lending rates tended to be lower, so there was no incentive to the banks to make loans. Private sector borrowing from the domestic banks and financial institutions accounted for only 11% of domestic credit in 1983 and under 3% of GDP.

The weaknesses in the export sector, and lack of foreign saving, led to import compression: the share of imports in GDP fell to less than 3% in 1983 (see Chapter 9, Table 9.4). As most tradeable capital goods were not produced domestically, this inevitably emerged as an important constraint on investment. It was one of the principal causes of the lack of investment in the mining industry during the 1970s. Ashanti Goldfields Corporation (AGC), the largest of the gold mining companies, was profitable in the 1970s despite the trend in the real exchange rate (this was offset by the increase in the world gold price) and AGC's after-tax profits plus provision for depreciation were more than sufficient to finance its capital expenditure programme. But AGC was unable to implement this programme (actual capital expenditures were only 60% of budgeted expenditures during 1975–80) mainly because of the constraints imposed by the import licensing system, which arose as a result of both the shortages of foreign exchange and bureaucratic problems arising from the manner in which the licensing system was implemented (Republic of Ghana, 1981).

Foreign-exchange shortages not only affected the availability of capital goods but also imported intermediate inputs, with the result that many firms, particularly in the manufacturing sector, were unable to operate at optimum capacity. Capacity utilization in manufacturing fell to 26% in 1980 (*Quarterly Digest of Statistics,* 1983: 9 and Chapter 13, Table 13.4), providing a further disincentive to investment.

Private sector investors were also deterred because the risks of investment were exacerbated by the extensive system of administrative controls imposed on the economy (which made the commercial viability of firms vulnerable to bureaucratic interference), by perceptions of government hostility towards private business and by acute political and economic instability (Rimmer, 1992).

The ERP 1983–95

Investment Policies of the ERP The Economic Recovery Programme (ERP) begun in 1983 involved a radical change of direction in economic policies. This entailed a shift in the focus of public investment, a much more accommodating policy stance towards private investors, including foreign investors, and the replacement by market forces of administrative controls over the allocation of resources. The policy reforms most pertinent to investment were the following.

First, the government made a major effort to increase public saving and to reduce its domestic borrowing requirement, with the aim of releasing resources for use by the private sector. Public sector borrowing from the domestic banking system was reduced from 16% of GDP in 1983 to 7.3% in 1990 (IMF, 1994), although it subsequently rose sharply when public sector deficits increased in the 1990s. Secondly, there was an increase in public investment, facilitated by an inflow of external donor finance. Public investment was concentrated on the rehabilitation of the physical infrastructure, rather than on industries producing marketable output. It was therefore potentially complementary to private capital, rather than a competitor.

Thirdly, pricing reforms and the liberalization of external trade and domestic goods markets induced major sectoral shifts in price incentives for investment. The beneficiaries included the export industries, while the losers included formerly protected manufacturing industries. Fourthly, real exchange rate devaluation and interest rate increases removed the implicit subsidy on, and raised the real cost of, imported capital goods and bank credit. However, tariff rates on imported capital goods (for those firms not eligible for exemptions) were reduced from 30% in 1985 to 20% in 1986, 15% in 1988 and 10% in 1990 (Leechor, 1994: 166).

Fifthly, legislative changes were enacted to improve incentives for, and enhance confidence among, private investors. An amended investment code was enacted in 1985 which, together with fiscal incentives for eligible investors, allowed unrestricted repatriation of profits and debt-service payments and provided guarantees against expropriation. The 1976 investment policy decree, which limited foreign equity holdings in large-scale industries, was repealed. Legislation covering the mining industry underwent a major revision with the enactment of the 1986 mining law. This established a fiscal and regulatory regime comparable to that in other countries with important mining industries, and removed the requirement for government majority shareholdings in mining companies (UNIDO, 1991). Investment regulations were further liberalized with the enactment of the Ghana Investments Promotion Centre Act in 1994. This removed the need for investors to obtain government approval for projects satisfying conditions set out in the Act, reduced the minimum capital requirements for foreign investment in joint ventures and introduced a more uniform set of fiscal incentives for investors (World Bank, 1995: 2).

Sixth, corporate tax rates were reduced by a series of tax changes beginning in 1988. Nominal income tax rates for agriculture, manufacturing and other sectors were reduced from 55% in 1988 to 35% in 1991. Capital gains taxes were also sharply reduced in 1991 (Kapur *et al.,* 1991: 16). Finally, the government in recent years has initiated efforts to attract foreign investment through, *inter alia,* trade fairs and investment promotion tours to the developed countries and the Far East.

The Investment Response to the ERP Despite the policy reforms outlined above, investment levels during the ERP were modest at best. Public sector investment recovered, but only from a very low base, while private investment remained depressed. By the mid-1990s, total investment amounted to around 15% of GDP. Although this was an improvement on the late 1970s and early 1980s, investment levels in Ghana were only about half those of the more dynamic developing countries in Asia.

The inflow of external finance enabled public investment to increase from the low levels to which it had fallen in the early 1980s. It rose steadily to over 10% of GDP in 1994, with an average during the ERP (1984–94) 7.5% of GDP. It was mainly concentrated on the rehabilitation of the communications infrastructure, public utilities and social services.

It took several years before the ERP stimulated any significant increase in private investment. It averaged 3.6% of GDP during 1984–7, barely higher than in the early 1980s. The mining boom lifted it to an average of 6.1% of GDP during 1988–91, but this was not sustained. Private investment fell back to 4.5 per cent of GDP in 1992–4 as major mining projects neared completion.

The average level of private investment during the ERP was 4.8% of GDP, only slightly higher than it had been before the introduction of the ERP and well below levels recorded in other parts of the developing world, including Africa. However, although the share of private investment in GDP remained low during the ERP, in absolute value, private investment was around 50% higher in 1994 than it had been in the early 1980s, given the growth of the economy.

The only sector which did manage a substantially higher increase in private investment was gold mining. A major expansion programme by AGC, and the construction of several new mines by foreign companies, entailed cumulative capital expenditures amounting to over $570 m. during 1986–92, and accounted for 35–40% of all private investment in this period. Investment in the industry was actuated by the liberalization of access to imports and foreign exchange, the incentives and guarantees provided by the 1986 Mining Law, and the extension of loans and equity finance to three of the mining companies by the World Bank's subsidiary, the International Finance Corporation (IFC).

There was some investment in the cocoa industry in the form of replanting and new planting of trees. COCOBOD data indicate that the annual plantings/replantings during the 1983/84 to 1991/92 cocoa seasons averaged 10,000 hectares, more than four times higher than in the 1970s. Field surveys in 1987 reported that replantings in the mid-1980s accounted for between 20% and 25% of cocoa trees (Bateman *et al.*, 1990: 320; Commander *et al.*, 1989), although data from COCOBOD suggest a lower percentage.

The ERP did not stimulate much investment in manufacturing. Some of the larger manufacturers, such as the breweries, took advantage of the increased availability of foreign exchange to upgrade capital equipment, but few new factories were established. A survey of 200 manufacturing firms reported that their annual investment between 1983 and 1990 averaged just under 10% of their 1991 capital stock (Baah-Nuakoh and Teal, 1993). There was some private investment in hotel construction, the timber industry, and especially real estate and residential construction, but little evidence of much investment in other sectors.

Apart from the mining sector, the ERP failed to attract a strong inflow of foreign investment. New investments by foreign companies were limited to relatively few projects, several of which were partly financed by the IFC.

Why has Private Investment Remained Depressed? The failure of private investment to respond with vigour during the ERP, despite the recovery of the economy and the implementation of policy reforms intended to increase incentives and opportunities for private investors, requires an explanation.

The single most important determinant of private investment is usually considered to be demand for output, as in the accelerator theory of investment (Greene and Villanueva, 1991; Oshikoya, 1994; Severin and Solimano, 1993). But the weakness of private investment in Ghana during the ERP cannot be attributed to lack of demand. Real aggregate expenditures were 40%

higher in 1994 than in 1980 (their previous peak), while growth averaged 5% per annum between the start of the recovery in 1983 and 1994 (data from World Bank, 1996, and 1995: 79).
Ceteris paribus, the growth in demand should have given firms an incentive to expand, or at
least rehabilitate, their capital stock. It is difficult to identify a single causal factor for the weakness of private investment, but three different factors provide possible partial explanations: relative price changes, credit constraints, and investment risks.

Relative Price Changes The policy reforms of the ERP, in particular real exchange depreciation, real interest-rate rises and the reduction of trade barriers, induced changes in relative prices
which shifted incentives against investment in large-scale capital-intensive production. The real
purchase cost of capital goods (ie capital goods prices relative to average output prices in the
economy) rose sharply in 1984 because of the real exchange-rate devaluation, and was almost
100% higher during 1984/91 than it had been during the early 1980s (Brownbridge, 1995). Real
lending rates also increased, although they were only occasionally positive (in 1985 and 1989)
before 1991.

Table 7.2   **Real Capital Goods Price Index and Real Lending
Rates. Period Averages: 1975–93 (1975 = 100)**

Period	Real Cost of Capital Goods	Real Lending Rate (%)
1975–79	76	–21.0
1980–83	56	–26.7
1984–87	105	–7.7
1988–91	103	0.5
1992–93	91	13.2

Notes: The real cost of capital goods is calculated as the GFCF deflator divided by
the GDP deflator; i.e. capital goods prices deflated by output prices. Real
interest rates are derived by adjusting the maximum nominal interest rate for
bank lending to 'other' sectors by the annual rise in the GDP deflator.

Sources: *Quarterly Digest of Statistics* and *International Financial Statistics* for GFCF
and GDP deflators; Bank of Ghana for nominal lending rates.

Relative price shifts did not adversely affect the mining industry, which is highly capital-
intensive, because its output is exported and its capital expenditures are externally financed. But
they did reduce incentives to invest in the other major capital-intensive sector in the economy,
manufacturing, in which profitability was squeezed between higher input costs and increased
competition from imports (Fontaine, 1992). Incentives have favoured small-scale labour-intensive production, especially in services, where the fixed capital employed is often minimal and
where much investment is of a nature which may not be captured in official statistics.

Credit Constraints Domestic private investors have faced financing constraints in bank credit
markets. Although bank credit is not the optimal form of finance for capital investment, there are
few alternative domestic sources, other than retained profits, available in Ghana. Bank lending
in current prices to the private sector rose between the start of the ERP and 1992, but the rate of
expansion was constrained by the Bank of Ghana's monetary policies (credit ceilings up to 1991,
open market operations and liquid asset ratios thereafter). Since the start of the ERP bank credit
to the private sector averaged less than 5% of GDP. Furthermore, although lending to the private
sector rose in nominal terms, it registered very little increase when adjusted for the cost of
capital goods.

The supply of new loans was further curtailed because of the accumulation of non-performing loans in the asset portfolios of the banks. By 1989, 41% of bank loans (to both SOEs and the private sector) were not being serviced and therefore could not be recycled to new borrowers (Kapur *et al.*, 1991: 60–61). The banks' non-performing assets were removed from their balance sheets in 1989/90, but since then the banks have been reluctant to extend loans to all but the most creditworthy of borrowers for fear of a recurrence of bad debts. The high nominal interest rates prevailing in the 1990s (lending rates rose to almost 40% in 1993/4), which increase the risks of loan default, have also deterred the banks from expanding lending to the private sector.

Table 7.3   Bank Claims on the Private Sector 1980–94 (% of GDP)

1980–83	3.4
1984–87	4.3
1988–91	4.1
1991–94	4.8

Note: Includes both the primary and secondary banks.
Source: Claims on the private sector from Bank of Ghana; GDP from *Quarterly Digest of Statistics*.

The extent to which private sector investors were rationed out of credit markets because of the credit ceilings is difficult to judge. Shortage of credit was cited by firms in a number of surveys as being among the most important constraints on their expansion (Baah-Nuakoh and Teal, 1993; Steel and Webster, 1992; World Bank, 1991), although many firms denied credit may not have been regarded as creditworthy by the banks. However, this explanation for the weakness of private investment during the ERP is less applicable to foreign investors, most of whom would not normally borrow on the domestic financial market.

The credit constraints experienced by the private sector suggest that one of the mechanisms through which structural adjustment programmes are intended to facilitate private investment did not work in Ghana. Policy reforms aim to reduce public domestic borrowing and increase deposit mobilization so as to enable an expansion of financial resources available to the private sector. Public sector domestic bank borrowing in Ghana was reduced during the 1980s, but the money supply continued to grow rapidly, fuelled by inflows of foreign exchange (partly to finance public investment projects) combined with the Bank of Ghana's strategy of building up net foreign reserves (Younger, 1992), and by losses incurred by the banks as a result of the revaluation of their external liabilities following exchange rate devaluations (Bhatt, 1993). During 1992/4 increased public sector borrowing also contributed to monetary growth. Moreover, raising deposit interest rates had only a limited impact in mobilizing financial saving: the financial system remained shallow with M2 amounting to only 18.7% of GDP in 1994. Consequently tight restrictions on bank lending to the private sector were necessary to avoid fuelling inflationary money supply growth.

Investment Risk The sensitivity of private investment to perceptions of risk has been highlighted by a number of recent theoretical contributions to the investment literature (e.g. Rodrik, 1991). Macroeconomic imbalances were reduced to some extent during the ERP in the 1980s, but economic variables of crucial importance for long-term investors, in particular domestic prices and the exchange rate, have not been stable. The fluctuating inflation rate and rapid depreciation of the exchange rate must have exacerbated the risk of long-term investment. High nominal interest rates are likely to have further heightened investment risk.

Macroeconomic conditions aside, the adoption of market-orientated policies under the ERP should have strengthened the business climate in Ghana. Nevertheless it appears that confidence among private investors remained fragile. Aryeetey (1994) contends that Ghanaian investors have avoided committing resources to long-term investments because they are not convinced that the government is committed to liberal economic policies, in particular because of its record of arbitrary actions against businessmen, including the confiscation of assets, in the late 1970s and early 1980s. Although markets have been liberalized, some of the legislation giving the government the power to intervene remains on the statute books, and only a few firms in the public sector have been privatized.

The hypothesis that political and economic risks were a significant deterrent to private investment is inevitably speculative, given that investors' perceptions cannot readily be measured. Much of the evidence is anecdotal (Tangri, 1992). However, the gold mining industry, which has attracted by far the largest volume of investment of any industry, has been insulated from some of the sources of risk facing other sectors of the economy. The viability of its operations is less vulnerable to developments in the domestic economy because all earnings and a large share of costs are in foreign exchange, while the financial involvement of the World Bank in three of the gold mining companies makes it unlikely that the government would introduce changes to the fiscal or regulatory regime which would jeopardize the viability of the industry.

3. Saving

Trends in Gross Domestic Saving (GDS) and Gross National Saving (GNS)
Table 7.4 shows average ratios for GDS, private and public saving, foreign saving and GNS for the periods 1974/9, 1980/85, and 1986/93. These periods correspond with different socio-economic and political regimes experienced in Ghana.[2] Despite the fact that the ERP began in 1983, financial reforms did not start until 1986 with the launching of the Financial Sector Adjustment Programme (FINSAP). The table shows that in the period 1974/9 the average GDS ratio was about 8.7. This fell to 5.03 between 1980 and 1985, and rose slightly to 5.17 during the 1986-93 period. Similar trends were observed in GNS.

Although saving ratios for sub-Saharan African (SSA) countries have been low and deteriorating over the last two decades, Ghana's performance was far below the regional average. SSA countries' gross domestic saving as a ratio of GDP declined from an average of 18.9% during the 1974–9 period to 13.4% over the 1980–85 period, and then fell to 12.7% for the period 1986–90 (see UNECA, 1996).

Table 7.4   Annual Average Saving Ratios for Ghana: Selected Periods

Period	GDS Ratio Average	Private Saving Ratio	Public Saving Ratio	Foreign Saving Ratio	GNS Ratio
1974–79	8.69	14.14	–5.72	3.09	8.30
1980–85	5.03	7.33	–2.30	5.49	4.34
1986–93	5.17	–0.15	5.31	6.41	6.43

Source: Computed from *Government Budget Statement,* and *Quarterly Digest Of Statistics,* various issues.

Private and Public Saving With regard to private and public sector saving, the picture that emerges is one of opposite trends. Whilst public saving was consistently negative between 1974

---

[2] Period one, 1974–9, reflects years of political stability until the military upheaval in 1979 with the execution of nine high-ranking government officials including three former heads of state, and the subsequent inception of well-intentioned but misguided policies. The second period covers the pre-FINSAP years of 1980–85, whilst the third period covers the FINSAP years.

and 1983, private saving was consistently positive from 1974 until 1987, although generally declining. The picture that emerges from Table 7.4 is one of low domestic saving. Foreign saving increased consistently, as a result of the foreign inflows that accompany structural adjustment programmes. These figures suggest that Ghanaians were generally unable to sustain the saving rates argued by Arthur Lewis and Walt Rostow as being vital for economic take-off. These trends show that much of the investment financing in Ghana since the financial sector reforms in 1986 came from foreign sources.

The rising trends in foreign resource inflows to Ghana vis-à-vis the declining trends in private saving with questionable public saving (as discussed below) raise the issue of the sustainability and effectiveness of foreign saving in economic growth. Analytically, whilst foreign saving should complement domestic saving to increase the volume of productive capacity, rising foreign inflows in Ghana have been associated with reduced national saving. Ghana's experience so far supports Griffin's empirical analysis that foreign inflows tend to displace rather than complement domestic saving (Griffin, 1970).

The inverse relationship between foreign saving and domestic resource mobilization is disturbing, since this mode of raising resources is not sustainable. New external resource inflows cannot continue indefinitely and even if external finance were to be available for an extended period, this would have serious implications for the sustainability of the growth process. Debt servicing is already putting considerable strain on Ghana's export earnings (see Gockel, 1995). As more of the country's export earnings are diverted to debt service future growth prospects are jeopardized. Furthermore, the Third World debt crisis showed that Latin American and African countries that depended on external finance to promote economic development in the 1960s and 1970s had their growth disrupted, whilst the Asian countries that relied on domestic sources and export earnings for investment financing were more successful. Worst still is the aid fatigue in donor countries. Both multilateral and bilateral donors' perception of value for money in Ghana is low, and as shown in Chapter 10, Table 10.1, real aid inflows have declined in the 1990s. There is global competition for investible resources and the indications are that with a host of factors that have combined to make Africa, including Ghana, an unstable economic environment, sub-Saharan Africa could be crowded out or marginalized so far as foreign resource inflows are concerned. Discussing this theme against the background of certain pronouncements and actions taken by the Government of Ghana, the World Bank (1995: 212) in a policy research report summed the situation up as follows:

> More damaging to Ghana's credibility . . . were actions that the government took against some businesses. In 1987–88, for example, the government took the principal domestic tobacco company from one set of private owners and gave it to another, changing the name from International Tobacco to Meridian in the process. Moreover, as Leith and Lofchie (1993) report, in the early years of the Rawlings regime, people's defense committees were set up to monitor and arrest business people suspected of "counterrevolutionary" activity. Actions such as these would have severely undermined the credibility of a government with investors.

Consequently, it cannot be overemphasized that not only has Ghana to create a credible investment environment but it must also assume responsibility for financing, to a large extent, the investment required to achieve sustained real GDP growth.

Financial Saving Although the institutional framework of banks in Ghana appears adequate, at least in terms of the sheer physical presence and outward diversification of banks, an examination of macrofinancial data suggests that the impact of the banking system on financial saving is less than might have been expected. Table 7.5 shows financial saving indicators. The figures show that the M2/GDP ratio was generally low and declined between 1977 and 1985. Similarly, the QM/GDP ratio was also low and exhibited a declining trend. It is worth noting that the

declining trend in the QM/GDP ratio coincided with the era of repressive policies of the late
1970s and early 1980s that tended to discourage the holding of assets with banks. Thus, in spite
of the proliferation of banks, savings and time deposits fell to their lowest level since 1960 (see
Gockel, 1995).

Table 7.5   Selected Indicators of Financial Depth 1970–96

Year	M2/GDP	M1/GDP	QM/GDP
1970–73	21.1	14.7	6.4
1974–77	26.1	19.4	6.8
1978–81	20.1	16.0	4.2
1982–85	13.5	10.8	2.7
1986–89	17.0	13.0	4.0
1990–92	14.7	10.67	4.0
1993–96	18.5	12.8	5.5

Note: M1=currency plus demand deposits; M2=M1+time deposits and savings deposits; QM,
quasi-money=time deposits plus savings deposits.
Source: Gockel (1995) and Bank of Ghana, *Quarterly Bulletin,* various issues.

Determinants of Public Saving

The trends in public saving are intriguing for several reasons. The negative public saving before
the inception of the ERP can be traced to fiscal indiscipline. Total revenues were not enough to
cover government recurrent expenditures, let alone total expenditures. Table 7.6 shows that total
revenue was consistently lower than total expenditure during the 1974–85 period, and would
have remained so but for the use of the proceeds of divestiture as balancing items in the budget.
From 13.89% of GDP in 1974, total revenue fell to 5.57% in 1983. This trend was halted in
1984 and an increasing trend emerged, so that by 1994 total revenue was as high as 24% of GDP
(tax revenue amounted to about 16% of GDP). In the earlier period, although public expenditure
as a percentage of GDP was declining, the fall in revenues was so fast that recurrent expenditure
on its own exceeded revenue between 1974 and 1985.

Table 7.6   Selected Fiscal Ratios 1974–96

Year	Total Revenue GDP Ratio	Recurrent Expenditure GDP Ratio	Total Expenditure GDP Ratio	Deficit/Surplus GDP Ratio
1974–78	12.6	14.78	10.29	–10.7
1979–82	6.04	11.27	13.92	–7.89
1983–85	8.57	8.96	10.79	–2.22
1986–91	14.57	10.63	14.00	0.90
1992–96	20.68	16.16	21.69	–1.26

Note: The periods are selected on the basis of various socio-economic regimes, viz. 1974–8 pre-revolutionary era;
1979–82, revolutionary era; 1983–6 ERP era but without FINSAP; 1986–91, ERP cum FINSAP but still under
military regime; and 1992–6, the constitutional era.
Source: Calculated from Budget Statement, various issues.

An interesting development is the increasing role that 'Grants' and 'Other Revenues' have come to play in public saving. From about 1% and 0.5% of total revenue in 1982 and 1983 respectively, grants accounted for about 4% of revenue in 1984 and 1985 and increased to 10.4% in 1990. Although the fraction of grants in total revenue dropped between 1991 and 1994, it was nevertheless a significant item.

Similarly, 'Other Revenues' and proceeds from the sale of State-owned enterprises (divestiture receipts) now form substantial parts of government revenue. Indeed, an assessment of the share of divestiture proceeds and grants in total revenue in recent years shows that, without these sources of revenue, government budgets would have remained in deficit. In terms of tax revenue alone, the government budget is still in deficit. While the government was able to raise an increasing proportion of GDP in tax revenue after 1984, such revenues were used to finance higher recurrent expenditures. Table 7.7 provides a summary of government budgets for 1990–96.

Table 7.7   Summary of Government Budgets 1990–96 (¢ bn)

Year	Total Revenue	Total Expenditure	Budget Out-Turn: Surplus or Deficit	Budget Out-Turn Less Divestiture Proceeds	Budget Out-Turn Less Divestiture Proceeds & Grants
1990	267.2	264.0	3.2	3.2	–24.6
1991	395.5	351.6	43.9	39.1	2.8
1992	366.3	511.0	–144.6	–150.6	–183.3
1993	725.2	822.5	–97.3	–184.2	–250.8
1994	1216.3	1149.6	111.7	–161.6	–201.1
1995	1784.6	1732.0	52.6	–59.2	–153.0
1996	2268.5	2410.5	–142.0	–318.3	–395.1

Source: Derived from Budget Statement, various issues

The use of divestiture receipts to finance government expenditure on a large scale is worrying. Recalling the fact that expenditures are largely biased towards recurrent expenditure, one wonders if there is much rationale in selling public assets like the Ashanti Goldfields and other profitable SOEs only to use the proceeds for expenditure that is not income generating. Divestiture receipts used to finance recurrent budgets are not a sustainable source of revenue. The realized public saving and fiscal surpluses are no indication of sustainable fiscal performance since tax revenue *per se* is inadequate to cover expenditure.

Reasons for Weak Savings Mobilization before the Financial Reforms

Low savings mobilization prior to the 1986 FINSAP can be explained by several factors: low interest rates; credit controls, reserve requirements, unorthodox monetary policies and bad legislation.

Low Interest Rate Policies Before the inception of the financial reforms in 1986, there was no clear policy to mobilize savings. The then received wisdom was that low interest rates would induce investment, which in turn would increase output and employment, and consequently lead to higher saving. Interest rates were seen as the cost of investible resources and saving was regarded as being predominantly income-determined.

The practice was for the Bank of Ghana to set minimum rates for deposits and to place ceilings on lending rates. Once determined, these rates were allowed to remain for extended periods of time without adequate allowance for changes in the real sectors of the economy.

The policy of low interest rates in Ghana appears to have caused more distortions than the market imperfections it was designed to overcome. As the low rates were fixed for extended periods of time without regard to high rates of inflation, real interest rates became negative. That is, interest rates were determined by fiat rather than by market forces and rose less rapidly than the rate of inflation which increased from 20.3% in 1972 to 122.8% in 1983. The general consequence of high inflation and negative real interest rates was to reinforce the disincentive to dealing in financial assets by both banks and other wealth-owning units. As time and savings deposits became unattractive, funds were channelled into physical assets and foreign assets, and inflation exacerbated financial shallowing.

Although the Bank of Ghana offered to reimburse the banks for the negative interest rate differentials in the cases where deposit rates exceeded lending rates, the offer nevertheless did not take into account other expenses incurred in handling banking transactions. The adverse effect of such policies discouraged banks from adopting competitive savings collection strategies such as advertisements to entice potential savers, and from introducing new savings instruments with differential interest rates according to maturity profile. Instead, they refused to accept deposits and literally turned away prospective savers once they realized they did not have profitable uses for funds. Hence, the increasing disintermediation and lower financial ratios. Banks were reluctant to collect savings just as the people were reluctant to save. This could be expected to lead to a reduction in financial saving, which was reflected in a declining M2/GNP ratio.

Simultaneously, the expected real price of credit declined with inflation and an abnormally high demand for credit was generated; negative interest rates encourage the demand for funds not only for investment purposes but for the purchase of real assets. The borrower's real debt burden was reduced and transferred to the banks. As a result, the banks had to invoke other considerations besides the Bank of Ghana's credit policy in the granting of loans. The tendency was to increase collateral requirements and/or to succumb to political pressures and corruption. Credit allocation became inefficient, and average rates of return on investment were reduced below the maximum attainable, thus discouraging banks from active intermediation, especially in the collection of interest-bearing deposits.

Ghana's pre-FINSAP interest-rate policy tends to confirm McKinnon's (1973) and Shaw's (1973) views that financial repression, especially under inflationary conditions, is bound to stimulate demand for physical wealth and for consumption, as well as causing capital flight. The establishment and development of a viable financial system capable of mobilizing saving becomes more difficult.

Credit Controls Credit ceilings and sectoral credit controls appear to have been one of the major instruments of the Bank of Ghana's financial policy until 1990. The ceilings were bank-specific and each bank's ceiling was categorized into a) credit to the rest of the economy and b) credit to the government and to cocoa financing. Credit was measured in gross terms without allowance for debt provisions. In addition, the Bank of Ghana also prescribed sectoral credit limits for all productive sectors of the economy. Such limits took the form of a permissible percentage increase in the outstanding credit of each bank to a given sector. By implication, when all sectoral credit limits were summed, the total was equal to each bank's credit ceiling.

Ostensibly, credit ceilings and sectoral credit controls attempted to curb inflation, whilst allowing official selectivity in credit allocation intended to promote a specific pattern of investment and growth. The designated priority sectors were the export, agriculture and manufacturing sectors. Whilst these policies characterized the 1970s, so important had the policy of giving directives to the banks become that the Bank of Ghana noted in its 1983 *Annual Report* (pp.12–14):

> To give more concrete expression to its agricultural policy, the PNDC Government adopted policy measures which sought to increase the level of credit to the agricultural sector . . . all

commercial banks were required to lend at least 20% of their total loan portfolio, as at every reporting date, to the agricultural sector. This proportion was meant to comprise at least 12.5% of that portfolio to the small-scale farmers and at least 7.5% to other farmers. . . . Where, for some reason, a bank was unable to comply, it was required to transfer to the Agricultural Development Bank (ADB) such amounts as would bring their total lending to the agricultural sector to the required proportion. Such transfers, however, would not attract any interest.

Although credit ceilings and sectoral credit controls were relatively easy to administer, their use added further distortions in financial intermediation. Together with low interest rates, they produced dis-incentive effects on the banking system and discouraged banks in the collection of savings once they had attained their ceilings. Once the banks refused to accept further interest-bearing deposits, this would tend to encourage intermediation outside the banking system, capital flight and/or the acquisition of durable goods. Credit ceilings tend to limit competition as credit is allocated on the basis of historical market shares, not according to lending opportunities. Similarly, they limit the scope for borrowers to switch between banks.

Further aggravating the disincentive to collect savings was the absence of suitable liquid investment opportunities in which banks could invest excess funds not channelled into credit. Except for the limited amount of bills that the Bank of Ghana issued to allow banks to meet their secondary reserve requirements, banks did not have other suitable outlets for funds. Even then, on many occasions the bills issued were insufficient to meet the secondary reserve requirements. As excess cash reserves were not eligible to fulfil secondary reserve requirements and as these cash reserves earned no returns, the banks were further discouraged from competition for deposits. They tended only to accept demand deposits on which no interest was paid.

Reserve Requirements The Bank of Ghana had broad powers to specify the nature and level of reserve and liquid asset requirements. In its monetary management, the Bank of Ghana imposed reserve ratios for cash and secondary liquid assets. The cash reserve requirement was a two-tier system: one for demand deposits and another for time and savings deposits. These were to be held as either cash in tills or balances with the Bank of Ghana; such deposits earned no interest.

Unlike reserve requirements in the industrialized countries which are typically low, often less than 10%, reserve requirements in Ghana averaged over 50% by 1983 and about 32% between 1987 and 1989. The effects on the banking system of such high reserve requirements are two-fold. First, a substantial amount of the available funds is directed away from potential borrowers. These potential borrowers have to look elsewhere for funds, and the indications were that in Ghana there was a growing informal financial sector (see Aryeetey and Gockel, 1991; Gockel, 1995). Secondly, when banks are forced to hold large amounts of low or zero-yielding assets, distortions to interest rates arise, and where it is possible there will be increases in the margin between deposit and lending rates. In Ghana, while both rates were largely controlled, the minimum deposit rate tended to become the maximum. Moreover, the banks resorted to high service charges to borrowers.

To sum up, the Bank of Ghana's monetary policy instruments reinforced one another in accentuating distortions in financial intermediation making investment in financial assets less attractive, and so discouraging savings mobilization. It was apparent that credit ceilings and selective credit controls, like low interest rate policies, caused banks to hold excess cash as lending under such prescribed conditions was unprofitable. Severe misallocation of resources ensued, competition among banks was inhibited and the development of an interbank market retarded. Financial intermediation became shallower with a risk-aversion demand for physical wealth, increased informal financial activities and capital flight. This was reflected in the low and declining M2/GDP ratio.

Unorthodox Monetary Policies and Bad Legislation Unorthodox monetary policies and certain legislation were intended to mop up excess liquidity, halt inflation and instil accountability in financial transactions. The measures relating to currency comprised: a) demonetization of the existing currency on 27 March 1979; and b) demonetization of ¢50 notes in circulation in 1982. Many people lost their lives in the demonetization exercises as there was a rush to exchange old currencies for new ones before the deadline. With the ¢50 notes, no compensation was paid until 1990, by which time many people had lost the receipts given to them when their notes were taken in. The Secretary of Finance and Economic Planning, Dr Kwesi Botchwey, admitted in an interview with *West Africa* magazine (10–12 January 1994, p.27) 'it is true that the PDNC in 1982–83 did take some decisions that affected banking confidence especially through the withdrawal of the ¢50 notes and the way that this was conducted'.

The loss of confidence in the banking system and in the financial system as a whole was further aggravated by a series of laws and policy directives between 1979 and 1982. These included: the freezing of all bank deposits exceeding ¢50,000 and the investigation of holders for tax liability and corruption and fraud; the recall of bank loans for the financing of trading inventories; and the introduction of compulsory payment by cheque for all business transactions in excess of ¢1,000. Worse still was the infamous AFRC Decree 17 enacted on 27 August 1979 but with retrospective effect from 4 June 1979. Essentially, the decree empowered the revolutionary government to call for any person's bank or other financial statement without his/her knowledge or approval. The financial institution had no power to deny the revolutionary officials access to such information. Consequently, many people came to consider the holding of normal financial assets a perilous undertaking as people like market women and businessmen were investigated and imprisoned. Not surprisingly, firms and households responded by reducing their deposits and rechannelling them into the holding of physical assets such as building materials. Not only did confidence-sensitive monies evaporate from the banking system but people who would ordinarily save with banks thought it wiser not to do so (Aryeetey and Gockel, 1991).

The loss of confidence in the banking system was further worsened by high costs in terms of time taken to make withdrawals and deposits. In large centres, transactions which would ordinarily have taken about 10 minutes to complete in a UK bank, could take as long as two hours in a Ghanaian bank. For workers in rural areas where bank diffusion is less, travel time to and from the bank had to be added to the waiting time at the bank. The indications were that in such cases, on pay days, people spent virtually the whole day making withdrawals, at the cost of their jobs. The situation was especially time-consuming for market women and businessmen who deal in large amounts of cash every day. As most of them were not prepared to waste half a day making deposits or withdrawals, they tended to keep cash in holes in the market place or at home.

Financial Saving under Financial Reforms

It was against the above background that financial reforms were formulated in 1986, intended to lead to increased domestic saving and greater efficiency of credit allocation and resource use, and to put an end to capital flight. The financial sector adjustment programme (FINSAP) freed interest rates and the allocation of credit from bureaucratic control. Unfortunately whilst this financial deregulation was inspired by theoretical analysis and by the success story of South Korea and other East Asian countries (at least until 1997), Ghana's experience has yet to improve domestic resource mobilization significantly (see Table 7.5 above).

The question raised is: why has Ghana's experience with financial reform not yet yielded the expected results, particularly increased financial resource mobilization? A straightforward answer to this question is the general lack of public confidence in the financial system. This confidence factor, which also affects the investment response, can be traced to macroeconomic instability, the lingering effects of socio-political uncertainty and the unorthodox policies discussed above. Macroeconomic instability is reflected in the intractability of inflation and the persistent depreciation of the cedi. Although inflation has been brought down from the record high of about 123% in 1983, it has remained a major problem since the inception of the ERP (see Chapter 1).

The intractability of inflation and the successive declines of the cedi have meant that nominal interest rates have been at high levels in order to achieve positive real rates. Whilst a detailed study is yet to be done of the impact of the high lending rates on cost-push inflation, discussions with private investors and the executives of the Private Enterprises Foundation suggest that the very high nominal rates make business firms reluctant to use loans for investment purposes. The indications are that the high lending costs tend to add to the production costs and raise the prices of locally produced commodities.

Table 7.8 shows the trends in average annual interest rates for the period 1990–96. An examination of these trends shows that whilst nominal rates were generally high, inflation meant that real deposit rates were largely negative although real lending rates were positive. The spread between borrowing and lending rates was high. With such rates of interest, there is still little incentive to save with banks.

A further development is the emergence of currency substitution or dollarization. Income earners now tend to buy foreign currencies as a way of storing wealth. As is to be expected, those savings which would normally have been made in cedis are now made in hard currencies. So rife has dollarization become that the Bank of Ghana since early 1997 has included foreign currency holdings in the definition of money, and has consequently directed banks to maintain 8% cedi reserves against their holdings of foreign currencies.

Table 7.8   Interest-Rate Structure (%)

Year	Nominal Saving Rate	Nominal Lending Rate	Nominal Treasury Bill Rate	Real Saving Rate	Real Lending Rate	Real Treasury Bill Rate
1990	18.0	30.25	21.8	–14.0	–5.1	–11.2
1991	20.0	31.5	29.2	1.3	11.4	9.5
1992	16.0	29.0	19.4	5.5	17.3	8.5
1993	23.0	39.0	31.0	–2.0	11.2	4.8
1994	23.0	38.0	27.3	–1.5	10.5	2.0
1995	25.1	41.8	35.8	–26.8	–17.0	–20.5
1996	31.5	47.7	41.7	–0.9	–21.6	6.8

Note: Real Interest Rate is calculated using the formula $R=(1+r)/(1+P^*)-1$, where R is real rate, r is the nominal rate and P^* is the rate of inflation.

Source: Nominal rates are from Bank of Ghana records.

In addition, under the ERP, saving efforts were compromised by structural adjustment policies that emphasized retrenchment, embargoes on public sector employment and divestiture with the accompanying lay-offs. In such circumstances, not only would those made redundant lose their income-earning capacity, but dis-saving would take place as they used past savings for subsistence. This was made worse by the absence of formal protection schemes against fluctuations in consumption, and the subsequent reliance on the extended family (Gockel, 1996).

4.   Conclusion

Investment by both public and private sectors declined to low levels during the 1970s and early 1980s. At the same time saving by the public authorities collapsed and private saving dropped sharply. The economy experienced a dramatic financial shallowing and the real volume of bank intermediation fell. The responsibility for these developments can, in large measure, be plausibly attributed to misguided government policies.

Government policy had attempted to stimulate investment by providing protection from imports, granting credit at low (often negative) real interest rates and making fiscal concessions to selected firms. Purchasers of imported capital goods also benefited from the overvalued exchange rate. These incentives were offset, however, by a number of severe deterrents and constraints. Demand on the domestic market stagnated, while trade and exchange rate policies discouraged investment for export. Firms faced acute constraints in credit and foreign-exchange markets, partly because of excessive government borrowing and partly because economic policy discouraged saving, deposit mobilization and foreign-exchange earnings. Throughout the 1970s, interest-rate controls, credit controls and high bank reserve ratios tended to reduce the incentives for people to save and make deposits and for banks to seek new deposits. Then in 1979 and 1982 currency operations which amounted to confiscation as well as the official probing of private bank accounts contributed to the undermining of all confidence in the organized monetary and banking systems.

One of the objectives of the ERP begun in 1983 and the ensuing financial reforms was to stimulate a revival of investment. Public investment, facilitated by inflows of external finance, increased and by 1994 reached 10% of GDP. But despite the economic reforms and a recovery of the economy, private investment outside the gold mining industry remained depressed, averaging less than 5% of GDP between the start of the ERP and 1994. This weakness of private investment is probably due to a combination of factors. Exchange-rate devaluation and interest rate rises shifted incentives against investment in capital-intensive products, especially those supplying the domestic market. The private sector continued to face constraints in domestic credit markets and investors may have been deterred by the risks arising from macroeconomic instability and political concerns. These impediments to some extent reflect inevitable conflicts between the stabilization and growth objectives of the ERP, but they were made more acute by the lack of effective monetary control and by the low level of saving and the shallowness of the financial system. Domestic/national savings rates have remained very low during the ERP, averaging less than half the investment rates.

The policy priorities should be to boost private investment to levels of around 10–15% of GDP and to raise national saving to levels which are much closer to total investment levels. Increased private investment is essential if economic growth rates are to be increased to levels where significant reductions in poverty can be achieved, while increased domestic resource mobilization is needed to ensure that an expansion of investment levels does not entail a dependence on unsustainable rates of foreign capital inflows.

To achieve these two inter-related objectives it will be necessary to improve macroeconomic management, and in particular to reduce inflation and the instability in the nominal exchange rate. Greater macroeconomic stability should benefit private investment by reducing some of the risks involved, allowing entrepreneurs to make long-term plans with greater confidence and also reducing the reluctance of the banks to lend to the private sector. It should also encourage greater financial savings if the public are more confident that financial assets will retain their real value. In addition, it is necessary for public saving to be increased, preferably through a reduction in the less productive components of public expenditure and enhanced efforts to collect taxes. Whether macroeconomic policies alone will be sufficient to raise saving and investment to the levels needed for sustained developed must be open to doubt, however. There is a diverse range of microeconomic, institutional, and structural constraints to increased saving and investment in Ghana, for example a lack of managerial and entrepreneurial skills in the business sector. A medium-term objective should be to identify these constraints and to devise effective policies to tackle them.

If economic policy is to contribute to an expansion of private investment, it will be essential to reduce public-sector borrowing in order to free up financial resources for the private sector. But if financial resources are to grow significantly it would seem necessary that some measures be taken to restore confidence in the monetary system. Confidence is a necessary condition for financial development and financial development is a necessary condition for sound economic development. Some reassurance needs to be given that an exercise like the 1982 demonetisation of ¢50 notes and the freezing of bank accounts in excess of stated amounts will never recur. Without such assurances Ghanaians will find it hard to trust their domestic currency and the whole process of mobilizing resources for investment will continue to be impaired.

References

Aryeetey, Ernest (1994) 'Private Investment Under Uncertainty in Ghana', *World Development* Vol . 22, No. 8.

Aryeetey, E. and Gockel, F. (1991) *Mobilizing Domestic Resources for Capital Formation in Ghana: The Role of Informal Financial Markets.* AERC Research Paper 3. Nairobi: AERC.

Baah-Nuakoh, Amoah and Teal, Francis (eds) (1993) *Economic Reform and the Manufacturing Sector in Ghana Final Report.* The Africa Regional Program of Enterprise Development. Washington, DC: World Bank.

Bank of Ghana, various years, *Annual Report.*

Bateman, Merrill J., Meeraus, Alexander, Newbery, David M., Okyere, William Asenso and O'Mara, Gerald T. (1990) *Ghana's Cocoa Pricing Policy.* Policy, Research and External Affairs Working Papers, WPS 429. Washington, DC: World Bank.

Bhatt, V. V. (1993) 'On Financial Sector Reform and Development: A Case Study of Ghana', *African Review of Money, Finance and Banking,* Special Supplement to *Savings and Development.*

Brownbridge, Martin, (1995) 'Credit Supply, Monetary Policy and Structural Adjustment in Ghana', *African Review of Money Finance and Banking,* 1–2.

Commander, Simon, Howell, John and Seini, Wayo (1989) 'Ghana 1983–87', in Simon Commander (ed.) *Structural Adjustment and Agriculture: Theory and Practice in Africa and Latin America.* London and Portsmouth, NH: ODI/James Currey and Heinemann.

Fontaine, Jean-Marc, (1992) 'Bias Overkill? Removal of Anti-Export Bias and Manufacturing Investment: Ghana 1983–89, in R. Adhikhari, C. Kirkpatrick and J. Weiss (eds) *Industrial and Trade Policy Reform in Developing Countries.* Manchester: Manchester University Press.

Gockel, A. F. (1996) *The Formal Social Security System In Ghana.* Accra: Friedrich Ebert Stiftung.

Gockel, A. F. (1995) 'The Role Of Finance In Economic Development: The Case Of Ghana', Ph.D Thesis, University of Manchester.

Greene, Joshua, and Villanueva, Delano (1991) 'Private Investment in Developing Countries', *IMF Staff Papers* Vol. 38.

Griffin, K. (1970) 'Foreign Capital, Domestic Savings And Economic Development', *Bulletin of Oxford University Institute Of Economics and Statistics,* Vol. 32, No. 2, May.

Huq, M. M. (1989) *The Economy of Ghana.* London and Basingstoke: Macmillan.

International Monetary Fund, *International Financial Statistics Yearbook.* Washington DC (various years).

Islam, Roumeen and Wetzel, Deborah L. (1994) 'Ghana: Adjustment, Reform and Growth' in William Easterly, Carlos Alfredo Rodriguez and Klaus Schmidt-Hebbel (eds) *Public Sector Deficits and Macroeconomic Performance.* Oxford: Oxford University Press.

Kapur, Ishan, Hadjimichael, Michael T., Hilbers, Paul, Schiff, Jerald and Szymczak, Philippe (1991) *Ghana: Adjustment and Growth 1983–91.* Occasional Paper 86. Washington, DC: International Monetary Fund.

Konings, Piet (1986) *The State and Rural Class Formation in Ghana: A Comparative Analysis.* London: KPI.

Killick, Tony (1978) *Development Economics in Action.* London: Heinemann Educational Books.

Leechor, Chad (1994) 'Ghana: Frontrunner in Adjustment', in Ishrat Husain and Rashid Faruqee (eds) *Adjustment in Africa: Lessons from Country Case Studies.* Washington, DC: World Bank.

McKinnon, Ronald I. (1973) *Money and Capital in Economic Development.* Washington, DC: The Brookings Institution.

McKinnon, Ronald I. (1988), 'Financial Liberalisation in Retrospect: Interest Rate Policies in LDCs', in Gustav Ranis and T. Paul Shultz (eds) *The State of Development Economics: Progress and Perspectives.* New York: Basil Blackwell.

Oshikoya, T. W. (1994) 'Macroeconomic Determinants of Domestic Private Investment in Africa: An Empirical Analysis', *Economic Development and Cultural Change* Vol. 42, No. 3.

Republic of Ghana Statistical Service, *Quarterly Digest of Statistics* Accra, Government of Ghana, various issues.

Republic of Ghana (1981) *Budget Statement.* Tema: Ghana Publishing Corporation.

Rimmer, Douglas (1992) *Staying Poor: Ghana's Political Economy 1950–1990.* Oxford: Pergamon Press.

Rodrik, Dani (1991) 'Policy Uncertainty and Private Investment in Developing Countries', *Journal of Development Economics* Vol. 36.

Severin, Luis and Solimano, Andres (1993) 'Debt Crisis, Adjustment Policies and Capital Formation in Developing Countries: Where Do We Stand?', *World Development* Vol. 21, No. 1.

Shaw, E. S. (1973) *Financial Deepining in Economic Development.* New York: Oxford University Press.

Steel, William F. and Webster, Leila M. (1992) 'How Small Enterprises in Ghana have Responded to Adjustment', *The World Bank Economic Review* Vol. 6, No. 3.

Tangri, Roger (1992) 'The Politics of Government-Business Relations in Ghana', *Journal of Modern African Studies* Vol. 30, No. 1.

UNECA (1996) *Mobilizing Domestic Financial Resources For Africa's Development: Retrospects and Prospects*. Addis Ababa: UNECA, Socio-economic Research and Planning Division,

United Nations Industrial Development Organisation (1991) *Investors Guide to Ghana*. Vienna: UNIDO.

World Bank (1991) *Ghana Progress on Adjustment*. Washington, DC: World Bank.

World Bank (1992) *Ghana 2000 and Beyond*. Washington, DC: World Bank.

World Bank (1995) *Ghana Growth, Private Sector, and Poverty Reduction*. Washington, DC: World Bank.

World Bank (1996) *World Tables*. Washington, DC: World Bank.

Younger, Stephen D. (1992) 'Aid and the Dutch Disease: Macroeconomic Management When Everybody Loves You', *World Development* Vol. 20, No. 11.

III The External Sector

8

Exchange Rate Policy
& the Balance of Payments
1972–96

JANE HARRIGAN
& ABENA D. ODURO

1. Introduction

Ghana's exchange rate and balance of payments policies have see-sawed between controls and liberalization during most of the period since independence. An economic reform programme was agreed upon with the Bretton Woods institutions in 1966 in response to a balance of payments crisis. It was implemented between 1967 and 1971 but was suspended in 1972. The abortion of the reforms was largely due to the emergence of fiscal imbalances and balance of payments difficulties, the failure to prevent the real exchange rate from appreciating, and the susceptibility of the Ghanaian economy to fluctuations in cocoa prices.[1] Since 1972 Ghana's exchange rate and balance of payments policies fall into distinct regimes; 1972–83 and 1983 onwards.

Section 2 below analyzes exchange rate policy between 1972 and 1983, when a quantity-controlled regime was operated. This involved a fixed exchange rate subject to infrequent devaluations, with surrender laws, exchange rationing and currency inconvertibility. In the face of rapid inflation caused by expansionary fiscal and monetary policy, the real exchange rate became significantly overvalued, discouraging exports and making imports artificially cheap. In order to contain the balance of payments, quantitative controls were applied to imports. This resulted in a low level of balance of payments equilibrium as import strangulation reduced GDP.[2]

Section 3 will look at exchange rate policies since 1983 when a programme to boost and diversify exports was introduced in order to correct underlying external payments problems, as part of a donor-supported economic recovery programme (ERP). Under the ERP Ghana has moved towards a floating exchange rate mechanism for correcting external payments problems. A series of exchange reform measures were implemented, which included step-wise devaluation in the period 1983–6, the introduction of a foreign-exchange auction in 1986, legalizing the parallel exchange market through the introduction of foreign exchange bureaux in 1988 and the establishment in 1992 of an interbank market. This gradualism and incrementalism has helped to depoliticize the issue of exchange rate devaluation.

---

[1] For a discussion of the reforms of the earlier period see Jebuni *et al.*, 1994 and Jebuni (1996).

[2] Theoretical models of the balance of payments suggest that fiscal budget deficits, excess money supply, excess of private investment over saving and appreciating real exchange rates will cause balance of payments deficits. Controls on the current and capital account may contain the deficit, which can then manifest itself as rising domestic inflation. However, these controls, especially quantitative trade controls, will not correct the underlying cause of the balance of payments problems.

Reform of the exchange rate mechanism has been accompanied by import liberalization. Although depreciation of the exchange rate has helped to boost exports this has not been sufficient to cover the surge in imports since liberalization. Hence, the foreign-exchange auction was heavily dependent on foreign exchange supplied by donors supporting the ERP. Foreign sources financed 40.6% of the auction in 1986, increasing to 69.3% in 1988. Without this, exchange rate depreciation would have been even more dramatic. This begs the question as to whether the price-controlled payments regime has become over-dependent on foreign inflows and whether it is sustainable in the absence of extensive export diversification.

Since 1992 macro instability has re-emerged in the form of expansionary fiscal and monetary policies leading to escalating inflation. This has caused appreciation of the real exchange rate, which has also been exacerbated by the Dutch Disease effects of donor foreign-exchange inflows. Appreciation is further hampering the ability to expand the export base and it remains to be seen whether import controls will be reintroduced to contain the balance of payments.

Section 4 will review the empirical literature on the determinants of Ghana's exchange rates, including the parallel market premium and the effects of exchange-rate changes on output, exports and inflation. It will also discuss the results of our own regressions which show that an increase in the parallel market premium had a negative effect on exports and on government revenue.

Section 5 will discuss the evolution of the balance of payments since 1972 and show that its structure has changed significantly under the ERP. In the pre-ERP period import controls produced a trade balance surplus, and hence a sustainable current account deficit. Furthermore, restrictions on transfers and the capital account meant that reserve depletion to support the fixed exchange rate was not required. Under the ERP, a combination of import liberalization, failure to diversify the export base and declining terms of trade have meant that both the trade account and the current account have registered large deficits. These have been bridged by large surpluses on the capital account in the form of foreign loans to support the ERP. The resultant dependency on foreign capital leaves the economy in a vulnerable position. Thus, successful import and foreign-exchange liberalization remains heavily dependent on foreign loans and grants whilst, in the absence of export diversification, the economy's demand for foreign exchange continues to exceed domestic capacity to generate it.

2. Exchange Rate Policy 1970–82

During the 1960s the Bretton Woods system supported the policy of fixed exchange rates. Adjustment of the parities was only supposed to occur when there was a fundamental balance of payments disequilibrium. The choice of a fixed exchange rate regime in Ghana was therefore consistent with the thinking of the times. However, the breakdown of the Bretton Woods system and the shift to floating exchange rates by most industrialized countries in 1973 and the acceptance of the principle of floating exchange rates by the International Monetary Fund did not initiate any changes in thinking about exchange rate policy in Ghana.[3] The policy of fixed exchange rates was maintained until the second half of the 1980s. This fixed exchange rate regime was characterized by four main features: a highly overvalued official exchange rate; an active parallel market in foreign exchange; capital controls; and an allocation of foreign exchange based on import licences issued by the Import Programming and Monitoring Committee. Licences favoured industrial inputs over agricultural inputs and consumer goods.

There was extreme hesitance on the part of most governments during this period to alter the exchange rate because of concern about adverse political repercussions. The devaluation of the cedi in December 1971 (which was long overdue) was preceded by several months of discus-

---

[3] The exception was a brief attempt at exchange rate devaluation and import liberalization under IMF guidance in 1971–2 which failed because of lack of donor support.

sion. The devaluation package eventually put together was determined not only by balance of payments considerations but also by concerns to alleviate the impact of the devaluation on the restive urban population. Not more than six weeks after the devaluation the government was ousted in a military coup and the currency revalued by 29% (Table 8.1).

In retrospect it appears that by revaluing the currency the new government was effectively tying its hand against the active use of the exchange rate as a policy instrument. This choice was made clear in the Five-Year Plan for the period 1975/76 to 1979/80 where it was stated that the conditions for a successful devaluation did not exist.[4] Thus even though it was realized that changes in the prices of tradeables relative to non-tradeables were required, this was to be achieved through the use of *ad valorem* and purchase taxes.

A policy of fixed exchange rates will be successful in preventing real exchange-rate misalignment if it is accompanied by restrained fiscal and monetary policies that will not fuel excess demand and introduce inflationary pressures in the economy. If the fiscal and monetary policies are not consistent with the parity, it is necessary that the parity be adjusted. Alternatively, a fixed exchange rate regime and expansionary policies can be pursued by using rigorous import controls in an attempt to control the balance of payments. Problems of compatibility between the fixed exchange rate and the macroeconomic policy stance emerged in the mid-1970s as the domestic inflation rate accelerated above the rate of the major trading partners and the real exchange rate began to appreciate (Table 8.1). Access to foreign exchange was restricted as the demand for it exceeded supply and tight import controls were introduced (Jebuni *et al.*, 1994). The trade and exchange controls encouraged the development of a parallel market for foreign exchange and a large black market premium began to emerge in 1975 (Table 8.1). Import controls also led to rent-seeking and to shortages of imported raw materials and inputs which contributed to the deteriorating performance of the manufacturing and agricultural sectors (Nyanteng, 1980; MDPI, 1974).

The nominal exchange rate was not adjusted until 1978. By then it had become severely overvalued and the black market premium had widened substantially. Following the 1978 devaluation the nominal rate remained fixed until 1983. Concerns about the political repercussions of the devaluation were again responsible for the delay in adjusting the nominal rate even though it was clear it had to be done.[5]

3.   Exchange Rate Policy 1983–93

The period 1983–93 marks another distinct phase in Ghana's exchange rate policy. By 1983 the options open to policy-makers were limited. It was clear that adjustment of the exchange rate was required if sharp deflation of the economy was to be avoided. Deflation of the economy would have been a suicidal choice since real GDP and real per capita incomes had shrunk dramatically in the eight years since 1975. Maintenance of the rate at its 1978 levels could only happen if there was an inflow of foreign grants to finance the budget and ease the shortage of foreign exchange in the the economy. The foreign inflows, however, were not forthcoming from potential donors without accompanying reforms, one of which was exchange rate reform.

An underlying objective of the donor-supported ERP launched in 1983 was the dismantling of price and trade controls and liberalization of the economy. In terms of reforms to the foreign-

---

[4] This view is contested by Ghartey (1987) who estimated import and export elasticities using data from 1959–76 and found that the Marshall-Lerner conditions held for Ghana, suggesting that devaluation would have been an appropriate policy tool. He found, however, that in the event of devaluation adjustment in the import sector would be slow and difficult, and so in order to benefit from devaluation policy-makers would need to concentrate on the export sector.

[5] Except for the devaluation of 1967, all devaluations had been associated with forced changes in governments. A justification of the 1972 coup had been the December 1971 devaluation. The 1978 devaluation occurred after Acheampong, the leader of the 1972 coup, had been replaced in a palace coup.

Table 8.1   Exchange Rates and Macroeconomic Indicators

Year	Nominal Exchange Rate[a] ¢ per US$	Real Exchange Rate[b] ¢ per US$	Black Market Premium	Real Exchange Misalignment	Fiscal Deficit GDP Ratio	Inflation Rate %
1971*	1.82	100.44	0.96	–12.2	2.31	9.28
1972*	1.28	112.75	1.28	–21.4	4.32	10.04
1973	1.15	110.31	1.29	–4.8	7.07	17.51
1974	1.15	103.64	1.50	–7.1	4.08	18.35
1975	1.15	80.22	1.73	–14.0	7.99	29.68
1976	1.15	55.01	2.53	1.5	9.07	56.34
1977	1.15	26.38	8.00	42.3	10.86	116.25
1978*	2.75	25.14	5.93	38.2	7.99	73.16
1979	2.75	28.62	5.67	89.4	6.64	54.49
1980	2.75	21.77	5.77	67.8	7.10	50.09
1981	2.75	10.99	9.54	134.0	6.35	116.45
1982	2.75	9.38	22.42	87.7	5.05	22.31
1983	30.00	13.34	8.686	67.8	2.45	128.71
1984	50.00	38.89	2.687	8.6	1.50	39.67
1985	60.00	54.36	2.415	0.0	1.59	10.31
1986	90.00	69.52	2.074	15.2	–0.59	24.60
1987	176.09	92.92	1.380	17.4	–1.19	39.81
1988	229.89	91.71	1.367	4.3	–0.94	31.34
1989	303.03	102.53	1.280	13.9	–1.27	25.22
1990	344.83	93.53	1.056	–3.8	–0.63	37.24
1991	390.63	89.46	N/A	–2.2	–1.96	18.03
1992	520.83	97.20	N/A	–6.0	3.41	10.06
1993	619.67	117.22	N/A	15.0	2.45	24.96
1994	1052.63	140.1	N/A	N/A	2.3	24.8
1995	1449.28	104.4	N/A	N/A	0.7	74.34

Note: [a] End of Period.
   [b] Calculated as $(E.P^*)/Pd$ where E is the average nominal exchange rate, P^* is the wholesale price index of the USA, and Pd is the domestic consumer price index.
   * is the year in which the official exchange rate was changed. For both 1971 and 1978 the devaluation occurred in the last quarter of the year.
   An increase in the real rate indicates depreciation.
   Exchange rate misalignment is defined as the percentage-deviation of the real exchange rate from the estimated real equilibrium exchange rate.
Source: Nominal exchange rate obtained from IMF *International Financial Statistics Yearbook 1995*, Washington, DC.
   Estimates of real exchange rate misalignment obtained from Elbadawi and Soto (1995)
   Ratio of parallel to official exchange rates obtained from Kapur *et al.* (1991).
   Parallel market rates for 1970–82 obtained from Stryker (1990).
   Fiscal deficit ratios: 1970–90 calculated using data from Statistical Services *Quarterly Digest of Statistics*, various issues, 1991–5 obtained from ISSER, various issues.

exchange regime there were four main objectives: to realign the official exchange rate; to achieve a convergence of official and parallel rates; to absorb the parallel market into the legal market; and to allow demand and supply to determine the rate and allocation of foreign exchange (Dordunoo, 1994).

As in earlier years, the political implications of devaluation were a major consideration. Consequently the transition to a liberalized exchange rate regime was begun gradually in 1983 with the announcement of a system of bonuses and surcharges. The effect of these was to institute a multiple exchange rate system. Traditional exports and imports of crude oil, essential raw materials, basic foodstuffs and capital goods were subject to a rate of ¢23.375 = US$1.00. The rate for non-traditional exports and other imports was ¢29.975 = US$1.00. The exchange rate was unified six months later at a rate of ¢30 = US$1.00.[6] Once the initial large exchange rate adjustment had been introduced, it was followed by more frequent adjustments of the rate based on a quarterly purchasing power parity principle of exchange rate determination and by January 1986 the cedi stood at ¢90 = US$1.00.

Nominal and real depreciations were accompanied by a decline in the parallel market premium. However, the continued existence of the premium was suggestive of distortions in the incentive framework, due to the trade and exchange controls still in place. The introduction of the foreign-exchange auction in September 1986 was the first step in moving towards a market-determined exchange rate. It also aimed to divert foreign exchange held outside banks into the banking system. An official two-tier system was introduced, whereby imports and exports of selected goods were subject to the official fixed rate whilst the remaining two-thirds of Ghana's external transactions were subject to the weekly auction rate. The two-tier system was unified in February 1987 at ¢150 per US dollar with all transactions settled at the weekly auction rate. The primary objective of the Dutch auction was to narrow the spread between the parallel and official exchange rates. This gap needed to be closed in order to prevent rapid depreciation in the auction rate, to prevent exchange seepage from the auction to the parallel market, to improve export incentives, and to reduce smuggling and capital flight.

Despite considerable institutional and financial support, particularly in the form of external foreign-exchange assistance for the economic reform programme,[7] the auction behaved erratically and took over 210 auctions and four years to achieve its objectives (Dordunoo, 1994). It was not until 1990 that the official and parallel rates were virtually unified. As predicted by theory (Grilli and Kaminsky, 1991) the auction was initially characterized by increased instability. In the initial few auctions the exchange rate rapidly depreciated from ¢128 to the $ to ¢145 to the $. Thereafter movements became smoother with less than 1% depreciation in most weeks. The number of bids also steadily increased with the inclusion of more consumer goods in the auction.

Econometric evidence reveals that the auction exchange rate was heavily influenced by the previous week's rate and by unmet demand at the previous auction (World Bank, 1989: Annex D). In terms of distribution of auction funds by sector between 1986 and 1988 industry was the largest recipient receiving about half, whilst agriculture received less than 10% (*ibid*).

The third phase of the exchange reform process began in February 1988 when the parallel market was legalized with the establishment of foreign-exchange bureaux. These bureaux were

---

[6] The devaluation of October 1983 was really a 26% devaluation of the exchange rate for traditional exports and imports of crude oil, essential raw materials, basic foodstuffs and capital goods, and a 15% devaluation for non-traditional exports and other imports.

[7] In contrast to the unsuccessful auction system introduced in Zambia, Ghana's auction succeeded for two reasons: adequate foreign-exchange support from foreign sources (Chhibber and Shafik, 1991) and the government's ability to adjust and fine tune the auction (Martin, 1993: 148–9). At key stages in the auction Ghana was able to satisfy the surge in demand for foreign exchange caused by import liberalization by borrowing from Standard Chartered Bank.

authorized to trade in foreign currency without having to verify the source of the foreign exchange or the purpose for which it was demanded. The aim of the bureaux was to attract additional foreign exchange to official channels, to facilitate the acquisition of small amounts of foreign exchange on a daily basis and to bring about convergence between the parallel and auction rates. By the end of 1988 over 70 bureaux had been established. Further development in the process of liberalization of the exchange rate was the introduction of a wholesale auction in 1990 which was replaced by an interbank market in 1992.[8] The main achievement of the wholesale auction and interbank market was to largely eliminate the gap between the auction and bureaux exchange rates, a feat which took over five years to achieve (see Table 8.1).

The initial decision taken in 1983 to adjust the exchange rate at discrete intervals was successful in addressing the problem of exchange rate misalignment without generating a severe contraction of economic activity. A major concern about devaluations is that they may be contractionary. This is because, in order for a real depreciation to be achieved, it is necessary to have accompanying restrictive fiscal and monetary policies and restraints on nominal wage increases. The devaluations begun in 1983 were not accompanied by contractions in output for various reasons. First, the devaluations allowed the nominal exchange rate to rise towards the parallel rate which already influenced prices and costs in the domestic economy (Chhibbber and Shafik, 1992). Secondly, the devaluation was accompanied by inflows of foreign exchange from donors supporting the ERP which increased the supply of raw materials, spare parts and capital goods. The shortage in the supply of these items had been a constraint on the expansion of production. Thirdly, the fiscal policy emphasized expenditure control within the context of revenue generation. Fortunately revenues rose after 1984, so that expenditures also increased in both real terms and as a share of GDP.

The slow move to a market-determined exchange rate was accompanied by a gradual liberalization of import controls and tariffs. To increase the supply of foreign exchange to match the increased demand caused by import liberalization, new surrender regulations made non-traditional exporters immediately lodge all export earnings in a commercial bank while other export proceeds had to be lodged with the Bank of Ghana.[9]

By the early 1990s a degree of de-politicization of nominal exchange rate changes had occurred via the gradual shift to a floating exchange rate mechanism. Government policy affected the nominal exchange rate not directly by fixing the rate but indirectly through fiscal and monetary policy. Recently intervention has been in the way of increasing the supply of foreign exchange on the market in order to curtail the depreciation of the nominal exchange rate because of concerns about the inflationary impact. The government, however, has asserted its commitment to achieving balance of payments objectives via appropriate fiscal, monetary and exchange rate policies rather than through heavy intervention in the exchange market or the reintroduction of quantitative controls on the current account (World Bank, 1995).

4. Determinants of Exchange Rates and the Effects of Exchange Rate Policy

Stability of the nominal exchange rate between 1970 and 1982 was achieved at the expense of an overvalued exchange rate that eroded the competitiveness of the import-substituting and export sectors. Estimates of the extent of real exchange rate misalignment found that the real exchange rate was undervalued from 1971 to 1975, whereafter it became grossly overvalued (Elbadawi

---

[8] The interbank market enabled authorized dealers, i.e. both banks and bureaux, including the Bank of Ghana, to trade in foreign currencies amongst themselves and with end-user customers.

[9] More recently, in a bid to stimulate non-traditional exorts, the export retention regime has been modified to the extent that only gold and cocoa exporters, not non-traditional exporters, are required to surrender their foreign exchange.

and Soto, 1995; see also Table 8.1). Islam and Wetzel (1994) attribute much of the real exchange rate appreciation that occurred between 1972 and 1982 to rising public sector expenditures and argue that the appreciation would not have occurred if public sector expenditure had remained contained.[10]

Another important determinant of the real exchange rate has been the inflow of foreign grants and loans in support of the ERP from 1986 onwards. In the period 1989–94 this led to real exchange rate appreciation (Table 8.1) through Dutch Disease effects (Younger, 1992a). Estimates of the real exchange rate facing exporters find that it appreciated sharply between 1989 and 1991. It has remained appreciated compared with its 1989 values despite a slight depreciation between 1992 and 1994 (CEPA, 1996). The increased inflow of foreign exchange has been too strong to sterilize, leading to rapid growth in M_2 and demand-pull inflation for non-tradeable goods.[11] Younger has argued that these capital inflows should be regarded as a permanent positive shock and that in order to cure inflation the increased money supply should be diverted into increased imports. In order for this to take place he argues that the real exchange rate should be allowed to appreciate further (through nominal appreciation rather than through domestic inflation) and that nominal devaluations in Ghana have been excessive.[12]

The danger of such a strategy, however, is that it would undermine the competitiveness of exports and import substitutes, leading to declining tradeables production and even greater aid dependence, causing vulnerability to fluctuations in capital inflows which may turn out not to be permanent. For a long time the strategy suggested by Younger was resisted by the Bank of Ghana. Bank of Ghana staff argue that the cedi's value should be allowed to reflect underlying domestic economic conditions, and that the root causes of inflation, such as recent government deficits and structural constraints on supply, should be tackled instead. However, in 1995 some intervention occurred in the market to restrain the nominal depreciation of the currency. This was because of the government's desire to use the exchange rate more as a nominal anchor against inflationary expectations than as a means of maintaining competitiveness in the tradeable goods sector.

Several studies of the real exchange rate in Ghana have found it to be an important determinant of output, exports and imports. A study by Jebuni, Sowa and Tutu (1991) found that the real exchange rate was an important explanatory variable for output, with appreciations in the rate causing a decline in output. The same study found that depreciation of the real exchange rate had a positive effect on exports and a negative effect on imports. The real exchange rate is also an important determinant of developments in the non-traditional export sector where real appreciations discourage this category of exports (Jebuni *et al.*, 1992). These results suggest that the appreciation of the real exchange rate in the 1970–82 period was important in explaining the decline in output and exports. Likewise, the discrete devaluations and the move to a floating exchange rate that took place after 1982 prevented gross misalignment and has had a positive influence on exports and output.

Another significant feature of the exchange rate system in Ghana has been the gap between the official exchange rate and the parallel market rate, i.e. the parallel market premium. During the 1970s an active parallel foreign-exchange market developed. This market, although illegal,

---

[10] This is because increased government spending caused inflation by pushing up the prices of non-tradeable goods and the black market premium which made imported inputs more expensive and raised the price of goods using these inputs.

[11] Capital inflows have also enabled the purchase of imports for the promotion of domestic output which helps to muffle the demand-pull inflationary effects. One important issue is whether the government has used foreign exchange inflows productively to alleviate the inflationary pressures of Dutch Disease. The effects of capital inflows on inflation and the real exchange rate thus become an empirical issue. Younger assumes that this effect is not strong enough to outweigh the inflationary effects.

[12] Hence, Younger concludes that inflation has remained high because of attempts to maintain the real exchange rate in the face of strong capital inflows.

was a price-clearing flexible regime with convertibility and no quantity rationing. This illegal market developed partly because of the increasing official import controls. Black market foreign currency was demanded predominantly to finance smuggled imports rather than for capital flight. A parallel market in foreign exchange also developed in order to avoid taxation and the foreign currency surrender laws. As official import strangulation intensified, the premium widened particularly over the period 1976–83. Since 1983 the discrete devaluations and evolution to a market-determined official rate have been successful in achieving unification of the exchange market through the elimination of significant differentials between the parallel and official rates (Table 8.1).

Several studies have been conducted to identify the determinants of the parallel market premium in Ghana. Chhibber and Shafik (1991) used a model which simultaneously determines the rate of inflation and the parallel market exchange rate premium and links them to the monetary, fiscal and real sides of the economy through several channels. The model was estimated with data from 1965–88 using two-stage least squares regressions. They found that the premium was determined by: the real effective official exchange rate,[13] with devaluation of the latter reducing the premium; interest rate differentials between Ghana and the rest of the world, with widening differentials causing an increase in the premium;[14] and uncertainly about future official exchange rates, with expectations of official devaluation causing the premium to decline.

Gyimah-Brempong (1992) used quarterly data from 1972–87 and a four-equation simultaneous model within a smuggling framework to investigate the determinants of the parallel market exchange rate. He argues that official exchange rate policy affects the parallel market rate both directly and indirectly. The direct effect works through official devaluation and exchange law enforcement and policing effects. Increased enforcement and policing of exchange laws decreases the supply of foreign exchange to the black market more than it decreases demand, resulting in depreciation of the domestic currency on the black market and a widening premium. The indirect effect works through changes in imports and exports and hence the supply and demand for black market foreign exchange. A similar argument has been made by May (1985).

Gyimah-Brempong, like Chhibber and Shafik, finds that devaluation of the official exchange rate leads to an appreciation of the domestic currency in the black market and hence a reduction in the premium. This is because official devaluation increases exports and hence capacity to import, which reduces pressure on the domestic currency in the black market. Anything which increases official exports and hence causes foreign-exchange supplies to expand, enabling increases in official imports, will have a similar effect.[15]

Islam and Wetzel (1994) estimated that fiscal deficits in Ghana have increased the black market premium. This is because increased government tradeables consumption reduces the supply of foreign currency to the private sector, so pushing up the black market price of foreign exchange. Wetzel and Islam concluded that from 1977 to 1983 the large public sector deficit was the most important factor affecting the black market premium. The premium fell in the mid and late 1980s as fiscal deficits were curbed.

We have carried out our own regression analysis for the period 1963–91 to test the hypothesis that increases in the parallel market premium have negative effects on exports and government

---

[13] Younger (1992b: 389) disagrees. He found no evidence that official devaluations caused changes in the parallel exchange rate during the controlled trade regime of 1974–86.

[14] Chhibber and Shafik (1991) argue that the significance of the relative interest rate variable shows that, as long as Ghana's real interest rates diverge widely from world rates, there will be a parallel market premium. Hence, exchange rate unification requires an opening up of the capital account so that there is legal arbitrage between cedis and foreign assets. Moves towards full convertibility of the cedi have taken place since 1992.

[15] The wider the gap between desired imports and actual official imports, the greater the demand for foreign exchange in the parallel market, which increases pressure on the domestic currency, leading to depreciation of the black market rate and an increased premium.

revenue. According to our estimate, the premium was found to have a significant negative effect on the ratio of exports to GDP. A 10% increase in the premium would cause exports as a proportion of GDP to decline by 3.3%. Further, the source of financing for parallel markets is usually through the underinvoicing of exports and the overinvoicing of imports, and hence, a proportion of economic activity is not being captured by the tax system. Indeed, our estimates of the effect of the black market premium on government revenues support the hypothesis that the emergence of a parallel market in foreign exchange adversely impacted on revenues. A 10% rise in the parallel market premium would be accompanied by a decline of 3.1% in real revenues.

Another important question concerning the effects of exchange rate policy is whether the nominal devaluations that have occurred since 1983 have led to cost-push inflation through increased import prices. There is considerable controversy surrounding this question in Ghana. Chhibber and Shafik (1991) and Toye (1995) argue that this has not been the case since most prices had already adjusted to the parallel exchange rate.[16] Chhibber and Shafik also found that official devaluation has a positive effect on the budget deficit because the government is a net supplier of foreign exchange to the economy. The government's supply of foreign exchange also increased with devaluation since a larger proportion of transactions occurred through official channels. This improvement in the budget deficit reduced monetization of the fiscal deficit and hence inflation. By reducing the budget deficit, it is argued that devaluation also boosted private sector growth, since there was less need for government borrowing which crowds out the private sector. These growth effects also contributed to reduced inflation.[17] Since nominal devaluations did not fuel inflation, they enabled a substantial real devaluation to take place.

Pinto (1989) reaches a different conclusion. Unlike Chhibber and Shafik, he argues that the government is a net buyer, rather than seller, of foreign exchange, such that devaluation in an attempt to unify the parallel and official exchange rates worsens the budget deficit which is monetized and hence leads to inflation.[18] Younger (1992b) reaches a less extreme conclusion than Chhibber and Shafik or Pinto. Using data from 1974–86, when severe exchange controls were in place, he found that devaluation of the official exchange rate had a statistically significant but very small effect on the CPI, with elasticities between 6% and 10% and with the impact occurring within three months.[19]

Several other effects of exchange rate devaluation deserve mention. First, devaluation has pushed up the domestic currency cost of debt service and other foreign exchange-denominated payments in government budgets. This has been particularly significant since 1983 when government debt to external agencies has been increasing (see Chapter 10). Secondly, devaluation increases the cost of working capital which has been in tight supply because of the IMF credit squeeze. Thirdly, small entrepreneurs, who were meant to be a leading source of growth, have found it hard to borrow enough local currency to purchase foreign exchange in the auction and to

---

[16] Chhibber and Shafik (1991) found in their estimation of an inflation equation that the parallel exchange rate was far more significant than the official rate and was the relevant cost-push variable.

[17] The inability to control inflation during the ERP can be attributed to: the inability to sterilize grant and loan inflows in support of the ERP, which led to rapid growth in the money supply; the emergence of fiscal deficits in the 1990s; and the failure to address fluctuations in food production which accounts for 50% of the official CPI (Sowa, 1994).

[18] Overvaluation acts as an implicit tax on exports since the government purchases exporters' foreign exchange at the official price which is lower than the market clearing rate. Devaluation means that revenue from cheap purchase of export earnings is lost. The premium of the free market over the official rate provides an alternative to using inflation, i.e. tax on domestic money, to finance the fiscal deficit such that unification takes away an implicit tax instrument. The costs of this implicit tax, however, are disincentives to exports, leading to import compression and reduced output.

[19] Younger argues that, even though the elasticity is small, the rapid impact means that large devaluations will produce inflation that is palpable to the person on the street, hence the government's political resistance to devaluation prior to 1983.

buy imported capital goods. Finally, rapid depreciation has led to general business uncertainty which has inhibited the private sector investment needed to increase productivity (Aryeetey, 1994).

5.   The Evolution of the Balance of Payments

The mismatch between the macroeconomic policy stance and exchange rate policy in the period prior to 1983 necessitated the imposition of controls on the capital and current accounts. The persistent deficit in the services account required that, for a sustainable current account deficit to be achieved, the trade account had to be in surplus. This was necessary because official transfers were outside the control of domestic policy-makers. Quantitative restrictions on imports were imposed to achieve trade balance surpluses and restrictions were imposed on the transfer of dividends, profits and salaries in order to contain the services account deficit. The maintenance of the import restrictions made it possible for a positive resource balance to be recorded in some years between 1970 and 1982 (Table 8.2). This balance, however, was achieved at a low-level equilibrium. Between 1970 and 1981 the exports/GDP ratio fell from 20.7% to 3.6% whilst the import ratio fell from 18.5% to 3.6% (Armah, 1993). Import rationing combined with capital controls meant that depletion of official reserves to support the fixed exchange rate was more or less contained.

The capital account of the balance of payments behaved erratically in the period 1971–82, registering a surplus in six years and a deficit in six years. Direct foreign investment remained positive throughout most of the period, averaging US$ 16.2 million per annum. The overall capital account went into deficit in 1972 and 1973, due to the interruption of external loans following the government's announcement in February 1972 of the suspension of all repayments on medium-term debt. This explains why the 1972 overall capital account deficit of US$ 77.8 m. was the largest of the period. Throughout the period the overall balance was in surplus in only four of the twelve years, and this was predominantly due to trade surpluses rather than capital inflows. There was not extensive recourse to external financing or aid during the 1972–82 period.

There have been significant changes in the structure of the balance of payments since 1983. These changes may be explained largely by the response to policy changes including exchange rate reform. The basic feature of the post-1983 balance of payments is the replacement of the trade balance surpluses of the 1970s with deficits in the trade and services accounts in most years, whilst net private transfers have been constantly positive since 1984.

In contrast to the 1970–82 period, the experience since 1983 has been one of the almost continuous deficits. The process of trade and payments liberalization has been important in this respect. The trade balance deficits were due to an increase in import values that was faster than the increase in export values. Import volumes increased dramatically with the removal of quantitative restrictions and the surge of external flows to finance capital and intermediate good imports.

The depreciation in the real exchange rate was important in encouraging an expansion in traditional and non-traditional exports (Jebuni *et al.,* 1991, 1992). The export retention scheme has also become instrumental in eliciting a positive supply response from non-traditional exports. Initially non-traditional exporters could retain 20% of their export earnings primarily for the importation of inputs. The percentage retained was increased to 35% in 1987 and a 100% retention was introduced in 1992. The restrictions placed on how the retained earnings were to be spent were also relaxed over time. However, the weakness in the gold and cocoa markets, reflected in declining terms of trade, dampened the positive impact the expansion of export volumes of these commodities had on export values. Although cocoa exports nearly doubled between 1983 and 1989 the price of cocoa fell by over 50% over the same period causing a loss of $US200 m. in cocoa sales in 1989 (Adedeji, 1990). Import values thus grew faster than exports.

Table 8.2 The Balance of Payments (US$m.)

	1971	1972	1973	1974	1975	1976	1977	1978	1979	1980	1981	1982
Trade Balance	-33.6	161.4	212.9	-29.2	150.4	88.8	29.4	112.5	262.6	195.3	-243.6	18.3
Net Non-factor Services	-76.0	-45.1	-82.8	-143.8	-141.1	-147.9	-132.7	-189.3	-161.1	-159.7	-172.5	-120.8
Net Factor Services	-36.5	-21.4	-15.9	-22.6	-36.4	-41.8	-34.9	-27.4	-58.3	-86.0	-87.7	-88.6
Transfers (Net)												
Private	-8.7	-2.9	-6.3	-3.6	24.3	-4.3	-6.1	-5.1	-2.6	-3.3	-4.2	-1.2
Official	9.0	16.2	18.8	27.8	20.3	31.0	64.6	63.4	81.4	82.9	87.2	83.7
Current Account	-145.8	108.2	126.7	-171.5	17.6	-74.0	-79.7	-45.9	122.0	29.2	-420.8	-108.6
Direct Investment	30.6	11.5	14.4	10.5	70.9	-18.3	19.2	9.7	-2.8	15.6	16.3	16.3
Other Long-term capital	34.4	36.9	17.0	-2.0	22.0	4.9	69.7	83.9	88.4	48.5	77.5	111.8
Capital Account	111.2	-77.8	-18.6	29.6	88.8	-63.4	71.2	-0.1	-52.1	-30.5	132.5	99.1
Overall Balance	-34.6	30.4	-108.1	-141.9	105.6	-137.4	-8.5	46.0	69.9	-1.3	-288.3	-9.5
Resource Balance	-109.6	115.9	130.1	-173.0	9.3	-59.9	-103.3	-76.8	101.5	35.6	-416.1	-102.5

Table 8.2 cont'd.

	1983	1984	1985	1986	1987	1988	1989	1990	1991	1992	1993	1994	1995
Trade Balance	-60.6	32.9	-36.3	60.9	-124.7	-112.4	-195.0	-308.3	-321.1	-470.3	-664.3	-342.1	-256.6
Net Non-factor Services	-96.2	-119.1	-129.5	-187.9	-165.1	-183.6	-195.2	-216.1	-223.7	-261.0	-299.8	-272.6	-129.2
Net Factor Services	-89.7	-114.9	-110.5	-110.6	-131.9	-138.3	-130.7	-119.8	-128.8	-115.2	-112.3	-110.9	-118.6
Transfers (Net)													
Private	-1.8	21.6	32.6	72.1	201.6	172.4	202.1	201.9	219.5	254.9	261.2	271.0	263.2
Official	74.2	141.2	109.5	122.5	123.2	196.1	220.2	213.8	201.4	213.8	256.2	200.8	260.0
Current Account	-174.1	-38.8	-134.2	-43.0	-96.9	-65.8	-98.6	-228.5	-252.7	-377.8	-591.8	-254.6	-144.6
Direct Investment	2.4	2.0	5.6	4.3	4.7	5.0	15.0	14.8	20.0	22.5	125.0	233.0	106.5
Other Long-term capital	31.4	202.2	39.5	142.0	227.7	178.9	165.2	319.0	353.5	253.4	517.6	248.7	355.6
Capital Account	1.2	74.4	148.3	-17.8	237.1	246.9	254.2	333.8	391.9	274.0	630.1	478.8	396.7
Overall Balance	-172.9	35.6	141.0	-60.8	140.2	181.1	155.6	105.3	136.7	-122.8	53.3	172.1	265.5
Resource Balance	-156.8	-86.2	-165.8	-127.0	-289.8	-296.0	-390.2	-524.4	-544.8	-731.3	-964.1	–	–

Source: IMF, *International Financial Statistics Yearbooks*, various issues.

The current account has been in deficit in all years since 1983. However, the current account deficit to GDP ratio declined substantially between 1986 and 1991. This improvement was largely due to the expansion in both official and private transfers. In most years since 1984 the surplus on the transfer account has been larger than the trade balance deficit. Donor support for the Economic Reform Programme led to substantial increases in concessional flows into the economy. These flows are quite volatile since they are determined not only by domestic economic policy but also by the perceptions and domestic policies in the source countries. A decision of the donors to withhold grants to Ghana will instantly create a balance of payments crisis since the domestic capacity to generate foreign exchange still lags behind the demand for it.

Net private transfers have remained positive since 1984 in sharp contrast to the deficits of the earlier years. These remittances increased quite rapidly between 1984 and 1993. The improvement may be attributed to the currency devaluations and the declining black market premium. The net impact of these flows on the current account is quite large since in some years they have been greater than the net official transfers. These private remittances have been an important source of private investment in the Ghanian economy during the ERP period.

The services account deficits have increased quite dramatically since 1984 because of debt servicing.[20] The factor services deficit remained large between 1983 and 1995, particularly in the mid-1980s as repayments were being made on loans incurred mainly from the IMF. The current efforts being made to increase tourism are crucial if the size of the deficits on the services account is to be reduced.

The current account position worsened in 1992–3. Expansionary fiscal policies and increases in the money supply fuelled aggregate demand. The current account deficit to GDP ratio increased to 5.4% in 1992 and 9.2% in 1993. Examination of the balance of payments account shows a worsening of the current account deficit because of large increases in the trade balance deficit.

In the 1983–93 period of economic reform the capital account registered a large surplus in all years except 1986. This was due to high levels of long-term capital inflows, largely in the form of loans to support the Economic Recovery Programme. Inflows of long- and short-term capital have enabled the overall balance to register a surplus in most years, despite a persistent current account deficit, enabling substantially larger holdings of international reserves. The inflow of long-term loans increased in 1984 and 1986–7. The importance of foreign capital is shown by the fact that between 1984 and 1994 total external debt outstanding increased from 25.9% of GDP to 92.3%.

In the early years of the ERP, Ghana's creditworthiness was poor and it was hard to attract long-term concessional finance. Hence, the government relied heavily on short-term borrowing from the IMF and other commercial sources. The share of short-term credit in total external debt rose from 20.1% in 1982 to 40.7% by 1985. As implementation of the recovery programme progressed creditworthiness improved and the share of long-term concessional loans increased in the mid-1980s. Direct foreign investment, on the other hand, has been slow to respond to the reform programme; it averaged only $9.6 m. in the period 1983–92 but registered a sharp increase to $125 m. in 1993 mainly due to investment in gold mining.

The persistence of the current account deficit throughout the 1983–95 period and the importance of capital inflows beg the question as to whether the import and foreign exchange market liberalizations would have been sustainable in the face of a decline in foreign loans and transfers, particularly in view of the declining international cocoa prices and the failure to diversify the export base significantly. Indeed, export diversification was hampered in the early 1990s due to real exchange rate appreciation caused by the Dutch Disease effects of the foreign capital inflows (Younger, 1992a). Hence, one legacy of the ERP seems to have been a change in the structure of the balance of payments which has created an aid-dependent economy.

---

[20] Chapter 10 provides details of the debt build-up since 1983 which has had a significant impact on the net factor services account of the balance of payments.

6.   Conclusions

Between 1972 and 1982 Ghana ran a quantity-controlled trade and payments regime with controls on the current and capital accounts. The exchange rate was fixed, which, in the face of inflationary fiscal and monetary policies, led to exchange rate overvaluation. This discouraged exports which in turn led to quantity-controlled import compression. Trade surpluses were recorded in most years and the current account and overall balance also recorded a surplus in many years. But this was at a low-level equilibrium as import compression reduced output. An active parallel foreign exchange market also developed with a high premium.

Since 1983 the foreign trade and payments regime has been gradually liberalized through a series of institutional reforms which have resulted in gradual devaluation that has helped to overcome exchange rate overvaluation. The parallel market has been legalized and the premium largely eliminated. In recent years a return to expansionary fiscal and monetary policies combined with large inflows of external resources has led to the re-emergence of exchange rate overvaluation.

Several important empirical relationships have been established between the exchange rate and other macroeconomic variables. The real effective exchange rate has been partly determined by the size of the fiscal deficit, and since 1986, by large inflows of external resources which have led to Dutch Disease effects. The real exchange rate, in turn, has been an important determinant of output, exports and imports with depreciations having a positive effect on exports and output and a negative effect on imports. Various studies have found the parallel foreign-exchange market premium to be determined by: the real official exchange rate, and uncertainty regarding changes in this rate; interest rate differentials; exchange law enforcement; any policies that increase exports and hence the capacity to import; and government fiscal deficits. Our regressions found that this parallel market premium had a significant negative effect on the ratio of exports to GDP and on government revenue.

One area of controversy is whether the official devaluations have been inflationary. Most studies suggest not. This hinges on the assumption that the government is a net seller of foreign exchange such that devaluation reduces the government budget deficit and hence reduces fiscally induced inflation. Pinto (1992), however, reaches the opposite conclusion based on the assumption that the government is a net buyer of foreign exchange. Whether or not the government is a net seller or buyer in any given year is an empirical question that merits further investigation.

Import liberalization combined with declining terms of trade has led to trade deficits and current account deficits throughout the 1983–95 period. This means that support for imports and for the currency in the auction market has been highly dependent on inflows of foreign loans and grants in support of the ERP. This begs the question as to whether, in the face of declining terms of trade and the failure to significantly diversify the export base, liberalization of the trade and payments regime would be sustainable in the absence of donor inflows of resources. Indeed, changes in the structure of the balance of payments accounts under the ERP seem to have created a more vulnerable dependency relationship between Ghana and its main donors.

References

Adedeji, A. (1990) *A Preliminary Assessment of the Performance of the African Economy in 1989 and Prospects for 1990.* Addis Ababa: ECA.

Armah, B. (1993) 'Trade Structure and Employment Growth in Ghana, A Historical Comparative Analysis: 1960:89', *African Economic History*, Vol. 21.

Aryeetey, E. (1994) 'Private Investment Under Uncertainty in Ghana', *World Development*, Vol. 22, No. 8.

CEPA (1996) *Macroeconomic Review and Outlook.* Accra: CEPA.

Chhibber, A. and Shafik, N. (1991) 'The Inflationary Consequences of Devaluation with Parallel Markets: The Case of Ghana' in *Economic Reform in Sub-Saharan Africa.* Washington, DC: World Bank.

Dordunoo, C. (1994) *The Foreign Exchange Market and the Dutch Auction System in Ghana.* African Economic Research Consortium Research Paper No.24: Nairobi: AERC.

Elbadawi, I. A. and Soto, R. (1995) 'Real Exchange Rates and Macroeconomic Adjustment in Sub-Saharan Africa and Other Developing Countries'. Paper presented at Bi-Annual Research Workshop of the African Economic Research Consortium, Johannesburg.

Ghartey, E. E. (1987) 'Devaluation as a Balance of Payments Corrective Measure in Developing Countries: A Study Relating to Ghana', *Applied Economics*, Vol. 19: 937–47.

Government of Ghana, *Quarterly Digest of Statistics*, various issues.

Grilli, V. and Kaminsky, G. (1991) 'Nominal Exchange Rate Regimes and Real Exchange Rate: Evidence from the US and Great Britain 1985–86', *Journal of Monetary Economics*, April.

Gyimah-Brempong, K. (1992) 'Exchange Control and Black Market Exchange Rate in Ghana: A Simultaneous Equation Approach', *East African Economic Review*, Vol. 8, No. 1.

IMF (1995) *International Financial Statistics Yearbook.* Washington DC: IMF.

ISSER, *The State of the Ghanaian Economy*, various issues.

Islam, R., and Wetzel, D. (1994) 'Ghana: Adjustment, Reform and Growth' in W. Easterly, C. Rodriguez and K. Schmidt-Hebbel (eds), *Public Sector Deficits and Macroeconomic Performance.* Washington, DC: World Bank.

Jebuni, C.D. (1996) 'Governance and Structural Adjustment in Ghana' in L. Reischtuk and I. Atiyas (eds) *Governance and Leadership and Communication. Building Constituencies for Economic Reform.* Washington, DC: World Bank.

Jebuni, C.D., Oduro, A., Asante, Y. and Tsikata, G. K. (1992) *Diversifying Exports. The Supply Response of Non-Traditional Exports to Ghana's Economic Recovery Programme.* London: Overseas Development Institute/University of Ghana.

Jebuni, C.D., Oduro, A. D., and Tutu, K.A. (1994) 'Trade and Payments Regime and the Balance of Payments in Ghana' *World Development*, Vol. 22, No. 8.

Jebuni, C.D., Sowa, N. K. and Tutu, K. A. (1991) *Exchange Rate Policy and Macroeconomic Performance in Ghana.* Research Paper No. 6. Nairobi: African Economic Research Consortium.

Kapur, I., Hadjimichael, M. T., Hilbers, P., Schiff, J. and Szymczak, P. (1991) *Ghana: Adjustment and Growth.* IMF Occasional Paper No. 86. Washington, DC: IMF.

Martin, M., (1993) 'Neither Phoenix nor Icarus: Negotiating Economic Reform in Ghana and Zambia, 1983–1993' in T. Callaghy and J. Ravenhill (eds) *Hemmed in: Responses to Africa's Economic Decline.* New York: Columbia University Press.

May, E., (1985) *Exchange Controls and Parallel Market Economies in Sub-Saharan Africa: focus on Ghana.* World Bank Staff Working Paper. Washington, DC: World Bank.

MDPI (1974) *Utilisation of Installed Capacity in Ghanaian Manufacturing Industry.* Accra: Management Development and Productivity Institute.

Nyanteng, V. K. (1980) *The Declining Cocoa Industry: An Analysis Some Fundamental Problems.* Technical Publication Series, No. 40. Institute of Statistical, Social and Economic Research, University of Ghana, Legon.

Pinto, B. (1989) 'Black Market Premia, Exchange Rate Unification, and Inflation in Sub-Saharan Africa', *The World Bank Economic Review*, Vol. 3, No. 3.

Sowa, N. (1994) 'Fiscal Deficits, Output Growth and Inflation Targets in Ghana', *World Development*, Vol. 22, No. 8.

Stryker, J. Dirck (1990) *Trade, Exchange Rate and Agricultural Pricing Policies in Ghana.* World Bank Comparative Studies. Washington, DC: World Bank,

Toye, J. (1995) 'Ghana' in Mosley *et al., Aid and Power: The World Bank and Policy-Based Lending*, 2nd edition, Vol. 2. London and New York: Routledge.

Werlin, H. (1994) 'Ghana and South Korea: ExplainingDevelopment Disparities. An Essay in Honour of Carl Rosberg', *Journal of Asian and African Studies*, Vol. XXIX, Nos. 3–4.

World Bank (1989) *Ghana: Structural Adjustment and Growth,* Report No.7515-GH. Washington, DC: World Bank.

World Bank (1995) *Ghana's Growth, Private Sector, and Poverty Reduction, A Country Economic Memorandum.* Report No.14111-GH. Washington, DC: World Bank.

Younger, S., (1992a) 'Aid and Dutch Disease: Macroeconomic Management When Everybody Loves You', *World Development,* Vol. 20, No. 11.

Younger, S. (1992b) 'Testing the Link Between Devaluation and Inflation: Time Series Evidence from Ghana', *Journal of African Economies,* Vol. 1, No. 3.

9 Performance of the External Trade Sector Since 1970

ABENA D. ODURO

1. Introduction

Despite the shift to a liberalized trade regime in Ghana and most other African countries the debate about the appropriate trade strategy for development still continues. In the 1960s the trend in thinking amongst development economists favoured the adoption of inward-oriented trade strategies. Import-substitution industrialization was forcefully espoused by writers such as Prebisch (1959) because of scepticism about the growth and development prospects of low-income countries if they remained producers and exporters of primary products. A second group of economists argued for more outward-oriented trade strategies that did not discriminate against exports (Krueger, 1978 and Balassa, 1978). This strategy was preferred because it would encourage competition and efficiency.

The 1980s saw a swing towards more open trade regimes by several African countries. This shift coincided with the adoption of the economic reform programmes of the Bretton Woods institutions which have been proponents of open trade regimes. The position of the latter was reinforced by the superior performance of the Asian newly industrializing economies that had made the transition from inward- to outward-oriented trade regimes as compared with the lacklustre performance of those countries that had maintained inward-oriented trade regimes. However, the results of studies on the links between trade and growth are ambiguous.

Despite the adoption of trade liberalization programmes by many African countries the question of the appropriate trade regime is still not settled. The basic concern is whether trade liberalization is the best means to help African countries achieve their development objectives. Improvement in the standard of living is a basic development objective of African countries. This can be achieved by improving productivity and structural transformation of the economy, in other words, diversifying the structure of production and exports, reducing the size of the subsistence economy, increasing the monetization of the economy, enhancing the provision of social services, etc. The development process can be stalled if there is an inadequate supply of foreign exchange to meet domestic requirements (Chenery and Strout, 1966). Appropriate trade and exchange rate policies are necessary components of any economic policies package to reduce the instances of destabilizing balance of payments disequilibrium.

This chapter examines the performance of Ghana's external trade sector and assesses its trade policy, by determining whether the policies followed were appropriate and adequate. The conclusion is that the trade and macroeconomic policies implemented prior to 1983 were not successful in reducing the foreign exchange bottleneck. This is because the policies were inappropriate and inadequate. They were inappropriate because the wrong instruments were assigned to objectives, and they were inadequate because the number of instruments was less than the number of policy targets.

The chapter is divided into two broad sections. The first examines trade and exchange rate policy and the external trade sector prior to 1983 and the second considers the experience since 1983. The analysis will proceed by first setting out the policy objectives for the external trade sector. This is followed by a discussion of policy implementation and the developments in the sector. The analysis concludes by considering the issues of policy consistency and the appropriateness of policy instruments.

2. Trade and Exchange Rate Policy 1970–82

The Objectives of Trade Policy

In most documents stating government objectives and policy, the availability of foreign exchange was identified as a major constraint facing the economy (see, for example, the Two Year Plan for the period 1968/69–69/70 and the Five Year Development Plan for the period 1975/76–79/80). Expansionary fiscal programmes quickly hit a balance of payments bottleneck because of certain features of the economy, namely, the high commodity concentration of exports, the import-dependent nature of the economy and the dependence of government revenues on international trade taxes.

Cocoa was the largest export earner and developments in export revenues were very sensitive to changes in cocoa earnings. The capacity to import was constrained to a large extent by changes in cocoa earnings because revenues from merchandise trade accounted for a large proportion of gross foreign exchange inflows. Merchandise exports accounted for approximately 72% of these inflows in 1970 and approximately 85% in 1975. Since cocoa earnings averaged about 65% of the total merchandise exports, in some years cocoa earnings constituted approximately 45% of the foreign exchange inflows. In addition, the manufacturing sector was highly dependent on import of raw materials,[1] hence, capacity utilization and the performance of the sector were dependent on the availability of foreign exchange.

The contribution of trade taxes to central government revenue ranged between 47% and 64% between 1970 and 1975. It rose to about 85% in 1979. Changes in cocoa export earnings influenced trends in government revenues because cocoa duties dominated international trade taxes. The performance of the export sector also impacted on the ability to raise taxes from the import trade and the manufacturing sector, because the volume of imports and manufacturing production were determined by the capacity to import.

In order to address these structural weaknesses, trade policy instruments were used during this period to deal with three major sets of objectives. These were as follows:

Reducing the Balance of Trade Constraint Export values were to be increased through rising volumes and export diversification. Expansion of non-traditional exports was an objective of both the Two Year Plan of 1968/69–70/71 and the One Year Plan.[2] In the Five Year Plan it was stated that

> More systematic and effective methods will be exploited in terms of increasing earnings of foreign exchange through exports of larger volume, higher quality, and greater diversification as to both items and markets (Republic of Ghana, 1977: 22).

---

[1] The share of imports in total raw materials requirements for medium and large-scale industries in 1979 and 1980 averaged 69% and 73.3% respectively.

[2] Non-traditional exports are defined as all exports excluding cocoa beans and products, timber, minerals, coffee, sheanuts and electricity.

With regard to imports, the policy emphasis during most of the period was on containing import demand within the bounds prescribed by the availability of foreign exchange, and on the allocation of foreign exchange to priority areas. The import requirements of the non-traditional exports sector were to receive priority.

Changing the Structure of Production The policy of import restraint was to be supported by an increase in the share of manufacturing in Gross Domestic Production behind protective barriers,i.e. import substitution. The expansion of manufacturing GDP was expected to be accompanied by an increase in manufactured exports as part of the export diversification strategy.

Revenue Objectives Government tax revenues were to be increased within the context of an expansion in the revenue base. In particular, there was a need to diversify government revenues from cocoa taxes. For example the revenue proposals of the 1973/74 budget were determined by the need to . . . 'attack systematically the excessive dependence of Government's fiscal operations on revenue derived from cocoa duties' (Republic of Ghana, 1973: 1).

Implementation of Trade Policy

A feature of the period was the rapid and frequent changes in the policy instruments. This unstable policy framework created uncertainty. The major sets of instruments employed were trade taxes, other fiscal instruments and quantitative and exchange controls. Trade taxes, in particular import taxes, were earmarked to achieve the revenue objectives. Other fiscal instruments, for example income-tax rebate schemes and tax waivers, were to be used to create incentives to encourage non-traditional exports to deal with the balance of trade objectives. Quantitative restrictions were to control imports in order to protect domestic industry. Adjustments in the number and intensity of use of the trade policy instruments in an attempt to achieve all three objectives simultaneously were made within the context of a fixed exchange rate regime.

Quantitative Restrictions and Exchange Controls Quantitative restrictions were implemented through the issue of import licences that were not auctioned or resalable. There were three types of licences. The Open General Licence (OGL) allowed registered importers to import freely the item specified on the licence. The Specific Licence required prior authorization before the goods were brought in. The Special Unnumbered Licence, later renamed the Special Licence, allowed imports to be brought in by importers who had access to their own foreign exchange.

The import liberalization begun in 1967 had, by 1970, allowed almost half of the imports to enter using the OGL. The currency was devalued in December 1971 as part of a package to deal with the balance of payments problems arising from an expansionary fiscal regime and import liberalization. The rate of devaluation was reduced in February 1972 when the currency was revalued. The import liberalization could not be maintained under these circumstances and import controls had to be introduced to prevent a deterioration in the balance of payments.

In 1972 most items were transferred to the Specific Licence lists and the importation of about 150 items were either restricted or banned. By the end of 1974 the OGL could be used only to import trade samples, gifts and personal effects.

In the 1973/74 budget, the government recognized that the reduction in import values in 1972 had been due mainly to the import controls imposed that year. It was stated that the balance of payments objectives were not to be achieved by the use of quantitative restrictions but through the encouragement of exports particularly non-traditional exports. The role of direct controls was to restructure imports in conformity with economic policy, i.e. to achieve, among other things, the protection of domestic industry. In the Five Year Plan for the period 1975/76 to 1979/80, this role of direct controls was reiterated. However, despite these assertions, direct controls were resorted to increasingly for balance of payments purposes. This was because of the government's failure to pursue appropriate macroeconomic and exchange rate policies to complement the export promotion package.

During the 1970s import programming took prominence. Import licences were to be allocated on the basis of the programme that had been drawn up. In most years the value of import licences issued was greater than the planned import values, and the value of actual imports exceeded those planned (Jebuni *et al.*, 1994). The response to the failure to issue import licences within the limits prescribed by the programme was to declare the licences invalid. This created a great deal of uncertainty. For example, the face value of import licences for which no letters of credit were established was reduced by half in 1974, and in 1975 import licences were revoked.

The special unnumbered licences had a particularly chequered history. They were abolished in 1974, re-introduced in 1975, and in 1977 their use was restricted to specified import categories. They were completely withdrawn in 1978 but re-introduced in 1980 as Special Licences. The frequent changes in the use of this category of licences made planning by the private sector hazardous.

Exchange controls in operation prior to 1970 were maintained, and operated alongside the import licensing system. All invisible payments had to be approved by the Exchange Control Department of the Bank of Ghana. Export proceeds had to be collected and repatriated to Ghana within sixty days of shipment, and their foreign exchange was required to be deposited with the commercial banks.

Taxes on Imports The stated policy objective guiding the use of import taxes was revenue generation. Problems were encountered in trying to attain revenue targets, largely because the structure of the tariff schedule made possible tax evasion through the misclassification of goods. The use of *ad-hoc* tax exemptions was another reason. The attempts to solve these problems created a tax system that was highly unstable because of the frequent changes in tariff schedules. Major tariff schedule restructuring was announced in the 1972/73, 1973/74, 1977, 1979 and 1980 budgets. The main reason for the changes was to achieve revenue targets. However, the actual duty collection rates remained consistently below those expected.

Taxes on Exports Taxation of the export sector is synonymous with taxation of cocoa. Cocoa contributed approximately 90% of the total export tax revenue between 1970 and 1982. The cocoa tax rate ranged between 36% and 60%. This contrasts with an average non-cocoa tax rate of less than 1% in the same period. The government's cocoa revenue consists of the difference between the world price and the producer price after taking account of the costs of the Cocoa Marketing Board (COCOBOD). Since neither the world price nor the costs of the marketing board remained stable, the export tax rate fluctuated considerably. Two problems emerged. The first was that, because of revenue considerations, the farmers invariably bore the burden of the falls in world prices and the increases in marketing costs (Table 9.1). The inability to maintain real prices indicates that short-term revenue considerations took precedence over long-term balance of payments and revenue objectives. Secondly, since the marketing costs were not directly within the government's control it could not predict its cocoa revenues with any certainty. An extreme example of this predicament occurred in 1981 when producer prices were increased to encourage cocoa exports (but the exchange rate was not adjusted as world prices fell). The difference between the world and the domestic price was absorbed by marketing costs, leaving virtually nothing for the government.

Export Promotion An export promotion package was introduced in 1969 to encourage an increase in manufactured exports.[3] It was later extended to other non-cocoa exports. The package of incentives was basically an attempt to counteract the adverse impact of the import trade regime on exporters.

The export promotion policy was also characterized by some degree of instability and uncertainty with the removal and re-introduction of components of the package. New incentives were added to the package over time. An important one was the foreign-exchange retention scheme which became operational in 1982. This allowed exporters of non-traditional exports to retain a percentage of their foreign earnings specifically to purchase machinery, equipment, spare parts and raw materials required in the production of exports.

---

[3] Jebuni *et al.* (1992) provide a detailed discussion of the evolution of the export promotion package.

Table 9.1   Export and Import Tax Collection Ratesa and Cocoa Prices

	Percentage			Cedis Per Metric Tonne			
Year	Import Tax Rates[b]	Export Tax Rates	Average FOB Cocoa Export Price[c]	Producer Price[c]	Costs of Cocoa Marketing Board[c]	Cocoa Export Duty[c]	Real Producer Price[c,d]
1970	25.75	37.23	642.9	292.7	79	271.2	229.00
1971	27.37	33.73	688.8	292.7	88	308.1	156.80
1972	16.40	21.16	824.2	365.9	145.9	312.4	228.54
1973	18.81	12.98	1294.2	439.0	211.0	644.2	231.20
1974	12.74	20.96	1688.0	548.8	314.0	825.2	230.07
1975	11.50	34.12	1526.0	585.4	397.0	543.6	162.64
1976	12.82	11.51	2596.0	731.7	336.0	1528.3	100.0
1977	12.61	24.11	3942.0	1333.3	1071.0	1537.7	124.36
1978	18.29	18.10	10396.0	2666.7	1492.0	6237.0	141.99
1979	17.42	66.50	9120.0	4000.0	2120.0	3000.0	159.21
1980	12.90	20.20	6300.0	4000.0	3573.0	–	74.75
1981	18.81	16.22	5000.0	12000.0	5200.0	–	159.49
1982	22.95	0.10	–	12000.0	–	–	84.38

[a]   Collection rates are calculated as import (export) revenues divided by import (export) values.
[b]   Comprises import duties, sales tax on imported goods and purchase tax.
[c]   Crop year, i.e. October to September.
[d]   The real producer price is the nominal price deflated by the consumer price index (1976/77=100).
n/a   not available
Source: Calculated by the author from Statistical Services, *Quarterly Digest of Statistics,* various
            issues. Nominal producer prices, costs of Cocoa Board and average fob export price
            obtained from Cocoa Marketing Board.

Other Policy Instruments The system of prior cash deposits was re-introduced in 1974 and remained until 1981. This required the importer to deposit with the Bank of Ghana a percentage of the value of the import licence before it could be issued. The structure of the cash deposit scheme favoured non-consumer goods imports as against consumer goods. Particular items, for example, fertilizers and crude oil required no prior cash deposit. Credit controls and differential lending rates were also used to regulate imports. The import sector was designated a non-priority area and on occasion directives were sent out limiting the credit that could be allocated to the sector. There was a decline in the share of commercial bank credit going to finance the import trade during this period. From 1979, credit to finance exports exceeded that for imports by a significant margin. The lending rate to finance the import trade was higher than that charged to exporters between 1978/79 and 1980/81, namely 18% as against 13%.

Performance of the External Trade Sector
The period 1970–82 saw a deterioration in the external trade sector that became pronounced after 1975. The trade balance surpluses recorded in most years hide the extent of the deteriora-

tion (Table 9.2). These surpluses were the outcome of import contraction through the use of quantitative restrictions rather than of improved export performance. A better picture of the state of the external trade sector can be obtained by examining trends in export and import volumes, trade ratios and the extent of export diversification.

Both import volumes and the import to GDP ratio registered continuous declines, particularly after 1974. The trend in the export/GDP ratio and the export volume index was downward, particularly from 1973. Despite the reversal of the decline in export volumes beginning in 1980, the index in 1982 was approximately 52% of its 1970 values (Table 9.2). Ghana's share of world exports declined by 68% between 1970 and 1982, and its share of world cocoa exports more than halved during the same period.

Table 9.2   Indicators of External Trade Sector Performance: 1970–82

| Year | Volume Indices: | | | | | Share of Total | | | | |
| | Eports US $m. | Imports US $m[a] | Trade Balance | Cocoa Exports | Total Exports | Imports | Percent of GDP: | | Exports: | |
							Exports	Imports	Cocoa	Principal[b]
1970	427.0	280.3	–40.4	156.87	220.9	256.9	19.28	16.94	72.04	90.64
1971	334.6	368.2	–33.6	140.41	155.2	215.8	13.78	15.16	67.91	91.38
1972	384.3	222.9	161.4	170.62	186.5	111.5	18.16	10.53	59.72	87.29
1973	585.0	372.1	212.9	191.97	169.2	132.8	19.54	12.43	56.99	94.17
1974	679.0	708.2	–29.2	133.12	139.5	179.1	16.73	17.45	64.36	93.76
1975	801.0	650.5	150.4	125.10	142.8	155.4	17.44	14.16	69.38	91.72
1976	779.0	690.3	88.8	127.29	149.7	149.6	13.73	12.16	63.60	83.81
1977	889.6	860.2	29.4	98.22	123.3	155.4	9.16	8.86	69.19	87.41
1978	892.8	780.3	112.5	82.91	101.6	128.8	7.49	6.54	71.15	87.14
1979	1065.7	803.1	262.6	73.54	96.8	97.9	10.38	7.83	75.63	90.67
1980	1103.6	908.3	195.3	100.00	100.0	100.0	7.08	5.83	64.27	87.16
1981	710.7	954.3	–242.6	70.52	103.1	112.7	2.69	3.62	45.37	67.86
1982	607.0	588.7	18.3	86.77	116.5	64.4	1.93	1.87	51.30	69.1

Notes: [a] Float on board.
          [b] Principal exports comprise exports of cocoa beans and products, timber and minerals.
Sources: IMF, *International Financial Statistics Yearbook, 1985*, Washington, DC; Statistical Services, *Quarterly Digest of Statistics*, various issues; IMF Data files.

Very little export diversification occurred during this period. Estimates of commodity concentration ratios found that there was no significant change in either the Hirschman or Entropy indices (Jebuni *et al.*, 1992). The share of principal exports (i.e. cocoa beans and products, timber and minerals) in total exports ranged between 87% and 93% for most of the period (Table 9.2). The fall in the share of the principal exports below historical levels in 1981 and 1982 was not indicative of the beginning of a successful diversification strategy. The falling shares were due largely to contracting cocoa export volumes compounded by declining world cocoa prices, rather than a rapidly expanding non-traditional export sector.

The industrial countries are the major destinations of Ghana's exports, and this did not change dramatically during the period 1970–82. The narrow production base and structure of exports, as well as the limited and relatively expensive transportation links, pose barriers to market diversification particularly within the West African region.

Poor export performance cannot be wholly explained by unfavourable conditions in the international economy. It was during the 1970s that the East Asian countries emerged as significant exporters of manufactured goods. Ghana's failure to maintain its share of the expanding world market through export diversification is largely due to domestic policy failure.

Thus the balance of trade objectives of trade policy were not achieved. Neither were the other two targets, namely, increasing government revenues and changing the structure of production. Real government revenues in 1982 were approximately 14% of their 1970 levels. The revenue/GDP ratio declined from 19.3% in 1970 to 5.62% in 1982. The share of export and import duties in total revenues fell as the export and import tax base shrank. In 1982 the contribution of trade taxes fell to approximately 13%.

The share of manufacturing output in real Gross Domestic Product declined to 7.4% in 1982 from the peak of 13.92% in 1975. Real manufacturing GDP was approximately half its 1975 value in 1982. The export orientation of the sector also deteriorated. The share of exports in manufacturing GDP declined from the peak of 42% in 1972 to 23.6% in 1982 (Baah-Nuakoh *et al.*, 1996).

The poor performance of the external trade sector during this period can be explained largely by conflicts in the objectives and inappropriate policy measures.

Assessing the Impact of Trade Policy on the External Sector

Conflict in Objectives The balance of trade objectives and the structure of production objectives were inconsistent. At the outset it could not be expected that a policy to expand the manufacturing base through import-substitution industrialization would automatically be accompanied by an increase in manufactured exports and therefore a diversification of exports. Theoretical and empirical work shows that import tariffs are a tax on the export sector (Clements and Sjaastad, 1984; Oyejide, 1986; Jebuni *et al.*, 1992). Estimates of the incidence of import taxes found that approximately 74–85% of the import tax in Ghana is shifted to the export sector (Jebuni *et al.*, 1992). The import-substitution strategy introduces an anti-export bias that can only be counteracted by an effective export promotion package. Unfortunately the export incentive packages were ineffective in counteracting the impact of the import-substitution strategy on the export sector, thus reducing the likelihood of achieving the export diversification objective and also the objective of expanding export volumes.

When there is a conflict among objectives, two things may happen to policy priorities. Policy objectives may be redefined as policy-makers consciously choose to drop one of the objectives. The alternative is an unconscious decision not to actively pursue a set of objectives even though they may continue to form part of the stated overall policy objectives.

During the 1970s despite several documents propounding export growth and diversification as objectives, the unconscious policy action was to drop them as objectives. That the objective to address the balance of trade issues through export expansion was accorded the lowest priority is clear from the implementation of policy. The export promotion scheme suffered from several shortcomings. The first was slowness in implementation. A second was failure to inform potential exporters about the various components of the package, and a third was failure to adopt supportive exchange rate and macroeconomic policies (Jebuni *et al.*, 1992).

The weakness of the trade balance and the susceptibility of the economy to foreign exchange crises hinged on the pivotal role of one export commodity, cocoa. An export promotion programme that encouraged export diversification and faster growth in volumes was crucial. The low priority given to promoting exports was a major policy failure during this period.

Inappropriate Policy Instruments Maintaining an exchange rate that does not become overvalued is important to ensure that incentives for exporting are maintained. A depreciated real exchange rate not only encourages exports but provides protection to the import-substituting sector. The real exchange rate may be prevented from appreciating by adjustments in the nominal rate, and/or supportive monetary and fiscal policies to control inflationary pressures. When the nominal exchange rate is fixed, fiscal and monetary restraint is required to prevent the real rate from appreciating. If monetary expansion exceeds what is necessary to support the exchange rate an adjustment in the nominal rate is required.

The expansionary fiscal and monetary policies of the 1970s and early 1980s that fuelled aggregate demand were not compatible with the fixed exchange rate policy. The real exchange rate appreciated, discouraging exports (see Chapter 8 in this volume). Since Ghana was a large exporter on the world cocoa market, an optimal policy would have been a tax on cocoa exports. An appreciating real exchange rate is not the best measure in these circumstances to tax the cocoa sector. The appreciating real exchange rate would constrain cocoa exports and also discourage non-cocoa exports. A preferred combination of trade policy instruments would have been a depreciated real rate to encourage non-cocoa exports and an export tax on cocoa.

The expansionary short-term fiscal programmes always pushed the economy to the brink of a foreign exchange crisis. The policy response was to tighten quantitative restrictions. The trade and exchange controls were relied upon to keep import demand within the capacity to import. The controls were inappropriate instruments to deal with the balance of trade situation, because they did not address the cause of the decline in the capacity to import. These controls coupled with the appreciating real exchange rate encouraged the development of a parallel foreign exchange market and smuggling. Significant quantities of cocoa exports were diverted to unofficial channels during this period.

To deal with the balance of payments implications of the inconsistent policies, policy instruments were resorted to which compounded the disincentive to export and the balance of payments problem. The low priority given to the export sector was a result of the government having to deal with the recurring foreign exchange crisis because of the failure to depreciate the nominal exchange rate, whilst it pursued expansionary fiscal programmes. The interplay of these forces resulted in a trade regime that was biased against the export sector.

Another major policy blunder was assigning trade taxes to achieve two objectives. Trade taxes were to be used to serve revenue purposes as well as to bring about a *de facto* devaluation.[4] Trade taxes could not be effectively used to perform the latter function because the policy bias was towards revenue generation. Import tax rates were continuously adjusted to satisfy the government's revenue objectives. Ironically concerns about revenue generation also made it impossible to implement a realistic cocoa pricing policy. To try to maintain cocoa revenues, the producer price of cocoa was not adjusted by enough to prevent a fall in real prices.

The increasing use of direct controls in response to the deteriorating balance of payments situation undermined the performance of the manufacturing sector, as the supply of necessary imports was kept below the desired levels. The contraction of import volumes through the use of direct controls also made it difficult for revenue targets to be achieved. The choice of trade policy objectives and the implementation of trade and macroeconomic policies failed to create a system of incentives that would encourage a change in the structure of the economy. Instead they contributed to reinforcing the features of the economy, such as a narrow range of primary exports, that increased its susceptibility to foreign exchange crises.

3.   Trade Policies under the ERP

The deterioration in the performance of the external sector in the 1970s was a reflection of the overall decline in economic performance. Real Gross Domestic Product in 1983 was a fraction of its 1970 values. Government's capacity to influence economic activity was severely eroded as

---

[4] In the Five-Year Plan import taxes were expected to be used to achieve a *de facto* devaluation.

its revenue base contracted. The increasing use of controls, rather than increasing the government's grip on the economy, encouraged a flourishing parallel economy. The policy actions of the past could not be maintained without increased access to foreign exchange. The potential sources of external finance, i.e. the Bretton Woods institutions and the international donor community, were not willing to lend to Ghana without a change in policies.

The economic reforms (known in local parlance as the economic recovery programme (ERP)) launched in 1983 were aimed at reversing the economic decline of the previous decade and reducing the foreign-exchange constraint on the domestic economy. An important feature of the programme which distinguishes it from the earlier set of policies was that it was clearly outward-oriented.

Policy Objectives for the External Trade Sector

The external sector objectives at the start of the ERP were to restore incentives for the production of exports and increase the overall availability of foreign exchange, and to improve the foreign-exchange allocation mechanism and channel it into selected high priority areas (Republic of Ghana, 1983). The expansion of the non-traditional export sector was an important component of the overall strategy to reduce the foreign-exchange constraint on the economy. The evolution of instruments to achieve these objectives were also policy targets in themselves. The long-term objective was to substitute price instruments for quantitative restrictions and to create a liberalized trade regime.

The Implementation of Trade Policy

The trade liberalization process was implemented in phases. Using the classification developed by Krueger (1978), the period since 1983 can be classified into three phases (see also Jebuni *et al.*, 1994).

Transition to Import Liberalization, 1983–86 In contrast to the earlier period, trade policy was conducted within the context of a continually adjusting exchange rate. The first step taken in the liberalization process was a depreciation of the real exchange rate, achieved initially not by means of a devaluation of the nominal exchange rate but by maintaining the nominal rate at its August 1978 level and introducing a system of bonuses and surcharges. The choice of this method was determined by concerns about the political repercussions of an outright devaluation. However, six months later, in October 1983, the system of bonuses and surcharges was replaced by a nominal devaluation. Between October 1983 and September 1986 real depreciation of the exchange rate was achieved largely through frequent nominal devaluations. The ratio of the parallel to the official exchange rate declined sharply as the nominal rate was devalued (see Table 8.1 in Chapter 8).

Import tariff rates were adjusted downwards in 1983. The tax schedules were 10%, 20%, 25% and 30%, compared with schedules of 35%, 60%, and 100% in 1982. The tariff schedules remained fairly stable until 1986, when the import duties on consumer goods and the sales tax on luxury imported goods were reduced (Jebuni *et al.*, 1994). The import licensing system and import programming were maintained. The largest proportion of the foreign exchange to finance imports was expected to come from foreign sources, i.e. donors supporting the ERP.

The set of incentives announced in 1983 for the non-traditional export sector did not differ significantly from the earlier ones. The main difference was the removal of the export bonus scheme of the export promotion programme when the bonuses and surcharges were announced.

The nominal devaluations made possible increases in nominal cocoa producer prices that translated into real cocoa price increases without jeopardizing government revenues. The policy objective was to improve the farmer's share of the world cocoa price in order to encourage replanting and rehabilitation of the tree stock.

Import Liberalization, 1986–89 The second stage of the liberalization process began in 1986 with the re-introduction of a formal dual exchange rate system. The rate at the first window was the prevailing official exchange rate set in January of that year and governed the purchase of essential raw materials and crude oil, all official transactions and cocoa earnings. The rate at the second window was determined by weekly foreign-exchange auctions organized by the Central Bank. The official exchange rate market was unified in early 1987 when all transactions were made subject to the auction rate. In 1988 the exchange rate system was liberalized further with the establishment of foreign-exchange bureaux that allowed individuals to trade freely in foreign exchange at spot rates. The real exchange rate depreciated and the gap between the nominal and parallel exchange rates was reduced (see Table 8.1 in Chapter 8).

There was re-definition of import licence categories in 1986 when the new exchange rate system was introduced. The 'A' licence allowed the holder to bid for foreign exchange at the foreign-exchange auction and restrictions were put on the type of goods that could be imported using the licence. The second licence was the 'S' licence. Holders of this licence could not bid for foreign exchange at the auction. The third licence was issued to government organizations for the importation of essential goods and services. Liberalization of the trade regime continued in 1987 with the transfer to the auction of about 70% of the goods which were previously not eligible for the auction. The process was completed in 1988.

The import tax rates on consumer goods were raised in 1987. However, there was a scaling down of import tax schedules in 1988 by between 5 and 15 percentage points, bringing import tariff rates to between 10% and 25%. Sales taxes on imported goods were reduced by 10 percentage points.

The foreign-exchange retention scheme was liberalized further in 1987 when the percentage of export earnings that could be retained was increased from 20% to 35%. Restrictions on the use of the retained earnings were relaxed over time.

The nominal producer price of cocoa was increased, despite the fall in world cocoa prices. These nominal price increases translated into real price increases until the 1987/88 crop year. The cocoa tax rate, i.e. the ratio of cocoa duties to cocoa export earnings, declined.

Liberalized Trade and Exchange Rate Regime 1989 to the present A wholesale foreign-exchange auction replaced the retail auction in 1990, and was itself replaced by an interbank market in 1992. Unification of the exchange rate regime through the virtual disappearance of a wedge between the nominal and parallel market rates was achieved by 1992. However, the real rate began to appreciate in 1990 and remained appreciated compared with its 1989 values until 1993 (Table 8.1 in Chapter 8).

In 1989 the import licensing system was abolished because it was considered redundant, given the developments in the exchange rate system. Import licence levies were also removed at the same time. Further liberalization occurred with the decline in import tax rates on raw materials and capital goods by 5 percentage points in 1990. The sales tax on imported basic consumer goods was reduced between 1989 and 1994. At the same time protective duty rates were introduced for specific goods in 1990 and again in the 1994 budget. These taxes were to alleviate the concerns of the import-substituting firms which were finding it difficult to compete in the new liberalized environment.

The export incentive package was made more attractive with some of the incentives becoming more generous. For example, there was an increase in the income tax rebate in the 1991 budget. The export retention scheme was phased out. Non-traditional exporters can now receive their foreign exchange over the counter from any authorized commercial bank.

The price incentive to the cocoa sector was not maintained during this period. Real producer prices began to fall in 1988/9. The increases in the nominal producer prices have been constrained largely by the fall in world cocoa prices and the government's attempt to maintain revenues.

The reduction in import tariffs and export tax rates, and the depreciation of the real exchange rate, reduced the anti-export bias in the trade regime. The trade bias indicator is suggestive of substantial improvements in the regime between 1983 and 1988. However, the incentives to the

export sector were not maintained between 1990 and 1992 when the real exchange rate appreciated.

Performance of the External Trade Sector

In contrast to the earlier period, the trade balance since 1983 has tended to register deficits rather
than surpluses. These open deficits have occurred as both the export and import-GDP ratios
have risen (Table 9.4).

Table 9.3   Trade Policy Variables 1983–94

Year	Import Tax Rates[a]	Export Tax Rates	Cocoa Tax Rate	Non-Cocoa Tax Rate	Bias in Trade Regime[b]
1983	17.26	28.69	70.18	2.16	1.64
1984	14.95	21.73	31.08	5.21	1.46
1985	13.96	27.38	44.51	2.29	1.56
1986	13.82	18.12	33.17	0.77	1.39
1987	12.24	18.34	39.77	0.03	1.37
1988	13.55	11.89	28.51	0.00	1.28
1989	18.11	11.34	30.08	0.00	1.33
1990	16.44	8.95	18.28	0.00	1.27
1991	15.64	8.18	23.54	0.87	1.25
1992	13.34	8.74	28.49	0.70	1.24
1993	12.44	5.30	19.91	0.42	1.18
1994	14.12	14.80	50.08	–	1.33

Notes: [a] Comprises import tax rates, sales and purchase taxes.
           [b] The bias in the trade regime is defined as $En(1+tm+q)/En(1-tx+s)$ where En is the nominal exchange rate, tm is the
           import tax rate, q is the import premium, tx is the export tax rate and s is the export subsidy rate. A value greater
           than one indicates the existence of an anti-export bias.
Sources: Statistical Services, *Quarterly Digest of Statistics,* various issues; Bank of Ghana *Quarterly Economic Bulletin.*

There was a substantial across-the-board rise in exports between 1983 and 1988, with the
principal exports (i.e. cocoa, timber and minerals) and the non-traditional exports responding
positively to the improved incentive structure. The increase in total exports can be explained by
the depreciation of the real exchange rate and the increased availability of imports made possible
by loans and aid inflows (Jebuni *et al.,* 1992). The number of enterprises involved in exporting
non-traditional items increased during the first six years of the programme. The depreciating real
exchange rate and export incentives also encouraged enterprises that were not already exporting
to do so (*ibid.*).

Although export volumes more than doubled between 1984 and 1988, the growth in export
values was much less. This was because of the decline in world cocoa and gold prices. World
cocoa prices fell from 1984 until 1992, and by 1989 were less than half their 1984 values. The
performance of the export sector between 1988 and 1992 was lacklustre. The export/GDP ratio
fell and export volumes stagnated, not rising above their 1988 levels. This was largely because
of the poor growth of cocoa export volumes (ISSER, 1991 and 1994).

Prior to 1995 only limited progress had been made in export diversification, with not much
success in reducing the share of primary products in total exports. Cocoa, timber and minerals
still make up approximately 85% of total exports. However, the over-dependence on one com-

Table 9.4   Indicators of Performance of the External Sector: 1983–95

Year	Exports US $m.	Imports US $m[a]	Trade Balance	Volume Indices: 1980 = 100			Percent of GDP:		Share of Total Exports		
				Cocoa Exports	Total Exports	Imports	Exports	Imports	Cocoa	Principal	Non-Traditional
1983	439.1	499.7	–60.6	67.64	84.0	58.2	2.11	2.40	41.64	67.33	–
1984	565.9	533.0	32.9	59.12	85.7	73.9	7.53	7.09	70.47	94.02	–
1985	632.4	668.7	–36.3	64.97	103.7	82.2	10.02	10.60	65.86	88.28	–
1986	773.4	712.5	60.9	83.23	114.9	93.9	13.49	12.43	58.52	82.86	3.07
1987	826.8	951.5	–124.7	84.60	123.8	106.0	18.00	20.71	59.23	91.35	3.38
1988	881.0	993.4	–112.4	85.89	189.0	111.0	16.96	19.12	56.07	95.00	4.80
1989	807.2	1002.2	–195.0	105.19	166.6	118.9	15.38	19.09	49.60	83.20	4.30
1990	890.6	1198.9	–308.3	104.15	176.9	122.1	14.30	19.26	40.21	82.51	7.00
1991	997.6	1318.7	–321.1	94.41	182.5	131.8	14.25	18.84	34.73	82.51	6.27
1992	986.3	1456.5	664.2	86.87	188.5	134.8	14.33	21.16	30.67	81.62	6.93
1993	1063.6	1728.0	342.2	99.68	n/a	n/a	17.34	28.51	26.60	85.24	6.74
1994	1234.7	1579.9		92.39	–	–	22.63	31.80	25.9	86.84	9.72
1995	1431.2	1687.8	–256.6	–	–	–	25.00	–	29.5	88.20	–

Note: [a] Fob values
Sources: Statistical Services, *Quarterly Digest of Statistics*, various issues; IMF, *International Financial Statistics Yearbook 1995*. Data on non-traditional export values used to calculate export shares obtained from Ghana Export Promotion Council.

modity, cocoa, for foreign exchange, that was a feature of the 1960s and 1970s, no longer prevails. Gold exports now dominate merchandise exports, but do not make up more than half of total merchandise earnings as did cocoa in earlier years (Table 9.4). Gold production, unlike that of cocoa, is dominated by large transnational corporations; thus the increase in gross foreign-exchange flows from gold does not imply a commensurate increase in net flows because of profit repatriation and salary payments to expatriate staff.

The share of non-traditional exports tripled between 1986 and 1994, although the years 1990 through to 1993 did not see much change in these shares (Table 9.4). There was very little change in the number of non-traditional products exported and their export values between 1990 and 1992. However, some diversification in the structure of non-traditional exports has occurred. The share of agricultural exports declined from 74.8% in 1986 to 32.9% in 1994 (ISSER, 1991 and 1994). However, this cannot make much of an impact on the structure of total exports because of the small share of non-traditional exports. Diversification of the commodity structure of exports, especially towards manufactured goods, is necessary for several reasons. The prices of manufactured goods on the world market are more stable than those of primary products. Secondly, export earnings instability in Ghana can be explained by the lack of commodity diversification (Jebuni *et al.*, 1992).

Not much market diversification has occurred during this period. Official estimates of the direction of trade show that in 1994 the proportion of exports going to the ECOWAS market was approximately 3%, and imports from the region, excluding those from Nigeria, were about 1%. Imports from Nigeria are dominated by oil. Including Nigeria, the ECOWAS share of imports was 7% in 1994. These figures do not differ significantly from the 1980 shares. Sluggish growth, political instability and non-tariff barriers can explain the low shares of regional trade. Even though regional markets take a small proportion of total exports, they absorb a fairly large share of Ghana's non-traditional exports. A survey of manufacturing firms conducted in 1992 found that approximately a third of these exports were sold in ECOWAS markets (Tutu and Oduro, forthcoming). This suggests that opening up the ECOWAS market may be important in Ghana's effort to diversify into manufactured exports.

Despite the depreciation in the real exchange rate, import volumes increased continuously during the first two phases of the liberalization programme. This was because the increase in foreign loans and grants once the reform programme got under way made possible an increase in the supply of import licences. The initial surge in imports in 1984 was not to satisfy consumer demand, but was largely to supply raw materials and spare parts to the productive sectors of the economy.[5] Secondly, a *de facto* devaluation had already occurred in the parallel foreign-exchange market and most prices were determined by those rates. Import volumes have continued to increase as real incomes have risen and foreign inflows have continued. The foreign inflows have made possible the expansion of imports beyond the limitations of the domestic supply of exports.

Assessing the Trade Liberalization Programme

Conflicts in Objectives A major difference between the implementation of trade policy before and after 1983 is the policy objectives. Unlike the earlier period when trade policy instruments were earmarked to achieve three objectives, the focus since 1983 is on influencing the volume and pattern of trade, in particular increasing the availability of foreign exchange through the expansion of both traditional and non-traditional exports. An advantage of this is that conflicts between objectives have been minimized.

Since 1990, however, the issues of protection and revenue generation have again become

---

[5] The share of consumer imports declined by 10 percentage points between 1983 and 1984, rose in 1985 but declined again in 1986 by 9 percentage points. The import licensing succeeded to a degree in directing imports towards the provision of inputs and supplies for the rehabilitation of the infrastructure.

important. Protective tariffs were introduced in response to demands from the manufacturing sector which has found it difficult to compete in the liberalized environment. The difficulties of the manufacturing sector are due largely to the weak production and technological base of domestic manufacturing (Jebuni *et al.*, 1992; and Baah-Nuakoh *et al.*, 1996). Revenue considerations have also become increasingly important since 1990 when the fiscal discipline of the early years of adjustment was relaxed and government spending increased.

Appropriateness of Policy Instruments The possibility of a reversal of the trade liberalization programme depends upon two possible outcomes. The first is whether liberalization will create unsustainable balance of payments deficits (i.e. whether it is balance of payments-compatible). The second is whether the fiscal position will deteriorate (i.e. fiscal compatibility).

Liberalization of the trade regime will tend to worsen the balance of payments position because as import duties are reduced the price level falls and real money balances increase. The latter can cause the balance of payments to deteriorate. Reversal of the liberalization exercise can be avoided if it is accompanied by policies that restrain the increase in real money balances. A devaluation, an increase in indirect taxes, or contractionary fiscal and monetary policies are appropriate to support the liberalization to ensure that it is payments-compatible.

In Ghana trade liberalization began when the balance of payments was in a weak position. A liberalization that further weakened the balance of payments could not be sustained. Problems of macroeconomic incompatibility were initially avoided through real devaluations, the initial fiscal restraint that characterized the economic reform programme, the widening of the tax base and the inflows of external financing. The budget deficit-GDP ratio declined from 1983 to 1985, after which surpluses were recorded until 1992. The fiscal discipline reduced expansionary pressures on the money supply. By the time the pace of the liberalization had quickened in 1989, the budget was already in surplus. Aid flows increased in each year from 1985 to 1989. There was a substantial build-up of international reserves between 1983 and 1986; they declined in 1987 and 1988 but picked up again in 1989. Thus the current account deficit inclusive of official transfers decreased between 1985 and 1989.

However, from 1989 certain indicators suggest that the liberalization programme was becoming payments-incompatible. The real exchange rate appreciated in 1990 and 1991. This has been explained as a Dutch Disease effect arising from the inflow of external resources to finance government spending (Younger, 1992). For a full discussion see Chapters 1 and 10. The current account deficit began to rise significantly and continued to do so until 1993. The payments incompatibility was accommodated by the continued inflow of grants that allowed the current account deficit to be lower than it otherwise would have been.

Fiscal incompatibility occurs if trade liberalization reduces trade and total revenue. The liberalization will be reversed if there are no immediate alternative sources of revenue. The response to the emergence of fiscal incompatibility could be either to increase trade taxes to their pre-liberalization level or to run a budget deficit which, if financed by borrowing from the banking system, would increase money supply and worsen the balance of payments position.

The liberalization was fiscally compatible between 1983 and 1989. Real government revenues and real international trade revenues increased continuously. Analysis of the impact of the trade liberalization on government revenues found that it had an expansionary effect between 1984 and 1986, despite the decline in tariff schedules. This was because of rising import volumes and the depreciating exchange rate. Further reduction in tariff rates and sales taxes in 1988 and 1990 was accompanied by an increase in nominal revenues. The exchange rate adjustments have been important in ensuring that revenues did not decline with liberalization. Apart from the exchange rate effects, the widening of the tax base and the reduction in dependence on trade taxes as a source of revenue made possible a reduction in tariff rates without incurring severe fiscal problems.

Since 1990, although real government revenues have also been rising, they have also been fluctuating, i.e. rising in one year and falling in the next. The revenue-GDP ratio has followed a similar pattern. Real revenues from international trade hardly changed between 1990 and 1994 although they remained below the 1989 values. This is because of the fall in real cocoa export duties due to the decline in world cocoa prices.

The response to the emerging macroeconomic incompatibility since 1990 has not been to re-introduce import licensing, but to introduce special taxes. Protective duties were introduced in the 1990 budget although their rates were later reduced. Specific taxes were introduced in 1994 to create a level playing field for some firms. In 1995 the sales tax was replaced by the value added tax, and the rate increased from 15% to 17.5% as a revenue generating measure. However, the sales tax had to be re-introduced because of problems in implementing the VAT, and because of its effect on the price level and the failure to increase revenues significantly.

Despite the tax increases, many of which were domestic taxes, there have been no major policy reversals in the trade liberalization programme. This is largely because of the continuing inflow of foreign resources, though not always at the rate expected by government. If government spending is not controlled, the need to curb budgetary deficits and emerging balance of payments deficits will require increases in international trade taxes. This would imply some reversal of the trade liberalization programme. It might benefit the import-substituting sector but would undermine the policy of export promotion unless effective countervailing policies are introduced.

The discussion has so far focused on issues of policy compatibility. Another aspect of particular relevance is whether trade and exchange rate policy alone is adequate to deal with the performance of the external trade sector. The answer has to be in the negative. The creation of an environment conducive to the expansion of the tradeable goods sector is critical. Trade and exchange rate policies, monetary and fiscal policies, sectoral policy and the state of the physical infrastructure are necessary ingredients in creating a favourable environment for the production of tradeables. There is a debate as to whether trade liberalization will encourage exporting. It can do so if quantitative restrictions are lifted, thus easing any bottlenecks in the supply of imported inputs, if tariffs on imported inputs used in the production of exports are reduced, and if that reduction improves the prices of exports relative to non-tradeables. If the liberalization is accompanied by a depreciation of the exchange rate this should also encourage exporting. Liberalization will most likely encourage an increase in export orientation, i.e. the share of output sold abroad. It will not necessarily cause an increase in the productive capacity of the tradeables sector. A liberalized regime exposes the importables sector to international competition. If anything, trade liberalization can trigger a collapse of enterprises especially within the import-substituting sector. The probability of this happening is greater the more dependent the existence of these enterprises is on high protective barriers. Ghana's production base, particularly in the manufacturing sector, was badly battered during the period of economic controls. The mining sector was similarly affected, but has been able to bounce back because of the substantial inflows of loans and foreign direct investment to that sector. The manufacturing sector has not been so privileged.

In addition to the reduction in the bias in the trade regime against exporting, enterprises in the manufacturing and agricultural sectors will require assistance (financial and technical) to enable them respond to the new incentive structure. The existence of non-price constraints (for example, the high cost of capital and obsolete machines) can explain the dissatisfaction expressed by enterprises in the import-substituting sector against the trade liberalization programme. Such dissatisfaction can be another source of pressure on policy-makers to reverse the liberalization process. These non-price constraints can also partly explain the limited export diversification that has occurred.

Trade controls will not solve the problem faced by producers in the current liberalized regime. A controlled trade regime tends to encourage the production of importables and discourage exportables. This was Ghana's experience prior to 1983. During a controlled regime deliberate effort needs to be made to counteract the disincentive to exporting. The import-substituting phase can be viewed as a preliminary stage before a country embarks on an export promotion programme as manufacturing capacity is created. Unfortunately this was not Ghana's experience. The period of trade controls left the productive base of its tradeable goods sector bereft of the capacity to compete. The difficulties of the past in managing a controlled regime suggest that Ghana should not go down that path again. As it is a signatory to the agreement of the World Trade Organization, there is unlikely to be much leeway for the re-introduction of controls.

4.   Conclusions and Lessons for the Future

Several lessons emerge from Ghana's experience. The first is that the performance of the export sector is crucial for any import-dependent developing country such as Ghana. Policies to deal with balance of payments problems will not succeed in the long run if the focus is on constraining import demand rather than on managing imports within the context of an export expansion programme.

In import-dependent developing economies with a narrow export base, an exchange rate policy that prevents appreciation of the real rate is necessary to address balance of payments issues. In the period prior to 1983 not enough importance was given to the role of the real exchange rate in providing incentives to the production of tradeables. The difference in exchange rate policy between the two periods and the contrasting performance of exports attest to the importance of the exchange rate.

The extent to which any set of policies will be achieved and an appropriate set of instruments chosen to achieve those objectives depends upon whether policy objectives conflict with one another. If there are conflicts among policy objectives it is likely that none will be achieved because of a wrong assignment of instruments. This occurred in Ghana during the 1970s when three objectives, namely, strengthening the trade balance, changing the structure of production and realizing revenue, were pursued using trade policy instruments. Since the launching of the ERP in 1983, the conflict of objectives has been minimized with focus placed on the objective of stimulating exports. However, in the 1990s incompatibility of objectives has again re-emerged. Expansionary fiscal and monetary policies have placed pressure on the balance of payments making import liberalization balance of payments incompatible as well as placing pressure on the government budget making import liberalization through reduced tariffs fiscally incompatible. However, to date fiscal and balance of payments incompatibility has been accommodated by donor inflows meaning that a major reversal of trade liberalization has not occurred. Whether such a situation is sustainable given volatility in donor grants remains an open question.

The trade liberalization of the ERP was gradually implemented in three phases. Export volumes increased but due to the decline in world gold and cocoa prices export value growth was disappointing. Along with the surge in imports this created a balance of trade deficit. There was also limited progress with export and market diversification although in the mid-1990s there was some improvement.

Trade and exchange rate policies are necessary but not sufficient to influence the volume of imports and exports. The experience of the 1970s shows that trade controls can reduce export and import volumes. The reverse does not hold, however. The experience of the 1980s and 1990s so far shows that increases in export and import volumes require more than just a liberalization of the trade regime. The success of trade liberalization also depends on the existence of complementary policies to help the tradeable goods sector respond to the new liberalized regime, which it cannot do if it is faced with capacity constraints. Removing import restrictions and reducing tariff rates are not sufficient to assist enterprises in overcoming these problems. The potency of the trade liberalization to stimulate the tradeables goods sector will be enhanced by supportive fiscal, monetary, sectoral and investment policies.

The expansion of the tradeables sector is critical because the continued flow of external financial resources cannot be guaranteed. The economic reform programme, including import liberalization, has been sustained largely by these flows particularly in the early years of the programme. In order to rid Ghana of the plague of the foreign-exchange constraint, it is essential that it should be able to generate a growing proportion of its foreign-exchange requirements.

References

Baah-Nuakoh, A., Jebuni, C. D., Oduro, A. D. and Asante, Y. (1996) *Exporting Manufactures from Ghana: Is Adjustment Enough?* London: Overseas Development Institute.

Balassa, B. (1978) 'Export Incentives and Export Performance in Developing Countries: A Comparative Analysis', *Weltwirtschaftliches Archiv,* Vol. 114.

Bhagwati, J. D. (1968) *The Theory and Practice of Commercial Policy Departures from Unified Exchange Rates.* International Finance Section, Princeton University, Princeton, NJ.

Chenery, H. and Strout, A. M. (1966) 'Foreign Assistance and Economic Development', *America Economic Review,* Vol. 56.

Clements, K.W. and Sjaastad, L.A. (1984) *How Protection Taxes Exports.* London: Trade Policy Research Centre.

ISSER *The State of the Ghanaian Economy.* ISSER, University of Ghana, Legon (various issues).

Jebuni, C. D., Oduro, A. D., Asante, Y. and Tsikata, G. K. (1992) *Diversifying Exports. The Supply Response of Non-Traditional Exports to Ghana's Economic Recovery Programme.* London: Overseas Development Institute/University of Ghana.

Jebuni, C. D., Oduro, A. D. and Tutu, K. A. (1994) 'Trade and Payments Regime and the Balance of Payments in Ghana', *World Development* Vol. 22, No. 8.

Krueger, A. (1978) *Liberalisation Attempts and Consequences.* New York: National Bureau of Economic Research.

Oyejide, T. A. (1986) *The Effects of Trade and Exchange Rate Policies on Agriculture in Nigeria.* Research Report No. 55. Washington, DC: International Food Policy Research Institute.

Prebisch, R (1959) 'Commercial Policy in the Underdeveloped Countries', *American Economic Review Papers and Proceedings* Vol. 49.

Republic of Ghana (1973) *Budget Statement,* Accra.

Republic of Ghana (1977) *Five Year Development Plan for the Period 1975/76-1979/80,* Part I. Accra: Government Printer.

Republic of Ghana (1983) *Statement of the Economic Recovery Programme.* Accra: Government Printer.

Tutu, K. A. and Oduro, A. D. (forthcoming) *Trade Liberalisation in Ghana.*

Younger, S. D. (1992) 'Aid and the Dutch Disease: Macroeconomic Management when Everybody Loves You', *World Development,* Vol. 20, No.11: 1587–97.

10 Aid, Debt & Growth

JANE HARRIGAN
& STEPHEN YOUNGER*

1. Introduction

Do foreign capital flows promote economic growth in developing countries? This question is the subject of a long-running debate in the economics profession, and we revisit it for the case of Ghana in this chapter. In theory, it is sensible to consider the effects of public capital flows, primarily aid, as distinct from private flows. The motivations for the two are quite different, so one might well expect their effects to differ as well. Nevertheless, the bulk of the chapter considers only aid flows, as private capital flows have been extremely limited in Ghana. We do, however, extend the standard discussion of aid flows to the question of Ghana's debt, the vast majority of which has resulted from aid flows, and its implications for economic growth.

The early logic of foreign aid was straightforward: poor countries lack capital, so if wealthy countries transfer capital to them, they should grow out of poverty. For a variety of complex political-economic reasons, the wealthy countries provided us with the possibility to test this proposition empirically. Since the 1950s, net aid flows to developing countries have grown from near zero to $50-60 billion per year in the 1990s. Yet a remarkably wide range of economic analyses, reviewed in section 2, have produced ambiguous results as to whether aid has a positive impact on economic growth in the recipient countries.

How have these considerations played themselves out in Ghana? For many years and for reasons discussed in section 3, Ghana received average to below-average aid flows. By the early 1980s, it had become something of a pariah, a country where most donors had little hope that aid monies could promote economic development. Yet a remarkable reversal of economic policies, beginning with the Economic Recovery Programme (ERP) launched in 1983, brought a flood of aid in the 1980s and 1990s, reaching as much as $50.00 per capita (1987 US$). Both Ghanaians and donors should ask themselves, has this aid done any good? In the light of the theory that follows, we should be careful to define what we mean by 'any good'. In the worst of cases (from the donors' perspective), the aid has allowed Ghanaians to increase their consumption, and that may be a laudable result, depending on whose consumption rose. In addition, aid for specific development projects, such as immunization programmes, may well have improved social welfare. But the subject of this chapter is more demanding: has the aid increased economic growth? After laying out a theoretical framework in section 2, we try to answer this question in the case

*We are grateful for comments received from Tony Killick, Ernest Aryeetey, Martin Brownbridge and the participants at the authors' conference held in Accra, April 24–25, 1997.

of Ghana in section 3. Section 4 reviews the aid strategies of Ghana's principal donors and explores some of the problems Ghana has encountered in implementing aid-funded projects. Section 5 asks whether aid has improved social welfare in Ghana, which many would argue is the major aim of aid flows. Section 6 then considers the question of the impact of Ghana's growing external debt on future growth. The results are not unequivocal, but there is much to be learned from the particular circumstances found in Ghana's experience.

2.   Aid Flows and Growth: General Considerations

Theory

Economists' thinking about economic growth has changed considerably over the past 40 years. A brief review of this thinking helps fix ideas for our interpretation of capital flows and growth in Ghana. Early models of economic growth concentrated on factor accumulation. The most influential of these is due to Solow (1956). In the Solow model, output is a function of labour and capital, so economic growth depends on the accumulation of these inputs. Since we are usually more concerned with growth in output per capita than output itself, the key factor is capital. Economies that accumulate capital rapidly, i.e. have high saving and investment rates, will have rapid per capita output growth. The role of foreign capital flows, including aid, is straightforward in this model: by adding to the pool of savings, foreign capital allows a higher investment rate (Rosenstein-Rodan 1961). Thus, there should be a direct link between such flows and growth (at least in the short to medium term in the case of the Solow model).

The simplicity of this argument was and continues to be persuasive in development economics, yet it is subject to criticism on several counts. First, the Solow model assumes that the savings rate is exogenous and that the aid flows go to savings. In practice, there is reason to believe that the recipient economy may alter its savings rate in response to the aid flows. If we consider a simple Ramsey model in which the savings rate is endogenous, for example, the optimal response of a recipient country to a permanent increase in aid flows is to reduce its own savings proportionately (Blanchard and Fischer, 1989). That is because, at the optimum, the marginal product of capital should equal the internal discount rate, and the flow of aid cannot change either of these. Thus, it is not optimal to accumulate more capital despite the foreign saving, so the domestic economy offsets it by reducing its own savings by the same amount as the aid flow, yielding no change in GDP (but an increase in consumption equal to the aid flow).

In practice, there are two ways in which the foreign savings could be diverted to consumption. The simplest is that the recipient government spends the funds for something other than their intended use, e.g. it uses the aid funds to pay salaries rather than construct a road, so increasing consumption rather than investment. A second possibility is that the government funds the intended investment project, but reduces capital spending out of its own funds, so that the capital stock does not increase as much as if the government had not reacted to the aid flow. Mosley *et al.* (1987) call this the 'fungibility' problem. In addition, even if the government's behaviour does not counteract the effect of the aid flow, there may be general equilibrium effects that do so. This has been called the 'Dutch Disease' problem in the case of the real exchange rate, and 'crowding out' in the case of the capital markets. In the Dutch Disease, aid flows increase the supply of foreign exchange which appreciates the real exchange rate. This, in turn, discourages export production, which may have external benefits not associated with the aid. As for crowding out, aid flows usually go to governments, so they permit an expansion of the public sector, *ceterus paribus*. But if the public sector grows, it must absorb resources that otherwise would have gone to other sectors: it must crowd them out. If this is effected through tight monetary policy, it may crowd out investment, again reducing the intended impact of the aid flow on the capital stock (Younger, 1992).[1]

---

[1] This crowding-out effect only has a negative effect on growth if it is assumed that the public sector is a less efficient investor than the private sector. Also, especially in low income economies, increased public investment, e.g. in infrastructure, may 'crowd-in' private investment (Taylor, 1993).

Even if the capital flows increase the savings and investment rate, there are further reasons why they may not lead to a permanent increase in economic growth. The projects that the aid finances may have low rates of return so that the intended increase in productive capital is less than the value of the aid. Also, even if the gross aid flows are maintained, the net flow may fall if the aid comes in the form of loans rather than grants. In this case, a past history of aid flows increases the recipient's debt burden. There is a large literature on the potential for foreign debt to discourage investment in a debtor country (Krugman, 1988; Bulow and Rogoff, 1991), but it is almost exclusively concerned with commercial bank credits rather than debt to multilateral agencies or other governments. The aid literature, on the other hand, mostly ignores the debt problem, implicitly assuming that aid flows are grants rather than loans. While it is true that much official capital has a substantial grant element, it is rarely 100% grant, and it is sometimes close to commercial terms (in the case of IMF stand-by agreements, for example). Thus, today's aid flows can be tomorrow's debt burden, presenting a potential conflict between more growth today versus less tomorrow.

Finally, there is the declining marginal product of capital. If an economy accumulates capital faster than labour (which it must do to increase output per capita in the Solow model), the marginal product of capital declines, reducing the amount of extra growth that the economy gets for each extra unit of savings. In the long run, this problem is sufficiently severe that a higher savings rate will not produce any extra growth. Eventually, the extra capital that the higher savings rate produces is only just sufficient to keep capital's growth rate equal to labour's growth plus depreciation, so that growth per capita ceases. This simple observation has spawned a huge new literature on endogenous economic growth models, starting with Romer (1986) and Lucas (1988). These models are all firmly neoclassical. Like the Solow model, production functions are concave (usually with constant returns to scale); agents optimize; and markets clear. Nevertheless, each model adds some mechanism by which a steady accumulation of capital does *not* erode its marginal product. An early mechanism was 'learning-by-doing'. As the physical capital accumulates, workers learn how to work with it and thus improve their own productivity (or human capital). The increased productivity of labour can give each new unit of capital enough effective labour units to work with for its marginal product not to decline. As a result, output per capita can grow indefinitely. More recent models make technological progress a function of the stock of capital by arguing that the existing stock represents the economy's accumulated experience at innovation, and such innovation is aided by experience. That is, innovation breeds further innovation, and does so increasingly efficiently. This, too, leads to a result where the economy can accumulate capital without reducing its marginal product. Another possibility is that the savings rate is endogenous and dependent on aid flows or some factor that they can influence. Suppose that an extremely poor economy cannot save because it must dedicate all of its output to consumption to survive. Then an amount of aid sufficient to raise the equilibrium income per capita could allow domestic residents to begin saving, and this would start a process of self-sustained growth.

The 'new' growth economics is abstract and thus more difficult to relate directly to aid flows, but it does suggest new mechanisms for sustained economic growth that are consistent with market-clearing economics. In general, these models lead us to ask: to what extent has the physical capital associated with aid flows helped recipient countries

(i) to improve their human capital through learning-by-doing;
(ii) to improve the state of their technology through improved innovation; or
(iii) to improve their domestic savings rate.[2]

---

[2] Younger (1992) argues that these ideas provide another reason for a lack of correlation between programme aid and growth. Programme aid provides balance of payments support (foreign exchange) to the domestic economy. If the exchange rate is market-determined then the aid flow will cause it to appreciate, thus reducing incentives for exports, producing a Dutch Disease problem. If, in turn, production for export is an important mechanism for learning-by-doing and technological innovation, then the aid flow may reduce the positive externality and thus the possibility for long-term growth.

Developing countries may never reach the steady-state long-run equilibrium of the Solow model or the transition period might be very long. Both the Solow model and the new endogenous growth models are equilibrium models, in the sense that prices clear markets continuously. By contrast, there is a disequilibrium tradition in macroeconomic modelling for developing countries that assumes that important markets do not clear. The best known of these is the Two Gap Model (Chenery and Strout, 1966). They hypothesize that a developing country may face a savings-investment gap, where domestic saving is inadequate to finance the optimal level of investment, or a foreign-exchange gap, where the earning of foreign exchange is inadequate to finance the level of imports needed for investment activities. Foreign aid can help to bridge either of these two gaps because it represents savings and usually comes in the form of foreign exchange. This can spur investment and growth, and may not be subject to the declining marginal product of capital that is so important in the Solow model, because in the presence of non-market clearing, either savings or foreign exchange are rationed, and aid that alleviates this rationing will not drive down the equilibrium marginal product of capital.

Empirical Results: Cross-country Studies

At the same time that the theoretical endogenous growth literature has pushed beyond the traditional Solow model, another empirical literature has emerged to examine the determinants of economic growth in the context of the Solow model (Sala-i-Martin, 1994 and Levine and Renelt, 1992, survey this literature). Even though there are now hundreds of empirical papers on economic growth, there are relatively few that focus on foreign aid. Two papers by Boone (1995, 1996) generated an important debate. Boone includes the ratios of aid flows (as calculated by the OECD) to GDP as one of the independent variables in his growth equation. Thus, his work applies directly to this chapter: what is the relationship between aid flows and growth? His study, like all the growth regressions, uses a cross-section of many countries, so the results relate to Ghana only in so far as it is a 'typical' developing country. But they are striking. First, Boone (1995) finds no relation between aid flows and either the savings rate (foreign plus domestic savings over GDP) or economic growth. This result is consistent with earlier, less econometrically sophisticated empirical results in Mosley *et al.* (1987), Griffin (1970), and Weisskopf (1972), all of which found little impact of aid on growth or capital accumulation. Further, Boone (1996) finds that the coefficient on aid flows in a reduced form equation for investment over GDP is zero and for consumption over GDP is one, suggesting that aid flows go entirely into consumption, regardless of the aid's stated purposes. Again, these results are similar to the earlier empirical results of Griffin (1970) and Mosley *et al.* (1987). This suggests that domestic actors, most importantly the government, alter their behaviour in response to the aid flow such that its net impact is to increase consumption rather than savings or investment.

It is important to note, however, that there are also a number of empirical studies which find a positive correlation between aid and growth (Papnek, 1973; Dowling and Hiemenz, 1983; Gupta and Islam, 1983; Mosley *et al.*, 1992; Mosley, 1995). Also, all of the cross-country empirical studies have been subjected to considerable methodological criticism.[3]

Two papers written in response to Boone also suggest that there may be important exceptions to his results. Mosley (1995) finds that aid has had a significant impact on growth rates in some very poor countries. He hypothesizes that these governments have sufficiently small tax bases and large debt burdens that 'fungibility' is not an option for them: they do not have enough domestically financed resources to offset the donors' expenditures on investment projects. This is consistent with Boone's (1995) result for the 14 poorest countries in his sample, which also

---

[3] For a survey of the criticisms see White, 1992. Problems include: measurement difficulties; equation specification errors including simultaneity bias; and the underlying assumption of a homogeneous structure that is being estimated, e.g. the parameters of the model are assumed to be identical across the sample of countries.

show a positive correlation between aid and growth. Thus, aid to governments with little room to manoeuvre may have the desired impact on growth. Burnside and Dollar (1997) examine a different exception. They find that even though aid flows in general are not correlated with growth, aid flows to countries with sound macroeconomic policies do have a positive effect.

Because all of the above literature is based on cross-country regressions, it is impossible to apply it directly to the case of Ghana, except in so far as Ghana is a typical country in the sample. But the general observations help as we try to interpret Ghana's experience with aid and growth in the following section. This interpretation must be set against the background knowledge that theory remains divided regarding the impact of aid on growth, whilst empirical evidence, producing diverse and varied results, is ambiguous.

3. Ghana's Experience with Aid, Capital Flows, and Growth

Foreign Aid and Economic Growth
Formal statistical analysis of the relationship between aid flows and economic performance is difficult for a single country. Time series data are more likely to pick up the business cycle induced by a change in an exogenous variable than the long-term relationship that is of greater interest.[4] For the record, Table 10.1 shows the time series for aid flows and Tables 1.1 and 1.2 in Chapter 1 show the growth of GDP. There is no apparent relationship between these variables. The correlation coefficients between real GDP growth and aid flows divided by GDP are positive (0.12) but insignificantly different from zero.[5]

More generally, it would be difficult to argue that Ghana ever experienced self-sustained economic growth during any period after independence and before the ERP was launched in 1983. On average, growth in per capita GDP was –1.5% between 1960 and 1983. Growth was slightly positive during the 1960s (0.6% per capita), but fell to –1.8% per capita for the 1970s. While there were brief periods of more rapid growth, they were due to either business cycle perturbations or recoveries from drought. In the early 1960s, for example, growth was moderate, but it was driven by unsustainable public expenditures which ended in a balance of payments and debt crisis in 1965 and a subsequent recession. Growth briefly picked up again with the Busia government in 1969, again spurred by greater public spending and high international cocoa prices, but this also proved short-lived, ending with the 1972 balance of payments crisis and the Acheampong coup. From that year until the ERP, the economy shrank in many years. Only after 1984 has the economy grown steadily in per capita terms, albeit at a moderate pace of 4 to 5% per year, or 2% per capita. It is also true that aid flows have been substantially higher than normal in the ERP period, a fact that drives the positive correlation noted above. Indeed, the correlation between aid flows and growth is much higher, 0.322, for the period 1983–94 than for the entire post-independence period.[6] Whether or not this correlation reflects causation is an important point, to which we return below.

While growth was disappointing prior to 1983, aid flows have varied over time, with little apparent impact on growth, except for the most recent decade. Table 10.1 shows official development assistance as a share of GDP and in constant US$ per capita for Ghana, sub-Saharan Africa (excluding Nigeria and South Africa), and low-income developing countries in general. Until the mid-1960s, aid flows were relatively unimportant in Ghana. There was little interest in aid on the part of both Ghanaians and potential financiers. On the Ghanaian side, the Nkrumah government was suspicious of the mostly likely donors, Britain and the United States, an under-

---

[4] That is why the empirical studies on economic growth use cross-section data.
[5] Some authors argue that the relevant correlation is between changes in aid flows and growth, because that eliminates the impact of 'persistent' aid. This correlation is actually negative for Ghana, –0.018, though not significantly different from zero.
[6] Though it is still not significantly different from zero.

Table 10.1   Official Development Assistance to Ghana, sub-Saharan Africa, and Low Income LDCs, 1960–94

Year	ODA per capita (1987 US$)			ODA/GDP (%)		
	Ghana	Sub-Saharan Africa	Low-Income LDCs	Ghana	Sub-Saharan Africa	Low-Income LDCs
1960	1.44	5.42	5.67	0.002	0.012	0.028
1961	1.40	7.79	6.87	0.002	0.017	0.037
1962	2.72	8.92	7.06	0.004	0.019	0.038
1963	7.93	8.67	7.58	0.012	0.016	0.038
1964	8.55	12.02	7.23	0.012	0.024	0.033
1965	18.73	13.61	7.41	0.022	0.025	0.032
1966	20.88	12.23	6.89	0.025	0.022	0.031
1967	17.03	12.36	7.29	0.026	0.023	0.034
1968	18.83	8.86	5.63	0.031	0.016	0.027
1969	24.28	11.12	6.10	0.036	0.020	0.028
1970	19.10	10.59	6.40	0.027	0.019	0.027
1971	17.40	11.44	6.85	0.023	0.020	0.028
1972	16.79	11.59	6.79	0.028	0.019	0.028
1973	10.05	12.06	7.63	0.017	0.018	0.030
1974	7.43	14.27	8.37	0.013	0.021	0.035
1975	22.56	21.08	9.42	0.045	0.032	0.040
1976	10.76	18.86	8.33	0.023	0.030	0.038
1977	14.16	20.25	8.25	0.029	0.031	0.035
1978	16.17	24.84	10.25	0.031	0.036	0.047
1979	20.93	27.55	10.16	0.042	0.040	0.046
1980	20.48	27.41	10.43	0.043	0.037	0.046
1981	13.67	24.44	9.14	0.034	0.037	0.045
1982	12.57	24.25	8.04	0.035	0.040	0.041
1983	9.35	22.31	7.58	0.027	0.038	0.037
1984	17.22	23.54	7.57	0.049	0.045	0.037
1985	15.22	25.43	7.95	0.044	0.054	0.039
1986	27.89	30.29	9.42	0.063	0.057	0.046
1987	30.21	33.34	9.92	0.081	0.058	0.050
1988	39.32	35.33	10.10	0.111	0.063	0.051
1989	45.18	34.53	9.82	0.137	0.065	0.051
1990	33.11	33.76	10.38	0.090	0.062	0.053
1991	49.79	33.49	11.59	0.125	0.062	0.062
1992	33.91	34.82	11.54	0.090	0.065	0.061
1993	32.75	30.73	10.34	0.102	0.063	0.055
1994	27.83	32.59	10.81	0.069	0.070	0.051

Note: [a] Data for sub-Saharan Africa exclude Nigeria and South Africa.

standable position, given the country's recent emergence from colonial rule. What's more, the new nation had inherited substantial foreign-exchange reserves, little debt, and a small public sector from the colonial government, so the needs for foreign exchange and budgetary support were limited, at least until the 1961 balance of payments crisis. After 1961, there was more interest on the part of the Ghanaians in attracting foreign aid, but by that time, the government's increasingly strident criticism of Britain and the US put off major Western donors. Nkrumah did attract some support from the Eastern bloc, but Krassowski (1974) reports that relations between the CPP government and Russian advisers soured early on in the programme, limiting disbursements.[7]

Aid flows increased in the second half of the 1960s and as a share of GDP exceeded shares for low-income developing countries and sub-Saharan Africa (Table 10.1). The NLC government that ousted Nkrumah in 1966 showed itself to be more favourable to foreign interests. It agreed to reschedule the substantial medium-term debts that the CPP government had accumulated. It also signed an agreement with the IMF in response to the balance of payments crisis in 1965/6, agreeing to devalue the cedi and rein in public expenditures. These measures, along with a less belligerent rhetoric, brought increased foreign assistance, especially programme aid to support the balance of payments. Yet this aid was not able to overcome the recessionary effects of the policy changes, particularly reduced public spending, so that this period was one of increasing aid flows and stagnant growth. One possible explanation for the lack of impact is the allocation of a significant amount of the aid flows to clearing commercial credits and arrears following the debt crisis of 1965/6.

The 1970s were an interesting if discouraging period in Ghana. More recent experience with policy-based lending has made us associate Washington-style reform with increased aid flows, yet that correlation clearly fails in the 1970s in Ghana. That decade saw consistent application of bad economic policies in Ghana and correspondingly poor economic performance. But even though aid flows declined in the first part of the decade, the second half brought a more than compensating increase. Three different factors seem to be behind this phenomenon, all but one of which were global in scope. First, the world became more interested in Africa for geo-political reasons. Competition between the East and West for Africa's loyalty became more pronounced in this period. Many newly independent countries began to distance themselves from the colonial powers, and the perceived value of Africa's mineral resources rose with the post-OPEC commodity price booms. Secondly, donors began to recognize the severity of Africa's poverty relative to other developing countries and responded with increased aid flows. (Table 10.1 shows that aid flows per capita grew more rapidly in Africa, excluding Nigeria and South Africa, than in all low-income developing countries from 1974 onward.) Ghana appears to have benefitted from this general trend toward greater assistance to Africa. Official development assistance (ODA) as a share of Ghana's GDP rose in the second half of the 1970s. However, Ghana had still not caught up with many other developing countries in terms of aid flows. Aid as a share of GDP remained below the shares for low-income LDCs and for sub-Saharan Africa for most of the period, whilst ODA per capita was significantly below that for sub-Saharan Africa (Table 10.1). Thirdly, the development community began to lose confidence in economic growth as the engine for poverty reduction and shifted its emphasis towards more direct interventions to satisfy basic human needs. This weakened the link between good economic policy and aid flows to some extent.

---

[7] The one exception to this general pattern was the Volta River Project partly funded by the World Bank, Britain and the US with $US 75 m. in aid flows, the principal product of which was the dam on the Volta River at Akosombo. The project was profitable (Killick, 1978; Krassowski, 1974) but it was an enclave project. This highlights the argument of the new growth economics: a one-off investment, even if profitable, does not lead to long-term growth if it does not foster some behaviour or externality that offsets the falling marginal product of capital. Enclave investments like the Volta project do not have such a mechanism.

Political factors particular to Ghana also influenced aid flows during the decade. Some of the aid flows that Ghana received during the NLC government, particularly credits from the IMF, and rescheduled medium-term debts began to fall due in the early 1970s, reducing the net flow of resources. More importantly, the Acheampong government's decision to repudiate some of Ghana's commercial debts on the grounds that they were contracted irregularly brought a sharp response from bilateral donors in 1973 and 1974.[8] This was later compensated by a one-off increase in assistance in 1975 when Ghana agreed to yet another rescheduling that honoured the doubtful debts, but again, those funds probably benefitted the commercial creditors much more than Ghana. Nevertheless, the agreement does appear to have cleared the way for Ghana's participation in the global increase in aid flows to Africa, so that by the end of the decade per capita aid was again at the levels of the late 1960s. This does not appear to have helped promote economic growth, however, as the economy continued its slide. What's more, the aid came more as multilateral loans than grants, so foreign debts grew substantially, from US\$895 m. in 1975 to US\$1,407 m. in 1980 (see Table 10.4). Despite a low debt-service ratio, Ghana faced difficulties servicing debt by the end of the 1970s. In 1979 arrears on payments of short-term loans amounted to US \$432 m. and the international financial institutions began to refuse further credit. As the macro crisis of the late 1970s and early 1980s intensified, large overall balance of payments deficits were incurred, gross official reserves were depleted and external payments arrears continued to accumulate, reaching US \$577 m. by the end of 1982, equivalent to over 90% of export earnings. Between 1973 and 1983 Ghana's sources of external financing also narrowed to a small number of donors, the World Bank in particular.

The early 1980s brought a gradual reduction in the flow of aid to developing countries and to Africa, and this change was much more accentuated in Ghana (Table 10.1). To some extent, the political turmoil of the time and the strident nationalism of the Rawlings governments (pre-ERP) put donors off. More importantly, the gravity of the economic and social collapse and the inability of the public sector to perform even its most basic functions made it seem that any money spent in Ghana would be wasted. Unlike earlier periods, there was a correlation between growth and aid flows at this time, but it is difficult to believe that it was declining aid causing declining growth rather than the other way around, or more precisely, that the factors that caused the economic crisis also caused donors to lose hope for Ghana.

The same despair that affected potential donors also began to influence Ghanaian policy-makers who slowly came to accept the necessity of a radical change in economic policy, if only to get access to foreign financing. With the 1981-83 drought driving the economy to unimaginable lows, the PNDC agreed to an IMF programme that included all the typical Washington policies, including a massive devaluation and a tightening of the budget deficit (see Chapter 1 of this volume). Unlike many other adjusting countries, Ghana persisted with these policies, intensifying its efforts to liberalize the economy and maintaining a strict fiscal discipline for the remainder of the decade. There is a debate about the effectiveness of these policies in terms of the economy's performance, but it is clearly true that their pursuit made Ghana something of a favourite among donors. By the end of the 1980s, aid flows had increased substantially, to the point where Ghana was receiving significantly more aid per capita and as a proportion of GDP than the average for other developing countries in Africa and elsewhere (Table 10.1). At the same time, economic growth has recovered and remained consistently positive for the first time since the early 1960s. The question is, does this correlation reflect causation? Did the aid flows cause the growth, either entirely or in part?

Based on the theoretical discussion in section 2, there are several reasons to believe that increased aid flows have had a positive impact on growth in Ghana, at least during the early years of the ERP. One is that programme aid flows were attached to conditions requiring important improvements in economic policy (see Chapter 1), a point that we return to below. More

---

[8] The commercial creditors had not lent any fresh funds to Ghana since the 1965 crisis.

directly, at the beginning of the ERP, neither fungibility nor Dutch Disease were probably problems for the aid flows. Recall that the main problem with fungibility is that, in response to an aid flow intended to finance an investment, the government reduces its own investment spending and increases public consumption. In the case of Ghana, government spending had dropped to extremely low levels in the early 1980s and capital spending had almost disappeared.[9] Thus the government could not have reduced it in response to increased aid flows.

Furthermore, both the foreign exchange and the capital markets were strictly rationed at the time the ERP began, so the additional availability of foreign exchange and savings probably served only to relieve the rationing, with little effect on market prices (the exchange and interest rates), thus avoiding any Dutch Disease or crowding-out problems. Moreover, the rationing of foreign exchange and funds for investment also implies that some sort of disequilibrium model (e.g. the two-gap model) was appropriate for the time. When foreign exchange or capital are not rationed by price, it is possible to increase their supply without reducing their marginal product, so the Solow calculus did not apply either. Thus, even though it is difficult to prove to a sceptic, it seems entirely plausible that the aid flows which came at the beginning of the ERP contributed to the initial economic recovery by filling substantial gaps in foreign exchange and capital availability. This is consistent with the types of aid that Ghana received at the time, most of which supported the reconstruction of basic infrastructure and imports of spare parts and capital equipment necessary to rehabilitate a significant portion of the capital stock. Certainly the share of capital spending in the government budget and in GDP (see Table 6.1, Chapter 6) and the share of total investment to GDP (Table 1.2, Chapter 1) rose substantially in the first years of the ERP, by amounts roughly equal to the increased flow of foreign capital, suggesting that, in Ghana's case, increased foreign savings did not lead to a reduction in domestic savings, contrary to Mosley *et al.'s* (1987) findings for developing countries in general, but consistent with both Boone's (1995) and Mosley's (1995) results for poor countries or highly constrained governments.

By the late 1980s and early 1990s, however, the situation had changed considerably. By then, the government had made most of the highest return public investments, the infrastructure had been rehabilitated and markets were working relatively well again. More importantly, liberalization of the foreign-exchange market and the financial markets meant that prices now rationed the markets rather than government controls, so the two-gap view of foreign-exchange flows was no longer appropriate. Instead, the substantial flows of foreign funds to Ghana were appreciating the real exchange rate, reducing incentives for exporters. Furthermore, the government's attempt to sterilize the monetary effects of substantial programme aid flows through tight credit ceilings and (later) 'mopping up' open market operations made domestic credit to the private sector scarce, thus limiting investment.[10] Thus, once the key markets were functioning normally, the Dutch Disease problem of foreign aid cited by Mosley *et al.* (1987) and Younger (1992) became a reality and presented an important policy dilemma. Acceptance of continued foreign aid flows threatens to crowd out exports and private investment (if monetary policy remains tight).[11] Yet recalling the main lesson of the new growth theory, one must ask where the sort of non-convexities (e.g. learning-by-doing) that make self-sustaining growth possible are more likely to be found: in the public sector, through which virtually all aid is channelled, or in exports? This is not an easy question to answer. Obviously it depends on the quality of public expenditures, an issue that we cannot address without much better information on public activities, and on the government's ability to raise funds elsewhere for expenditures that it can make productively. For example, aid may be a better source of finance for government expenditure than taxes which are

---

[9] The small amount of recorded capital spending probably only paid salaries.
[10] As explained in Younger (1992), allowing the aid flows to increase the money supply would cause greater inflation, but would shift the burden of the crowding out to consumption rather than investment. This appears to have happened in the 1990s.
[11] This assumes full employment or bottlenecks and capacity constraints.

highly distortionary, for example import tariffs. On the other hand, the answer also depends on the extent to which production for export provides adequate possibilities for accumulation of knowledge capital and learning-by-doing. We are not aware of any evidence on this point, but the East Asian experience suggests that exports are an effective engine for growth, so that the aid flows may in fact be compromising prospects for self-sustained growth by crowding exports out.

The return of macro instability in the 1990s, in the form of real exchange rate instability, rapid money supply growth, inflation, and a return to government budget deficits (Chapter 1) has had a negative effect on aid flows which have declined as a share of GDP and in per capita terms (Table 10.1). At the same time, GDP growth rates have slowed. The slow down in donor disbursements of funds had negative effects on targeted balance of payments and government budget performance. In particular, a significant drop in commitments in 1992 signalled donor dissatisfaction with the government's inability to meet macroeconomic targets, notably the overshoot in the budget deficit in the election year, and led to balance of payments capital account problems.

Aid, Policy Reform, and Growth

One further way in which aid may influence economic growth is through its influence on economic policy. Several recent papers, including three broad reviews of aid and economic performance in Ghana (Aryeetey, 1995; Leechor, 1994; and Sowa and White, 1997), argue that aid makes good policy possible, and good policy promotes economic growth. This is consistent with the Burnside and Dollar (1997) empirical finding that aid flows to countries with sound macroeconomic policies have a positive growth effect. This argument does not fit neatly into traditional growth theory, which usually assumes that the economy is efficient and that policy does not distort this, but it is appealing in the African context, where governments have done much to thwart economic growth. Nevertheless, the reasoning raises questions about where the credit for growth lies: with the aid or the policy. If it is not the inflow of foreign capital *per se* that yields higher growth, but good policies provoked by aid, then presumably governments could choose the good policies without accepting the aid, and have just as beneficial an impact on growth. This brings us dangerously close to the argument that the main benefit of aid (in terms of economic growth) is that it buys influence with recipient governments, encouraging them to choose policies that they should have chosen anyway.[12] The argument also presents an empirical problem. Because Ghana's increased aid flows are highly correlated with improved policy, it is impossible to sort out which is actually causing the growth that we observe: the aid monies or the associated policy reform.

In any event, it seems undeniable that donors have influenced policy since 1983, in two distinct ways. First, there is conditionality attached to programme aid, which became a rapidly increasing share of aid flows to Ghana in the 1980s. This certainly prompted the initial ERP reforms, and several important policy changes since then, though one must recognize that conditions can be (and have been) circumvented. Secondly, at certain critical moments when the government has been tempted to reverse the reforms, donor willingness to supply additional funds has helped it to stay the course. In this section, we focus on the second type of influence since other chapters in this book treat the question of policy choice and growth extensively.

Ghana has faced important balance of payments problems at several times during the post-ERP period. With each crisis, there was the temptation to roll back some of the reforms, particularly those related to the foreign-exchange market and import decontrol, but the provision of aid helped prevent this. The sharp depreciation of the cedi that accompanied the advent of the auc-

---

[12] Harrigan (1988) argues that programme aid does indeed buy influence by encouraging the government to change policies which it is reluctant to change because of potential loss of political support from those powerful interest groups that will lose out due to policy reform. Hence, the relationship between donor and recipient is one of policy bargaining rather than pure policy dialogue.

tion and the fall in cocoa prices that began in the 1987/8 season are the most important examples.

Foreign loan and grant inflows provided important support to the foreign-exchange auction introduced in 1986. Foreign sources of finance for the auction increased from 40.6% in 1986 to 69.3% in 1988 (Jebuni *et al.*, 1994), easing pressure on the exchange rate, whose depreciation was (and is) controversial. Ghana also satisfied auction demand for foreign exchange at key stages by borrowing from Standard Chartered Bank, loans that would not have been possible without the expectation of future donor support.

When cocoa prices fell sharply and apparently permanently in 1988, donors moved to fill the gap left in the balance of payments, thus avoiding both strong exchange rate movements and reductions in imports. Indeed, import volume increased continuously between 1983 and 1990, much of it financed by large capital inflows in the form of both programme aid and budgetary support. By 1986 external resources, including suppliers' credits and bilateral inflows, financed 54.3% of total imports. The import liberalization programme has not, therefore, been constrained by the performance of the export sector. This contrasts with the abrupt end of the 1967–71 IMF liberalization programme following the 1971 decline in cocoa prices. It also contrasts with other countries' experiences. Martin (1993) has made an interesting comparison of Ghana's and Zambia's adjustment programmes. One of his central arguments is that more favourable levels of foreign financing helped in the success of Ghana's programme, particularly the exchange auction and import liberalization, in contrast to the disappointing outcomes of such programmes in Zambia. Another significant feature of Ghana's ERP was the government's success in fine-tuning the availability of external finance by filling temporary shortfalls with short-term bridging loans. This helped pay for oil imports, supported the foreign-exchange auction, prevented arrears to the IMF, and enabled long-term planning of imports and debt service. Ghana was able to repay these bridging loans on time mainly by using IMF funds.[13] Higher gross financial inflows to Ghana also enabled it to pay most of its debt service on schedule and to reduce arrears, in contrast to Zambia (*ibid.,* 154).

In sum, increasing donor support has helped to buffer the impact of external and policy-related shocks on the economy, thus making it easier for the government and Ghanaians in general to survive those changes without resorting to the sorts of controls that sank the economy in the 1970s. This led to a period of unusual macroeconomic stability during the 1980s. Indeed, the most striking thing about the relationship between aid flows and growth is not their correlation, but the fact that, for the first time in the country's history, growth has been steady since the mid-1980s, precisely the period when aid flows have increased. Such stability probably has a positive impact on investment decisions (Pindyck, 1991), though it has been swamped by other effects.

Another aspect of the increased aid flows has been the expansion of public spending. Between 1983 and 1991 grants to support the budget rose from being equivalent to 0.55% of domestic revenues to 10.23%, with government spending increasing in line. The overall effect of this increase is difficult to gauge. On the one hand, some of the additional spending has gone to the rehabilitation of ports, roads, and communications, the kinds of infrastructure investment that might crowd in private investment. In addition, public funding for education and health, both areas where the growth regressions suggest that increased investment leads to higher growth, have also increased. In neither case, however, have the changes been dramatic. At the same time, we have already noted that increased public expenditure combined with tight monetary policy can crowd out private investment (Jebuni *et al.*, 1994; Aryeetey, 1994). Furthermore, some of the increased expenditure has gone to items whose growth impact is doubtful, particularly civil service salary increases.

---

[13] New loans remained available even in 1987–8 when IMF and World Bank programmes were temporarily halted because programme targets could not be met in the face of declining cocoa prices.

Foreign Direct Investment and Economic Growth

Even though aid flows have been the dominant source of foreign savings in the Ghanaian economy, foreign direct investment (FDI) once played an important role. During the CPP government, the importance of FDI was roughly comparable to that of aid flows. Killick (1978) notes that Nkrumah recognized the conflict between his plans for a rapid, capital-intensive, Soviet-style industrialization drive and his own perception that Ghanaian entrepreneurs could not manage such enterprises or that, if they did, they would become too powerful. His solution to this problem was a strategy in which foreign firms would be allowed to operate large industrial enterprises, while smaller trading and manufacturing operations would be reserved for Ghanaians. Foreign investment basically followed the import substitution model, with protective tariffs allowing foreign firms to establish monopolistic conditions within the country in a pattern that was common for the times. In this regard, we should recall that Ghana was then a middle-income country, with one of the larger domestic markets in Africa, so there was good reason for foreign firms to establish themselves behind the tariff barriers.

The attraction was short-lived, however. With increasing balance of payments problems, the government prohibited repatriation of profits in 1965. While the controls had the short-run effect of increasing FDI, because companies were forced to reinvest their profits, the policy scared off many existing and potential investors. The NLC government did remove the controls, but, facing another payments crisis, the Busia government applied them again in 1970, causing another temporary spike in FDI. The Acheampong nationalizations were the final nail in the coffin, basically killing any interest in further investments in Ghana.

The other interesting aspect of FDI in Ghana is found in the 1980s. Despite the substantial policy change and the strong support of donors, foreign private investment has not returned to Ghana. Apart from the government's sale of part of Ashanti Goldfields in 1993 and 1994 to foreign mining interests, the ERP has generated very little FDI. This situation may have important implications for Ghana's long-term growth. If the key to sustained growth is learning-by-doing or expansion of the stock of knowledge capital, then developing economies have the advantage that they do not have to generate the knowledge themselves, but can simply acquire it from developed countries. This permits rapid improvements in technology, which in turn permits rapid growth. This sort of mechanism appears to have operated in the rapidly growing Asian economies. This is the advantage of FDI over aid flows: it brings improved technology along with the capital. The disadvantage is that it comes on commercial terms: investing firms expect to make a profit at market rates and expect (at some point) to repatriate it, while aid flows contain a grant element. In any event, this mechanism is sorely lacking in Ghana. Indeed, the industries where there has been foreign investment, gold mining recently or the VALCO smelter in the 1960s, are basically enclaves where the sorts of externalities that drive growth models are unlikely to operate. Thus, with the possible exception of the import-substitution investments in the early 1960s, there is little reason to believe that FDI has played a significant role in Ghana's economic growth.

4.   Aid Strategies of Principal Donors

Changes in Aid Strategies

During the late 1960s and again in the late 1970s, as aid flows increased, donors began to diversify their project portfolios in Ghana. In addition to infrastructure development, emphasis was placed on the productive sectors and poverty alleviation, with a growing number of donor-funded projects in the agricultural sector, where the majority of the poor were located, as well as in health and education.

During the 1980s multilateral donors, in particular the World Bank, played a large role in Ghana (Table 10.2), and policy-based programme lending, as opposed to traditional project lend-

Table 10.2   Share of Net Multilateral ODA in the Total (%)

Year	Ghana	Sub-Saharan Africa	Low-Income LDCs
1960	0	2.6	0.4
1961	0	6.0	0.3
1962	0	11.0	2.4
1963	5.6	16.4	6.4
1964	5.0	16.8	8.6
1965	4.3	13.7	8.8
1966	-1.9	16.2	9.4
1967	-2.2	14.2	11.7
1968	n.a.	n.a.	n.a.
1969	15.5	30.3	15.5
1970	13.6	36.1	15.5
1971	12.3	34.1	16.6
1972	15.3	32.7	16.7
1973	12.2	38.2	18.2
1974	29.7	32.0	18.9
1975	13.5	26.9	20.4
1976	46.9	27.3	20.3
1977	38.5	26.9	20.6
1978	32.5	31.7	20.3
1979	34.9	29.8	21.2
1980	28.6	29.8	22.3
1981	27.6	30.0	22.9
1982	51.1	27.7	24.0
1983	47.3	28.1	24.5
1984	58.1	29.8	24.6
1985	54.6	31.8	24.7
1986	66.1	31.9	22.8
1987	70.0	33.2	23.5
1988	57.2	32.9	24.6
1989	51.0	36.6	26.2
1990	52.9	38.1	25.8
1991	48.6	40.6	27.2
1992	46.0	42.8	28.9
1993	49.9	41.2	29.9
1994	39.9	44.3	31.8

Note: [a] Data for sub-Saharan Africa exclude Nigeria and South Africa.

ing, increased in importance. This shift has brought with it a donor emphasis on macroeconomic reform and economic growth implemented through stabilization and structural adjustment in the form of the Economic Recovery Programme (ERP). The ERP consisted of three phases: stabilization, rehabilitation and liberalization. Hence during much of the 1980s donor policy conditionality as well as donor-funded projects concentrated on rehabilitating the social and economic infrastructure. From the mid-1980s onwards donors also supported civil service reform and the creation of an enabling environment for the private sector.

The signing of the second World Bank Structural Adjustment Credit (SAC) in 1989 signalled a change of strategy with a shift away from stabilization issues, not just by the Bank but also by other donors. It was acknowledged that the first phase of the ERP had done little to alleviate poverty, which brought a new concern for the social dimensions of adjustment. The second SAC agreement stressed the need to tackle long-term issues of poverty, rapid population growth and food security. This was reiterated in the 6th meeting of the Donor Consultative group in 1991 which set the issues of employment generation and provision of social services as priorities. Hence in the 1990s there has been a clear consensus and the establishment of a common agenda between donors and government on the need to alleviate poverty. In 1993 the World Bank produced its own document outlining its approach to poverty reduction via enhanced investments in human capital, improving the framework for private sector participation and targeting policies and aid towards those sectors in which the poor were located, particularly the agricultural sector. It was hoped that such an approach would bring accelerated growth with poverty reduction (World Bank, 1993).

Another change in aid policies that has occurred in the 1990s is a concern for sector-level strategies. Many donors, including the World Bank and the European Union, have acknowledged that the past emphasis on stabilization and macropolicy ignored sector-level constraints on private sector activities, producing a disappointing private sector response to the ERP and a failure to bring about structural change and diversification of exports. Current donor programmes and projects are geared much more strongly towards sectoral developments, particularly within the agricultural sector because of the emphasis on poverty reduction and because agriculture still accounts for a major share of GDP and employs the bulk of the population. The strategy for the agricultural sector is to provide an enabling environment to stimulate private sector-led production and growth and to improve social welfare. This is to be done through donor and government projects to provide economic and social services (e.g. health and agricultural services), physical infrastructure (roads, power, telecommunications), and soft infrastructure (e.g. transport).

Principal Donors in the 1990s

Table 10.3 shows aid flows from Ghana's principal donors over the period 1989–94. During this period the World Bank has been by far the largest donor providing US$1,027 m., followed by Japan, the UK and Canada. Ghana's dependence on the World Bank for long-term aid flows (52% of the total in 1985) was much greater than the average for sub-Saharan Africa. The World Bank has been a dominant donor since 1983 not just because of the size of its disbursements, but also because government commitment to the Bank's programme of reform under the ERP has acted as a green light for other donors signalling that the government is committed to policy reform. In addition, the Bank has re-activated and led the Ghana Consultative Group which provides a forum for the co-ordination of aid programmes and policies, such that the Bank has effectively taken responsibility for co-ordinating the country's aid programme. Reliance on the World Bank has brought with it an increased share of quick-disbursing non-project programme loans in total aid flows. Between 1983 and 1985, 60% of Bank disbursements took this form, declining to 40% between 1986 and 1990.

Table 10.3   Official Development Assistance from Principal Donors 1989–94 (US$ m.)

	1989	1990	1991	1992	1993	1994	Total 1990–94
The World Bank	NA	196	150	192	206	283	1,027
Japan	98	72	116	71	90	104	453
United Kingdom	60	54	38	48	26	27	193
Canada	37	38	50	35	34	22	179
Germany	23	6	18	32	48	63	167
African Development Bank	NA	41	10	28	37	30	146
USA	21	23	16	32	31	41	143
France	9	6	9	13	44	60	132
Netherlands	18	14	9	9	22	24	78
Commonwealth Development Corporation	NA	6	16	4	4	37	67
Denmark	4	1	3	5	9	33	51
Italy	9	15	7	10	6	10	48
United Nations Development Programme	NA	9	12	9	6	NA	36
International Fund for Agricultural Development	NA	2	3	3	5	12	25
Arab Bank for Economic Development in Africa	NA	0	2	2	3	6	13

Source: Government of Ghana, 1996b.

Problems with Project Implementation

Between 1978 and 1982 aid commitments and disbursements to Ghana declined. This was partly due to donor dissatisfaction with project performance. There were several reasons for this (Aryeetey and Oduro, 1996). First, the government's declining revenue base made it difficult for it to finance local project costs. Secondly, the shortage of foreign exchange made it difficult to obtain imported raw materials and spare parts which slowed down project implementation. Thirdly, government policies, such as low cocoa producer prices and the macroeconomic imbalance, adversely impacted on projects. Fourthly, the brain drain reduced qualified personnel and hampered project implementation capacity as did lack of inter-ministerial co-ordination.

Many of these problems persisted, and in some cases intensified, as aid flows dramatically increased in the ERP period and Ghana reached a point of aid saturation. This was reflected in a very low level of project aid commitments actually disbursed. One particular problem has been lack of counterpart funds due to over-ambitious Ministry of Finance revenue projections and rapid inflation and exchange rate depreciation leading to under-estimation of local costs. Another problem has been time-consuming procurement and tendering procedures. Logistical difficulties, such as infrastructure problems and the need to consider environmental impact, have also delayed project implementation.

A recent debt and aid strategy document (Government of Ghana, 1996a) has outlined measures to speed up the process of aid utilization. This is to occur through: timely provision of adequate matching funds; easing the procurement process; improving monitoring and supervision; improving knowledge of donor procedures; and improving the timing of aid commitments. In addition, the document also emphasizes fostering self-reliance, mobilizing adequate aid resources and increasing the amount of aid channelled to the private sector.

5.   Aid and Social Welfare

So far this chapter has concentrated on the relationship between aid flows and economic growth. Growth, however, is not the only objective of donors and the government. Other important objectives of aid include improving social welfare indicators, alleviating poverty and, in some cases, improving income distribution. It is extremely difficult to know whether aid flows have achieved the above objectives as very few impact studies have been conducted. Table 3.2 in Chapter 3 shows that fertility rates, life expectancy, infant mortality, adult literacy, and primary and secondary school enrolment rates all improved between 1960 and 1994. Whilst social welfare indicators steadily improved, per capita aid flows have been erratic (Table 10.1), making it difficult to attribute the improved welfare to aid. Undoubtedly, however, certain donor policies, such as the emphasis on primary health care, in particular the immunization programme, have helped to reduce the infant mortality rate and improved life expectancy at birth (Aryeetey and Oduro, 1996).

An important question is whether the donor-supported ERP with its stabilization and structural adjustment programmes has been associated with a decline in social welfare. Detailed analysis (Stewart, 1995) of quality of life indicators during the ERP shows deterioration in the first half of the 1980s with some rather mixed recovery in later years when donors started to concentrate more on the social dimensions of adjustment. It should be noted, however, that the severe drought of the early 1980s had a major impact on poverty and social indicators and that the recovery in later years was partly due to the end of the drought and the return of macroeconomic stability. One particularly disquieting feature is the fall in both primary and secondary school enrolment rates in the early and mid-1980s as donor conditionality resulted in cost recovery measures.

Despite the initial decline in welfare indicators, both macro and meso policies since 1983 have had positive effects on the poor, although not all of the poor have benefited and for many the benefit has been small (Stewart, 1995). This contrasts with many other developing countries. The positive effects arose because the ERP was expansionary, producing rising incomes and increased government expenditure. Aid has played a major role in this respect. Stewart provides five reasons for this. First, the policy conditionality accompanying programme aid meant that, following prolonged stagnation and economic mismanagement, donor-guided reform produced positive growth results. Secondly, the ERP was generously financed by donors, meaning that net resources were not needed for debt repayments. Thirdly, both donor conditionality and donor technical assistance have resulted in a large increase in government revenue, so that government expenditure was able to increase whilst simultaneously enabling the government to reach its deficit reduction targets. The tax ratio increased from 5% of GDP in 1983 to 11.6% in 1990. This enabled a rise in the ratio of public expenditure to GDP from a low of 8% in 1983 to 13% by 1990 and 23% by 1995. At the same time the social allocation ratio[14] rose from 29% in 1981 to 34.7% in 1990.[15] As a result, real expenditure per capita on education rose by 51% and on health by 66% between 1983 and 1990. Fourthly, government expenditure has been directly boosted by donor funds. Between 1983 and 1991 donor grants to support the budget rose from being equivalent to 0.55% of domestic revenues to 10.23%. These inflows enabled the government to increase

---

[14] The social allocation ratio is the share of total government expenditure going to social sectors, broadly defined to include any expenditure that might benefit the poor, including food subsidies and employment schemes.

[15] However, as discussed in Chapter 16, social expenditure ratios declined in the 1990s with such expenditures crowded-out by public sector interest payments.

expenditures beyond what domestically generated resources would have allowed. By 1990 donor assistance constituted 62% of total budget expenditure and 88% of total development budget expenditure, although these shares fell slightly in the 1990s (see Tables 5.3 and 5.4 in Chapter 5). In particular, these inflows helped to avoid a decline in social sector expenditures such as often accompanies stabilization and adjustment programmes in developing countries. This is illustrated by the fact that aid inflows have become increasingly important in financing Ghana's social sector expenditures (see Chapter 16 for a more in-depth discussion of this issue). The ratio of social sector ODA spending to government social expenditure was 7.1% in 1988 rising to 34.6% in 1991 (Aryeetey and Oduro, 1996). Finally, apart from budgetary support, donor flows have also supported the balance of payments, making possible an increase in the availability of necessary raw materials, spare parts and consumables far above what domestically generated resources could have provided, thus resulting in economic expansion and hence rising incomes and rising government expenditure.

Although social welfare indicators temporarily declined in the first half of the 1980s and although by the end of the decade donors and government were concerned about the fact that, whilst the ERP had helped the poor, much more could have been done in terms of poverty reduction, it is important to bear in mind the counter-factual. The above analysis suggests that, in the absence of the policy reform conditions and massive aid flows that accompanied the ERP, social welfare would undoubtedly have deteriorated even further and poverty would have increased. This is especially true when one bears in mind the sharp deterioration in Ghana's terms of trade during much of the reform period.

One concrete way in which donors have tried to improve social welfare in Ghana, which coincides with increased donor concern for the social dimensions of adjustment and poverty from the late 1980s onwards, is through the Programme to Mitigate the Social Costs of Adjustment (PAMSCAD). First proposed in 1987 but launched in 1991, PAMSCAD consisted of a large number of projects financed by multiple donors and by the government. PAMSCAD had generous donor financing with a planned expenditure of US$84 m. or 6-8% of the annual cost of international support for the ERP. Despite this, it is generally acknowledged that PAMSCAD has been a failure (Aryeetey and Oduro, 1996; Stewart, 1995; World Bank, 1991; Government of Ghana, 1991). Long delays in getting started, complex administrative systems, and poor targeting of the poor meant that it had an insignificant effect on poverty. Projects were concentrated in urban areas rather than in rural areas where most of the poor were located. Disbursement from donors was low, the government was slow in releasing counterpart funds, and the large number of projects exceeded donor and government implementation capacity. Rather than reaching the poorest, PAMSCAD provided institution building, vehicles, and some social infrastructure and financed civil service retrenchment payments. In addition, the *ad hoc* programme failed to develop a long-term automatic mechanism to deal with the social costs of economic adjustment.

6. Aid, Debt, and Economic Growth

The previous sections have treated aid flows as if they were grants, consistent with the aid literature. Even though much aid comes on soft terms, the grant element is seldom 100%, and for some sources, such as the IMF's stand-by facilities, the terms are almost commercial. Thus, one must consider the implications of the liabilities that accompany aid flows for recipient countries. In section 3, we have already seen that Ghana suffered a debt crisis in the 1960s, long before they were common. Nevertheless, it was only after the advent of the ERP that debt levels began to increase substantially. This has caused some alarm among policy-makers (and their critics) in Ghana; we therefore devote most of our attention to the years after 1983, with emphasis on the sustainability of Ghana's foreign debts.

It has already been noted that in the first couple of years of the 1980s Ghana suffered a debt crisis with accumulated external payments arrears reaching US$577 m. by the end of 1982. This debt crisis was precipitated by the same factors that created debt distress in many other developing countries at the time, namely, the sharp 1979 increase in oil import prices and the declining terms of trade; the large rise in international interest rates; recession in the West, leading to protection and reduced aid flows - aid inflows fell dramatically in 1981 and 1982 to less than a quarter of their 1980 levels; and domestic policy mismanagement (Parfitt and Riley, 1989).

Key objectives of the ERP were to increase debt repayments so as to eliminate arrears, restore international creditworthiness, build up foreign reserves and use foreign finance to rehabilitate the infrastructure. In the initial 1983–6 phase of the ERP Ghana's creditworthiness was low and it was difficult to attract concessional long-term finance. Reliance was therefore placed on short-term borrowing from the IMF in the form of three successive stand-by agreements, and other commercial sources. The share of short-term credit in total external debt increased from 20.1% in 1982 to 40.7% by 1985, with the IMF providing around 60% of inflows to Ghana in this period and the World Bank providing only 14%. The recourse to short-term non-concessional finance is reflected in the increase in interest rates and the decline in the grant element between 1980 and 1985 and the peaking of the debt service ratio at 13.5% in 1986 (Table 10.4). The short-term IMF loans created major debt-servicing problems in 1987 and 1988 (Toye, 1991: 160). Hence, a key role for the IMF under ERP II was assistance with debt rescheduling to overcome the debt hump. This occurred by allowing Ghana access to concessional IMF facilities, namely the Extended Fund Facility (EFF) and the Structural Adjustment Facility (SAF) in 1987 and the even more favourable Extended Structural Adjustment Facility (ESAF) in 1988. Together these represented a huge package of IMF loans on softer terms worth SDR 506 million. They did not, however, prevent net repayments to the IMF throughout 1987–92 although they did reduce these flows.

One worrying aspect of this situation, however, is that aid and loans are now helping to finance debt repayments rather than investment (or even consumption), the same problem that occurred in the late 1960s. There is a risk of a type of Ponzi game developing in which donors lend so that governments can meet their debt-service obligations rather than investing in productive assets.[16] Clearly, Ghana has not reached that point yet, mainly because the debt restructuring of the late 1980s improved the terms of its debt enormously. As its creditworthiness improved and some arrears were cleared under successive IMF programmes, the share of long-term concessional loans in financing the ERP increased, particularly from multilateral sources. Between 1986 and 1992 average interest on new commitments fell from 4.7% to 0.8.%, the grant element rose from 39.4% to 76.7% and the debt-service ratio fell from 13.5% to 9.9% (Table 10.4). By 1990 most arrears had been cleared and holdings of foreign exchange had increased.

Recently Ghana has continued to service debt without rescheduling, although external payments arrears of US $93 m. emerged in 1994. At the end of 1994 its external debt outstanding, excluding IMF obligations, stood at $4.8 billion, nearly 80% of GDP. Bilateral official creditors accounted for 23%, multilaterals 70% and the remainder was owed to private creditors. Although the debt stock is growing each year, the debt-service burden is predicted to fall by the late 1990s because of increased concessionality (World Bank, 1995b). The debt-service burden appears sustainable and Ghana is currently retiring about US $150 m. of debt every year.

The heavy reliance on external inflows during the ERP has, however, had its costs. Debt servicing is increasing the current account deficit. Between 1995 and 1997 debt-service obligations, including reduction of arrears, were projected at US $1.0 billion (World Bank, 1995b: 69). Debt servicing also places a heavy burden on the government budget, made worse by devaluation which increases the domestic currency cost of debt. By 1993 interest on public debt, both domestic and foreign, amounted to 17.8% of government spending. These high payments have restricted much needed public sector investment and crowded out social expenditures (see Chapter 16).

---

[16] A Ponzi scheme is one in which an investor finances a project not with its own returns, but by borrowing fresh funds on which it will eventually not be able to provide a return.

Table 10.4 Ghana's Foreign Debt 1970–94 (US$ m.)

	1970	1980	1982	1985	1986	1987	1988	1989	1990	1991	1992	1993	1994
Total debt stocks (EDT)	N/A	1,407	1,475	2,226	2,726	3,262	3,048	3,296	3,761	4,209	4,477	4,835	5,389
Long-term debt stocks (LDOD) of which:	521	1,171	N/A	1,337	1,754	2,276	2,214	2,361	2,705	2,992	3,131	3,621	4,107
Official Multilaterals	10.2%	23.8%	36.0%	39.4%	44.6%	50.1%	59.4%	62.6%	68.0%	69.2%	70.0%	66.2%	65.0%
Official Bilaterals	53.6%	64.29%	49.0%	45.1%	38.9%	34.6%	26.1%	26.7%	23.85%	22.4%	22.6%	25.0%	25.7%
Private	36.3%	12.0%	15.0%	15.5%	16.5%	15.4%	14.5%	10.6%	8.2%	8.3%	7.6%	7.8%	8.5%
Disbursement	44	249	98	313	416	515	618	561	483	609	398	484	422
Net Resource Transfers[a]	79	135	60	167	378	298	352	384	687	859	500	552	1,197
Average terms of new commitments													
Interest %	2.0%	1.4%	5.1%	3.5%	4.7%	2.9%	1.1%	3.2%	2.5%	2.6%	1.8%	3.1%	3.5%
Grant elements %	66.8%	74.1%	36.0%	52.2%	39.4%	57.8%	69.9%	54.9%	62.8%	61.0%	76.7%	56.7%	51.8%
Total Debt-Service[b]	N/A	159	111	165	232	418	552	453	356	295	321	303	343
EDT: GNP %	N/A	31.6%	36.6%	50.3%	48.8%	66.2%	60.2%	64.2%	65.7%	66.9%	68.4%	81.0%	101.5%
Debt-service Ratio[c]	N/A	5.0%	9.0%	12.9%	13.5%	12.8%	13.2%	12.8%	10.6%	9.9%	10.6%	9.8%	8.3%
Total Debt-service Ratio[d]	N/A	13.1%	15.6%	24.3%	28.4%	46.0%	57.2%	50.6%	35.9%	27.0%	28.4%	24.7%	24.6%

Note: a) Net flow of long-term debt (excluding IMF) plus net direct foreign investment plus grants minus interest on long-term debt minus profit remittances.
b) Interest plus principal repayments.
c) Interest: exports of goods and services.
d) Principal and interest on long-term debt plus IMF repurchases and charges plus interest on short-term debt: exports goods and services.

Source: World Bank: *World Debt Tables 1992–1996.*

Another cost of debt has been macroeconomic instability, due to high growth in the money supply. Between 1986 and 1995 money growth was rapid, whilst at the same time, despite the reduction in government borrowing, the private sector was crowded out of credit markets. The major source of monetary growth during the ERP was the domestic currency counterpart of Bank of Ghana (BoG) repayments of foreign-exchange loans contracted by the government and parastatals. This appears under the revaluation account in the BoG monetary statistics (see Table 1.5 and discussion in Chapter 1). It has been the biggest contributor to M2 growth in every year during 1986–94 except 1991 and 1992. The revaluation account is effectively a domestic currency loan by the BoG to the public sector, and represents a form of quasi fiscal deficit.

As a percentage of GDP the revaluation account declined from its peak in 1986 to 14.7% in 1993. Its rise and then fall is mirrored by changes in the BoG's Net Foreign Assets (NFA) (see Table 1.5). The BoG's repayments of public sector debt in the mid-1980s had a big impact on its NFA which rose to 24% of GDP in 1986 (the BoG used its own foreign assets to repay someone else's foreign liabilities). The balance of payments surpluses accumulated after 1986 substantially improved the NFA position, rapidly during 1986-89 and more slowly since then. By 1993 the NFA had been reduced to –6% of GDP. But even this can be seen as a form of quasi fiscal deficit, because the rise in NFA was mainly funded by issuing liabilities to the general public (base money) rather than by real public sector savings: i.e the accumulation of foreign-exchange reserves was financed by borrowing from the private sector. There is an asymmetry in the BoG's dealings with the public sector: it ran down its NFA during 1983–6 by extending credit to the public sector through the revaluation account, but the rebuilding of its NFA after 1986 was not predominantly funded by the repayment of debt from the public sector.

It is the change of 18 percentage points of GDP in the Net Foreign Assets of the BoG which occurred after 1986 which gives rise to the arguments about Dutch Disease. The accumulation of foreign reserves after 1986 was to some extent simply a necessary correction of the effects of the revaluation account debt repayments which preceded it, rather than the result of an exogenous rise in foreign capital inflows. Had the Bank of Ghana not repaid the public sector foreign debt in the mid-1980s it would have had less need to accumulate the large balance of payments surpluses since 1986. Before it doubled in 1986, the BoG's NFA in 1985 was only –12.5% of GDP. Had the 1986 fall in NFA not occurred, the BoG could have improved its NFA by less than 1% of GDP a year and still have ended up at the same level as was actually recorded in 1993. Furthermore, had the foreign debt repayments not been made, there would have been less need for so much IMF credit in the early part of the ERP (which was partly used to make the repayments) and less need for World Bank and donor loans thereafter (which were partly used to repay the IMF credits). Consequently, the underlying cause of the high rates of M2 growth can be attributed to the quasi fiscal deficits funded by the Bank of Ghana in the early part of the ERP rather than to exogenous inflows of foreign capital. Whether these quasi fiscal deficits could have been avoided, or even reduced, is a different matter.

Although Ghana in recent years has had a good debt record, having avoided rescheduling in order to maintain access to new export credit loans, there is still scope for considerable debt forgiveness. Cancellation of all remaining aid debt would save US $30-40 m. a year, and cancelling 100% of the non-concessional debt contracted before 1986 would save US $50 m. a year (Martin, 1993: 171). Ghana would also benefit if creditor governments refinanced the debt service with additional grants; accepted payment in local currency; or converted their debt into equity, development or environmental projects (*ibid.*). Ghana's commercial creditors, however, are unlikely to undertake debt equity swaps, given the country's good repayment record. Given its large debt-service burden to multilateral organizations (about US $200 m. per annum), in particular the IMF and the World Bank, there is also scope for these organizations to provide net inflows on softer terms to refinance the debt servicing, for example through faster and larger disbursements of IMF ESAF loans.

Since 1987, when the Aid and Debt Management Unit in the Ministry of Finance was established, Ghana has been improving its debt management strategy. Data on debt, including parastatal debt, have been compiled, and ceilings have been placed on government-guaranteed non-concessional external loans in the 1–12 years' maturity range in order to reduce debt-servicing obligations in the medium to long term and to increase reliance on long-term funds. In its recent debt and aid strategy document (Government of Ghana, 1996a) the government announced a strategy for the management of a sustainable debt profile. This includes measures to reduce the severity of indebtedness, improve the monitoring of the future growth of debt, reduce the existing debt stock, and limit non-concessional loans.

7. Conclusions

Aid flows to Ghana since independence have been erratic and have been determined by a variety of exogenous and domestic factors. Ghana received little aid in the first half of the 1960s, except for the Akosambo Dam and related projects. Aid picked up in the second half of the 1960s but growth remained stagnant. Flows again declined in the first half of the 1970s but recovered later in the decade, although economic performance continued to deteriorate. Despite the recovery in aid, Ghana had still not caught up with most other developing countries in terms of aid flows. This changed in the 1980s. Although as with other developing countries, aid fell in the opening years of the 1980s, with the launching of the ERP in 1983 Ghana became the darling of the aid donors, a situation which continued until macroeconomic instability returned in the 1990s and both growth and aid flows fell.

The strategies of Ghana's principal donors have changed considerably over the decades. In the 1960s most donors concentrated their resources on infrastructure projects, but in the 1970s diversified to focus on poverty alleviation investments in health, education, and agriculture. The 1980s was a decade of structural adjustment, with donors concentrating their programme aid on macroeconomic stabilization and project aid on infrastructure rehabilitation. The 1990s have brought a renewed concern for poverty, neglected during much of the previous decade, and an emphasis on sector level strategies, particularly in the agricultural sector. Since the late 1970s, the World Bank has become the dominant donor in Ghana.

Ghana has suffered from a number of implementation problems with project aid which mean that aid disbursements have been significantly below commitments. Problems include: lack of counterpart funds; foreign-exchange shortages; adverse policies; and lack of qualified personnel. This has been particularly true during the ERP when Ghana reached a point of aid saturation. In 1996 measures were introduced to speed up aid utilization.

Although the subject of this chapter is aid, we have also looked briefly at private flows in the form of Direct Foreign Investment. Since controls were introduced in 1965 there has been a lack of DFI in Ghana and, with the exception of investment in gold mining, DFI has not recovered during the ERP. This suggests that Ghana is missing out on an important source of potential growth, namely, the technical progress and learning-by-doing that DFI often brings.

Theory and empirical evidence produce ambiguous conclusions regarding the impact of aid flows on economic growth in developing countries in general. There are a number of reasons why the impact of aid on growth might be disappointing: low rates of return on the use of the aid funds; offsetting adjustments in recipient governments' savings behaviour (fungibility); offsetting general equilibrium effects of foreign capital flows (crowding out of local investment and Dutch Disease); a declining marginal product of capital; and discouragement of investment from a debt overhang. In the case of Ghana, few of these possible explanations ring true, at least during most of the ERP period when aid flows increased dramatically and were correlated with increased growth rates. In earlier periods growth was erratic and not clearly correlated with aid flows but in the 1983-94 period the correlation coefficient was 0.322.

Estimating rates of return to the projects and programmes financed by aid is a huge task. We are not aware of any attempt to do this, nor have we attempted it here, so we cannot say much about this factor.

Fungibility during the ERP appears to have been limited, as evidenced by the similar increases in foreign aid and investment. This is probably due to the extremely limited room for manoeuvre that the Ghanaian government has in its budget. Domestic revenues enable it to do little more than pay the wage bill, service its debt and provide counterpart funds.

General equilibrium effects have been more problematic. Although there was little evidence of Dutch Disease effects or crowding out during most of the 1980s, the combination of expansive fiscal policy with tight monetary policy (as the government tried to sterilize aid inflows) in the last few years of the decade probably crowded out private investment. More recently, the relaxation of monetary policy (and the consequent inflation) have eased the pressure on the financial markets somewhat, but at the cost of an appreciating real exchange rate and the consequent Dutch Disease. If the potential for rapid economic growth in Ghana lies in labour-intensive, export-oriented manufacturing, this is a worrying development.

As for a declining marginal product of capital, capital accumulation has been so limited in Ghana that this can hardly be a problem. At the same time, one would be hard pressed to argue that the aid-financed investments have led to the kind of non-convex dynamics that feature prominently in the new growth economics. Investment levels, particularly in the private sector, remain far too low for either factor to have much effect.

Finally, there is the debt overhang. While it is true that Ghana has accumulated a considerable amount of foreign debt in the past 20 years, and suffered a debt crisis in the early 1980s, the concerted efforts to restructure those debts on much softer terms from the late 1980s onwards have helped to reduce their real burden significantly, to levels that appear manageable. Certainly, the figures to concentrate on are not the debt-to-GDP numbers, which look alarming, but some measure of the debt's servicing cost, which is much lower because of the debt's concessional terms.

Given that the problems which often nullify the effects of aid on growth do not seem to apply to Ghana during much of the ERP period, we can identify several possible ways in which aid may have helped to promote growth in this period. First, aid undoubtedly helped to bridge domestic savings and foreign-exchange gaps in the early years of the ERP. Secondly, aid helped to boost government spending, particularly on health, education and much needed investment. Thirdly, aid in the form of programme loans contributed to economic recovery by improving economic policy. In addition, aid helped the government to persist with the reform programme in the face of exogenous shocks, in particular by helping to provide financial support for the foreign-exchange auction and for import liberalization. By helping to prevent the reversal of such reforms, aid enabled the government to survive shocks without resorting to the controls that sank the economy in the 1970s.

The lack of impact studies means that it is hard to tell if, over the period since 1960, aid has improved social welfare in Ghana. Social welfare indicators have steadily improved but aid flows have been erratic. Some aid programmes, such as those in the primary health sector, have, however, undoubtedly improved certain welfare indicators.

Firmer conclusions can be reached for the ERP period. Although quality of life indicators initially deteriorated, they recovered as donors started to focus on the social dimensions of adjustment. Meso and macro policies which were introduced under the donor-supported ERP have also had a positive effect on the poor, although for many the benefits were small. The ERP policy reforms, supported by generous donor funds, promoted growth which improved incomes and welfare. Donor-guided reforms also helped to increase government revenues substantially, enabling public expenditure as a percentage of GDP and the social allocation ratio to rise. This brought with it a marked increase in real health and education expenditure. In addition, much of this expenditure was directly donor-funded. The donor-funded PAMSCAD has, however, produced disappointing results.

Although Ghana's donors would probably argue that they did things in the right order, with macro stability coming first and targeted interventions later, by the 1990s they acknowledged that although the ERP helped the poor, much more could, and should, have been done to alleviate poverty during the adjustment period. Hence in the 1990s, government and donors developed a new consensus which emphasized growth with poverty reduction.

References

Aryeetey, E. (1995) 'Aid Effectiveness in Ghana', Institute of Statistical, Social and Economic Research, University of Ghana, Legon (mimeo).

Aryeetey, E. and Oduro, A. (1996) 'The World Bank in Ghana: 1962–1994', unpublished paper, ISSER, University of Ghana, Legon.

Aryeetey, E. (1994) 'Private Investment Under Uncertainty in Ghana', *World Development*, Vol. 22, No. 8.

Blanchard, Oliver, and Fischer, Stanley (1989) *Lectures on Macroeconomics*. Cambridge, MA: MIT Press.

Boone, Peter (1995) 'Foreign Aid and Economic Growth', draft, London: Centre for Economic Performance.

Boone, Peter (1996) 'Politics and the Effectiveness of Foreign Aid', *European Economic Review* Vol. 40.

Bulow, Jeremy, and Rogoff, Kenneth (1989) 'The Buyback Boondoggle', *Brookings Papers on Economic Activity* Vol. 2: 675–98.

Burnside, C. and Dollar, D. (1997) *Aid Policies and Growth*. Washington, DC: World Bank, Policy Research Department.

Chenery, Hollis, and Strout, A. M. (1966) 'Foreign Assistance and Economic Development', *American Economic Review* Vol. 56: 679–733.

Chhibber, A. and Shafik, N. (1990) 'Exchange Rate Reform, Parallel Markets, and Inflation in Africa: The Case of Ghana', *World Bank Working Papers* No. 427, Washington, DC.

Dowling, J. M. and Hiemenz, U. (1983) 'Aid, Savings and Growth in the Asian Region', *The Developing Economies*, Vol. XXI, No. 1, March.

Government of Ghana (1996a) *Ghana's Aid and Debt Management Policies Strategies*. Accra: Aid and Debt Management Unit, Ministry of Finance.

Government of Ghana (1996b) *Compendium of Donor Policies and Procedures*. Accra: Ministry of Finance.

Griffin, Keith (1970) 'Foreign Capital, Domestic Savings, and Economic Development', *Bulletin of the Oxford University Institute of Economics and Statistics*, Vol. 32: 99–112.

Gupta, K. and Islam, M.A. (1983) *Foreign Capital, Savings and Growth: An International Cross-section Study*. Dordrecht, Holland: Reidel Publishing Company.

Harrigan, J. (1988) 'Alternative Concepts of Conditionality', *Manchester Papers on Development*, Vol. IV, No. 4: 451–71.

Jebuni, C., Oduro, A. and Tutu, K. (1994) 'Trade and Payments Regime and the Balance of Payments in Ghana', *World Development*, Vol. 22, No. 8.

Killick, Tony (1978) *Development Economics in Action: A Study of Economic Policies in Ghana*. London: Heinemann Educational Books.

Krassowski, Andrzej (1974) *Development and the Debt Trap*. London: Croom Helm.

Krugman, Paul (1988) 'Financing vs. Forgiving a Debt Overhang', *Journal of Development Economics* Vol. 29: 253–68.

Leechor, Chad (1978) 'Ghana: Frontrunner in Adjustment', in I. Husain and R. Faruqee (eds) *Adjustment in Africa: Lessons from Country Case Studies*. World Bank Regional and Sectoral Studies. Washington, DC: World Bank.

Levine, R., and Renelt, D. (1992) 'A Sensitivity Analysis of Cross-country Growth Regressions', *American Economic Review* Vol. 82: 942–64.

Lucas, Robert E. (1988) 'On the Mechanics of Economic Development', *Journal of Monetary Economics* Vol. 22: 3–42.

Martin, M. (1993) 'Neither Phoenix nor Icarus: Negotiating Economic Reform in Ghana and Zambia 1983-92' in T. Callaghy and J. Ravenhill (eds) *Hemmed in: Response to Africa's Economic Decline*. New York: Columbia University Press.

Mosley, P., Hudson, J., and Horrell, S. (1987) 'Aid, the Public Sector, and the Market in Less Developed Countries', *Economic Journal* Vol. 97: 616–41.

Mosley, P., Hudson, J., and Horrell S. (1992) 'Aid, the Public Sector and the Market in Less Developed Countries: A Return to the Scene of the Crime', *Journal of International Development*, Vol. 4, No. 3, February.

Mosley, P. (1995) 'Aid Effectiveness: A Study of the Effectiveness of Overseas Aid in the Main Countries Receiving ODA Assistance', unpublished paper, University of Reading.

Papanek, G. F. (1973) 'Aid, Foreign Private Investment, Savings and Growth in Less Developed Countries', *The Journal of Political Economy*, No. 81.

Parfitt, T. and Riley, S. (1989) *The African Debt Crisis*. London and New York: Routledge.

Pindyck, Robert (1991) 'Irreversibility, Uncertainty, and Investment', *Journal of Economic Literature* Vol. 29: 1110–48.

Romer, Paul M. (1986) 'Increasing Returns and Long-run Growth', *Journal of Political Economy* Vol. 94: 500–21.

Rosenstein-Rodan, P. N. (1961) 'International Aid for Underdeveloped Countries', *Review of Economics and Statistics*, Vol. 43, No. 2, May.

Sala-i-Martin, Xavier (1994) 'Cross-sectional Regressions and the Empirics of Economic Growth', *European Economic Review* Vol. 38: 739–47.

Solow, Robert (1956) 'A contribution to the theory of economic growth', *Quarterly Journal of Economics* Vol. 70: 65–94.

Sowa, N. K., and White, Howard (1997) 'An Evaluation of Netherlands Cofinancing of World Bank Activities in Ghana, 1983–1996', unpublished mimeo.

Stewart, F. (1995) *Adjustment and Poverty: Options and Choices*. London and New York: Routledge.

Taylor, L. (1993) *The Rocky Road to Reform: Adjustment, Income Distribution and Growth in the Developing World.* Cambridge, MA: MIT Press.

Toye, J. (1995) 'Ghana' in Mosley *et al. Aid and Power: The World Bank and Policy-Based Lending*, 2nd edition, Vol. II. London and New York: Routledge.

Weisskopf, Thomas (1972) 'Impact of Foreign Capital Inflows on Domestic Savings in Underdeveloped Countries', *Journal of International Economics* Vol. 2: .25–38.

White, H. (1992) 'The Macroeconomic Impact of Developing aid: A Critical Survey', *Journal of International Development*, Vol. 4, No. 3, February.

World Bank (1991) *Ghana Progress on Adjustment.* Washington, DC: World Bank.

World Bank (1993) *Ghana 2000 and Beyond. Setting the Stage for Accelerated Growth and Poverty Reduction.* Washington, DC: World Bank.

World Bank (1995a) *World Data* (disk). Washington, DC: World Bank.

World Bank (1995b) *Ghana: Growth, Private Sector and Poverty Reduction. A Country Economic Memorandum.* World Bank, Washington, DC.

Younger, Stephen D. (1992) 'Aid and the Dutch Disease: Macroeconomic Management When Everybody Loves You', *World Development* Vol. 20, No. 11.

IV Factor Markets

11 Intervention & Liberalization: Changing Policies & Performance in the Financial Sector

ERNEST ARYEETEY
MACHIKO NISSANKE
& WILLIAM F. STEEL

1. Introduction

Ghana has moved from an interventionist to a liberalized financial policy regime over the last three decades. Neither approach has successfully developed the financial sector's ability to support socio-economic goals, however. Financial intermediation has been persistently limited and inefficient, and the formal financial system has been unable to make deposit and credit facilities widely available. This chapter analyzes the performance of the financial system under the different regimes, focusing on key indicators such as asset and liability structures, credit characteristics, and efficiency. Apart from the fact that macroeconomic environments continue to be hostile to the development of efficient financial systems, the failure to achieve markedly different results under different regimes is explained in terms of the failure of both repressive and liberal regimes to address underlying structural and institutional constraints.

The financial sector policies adopted have undoubtedly been influenced by changes in general development thought. Indeed, the Ghanaian experience shows a remarkable attachment to prevailing orthodoxy in the development of policy. When it was fashionable in the development literature to advocate interventionist policies in the financial sector in order to achieve more redistributional goals in the 1970s, these also became the cornerstone of Ghanaian policies. Later, in the 1980s, as the wind of change blew and a new orthodoxy of financial liberalization began to reign throughout the developing world, the financial sector again became a major arena for policy experimentation.

The shifts in the financial sector regime in Ghana have also often been propelled by a domestic dissatisfaction with the performance of the system. Dissatisfaction with the system has often coincided with shifts in the political regime, often a move from a civilian to military regime or the reverse. Thus, the takeover by the military of the reins of power in 1972 from the civilian Busia administration was accompanied by tighter policies and the institution of more pervasive controls in an attempt to counter the effects of the reversal of the devaluation that pre-empted the fall of the Busia Government. The period of the most significant intervention (1972–8) was also marked by considerable governmental interest in the development of small businesses and small-scale agricultural projects. The lack of success with intervention paved the way for the liberal reforms that began in 1985.

2. Approaches to Financial Policies

While there is general agreement on the potentially vital contribution of the financial system to growth and development, economists are generally divided on the appropriate policy to foster financial sector development. It is accepted that, besides providing a medium of exchange and payment system, financial systems can contribute to savings, investment and growth by mobilizing and allocating investible resources and transforming risks and maturities. Goldsmith's (1969) study demonstrated an empirical association between economic growth and the increasing size and complexity of the financial system, i.e., 'financial deepening'. Similarly, Gertler and Rose (1994) argue that economic growth and financial sector development are mutually dependent, and Galbis (1977) suggests that financial development is a prerequisite for take-off into self-sustained economic growth.

Financial sector development should imply that financial resources are made available for real sector development. In most developing countries, financial systems are not developed to play this vital role of intermediation. Only some segments of the real sector receive credit, but they are not necessarily the most efficient users of capital. The markets are often extremely fragmented, with the various segments serving distinct groups of clients with similar characteristics and needs, without functional direct and indirect linkages and interaction among the market segments (Nissanke and Aryeetey, 1998). Ghana is a typical case. Fragmentation of the financial system in Ghana, as in most of sub-Saharan Africa, makes it difficult for the financial sector to fulfil its potential to facilitate growth of the real sector of the economy.

Fragmented financial markets have little interaction or flow of funds and information between the different segments, as indicated by the wide differences in interest rates and risk-adjusted returns among lenders. Fragmented markets have difficulty in intermediating between savers and investors, thus limiting the funds available for investment in the real economy. In particular, in sub-Saharan Africa, both formal and informal segments of the financial system serve a very narrow market niche. Demarcation of the boundaries of their specialization is determined by each lender's attempts to mitigate the problem caused by asymmetric information associated with moral hazard and adverse selection, and to contain risks and transaction costs. In this situation, differences in the structure of deposits mobilized and credit facilities offered by both formal and informal financial units tend to be associated with distinct socio-economic groups whom they largely pre-select on the basis of the availability of information and means of managing risks. Explanations for shallow, fragmented financial markets are thus often found in these structural and institutional constraints and environments: high transaction costs and default risks, problems with maturity transformation, inadequate complementary institutions such as insurance and legal contract enforcement, and poor supervisory and regulatory systems (Nissanke and Aryeetey, 1998).

These structural problems have not received due attention by either those who advocated interventionism in the 1960s and 1970s or those who called for liberalization in the 1980s in formulating policy environments for financial sector development.

Interventionism

Early forms of intervention were derived from the perceived large scale of market failures in finance, which were closely associated with the prevailing market structures and the nature and ownership of banking institutions at the time. Directing the allocation of credit and controlling interest rates were the common response of newly independent sub-Saharan African countries in the 1960s and 1970s to the financial systems they inherited and their aspirations for rapid economic growth. Colonial banks were foreign-owned, oriented towards import-export trade, and monopolistic. Governments tried to redirect the allocation of financial resources towards domestic investment through direct credit controls and specialized development banks. Establishment of state-owned banks and ceilings on lending rates and spreads were intended to counteract foreign banking monopolies and to enable governments to finance development expenditures at low cost.

The approach adopted was consistent with the emphasis of growth and development theory in the 1960s on capital accumulation and with the socialist perspective that 'decentralized finance . . . is exorbitantly expensive . . . elicits too little in savings, pays too little attention to the consumer welfare of succeeding generations . . . [and] allocates savings badly...biased by indifference to externalities of private investment, by hostility to public goods, by undervaluation of human capital' (Gurley and Shaw, 1967).

Critique of Financial Repression

Government control of and direct intervention in the financial sector was criticized as a cause of underdeveloped, inefficient financial systems by the *financial repression* school (McKinnon, 1973; Shaw, 1973; Fry, 1982, 1988). Besides shifting the allocation of investible funds from the market to the government, government financial controls implicitly taxed financial markets and, in many countries, the banking system became a means of financing budget deficits and covering the operating losses of parastatal companies (Popiel, 1994). Measuring the revenue from repression as the difference between foreign and domestic costs of government borrowing, Giovannini and De Melo (1990) estimated that the unweighted average of 'financial repression tax revenue' in 24 countries across different continents, including Africa, amounted to 2% of GDP for the period 1974–87.

According to McKinnon (1973) and Shaw (1973), repressive financial policies, particularly interest rate ceilings, retard investment and growth by discouraging savings and inhibiting financial deepening. They argue that liberalization would stimulate greater savings mobilization and efficiency through more competitive markets, and would eliminate the spillover of demand from repressed formal financial markets into parallel markets. Fry's (1988) empirical findings using pooled time-series data for seven Asian countries are presented as evidence supporting the McKinnon-Shaw proposition that financial liberalization increases savings.

Recent Conceptual Developments: Imperfect Financial Markets

The financial liberalization approach to financial sector development implicitly assumes that financial markets will function efficiently in the absence of restrictive policies (apart from prudential regulation and supervision). In contrast, another school of thought emphasizes *market failures* as a principal cause of poor financial market development (Stiglitz and Weiss, 1981; Stiglitz, 1989). High transaction costs due to *imperfect information* and difficult *contract enforcement* lie at the root of these market failures, inhibiting the ability of interest rates to achieve market equilibrium; *adverse selection* occurs when higher interest rates discourage borrowers with sound investments at reasonable rates of return and risk, leaving eventually only those applicants with high-risk investments that promise high returns. High interest rates may also increase demand for loans simply to pay interest on previous loans or to avoid bankruptcy rather than to finance working capital or investment. Furthermore, higher interest rates generate a *moral hazard* problem as the incentive to default grows with the rising costs of servicing a loan relative to the detrimental effects of default on creditworthiness and reputation.

Thus, the level of interest rates affects the risk composition of loan portfolios and lenders may well choose not to raise interest rates to clear the market when faced with excess demand for credit, because of concern about greater risk. Instead, they may opt to select borrowers through non-price rationing. As a result, market equilibrium may be characterized by credit rationing even in the absence of interest rate ceilings and direct credit allocation, and free markets do not ensure Pareto efficient allocation, nor do policies that move the economy closer to market solutions. Stiglitz (1994:19) argues that there may be some 'circumstances in which some amount of financial repression may actually be beneficial'. Furthermore, the existence of informal financial institutions may stem from their ability to solve the problems of imperfect information and contract enforcement in relation to their specific clientele, whereas the inability of formal financial institutions to overcome these problems limits the scope of their operations (Steel *et al.*, 1997; Hoff and Stiglitz, 1990).

3.   Interventionist Financial Policies and Performance before 1985

As seen above, it might be argued that there is always a distinction between intervening in order to assist the market to function and intervening to replace the market (Stiglitz, 1996). The interventionist policies that dominated financial sector development in the 1960s and 1970s were generally more of the latter type.

Institutional Development

The government's interventionist approach began under 'self-rule' in 1953 with the establishment of Ghana Commercial Bank for both political and economic objectives. The two foreign banks at the time were seen to favour well-established foreign firms and to neglect indigenous farmers and small entrepreneurs in granting loans and advances. Subsequently, the financing needs of specific sectors were addressed by establishing state-owned development banks: the National Investment Bank (1963), the Agricultural Development Bank (1965), and the Bank for Housing and Construction (1973). The Bank of Ghana was established in 1957 to supervise all other banks (replacing the role of the West African Currency Board). Direct intervention of state institutions in channelling credit paralleled the statist approach to investment under Nkrumah.

Government interest in small clients during the 1970s fostered another generation of specialized banks: the Co-operative Bank, the National Savings and Credit Bank, the Social Security Bank, and rural unit banks.[1] This emphasis on directed credit was consistent with the approaches of international agencies at the time, particularly as a means of satisfying the basic needs of low-income households and providing them opportunities for self-enhancement (Streeten, 1979). By 1985, eleven commercial, development and merchant banks were operating in Ghana, seven of them state-owned.

Government intervention to overcome the perceived slow pace of private banking also took the form of pressure on state-owned banks to increase the number of branches. The total number of bank branches more than doubled in the 1970s, reaching 466 (including rural banks) by 1985. Despite efforts to disperse bank branches, they remained concentrated in the population and economic centres of Greater Accra and Ashanti, which accounted for 32% of all bank branches in 1988, while Accra alone accounted for 67% of all deposits.

Financial Policies

Financial policies became most repressive following the 1972 military takeover from the civilian Busia administration, which had begun a programme of liberalization with a major devaluation in 1971. Controls on all sectors of the economy were substituted for market forces and tightened as weak macroeconomic management fostered rising inflation.

Portfolio Management Policies before 1985 The largely state-owned banking system was directed to channel credit to what were called 'the productive sectors' of the economy, using a mix of interest rates and selective credit controls and ceilings. Credit management policies were dictated by the fact that 'in spite of the high liquidity in the system, the productive and priority sectors in the economy were not receiving adequate institutional credit' (Bank of Ghana, 1980). As many as eleven borrower-categories for the sectoral distribution of loans and advances were identified for the purpose of directing credit.

With regard to interest rate policy, the Bank of Ghana adjusted all rates periodically in order to promote increases in the level of investment among different sectors. In 1973, for example,

---

[1] First launched in 1976, 128 were eventually established, owned and managed by members of the local community. Many became financially distressed or inoperative, but with rehabilitation efforts in the 1990s, 60 were ranked by the Bank of Ghana in 1996 as performing satisfactorily and another 47 as mediocre. Their primary success has been in savings mobilization, accounting for 27% of total formal deposits mobilized in 1993.

the lending rate was fixed at a maximum of 10%. In 1980, the Bank of Ghana indicated that it was adjusting interest rates downwards in order to make it easier for institutional funds to flow to the productive and priority sectors without removing the banks' incentive to attract more deposits. In 1983, it again directed that the commercial banks should charge a preferential interest rate of 8% per annum (instead of the general 9% at the time) on loans and advances to small-scale farmers, whose operations required funds not exceeding a total of ¢50,000.

The policy for sectoral credit allocation was for the Bank of Ghana to prescribe credit ceilings for the 11 different borrower-categories in the form of permissible percentage increases over each bank's prevailing loans and advances. As late as 1984, for instance, the Bank directed that since control of bank lending to the non-government sector was the most important monetary policy consideration, export trade would remain classified as a *special sector,* exempted from any limitations on credit expansion, while agriculture, manufacturing, construction, transport, storage and communications continued to be *priority sectors,* for which a maximum of 20% increase in commercial bank credit was allowed. For all others, credit could not rise beyond 5% of the previous year's credit.

Performance of the Financial Sector before Reform

At the beginning of the 1980s, it became clear to the authorities that the financial system was incapable of delivering the financial services, though the number of institutions and branches had increased rapidly in the 1960s and 1970s. Aside from failing to mobilize resources for growth and development efficiently, it was also failing in its supportive role to the development of the monetary sector. The failures of the system were best reflected in the way various policies became dysfunctional and were often ignored in the operations of the institutions. Broader macroeconomic indicators showed that Ghana lagged behind other African nations in terms of financial depth.[2] Indeed, the negative impact of repressive policies on financial sector development was most clearly seen in the halving of financial depth, as measured by the ratio of money supply (M2) to GDP, from over 25% in 1977 to only 12% in 1984 (see Figure 11.1). Between 1977 and 1984, most other indicators of the development of the financial system declined in size (measured as a percentage of GDP); demand deposits fell from 11.6% to 4.6%, savings and time deposits from 7.1% to 2.6%, and domestic credit from 38.8% to 15.6%.

Fig. 11.1: Indicators of Financial Deepening in Ghana 1976–96

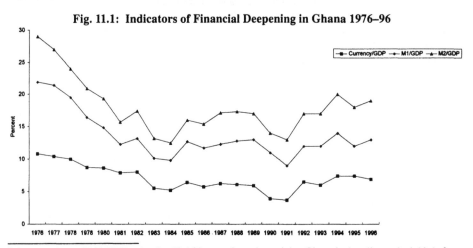

---

[2] A comparison of M2/GDP ratios for 10 African nations showed that Ghana had earlier ranked third after Ivory Coast and Kenya in 1977. By 1978, it ranked fifth after Kenya, Ivory Coast, Togo and Senegal, sixth in 1979, seventh in 1980, and ninth in 1981 and 1982. Between 1983 and 1986, Ghana remained at the tail end of the rankings (Aryeetey *et al.*, 1992).

In domestic finance, as in foreign-exchange markets, an increasing share of transactions took place outside the official, highly regulated institutions. Informalization of financial markets paralleled the decline of the formal real sectors under pervasive controls, a massively overvalued exchange rate, and scarcity of foreign exchange through official channels.

Liability and Asset Structures The dominance of items of short-term maturity in the consolidated balance sheets of banks was considerable. By 1984, almost 70% of the banking system's liabilities originated from demand and savings deposits. While the commercial banks on average had ratios of 60%–70% in the 1980s, the development banks followed with ratios of between 50%–60%, and the merchant banks had slightly lower ratios. 'Other liabilities'[3] were also significant to the banks. These constituted about 18% of total liabilities in 1977, 30% in 1979, and by 1983 even made up about 40% of total liabilities for a small number of banks. Their growth in the early 1980s showed the reliance on borrowing from various sources, in the face of shrinking business for the development banks and a declining deposit base. The capital adequacy ratio of banks, measured as the ratio of paid-up capital to total deposit liabilities, was not to be less than 5%. In general, however, very few banks achieved ratios in excess of 5% before 1984. Many had smaller ratios.

Similar to the trend above, the assets of the banking system before the reforms were characterized by low lending volumes in very short-term instruments. Most lending at the time was undertaken by the development banks, whose loan/deposit ratios exceeded 80%, mainly funded from short-term borrowing. In the decade prior to the reforms, the loan/deposit ratio averaged 50% for the indigenous commercial banks and 45% for the expatriate banks (the equity/loan ratios were 15% and 32%, respectively).

The banks argued that the lack of term lending in their asset structures was dictated by the need to match the maturity structure of their assets to the maturities of their liabilities. Because savings deposits in Ghana were operated almost like current accounts, banks argued that substantial medium- and long-term lending was inconsistent with the liquidity status needed to retain depositors' confidence. Hence they maintained a significant proportion of assets in highly liquid form with acceptable collateral, and securities of different maturities were not readily substitutable.

Despite substantial excess demand by the priority sectors and credit controls intended to channel funds to them, all of the commercial banks held substantial excess reserves in the form of cash and government paper, far above the Bank of Ghana's minimum reserve requirement. Excess reserves averaged about 15% of total deposit liabilities in the decade prior to the reforms, with about 5% in cash reserves and 10% in government paper. One explanation for the excess reserves during this period was the low return to lending to the priority sectors. Credit and interest rate controls prevented banks from making and pricing loans according to a ranking of risks and returns. In these circumstances, holding cash with no return was preferable to lending at spreads insufficient to cover costs.

Holding cash but without 'creditworthy' customers, the banks did not put in place effective savings mobilization schemes. They sometimes discouraged prospective savers from opening interest-bearing accounts, often using various administrative ploys.

Impact of Portfolio Management Policies on the Direction of Credit The fixed interest rates, credit ceilings and mandatory guidelines turned out to be ineffective in directing credit (Aryeetey *et al.,* 1992). Basically, the government's macroeconomic objectives which underpinned the sectoral choices (real economic growth and abatement of inflation) did not necessarily coincide with the microeconomic considerations of the banking sector. The banks were more interested in resolving the conflict between profitability and liquidity against the background of risks, creditworthiness and investment opportunities. Quite often, directives from the Bank of

---

[3] Other liabilities represent low-cost and short-term credit, marginal requirements, and provisions for taxation and pay-roll deductions.

Ghana to the banks to allocate more to the priority sectors were not accompanied by any incentives to the banks, bearing in mind the fact that these sectors were considered by most bankers to be high-risk sectors. Moreover, the sectoral guidelines and mandatory targets were often applied to the entire banking system irrespective of the individual banks' specialization. Similarly, the method of directing an expansion coefficient at domestic credit and the sectoral distribution tended to freeze the institutional structure of loans and advances prevailing at the reference date.

There was subsequently a reduction of credit to the priority sectors. For example, loans and advances to the agricultural sector experienced a 4.4% decline between 1980 and 1981, despite the fact that credit guidelines permitted a 50% increase over the previous year's level. Again, credit to the 'special' export and 'priority' manufacturing sectors showed in the same period increases of only 7.8% and –0.3% respectively. Credit to the commerce sector, on the other hand, recorded a 53% increase against the permitted 10% increase. In 1982, the Bank of Ghana reported that,

> lending to most sectors, especially the designated priority sectors, fell far short of permitted limits. In the case of agriculture, for instance, the previous ceiling of 100% increase was lifted completely in September 1981 to encourage the banks to increase lending to the sector. Despite this encouragement, credit to agriculture rose by only 36%. Similarly, lending to the manufacturing sector increased by only 20% compared with the permissible ceiling of 75%, while credit to the export trade sector even declined (Bank of Ghana, 1982).

Figure 11.2 shows how rapidly lending to other sectors (mainly trading) rose against the growth of agricultural credit.

Figure 11.2: Sectoral Distribution of Credit

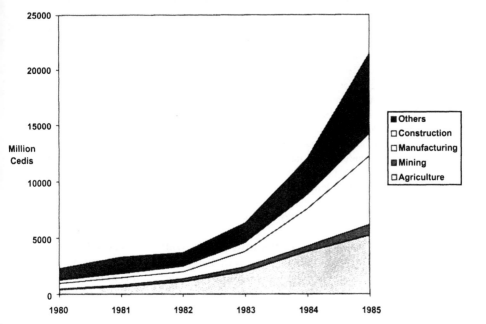

Indigenous small businesses received on average the smallest loan amounts and the smallest share of credit. Small foreign companies were limited by law in the amount of borrowing they could do, hence a small share in the total portfolio. Proportionately, the most favoured groups were the state-owned enterprises and limited liability companies (both indigenous and foreign). The public institutions had government backing and were mainly served by the Ghana Commercial Bank and the Social Security Bank, and tended to have some prior approval from government. Again these two banks dealt with the indigenous limited liability companies, while the two expatriate banks at the time 'dealt largely with foreign-owned companies'.

Relaxation of Enforcement

As monetary and credit restrictions during the mid-1970s proved ineffective in restraining growing inflationary pressures, let alone in achieving socio-economic goals, it was not surprising that this led to unrest. Following a 'palace coup' within the Supreme Military Council in 1978, enforcement of controls was relaxed somewhat. Without announcing explicit policy changes, the central bank eased its grip on the banks in implementing credit controls. Banks ignored sectoral credit ceilings with impunity.

The relaxation in enforcement between 1978 and 1985 did not, however, constitute a philosophical shift away from the interventionist approach. The approach was more one of 'muddling through', with restrictive policies on the books but little observation or enforcement. At the same time, several sporadic interventions after the PNDC took over in December 1981 undermined confidence in the banking system and led to financial disintermediation. These included a currency conversion in 1979, demonetization of the ¢50 note in 1982, freezing bank accounts over ¢50,000 in 1982 pending investigation for tax liability, and requiring business transactions over ¢1,000 to be paid by cheque.

Impetus for Reform

By the beginning of the 1980s, the banks needed recapitalization after years of poor asset management and the non-repayment of loans to state-owned enterprises. Despite nominal efforts to channel credit to small farmers and entrepreneurs, the state had become the largest beneficiary of a financial system that had become primarily an instrument of taxation. Implicit taxation of the financial system in Ghana was estimated at a relatively high 4.7% of GDP for 1978–8, accounting for 61% of government revenue (Chamley and Honohan, 1990). The legacy of repressive financial policies was that deposits drawn from the general population went to provide cheap credit to the public sector.

When drought aggravated the growing economic crisis in 1983, the PNDC government began considering major economic reform to reverse the situation and restore Ghana to favour with international lenders. At the time, the approach to development by influential bodies such as the World Bank and the International Monetary Fund emphasized reliance on the market for allocation of resources, including financial resources. Directed credit was deemed ineffective in achieving its objectives, and liberalization of financial markets was considered to be essential (Adams, 1984; Caprio et al., 1994). Hence it was clear to Ghanaian policy-makers both that controls were proving ineffective and that liberalization would be necessary to obtain the international assistance needed to finance balance of payments and budget deficits.

4.   Financial Policy Reforms and Performance after 1985

The initial focus of Ghana's Economic Recovery Programme in 1983–5 was on liberalizing foreign-exchange markets through devaluation and elimination of import licensing, removing price and distribution controls, and stabilizing the fiscal deficit. Financial markets were affected by the introduction of auctions for foreign exchange (in 1986) and Treasury bills (in 1987) and by decontrol of interest rates on lending and deposits (in 1987) and of sectoral credit controls (in

1988, except for agriculture). In 1988 private foreign-exchange bureaux were permitted, and Bank of Ghana bills were introduced as interest-bearing instruments that banks could hold.

While these reforms opened up financial markets, consistent with thinking on the negative effects of financial repression, they also exposed weaknesses in the regulatory infrastructure:

> Before 1989, norms for minimum capital adequacy and prudential lending were not clearly defined by law. Banks failed to apply uniform accounting standards. . . . They had no legal obligation to build up loan-loss reserves, and as a result, virtually all of Ghana's banks had excessive concentrations of risk, insufficient capital, unrecognized loan losses, and reported inflated profits. (World Bank, 1994b)

In 1989, attention shifted to bank restructuring, the legal and regulatory framework, and the supervisory capabilities of the central bank, with support from the World Bank-funded Financial Sector Adjustment Programme (FINSAP). The Banking Law was amended to provide a stronger prudential base in terms of minimum capital, reporting and lending guidelines. In 1990 non-performing loans were removed from bank portfolios to a separate recovery agency, in exchange for FINSAP bonds issued by the Bank of Ghana. A new Bank of Ghana law in 1992 provided stronger regulatory and supervisory powers. At the same time, entry of new banks and non-bank financial institutions was encouraged, especially through new laws in 1993 to support development of leasing, housing finance, and nine categories of non-bank financial institutions.

Portfolio Management Policies

Monetary and financial policies during the reform period had both stabilization and resource allocation objectives. In 1990–91 a predominant concern was to bring down inflation by controlling growth of the money supply and soaking up liquidity. Consistent with the liberalization approach, this was accomplished increasingly through interest rates and open market operations, while sectoral and bank credit ceilings were phased out from 1988 to 1992. Lending rates became positive in real terms in 1989 and 1991 (after more than a decade of negative real rates, except briefly in 1985), currency in circulation declined relative to GDP, and inflation fell to 10%.

Nevertheless, reserve requirements became an important tool of monetary management. The total ratio of reserves to deposits was raised from 25% in 1988 to 42% in 1990, with the composition shifting from 22% cash reserves and 20% secondary reserves in 1990 to 10% cash and 32% secondary in 1993 (World Bank, 1994b). In the latter year, with inflation rising following an increase in the fiscal deficit and money supply in 1992, secondary reserve requirements were raised to 52%, with the cash reserve ratio at 5%. Initially, the excess of actual over required reserves diminished from the high rates that had characterized the 1980s. But holdings of secondary reserves rose even faster than required in 1991–3, as interest rates rose on government paper.

The entire interest rate structure — Treasury bills, bank lending rates, and deposit rates — initially moved upward during 1984–7, then stabilized in 1988–9. But excess liquidity remained in the system, and Treasury bill rates rose substantially in 1990–91 in an effort to bring down inflation, while banks lowered their deposit rates. The result was an increase in the interest rate spread (Figure 11.3). While the spread subsequently narrowed somewhat, it remained relatively high, contrary to the expectation that increased competition and productivity among banks would lead to greater efficiency and lower spreads.

Developments in Liability Structures

Short-term liquid instruments continued to dominate the liability structure of the banking system after the reforms, albeit with some decline and greater variation across banks. Demand deposits fell from 70% of total bank liabilities in 1983 to 57% in 1991, ranging from 45% to 85%, with

Figure 11.3: Interest Rate Spread

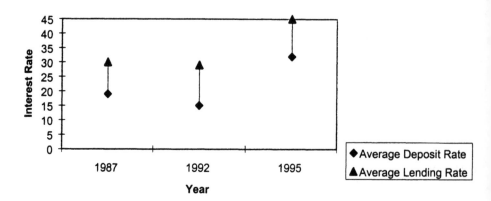

commercial banks at the higher end. For some banks, however, the main source of growth in their capital base after the reforms was increased capital from shareholders, rather than deposit mobilization. Most of the deposit instruments held were for very short periods and with low returns relative to inflation and interest rates on Treasury bills. The structure of savings instruments held has been as in Table 11.1, showing insignificant variation in the composition of deposits. There are indications of some revival in savings mobilization, but this has been slow and inconsistent. Studies with branch level data showed inconsistent growth in numbers of depositors and deposit sizes over a three-year period (1990–93) following the implementation of some reforms (Aryeetey, 1996). The slow growth of savings is indicated by the slow growth of the M2/GDP ratio which averaged 17% in 1990–95. At the end of 1996 it was only 19.4% (see Figure 11.1).

Table 11.1   Allocation of Total Formal Private Savings (%)

Year	Money Market Instruments[a]	Savings Deposits	Time Deposits	Total
1989	46.8	42.7	10.4	100
1990	44.3	46.7	8.9	100
1991	33.1	55.6	11.1	100
1992	35.8	48.5	15.5	100
1993	53.2	41.5	13.5	100
1994	48.2	44.2	7.6	100
1995	48.9	40.2	10.9	100
1996	51.0	39.8	10.2	100

Note: [a] Include Bills and Stocks
Source: Calculated from Bank of Ghana figures.

The growth in shareholders' funds reflected recapitalization of banks as a major component of the banking sector reform programme (FINSAC). Since 1988, average shareholder capital has been well above the 5% minimum (but usually below 15%). State-owned development banks averaged a relatively high 12%, as a result of government recapitalization schemes.

Despite the emergence of two discount houses, short-term borrowing remained negligible. The possibilities for long-term borrowing appear to have shrunk with the reforms. Only half the banks (mainly the former development banks) had any long-term borrowing commitments in 1992.

Trends in Assets

The development banks showed the most significant change in the composition of assets following the reforms, reflecting their previous difficulty in matching assets with liabilities. They gradually diversified their portfolios by reducing the volume of loans with maturities over three years by 20% from 1988 to 1991 in favour of short-term loans.

The commercial banks built up their foreign assets substantially following the reforms, which permitted them to offer foreign-denominated accounts to citizens. Despite some reduction in the claims of commercial banks on the government and the public sector, lending to the public sector has remained very important (Table 11.2). The high share of 'other assets', including fixed assets and highly liquid instruments, meant that relatively little was allocated to productive activities.

Table 11.2   Distribution of Total Domestic Credit (%)

Year	Central Government	Public Enterprises	Private Sector	Financial Sector
1986	64.2	16.9	15.5	3.2
1987	76.4	9.8	11.4	2.4
1988	75.8	4.13	16.9	3.2
1989	45.2	16.9	34.1	3.7
1990	47.1	11.8	37.4	3.5
1991	68.7	12.0	19.3	–
1992	68.3	10.8	20.7	–
1993	72.8	8.8	18.4	–
1994	62.7	14.7	22.6	–
1995	60.6	12.8	22.6	–
1996	54.8	10.2	34.8	–

The sectoral allocation of loans and advances has continued to shift steadily away from agriculture, whose share fell from over 30% in 1983–4 to under 10% in 1992–3. The share of manufacturing rose at first from around 20% during 1980–83 to over 30% in 1988–90, but then fell back to around 25%. Commercial bank credit went overwhelmingly to large enterprises, estimated in one survey at 74% of the loan portfolio (Aryeetey, 1996).

Competition after the Reforms

The new policy and legal environment stimulated the entry of a variety of both bank and non-

Figure 11.4: Sectoral Distribution of Credit After Reforms

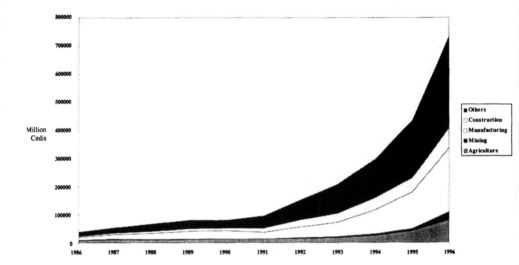

bank financial institutions (NBFIs), which substantially broadened the range of instruments and choices available. Two private merchant banks and a stock exchange were licensed in 1990, and a commercial bank in 1991. There are currently 17 banks in Ghana as against 11 at the start of the reforms. The 1993 Financial Institutions (Non-Banking) Law fostered the entry of four leasing companies, two savings and loan companies, two building societies, a venture capital company, a finance house, and a mortgage finance company by 1995, in addition to the two discount houses that had already been established in 1987 and 1991.[4]

The new NBFIs introduced a wider variety of financial products to compete with the commercial banks, which have, at best, only re-packaged their traditional financial products of current accounts, savings accounts, time deposits, and a select number of bonds and bills. But the formal NBFIs were competing largely for the same large-scale clients of the commercial banks, with relatively little impact in broadening the range of clients with access to formal financial services.

Private Sector Access to Finance

As a result of extraordinarily high reserve requirements by international standards and voluntary holdings of excess secondary reserves, the availability of credit to the private sector remained low (averaging about 4% of GDP during 1987–92, compared with 9% in Malawi, 20% in Kenya, and 50% in Indonesia). In response to the weak response of private investment and increasing complaints about the lack of finance from the general public, various special credit programmes were put in place. These include the Fund for Small and Medium Enterprise Development (FUSMED), the Rural Finance Project, the Credit Guarantee Scheme, and the Private Enterprise and Export Development project. FUSMED, for example, was a credit line of $25 m. channelled through the Bank of Ghana for on-lending at a cost reflecting the average cost of 180-day

---

[4] The NBFI Law also covers 128 rural banks and 250 credit unions which already existed (not all of them active). They are being strengthened through the Association of Rural Banks and the Credit Union Association, in preparation for being brought under the provisions of the law.

deposits mobilized by the banks. Other components of the project included training and technical assistance to improve banks' skills in project appraisal, monitoring and supervision of small- and medium-scale enterprise (SME) loans.

Nevertheless, the banks have not substantially changed their approach towards appraising creditworthiness. They apply the same technical requirements of feasibility studies, audited accounts, and legally documented property as collateral to SMEs as to large firms, even though these are beyond the capabilities of most of the SMEs targeted by the special programmes (Duggleby, 1992). Although banks rank collateral low compared with project viability as a criterion for appraising applications, in practice the collateral requirement serves to screen out most potential SME applicants.[5] As a result, banks perceive a lack of demand from creditworthy SMEs, even though survey evidence indicates excess effective demand for credit from the indigenous private sector (Aryeetey *et al.*, 1994).

Ironically, efforts to strengthen the banking system through stricter portfolio quality requirements by the Bank of Ghana may have restricted the access of SMEs by leading to increased centralization of decision-making (at least initially) and greater risk aversion. Most banks indicated that collateral requirements could be relaxed if a sound loan insurance or guarantee fund were available (Aryeetey *et al.*, 1994), though experience suggests that such schemes have negligible impact because the banks lack confidence in them, demand excessively high coverage, and do not substantially change their attitude toward SME clients.

Informal Financial Institutions

Informal financial institutions flourished during the reform period. These include trade credit, savings and credit associations, savings collectors, moneylenders, and non-governmental organizations (NGOs) engaged in credit.[6] For example, the average number of clients per savings collector rose from 155 in 1990 to 290 in 1992 and average monthly deposits grew by 64% (as against inflation of 35%) (Steel *et al.*, 1997). The average number of loans approved by moneylenders went up, while their interest rates softened, indicating that the supply of funds was increasing even faster than the demand. This increase in informal financial sector activity and competition was associated more with the increase in real sector activity during the adjustment period·than with financial policy reforms *per se*. That is, increased activity in markets due to elimination of controls and increased foreign borrowing meant that traders had more money to save and to lend (either to business clients or to borrowers).

The evident ability of informal financial markets to capture much of the increased economic activity runs counter to the expectation of the financial repression hypothesis that financial liberalization would lead formal financial markets to deepen and absorb the spillover into informal financial markets. The explanation is that Ghana's financial markets remained dominated by imperfections owing to lack of information, difficult contract enforcement, and inadequate risk management instruments. Well into the 1990s, the commercial banks were still trying to improve portfolio performance and efficiency in dealing with their traditional large-scale customers. High returns on government paper and weak competition gave them little incentive to innovate in reaching new, smaller clients. The specialized, character-based techniques of informal financial institutions continued to give them a comparative advantage in managing the costs and risks of small transactions with the majority of the population.

---

[5] Difficulties enforcing collateral have led banks to document it thoroughly up front, imposing fees that can amount to as much as 1% of the loan amount and adding several weeks to processing.

[6] Both rotating savings and credit associations and savings collectors are known in Ghana as *susu*. In *susu* associations, members pay set amounts at regular intervals into a common pool, which goes to each in turn. *Susu* collectors take a fixed daily deposit from individual clients and return the accumulated amount at the end of the month, minus one day's deposit as commission. They are particularly important in helping market traders to set aside a portion of daily profits for working capital to re-stock at the end of the month.

Informal institutions innovated in seeking new clients. In the late 1980s, registered *susu* companies used informal savings collection techniques to mobilize substantial deposits by promising depositors credit after six months of regular deposits. Most of these collapsed because of poor management and inability to meet increasing demands on their liquidity, but some re-emerged under the new NBFI Law as Savings and Loan Companies. In the mid-1990s, *susu* clubs emerged as privately-run savings and credit associations. NGOs also moved increasingly into financial activities, with innovations such as the inventory credit scheme of TechnoServe, which enabled farmers to set aside part of their crops during the harvest season for credit which could be repaid by selling the crop at a higher price during the off season.

5.   Constraints on Financial Market Development

The performance of Ghana's financial system has not differed greatly between the interventionist and liberalized policy regimes. While the range and competition of financial institutions are undoubtedly greater today than in the 1970s, the system remains fragmented, financial depth has recovered little from the sharp decline of the early 1980s, short-term liabilities and assets continue to dominate, and high spreads do not betoken improved efficiency. While the regulatory infrastructure and portfolio monitoring have improved, the legal infrastructure for collateral documentation and contract enforcement has not.

Explanations for the apparent similarity in performance under different financial policy regimes include the macroeconomic environment and underlying structural and institutional constraints. The decline in financial depth in the late 1970s and early 1980s can be attributed as much to macroeconomic instability (including high inflation, falling income per capita, and a highly overvalued exchange rate) as to the legacy of repressive financial policies (Montiel, 1994). Financial reforms were part of the overall Economic Recovery Programme, which was successful in bringing the fiscal deficit below 5% of GDP in 1991 and inflation down to 10%, setting a more stable stage for developing the financial sector. Other reforms carried out concurrently with financial reform included the liberalization of foreign-exchange markets, trade policy reforms, and public enterprise reforms (though privatization of state enterprises proceeded very slowly).

Despite these efforts to establish a sound policy environment, a surge in expenditures in the 1992 election year ushered in a new period of relatively high fiscal deficits and inflation (averaging 13% of GDP and 40%, respectively, over 1993–6; World Bank, 1997). Money supply grew by 53% in 1992, after growing less than 14% in the two preceding years. Efforts to finance these deficits and to control inflation by limiting monetary growth resulted in exceptionally high interest rates on government paper, giving banks a low-risk route to profitability and leaving little incentive for the banking system to expand its private sector clientele and become more efficient.

Worldwide evidence indicates that macroeconomic stability is a condition for successful financial sector reform. Countries with macro stability are better able to avoid high interest rates, fluctuations in real exchange rates, and insolvency among firms and banks (World Bank, 1989). For example, with low inflation, Malaysia's M2/GDP ratio rose from 31% in 1970 to 75% in 1987. In contrast, high-inflation countries have tended to experience slow or negative growth in financial depth. For example, the far-reaching financial sector reforms in Argentina, Chile, and Uruguay during the mid-1970s generally produced undesirable effects in the banking sector and failed to improve financial sector efficiency (Diaz-Alejandro, 1985). Ghana's failure to maintain control over macroeconomic variables has more in common with the latter examples than the former.

Furthermore, Ghana's financial reforms have evidently had little impact on the underlying market failures that characterize the imperfect information paradigm of Stiglitz and Weiss. The lack of adequate information makes different lenders perceive different borrowers differently, leading them to adopt screening, monitoring and contract enforcement methods suited to a narrow group of clients. There has been some increase in the array of non-bank financial institutions with specialized products, such as leasing and discounting. But financial markets have remained highly fragmented, with little flow of funds, information or clients between segments. The lack of credit bureaux and of good interbank co-operation makes it difficult for banks to evaluate new applicants and for the latter to establish a reputation. The majority of the population still lacks access to formal bank and non-bank financial institutions, and continues to depend on informal financial institutions that use character-based techniques and localized information.

One reason for the persistent fragmentation is the continuing difficulties faced by would-be borrowers in obtaining legal title to land to use as collateral and by lenders in enforcing contracts through the judicial system. Furthermore, most bank staff lack the skills to market financial services more aggressively in a more competitive environment, especially those in government-owned banks that historically operated in monopolistic markets and had fairly simple appraisal techniques.

6.   The Road Ahead

Ghana's experience demonstrates that, on the one hand, interventionist financial policies are largely ineffective in facilitating the growth of priority productive sectors, and, on the other hand, simply liberalizing restrictive policies alone is not sufficient to stimulate a deeper, efficient, more integrated financial sector. The impact of financial policy reforms depends on complementary efforts to achieve macroeconomic stability and to reduce underlying structural and institutional constraints. Ghana has had only limited success in achieving these basic conditions, and financial sector performance under liberalization has progressed slowly, at best.

Ghana's ability to achieve faster economic growth led by private sector investment depends in large part on developing efficient financial intermediation that mobilizes savings from a wide range of the population and makes it available to private investors and businesses of all sizes. Progress toward this goal will depend first of all on restoring macroeconomic stability, especially by bringing public expenditures and deficit spending under control to relieve pressure on the money supply, interest rates, and inflation. Otherwise, banks will have little incentive to extend lending to the private sector and financial resources will continue to flow overwhelmingly to the government at the expense of the private sector.

Nevertheless, Ghana's experience also shows that macroeconomic stability and financial liberalization are not sufficient to improve financial sector performance significantly. Complementary efforts will be needed to reduce market imperfections related to information availability and contract enforcement — for example, credit bureaux and other means of sharing information on client creditworthiness, legal reforms to simplify land titling, and special commercial laws and courts to settle disputes and enforce claims.

Successful financial sector development in Ghana will also have to incorporate informal and semi-formal financial institutions better in order to increase resource mobilization and financial services in the economy as a whole. These institutions have proved able to reach the lower-income households, farmers, and microenterprises that have remained beyond the reach of the banks. But their dependence on localized information and personal contact makes it hard for them to become formal and reach a larger scale. The first step would be to clarify the legal and regulatory situation for informal and semi-formal institutions that are not covered in the NBFI Law. Small savings and credit associations based on common bonds and one-on-one transactions, such as *susu* groups and collectors, can be recognized as informal and beyond the purview of the authorities, though perhaps encouraged to self-regulate and to associate with formal financial intermediaries. Larger institutions that serve the general public, such as NGOs, may be brought under some degree of regulation, especially if they want to engage in savings mobilization as well as credit.

A clearer legal and regulatory framework would facilitate greater integration between different segments of the financial system, reducing fragmentation and increasing system-wide efficiency of intermediation. For example, the banks could establish closer links with *susu* collectors and NGOs, which could more effectively mobilize savings and dispense credit in small amounts if they had access to bank credit. Growing small enterprises could better access bank finance if they could establish acceptable track records with micro finance institutions.

Additional support may be warranted to strengthen the capabilities of rural and micro finance institutions to expand their outreach while moving to higher levels of sustainability. International evidence shows that informal, character-based techniques can be adapted to achieve high rates of loan and cost recovery and to increase the outreach of their operation (Christen *et al.*, 1994; Otero and Rhyne, 1994). A number of Ghana's rural and micro finance institutions formed an Action Research Network in 1996 to share information on best practices and attempt to develop the industry, for example through shared training programmes.

Technical assistance to improve capabilities is needed at all levels to improve efficiency, innovation, and competitiveness. Bank staff need new skills to develop and market new financial services in an increasingly competitive market. NGOs engaged in credit likewise need to learn commercial methods and financial management to assure cost recovery and sustainability. Credit unions, rural banks, and *susu* collectors could benefit from assistance in their efforts to build strong apex structures, which could facilitate supervision as well as strengthen their market segments.

References

Adams, D. W. (1984) 'Are the Arguments for Cheap Agricultural Credit Sound?' In D. W. Adams, D. H. Graham and J. D. Von Pischke (eds) *Undermining Rural Development with Cheap Credit.* Boulder, 10: Westview Press.

Aryeetey, E. (1994) *Financial Integration and Development in Sub-Saharan Africa: A Study of Informal Finance in Ghana.* Working Paper 78, London: Overseas Development Institute.

Aryeetey, E. (1996) *The Formal Financial Sector in Ghana After the Reforms.* Working Paper 86, London.

Aryeetey, E., Asante, Y. and Kyei, A. Y. (1992) 'Mobilizing Domestic Savings for African Development and Diversification: A Ghanaian Case Study'. Oxford: International Development Centre, Queen Elizabeth House, mimeo.

Aryeetey, E., Baah-Nuakoh, A., Duggleby, T., Hettige, H. and Steel, W. F. (1994) *The Supply and Demand for Finance Among SMEs in Ghana.* World Bank Discussion Paper 251. Washington, DC: World Bank, Africa Technical Department.

Bank of Ghana (1975) *Annual Report 1974/75.* Accra: Bank of Ghana.

Bank of Ghana (1980) *Annual Report.* Accra: Bank of Ghana.

Bank of Ghana (1982) *Annual Report.* Accra: Bank of Ghana.

Caprio, G., Jr., Atiyas, I. and Hanson, J. (eds) (1994) *Financial Reform: Theory and Experience.* Cambridge: Cambridge University Press.

Chamley, Christopher and Honohan, Patrick (1990) *Taxation of Financial Intermediation: Measurement Principles and Application to Five African Countries.* World Bank WPS 421. Washington, DC: World Bank.

Christen, R. P., Rhyne, E. and Vogel, R. C. (1994) *Maximizing the Outreach of Microenterprise Finance: The Emerging Lessons of Successful Programs.* Consulting Assistance for Economic Reform (CAER) Paper. Washington, DC: IMCC.

Diaz-Alejandro, C. (1985) 'Good-Bye Financial Repression, Hello Financial Crash', *Journal of Development Economics,* Vol. 19: 1–24

Duggleby, T. (1992) 'Best Practices in Innovative Small Enterprise Finance Institutions', in William F. Steel (ed.) *Financial Deepening in Sub-Saharan Africa: Theory and Innovations.* Industry and Energy Department Working Paper, Industry Series Paper No. 62. Washington, DC: World Bank.

Fry, M. J. (1982) 'Models of Financial Repressed Developing Economies', *World Development,* Vol. 10, No. 9.

Fry, M. J. (1988) *Money, Interest, and Banking in Economic Development.* Baltimore, MD and London: Johns Hopkins University Press.

Galbis, V. (1977) 'Financial Intermediation and Economic Growth in Less-Developed Countries: A Theoretical Approach', *Journal of Development Studies,* Vol. 13: 58–72

Gertler, M. and Rose, A. (1994) 'Finance, Growth and Public Policy', in Caprio *et al.*

Giovannini, A and de Melo, M. (1990) *Government Revenue from Financial Repression.* Policy, Research and External Affairs Working Papers. WPS 533. Washington, DC: World Bank, November.

Goldsmith, R. W. (1969) *Financial Structure and Development.* New Haven, CT and London: Yale University Press.

Gurley, J. G., and Shaw, E. (1967) 'Financial Development and Economic Development', *Economic Development and Cultural Change,* Vol. 15, No. 3, April: 257–65.

Hoff K. and Stiglitz, J. E. (1990) 'Imperfect Information and Rural Credit Markets — Puzzles and Policy Perspectives', *The World Bank Economic Review,* Vol. 4, No. 3.

McKinnon, R. I. (1973) *Money and Capital in Economic Development.* Washington, DC: The Brookings Institution.

Montiel, P. (1994) 'Financial Policies and Economic Growth: Theory, Evidence and Country-Specific Experience from Sub-Saharan Africa'. Paper Presented at the African Economic Research Consortium Biannual Workshop, Nairobi, May.

Nissanke, M. and Aryeetey, E. (1998) *Financial Integration and Development in Sub-Saharan Africa.* London and New York: Routledge.

Otero, M. and Rhyne, E. (1994) *The New World of Microenterprise Finance.* West Hartford, CT: Kumarian Press.

Popiel, P. A. (1994) *Financial Systems in Sub-Saharan Africa; A Comparative Study.* World Bank Discussion Papers 260, Africa Technical Department Series. Washington, DC: World Bank.

Shaw, E. S. (1973) *Financial Deepening in Economic Development.* New York: Oxford University Press.

Steel, W. F., Aryeetey, E., Hettige, H. and Nissanke, M. (1997) 'Informal Financial Markets Under Liberalization in Four African Countries', *World Development* Vol. 25, No. 5.

Stiglitz, J. E. (1989) 'Financial Markets and Development', *Oxford Review of Economic Policy,* Vol. 5, No. 4.

Stiglitz, J. E. (1994) 'The Role of the State in Financial Markets', in *Proceedings of the World Bank Annual Conference on Development Economics 1993.* Washington, DC: World Bank.

Stiglitz, J. E. (1996) *The Role of the State in Financial Markets: Proceedings of the World Bank Annual Conference on Development Economics.* Washington, DC: World Bank.

Stiglitz, J. E. and Weiss, A. (1981) 'Credit Rationing in Markets with Incomplete Information'. *American Economic Review,* Vol. 17.

Streeten, P. (1979) 'From Growth to Basic Needs', *Basic Needs Strategy as a Planning Parameter.* Berlin: German Foundation for International Development.

World Bank (1989) *World Development Report 1989: Financial Systems and Development.* Washington, DC: World Bank.

World Bank (1994a) *Adjustment in Africa: Reforms, Results and the Road Ahead,* Policy Research Report. New York: Oxford University Press.

World Bank (1994b) *Ghana Financial Sector: Missing Links between Savers and Investors.* Report No. 13423-GH. Washington, DC: World Bank.

World Bank (1997) *African Development Indicators.* Washington, DC: World Bank.

12 Labour & Employment under Structural Adjustment

BEN FINE
& KWABIA BOATENG

1. Introduction

For Ghana, as for other developing countries, the labour market poses a, if not the, major problem for the economy and for policy-making. Within the labour market itself, there is the persistent challenge of generating sufficient jobs to absorb a growing labour force and to avoid mass unemployment, especially amongst the young. There are macroeconomic issues of stabilizing growth in money wages in order to hold down inflationary pressures. Wage differentials both within and between the public and private sectors are significant in allocating scarce skills to their most effective use. The creation of more skills within the workforce is also a precondition for growing productivity. The labour market is the most important source of income and so has a crucial influence on the distribution of income and poverty. Not surprisingly, the labour market is highly politicized with the formation and activities of trade unions.

Satisfactory consideration of these issues depends upon both the availability of adequate statistics and the deployment of appropriate analytical framework and theory. Each of these has been far from satisfactory in the Ghanaian context. In the first section of this chapter, some consideration is given to the data that can be used in studying the Ghanaian labour market. Whilst severe reservations are expressed about their reliability, one conclusion can be drawn — that the labour market is highly heterogeneous and fragmented. This is taken up in the following section which covers recent developments in labour market theory which, it is argued, has been insufficiently sensitive to the differentiation between labour markets, particularly in the sense that different labour markets are not only structurally separated but also function in different ways. This is confirmed in the next section in the Ghanaian context by considering a number of specific issues within the labour market, especially the role of informal employment and of apprentices. The final section points towards an alternative to much of the existing and orthodox treatment of labour markets. It suggests that analysis needs to be placed within the context of a developing economy in which the exercise of market power within the labour market is significant but uneven. By the same token, policy initiatives within and around the labour market must directly address economic and political realities and the goals of development, including industrialization, rather than resting upon the simple nostrum that labour markets will work better the more they are allowed to conform to the ideal of perfect competition.

2. The Bare Statistics

Two severe handicaps have plagued the study of labour markets in Ghana — inadequate data and inappropriate theory. Each alone is debilitating; taken together they are devastating. Analytical issues will be examined in later sections. Consider first the data.[1] The last census was undertaken in 1984 with estimates of the potential labour force, and participation rates, subsequently dependent on projections or less comprehensive surveys, see Table 12.1.[2] The Ghana Statistical Service, GSS, last published figures for employment for 1992 with the latest monthly data from the Employment Market Report appearing for July 1987.

Table 12.1   Estimated Annual Growth of the Labour Force 1960–2000

Year	Total	Males	Females
1960–65	1.92	2.18	1.57
1970–75	2.08	2.22	1.90
1980–85	2.66	2.94	2.26
1985–90	2.76	3.05	2.32
1990–95	2.99	3.14	2.76
1995–2000	3.10	3.25	2.87

Source: UN, *African Statistical Yearbook 1990/91.* Part 2.

Quite apart from the frequency with which data are collected, the range of variables included is extremely limited. The *Quarterly Digest of Statistics* covers only two major items — recorded levels of employment and the corresponding average earnings per employee within the so-called formal sector. As the latter certainly comprises a minority share of overall employment, and there are no systematic data on the informal sectors, the available statistics provide only a partial and skewed picture of the labour markets. Last, and by no means least, the reliability and even credibility of the data that are made available need to be considered. The *Quarterly Digest* for March, 1993, for example, reported a mere 123,000 employees in the public sector throughout Ghana, a figure that even government officials themselves were not prepared to accept. Further, Boateng (1996b) has suggested that unemployment has increased from an estimated 6% in 1960 to over 35% in 1995. Yet, the number of registered unemployed has barely changed over the past decade, given the limited incentive to register at employment centres.

Such problems could be replicated many times over. Of course, even with reliable and regularly collected data, there can be conceptual problems and problems of interpretation, particularly when, for example, it comes to unemployment. What exactly do we mean by (un)employed? This is especially germane in the Ghanaian context. As will be seen, there does appear to have been a considerable shake-out of formal employment from both the public and the private sectors over the past decade. If, however, for example, as is common, previously high levels of public sector employment are interpreted as representing the exercise of political favour and commitment without necessarily involving work other than in the formal occupation of a job, then much of such formal employment has closer resonances with welfare payments than wage labour. Yet, those on welfare benefits would not be considered to be employed in most circum-

---

[1] Much of the following draws upon Boateng (1996a). It is not possible here to provide a full account of the labour market statistics that are available, nor their strengths and weaknesses.
[2] Of these, the most important for examining labour market issues is the Ghana Living Standards Survey, although it is limited by only covering the years 1987/8, 1988/9, and 1991/2. There are also problems of its consistency over the three survey periods. Nonetheless, despite being motivated by the slightly different issue of examining the incidence of poverty, the GLSS has much to offer in labour market analysis, a potential that has been neglected or wasted as is revealed in later discussion.

stances, although this can also occur in a sense in advanced countries in order to massage the unemployment figures.[3]

With much hesitancy and trepidation, selective data on the labour market are reproduced below. Formal sector employment in Ghana is defined as that recorded in establishments employing five or more workers. Table 12.2 shows the overall numbers of those so formally employed and their distribution by share across economic sectors and by public and private sectors.

Table 12.2   Distribution of Formal Sector Employment in Ghana ('000)

	Overall			Public			Private		
	1970	1980	1990	1970	1980	1990	1970	1980	1990
Agric. hunting, forestry	48.9	54.9	19.0	43.6	51.1	17.8	5.3	3.8	1.2
Mining & quarrying	25.2	23.8	12.9	11.7	23.3	12.0	13.5	0.5	0.9
Manufacturing	52.8	35.1	28.7	15.1	13.1	6.3	37.7	22.0	22.3
Utilities[a]	14.8	6.6	4.0	14.8	6.6	4.0	–	–	–
Construction	50.0	22.4	10.3	35.2	19.4	6.9	14.8	3.0	3.7
Trade	35.9	22.1	10.7	20.0	14.3	6.8	15.9	7.8	3.9
Transport, communication	32.5	17.0	9.6	31.3	15.9	8.7	1.2	1.1	0.9
Finance[b]	–	11.0	4.4	–	9.6	4.0	–	1.4	0.4
Services[c]	137.8	145.9	123.8	116.2	137.9	122.9	21.6	8.0	0.9
Total Employment	397.9	338.8	223.7	287.9	291.2	189.4	110.0	47.6	34.2

Notes: [a] Utilities include only electricity, gas and water.
              [b] Finance used to be classified with Services.
              [c] Services refer to social, community and personal services.
Source: Ghana Statistical Service, *Quarterly Digest of Statistics*, March 1993.

As such, although the share of formal employment is estimated to have been almost 45% in 1960, the total absolute figure for formal employment of 464,000 is estimated to have peaked at a level of only 7.3% of the labour force in 1985 (9.5% of labour demand) before falling to 186,000 in 1991 or 2.5% of the labour force (3.2% of demand). The corresponding figures for the public sector are 397,000 and 156,000, respectively. Private sector employment, however, experienced a dramatic fall in the second half of the 1970s, from 137,000 in 1975 to 48,000 in 1980, as well as falling from a peak of 79,000 in 1987 to a mere 30,000 in 1991.

Thus, prior to 1985, formal employment had been growing more slowly than the labour supply. Thereafter, it has been falling in absolute terms. Private sector formal employment has been falling more or less continuously since 1975. This has left the bulk of employment in the informal sectors. These are themselves a statistical and conceptual minefield, not least serving as a huge sump for those unable to obtain formal employment.[4] ISSER (1995) estimates that employment in the non-agricultural informal sectors increased from just over 1 to almost 3 million between 1960 and 1990. This would imply an increase of the informal sectors' share from 68% to well over 90%. Most informal employment, however, remains concentrated in agriculture,

---

[3] See Bartholomew *et al.* (1995) for a discussion in the UK context.
[4] See also Ninsin (1990) who describes the informal sectors as, 'an array of precarious economic activities which have become the haven of people seeking desperately to eke out a living because they are unable to secure wage or salaried employment in the formal capitalist sector' (p.60).

with its overall share of the economically active population estimated by the *African Development Report* of 1994 to have fallen from 64% to 58% between 1960 and 1970 but only to 52% by
1992.

The contentious and mixed nature of these figures is brought out by considering the proxi-
mate causes of their shifts over time. The period from 1960 to 1985 was marked by a policy of
creating high levels of public employment. When this policy was abandoned, indeed reversed in
the following period, formal public sector employment dropped considerably. In the case of
agriculture, for example, 10,000 employees were retrenched from the Ghana Cocoa Marketing
Board with arguably limited direct impact on output. On the other hand, the decline in formal
employment in the construction industry, from 18.6% and 12.6%, respectively, in 1960 and
1970, to a mere 4.2% in 1991 has been due to the partial liquidation of the State Construction
Corporation and the downsizing of the Public Works Department and the now privatized State
Housing Corporation. Most remaining employment in the construction industry has shifted into
the informal sectors. The mining and quarrying sector has witnessed steadily increasing output
since 1983 but employment levels have been falling, from 24,000 in 1983 to 17,100 in 1991, due
both to increasing capital-intensity in new companies and rationalization amongst the old.

In short, data on employment in the formal sector reflect a variety of processes from the
incidence of featherbedding, through productivity and output levels, to shifts into the informal
sectors. The problems with data on employment are compounded when examining (formal) wage
levels, for these inevitably aggregate and average over the more or less arbitrary employment
statistics. Set against an uneven inflation rate raising monthly nominal earnings by over a thou-
sand-fold between 1960 and 1991, real earnings had fallen steadily by 1984 to a fifth of their
level in 1960, falling most dramatically between 1975 and 1980, before rising to 40% in 1990 of
what they had been thirty years before, see Figure 12.1. Necessarily, these figures reflect the
high share of public sector employment. Given the very low levels of salaries from the mid-
1970s onwards, and the common knowledge of moonlighting, figures on average wages beg the
question of not only for whom but also for what.

Figure 12.1: Trends in Average Monthly Real Earnings per Employee

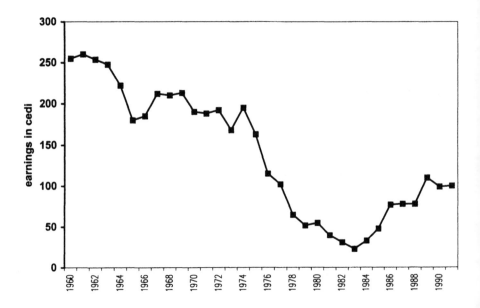

Furthermore, wage differentials within the public sector have been associated with a mixture of policies, motives and factors, each with their own rhythm — ranging from egalitarianism, minimum wages, efficiency, fiscal pressures, and political expediency. In this light, data concerning overall ratios of public and private sector remuneration have to be treated with considerable caution. The change in the ratio from 68.2% to 93.7% between 1988 and 1991, for example, is largely explained by the retrenchment of low wage workers in the public sector, especially agriculture. Earnings in financial services appear to be 50% less in the public than the private sector (see also Baah-Nuakoh *et al.*, 1996). For a developing country, the unusual differential in Ghana in favour of the private sector and against the public sector is all the more remarkable given the high proportion of graduates that work for government, as much as 94% of one sample of graduates.[5] Table 12.3 shows wage relativities and how they have changed between 1981 and 1991, with some corresponding figures for minimum wages and changes, generally declines, in employment.

Table 12.3   Average Monthly Earnings by Sector 1981–91

	1981	Relative Wage 1981	1991	Relative Wage 1991	% increase in wages 1981–91	% decline in employment 1981–91
Agric. forestry, fishing	503	1.02	39231	1.11	700	4.9
Mining & quarrying	859	1.74	27417	0.78	280	0
Manufacturing	689	1.40	34226	0.97	440	1.9
Construction	507	1.03	25738	0.73	450	3.1
Commerce	518	1.05	30189	0.86	520	3.2
Transport, storage & communication	624	1.27	39119	1.11	560	1.0
Finance, insurance	–	–	50016	1.42	860	(5.3)
Services	n.a	n.a	n.a	n.a	n.a	n.a
All sectors	493	1.00	35212	1.00	640	0.9
Minimum monthly wage[a]	300	0.61	11318	0.32	330	n.a

Note: [a] This is calculated as the daily minimum wage times 25 working days. ( ) indicates improvement. Percentages are annual averages.
Source: Ghana Statistical Service

The explicit purpose of these opening remarks has been to express grave reservations about the availability and use of Ghanaian labour market statistics. At the very least, any study that employs them should discuss their reliability and margins for error, preferably in the context of the theory or hypothesis that is being advanced and certainly relative to the estimation of, and confidence that is attached to, parameters within any regression. But there has also been an implicit purpose. This has been to provide a preface to the following discussion of labour market theory which itself is organized around the notion that it is inappropriate to understand the labour market in terms of a greater or lesser deviation from an idealized world of harmonious

---

[5] As reported in Commander and Ugaz (1994).

equilibrium between labour supply and demand. Even examining the problems raised by the construction and use of labour market statistics puts such a perspective in doubt.

3.   Recent Developments in Labour Market Theory — Are They Enough?

Over the past two decades, the economic theory of labour markets has changed substantially, and the impact of that change has increasingly been felt in the study of the labour markets of developing countries. Traditionally, in the post-war period, the overall working of the labour market has been tied to macroeconomic theory. Keynesian notions of effective demand have been deployed to determine the overall level of (un)employment, giving way in the mid-1970s to more pessimistic prognoses for the potential role of policy in the wake of the new classical economics and its assumptions of instantaneous market clearing and rational expectations, albeit in the context of uncertainty attached to exogenous shocks. Whilst this has rendered the (vertical) Phillips curve redundant, the notion of a natural rate of unemployment has persisted even if, at times, in the context of a non-accelerating inflation rate of unemployment, NAIRU. With the natural rate apparently rising from the mid-1970s across OECD countries, the notion of hysteresis in unemployment has evolved to explain its persistence at higher levels.

The macroeconomic policy underlying IMF stabilization policy has scarcely attempted to keep abreast of these already dated developments within macroeconomic theory, continuing to rely upon the simplistic framework suggested by Polak as long ago as 1957, in which the impact upon the workings of the labour market is, in any case, generally overlooked in the light of priority in adjusting the balance of payments. More recently, however, particularly in the light of the experience of economic adjustment in developing countries, closer attention has been given to the role played by labour markets — usually as a potential obstacle to adjustment. Here, the literature has not only caught up, to some extent, with the macroeconomic theory of the past, it has also incorporated some of the more recent developments in the relationship between the labour market and macroeconomic theory (Azam, 1994; Agenor, 1996).

These fall under the rubric of the new Keynesian economics or the micro foundations of macroeconomics. Here, the motivating idea is to explain why particular markets might not work perfectly in the sense of leading to instantaneous market clearing, even though the obstacles to their doing so are not necessarily taken as institutional or exogenous. Rather, markets might not clear because of, not despite, the optimizing behaviour of individual economic agents. An illustration is easily offered by way of efficiency wages — with firms paying more than they need to in an environment of surplus labour in order to enhance the productivity of their workforce. This can be motivated by the idea of raising the consumption of workers above bare subsistence but, in the context of developed economies, it has also been connected to the wish of employers to attract a higher quality of worker or to induce higher work effort, given the greater cost of being fired.

Ultimately, if based on individual optimization, these results depend upon imperfect and/or asymmetric information and transactions costs (whether in making or monitoring contracts). As such, they do not apply exclusively to, nor have they always originated analytically in, labour market theory. Exactly the same considerations apply to other markets, as in the market for 'lemons' (or second-hand cars), credit rationing, etc. There can, however, be knock-on effects from these markets on the labour market, as pricing affects the level of the real wage and output decisions affect the demand for labour. In addition, account has also been taken of traditional microeconomic notions of imperfect competition in labour and/or other markets in determining the quantity/price relationship and its implications for the macroeconomy. Trade unions, for example, can be perceived to exercise a monopsony in which wages are held above the market-clearing level in trading off the membership's real wage against the overall level of employment.[6]

---

[6] Solow (1990) shows in the context of game theory how it may also be optimal for the unemployed to adopt the custom of not undercutting the wages of the employed.

In short, the recent literature on labour markets and adjustment in developing countries has now come to accept, primarily drawing upon theory attached to developed economies, that the labour market works in a more complicated fashion than simply reflecting an inverse relationship between the real wage and the level of employment, with adjustment depending upon downward wage flexibility. The old view is summarized by Horton *et al.* (1994a: 3):

In this framework, therefore, the test for whether the labour market was working well would focus on whether the real wage fell sufficiently to maintain employment and output in the face of a reduction in total national expenditure.

In contrast, they posit a new framework in which there are alternative explanations for unemployment:

With persistent unemployment, therefore, the finger can point to at least one of three factors: imperfectly competitive product markets, aggregate demand feedback from real wages, or labour markets not working well (*ibid.*: 4).

Thus, as in structuralist macroeconomic models, falling real wages due to monopoly prices or lower money wages might lead to deficient aggregate demand. Significantly, the conclusion from the country studies collected in Horton *et al.* (1994b) is that the overall evidence is of downward real wage flexibility and, hence, too high wages cannot be blamed as the general cause of unemployment.[7]

A recent overview of the literature on the labour market and economic adjustment is provided by Agenor (1996), and it is worth briefly running over some of his results. He observes that studies of labour markets were previously attached to the medium or long term, with the focus upon rural/urban migration, the growth of the urban labour force, and the relationships between unemployment and poverty and between human capital and earnings. Devaluation or trade reform as a policy to improve international competitiveness has recently brought other issues to the fore. First, its effects, according to conventional Walrasian reasoning, depend upon immediate and sustained reductions in real wages for employment to be sustained, so that there are neither compensating increases in money wages nor an inflationary impetus. Secondly, at a disaggregated level, it is necessary for the switch in the composition of output in favour of exports to be accommodated by a corresponding shift of labour between sectors and, again, without this unduly disturbing the overall reduction in real wages (Edwards and Edwards, 1994).

Necessarily, then, the recent literature has addressed the disaggregation of the labour market, and it has done so in two different ways. On the one hand, it relies upon the traditional divisions inherited from the earlier literature. Agenor points to three segments, the rural/household sector, and the urban formal and informal sectors. These divisions depend upon a descriptive conventional wisdom, derived from standard models such as those of Lewis and Harris-Todaro. Within these, labour market structures are taken as given and as functioning in different ways. For Lewis, for example, rewards to the rural sector are at average as opposed to marginal product in the urban sector; for Harris-Todaro, the urban sector is non-clearing, inducing search or waiting unemployment, in response to the higher wages prompted by trade unions or the public sector.

On the other hand, this segmentation is complemented by one motivated by adjustment and/ or new developments in labour market theory. As observed, the former depends upon disaggregating by trading status of the products, and the latter upon considerations of efficiency wages, trade unions, search costs and voluntary unemployment for those with skills, and so on. Emphasis can be placed upon the interaction between disaggregated labour markets. If, for ex-

---

[7] See Nelson (1994). Agenor (1996: 316) also concludes, 'attempts at circumventing the role of unions in the process of wage formation are unlikely to have any significant effect on "flexibility" in most cases'.

ample, real wages are maintained in the formal sector, labour will be shed, depressing wages in the informal sector so that overall employment may even grow but at the expense of growing poverty and worsening income distribution (Addison and Demery, 1994). Similarly, if trade unions are powerful enough, they can engage in rent-sharing in those sectors where profitability is boosted by adjustment policies, both dulling their impact and explaining wage differentials across sectors of the economy.

This neat division between the old institutional literature and the more recent is, however, far too rigid. Agenor, for example, also works within the old tradition, especially when it comes to the role of wage and employment regulation and public sector employment. The latter, for example, is seen as more responsive to pay levels than to employment levels, although the emphasis in each has shifted over time. This could be explained on the basis of a rational choice approach to politics, but it is more usual to take government policy as given and to examine the implications for private sector employment through wage leadership in either direction and the availability of skills.[8]

It follows that the recent literature draws freely on a range of influences that can be variously combined — the exogenously given role of institutions and structures as well as those endogenously derived from various micro foundations. The thrust of the literature is towards a disaggregation of the labour market into separate segments, to recognize that each of these segments yields different outcomes according to which of the various factors are included, and to examine interaction between segments within a general equilibrium framework of supply and demand.

Elsewhere, Fine (1998), the analytical move towards disaggregating labour markets has been welcomed but the methodology under which it has been done has been equally criticized for a number of reasons. First, as the approach has been based upon micro foundations, it tends to be insensitive to broader historical and socioeconomic factors. At best, these are introduced as a further variable or as an exogenous constraint. Quite clearly, however, the dynamic and structure of an economy will depend upon the underlying economic and political relations, and their influence will be carried over into the structuring and functioning of labour markets. It is impossible for such considerations to be adequately captured, especially in the context of a developing economy undergoing adjustment, by more or less formal models organized around equilibrium.

Secondly, whilst the recent literature has recognized that labour markets are segmented and that they function differently, this is merely a consequence of a general theory in which different factors are either included or excluded. In contrast, it is argued here that each labour market segment is structured and reproduced differently from others, depending upon how the various factors interact with one another. The functioning and structuring of labour markets depend upon a host of society-wide factors such as education, legislation, economic structure and performance, trade unionism and gender relations. These interact, for example, to create rural labour markets that are very different from those to be found in technologically advanced sectors.

Thirdly, to a large extent a corollary of the first two points, there is a general neglect of the role of power in labour markets — other than through the proxy of differential access to markets, endowments and information. Even from this narrower frame of reference, the issue of power, interpreted as a degree of monopsony in the supply of jobs, has been subject to neglect. This is even so in the context of developed economies. In contrast, in papers on the UK economy, the impact of equal pay legislation on women's employment, and the impact of minimum wages in raising the level of employment, Alan Manning has been able to show theoretically, and estimate empirically, how labour markets function within the context of monopsony. On this basis, it is possible to explain what otherwise would appear to be empirical anomalies — that the UK is caught in a low wage, high unemployment equilibrium, that women's employment has increased

---

[8] Note, however, that Agenor (1996: 289) concludes that 'there also appears to be little correlation between the rates of growth of real wages in the public and private sectors'.

with equal pay, and that employment can even increase with rising minimum wages.[9]

Fourthly, especially in the context of developing economies, the categories used to examine labour market segments have been insufficiently nuanced both in conceptual and in empirical terms. Notions such as the rural/urban, formal/informal and public/private conflate a huge range of heterogeneous labour market structures whose nature differs both within and between countries. Consequently, the distinctions are dubious as a basis on which to examine empirical developments, unless they are endowed with a specific content rather than subject to a general theory.

It is against this critical assessment of labour market theory that we assess the recent literature on Ghanaian labour markets. This is followed by posing an alternative interpretation and research agenda.

4.   Surveying the Ghanaian Labour Market

In view of traditional approaches to the economics of labour markets, it is not surprising that empirical analysis should be motivated by measuring to what extent outcomes conform to, or diverge from, an ideal and harmonious interaction of supply and demand. In the context of Ghana, this is reinforced by the idea that structural adjustment and stabilization have benefitted the economy in general by moving it towards the market ideal. Given the policies adopted before the ERP, it is almost inevitable for labour as well as other markets to be interpreted as having benefitted from being liberalized.

Thus, Beaudry and Sowa (1994) seek to examine whether the ERP has worked through the labour market to reallocate and absorb labour. They predominantly draw upon the GLSS for 1987/8 alone. After an initial trawl of some average statistics on earnings and hours, they come to the conclusion (p.375):

> Although Ghanaian workers are mainly concentrated in the household sectors, especially in farming, market forces are apparent in the allocation and remuneration of labor. For example, hourly earnings are quite similar within rural areas and within urban areas, most people seem to be able to find a sufficient amount of work, and, on the basis of hourly earnings, women do not seem to be paid less than men.

These are truly astonishing results, which would appear to qualify Ghana as unique in the even-handedness of its treatment of the labour force. More detailed analysis based on regressions, however, only qualifies these results as far as these authors are concerned.

The first regression is based on a Mincer, human capital equation, ultimately with six sets of variables: the first set relates to human capital in the form of experience, schooling and training; the second is geographical; the third set of dummies is intended to capture information networks and discrimination as in Ghanaian nationals, head of household, regional migration, and seasonality; the fourth is current length of employment tenure by broad type of employment; the fifth is a union dummy; and the sixth is by broad sector.

Consider how the results are interpreted. It is found that unionization raises the wage by 60%, there is a premium for not working in farming (especially in the public sector) but that, overall, 'compensating differentials are related mostly to being off the farm, especially in the mining industry' (p.380/1). Nothing would appear to budge the authors far from their notion that the labour market is primarily clearing perfectly. Take seasonal work, for example. Since it is found that seasonal workers earn higher than average hourly wages, this suggests they 'enter the market only in good times and leave in bad times, indicating a relatively frictionless labor market' (p.379). It is difficult, however, to conceive of a labour market theory that does not predict higher wages in good times and lower wages in bad times. No implications can be drawn for the degree

---

[9] See Manning (1992) and (1996) and Machin and Manning (1996), for example, respectively. See also Manning (1995) and Fine (1998).

of friction. For the treatment of secondary jobs, closely related to seasonal employment, the finding that only 23% of those in employment are seeking extra work is taken as an indicator of satisfaction with hours worked. With 30% of the workforce engaged in secondary employment, an overall regression finds that primary and secondary jobs are paid at the same rate, interpreted as supporting a 'competitive interpretation of labor allocation' (p.385). If so, this raises the question of why workers (and employers) go to the inconvenience of multiple sources of employment.

Nor, of course, is such equality in wage rates for individuals inconsistent with an uncompetitive allocation of labour. It depends in part on the different levels of wages for different jobs and not only on whether individuals always get the same wage for what they do. Interestingly, when it is found with disaggregated regressions for farming that off-farm labour is paid more, this is interpreted as reflecting the costs of finding secondary jobs or the underestimation of farmers' own consumption. The latter is even used to argue that 'the differential against farming's hourly earnings is spurious — because of wages in the form of consumption in kind, for example — and secondary earnings should be taken as a true reflection of primary earnings' (p.390).

More examples of the anomalies in the work of Beaudry and Sowa could be given, and they are by no means the only ones to employ simple regressions to draw conclusions about the workings of the Ghanaian labour market in response to the ERP. There are more general points to be made about the procedure they adopt. First, they do use a general theory which is reducible to one or more single equations to be estimated with the inclusion of more or fewer variables. Consequently, all labour markets are structured and function in the same way — as competitive with or without frictions. Secondly, one equation is used to estimate wages, presumably reflecting the demand for labour; another is used to estimate hours of work or the supply of labour. Exactly the same independent variables are used in each case. This leaves in doubt the theory that is being tested — is it a supply curve, a demand curve, their interaction or both? Thirdly, whatever the theory, it is never tested against an alternative hypothesis of how the labour market works. The only test is of significance within the given theories. Fourthly, where there is significance in this sense for a variable that is taken as indicative of friction, every attempt is made to re-interpret the outcome in terms of some refinement of the frictionless interpretation. Fifthly, when all else has failed, some degree of friction is used to explain the outcome.

One of the conveniences, if weaknesses, of drawing upon the GLSS for estimating labour market equations is that it is not necessary to consider what is happening at the aggregate level, the overall levels of employment by sector. Beaudry and Sowa do suggest that real wages have tended to rise more with rising value added and in those sectors, such as agriculture, mining, and transportation, which it was intended should be favoured by the ERP. The one exception is services for which increasing share of value added has been associated with decline in wage relativity. This is explained by the influx of labour into services. A fuller account of the role of services, however, emerges from the World Bank (1995) report on poverty reduction which compares results from the GLSS between 1987/8 and 1991/2.

It finds that there has been a marked reduction in poverty, especially for female-headed and rural households.[10] This is seen as primarily due to the increase in self-employment in trade. First, in rural areas, the income share from farm self-employment has decreased from 69.2% to 62.3%, more than compensated for by an increase in non-farm self-employment from 14.8% to 21.5%. The latter is seen as having caused the decrease in poverty, although, of course, this cannot be deduced from the figures alone; if one share goes down, one or more must go up.

What the World Bank figures also show is that the share of the population in cocoa farming

---

[10] It is even claimed that female-headed households have become less likely to be in poverty, with a drop in share from 38.5% to 28.5% compared with the drop from 36.1% to 33.2% for male-headed households. Note, however, that the share of income from remittances to female-headed households has risen from 13.2% to 14.3% compared with 2.8% and 2.9% for male-headed households.

has increased from 2.3% to 11.8% with a corresponding reduction in the incidence of poverty from 42.7% to 32.0%.[11] Non-cocoa farmers have decreased from 72.6% to 55.5%, even more than the increase in cocoa farmers, so that the overall share of non-farm households has increased from 25.1% to 32.8%. Only for them is there a significant increase in the income gained from non-farm self-employment, from 42.4% to 50.0% of income (with a fall in income share from self-employment). In short, there appears to have been a shift of employment out of farming overall, even if into cocoa, with an increasing share of non-farm self-employment. On this basis, the World Bank (1995: 32/3) concludes that:

> The growth in domestic trading then appears to be driving the growth in employment, income and expenditures for rural groups. . . . While poverty continues to be a predominantly rural phenomenon, most of the poverty reduction has also come from the rural areas. Growth and increasing dependence on non-farm self-employment income, particularly from trading and manufacturing, appear to drive the reduction in poverty.

At first sight, this appears to be borne out by the increasing share of rural self-employment in wholesale and retail trade, from 49.9% to 55.2%. However, this is based on an increase in the share of non-farm in rural self-employment from 11.0% to 12.8%. In other words, the share of rural self-employment trading has merely increased from 5.5% to 7.1%. As the share of rural households has itself only increased from 65.8% to 66.8%, this implies an increase in the share of rural self-employment in trading in all households from 3.6% to 4.7%, a mere 1.1% increase. This hardly appears to be the basis on which to claim poverty reduction. Ultimately, the corresponding figures for rural manufacturing are for it to remain steady at 2.7% of all households.[12] So manufacturing does not appear to have driven the reduction in rural poverty.

Apart from error, the inevitable conclusion is that the way in which trading has contributed to poverty alleviation is through its general spread across rural households, rather than a specialization. Both poor and non-poor households alike have experienced an increase in income from non-farm self-employment and a decrease in farm self-employment income. Without going back to the raw data at the level of the individual household, it would appear that the poorer households are those that have low and falling income from farming which has been more than compensated for by an increase in trading activity — which, for the economy as a whole, grew by only 10% over the four-year period.

There is, however, a further problem with the figures. Decomposing the reduction in poverty into growth, redistribution and interaction components, only the first of these is found to be significant. Yet, how can trading activity decrease poverty in the absence of redistribution, given that trading does not produce anything? The only answer is in price effects as trading becomes cheaper but is measured on an old basis, or efficiency effects as fewer inputs are used per unit of trading. Given that the margins on trading have been squeezed by the numbers engaged in it, the overall conclusion to be drawn, confirmed by casual observation, is that trading has become a widespread form of distress employment, depended upon to complement any other source of income that is available to the poor.

Apart from Beaudry and Sowa, a sophisticated use of the GLSS from the point of view of economic theory and econometrics has been made by van den Boom *et al.* (1996). They examine the two-sided relationship between nutrition and productivity; higher nutrition increases efficiency, and higher productivity increases earnings and hence consumption. In addition, nutritional status is perceived to depend negatively on labour supply, as less time is available for

---

[11] Although, paradoxically, this has meant that cocoa farming's contribution to national poverty has gone up from 2.3% to 11.1% of the population.

[12] The share of rural households in manufacturing has *declined* from 37.3% to 31.4%, a *decline* in overall rural households from 4.1% to 4.0%.

domestic leisure and care. The model depends upon unconstrained labour supply as choices are made on hours of work and (food) consumption. Crucially, of course, this implies that there is a perfectly competitive labour market.

From the estimates, correcting for human capital and other factors, it is concluded that men and women have similar hourly earnings and that these respond positively both to food consumption and, to a lesser extent, to nutritional status. Moreover, earnings are negatively related to hours worked, although women moving into market employment would increase their productivity by 20% (with a similar gain for middle school enrolment). It is also found that there is a highly negative relationship between hours worked and the wage rate.

The latter is interpreted, as it must within the model adopted, as evidence of a backward bending labour supply curve, with workers freely choosing lower hours of work at higher wage rates, despite high levels of poverty and the chances of increased productivity and nutritional status through working more (even if sacrificing leisure). An alternative interpretation rests upon rejecting the assumption of a perfectly competitive labour market. Rather, the inverse relationship between hours of work and hourly earnings is liable to reflect monopsony and distress selling within the labour market. The more workers depend upon wage earnings for survival, the lower will be the wage that they are offered, which will, then, tend to decline with the hours worked but not as a consequence of choice at exogenously given wage rates.

Let us now turn more specifically to manufacturing employment, which in Ghana is dominated by small enterprises, those with less than thirty employees. Just four sectors — food, metals, textiles and garments, and woodwork and furniture — account for 77% of manufacturing enterprises and 65% of employment. A distinctive feature of these enterprises is their high level of dependence upon what are termed apprentices.[13] Many firms have apprentices only, with no purely wage-earning employees. Velenchik (1995) observes that the apprenticeship system is also distinguished by whether or not apprentices are paid a wage or pay a fee leading to a four-fold categorization. As most are paid a wage, the major exception being female seamstresses, she takes the key difference in Ghana to be the payment or not of a fee by the apprentice and seeks to explain it. This she does on the basis of market imperfections in which training is perceived as comprising both the acquisition of skills and the performance of work. The question is that of who is to finance the training, given that the skills acquired accrue to the apprentice. In an ideal world, it follows that the apprentice would pay either in the form of a fee or reduced wage levels, as does occur for wages in one category.

On the other hand, credit markets are not perfect so that apprentices (or their families) may not have access to credit and be unable to finance a period of training. Consequently, especially where firms themselves have access to credit (as measured by the use of a bank account), they are liable to fund their apprentices without charging a fee. The firms, however, face a problem of moral hazard in that, once trained, the workers may leave. This is less likely the more job-specific rather than general is the training received. Consequently, the observation that apprentices stay longer in firms where no fee is charged is explained by the associated training being more job-specific.

There is an alternative explanation based on market power within the labour market. The need to pay fees for training reflects monopsony power on the part of employers. Where fees are not paid, apprentices are fortunate enough to have found more favourable employment conditions which they are loath to leave. Significantly, larger employers are less likely to charge fees (and are more likely to have a bank account) and, presumably, are able to offer more secure and well-rewarded employment. Velenchik indirectly sets aside the possibility of employer power in the labour market by suggesting that the market for training is competitive, given the large number of firms offering it (p.474).

---

[13] According to JASPA (1989), 65.5% of the labour force in manufacturing in Accra is accounted for by apprentices.

To some extent, this is misleading since no account is given of the training that is offered in practice (p.473). There is reason to believe that it is limited. Sowa *et al.* (1992) find that most entrepreneurs have limited formal education, having mainly served as apprentices themselves. In any case, those with more formal education appear to be associated with poorer firm perform-ance. In addition, as shown by Riedel *et al.* (1989), many of the entrepreneurs engage in other activity, especially farming, suggesting that their commitment to, and capacity for, training their apprentices is far from strong.

Irrespective of the training on offer, the numbers offering it must be set against the numbers seeking work and the alternative opportunities open to them. Here, again, the evidence is not encouraging to a favourable interpretation of the apprenticeship system. It involves casual em-ployment and training, as described by Riedel *et al.* (1989: 64):

> The apprenticeship relationship is a relatively loose one between the two parties. . . . Appren-tices show up at the premises of their master in order not to miss the daily food the master is to provide or do not show up if another temporarily promising job is at stake . . . or if the family needs assistance. These absences are often fostered by the fact that there is not enough work at the enterprise, that there are no orders. Since apprenticeship is completely informal and no trade testing takes place, the learning period very often is ended if the apprentice feels there is nothing more to be learned and/or he wants to earn money for himself since he is usually only remunerated with food and minimal pocket money. The step then normally taken is the opening up of an own workshop, calling oneself a "master" and employing apprentices oneself.

Further, Sowa *et al.* (1992) find that, where output has increased in firms, this has not been associated with increased employment, suggesting excess capacity with a given workforce which is paid (or pays) accordingly. The relative absence of other forms of waged employment and the desire for apprentices to set up on their own account as soon as possible are also evidence of limited alternative employment opportunities.

In short, the point is not to deny the factors to which Velenchik refers. Training is more or less demanding, job-specific and funded in ways which relate more generally to access to credit.[14] But these considerations cannot be examined satisfactorily in the absence, let alone in place of, the effects of the balance of power in the labour markets. Furthermore, the impact of the various factors is uneven and they interact in different ways with one another; in welding, for example, access to appropriate tools is a further factor. As Riedel *et al.* (1989: 143/4) conclude:

> It is exploitative. The labour of the apprentice is virtually unpaid labour. He or she does receive "chop money" (for food and drink) but it is minimal . . . the quality of the training received is sometimes limited by the low educational and professional standard of the master. More serious, however, are the poor technological conditions of the enterprise.

This is a far cry from optimizing agents in the context of asymmetric information and differential access to credit.

Despite the paucity and poor quality of labour market statistics, there have been a number of investigations of wage equations for the Ghanaian labour market, although they are sometimes based on micro surveys. The point here is not to provide a comprehensive survey of these contri-butions nor to summarize the results of the studies, critical assessment of which would almost certainly render them of limited empirical validity. Rather, the intention is to show how complex and varied are the factors that are perceived to be operative within the labour markets even if they are placed within an orthodox framework. It should be added that the factors concerned are

---

[14] It quite clearly also serves in part as a privatized form of welfare provision to unemployed youth.

also liable to be extremely uneven in their incidence and mutual interaction.

Boateng (1997), for example, hypothesizes that formal public sector employment grows when there are cordial relations between government and trade unions, as reflected in low strike activity and the balance of political power.[15] Such employment growth, subject to overall economic growth and the government budget, could be accommodated by falling real wages. It is arguable, however, that the causal relations can run in the opposite direction, with the unions prepared to be more co-operative when their employment and wage goals are being met. They may also gain concessions from militancy as opposed to acquiescence. Boateng also examines the role of factors such as trade unions and skills on wage dispersion, differentials and flexibility in wages and employment. In another paper, Boateng (1996c) has studied sex differences in Ghana's labour market. Women's participation has decreased with greater access to education. But their share of formal employment has increased in line with the growth in the service sectors in which they are disproportionately represented. Wage discrimination is estimated at an average of 20%, and at its highest in the agricultural and informal sectors.

Jebuni *et al.* (1995) examine the labour markets in the context of structural adjustment. They distinguish between the public and private, the traded and non-traded, and the urban and rural sectors. They investigate the structure and flexibility of the labour markets and how they interact with product markets. They suggest that relative sectoral wages have remained inflexible but that differences between urban and rural wages reveal a mixed pattern. For them, a major problem is the failure of the private sector to create employment despite the retrenchment from the public sector. Even so, there appears to have been little mobility from the formal to the informal sectors, with those losing their formal jobs presumably preferring to wait for new opportunities to present themselves.

5.   Towards an Alternative

In brief, Ghana's labour markets have been characterized by a decline in formal sector employment, with the private sector failing to take up those displaced from the public sector despite considerably lower levels of real wages. The formal sectors exhibit heavy dependence on the sweated apprenticeship system, and are associated with fragmentation and low levels of investment and productivity. The major beneficiaries of employment under the ERP have been the informal sectors, especially those attached to trading. In addition, however, these broad conclusions need to be qualified by emphasizing how heterogeneous Ghanaian labour markets are in their performance and structures,[16] with limited synergy and/or linkages both within and between sectors of the economy.

Against this background, two very different approaches to the evolution of labour markets in developing countries need to be regarded with considerable suspicion. The traditional view linked with structural adjustment and stabilization would open up the following issues: are there institutional obstacles to labour market clearing, especially from trade unions and a privileged public sector; is aggregate demand sufficiently high; and are there imperfections in other (product) markets which impede clearing in the labour market? These concerns simply overlook the heterogeneity and complexity of the Ghanaian labour markets, attempting to reduce them more or less to a matter of relative prices alone. On this score, the most compelling evidence is entirely negative in so far as devaluation and trade reform have accompanied improvement in the relative position of the informal non-traded sectors, especially trading itself, whatever improvement there may have been in other sectors for which empirically isolating the quantitative impact of liberalization alone is excessively demanding.

---

[15] See also Jebuni *et al.* (1995) for a discussion of the caution of the trade union movement in the 1980s in view of the fear of repression.

[16] For empirical confirmation of the position adopted here, even if from different theoretical perspectives, of the need to approach Ghanaian labour markets in terms of their heterogeneity across a variety of factors, see Teal (1995 and 1996) and Collier and Garg (1997).

Equally, the notion that the level of aggregate employment can be put right by appropriate macroeconomic policies, whether conforming to the Washington consensus or not, is inadequate. Expanding aggregate demand and employment will, as conservative macroeconomists emphasize, be counterproductive if they merely featherbed nominal work at inflated wages. Judicious macroeconomic policy has to be combined with a more sophisticated understanding of, and attention to, how different sectors of the economy function and interact with one another.

The evidence on the growth of the informal service sectors is also highly inconvenient for the Lewis model of structural transformation, which has been shown to be questionable in other chapters of this volume. It could be argued that the ERP needs some considerable time to adjust the economy's structure back to its natural starting point. This aside, however, the shift from a rural to an urban economy through the transfer of surplus agricultural labour to industry is notable for its absence. There has even been a leap-frogging into tertiary employment in both formal and informal sectors.

In previous sections, considerable emphasis has been placed on the pervasive presence of monopsony in labour markets, or the balance of power in favour of employers. It has assumed, or is reflected in, a number of forms: the premium attached to jobs in the formal sectors; the apprenticeship systems; the extremely high levels of poverty leading to a desperate search for work; the corresponding straddling across a variety of working activities; the growth in low level trading; the low levels of productivity associated with inadequate nutrition; and, paradoxically, the relatively favourable position for female-headed households as a consequence of their activity in the informal sectors, which points to the limited opportunities in the formal sectors, the vast majority of which are taken by men.

In addition, other evidence can be hypothesized. The persistence of small-scale agriculture as a major source of income for a majority of households is a consequence of the limited opportunities for employment elsewhere in the economy. In rural areas, 30% of girls and 21% of boys aged between 7 and 16 are reported as economically active, keeping them out of school and from educational qualifications which would significantly enhance neither their chances of a job nor their rewards within one. The education system serves as credentialism for access to government jobs, otherwise encouraging flight of the most skilled and mobile to better paid jobs abroad.

The particular incidence of each of these and other factors in the structuring and functioning of labour markets will differ, as will the exact nature of the monopsony in the labour market. It is to be hoped that sufficient argument and evidence have been brought forward to persuade scholars to think again before setting aside, even precluding, consideration of such imbalance in the labour market. In the United States, it was impossible for the orthodoxy to accept that an increase in minimum wages could raise employment as had been observed empirically. As Dickens *et al.* (1995: 3) suggest in the context of monopsony power in the labour market:

> It is important, when constructing a theoretical model of the labour market to use as a basis for empirical work, to start from a framework in which the effect of minimum wages on employment can be positive or negative. The conventional approach often fails to satisfy this criterion as it generally works from the assumption that (in the absence of minimum wages) the labour market is perfectly competitive.

The same lesson needs to be learnt in studying Ghanaian labour markets.

Nor does the recent literature often place the labour markets within the broader context of economic development. Manufacturing growth and industrialization have faltered, rather than generating new investments, with progress under the ERP dependent upon utilizing existing capacity as imported inputs have become more freely available. There has been some displacement of labour from agriculture but it has been slow and it has been absorbed into services, especially trading, rather than manufacturing. Furthermore, much policy has been oriented towards promoting efficiency within each of the broad categories of formal and informal sectors.

This neglects what appears to be a negative synergy between them. In addition, as Lall and Wignaraja (1996) observe, only 'naturally' protected and traditional manufacturing exports and employment have been sustained with the ERP, otherwise domestic production has been wiped out in swathes by cheaper imports.

Consider, for example, the prospects for a large-scale investment in manufacturing. This requires growing and stable markets for output. If such an investment does materialize in a sector in direct competition with informal, labour-intensive production, the result is to absorb the market and swell the ranks of the under- or unemployed in the sector, depressing rewards and prices even for the large-scale investment (and inhibiting further such investments). It cannot be presumed, then, that large-scale manufacturing investment will enhance economic performance or employment generation unless it is accompanied both by sufficient demand and adequate wages and by conditions to prevent the surviving informal sectors from intensifying competition in product markets. There is no evidence, for example, even in the formal sectors that the major problem for employment is too high or inflexible real wages. For those who think otherwise, the appropriate question is to ask at what level of real wages would the labour market clear.

Similar conclusions can be reached should the formal serve as a source of inputs for the informal sectors or vice-versa.[17] Cheapening inputs to the informal sectors encourages entry and fragmentation of production, leading to high costs which at least moderate the benefits of the cheaper inputs. High costs of production in the informal sectors also have the effect of raising wage costs for a given level of subsistence.

Such stylized theory is not without precedents and empirical applications. At a macroeconomic level, Domar's contribution to the Harrod-Domar model was based on the notion that older, less productive investments would not harmoniously give way to the newer investments. Instead, they would retain part of the market, reducing the effective level of capacity utilization. At a microeconomic level,[18] throughout the world and historically, large numbers of small-scale firms serving a fragmented market have been associated with sweated labour conditions and the failure to innovate — despite apparent conformity to the classical conditions of perfect competition.

It cannot be pre-determined whether the Ghanaian economy is caught in such a vicious circle of decline or is heading for a virtuous circle of development. The analytical and policy implication is that particular developments have to be located systemically and specifically within their context. Certainly, the evidence from agriculture and trading is far from encouraging. In research and policy, too often has a virtue been made out of necessity. The importance of agriculture and the growth of trading and the informal sectors more generally have led to the view that they lead the economy and, consequently, should be subject to a wide range of support. In contrast, our emphasis would be put on promoting secure employment in formal sectors, whether through its expansion directly or through formalization of the informal. In particular, there is a need for much greater co-ordination of vertical integration, and further creation of synergy both within and between formal and informal sectors.

By the same token, much research, especially with a policy orientation, needs to adopt a more systemic approach, quite apart from incorporating a more broad-minded view of how the labour market might be operating, as previously argued. Strengthening support for the informal sectors may only lead to further inflows of the self-employed, fragmentation and short- and long-run static and dynamic inefficiencies. Provision of training may merely expand the numbers queuing

[17] In practice, the informal sectors are dependent on the formal sectors rather than vice versa, with limited forward linkages. See Baah-Nuakoh (1994) and Aryeetey (1996).

[18] A case study is provided by the British coal industry in the 1930s. Fine (1990) has shown how the proliferation of small-scale mines impeded the rationalization of the industry into fewer, larger, mechanized operations.

for jobs in the formal sectors.[19] It also follows that data have to be treated with care and conceptual premeditation. It is well-known that employment in the public sector has in the past combined elements both of work and of welfarism, and such influences no doubt persist. Consequently, the notion of employment has to be treated with considerable caution, and certainly not as the basis on which to calculate employment elasticities. To proceed in this fashion would, in a developed country context, be like treating the unemployed as employed on a wage equal to their benefit (in which, presumably, their unidentified marginal product of labour is equal to zero). Whether such problems and others can be disentangled on the basis of existing data is a moot point. They must, however, be addressed, otherwise we shall all prove poor masters and apprentices in economic and policy research, whoever pays for the training and work.[20]

---

[19] Thus, whilst Lall and Wignaraja (1996) point to the lack of technical capability in Ghanaian manufacturing, this needs to be investigated not only as a problem of shortage of skills but also as a lack of deployment of those skills that are or could be available.

[20] For an exemplary discussion of data needs and an investigation of labour markets in a policy context, see ILO (1996).

References

Addison, T. and Demery, L. (1994) "The Poverty Effects of Adjustment with Labor Market Imperfections", in Horton *et al.* Vol.1, (1994).

Agenor, P. (1996) 'The Labor Market and Economic Adjustment', *IMF Staff Papers*, Vol. 43, No. 2: 261–335.

Aryeetey, E. (1996) 'The Potential for Expanded Economic Activity from the Informal Sector', in IEA.

Azam, J. (1994) 'Recent Developments in the Developed-Country Literature on Labor Markets and the Implications for Developing Countries', in Horton *et al.* Vol. 1.

Baah-Nuakoh, A. (1994) *Policies and Strategies for Promoting Informal Sector Development in Ghana.* Legon Economic Studies, No. 9402,

Baah-Nuakoh, A. *et al.* (1996) *Review and Analysis of the Impact of Public Sector Wage Changes on the Ghanaian Economy.* University Consultancy Centre, Legon.

Bartholomew, D. *et al.* (1995) 'The Measurement of Unemployment in the UK', *Journal of the Royal Statistical Society*, Series A, Vol. 158, Part 3: 363–417.

Beaudry, P. and Sowa, N. (1994) 'Ghana', in Horton *et al.* Vol. 2.

Boateng, K. (1996a) 'Labour Market Information System in Ghana — An Overview', paper presented at the seminar on the 'Harmonisation of Labour Market Concepts in Ghana', Ministry of Employment and Social Welfare (October).

Boateng, K. (1996b) *Employment, Unemployment and Underemployment in Ghana.* Institute of Economics Affairs, Occasional Paper, No. 3. Accra: IEA.

Boateng, K. (1996c) 'Labour Market Discrimination Against Women in Ghana", *Journal of Management Studies*, Vol. 9.

Boateng, K. (1997) 'Institutional Determinants of Labour Market Performance in Ghana'. Technical Paper prepared for CEPA, Accra, (February).

Collier, P. and Garg, A. (1997) *On Kin Groups and Wages in the Ghanaian Labour Market.* White Paper Series, 97: 20. Centre for the Study of African Economies, University of Oxford.

Commander, S. and Ugaz, C. (1994) 'What Seems Right and What Seems Wrong with Ghana's Labour Market', *The Economic Bulletin of Ghana*, Vol. 4, No. 1: 129–41.

Dickens, R. *et al.* (1995) 'What Happened to Wages and Employment after the Abolition of Minimum Wages in Britain?', London School of Economics, mimeo.

Edwards, A. and Edwards, S. (1994) 'Labor Market Distortions and Structural Adjustment in Developing Countries', in Horton *et al.*, Vol. 1.

Fine, B. (1990) *The Coal Question: Political Economy and Industrial Change from the Nineteenth Century to the Present Day.* London: Routledge.

Fine, B. (1998) *Labour Market Theory: A Constructive Reassessment*, London: Routledge.

Horton, S. *et al.* (1994a) 'Labor Markets in an Era of Adjustment: An Overview', in Horton *et al.*, Vol. 1.

Horton, S. *et al.* (eds) (1994b) *Labor Markets in an Era of Adjustment*, Vols. 1 and 2, Washington, DC: World Bank.

IEA (1996) *Agenda '96, Preparing Ghana for the 21st Century: Some Economic and Social Issues.* Accra: Anansesem Publications.

ILO (1996) *Restructuring the Labour Market: The South African Challenge - An ILO Country Review.* Geneva: ILO.

ISSER (1995) *State of the Ghanaian Economy in 1994.* University of Ghana, Legon.

JASPA (1989) *From Redeployment to Sustained Employment Generation: Challenges for Ghana's Programme of Economic Recovery and Development.* Job and Skills Programme for Africa. Addis Ababa: ILO.

Jebuni, C. *et al.* (1995) 'Structural Adjustment and the Labour Market in Ghana', Final Report to the AERC, Johannesburg, December.

Lall, S. (1996) *Learning from the Asian Tigers: Studies in Technology and Industrial Policy.* London and Basingstoke: Macmillan.

Lall, S, and Wignaraja, G. (1996) 'Skills and Capabilities in Ghana's Competitiveness' in Lall.

Machin, S. and Manning, A. (1996) 'Employment and the Introduction of a Minimum Wage in Britain', *Economic Journal*, Vol. 106, No. 436: 667–76.

Manning, A. (1992) 'Multiple Equilibria in the British Labour Market', *European Economic Review*, Vol. 36, No. 7: 1333–65.

Manning, A. (1995) 'Developments in Labour Market Theory and Their Implications for Macroeconomic Policy', *Scottish Journal of Political Economy*, Vol. 42, No. 3, (August), pp. 250–66.

Manning, A. (1996) 'The Equal Pay Act as an Experiment to Test Theories of the Labour Market', *Economica*, Vol. 63, No. 250, (May): 191–212.

Nelson, J. (1994) 'Organized Labor, Politics, and Labor Market Flexibility in Developing Countries', in Horton *et al.* Vol. 1.

Ninsin, K. (1990) *The Informal Sector in Ghana's Political Economy.* Accra: Freedom Publications.

Riedel, J. *et al.* (1989) *Grass-Root Industrialisation in a Ghanaian Town.* London: Hurst.

Solow, R. (1990) *The Labour Market as a Social Institution.* Oxford: Blackwell.

Sowa, N. *et al.* (1992) *Small Enterprises and Adjustment: The Impact of Ghana's Economic Recovery Programme.* London: Overseas Development Institute.

Teal, F. (1995) *Real Wages and the Demand for Labour in Ghana's Manufacturing Sector.* White Paper Series 95: 7. Centre for the Study of African Economies, University of Oxford.

Teal, F. (1996) 'The Sizes and Sources of Economic Rents in a Developing Country Manufacturing Labour Market', *Economic Journal,* Vol. 106, July, pp. 963–76.

Van den Boom, G. *et al.* (1996) 'Nutrition, Labour Productivity and Labour Supply of Men and Women in Ghana', *Journal of Development Studies,* Vol. 32, No. 6: 801–29.

Velenchik, A. (1995) 'Apprenticeship Contracts, Small Enterprises, and Credit Markets in Ghana', *World Bank Economic Review,* Vol. 9, No. 3: 451–75.

World Bank (1995) *Ghana: Growth, Private Sector, and Poverty Reduction, A Country Economic Memorandum,* Report no 14111-GH, Washington, DC: World Bank.

V Sectoral Performance

13 The Industrial Sector & Economic Development

YAW ASANTE
FREDERICK NIXSON
& G. KWAKU TSIKATA*

1. Introduction

It is generally accepted that industrialization is a necessary but not a sufficient condition for the rapid and sustained development of poor countries. By industrialization we mean the development of a modern manufacturing sector which involves: the organization of production in business enterprises; specialization and the division of labour; and the application of technology to supplement and replace human labour. The manufacturing sector retains the characteristics of an 'engine of growth' — rapid productivity growth, dynamic increasing returns to scale, rapid technological change and various dynamic externalities (Weiss, 1988). Productivity growth in both the agricultural and service sectors requires inputs from the manufacturing sector, and if sufficient foreign exchange is not available for their importation, such inputs must be produced domestically. For most developing countries, the question is not *whether* but *how* to industrialize.

For many of these countries, the dominant industrialization strategy in the post-1945, post-independence period was import-substitution industrialization (ISI). In Latin America it had been stimulated earlier by global war and international depression, including the collapse of primary commodity prices and the abandonment of the primary commodity export-based model of development. ISI was given intellectual respectability in the post-1945 period by Latin American structuralist economists who, because they were 'export pessimists', saw ISI as the only way to break their economies' dependence on the vagaries of global commodity markets. In South Asia, sub-Saharan Africa and a number of South-East Asian economies, ISI was adopted in the immediate post-independence period as, in effect, a development strategy.

Ghana became independent at a time when industrialization was viewed as a key factor in modernization and development. The explicit objectives of industrialization were to exploit domestic natural resources, to form a base for developing other economic sectors, to satisfy the basic needs of the population, to create jobs, and to assimilate and promote technological progress and modernize society. Industrial strategy prior to the Economic Recovery Programme was characterized by (a) an emphasis on import substitution through high levels of effective protection, (b) a reliance on administrative controls rather than market mechanisms to determine incentives and resource allocation, and (c) a reliance on large-scale, public sector investment as the leading edge in industrial development. The emphasis on import substitution was partly a manifestation

---

* Our thanks are due to William Steel for comments on an earlier version.

of the post-independence drive to reduce economic dependence by manufacturing locally what was previously imported, and partly a consequence of balance of payments difficulties due to rapidly rising imports and stagnant export earnings. A policy environment of high protection evolved through tariffs and quantitative restrictions (Steel, 1972).

By the mid- to late 1960s, ISI as an industrialization strategy was widely seen to have 'failed'. The actual experience of ISI in the Latin American economies (Brazil, Mexico, Argentina) and the structuralist critique of that experience (for example, UNCTAD, 1964) in part gave rise to varieties of dependency theory (Kay, 1989) and a certain pessimism as to the possibilities for sustained development as long as the less developed countries remained a part of the global capitalist economy.

Neoclassical economists also produced a powerful critique of ISI (the seminal work is Little *et al.,* 1970), in part developing new analytical tools, for example, the concept of the effective rate of protection, to evaluate the alleged misallocation of scarce resources resulting from inappropriate interventions in factor and product markets. The resurgence in neoclassical development economics coincided with, and was no doubt stimulated by, the emergence of a small group of East and South-East Asian economies pursuing policies of export-oriented industrialization (EOI), from approximately the mid-1960s onwards.

The experience of Ghana with respect to the strategy of ISI was not radically different from that of other countries that had pursued a similar strategy. Steel's (1972: 226–7) critique of the experience of ISI concluded that, as of the late 1960s, 'Ghana's industrialisation and IS policies were extremely unsuccessful in establishing a structure and level of manufacturing output which could efficiently reduce foreign exchange requirements and stimulate growth of GNP'. Massive capacity underutilization was the consequence of inappropriate foreign-exchange policies and high levels of effective protection which stimulated the domestic production of final-stage assembly, 'non-essential' activities. Killick (1978) was also very critical of the strategy of ISI pursued by Ghana, arguing that '. . . a wide-ranging set of conditions conspired to limit the efficiency of the industrialisation drive', including over-optimism about the future growth of the economy, unselective and arbitrary protection, a variety of biases favouring capital intensity and processes with few linkages with other sectors, a deteriorating quality of investment decisions and sub-standard performance by state enterprises (Killick, 1978: 204–5).[1]

The launching of the Economic Recovery Programme (ERP) in April 1983 changed the macroeconomic and incentive framework within which industry had to operate. There has been a substantial improvement in the trade regime with the reduction in the anti-export bias (Jebuni *et al.,* 1992). The exchange rate policies pursued since 1984 have ensured substantial depreciation of the real exchange rate. The import control system has been completely liberalized and significant tariff cuts have been implemented. The cautious fiscal policies pursued between 1984 and 1989 ensured a decline in the fiscal deficit and thus contributed to dampening inflationary pressures. Other measures taken to improve the incentive framework include (a) the gradual removal of administrative and other bottlenecks, (b) a review of the tax structure as it relates to private investment, (c) the establishment of retention accounts (and foreign accounts) for individual companies for the retention of a portion of export earnings to finance imports of essential spare parts and raw materials or machinery, and (d) the liberalization of the financial system.

Despite the attention that manufacturing has received over the years, mining has been the major industrial activity in terms of earnings. The mining sector is currently the leading foreign-exchange earner in the Ghanaian economy. It has been one of the key beneficiaries in terms of policy initiatives and financing under the ERP. The turn-around in the sector has thus provided

---

[1] Similar outcomes are to be found both in developing countries in general and in other sub-Saharan economies, in particular. For surveys of the evidence see: Nixson (1982); Colman and Nixson, 1994, Chapter 8. On the question of choice of techniques in the Ghanaian manufacturing sector, see Forsyth and Solomon, 1977 and Forsyth *et al.,* 1980

some measure of justification for the Programme. At the sub-sectoral level, the gold industry has played the dominant role in terms of its investment and output impact on the economy and the 'modest economic growth which has occurred, especially after 1990, has essentially been a gold-industry-led growth' (Tsikata, 1995b). It is important to note that the extent of activities in the gold sub-sector renders it the key representative of the minerals sector. Recent ore discoveries, stretching from the Western to the Northern Regions of the country, indicate good prospects for the sector as a major potential contributor to economic growth.

This chapter discusses the manufacturing and mining sectors in the light of the problems and policies both before and after the implementation of the ERP. Section 2 focuses on the manufacturing sector and looks in particular at issues related to growth and structural change, sector performance, capacity utilization, employment, exports and future prospects. Section 3 discusses the mining sector with a focus on structure, performance, the environmental impact and prospects. Section 4 presents a summary and conclusions.

2.   The Manufacturing Sector and Economic Development

Structure of the Manufacturing Sector

As per capita incomes grow, economists have identified fairly consistent patterns of intra-sectoral change in manufacturing, with the proportion of output or value added accounted for by capital and intermediate goods (heavy industry) rising (for a survey of the literature, see Nixson, 1990). It is difficult to identify consistent patterns of change in Ghana's manufacturing sector, however, because of the instability and poor performance of both the economy as a whole and the manufacturing sector in particular.

The contribution of consumer goods to manufactured output (measured by the index of manufacturing production) did not change much between 1977 and 1994. It averaged 46.3% between 1977 and 1983, 47.1% between 1984 and 1990 and declined to 39.6% between 1991 and 1994. The share of petroleum refining declined from an average of 25.4% between 1977 and 1983 to 25.1% between 1984 and 1990, further declining to an average of 18.3% between 1991 and 1994.

Since 1977, the year in which manufacturing output peaked, the contribution of capital goods as a proportion of total manufacturing output has declined continuously. It fell from 4.4% of manufacturing output in 1977 to 0.9% in 1983. Since then, it has not risen beyond 1.2% and stood at 0.4% in 1994. Between 1977 and 1982, its contribution averaged 3.4%, whereas between 1991 and 1994 it averaged only 0.9%. The share of intermediate goods production, however, has increased from an average of 25.3% between 1977 and 1983 to 27.1% between 1984 and 1990. Between 1991 and 1994, its average share overtook that of consumer goods. Thus the ERP appears to have been accompanied by a shift in the structure of manufacturing away from the production of consumer goods, capital goods, and petroleum refining towards intermediate goods production.

This may be attributed to the boom in the construction industry. Between 1989 and 1995, the construction industry grew at an average annual rate of 9.8% compared with 3.8% for the whole of manufacturing (ISSER, 1996: 112). The boom in the construction sector may be attributable, among other things, to the following:

• from 1986 to 1993, the importation of building materials was zero-rated; there were no tariffs on them. In 1994, a concessionary rate of 10% was imposed.

• the liberalization of foreign exchange increased the foreign exchange available for the importation of building materials and enabled Ghanaians resident abroad to send remittances home for construction activities;

• the ERP also encouraged the formation of construction companies.

Significance tests of the means indicate that the share of capital goods in total manufacturing production fell significantly between the pre-ERP and post-ERP periods, while that of intermediate goods significantly increased the post-ERP period 1984–94, especially during 1991–2.[2]

Table13.1   Mean Percentage Contribution to Index of Manufacturing Production (1977 = 100)

Period	Petroleum Refining	Consumer Goods	Intermediate Goods	Capital Goods
1977–83	25.4	46.3	25.3	3.0
1984–90	25.1	47.1	27.1	0.8
1991–94	18.3	39.6	41.2	0.9
Pre ERP				
1977–83	25.4	46.3	25.4	3.0
Post ERP				
1984–94	22.6	44.3	32.2	0.8
T-Stat	1.2	0.8	2.0*	5.6***

***   Significant at the 1% level

*   Significant at the 10% level

Consumer Goods: Comprise food manufacturing, beverages, tobacco and tobacco products, textiles, wearing apparel and leather goods, paper products and printing, chemical products other than petroleum, and cutlery and other non-ferrous metal products

Intermediate Goods: Comprise sawmill and wood products, cement and other non-metallic mineral products, iron and steel products, and non-ferrous metal basic products.

Capital Goods: Made up of electrical equipment and appliances, and transport equipment.

Percentage contribution for each subsector was calculated as:

[(Weight$_i$/100)xIndex$_i$]/[(index for all manufacturing)] x 100

Source: Computed from *Quarterly Digest of Statistics.*

Although some linkages exist, particularly in the agro-industrial, wood, aluminium, and rubber subsectors, the sector as a whole lacks strong forward and backward linkages, both inter- and intra-sectoral. Linkages between the formal and informal sectors are similarly weak. The overall effect of this poor integration is the sectors' continued dependence on imported inputs. Firm-level data show that, apart from the wood subsector which imports 30.7% of its raw materials, the percentage ranges between 61% and 80% for the other sectors (Baah-Nuakoh *et al.*, 1996: 43, Table 10). The proportion of imported inputs is smaller for micro-enterprises and increases with enterprise size, although the proportion for large firms is smaller than for medium-sized firms. However, the increase in the share of intermediate goods in total output, especially from 1991 onwards, is *prima facie* evidence of growing linkages in the manufacturing sector.

Performance and Constraints

Output The policies adopted in the 1960s stimulated rapid growth of manufacturing output

---

[2] The data on the Ghanaian manufacturing sector are 'totally inadequate for in-depth analysis' (private communication from W.F. Steel). Whatever qualifications we may need to make with regard to the quality of the data, however, it is clear that the patterns of intra-sectoral change in the manufacturing sector have not followed the 'normal' line.

(averaging 13% per annum) and employment (averaging 8% per annum) (World Bank, 1984: 64). By 1970, manufacturing as a share of GDP had risen to 13%. Total industrial output as a percentage of GDP peaked at 21.5% in 1977. From 1977, however, the industrial sector began to lose its momentum. Between 1975 and 1979, the manufacturing sector declined at an annual average rate of –2.5%, but this worsened to –12.3% between 1980 and 1982. The fall in manufacturing output prior to the ERP was mainly due to the serious problems experienced by the balance of payments, beginning in the mid-1970s. Import capacity was determined principally by the level of exports, since capital inflows were negligible. Export earnings relied predominantly on cocoa and to a lesser extent on timber, gold and diamonds, all of which showed a downward trend. The sharpest decline in cocoa and gold production took place at a time when world prices were favourable (1976–9). Because of their high dependence on imports of raw materials, spare parts and equipment, manufacturing industries suffered heavily from the decline in import capacity.

The implementation of the ERP brought a positive change in the performance of the manufacturing sector. After six years of continuous decline, real manufacturing GDP experienced positive growth rates after 1984, but at a decreasing rate since 1988 (Table 13.2). The initial spurt in the growth of manufacturing after the implementation of the ERP was not sustained and came from a low base. The growth of manufacturing lagged behind that of GDP, leading to a declining share of manufacturing in GDP and therefore a lack of inter-sectoral structural change of the type usually associated with development (Nixson, 1990). The decline in the growth rate between 1988 and 1995 may be due to the fact that, while competitive industries continued to grow, uncompetitive ones began to decline or fold up in the more liberalized environment. The slowdown in the growth of the manufacturing sector was reflected in the growth rate of the whole industrial sector, which declined from 12.1% between 1984 and 1987 to 4.4% between 1988 and 1995.

Statistical tests conducted on the mean growth rates for both the manufacturing and industrial sectors indicate that the growth rates are significantly higher for the post-ERP period than for the pre-ERP period. The shares of manufacturing GDP and industrial GDP in total GDP are significantly lower for the post-ERP period as a result of their growth rates lagging behind that of GDP. It must be emphasized, however, that even though these shares have declined in the post-ERP period, this does not necessarily imply 'de-industrialization'. This is because industry was heavily protected in the pre-ERP era, thus raising manufacturing value added in domestic prices above what it would have been if measured in international prices, and, some would argue, exaggerating the relative importance of the manufacturing sector (Little *et al.*, 1970). A study by the World Bank (1984) showed that 40% of the firms in 1983 had negative value added at world prices. Closing them down would have yielded a net *real* benefit to the country, even though the loss of value added at (highly protected) domestic prices would have looked like 'de-industrialization'.[3]

The slowing down in the growth of real manufacturing GDP since 1988, in spite of the price incentives, suggests that appropriate trade and macroeconomic policies are necessary to bring about an improvement in the performance of the sector but are not sufficient to ensure that this performance is sustained or even improved upon. Other factors may be important in influencing the performance of the sector and even its ability to respond to the trade and exchange rate programmes which are put in place.

One important factor is the disappointing response of private investment in manufacturing during the ERP period. The ability to undertake the needed investment has been inhibited by a

---

[3] The debate on whether or not structural adjustment programmes have led to 'de-industrialization' in sub-Saharan Africa remains unresolved. See Stein, 1992; Lall, 1992; Meier and Steel, 1989 and World Bank, 1994b, for conflicting views.

number of factors. A survey of 116 firms in the manufacturing sector (Asante, 1995) indicated the following as significant constraints on private investment: macroeconomic instability; the problems of obtaining credit; the high cost of credit; and the high level of taxes.

Output growth performance has differed widely, however, among subsectors within manufacturing. With the exception of iron and steel products, transport equipment, textiles, and paper products and printing, all the other subsectors registered increased production immediately after the ERP relative to the period immediately preceding implementation of the reforms. However, the subsectors that recorded an impressive performance as far as production is concerned in the post-adjustment period were beverages, sawmill and wood products, cement, iron and steel (this subsector picked up impressively from 1992), and non-ferrous basic metal industries. By 1992, these five subsectors had attained levels of production greater than those registered in 1977. By 1994, the output of cement and other non-metallic mineral products was more than double its 1977 figure while that of iron and steel products was more than five times the 1977 figure (Table 13.2). As explained earlier, this may be due to the boom in the construction industry.

Table 13.2   Mean Output, Shares, and Growth Rates in the Manufacturing Sector

Period	Real GDP	Ind. GDP	Man. GDP	Shares			Growth Rates		
	(Millions of 1975 Cedis)			Ind./GDP	Man./GDP	Man./Ind.	Ind.	Man.	GDP
1971–79	5492.0	1043.8	671.8	19.0	12.3	64.5	–2.0	–1.1	0.4
1980–83	5126.2	695.5	462.8	13.5	8.9	65.7	–9.6	–12.0	–3.4
1984–87	5563.7	726.9	475.6	13.0	8.5	65.2	12.1	14.5	6.0
1988–95	7386.5	1053.9	641.4	14.3	8.7	61.1	4.4	2.6	4.6
Pre ERP									
1971–83	5379.5	936.6	607.5	17.3	11.2	64.9	–4.3	–4.5	–0.8
Post ERP									
1984–95	6778.9	944.9	586.2	13.9	8.7	62.5	7.0	6.6	5.0
T-Stat	4.6[a]	0.1	0.5	3.7[a]	4.1[a]	1.6	3.4[a]	2.6[b]	3.5[a]

Notes: [a] Significant at the 1% level
            [b] Significant at the 5% level
Source: Statistical Service, *Quarterly Digest of Statistics,* Various Issues

The subsectors whose outputs have declined significantly between the pre- and post-ERP periods include textiles, wearing apparel and leather goods, where high-cost, overprotected firms have had difficulty competing with liberalized imports. Subsectors whose outputs have increased significantly include sawmill and wood products and beverages, which are domestic-resource based.[4]

---

[4] As Greenaway *et al.* (1997; 1885) have noted, 'The motivation behind trade reform, and adjustment programmes more broadly defined, has been to improve the functioning of markets with a view to enhancing factor allocation and accumulation and ultimately improving economic performance'. The intra-sectoral shifts observed in Ghana following the implementation of the ERP are thus not unexpected. It should be noted, however, that according to Greenaway *et al.*, Ghana's post-liberalization macroeconomic performance has been below the sub-Saharan average.

Table 13.3   Mean Index of Manufacturing Production (1977 = 100)

Subsector	Weight	Period			Significance Test of Mean Differences		
		84–87	88–91	92–94	Pre-ERP 78–83	Post-ERP 78–83	T-Stat.
Food	15.00	40.6	54.6	72.2	62.3	54.3	1.0
Beverage	8.11	69.9	93.5	112.7	65.6	90.1	2.8[b]
Tobacco	7.75	59.3	53.9	44.3	51.4	53.3	0.4
Textiles, Wearing Apparel & Leather Products	13.71	21.0	32.4	32.0	41.8	28.1	1.6
Sawmill & Wood Products	7.22	73.6	96.5	114.6	58.1	93.1	3.2[a]
Paper products & Printing	1.94	66.8	50.9	53.1	67.6	57.3	1.3
Petroleum refinery	19.00	69.2	79.4	75.9	83.1	74.7	1.3
Chemical Products Other than Petroleum	6.56	40.5	58.0	80.5	30.3	57.8	2.6[b]
Cement & Other Non-Metallic products	2.98	50.8	104.1	199.8	58.6	110.8	2.0[c]
Iron & Steel Products	3.25	38.6	11.9	433.1	46.4	148.9	1.3
Non-Ferrous Metal Basic Industries	9.62	63.7	101.6	107.1	85.5	91.9	0.5
Cutlery & Other Non-Ferrous Metal products	0.49	38.0	53.1	97.0	29.8	59.6	2.2[b]
Electrical Equipment & Appliances	1.34	32.5	31.6	41.3	27.7	34.6	0.8
Transport Equipment	3.03	6.5	n.a	11.6	49.9	9.9	n.a
All Manufacturing	100.0	49.9	65.0	85.8	61.1	65.2	0.5

Notes: [a] Significant at the 1% level
[b] Significant at the 5% level
[c] Significant at the 10% level
Source: Ibid.

Capacity Utilisation There has been an increase in capacity utilization following the implementation of the ERP. The liberalization of the foreign-exchange market eased the flow of imported raw materials as well as essential spare parts, and permitted the replacement of obsolete machinery and plant in some cases.

After declining continuously from 40% in 1978 to 21% in 1982, capacity utilization in the manufacturing sector recovered temporarily to 30% in 1983 but declined again to 18% the following year. Since then, it has increased continuously, hitting 46% in 1993. Subsectors which are domestic resource-based, such as tobacco and beverages, wood processing, and food processing, showed remarkable increases in capacity utilization. According to Biggs and Srivastava (1996) the most consistent positive correlation between local resource intensity and capacity utilization and output growth is found in the wood products subsector.

Capacity utilization in the wood subsector increased from 20% in 1983 to 65% in 1993 where

Table 13.4 Capacity Utilization in Medium and Large-Scale Enterprise (%)

	1971	76	78	79	80	81	82	83	84	85	86	87	88	89	90	91	92	93
Metal	35	32	28	26	28	24	43	55	20	16	n.a	42	45	47	49	58	68	80
Electrical	n.a	29	32	31	18	19	37	44	8	33	30	36	40	11	13	12	12	24
Plastics	n.a	n.a	11	15	17	23	20	35	30	28	30	39	39	41	40	31	42	45
Vehicles Assembly	63	13	18	17	n.a	28	15	20	8	20	n.a	10	24	n.a	25	22	22	16
Tobacco & Beverages	62	55	50	28	30	31	n.a	65	20	40	40	45	58	60	65	75	75	76
Food Processing	n.a	40	41	23	30	25	n.a	25	23	31	36	42	60	51	55	57	49	52
Leather	56	46	31	31	21	26	18	26	12	22	n.a	15	20	15	12	7	10	10
Garments	40	47	38	25	30	24	20	25	20	26	27	25	35	25	22	30	35	53
Pharmaceuticals	40	43	25	17	17	17	20	35	n.a	17	n.a	26	33	33	30	28	25	40
Cosmetics	44	27	33	27	8	15	15	20	n.a	n.a	25	29	33	30	25	25	24	16
Paper	50	50	31	28	28	31	25	30	17	15	n.a	30	42	30	30	30	32	45
Non-metals	60	65	47	34	30	24	15	22	12	35	n.a	37	40	44	48	54	65	73
Chemicals	55	55	42	26	28	17	15	20	22	20	25	30	35	33	30	30	30	40
Rubber	n.a	36	22	18	16	20	27	22	15	16	23	28	38	43	48	51	49	54
Wood Processing	n.a	n.a	36	36	27	38	20	20	28	33	n.a	43	70	70	70	65	65	65
Textiles	78	86	40	32	21	20	10	16	17	20	17	24	33	41	35	45	67	41
All Manufacturing	52	43	40	33	26	25	21	30	18	25	30	31	40	38	37	41	45	46

Source: Statistical Service, Quarterly Digest of Statistics, Various Issues

the domestic component of inputs in this activity is about 90%. On the other hand, subsectors like textiles and garments were unable to reach high rates mainly due to the stiff competition they faced from imports, coupled with the high percentage of imported raw materials (73.4% for textiles and 65.9% for garments, Baah-Nuakoh *et al.*, 1996: 43).

Employment and Productivity[5] Employment generation has been one of the biggest challenges to the government since launching the ERP. Employment in the formal manufacturing sector declined from an average of 84,000 between 1975 and 1979 to 31,700 between 1980 and 1983. The decline was more pronounced in the private sector, where employment fell from 66,700 to 21,000 over the same period. Between 1983 and 1987, total formal employment increased to an average of 57,600 but declined to 30,200 between 1988 and 1991. The decline over this period fell more heavily on the public sector where employment decreased from 17,900 to 6,500. The reduction was the result, among other things, of:

- the retrenchment and redeployment of workers from the public sector and parastatal organizations;
- the removal of ghost workers from the payrolls of parastatal organizations;
- the collapse of some firms following the import liberalization policy;
- the divestiture of state-owned enterprises and subsequent rationalization by the new owners;
- the slow response of the private sector and new investment to the new policy changes;
- the low labour absorptive capacity of the new firms despite the policy changes (some of which were capital-intensive).

It must be emphasized that the data in Table 13.5 deal with formal sector employment and do not take into account the small-scale manufacturing enterprises (SME) some of which are doing very well. It is probable that the growth of the SME sector provides an important offset to the employment decline and probably adds to the output growth. Steel and Webster (1992) have found some evidence that small-scale enterprises in Ghana adapted successfully to structural adjustment. Teal (1995) also finds that the so-called micro firms (less than five employees) have grown rapidly in the post-ERP period. The World Bank (1994b) notes that a significant proportion of new entrants to the manufacturing sector have been small enterprises in the woodworking and metal-working sectors.

Labour productivity in the manufacturing sector (average value added per worker deflated by the manufactures wholesale price index) declined by about 43% between 1977 and 1981 (World Bank, 1984). This downward trend was largely due to constraints in laying off redundant labour in spite of the low rates of capacity utilization. The low wages, relative to the urban cost of

Table 13.5   Mean Employment in Formal Sector Manufacturing 1975–91

Period	Public '000	Private '000	Total '000	Public as % of Total	Private as % of Total
1975–9	17.3	66.7	84.0	20.6	79.4
1980–83	10.7	21.0	31.7	34.3	65.7
1984–7	17.9	39.7	57.6	31.4	68.6
1988–91	6.5	23.7	30.2	21.6	78.4

Source: Statistical Service, *Quarterly Digest of Statistics*, Various Issues.

[5] We acknowledge the major difficulties with employment statistics as suggested in Chapter 12. The trends discussed here, however, conform to estimations made by the government and the World Bank as in the relevant references.

living, provided little incentive to work. The compressed wage structure offered little reward to greater skills and productivity, especially in the public sector. The decline in employment in the face of rising output implies that labour productivity has increased, at least in the formal sector. There is some empirical evidence based on a survey carried out in 1992/3 of 70 large and medium-scale manufacturing enterprises (Acheampong, 1996; Acheampong and Tribe, 1997) that labour productivity has increased following the introduction of the ERP. The main factors responsible for this were the restructuring of firms, increased capacity utilization, the retraining of labour, the re-organization of labour to undertake new tasks and increased capital per worker.

Manufactured Exports The policies adopted prior to the ERP discriminated against export activities. Between 1975 and 1979, manufactured exports grew at an annual average rate of 12.1%. Between 1980 and 1983, however, they declined at an average rate of –18.6% (Baah-Nuakoh *et al.*, 1996: 4).

The large devaluations accompanying the ERP raised the profitability of exporting for a range of activities. As a consequence, a flurry of export activities was reported among several firms in Ghana, including agricultural equipment, beverages, furniture and aluminium products (Hettige *et al.*, 1991). Of the 116 firms reported in Asante's (1995) survey, 34 were exporters. Of the remaining 82, 53 expressed an interest in exporting.

Even though manufacturing output responded almost immediately with positive growth rates from 1984 onwards, there was a lag in the response of manufactured exports which did not register positive growth rates until 1986. This is partly because a firm established during the period of a liberalized trade regime with an incentive system which encourages exporting, is unlikely to move into exporting immediately as it again concentrates on the domestic market during the period when its costs are still high. It is also possible that it may take time to establish external marketing links, whereas the domestic market will be more easily identified.

Table 13.6   Composition of Manufactured Exports (%)

Period	Traditional[a] Man. Exp.	Food[b] Products	Basic[c] Manuf.	Misc.[d] Manuf.
	3-Year Moving Average			
1970–76	56.2	1.6	37.7	0.1
1977–83	44.1	1.9	45.7	0.8
1984–86	38.8	5.1	46.0	1.6
1987–90	44.5	3.6	45.9	2.1
Significance Test of Difference in Means				
Pre-ERP				
1971–83	49.2	1.8	42.4	0.5
Post-ERP				
1984–90	42.0	4.3	45.9	1.9
T-Stat	1.4	–2.8**	–0.6	–3.5***

*** Significant at the 1% level; **Significant at the 5% level

Notes: [a] Traditional manufactured exports are defined here as cocoa products and sawn wood exports.
  [b] Food products do not include cocoa products
  [c] Basic manufactures include veneers, plywood, aluminium, non-ferrous metals, etc.
  [d] Miscellaneous manufactures include furniture and furniture parts, clothing, etc.
Source: Calculated from Baah-Nuakoh *et al.*, 1996; Table 5.

Composition of Manufactured Exports Prior to the ERP, diversification of manufactured exports made little headway despite the importance attached to it by successive governments. Traditional exports (i.e. cocoa products and sawn timber) dominated manufactured exports between 1970 and 1982 (Table 13.6). These items averaged 56.2% of total manufactured exports between 1970 and 1976. This figure dropped to 44.1% between 1977 and 1983. There has been some diversification of manufactured exports since the ERP. Traditional manufactured exports declined to an average of 38.8% between 1984 and 1986, then increased to 44.5% between 1987 and 1990, suggesting that the diversification which took place earlier was being reversed. On the other hand, the share of food products increased from an average of 1.6% between 1970 and 1976 to 5.1% between 1984 and 1986 but declined to 3.6% between 1987 and 1990. It is clear that there is the possibility of expansion of manufactured exports through commodity diversification. The post-ERP performance of manufactured exports has not been impressive despite the substantial improvements in price incentives, implying the importance of other factors. The dominance of exports by a few product groups supports the argument that not only macro but sectoral policies will be necessary to increase manufactured exports, not only through an increase in the value of existing product groups but also through an increase in the number of product groups which are exported.

Constraints of Manufacturing and Recent Initiatives Despite the improved performance of the sector, some problems still remain, including the following:

- inadequate finance for working capital, rehabilitation and modernization;
- the large depreciation of the cedi has eroded the liquid resources which could have helped firms to undertake the necessary investments. In some cases, the depreciation has sharply inflated the cedi value of debts related to previous imports of machinery and equipment;
- the tight monetary policy pursued has increased the cost of credit;
- some of the enterprises operated under high protective barriers are now finding it difficult to cope with the more competitive market environment;
- macroeconomic instability.

In addition to the above factors, Teal (1995) argues that labour regulations, price controls and other obstacles to expansion have constrained output and export growth, especially in the case of wood products which is the major manufacturing export sub-sector. More generally, he argues that government-induced market failure explains the failure to develop manufacturing exports. Structural adjustment and liberalization are not complete in Ghana and government policy continues to have an adverse effect on the output of firms in the exportables sector in particular.

Although the general prognosis for the manufacturing sector appears pessimistic, there exists considerable potential for its future development. Ghana's accelerated growth strategy (a policy adopted in 1994) has as its goal encouragement of the private sector as a dynamic partner of government in the development process. To address the poor performance of the manufacturing sector which is expected to lead the way to accelerated growth, a number of policy initiatives have been taken by the government. These include the establishment of the Private Enterprise Foundation (PEF) under the Trade and Investment Project (TIP) and the ¢10 billion government-sponsored Business Assistance Fund (BAF) to assist distressed but potentially viable industries.

Within the Accelerated Growth Strategy, the industrial sector is supposed to embark on a policy of export-led growth and selective import substitution. Sectors identified under the strategy in view of their linkages to domestic resources include: the food and agro-industries, textiles, and wood processing and packaging. A number of projects and programmes have also been put in place to enhance the supply capabilities of exporters. These include: (i) the Medium Term Programme for Non-Traditional Exports (MTP-NTE); (ii) the USAID-sponsored Trade and Investment Programme (TIP); (iii) Private Enterprise and Export Development (PEED); and (iv) Funds for Small and Medium Enterprises Development (FUSMED).

The sector has responded favourably to the above programmes and policies. Although, as indicated earlier, the growth rate of the manufacturing sector has slackened since 1988, some subsectors have picked up strongly, suggesting that the potential exists. Likewise, capacity utilization has increased remarkably in some subsectors participating in the support programmes. There has also been some diversification of manufactured exports. The substantial increase in the share of intermediate goods especially since 1990 indicates growing linkages in the manufacturing sector.

Lall (1991: 121) has defined 'successful' industrialization as a process whereby capacity is built and utilized efficiently and growth is sustained over the longer term by increases in productivity and competitiveness, implying 'a certain *efficiency* and *dynamism* in the industrialisation process'. The 'basic building block of industrial success' is 'the attainment of static and dynamic efficiency at the firm level' (p.123). Firms have to invest time and effort in learning new skills in order to achieve static efficiency, but acquisition of skills and knowledge is the major determinant of dynamic efficiency, that is, adaptation to change, improved productivity performance and innovation. National industrial performance is determined by what Lall calls incentives, capabilities and institutions. Successful industrialization is characterized by direct but selective government intervention, and will display increasing depth and capability of manufacturing activity, with growing local content in physical, human and technological inputs (*ibid.:* 122).

'Successful' industrialization is thus explained by a combination of factors which interact in a complex way. It must remain an open question as to whether Ghana has the resources and technical capabilities, as well as the political will and commitment, to devise and implement the required policy package to achieve this objective.

3.   Developments in the Mining Sector

Structure of the Mining Sector and Initiatives Taken
The mining sector has been dominated by the gold industry over the years. In terms of foreign-exchange earnings, for example, the share of gold in total earnings from all minerals stood at almost 89% in 1980 and rose to 90% in 1994. A greater part of the discussion here is therefore devoted to the gold industry. Further justification for this approach stems from the fact that, unlike the gold sub-sector, there is a paucity of reliable information on all other mining activities.

Traditionally, the large companies Ashanti Goldfields Company (AGC), Goldfields Limited (GFL)) have operated only underground mines. However, by the early 1990s, new medium-sized firms introduced state-of-the-art open-cast mining technology. The latter is gradually becoming an acceptable technology in many depressed developing countries because of the overriding need for foreign exchange and employment generation. Although ecologically questionable, the cost-effectiveness of the technology is such that low-grade ore, which was unprofitable under the old technology, can now be economically mined. The large companies have recently added this technology to their line of operations.

At the institutional level, the Ghana Chamber of Mines plays a vital role in co-ordinating activities in the industry on behalf of its members. All the major firms in the industry are members. A key objective of the Chamber is the formulation of proposals for legislation, regulations, bye-laws and all other measures which might impact positively on the mining sector (Ghana Chamber of Mines, 1996a). In this regard, the Chamber, in collaboration with the Minerals Commission, has been instrumental in the formulation of policies for the industry. Under the ERP major initiatives taken include the following:

a)   removal of the minimum mineral duty which ranged between 5 and 10%; the minimum turnover tax of 2.5%; the 10% import duty, the foreign-exchange tax ranging from 35 to

75%, and the gold export levy of ¢3.00 p/oz of gold after 100,000 oz;

b) the 6% royalty charged on the gross values of minerals obtained was set to vary from a minimum of 3% to a maximum of 12%. There is also a flexible deferment clause which caters for exigencies faced by the companies;

c) the corporate tax which ranged between 50 and 55% was reduced to a flat rate of 35%; and

d) the import duty of 35% was replaced by an 'Import Subsidy Scheme' which exempted companies from payment of duties on plant and equipment, and from paying the selective Aliens Employment Tax.

Constraints and Performance in the Mining Sector

There was a precipitous decline in output and foreign-exchange earnings in all sub-sectors within the mining sector from the mid-1970s to the early years of the ERP. A World Bank report of 1984 identified the main causes of the decline in the 1970s as follows:

> The reasons for the decline in minerals production include shortages of foreign exchange to maintain and rehabilitate the mines; lack of capital investment for exploration and development; poor management and lack of mining skills; infrastructure deterioration, particularly shortages of rail capacity for manganese and bauxite; mining company financial problems due to the greatly overvalued currency and spiralling inflation; a declining grade of gold ore; . . . illegal panning and smuggling of gold and diamonds.

At the official and industrial levels, there is general agreement on the foregoing points as the true depiction of the causes of the decline. A more potent set of problems in the sector, especially in the gold subsector, stemmed from the harsh fiscal regime which impacted on overall performance. The 1980 report of the Quarshie Committee for Increased Gold Output in Ghana was emphatic on the impediments imposed on the industry by the prevailing fiscal regime. In the Committee's opinion, 'it appears the door has been completely shut to outside investment in the Gold Mining Industry'.

The pre-ERP provisions amended above were viewed by the industry with concern on two main points:

(i) they were seen as inherently too bureaucratic and, therefore, operationally too inflexible; and

(ii) the levies were deemed to be exorbitant and, therefore, as inhibiting the expansion of the sector. More specifically, the sharp decline in the gold industry (Table 13.7) from the mid-1970s to the early 1980s was attributed to the fiscal disincentives. Total output had fallen sharply from 516,000 oz. in 1976 to 285,000 oz. (44.8%) by 1983 when the ERP was launched.

At present (1997), the provisions with respect to royalty payments and the minimum minerals duty are such that, in practice, the companies pay the floor rate of 3%. Legally, the precise percentage depends on a company's operating cost. In addition to the reduction in the corporate tax rate, companies are allowed to capitalize all expenditures during reconnaissance, prospecting, and development, in accordance with the capital allowance (amortization) provision of the Law (Tsikata, 1995b).

Table 13.7   Gold Output in Major Mines: Pre-ERP (oz.)

Mine	1976	1977	1978	1979	1980	1981	1982	1983
AGC	361,512	265,684	237,935	232,156	232,036	252,408	268,040	243,194
Tarkwa	58,319	56,271	52,931	39,210	43,120	*	*	*
Prestea	83,761	79,894	95,263	82,102	77,400	*	*	*
Dunkwa	9,587	64	1,272	4,147	5,394	*	*	*
Konongo	3,199	4,282	998	61	400	*	*	*
SGMC						85,634	69,714	42,097
Total	516,378	406,195	388,399	357,676	327,683	338,042	337,754	285,291

Note: *SGMC comprised Tarkwa, Prestea, Dunkwa and Konongo. Disaggregated data not available.
Source: Tsikata, 1995b.

Post-1983 Performance

Total investment in the mineral sector between 1983 and 1992 stood at $844.57 m., of which $818.07 m. (97%) went to the gold subsector. The entry of Teberebie Goldfields presumably had a remarkable influence on the inflow of foreign direct investment in the gold industry. Except in 1985 when AGC underwent a major recapitalization at the cost of $171.40 m., investment was sluggish (Table 13.8). The bulk of investment occurred between 1989 and 1992, when Teberebie entered the industry. Total investment during this sub-period was $633.37 m., that is, 77% of the industry total for the entire period. The trend can partly be explained by growing investor confidence and the liberalized market conditions prevailing in the economy. Within an international perspective, increased demand for gold for both transactions and fabrication worldwide encouraged investors to step up production in order to increase sales revenue, even though gold prices were at best stagnant. It is worth noting that, since 1993, interest in the sector has been rising. The takeover of Tarkwa Goldfields (now Goldfields Limited, GFL) and Ghana Consolidated Diamonds Limited by South African mining conglomerates provides further proof of the growing investor confidence which must be vigorously promoted if the sector is to maintain its position as the leading foreign-exchange earner of the economy.

Output-Revenue Profile

One way of analyzing the policy impact on the mining sector is by evaluating the resultant output or sales revenue generated. The trends are compared for the periods before and after the inception of the reform programme. Taking 1980 as the base year, one observes a steady decline in output and, consequently, revenue during the period after 1980 (Table 13.9). Output dropped from 342,900 oz. in 1980 to 282,300 oz. by 1984, the lowest for the decade. A minor recovery, however, occurred in 1985, raising output to almost 300,000 oz., i.e. a 6.13% increase on the previous year's level. Output again dropped to 287,100 oz. the following year. By 1987, however, a major recovery was under way which eventually led to what can now be described as sustainable growth in the industry. Output expanded from its 1986 level of 287,100 to 329,000 oz. (i.e by 14%). The upward trend has continued ever since, reaching 845,900 oz. by 1991 and 1,261,400 oz. in 1993, almost 2.5 and 3.7 times the output recorded for 1980. A comparison of average growth rates for the pre- and post-reform periods shows a 0.75 average decline for 1981 and 1982 and a positive annual average rate of 14% between 1983 and 1994. A clearer picture of positive growth trends is provided by the 1987–94 data. This period of recovery and sustained growth recorded an average annual growth rate of 22.8% (Table 13.10).

Table 13.8   Total Investment in the Mineral Sector: Post-ERP
(Excluding Prospecting Companies) (US$m.)

Year	Gold	Diamonds	Manganese	Bauxite	Annual Total
1983	–	–	6.00	–	6.00
1984	–	11.40	1.30	–	12.70
1985	171.40	–	–	–	171.40
1986	3.69	–	–	–	3.69
1987	–	–	–	–	–
1988	9.61	–	–	–	9.61
1989	45.11	–	2.80	–	47.91
1990	210.29	–	–	5.00	215.29
1991	87.97	–	–	–	87.97
1992	290.00	–	–	–	290.00
Total	818.07	11.40	10.10	5.00	844.57

Source: Minerals Commission, Ghana Chamber of Mines and company data.

Table 13.9   Gold Production and Revenue Trends

Year	Output (oz.)	Output Growth Rate	Revenue (US$ '000)	Revenue Growth Rate	e_R
1980	342,904.20		202,350		
1981	338,041.75	–1.42	166,980	–17.48	12.33
1982	337,754.14	–0.09	126,590	–24.19	268.78
1983	285,291.45	–15.33	104,690	–17.30	1.11
1984	282,298.75	–1.05	99,300	–5.15	4.91
1985	299,615.38	6.13	93,840	–5.50	–0.90
1986	287,124.16	–4.17	107,134	14.17	–3.40
1987	328,955.81	14.57	147,791	38.06	2.61
1988	373,936.53	13.67	157,427	6.43	0.47
1989	429,475.84	14.85	174,797	11.03	0.74
1990	541,408.33	26.06	205,786	17.73	0.68
1991	845,907.85	56.24	303,480	47.47	0.84
1992	998,194.50	18.00	346.220	14.08	0.78
1993	1,261,424.26	26.37	453,636	31.03	1.18
1994	1,423,600.00	12.86	519,800	14.59	1.13

Source: Minerals Commission.

Table 13.10 Selected Period Averages

Period	Average Output (Q) (oz)	Average Growth of Output (%)	Average Revenue (US$ '000)
1980–82	339,566.70	–0.75	165,307
1983–94	613,102.74	14.00	226,169
1987–94	775,362.89	22.83	288,632
1987–89	377,456.06	14.37	160,045
1990–94	1,014,106.99	27.91	365,784

Source: Calculated from Table 13.9.

Another helpful approach is the sub-periodization of the years 1980–94 in order to ascertain the probable impact of the entry of new mines from 1990 onwards on the industry's growth. The period segmentations and the average values are given in Table 13.10.

A moderately positive average growth of 14% was realized during the period prior to the entry (i.e 1987–9) of the new firms. This tallies with the overall ERP period (1983–94) average growth of 14%. The rate almost doubled to 27.9% between 1990 and 1994 when the new firms entered the industry. Admittedly, a significant portion of the increase is also attributable to output expansion by AGC.

In terms of revenue growth, the average decline in growth during 1981 and 1982 was significantly larger than the average fall in output, that is, –20.83% and –0.75%, respectively (Tables 13.9 and 13.10). By implication, there was a tighter squeeze on development financing than would have been the case if a proportionate fall had occurred in revenue.

The recovery in the sector is clearly portrayed by revenue trends since 1990. Revenue, comprising total earnings, more than doubled from US$246.98 m. in 1990 to US$494.37 m. in 1993. The gold subsector recorded revenue of US$453.64 m. in 1993 as against US$202.79 m. in 1990. Table 13.11 shows details.

Table 13.11 Revenue Growth Trends 1990–3

	1990 Revenue ($mil.)	Growth %	1991 Revenue ($mil.)	Growth %	1992 Revenue (Smil.)	Growth %	1993 Revenue ($mil.)	Growth %
All Minerals:	247.0	25.0	353.6	43.1	392.1	10.9	494.4	26.10
Gold								
1. Aggregate:	202.8	–	303.5	49.6	346.2	14.1	453.6	31.0
2. Small-scale	6.3	–	3.8	–39.25	7.7	102.94	12.0	55.03
Diamonds								
1. Aggregate	17.0	–	19.6	15.3	19.7	0.23	18.5	–5.70
2. Small-scale Mining	–	–	17.4	22.15	15.5	–26.73	11.8	–7.42

Source: Derived from Mineral Commission Estimates

Prospects

Output Potential Output trends in the dominant firms and the respective ore reserve positions clearly indicate that the rising gold production is likely to continue for some time. Geologically, the potential stretches from the Western Region through Ashanti to the Northern and Upper Regions. Assuming no changes in national economic policies, based on 1994 levels of operation the industry is potentially capable of raising output from 1,423,600 to over 2.5 million oz. by 2000, a production capacity which makes the country potentially one of the major gold exporters. The latter output is about 26% more than the output of 2 million oz. projected by the industry. The difference can be explained by the productivity increases at AGC and the investments undertaken in surface mining. Total projected output from 1995 to 2000 is estimated at over 12 million oz. Gross earnings over the period are estimated at about $5.28 billion, yielding total tax revenue and royalty payments of $422 m. and $158 m. respectively under the conditions specified above. The total fiscal contribution (tax revenue + royalty payments) is expected to reach at least $580 m., accounting for 11% of gross earnings in the industry over the period. In the face of dwindling tax revenues from other sectors, the projected amounts will constitute a significant fiscal contribution to economic growth and development.

Table 13.12 Projected Values Based on 10% Growth of Output

	Output ('000 oz.)	Price[a] ($ p/oz.)	Earnings ($ mil.)	Tax Revenue ($ mil.)	Royalty Payments ($ mil.)
1994	1,423.6	–	519.8	–	–
1995	1,566.0	420	657.7	52.6	19.7
1996	1,722.6	420	723.5	57.9	21.7
1997	1,894.8	420	795.8	63.7	23.9
1998	2,084.3	420	875.8	70.0	26.3
1999	2,292.7	420	962.9	77.0	28.9
2000	2,522.0	500	1,261.0	100.9	37.8
Total[b]	12,082.3		5,276.3	422.1	158.3

Notes: [a] Price projections used have been obtained from World Bank, 1994a.
            [b] Projected totals are from 1995 to 2000.
Source: Minerals Commission and authors' calculations.

Investment Potential Investor interest in the gold industry continues to be keen. Within the operating firms, there is an increasing urge not only to undertake further investments but also to diversify technology to include surface mining. The three main reasons underpinning this potential investment trend are:

  (i) the seemingly more conducive investment climate that prevails in Ghana than can be found in other gold-producing areas in sub-Saharan and South Africa;

 (ii) the existing gold mining culture and pool of skilled miners and professionals in old mining districts such as Tarkwa, Aboso, Konongo and Bibiani and, probably more importantly, the low cost of production because of the relatively cheap labour force; and

(iii) fairly bright prospects in the international bullion market (World Bank, 1994a).

From a total of 619 applications submitted to the Minerals Commission between 1988 and April, 1995, 491 mining licences were approved. Of that number, 134 are for large concession companies, of which 99 are Ghanaian and 35 foreign companies. By sub-Saharan African standards, the degree of interest shown by foreign companies can, to some extent, be interpreted as a partial expression of growing confidence in the industry. This, in turn, requires constant assessment of the investment climate in order not only to sustain the interest, but also to find ways in which the country can derive maximum development benefits from the undertakings. Plausible evidence exists (Tsikata, 1995b) indicating that, with the ongoing investments by both old and new companies, it is feasible to attain output levels of over 3.3 and 5.4 million oz. by 2000 and 2005, respectively.

4. Summary and Conclusions

The implementation of the ERP brought about a dramatic change in the performance of the manufacturing sector. After six years of continuous decline, real manufacturing GDP has experienced positive growth rates since 1984. There has also been an increase in capacity utilization. The liberalization of the foreign-exchange market eased the flow of imported raw materials as well as essential spare parts and the replacement of obsolete machinery and plant in some cases. Formal manufacturing employment has declined during the adjustment period. However, the effects of the ERP have varied across subsectors. Some subsectors have performed well, e.g., those relying on local resources like wood industries and beverages, indicating that some linkages are being formed, whilst others like textiles, which were overprotected, have not been able to face the increased competition from imports.

However, the slowing down in the growth of real manufacturing GDP since 1988 in spite of the price incentives suggests that appropriate trade and macroeconomic policies are necessary to bring about an improvement in the performance of the manufacturing sector but are not sufficient to ensure that this performance is sustained. Other factors are important in influencing the performance of the sector and the longer-term issues of strategy and policy which may lead to successful and sustained industrialization are still matters of debate.

The minerals sector has been a key beneficiary of the policy initiatives under the ERP. The main provisions under the Minerals and Mining Law, 1986 (PNDC L.153) have provided the foundation on which investments in the mining sector, especially the gold subsector, currently stand. In particular, the 10% government equity participation is viewed by the industry as appropriate in insulating companies from unnecessary ownership crises and/or political interference which hitherto had seriously affected the efficiency of companies in which the state held a majority share. In addition, although some firms and the Ghana Chamber of Mines have complained about the royalty rate of 3% (minimum) as being high, in general most firms find the rate neither excessive nor distortionary.

More significantly, two provisions have tremendously enhanced the potential for profits and guarantees for repatriation, namely i) allowances for capital write-off and ii) permission for the retention of part of foreign-exchange earnings abroad.

There is no doubt that Ghana's mining sector, especially the gold subsector, has a bright future and is capable of contributing immensely to the national development effort. Although it is difficult to know what precisely the country's gold reserve position is, expert opinion and continuing ore discoveries tend to put the industry on a high ore-reserve ranking. According to some estimates, the industry, as currently constituted, seems capable of raising output to over 2.5 million oz. per annum by 2000. It could be further increased to over 4.0 million oz. per annum by 2005, based on a 10% average growth rate. Projected demand, supply and price of gold (World Bank, 1994a) indicate that increases in output from Ghana should be easily absorbed in the world market at relatively better prices than those that prevail at present.

An institutional nexus of co-operation between the Minerals Commission, the Ghana Chamber of Mines and the Environmental Protection Agency will be crucial in the government's formulation and implementation of policies which will ensure that a mineral-sector-based growth and development strategy is undertaken with due attention to environmental sustainability. Indeed, feasibility studies on the restoration of selected degraded mining areas show positive net social returns in the long run (Tsikata, 1995a).

In general, the ERP has removed most of the key constraints on the mining sector which in turn has become a prime mover in the country's economic growth effort. More specifically, the gold industry has played a significant role in macroeconomic growth since 1990. However, in terms of economic linkages, net foreign-exchange-earning capacity and environmental resources and the open-cast technologies being used, especially in gold mining, have serious repercussions for health and agricultural activities in the mining areas.

References

Acheampong, I. (1996) 'The Impact of the Economic Recovery Programme (1983–1990) on Industrial Performance in Ghana', PhD Thesis, University of Bradford, mimeo.

Acheampong, I. and Tribe, M. (1997) 'Restructuring Ghana's Manufacturing Sector: The Impact of Bureaucratic Retreat', mimeo.

Asante, Y. (1995) *Determinants of Private Investment Behaviour in Ghana.* Revised Final Report submitted to the African Economic Research Consortium, July.

Baah-Nuakoh, A., Jebuni, C. D., Oduro, A. D. and Asante, Y. (1996) *Exporting Manufactures From Ghana: Is Adjustment Enough?* London: ODI Research Studies.

Biggs, T. and Srivastava, P. (1996) *Structural Aspects of Manufacturing in Sub-Saharan Africa: Findings from a Seven Country Enterprise.* Discussion Paper No. 346. Washington, DC: World Bank.

Colman, D. and Nixson, F. (1994) *The Economics of Change in Less Developed Countries*, 3rd Edition. Hemel Hempstead: Harvester Wheatsheaf.

Forysth, D. J. C. and Solomon, R. F. (1977) 'Choice of Technology and Nationality of Ownership in Manufacturing in a Developing Country', *Oxford Economic Papers*, Vol. 29, No. 2: 258–82.

Forysth D. J. C., McBain, N. S. and Solomon, R. F. (1980), 'Technical Rigidity and Appropriate Technology in Less Developed Countries', *World Development*, Vol. 8, No. 5/6: 371–98.

Ghana Chamber of Mines (1996a) *The Dynamics of the Ghana Chamber of Mines.* Accra: GCM.

Ghana Chamber of Mines (1996b) *The Mining Industry in Ghana.* Accra: GCM.

Ghana Statistical Service, *Ghana Industrial Census 1987.*

Greenaway, D., Morgan, W. and Wright, P. (1997) 'Trade Liberalisation and Growth in Developing Countries: Some new Evidence', *World Development*, Vol. 25, No. 11, 1885–92.

Hettige, H., Steel, W. F. and Wayen, J. A. (1991) *The Impact of Adjustment Lending on Industry in African Countries.* Washington, DC: World Bank Industry and Energy Department.

IMF, *International Financial Statistics,* Various Issues.

ISSER (1996) *State of the Ghanaian Economy in 1995.* University of Ghana, Legon.

Jebuni, C., Oduro, A. Asante, Y. and Tsikata, G. K. (1992) *Diversifying Exports: Supply Response of Non-Traditional Exports to Measures under ERP.* London: ODI Research Report.

Kay, Cristobal (1989) *Latin American Theories of Development and Underdevelopment.* London: Routledge.

Killick, Tony (1978) *Development Economics in Action: A Study of Economic Policies in Ghana.* London: Heinemann Educational Books.

Lall, S. (1991) 'Explaining Industrial Success in the Developing World' in V. N. Balasubramanyam and S. Lall (eds), *Current Issues in Development Economics.* London: Macmillan.

Lall, S. (1992) 'Structural Problems of African Industry' in F. Stewart, S. Lall and S. Wangwe (eds) *Alternative Development Strategies in Sub-Saharan Africa.* London: Macmillan.

Little, I. M. D., Scitovsky, T. and Scott, M. (1970) *Industry and Trade in some Developing Countries.* Oxford: Oxford University Press.

Meier, G. M. and Steel, W. F. (eds) (1989) *Industrial Adjustment in Sub-Saharan Africa.* New York: Oxford University Press for the World Bank.

Nixson, F. (1982) 'Import-Substituting Industrialisation' in Martin Fransman (ed.), *Industry and Accumulation in Africa.* London: Heinemann.

Nixson, F. (1990) 'Industrialisation and Structural Change in Developing Countries', *Journal of International Development*, Vol. 20, No. 3: 310–33.

Steel, W.F. (1972) 'Import Substitution and Excess Capacity in Ghana', *Oxford Economic Papers*, Vol. 24, No. 2, July.

Steel, W. F. and Webster, L. M. (1992) 'How Small Enterprises Have Responded to Adjustment', *The World Bank Economic Review*, Vol. 6, No. 3: 423–38.

Stein, H. (1992), 'Deindustrialisation, Adjustment, the World Bank and the IMF in Africa', *World Development*, Vol. 20, No. 1: 83–95.

Teal, F. (1995) *Does 'Getting Prices Right' Work? Micro Evidence from Ghana.* WPS/95–19. Centre for the Study of African Economies, Oxford University.

Tsikata, G. Kwaku (1995a) *Economic Cost-Benefit Analysis of Reclamation of Small-scale Mining Activities.* (A Report for the World Bank).

Tsikata, G. Kwaku (1995b) *The Gold Sub-sector and Economic Growth and Development in Ghana.* A Report for the World Bank.

UNCTAD (1964) *Towards a New Trade Policy for Development.* Report by the Secretary General of UNCTAD. New York: United Nations.

Weiss, J. (1988) *Industry in Developing Countries, Theory, Policy and Evidence.* London: Routledge.

World Bank (1984) *Ghana: Industrial Policy, Performance and Recovery*, Vol. 1. Washington, DC: World Bank.

World Bank (1994a) *Market Outlook for Major Energy Products, Metals, and Minerals*. Washington, DC: World Bank.

World Bank (1994b) *Adjustment in Africa: Reforms, Results and the Road Ahead*. New York: Oxford University Press for the World Bank.

14 Agricultural Policy & the Impact on Growth & Productivity 1970–95

V. K. NYANTENG
& A. WAYO SEINI

1. Introduction

Throughout the period 1970-95, governments in Ghana — frequently with strong encouragement from external donor agencies and financial institutions — have attempted to transform agriculture through policy directives or the use of economic instruments directed at improving incentives to production. Despite some significant gains at different times, these attempts have been generally unsuccessful, partly because they have been inconsistently applied and partly because they have failed to address the formidable technical and institutional problems confronting agricultural improvement.

This chapter first describes the role of agriculture in the Ghanaian economy and the main characteristics of Ghana's farming systems. It then provides an overview of agricultural policy over a period of frequent political changes and examines data, on output growth and yields in particular, over the same period. It finally assesses the overall constraints on agricultural development in Ghana in order to explain the limitations of economic policy instruments alone in addressing long-term structural problems in the sector.

2. Role of Agriculture

Ghana is mainly an agricultural country since agricultural activities constitute the main use to which Ghana's labour and land resources are put. The country covers an area of approximately 23.9 million sq. km, about 57% of which is agricultural land. Only about 20% of this agricultural land was under cultivation in 1994, however.

Agriculture is a major contributor to the Gross Domestic Product (GDP). However, while the sector's contribution to GDP averaged about 55% in the first half of the 1980s, it has progressively declined to 41% in 1995. Agriculture also contributes to government revenue, mainly through duties paid on exports of selected agricultural commodities, particularly cocoa. The contribution of agriculture to total revenue has declined steadily from its peak of 26% in 1987 to an average of about 7.5% per annum between 1990 and 1995. The agricultural sector is also the main source of food supply for the large non-agricultural and mainly urban population. Agriculture also supplies raw materials to some agro-based industries in Ghana, for example, textiles and soap manufacturing.

The agricultural sector contributes to the country's foreign-exchange availability in two main ways: (i) through the export of agricultural commodities and (ii) by producing import-substituting food and raw materials. Until 1992, when gold superseded cocoa, agriculture accounted for the highest proportion of the total foreign-exchange earnings, with cocoa as the highest foreign-exchange earner. At present, cocoa ranks second to minerals in Ghana's foreign-exchange earning capacity (see Tables 9.2 and 9.4 in Chapter 9).

Agriculture employs the highest proportion of the country's economically active population (EAP) as farmers and fishermen in farm labour and other agricultural-related activities such as marketing, processing, etc. Although the proportion of the EAP in agriculture has continued to decline over several decades, it still exceeded 40% in 1995. However, the incomes of those working in the agricultural sector as employees and self-employed are among the lowest in the country (Boateng *et al.*, 1990).

3.   Main Characteristics

The country is divided into six distinct agro-ecological zones, namely the high rain forest, the semi-deciduous rain forest, the forest-savannah transition, the Guinea savannah, the Sudan savannah and the coastal savannah. The conditions of these zones limit the type of crops that can be successfully cultivated. In general, tree crops do better in the forest zones, while food crops do well in the transitional and savannah zones.

The major staple food crops include cereals, mainly rice and maize and starchy staples including yams, cassava and plantain. Industrial raw materials include cotton, oil palm, tobacco and bast fibre. The main export crop is cocoa for which Ghana was for a long time the world's leading producer. It lost its place as the largest producer of cocoa in the 1977/78 season, however, and its recorded share of world cocoa exports declined from 35% in 1961–5 to only 15% in 1981. After rising from 159,000 tonnes in 1983 to 247,000 tonnes in 1990, cocoa export volumes have stagnated and Ghana's current world market share is even smaller (13% in 1995) than it was in 1981.

Traditional crop farming systems still prevail in most of Ghana, particularly in food production where small-scale farming predominates. Over 90% of food production, for example, emanates from smallholdings of less than 3 hectares. Under traditional systems, land preparation is accomplished by slash and burn methods. The seed is obtained from the previous harvest. Usually several crops are intercropped often at random, particularly on the poorer subsistence farms. The land is cultivated for one or two seasons and then abandoned for several years when yields are observed to be too low, with cultivation shifting to 'new' land, or previously abandoned fields, leaving the abandoned land to regenerate its lost fertility by natural means. Thus, the traditional shifting cultivation systems depend mainly on natural soil fertility and very little on chemical fertilizers. The traditional systems work better in regenerating soil fertility in the forest zones than in the savannah zones with lower vegetative cover. The longer the land is allowed to rest, the higher the level of fertility generated. However, with increasing population pressure, the fallow period is being progressively shortened, resulting in lower crop yields where fertilizers are not used.

4.   Agricultural Policies, 1970–1995

Agricultural policy in Ghana can be discussed in terms of two contrasting periods, 1970–82 and 1983–95, neatly divided into the pre- and post-structural adjustment periods.

The period 1970–82 was probably the most difficult period in Ghana's history, characterized by political instability with its concomitant variations in economic policy which had drastic ramifications in the agricultural sector. The civilian government in power in 1970 sought to rescue the country from the stranglehold of the command economy that it inherited and return it to the market economy existing at the time of independence in 1957. Emphasis was placed on economic development based on reliance on the private sector as opposed to the heavy hand of the state that predominated in both agriculture and industry. Thus state-owned enterprises, machinery and equipment were sold to private entrepreneurs and the economy was returned to a private enterprise, market-oriented system. Experiments with import liberalization were carried out and small-scale and medium sized agricultural development was emphasized as opposed to large state farms in the government's economic programmes.

Conscious efforts were therefore made to reverse the expansion of state participation in agriculture that had led to the cutting back of the exiguous investment in small-scale farming. With regard to food production, the government actively promoted the production of rice in valley bottoms in the northern part of the country. Farmers were helped to purchase the agricultural machinery and equipment previously used on the state farms. The extension services were revived and strengthened to offer advice to small-scale farmers. The emphasis was on private ownership in small and medium-sized farm units with direct financing from the banks.

A major feature of agricultural policy in the early 1970s was the formation of single product development boards for commodities such as cotton, bast fibre, grains and cattle and meat. Policy-makers believed that the ingenuity of the peasant farmer could be further successfully exploited, as in the case of cocoa, by the establishment of development boards to offer advice and incentives and to oversee the production of the agricultural raw materials vital to the newly established factories. In order to protect farmers from income losses from productivity gains and over-production of these commodities, the government also instituted minimum guaranteed price schemes. Agricultural policies were supported by a massive rural development scheme, designed to provide the basic infrastructure of roads, water and electricity that would encourage people to stay in the rural areas rather than migrate to the overpopulated urban areas. In the cocoa subsector, the multiple buying system, involving several companies, was re-established to replace the monopoly enjoyed by the United Ghana Farmers Co-operative Council, which was subsequently dissolved.

The experiments of the early 1970s were short-lived, however. The overthrow of the civilian government by the military in 1972 led to the dismantling of the open market policies and the restoration of the command economy. Comprehensive import controls were resorted to, the scope of price controls was widened,and some imported consumer goods were subsidized. A monopoly system of cocoa purchasing (unitary buying system) was reintroduced in 1977.

At the same time, there was an upsurge of interest in raising agricultural production to the self-sufficiency level. This led to the institution of the Operation Feed Yourself (OFY) and the Operation Feed Your Industries (OFYI) programmes, which were to spearhead the campaign to increase food and agricultural raw materials production. Among the objectives of these programmes was an increase in small farm production through acreage expansion (Killick,1978). The OFY emphasized the production of cereals, mainly maize and rice, while the OFYI encouraged the production of cotton, kenaf and sugarcane among other agricultural raw materials.

The OFY was, in fact, relatively successful as Ghana became self-sufficient in rice production between 1974 and 1975 (Winch, 1976). The contribution of small farmers to rice self-sufficiency was insignificant, however, largely because they were not given the opportunity to participate in the rice scheme (Roberts, 1981). While the efforts in rice met with some success, the gains in food production were marked by a dramatic decline in cocoa production. Cocoa output fell by about 41%, from about 462,000 tonnes in 1972 to 271,000 tonnes in 1978.

Despite the major shifts in policy, the period 1970–75 was one of hope for agricultural development in Ghana. But the following period, 1976–82, turned out to be one of despair. Agricultural development in this period took place in an especially unfavourable macroeconomic and political environment (see Table 1.1 in Chapter 1). The period was characterized by a rapid expansion of money supply to finance the government's budget deficits. The money supply was expanded at an average annual rate of 28.5% between 1975 and 1977. Between 1974 and 1979, more than 70% of every budget deficit was financed by the creation of money. This led to the period of Ghana's highest inflation rates. Inflation rose from 3.5% in 1970 to 24.3% in 1974, and 41% in 1976 to reach 121.2% in 1977.

The high rates of inflation combined with continuing balance of trade deficits made the cedi so overvalued relative to other currencies that a lucrative black market in foreign currencies sprang up. Smuggling operations also became commonplace as farmers and entrepreneurs saw the benefits of illegally trading in the markets of neighbouring countries. There was a complete lack of incentive to produce in the primary and secondary sectors of agriculture and industry. Because agricultural inputs such as fertilizers and insecticides were subsidized, they became primary targets for smuggling into neighbouring countries where high prices more than compensated for the loss of their application in Ghana. The economy continued to decline into the early 1980s. Between 1972 and 1981, real GDP grew at an average rate of about 0.55%. By 1982, the high hopes of the early 1970s had given way to despair as shortages of essential commodities and basic spare parts needed to keep plant and machinery operating became commonplace and economic hardship became a reality. Agricultural mechanization, which had been on the upturn, suffered, particularly as basic spare parts required to maintain machines were lacking.

To compound the economic problems, the period was also punctuated by frequent changes of government. A palace coup reshuffled the military government in 1978. An unsuccessful coup attempt in May 1979 was followed by a violent but successful one the following month. In December 1981, the same group of military men successfully overthrew the constitutionally elected civilian government to which they had handed over power in October 1979.

By early 1983, the need to resuscitate the economy became urgent and in April 1983 the government launched a set of reforms under an Economic Recovery Programme (ERP) supported by an International Monetary Fund stand-by credit. This put in place a new era for agriculture. Nevertheless, the subsequent period (1983–95) can be characterized as one of renewed hope but eventual frustration.

The immediate priority in the ERP was to renew the process of economic growth and for this an essential requirement was revitalization of the export crop sector. Thus, the main feature in terms of agricultural policy was the increase in the producer price of cocoa relative to other crops. In addition, subsidies on input prices, particularly fertilizer, pesticides and farm equipment were eventually eliminated. In the more general area of the reform of public agricultural institutions, the main initiative was the reduction in budgetary costs to the government of the large parastatal sector and a drastic redundancy programme for the Ghana Cocoa Marketing Board.

The first phase of the ERP emphasized stabilization policies which sought to create incentives to stimulate the productive sectors of the economy by realigning relative prices (including the exchange rate and interest rates) in favour of domestic production of import-substitutes and exports, and by providing needed supplies through an import liberalization programme (World Bank, 1984). The strategy was also aimed at improving government finances and at lowering the rate of inflation by pursuing prudent fiscal, monetary and trade policies (see Chapter 1 for fuller discussion).

The second phase of the ERP consisted of a medium-term Structural Adjustment Programme (SAP) launched in 1986 and aimed at removing structural impediments from the economy in order to set it on a growth path. Its objectives included the following: to attain a 5% average annual growth rate of GDP; to bring the annual inflation rate down from 24.6% in 1986 to 8% by 1990; and to maintain balance of payment surpluses averaging about US$110 m. per annum. Under a third phase of the adjustment process (the liberalization and growth phase), which started in 1989, the major goals included the deregulation of commodity and service markets to reduce domestic price distortions as well as liberalization of export and import markets.

Being the largest sector of the economy, agriculture received a lot of attention in all phases of the ERP. In the first phase, the main objectives in agriculture were to achieve self-sufficiency in the production of cereals; to maintain adequate levels of buffer stocks of grains, particularly maize and rice; to ensure price stability and the provision of maximum food security against unforeseen crop failure and other natural hazards; and to increase the foreign-exchange earnings from agriculture mainly through the provision of incentives to cocoa farmers. The main feature of agricultural policy was the increase in producer prices, with particularly sharp increases for cocoa relative to other crops. With the help of the World Bank, the Agricultural Services Rehabilitation Project (ASRP), aimed primarily at rehabilitating agricultural services to enhance the achievement of government policy objectives in agriculture, was implemented. The first phase also incorporated institutional reforms in agriculture which, among other things, saw the establishment and strengthening of the Policy Planning, Monitoring and Evaluation Department (PPMED) of the Ministry of Agriculture to enhance the ministry's capacity to plan and follow through agricultural projects.

In addition, there were special programmes aimed at reorganizing and strengthening agricultural services. These included the National Agricultural Research Programme (NARP) aimed at rehabilitating and reinforcing agricultural research systems. A rural (agricultural) finance scheme was also implemented, aimed at addressing the credit needs of farming communities and expanding production capacity and employment in the rural sectors by providing finance for viable projects strengthening credit institutions operating in the rural areas. The International Fund for Agricultural Development (IFAD) also implemented schemes to help smallholders in the savannah and transitional areas of the country. USAID also assisted in the promotion of agricultural development through its Agricultural Productivity Promotion Programme (APPP) which aimed at improving productivity among food-crop farmers, mainly via the maintenance of feeder roads leading to these areas.

The second phase of the reforms (1986–8) emphasized increased productivity and internal price stability in the agricultural sector. The government actively promoted cereal production in pursuit of food security objectives. Thus, it raised the guaranteed minimum price for maize and rice every year and subsidies on farm inputs such as fertilizers, machinery and other agricultural chemicals continued, though on a much reduced scale.

Institutional reforms were also intensified in the cocoa sector during this phase. The Cocoa Sector Rehabilitation Project was implemented with World Bank financing, the main objective being to increase efficiency in the sector with respect to production and marketing. This involved a reduction in the size of the Cocoa Board and the passing of a greater share of the world price of cocoa on to producers. Unification of the extension services of the Board and the Ministry of Agriculture was also planned. The Agricultural Policy Co-ordinating Committeee (APCC) was set up in this phase to bring together all institutions dealing with agriculture.

Agricultural policy in the third phase of adjustment was implemented within the context of the Medium Term Agricultural Development Programme, 1991–2000 (MTADP). As part of the liberalization programme in this phase, the guaranteed minimum prices for maize and rice were abolished and all subsidies were removed including those for agricultural inputs, notably fertilizers, insecticides and fungicides. In addition, the procurement and distribution of these inputs which had hitherto been the responsibilty of the Ministry of Agriculture and COCOBOD, were privatized, the objective being to enhance competition and efficiency in agricultural input marketing.

The period 1983–95 was one of renewed hope. Growth in the economy took a positive turn, averaging about 4.2% per annum between 1983 and 1992; the rate of inflation was brought down drastically from its peak of 128.7% in 1983 to about 10.4% in 1985; there were increases in traditional exports, notably in the cocoa, mining and timber sectors. But it has been a period of frustration since 1992, as the expected accelerated growth failed to materialize and GDP fluctuated between 3.8 and 5.0% per annum between 1992 and 1995. Domestic prices of farm inputs doubled or tripled; and the inflation rate took an upward trend again, hitting an end-year level of over 60% in 1995. Many of the causes of these symptoms can be traced to the poor performance of the agricultural sector in this period and the weak supply response to the policy and institutional initiatives described above.

5.   Impact of Policy Reform on Growth

Tables 14.1 and 14.2 show succinctly how the economy and agriculture grew in response to the changes in policy from 1970–89. Clearly, the period 1970–76 was a time when both grew positively though moderately, at an average rate of 1.73% and 1.3% per annum, respectively. On the whole, there was a positive response to the policies emphasizing private sector development of agriculture as well as the OFY and OFYI policies that encouraged self-sufficiency in food and industrial raw materials production.

Table 14.1   Output of Selected Major Agricultural Commodities 1970–95

Commodity	Five-Year Period Averages ('000 metric tons)					
	1970/74	1975/79	1980/94	1985/89	1990/94	1995
Maize	452	304	334	573	823	1034
Rice	62	69	50	81	125	221
Millet	127	134	224	217	188	209
Sorghum	171	152	147	182	258	361
Cassava	2836	2198	2609	3059	5216	6612
Yam	791	569	488	1039	2052	2126
Cocoyam	1210	777	1205	1046	1140	1408
Plantain	1809	993	904	1151	1171	1638
Cocoa	405	309	223	222	280	310

Source: Nyanteng and Dapaah (1997a).

Table 14.2   Average Annual Real Growth of GDP and Agriculture (%)

	1970–76	1970–83	1984–89	1990–95
GDP	1.73	0.45	5.13	4.3
Agriculture	1.3	–0.5	3.6	2.0

Source: World Bank, *World Development Report,* (various years); Ghana Statistical Services, *Quarterly Digest of Statistics,* (various issues); Tables 1.1 and 1.2, Chapter 1.

However, after 1976 consistently negative growth rates wiped out the gains of the early 1970s, giving rise to stagnant average real growth rates for the economy (0.45% per annum) and negative average growth rates for agriculture (–0.5% per annum) for the entire period 1970–83. Indeed, in the country's most desperate years (1979 to 1983), the economy grew at an average rate of –3.31% per annum (Table 1.1, Chapter 1).

The wide fluctuations in the annual growth rates are reflected in considerable year-to-year fluctuations largely in accordance with the irregular rainfall pattern. For example, over the period 1982–8, the coefficient of variation (CV) for cassava was 0.45, maize 0.36, cotton 0.32 and yam 0.21 (Jebuni *et al.,* 1990). However, in general terms, agricultural output in the country declined over the period 1975–83, the last being a particularly bad year, with poor performance partly caused by a prolonged drought and bushfires. Since then, the general level of output has been upwards (Table 14.1).

With the structural adjustment programmes came renewed hope as reflected in the performance of the economy in the period 1984–89. With the economy growing at an average rate of 5.73% per annum, agriculture also grew at an average 3.6% per annum in this period, with much of the growth attributable to increases in cocoa production. This encouraging performance led to revised expectations of accelerated growth in the 1990s, which were ultimately to lead to frustration as average annual growth in both the economy and agriculture failed to improve in the first half of the 1990s. While the economy grew at an average of 4.3% between 1990 and 1995, agriculture grew at an average of about 2% per annum, both of them below their respective average growth rates between 1984 and 1989.

The period 1990–95 exhibited a direct relationship between the overall performance of the economy and agricultural growth. For instance, after 1990 there were wide fluctuations in the growth rate of GDP per capita around a declining trend largely because the agricultural sector was performing below expectations. GDP grew by 3.3% in 1990 but, following the excellent performance of agriculture which grew by 4.7% in 1991, economic growth rebounded to 5.3% in the same year (CEPA, 1996). The catastrophic performance of agriculture in 1992, when it grew by –0.6%, resulted in GDP growth of only 3.9%. With a significant improvement in food and livestock production, agricultural output in 1993 increased by about 2.8%, leading to an overall growth in real GDP of 5%. However, flooding as well as the disruptive effects of ethnic conflicts in the Northern Region and unfavourable climatic conditions during the harvest season brought decreases in agricultural output in 1994, resulting in GDP growth of only 3.8%.

The period 1990–95 witnessed relatively poor performance in the agricultural sector, with an average annual real growth rate of about 2%. While the share of agriculture in GDP remains large it nevertheless declined continuously in this period, from 43.5% in 1990 to about 41% in 1995. Table 14.3 shows the extreme fluctuations in agricultural growth during the period. Apart from 1991 when agricultural growth rebounded, largely for climatic reasons, from –2.0% the previous year to 4.7%, there was a general deterioration in the rate of change in agricultural sector output. It was only in 1995 that agricultural growth exceeded 4% again.

Table 14.3   Agricultural Growth and Contribution to Real GDP Growth 1990–95 (at constant 1975 prices)

	1990	1991	1992	1993	1994	1995	Period Average
Real Agricultural Growth	–2.0	4.7	–0.6	2.8	1.0	4.2	2.0
Agriculture's percentage contribution to real GDPGrowth	–27.8	38.8	–7.1	23.6	10.9	38.3	12.8

Source: Ghana Statistical Services, *Quarterly Digest of Statistics*, various issues, and 1995 Budget Statement.

Table 14.3 also shows the wide fluctuations in agriculture's contribution to GDP growth — a mirror image of the wide fluctuations in agricultural growth itself. Thus, agriculture's contribution to GDP growth was highest in 1991 and 1995 (over 38%), the years in which agricultural growth exceeded 4%.

The wide fluctuations in agricultural growth primarily reflect fluctuations in the weather, particularly rainfall on which Ghana's agriculture largely depends, and the performance of the food and livestock subsector which constitutes about 60% of agricultural output. In the period 1990–95, the average annual growth rate in the food and livestock subsector was a dismal 1.2%, consistently growing at a slower rate than the agricultural sector as a whole.

Despite the persistent poor performance in the food and livestock subsector, agricultural growth has benefited from modest growth in the second largest subsector, cocoa, which experienced an annual average growth rate of over 5.5% in the period 1990–95, consistently higher than the average growth rate of the agricultural sector as a whole. Despite this modest performance, growth in the cocoa sector has also shown marked variations from year to year, principally reflecting unstable climatic conditions and, to a lesser extent, changes in the real producer price of cocoa. From a peak growth of 13.9% in 1991, the growth of cocoa output fell dramatically to –7.2% in 1992 and grew by only a tenth of a percentage point in 1993. However, there was a remarkable turnaround in 1994 when cocoa output increased by 12.2%.

The producer price of cocoa has been an important factor in determining the amount of cocoa production in the country. The observed fluctuations in the growth in cocoa production could therefore be attributed, in part, to changes in the real producer price of cocoa. As shown in Table 14.4, the nominal price increases in the price of cocoa resulted in increases in real producer prices from 1984 to 1988. Thereafter, the nominal price increases resulted in mostly negative real producer price changes. Despite the annual upward revision of the nominal producer price of cocoa, the share of the farmer in the fob price of cocoa has always been less than 50% (Table 14.4).

Table 14.4   Nominal and Real Producer Prices of Cocoa
1984–95 (1981 constant prices)

Year	Nominal Prices			Real Prices	
	C/tonne	% change	% fob price	C/tonne	% change
1984	20000	66.7	34	5260	19.4
1985	30000	50.0	28	7148	35.9
1986	56000	86.7	27	10712	49.9
1987	85000	51.8	27	11628	8.6
1988	150000	76.5	35	15622	34.3
1989	165000	10.0	40	13723	–12.2
1990	174000	5.7	42	10567	–23.0
1991	224000	28.4	46	11495	8.8
1992	251200	12.1	49	11718	1.9
1993	258000	2.7	46	9631	–17.8
1994	308000	19.4	30	9207	–4.4
1995	700000	127.3	49	13122	42.5

Source: ISSER, 1996.

In spite of the fluctuations in output, the performance of the cocoa subsector has been generally encouraging, mainly because of the replanting after the years of drought and bushfires of the early 1980s and a change in government policy to increase significantly the nominal price paid to producers. The latter in particular helped to stamp out the smuggling of cocoa to neighbouring countries. Though the share of cocoa as a percentage of total export earnings continues to fall (see Table 9.4 in Chapter 9), it still constitutes an important foreign-exchange earner, ranking second only to gold exports since 1992. The fishery, forestry and logging subsectors of the agricultural sector, on the other hand, have remained virtually stagnant, managing an average annual growth rate consistently lower than growth in the sector as a whole in the period 1990–95.

On the whole, the supply responses to adjustment policies have been weak in agriculture although there have been some improvements in productivity in the 1990s. Exchange rate reforms and increases in producer prices initially helped to increase earnings from cocoa. The volume index of cocoa exports (1980 = 100) increased from 59.12 in 1984 to 105.19 in 1989 but declined to 92.39 by 1994 (see Table 9.4 in Chapter 9). Also, disease problems and climate change in the old cocoa growing areas have caused the cocoa frontier to move to less optimal conditions in the Western Region of the country. At the same time, the food subsector appears to have been weakened by the switch to price incentives for cash crops and by the increased cost of inputs, particularly fertilizers and labour. The major constraint, however, remains the low level of technological progress in the subsector as well as bottlenecks in the factor markets. These are now considered.

6. Constraints

To understand the weak supply response to incentives in agriculture, we need to consider the longer-term constraints on the sector. In the traditional farming systems which are still predominant, land and labour are the main production inputs. The productivity of these inputs is generally very low.

The trends in land productivity, as measured by yield per hectare of the staple crops in Ghana, are shown in Table 14.5. From 1970 to 1990, with the exception of 1982 and 1983, the yield per hectare of cereals, namely, maize, rice, millet and sorghum, was relatively stable. The trend generally turned upwards in 1991 and continued in that direction to 1995. During this period, the yield per hectare of rice increased by about 144%, millet and sorghum by about 83% and maize by about 33%. These increases in yield are partly attributable to revised methods of output estimation by the Ministry of Food and Agriculture as well as to increases in land productivity. It should be noted that these increased yields in the 1990s occurred despite declining input use in the face of reductions in input subsidies.

Table 14.5   Yield Per Hectare of Major Food Crops, 1970–95

Period	Food Crop (Five-Year Average, MT)							
	Maize	Rice	Millet	Sorghum	Yam	Cocoyam	Cassava	Plantain
1970–74	1.06	0.98	0.62	0.76	5.36	5.48	7.66	5.80
1975–79	1.04	1.02	0.60	0.72	5.24	4.84	8.08	5.82
1980–84	0.90	0.92	0.56	0.66	4.70	5.18	6.70	5.38
1985–89	1.14	0.94	0.68	0.72	5.70	4.78	7.56	5.56
1990–94	1.38	1.64	0.72	0.90	10.70	6.36	10.40	7.20
1990	1.20	0.90	0.60	0.60	7.40	5.70	8.40	6.20
1995	1.60	2.20	1.10	1.10	12.10	6.80	12.00	7.70
% change 1990–95	33	144	83	83	64	19	43	24

Source: PPMED, Ministry of Food and Agriculture, Accra.

However, rainfall was generally favourable in this period (1991–95), and in specific areas with direct external support, production and productivity increases appear to be sustainable. For example, small-scale farmers in the food-growing areas of the savannah-forest transition and the savannah agro-ecological zones have benefited from the IFAD smallholder schemes, and other farming schemes from non-governmental organizations such as the Sasakawa Global 2000 project, that provide credit for fertilizer and other farm inputs. For rice in particular, the introduction of high yielding varieties and the encouragement of moderate sized units rather than large-scale farming have improved farm management practices and, for that matter, yields. Also, the introduction of bonded farming, which restricts water flow in the peak rainy season and allows water to be retained on rice fields for the critical period of seed formation towards the end of the rainy season, has gone a long way to improve yields.

Among the major starchy crops, namely, cassava, yam, cocoyam and plantain, the yields per hectare also remained virtually stable from 1970 to 1989, except for 1982 and 1984 when they were relatively lower, as shown in Table 14.5. The yields took an upward trend in 1990, which continued steadily to 1995. During this period, the yield per hectare of yam increased by about 64%, cassava by about 43%, plantain by 24% and cocoyam by about 19%. Apart from favourable weather in this period, intensified extension education on the use of new varieties has helped to increase yields. The use of new cassava seeds developed by the International Institute of Tropical Agriculture has intensified in recent times. Pests and disease control have also been introduced to enhance the performance of the new varieties.

Despite the substantial increases in the yields of the staple crops during the first half of the 1990s, they still compare poorly with on-farm research findings and yields recorded in isolated farmers' fields, as shown in Table 14.6.

Table 14.6   Yields Per Hectare and Potential Yields of Major Staples

Crop	Metric Tonnes Per Hectare	
	Ave. Yield 1990–94	Potential Yield
Cassava	10.44	28.0
Plantain	7.20	10.0
Yam	10.70	14.0
Cocoyam	6.36	8.0
Maize	1.38	5.0
Rice	1.64	3.0
Sorghum	0.90	2.5
Millet	0.72	2.0

Source: Ministry of Agriculture, 1995.

The generally low level of land productivity can be attributed to poor farming practices such as shifting cultivation which, in the face of increasing population pressure, does not allow adequate restoration of soil fertility. In addition, land preparation, planting materials and weed management remain generally poor despite the modest increases in the average yields of staple food crops in the first half of the 1990s.

Population growth, in particular, is putting a lot of pressure on land use and productivity. The censuses of 1960 and 1970 put the population of Ghana at 6.7 and 8.6 million, respectively. The next census in 1984 indicated a population of 12.3 million, and is estimated to have reached 16.6 million in 1995. Thus, the population has nearly doubled in about 25 years (1970–95). *Ceteris paribus,* the pressure on the use of land suitable for agriculture, particularly in the immediate vicinity of the farming villages, is expected to have increased considerably and therefore the fallow periods involved in the predominant practice of shifting cultivation are expected to have been reduced appreciably. This is consistent with the observation that increases in agricultural production over several decades resulted from the expansion in area cultivated rather than from increases in yield (ISSER Series).

A related issue is the land tenure system which is still largely traditional with usufructuary rights predominating. Although many studies, for example Migot-Adholla *et al.* (1990), have concluded that the tenure systems do not pose a serious constraint on agricultural development so long as land remains abundant, it is doubtful whether they are sufficiently resilient to accommodate the transformation necessitated by more capital-intensive agriculture and long-term investments in soil conservation as land becomes increasingly scarce.

A major modern input that enhances crop yield quite substantially is fertilizer. This notwithstanding, the use of fertilizer in Ghana is generally very low and not widespread even when compared with some other sub-Saharan African countries. Fertilizers are not used in the cultivation of starchy crops (yam, cassava, cocoyam, plantain, etc.). They are applied, in limited cases, in the cultivation of rice and maize but not for millet and sorghum.

All the fertilizers used in the country are imported and the quantity imported annually is a fair indication of the extent of fertilizer consumption. The trend in fertilizer imports from 1970 to 1994 is shown in five-year averages in Table 14.7. The quantity of fertilizers imported has fluctuated widely, even when five-year averages are considered, from an average of about 12,000 tonnes per annum during the first half of the 1970s to 39,000 tonnes in the second half of the 1980s and down again to 24,000 tonnes in the first half of the 1990s. Fertilizers were not imported in some years (1981, 1983 and 1991) because of lack of import capacity in the case of the early 1980s, and because stocks were adequate to meet consumption in 1991.

Table 14.7   Five-Year Averages of Fertilizer Imports 1970–94

Period	Five-Year Average (Metric Tonnes)	% Change
1970–74	11,717	164
1975–79	34,474	192
1980–84	29,062	−16
1985–89	38,597	33
1990–94	23,494	−39

Source: Compiled from data from the Crop Services Department, Ministry of Food and Agriculture.

The significant drop in fertilizer imports and hence consumption is due partly to the removal of subsidies on fertilizer prices in 1990. Before then fertilizer subsidies were in the range of 40 to 80%. The reduced quantities of fertilizer imports in the 1990s reflects reduced consumption due to a substantial increase in open market prices. The policy of abolishing fertilizer subsidies therefore puts agricultural productivity, particularly of food crops, in danger of decline.

As shown in Table 14.8, real fertilizer prices increased by about 34% by 1992 after subsidies were removed in 1990. Since then, the price of fertilizer (represented in Table 14.8 by NPK, the most widely used fertilizer in Ghana) continued to increase substantially in real terms and almost doubled by 1994.

Table 14.8   Real Prices of Some Agricultural Inputs in Ghana 1989–95 (1990 Prices)

Year	Fertilizer (C/50kg.)	Insecticide (C/litre)	Fungicide (C/kg/)	Sprayers (C/unit)
1989	2881	823	274	31556
1990	4500	2585	2900	23000
1991	3811	2190	2965	63661
1992	6006	1991	2695	57873
1993	7269	1592	2526	46299
1994	8480	740	1356	37054
1995	6363	425	778	21270

Source: Computed from data from Crop Services Department, Ministry of Agriculture and COCOBOD

These price increases are much higher than the rate of depreciation of the currency or increases in charges affecting fertilizer costs (ISSER,1995), and are likely to have reduced further the already inadequate consumption of fertilizer in the country (Nyanteng and Dapaah, 1997).

Similarly, the removal of subsidies on insecticides and fungicides almost tripled their real prices, as shown in Table 14.8. These inputs are very important in the maintenance of established cocoa farms. Insecticides are used to control capsid which causes the swollen shoot disease, while fungicides are used to control blackpod disease. As a result of the increase in the price of insecticides, the quantity purchased by farmers decreased steadily from about 1.4 million litres in 1989 to only 159,000 litres in 1992 (ISSER, 1996). The consumption of fungicides also decreased from over 20 tonnes in 1989 to about 5 tonnes in 1993. Following pressure from cocoa farmer organizations, the prices of both insecticides and fungicides were reduced in 1994, implying their subsidization. The real price of the motorized sprayers used with the insecticides also more than tripled as shown in Table 14.8. Thus, the relatively disappointing performance of the agriculture sector in the 1990s could be attributed, in part, to the astronomical increases in the price of agricultural inputs that followed the removal of subsidies.

Another factor affecting land productivity is the manner in which land is prepared for crop cultivation. The predominant method of land preparation in Ghana is zero tillage. The vegetation is slashed and burned *in situ,* with some of the debris in some cases gathered and heaped in parts of the field prior to planting. The prepared piece of land is usually full of stumps, tree trunks and branches which occupy a substantial part of the farm. Consequently, the population of the cultivated crop is lower than is possible or recommended.

Planting materials used also affect land productivity. Although efforts are being made to introduce improved high yielding varieties of some of the staple crops, their adoption is not yet widespread. In spite of the fact that the traditional varieties are relatively low yielding, they are still preferred by many farmers because they are better adapted to the harsh environment and (poor) soil conditions in the country.

Weed management is, perhaps, the most important factor affecting land productivity in Ghana. The zero tillage method of land preparation is not an effective way to manage weeds. The number of times (three to four from planting to harvesting) that a farm has to be weeded, and the labour cost involved, result in many farmers neglecting or inadequately carrying out this activity. This usually results in high crop losses which can be as high as 100% in some cases.

Labour productivity is equally very low and this can be attributed to the primitive traditional tools used in agriculture. These tools include axes, cutlasses, several types of hoes and knives for land preparation, weed management and harvesting. Due to the undulating terrain, particularly in the forest zone, the predominantly small farm sizes and certain economic factors, the use of modern farm equipment such as tractors and the accompanying implements is not widespread. In fact in many instances, the few available tractors are used to transport human beings and farm produce rather than for farm work.

There are other constraints that contribute to the low level of productivity in Ghana's agriculture which are largely outside the perspective of the constraints related to direct production. They are attributable more to government policies and public actions rather than to the physical environment in which agriculture operates and the actions of farmers. These constraints relate to the marketing of both output and inputs, the low and dwindling levels of investment in agriculture, the poor types, quality and quantity of inputs used, and poor farmer education.

Policy Constraints

Marketing Constraints Finding outlets to dispose of the marketable surplus of food crops has been a major problem for farmers, often resulting in part of the produce rotting on the farms. This has had major negative effects on incentives to produce marketable surplus. As part of the solution to the problem, the Ghana Food Distribution Corporation (GFDC) was set up in 1971 to trade alongside the private traders, particularly providing market outlets to farmers located in remote areas. However, the GFDC was unable to perform its task efficiently, handling less than 10% on average of the marketable surplus of foodstuffs annually.

The policy of direct public involvement in the distribution of foodstuffs diverted attention from assisting the private traders to perform their activities efficiently and effectively. Public intervention in the food distribution network should be limited to helping the private traders to provide adequate market outlets for farm produce. In other words, the government should provide an enabling environment to facilitate the marketing of foodstuffs in the country.

A major constraint on the marketing of foodstuffs is the poor transport infrastructure. Ghana is said to have some comparative advantage in the production of several food crops at the farm gate but this is lost in the inefficient marketing system. Transportation alone is estimated to contribute as much as 70% to marketing costs. Poor transport infrastructure manifests itself in poor road conditions which sometimes render some roads impassable, particularly during the rainy season and in the lack of transport and the breakdown of vehicles in the process of moving commodities. Improving the rural road network would provide considerable incentives (through increased farm-gate prices) for the production of marketable surpluses (Nyanteng and Dapaah, 1993).

Another constraint relates to post-harvest storage losses. The storage losses of all food crops produced are estimated to be between 15 and 30% (Government of Ghana, 1995). The losses are highest with vegetables, followed by starchy crops, legumes and cereals in that order. A reduction of about 30 to 50% of the losses would significantly reduce the country's dependence on food imports needed annually to meet consumer demand. Farmers store the bulk of their food crops in traditional structures which are highly ineffective and cause heavy losses in both quantity and quality. The government has so far emphasized the development of a number of large-scale modern facilities for grain storage which are operated by the GFDC in strategic places in the country. Though private entrepreneurs, traders and farmers are permitted to use these facilities for a fee, the number and location of the facilities pose some problems including being out of easy reach of many farmers who would want to use them. An alternative is to adopt measures to improve the farm-level small-scale storage facilities (Nyanteng and Dapaah, 1993).

Investment in Agriculture Low investment in agricure is reflected in the low and dwindling share of agriculture in total government expenditure as shown in Table 14.9. This share has been falling since 1980/81 when it was 12.2%. By 1995, it had fallen to only 2.24%. The share of the development budget in the low agricultural budget, on the other hand, has fluctuated from year to year. At this stage of Ghana's economic development, when private sector support for agriculture is almost non-existent, public sector support is essential in order to provide the infrastructure and services required to stimulate private investment in agricultural production. Unfortunately, the share of the agricultural sector in the government budget is not only low and declining, but the bulk of it also goes on recurrent expenditure. Though some development expenditure of some Ministries (for example, Roads and Highways) directly or indirectly promotes agricultural development, the Ministry of Agriculture does not control the activities of those Ministries (Nyanteng and Dapaah, 1997).

Table 14.9   Share of Agriculture in Government Expenditure 1980–95

Year	% Agriculture Expenditure	Share of Total Agriculture Budget	
		% Recurrent	% Development
1980	12.2	72.2	27.8
1981	11.0	82.9	17.1
1982	10.9	86.0	14.0
1983	10.4	90.4	9.6
1984	5.0	70.9	29.1
1985	4.2	65.8	34.2
1986	1.9	82.8	17.2
1987	2.4	37.2	62.8
1988	4.7	46.9	53.1
1989	7.5	53.3	46.7
1990	3.5	65.2	34.8
1991	3.0	74.2	25.8
1992	2.9	62.7	37.3
1993	2.1	72.0	28.0
1994	2.2	64.2	35.8
1995	2.2	68.1	31.9

Sources: MOFA (1991,1995) *Agriculture in Ghana: Facts and Figures,* GSS (1993) *Quarterly Digest of Statistics,* Vol. 1, No. 9; World Bank (1991) *Ghana Progress on Adjustment,* Report No. 9475-GH, Washington, DC; Republic of Ghana, *Budget Statement for the Financial Year 1995.*

The financing of agricultural development tends to rely heavily on external or donor sources. For example, in 1996 and 1997, 91% and 88.5% respectively of the total budget for agriculture were expected to originate from donor sources. This situation does not demonstrate a high commitment on the part of the government to develop the agricultural sector.

Production Risks and Uncertainties A major constraint on Ghana's agricultural development is the risk and uncertainty involved in production. These are caused mainly by weather conditions, particularly rainfall and drought, not discounting factors such as the timely availability of inputs including labour. The rainfall is quite unreliable with respect to its onset, duration, intensity and amount, and the rainfall pattern is partly the cause of the considerable seasonal fluctuations in crop yields.

One policy instrument to address the rainfall problem has been to develop irrigation facilities throughout the country. The implementation of irrigation policy is very slow, however. In 1992, a total of 7,500 hectares or about 0.17% of the total land area cultivated was irrigated and, by 1994, this had increased to 10,500 hectares or about 2% of the area cultivated in that year (MOFA, 1995). Most of the irrigation facilities developed to date are large-scale schemes with major problems with effective utilization, maintenance and management. Thus government policy is now shifting towards the development of small to medium-scale schemes which can be operated and managed by farmer groups and communities (Nyanteng and Dapaah, 1997).

Production Incentives A major factor accounting for Ghana's sluggish agricultural performance is the reduction or in some cases elimination of incentives as a result of policy reforms. Yet Ghanaian farmers, in particular, the predominantly small-scale ones, do not have much opportunity to avoid or internalize the many risks and uncertainties which they face in production and post-harvest activities.

Government intervention in input procurement, supply and distribution as an incentive to farmers was abolished in 1990, giving way to privatization. The objective of this policy reform was to establish a competitive private market that would ensure availability and timely supply of inputs such as fertilizers, insecticides, fungicides and improved seeds at the farm gate. It was envisaged that the competition would induce efficiency in distribution, reduce costs and increase benefits to the farmers in the form of lower prices. The response of the private sector to the policy reform has been sluggish in the short run, resulting in decreased availability of inputs at the farm gate (Jebuni and Seini, 1992). Although the implementation of the privatization policy was carried out over a period of three years, the time was not adequate to allow for the private sector to take over in an effective manner (Nyanteng and Dapaah, 1993).

Another incentive which suffered under the policy reforms was the input price subsidy. In the past it was among the major incentive measures to encourage the use of modern and improved inputs. A subsidy on inputs is a tool which has been applied world-wide as an incentive because of its effectiveness in influencing the adoption of new technology, improving resource allocation and addressing income disparities between agriculture and other economic sectors. The prices of all inputs and services handled by public agencies were directly subsidized until the end of 1990. These included fertilizers, improved seeds, production credit as well as insecticides, fungicides, spraying machines and other simple hand tools used in cocoa cultivation.

Charging the real input price to farmers was expected to be matched by an increased output price determined by the market forces of supply and demand. However, the match has not been perfect, at least in the short run, as input prices have increased faster than output prices (Jebuni and Seini, 1992). The resulting decrease in the output-input ratio will, theoretically, reduce the use of purchased inputs. The mismatch of output and input prices has occurred in the short run because the level of competition in the private sector distribution of inputs that was expected to lower the farm-gate prices did not occur. The output price, in particular that of foodstuffs, has not increased as fast partly because of the competition from imports from cheaper sources following the trade liberalization policy under the structural adjustment programme.

The input price subsidy has been abolished partly because of its substantial financial burden on the government. However, the subsidy can be justified under certain conditions, for example, when a new technology is introduced. The successful adoption of a new technology by a few farmers conveys valuable information to their neighbours which promotes widespread adoption. When the benefits of the new technology have been adequately demonstrated by the early adopters, the subsidy can then be removed. In Ghanaian circumstances where traditional technologies are still extensively used and the adoption of improved technologies is extremely low, providing subsidies is a necessary condition to promote their adoption and extensive use, particularly by the predominantly small-scale and financially poor farmers.

Production credit Among essential farm inputs, the availability of credit is inadequate and this has constrained, to a large extent, the adoption and extensive use of modern agricultural inputs particularly, among small-scale farmers. Smallholders obtain production credit mainly from the informal financial market where friends, relatives, traders, moneylenders and private groups are the principal sources. Such sources provide mainly short-term loans which are used predominantly for consumption rather than for production. The interest rates have traditionally been quite high due partly to the high risk of granting the loans without adequate collateral and the high rate of default in repayment (Aryeetey and Gockel, 1991).

The policy aimed at providing formal credit to small-scale farmers in particular, and for agricultural development in general, eventually resulted in the establishment of the Agricultural Development Bank (ADB) in the early 1960s. In addition to the ADB, the commercial banks were obliged as a matter of policy to lend not less than 25% of their loanable funds to the agricultural sector and also at subsidized interest rates. These preferential policies aimed at providing further incentives to farmers, were also abolished in 1990. Subsequently, the interest rates for agricultural loans have been raised to levels comparable with those charged for non-agricultural loans. Agriculture is at a considerable disadvantage when it comes to commercial interest rate determination because of the high risk of agricultural production, the high rate of default in repayment which in part is the consequence of this risk, and the high cost of administering loans to the many small-scale farmers (Seini, 1997; Nyanteng and Dapaah, 1997).

The need for cash on the part of many of the predominantly small-scale farmers is highest immediately after harvesting. The situation forces many of them to sell their produce soon after harvest, flooding the market and consequently receiving prices which a few months later would have been more than double. A new system of assisting farmers to secure loans in the immediate post-harvest period has emerged. Under a co-operative inventory credit scheme, Technoserve, a private non-governmental organization, has worked out an arrangement with the ADB to provide loans to farmers using their stored produce as collateral. When the produce is sold later by the farmers themselves at a time when the market prices are quite high, they are able to pay back the loans with interest and still make reasonable net profits (Nyanteng and Dapaah, 1993).

7.   Conclusion

The pattern of agricultural policy in Ghana has varied from 1970 to 1995 with frequent changes in government and in the macroeconomic situation of the country. Though growth in agricultural production and increases in agricultural productivity have been the main objectives of the agricultural policies of the past and present governments, sustained success has eluded policy-makers on both counts. There have been wide fluctuations in agricultural growth which primarily reflect fluctuations in the weather on which Ghana's agriculture largely depends and also on the poor performance of the food crop and livestock subsector which constitutes about 60% of agricultural output. Land and labour productivity remains low and has been exacerbated by poor farming practices and low application of productivity-enhancing inputs, such as fertilizers and agrochemicals, particularly following the removal of their subsidies. There have been isolated areas of growth, however, and these suggest that appropriate technological inputs, if properly researched, can have a positive impact. In particular, the harvesting of water in valley bottoms for irrigation purposes as well as the intensification of agricultural extension in support of improved farming practices of the small-scale farmers suggest keys to wider improvement. At a broader policy level, it is now clear that practical solutions to the inadequate use or non-use of modern farm inputs in Ghana's agriculture need to be found without jeopardizing the positive impact of the market economy that has been established in Ghana under structural adjustment. To this end, measures to improve rural infrastructure such as roads, storage facilities as well as to initiate processing of farm produce and the provision of market information are absolutely essential.

References

Aryeetey, Ernest and Gockel, Fritz (1991) *Mobilizing Domestic Resources: Role of Informal Financial Sector.* AERC Research Paper No. 3. Nairobi: Initiative Publishers.

Boateng, E. O., Kanbur, R., and McKay, A. (1990) *A Poverty Profile of Ghana, 1987/88.* Social Dimensions of Adjustment (SDA) Working Paper No. 3. Washington, DC: World Bank.

CEPA. (1996) 'Towards Accelerated Agricultural Growth'. Accra: Centre for Policy Analysis (CEPA) (mimeo).

Government of Ghana (1989) *Medium Term Agricultural Development Programme 1991–2000.* Accra.

Government of Ghana (1995) *Ghana-Vision 2020.* Presidential Report to Parliament on Co-ordinated Programme of Economic and Social Development Policies.

ISSER (1992) *The State of the Ghanaian Economy in 1991.* University of Ghana, ISSER, Legon.

ISSER (1993) *The State of the Ghanaian Economy in 1992.* University of Ghana, ISSER, Legon.

ISSER (1994) *The State of the Ghanaian Economy in 1993.* University of Ghana, ISSER, Legon.

ISSER (1995) *The State of the Ghanaian Economy in 1994.* University of Ghana, ISSER, Legon.

ISSER (1996) *The State of the Ghanaian Economy in 1995.* University of Ghana, ISSER, Legon.

Jebuni, C. D. and Seini, A. Wayo (1992) *Agricultural Input Policies Under Structural Adjustment: Their Distributional Implications.* Cornell Food and Nutrition Policy Programme Working Paper 31. Cornell University, Ithaca, NY.

Jebuni, C. D., Assuming-Brempong, S, and Fosu, K. Y. (1990) *Ghana: Economic Recovery Programme and Agriculture.* Accra: USAID/Ghana.

Killick, Tony. (1978) *Development Economics in Action: A Study of Economic Policies in Ghana.* London: Heinemann Educational Books.

Migot-Adholla, S. E., Place, Franc, Benneh George and Atsu, S. Y. (1990) 'Land Tenure Issues and Agricultral Productivity in Ghana'. Paper presented at the Seminar on Land Tenure and Agricultural Productivity in Ghana, 13 June, Accra.

Ministry of Agriculture (1995) *Agriculture in Ghana: Facts and Figures.* Accra: PPMED.

Nyanteng, V. K. and Dapaah, S. (1993) 'Agricultural Development' in V. K. Nyanteng (ed.) *Policies and Options for Ghanaian Economic Development.* ISSER, Legon.

Nyanteng, V. K. and Dapaah, S. (1997) 'Agricultural Development', Paper presented at a Seminar on Policies and Options for Ghanaian Economic Development. ISSER, Legon. July.

Roberts, P. (1981) 'Rural Development and the Rural Economy in Niger, 1900–75' in J. Hefer, G. Williams and P. Roberts (eds). *Rural Development in Tropical Africa.* London: Macmillan.

Seini, A. Wayo (1997) 'The Impact of Policy Reforms on Ghana's Agriculture with Policy Analysis Matrix Applications'. A Report Prepared for the International Centre for Economic Growth. Nairobi and San Francisco (unpublished).

Sowa, N. K. (1996) *Adjustment in Africa: Lessons from Ghana.* Overseas Development Institute (ODI) Briefing Paper, 1996 (3).

Winch, F. E. (1976) 'Costs and Returns to Alternative Rice Production Systems in Northern Ghana: Implication for Output, Employment and Income Distribution'. PhD Thesis, Michigan State University, East Landing, MI.

World Bank (1984) *Ghana: Policies and Programmes for Structural Adjustment.* Washington, DC: World Bank.

VI Socio-Economic Development

15 The Evolution of Social Policy

ERNEST ARYEETEY & MARKUS GOLDSTEIN

1. Introduction

Government social policy is a vital complement to economic policy. In addition to providing the vehicle for human capital development, it also furnishes a social safety net to ensure basic welfare. While Ghana continues to lack a unified or well-articulated social policy, social programmes have existed in a variety of sectors since independence. This chapter examines the development of the various strands that make up the *de facto* social policy from the 1970s to the mid-1990s.

Based on the premise that poverty in Ghana has been largely regarded as a rural phenomenon, the history of social policy development has been a mixture of concrete actions and rhetoric in the pursuit of rural development.[1] The error in equating rural development with social policy has never been apparent to policy-makers, however. This aside, the commitment to rural development itself has often shown weaknesses, as illustrated by the fact that while various governments have emphasized rural development as a major policy goal, public investment allocations have continually suggested a considerable urban bias, at least until recently (see discussion of 'urban bias' in Chapter 2). Although there is a strong perception that this has started to change and that rural development has become a major thrust of government development policy today, the social development content has continued to be weak. Rural development is currently pursued with a mix of 'development projects' that are either sponsored by various donors or activated by various levels of government, i.e. local and central. The participation of donors is interesting in view of the substitution as well as complementarity in resources it entails.

Indeed, the clearest change in the provision of development projects and social services has been the growing significance of donors and NGOs to the process. Also important has been the increasing role of local government, following the national programme of decentralization, beginning in 1988. The growing role of donors and NGOs in the water, sanitation, health and education sectors in relation to that of government marks the most significant change in the development of social policy. We shall return to this theme as we discuss the institutional setting of social policy.

The relevance of poverty as a major concern for social policy in a developing country is derived from the fact that poverty remains the most significant social and economic concern. As

---

[1] See Gwendolyn Mikell (1991) for a comprehensive discussion of rural development policies and their equity dimensions.

Chapter 16 indicates, poverty received little or no systematic statistical study in Ghana before the era of structural adjustment. Hence, significant medium-term longitudinal comparisons are impossible. The conjecture that poverty has fallen in the rural areas as the country has experienced steady growth was first made by Kanbur and Mink (1994). But, as discussed in Chapter 16, poverty remains quite high even if it has come down in some areas. Some of the major features of rural poverty were revealed in a World Bank-co-ordinated participatory poverty assessment (PPA). This study was carried out in 15 communities in 9 of Ghana's 10 regions[2] (Norton *et al.,* 1995). The PPA identified a number of poor groups. First, it shed some more light on those at the very bottom of the distribution. This group is usually characterized by lack of access to productive assets, especially labour resources, due to such factors as widowhood, disability, or age. Secondly, social networks are important in avoiding poverty, and migrants tend to have below-average access to these.[3] Thirdly, in the rural North, a significant amount of seasonal poverty was found, with large portions of the community unable to diversify income sources (beyond the single growing season), and thus experiencing a lean season. Finally, female headship seemed to be associated with poverty in the North, but also seems to be linked with other causal factors, such as the inadequacy of a kin network.

The PPA also established that poverty was viewed as a community problem in rural areas. One of the major attributes of a poor community was inadequate access to natural resources — fertile soil, water, and fuelwood. Also important was access to public services. Finally, poor communities, especially those in the forest zones, were those that lacked adequate access to markets and transport infrastructure. The study also emphasized the perceived correlation between education and poverty. Respondents indicated that 'the capacity to educate children beyond the primary level was a frequent indicator of wealth for the urban and rural south' (Norton *et al.,* 1995: 6). These features all indicate what are perceived dimensions of poverty and hence what social policy should seek to address.

We shall discuss the policy evolution across different political regimes, the institutions that provide for social programmes, and some of the attempts at a co-ordinated social policy. The focus of our discussion mirrors the government's own policy emphasis, namely, health and education. Some policy attention, however, has been devoted to other components of social policy such as housing, water and sanitation, and social security and we mention these when possible.

The chapter is organized as follows. In section 2 we look at the semblance of social policy in the 1960s and 1970s, focusing on the subjugation of any notion of social policy to the broader agenda of rural development. This discussion is continued in section 3 with a look at social policy in the years of economic reform, where social policy has often been described as largely an afterthought. Section 4 focuses on the relevant institutions and actors, discussing their roles in effecting and enacting social policy. Section 5 discusses the chief tie that binds the institutions and policy — public spending. Here we discuss the impacts of recent reforms on health and education in terms of distribution and service effectiveness.[4] We conclude this section with a discussion of how donor spending seems to be replacing, not adding to, government spending in the social sectors. Given the apparent failures in social policy development, section 6 offers some priorities for developing the instruments of the state to target the populations that are in need.

---

[2] Part of this Participatory Poverty Assessment (PPA) entailed eliciting local communities' definitions of what constituted poverty. The exercise was useful for identifying highly visible but not numerically obvious target groups for social policy. It was also important for the qualitative analysis that identified target groups through their demographic characteristics, rather than using an expenditure-based line and then observing various correlates.

[3] There is growing evidence, however, that in urban areas also, social networks are being rapidly reduced among non-migrant populations.

[4] The authors acknowledge with thanks the use of useful material from Deborah Wetzel for this section.

2.   Social Policy in the 1960s and 1970s

The policies of Ghana's first post-independence government set several of the social policy themes that have persisted through numerous governments. First, governments have devoted considerable attention to talking about rural development problems while public investment patterns have suggested an urban bias. The significant push for industrialization, as seen in earlier chapters, led to the urban bias in the provision of social services. The starkest example of this was in housing policy, where all new government-subsidized units were in medium-to-large towns and cities.

Another pattern that emerged (and has been recently reversed) was a disproportionate emphasis on higher education. As real wages failed to rise during the early 1960s, the government began to focus on providing skills for the labour market and building the nation's human capital. The churches had led the pre-independence campaigns to provide both primary and secondary education, as well as health facilities. But these were found to be inadequate for the growing mass of people released from agricultural households in expectation of urban industrial jobs. Central government pushed resources increasingly into secondary and technical education, as well as university education, and exhorted local government bodies to invest in primary and middle schools. It considered secondary and technical education a priority for the industrialization push and observed that 'the stage has now been reached where educational policy must increasingly concern itself with the second great purpose of education, the teaching of skills and other attainments that are needed for the running of a modern economy' (GoG, 1964: 142). This does not, however, mean that the Nkrumah government generally overlooked primary education. Indeed, under Nkrumah's 7-year plan, it was expected that school enrolment would double in the period 1963–70, while central government investment in education rose from $10.8 m. to $122 bn at current prices. The policy of tuition-free primary education was introduced with the 1961 Education Act.

In the area of health, the government's emphasis after independence, as expressed in the 7-year plan, was shifted from urban hospital-based curative medicine to the development of 'an extensive network of mobile and static health facilities [that] will be made available to the rural population. It [was] intended that all medical workers trained in the period would have an orientation which would make it possible for them to make an effective contribution to rural health work' (GoG, 1964: 177). Greater interest was to be shown in preventive medicine, to be achieved through mass education programmes. Health services were available at a nominal fee only.

A third feature of social provision was also revealed during the Nkrumah era, i.e., the weakened state. The effectiveness of the education and health policies was eroded as the financial and human resources available to government contracted when economic growth decelerated, and later became negative. The decline in per capita incomes reduced the capacity of individuals to make contributions on their own. The majority of the population became increasingly dependent on the public sector to provide education and health services to them, precisely at the time that the capacity of the state to do so was weakening.

Rural Development under the Busia Administration (1969–72)

After the fall of Nkrumah in 1966, this weakening capacity sparked a growing interest in the relaxation of the role of the state. Bureaucratic and technocratic solutions were deemed to be unworkable in many situations. In line with the development thought that prevailed at the time, i.e. the emphasis on 'basic needs', large-scale agricultural enterprises were regarded as being incapable of ensuring adequate diets for the rapidly growing population. The view was growing that it was only by producing more of their own food that rural people could construct a buffer against malnutrition and rising food prices. This disillusionment had a broader reach than merely agricultural enterprises. Self-help efforts in which individuals and communities took greater control over the issues that affected their lives, were thought to constitute a more effective way of dealing with many of the problems of the poor. Through self-help activities the psychology of dependence could be replaced by a growing sense of self-reliance. It was believed that self-help initiatives could create a new sense of communal living as people worked together to accomplish things that they could not achieve alone. This view influenced the major development strategies adopted in Ghana in the 1970s, with rural development strategies attaching greater attention to economic services than to social services.

Under the theme of increasing self-reliance, the Busia Government embarked on a comprehensive rural development programme after 1970. This programme continued the practice of relegating social policy to a back seat. While there was an increase in social spending, more emphasis was placed on economic services, especially feeder road construction. There was extensive development of a network of feeder roads to link rural settlements to larger centres, an ambitious programme for rural electrification and an extensive rural water supply programme. In the area of health care the government built a number of health posts and health centres while rural housing projects were begun under a new public department.

The 2½-year period under Busia is generally regarded as one in which the most attention was paid to rural development before the 1990s. But it was also one in which relatively little was done with regard to social policy, by which specific social services would be targeted at clearly disadvantaged groups.

Rural Development under the Acheampong Regime (1972–8)

As with the earlier push for rapid growth, the interest in focusing on basic needs cut across political barriers. As happened under the Busia Government, the need to provide basic needs also influenced the military government that took over in 1972 as the new leaders expressed concern about high inflation and introduced such programmes as 'Operation Feed Yourself' (OFY) and 'Operation Feed the Nation'. These were essentially agricultural development programmes that provided households, both rural and urban, with subsidized planting material in order to double food production within a three-year period. Regional agricultural production targets were set, and these were to be achieved through the provision of extension services, technical support to farmers, and access to credit.

The OFY programme suffered from poor planning and a tendency to concentrate resources on large commercial farmers and the remaining state farms, while infrastructural bottlenecks remained. Mikell (1991) attributes the failure of OFY to the failure of policy-makers to recognize the importance of labour relative to land. Thus, once again, while development policy was targeted at rural populations, it ended in a greater allocation of resources to urban-based state institutions. The efforts at rural development as a social policy were not sustained, and by 1981 social spending made up only 33% of the total, having fallen from the earlier 46%.

Another side of the Acheampong effort was the adoption of an approach of integrated rural development. The best expression of how this was supposed to work is shown in the experiences of the Upper Region Agricultural Development Programme (URADEP). URADEP was designed and initiated in 1975 as one of several package programmes for all the regions of Ghana in consultation with international development agencies. URADEP had as its objective the development of the Upper Region through the provision of farm support services from specific service centres in order to increase agricultural production and farm incomes. It was designed to achieve incremental rates of agricultural production which would reach their peak in 1981, the terminal year for its original investment programme. In addition to direct farm support services, other social services including the provision of water and farmer education were part of the deal.

Throughout the implementation of URADEP, the production of most crops showed considerable variation, and by 1981, less than half of the crops had been able to achieve the expected increases (Aryeetey, 1985). For some crops, production by 1981 was substantially less than before the programme was initiated, thus compelling the World Bank review mission (Morris, 1980) to conclude that the return on the project was substantially less than forecast, and the project might have been barely successful in economic terms. In social development terms, the people also expressed considerable misgivings about its impact (Aryeetey, 1985). It is generally acknowledged that the integrated programmes that were implemented in the Volta and the Northern Regions also had little impact on the performance of the agricultural sector and the delivery of social services in rural areas.

3.   Social Policy under the ERP

At the time Rawlings took power at the end of 1981, in addition to the numerous economic problems outlined in Chapter 1, there were also enormous social problems. The major ones included food insecurity, inadequate housing and rising unemployment. The education and health systems had all but ceased to function through the loss of human capacity resulting from the brain drain of the time.

A major characteristic of the policy reforms put in place to tackle the problems was the relative absence of social considerations and targeting for various programmes. When the government sought to reform the education and health sectors, this reform was guided by the need to achieve macroeconomic stability and less by the need to reach particular groups. A philosophy that continuous growth following the liberal policies would eventually lead to a more equitable social distribution ensured that (at least initially) no special efforts were made to reach the poor. On the other hand, there were also barriers to the vocalization of any demand for social policy. This was due to the absence of a participatory process and somewhat doubtful ownership in the design of the reforms, as significant aspects of the reform process were placed entirely in the hands of a small number of technocrats interacting with the World Bank and IMF. We discuss below developments in the education and health sectors, as well as in rural development in general and the more targeted Programme of Actions to Mitigate the Social Costs of Adjustment (PAMSCAD). We shall suggest that the ineffective social sector reforms were the outcome of a lack of coherent social policy accompanying the economic reforms and illustrate this with a discussion of the reform ownership question. It should be noted, however, that the government and donors were by no means immune to the social effects the ERP was having. Indeed, they sought to make some provisions for general poverty reduction as we shall see later, with varying success.

The Educational Sector Reforms

Before the government embarked on radical educational sector reforms at the pre-tertiary level in September 1987, the educational system was regarded as running inefficiently and unable to justify the huge costs incurred in it by the state (Cobbe, 1991). Pre-tertiary education was seen to take an unnecessarily long time, which added significantly to the costs. School children were found to be acquiring knowledge which was not always the most relevant for developing future careers. Access to education facilities was highly skewed, in favour of urban groups and males. With these problems, the reform programme sought

- to expand and create a more equitable access at all levels of education;
- to change the structure of the school system, reducing the length of pre-tertiary education from 17 to 12 years and increasing contact hours between teachers and pupils;
- to improve pedagogic efficiency and effectiveness;
- to ensure that, in the education provided, increasing attention was paid to problem solving, environmental concerns, pre-vocational training and manual dexterity;
- to contain and partially recover costs; and
  to enhance sector management and budgeting procedures.

Indeed, the government, with support from the World Bank, invested significantly after 1986 in various projects to achieve the above objectives (see Chapter 6). But recent evaluations of the outcome of the reform programme suggest that, despite the objective of ensuring equitable access, access is still highly skewed in favour of urban areas (Kwapong *et al.*, 1996). In our discussion of public spending on the social sectors below, we shall use budget figures to attempt to measure this in a financial/usage sense.

Since the reforms were put in place, perceptions about the educational system suggest disappointment with the outcomes. There is a widespread perception that the entire educational system fails to live up to expectations (Kwapong *et al.*, 1996). Desirable learning outcomes have been recorded only in private and public schools located in large towns and cities, in sharp contrast to the low learning outcomes recorded in the majority of public schools in rural and other deprived areas. The increase in the number of rural schools has placed a severe strain on already thin resources. Glewwe and Jacoby (1992) reviewed data from the second round of the Ghana Living Standards Survey (GLSS) and found that school quality was marginal, as some supposedly educated respondents performed badly on basic aptitude tests. Two rounds (in successive years) of criterion reference tests given to sixth grade primary students in conjunction with a USAID project indicated that only 2% of students were able to answer more than 60% of relatively simple Mathematics and English questions correctly. This outcome is consistent with other surveys and anecdotal evidence that learning materials are frequently not used even when available and that actual student-teacher contact hours are very limited. Even though early evidence from the GLSS seemed to indicate that such problems began with the decline in school quality during the 1970s, there has been no evidence of any improvements.

Enrolment rates have been increasing in recent years. The net enrolment in primary school rose from 62% in 1987/8 to 74% in 1991/2. Net enrolment in secondary schools rose to 38% in 1991/92 from 32% in 1987/8 (GSS, 1995). Enrolment in secondary schools is far lower than expected. Geographic disparities in education are stark. Rural-urban distinctions show a significant discrepancy; while the national enrolment rate in primary school is 67.4%, the rural-only enrolment rate is 54%. Regional breakdowns yield the contrast of a 66.6% attendance rate in Greater Accra, against a 28.6% attendance rate in Upper East, or 29.8% in Upper West (ISSER, 1996). In terms of outcomes, the patterns are also similar. More than half of the overall population is illiterate (51.2%). This is concentrated in rural areas, where some 60% of the population is completely illiterate. Within these figures, however, is a very sharp gender division. The male illiteracy rate is 39.2% (for the entire country) while the female illiteracy rate is 61.5% (*ibid.*).

It has been suggested by educational experts that the reforms, which started at the Junior Secondary School (JSS) level, should have embraced the Primary School level (Kwapong *et al.*, 1996). They attribute the poor performance and low student achievement of Senior Secondary School (SSS) and JSS pupils to poor preparation in primary schools. The wholesale promotion of primary pupils through the basic education system and into the JSS implies that there is little regular monitoring of the performance of most school children until they are ready to enter the SSS. The situation is worsened in rural areas where the monitoring system is even weaker.

There is also a narrowing of access among the upper tiers of education. Only 30% of Junior Secondary School leavers can find places in Senior Secondary Schools. The remainder are expected to become either self-employed, apprentices, or enter technical and public vocational institutions. In reality, many become unemployed and unemployable with hardly any skills.

Measuring distribution in terms of facilities, there is an uneven distribution of qualified teachers across the country, with cities and large towns getting a disproportionately large share of qualified teachers. Even though as many as 82% of primary school teachers were formally trained by 1995, there remains a severe shortage of trained teachers in rural schools in view of the highly skewed distribution in favour of urban schools. Many teachers prefer not to live in the rural areas.

Another issue in education is costs. The costs associated with a child in school apart from tuition — uniform, books, travel, tariffs for structural works, parent-teacher association fees, etc. — all add up to a substantial burden for households. It is believed that the cost-recovery measures in education contributed to declining enrolment rates in some areas.

Kwapong *et al.* (1996) have attributed the continuing difficulties to a number of factors. In sum, inadequately trained staff, insufficient textbooks, insufficient classroom furniture, and similar factors all contribute to questionable educational quality. They suggest that the reform programme was hastily implemented without in-depth consultation with stakeholders. There has indeed been a significant outcry against the manner in which decisions about reforms were arrived at. Parents and the general public were hardly engaged in any meaningful discussion as the reforms were presented by the Ministry of Education as a *fait accompli* to the public.

The Health Sector Reforms

By 1986, as much as 75% of the Ministry of Health's recurrent budget went into the payment of wages and salaries, having climbed from 44% in 1978. The effect of the cutback on other goods and services for the sector was seen to have severely constrained primary health care at the community level by restricting the deliveries of essential supplies, mobile health units and field supervision. The strategy for improving the sector was to achieve a better balance in the budget and was designed to reduce costs by restricting the range of publicly supplied drugs to a limited and carefully selected number that could serve a large majority of cases seen, particularly in primary health facilities. Cost-effectiveness was the main criterion in the determination of beneficiaries. The early World Bank adjustment documents do not suggest any way for targeting the poor or the so-called majority.

More than a decade after this reform began, the public outcry against the reforms has continued to grow, with steady calls for the withdrawal of the 'cash-and-carry' system where patients receive treatment only after they pay for the service. A recent assessment of the sector (Kwapong *et al.*, 1996) suggests that the health system in Ghana still has varied problems that can be summarized as follows:

- people cannot access the health care they need, in both rural and urban areas;
- the quantity and quality of services are far less than users demand;
- scarce resources are used inefficiently;
- there are weak linkages among the public and private delivery mechanisms, and also between the centre and the health facilities in small communities;
- the health sector is under-funded, with annual average real per capita spending (in constant 1987 US$) remaining at just over $4.5 between 1975–84 and 1985–91.

The deficiencies in the health system translate into severe capacity constraints for the sector. Because the provision of various health services is not prioritized, health service delivery tends to be institution-based, thus granting only 65% of the population access to facilities. On average, a travel distance of 12 kilometres is required to reach a health centre. People must travel an average of 40 kilometres to reach a hospital. While it is recognized that access to health facilities has been limited in the last decade by the introduction of user charges, there is also the stark reality that the services for which users are being asked to pay are deteriorating rapidly, hence making it difficult to justify continuing payment. The poor links between public and private health facilities lead to an under-utilization of available health resources. An estimated 50% of medical practitioners in Ghana are in private urban practice, while no incentives are offered to encourage them to expand their outreach to rural areas.

Rural Development Projects under the Economic Reforms

The PNDC government and its successor NDC government will go on record for encouraging a major renewed interest in 'rural development projects', particularly through the local government system and through major growth in donor activities in rural Ghana in the past decade. Thus, in addition to ceded revenue from locally-generated taxes, the constitution obliges central government to redistribute 5% of the Gross National Revenue (Consolidated Fund) to the 110 District Assemblies, in such a way that disadvantaged districts receive relatively more, (based on a formula agreed with the assemblies) to augment their traditional sources of revenue.

The problem with recent central government-supported rural development projects, however, is that they seem to follow an 'unplanned' course, where allocation to various parts of the country is based on a rationale that is not very apparent. The trend has been for mainly rural districts to compete with one another for resources from both the central government and donors in the implementation of 'development projects'.

The government has embarked on a number of development programmes aimed at improving the infrastructure for development at the local level. They include the provision of electricity to all regional and district capitals, construction of access roads to link major cities and food-producing areas, provision of potable water sources to settlements, as well as rural sanitation programmes. Other areas of concentration include non-formal education, small business/enterprise promotion, and training in the development and use of locally available building materials.

To complement the efforts of government, bilateral and multilateral agencies continue to commit resources through programmes/projects, studies and technical co-operation, with the ultimate objective of enhancing the living conditions of the disadvantaged in society. A number of NGOs have also been actively engaged in a wide range of activities, especially at the community level, aimed at reducing poverty. It must be stressed, however, that for certain services (particularly water and sanitation), the role of donors and NGOs has grown so significantly, in relation to that of the government, that the service provision is generally seen to be driven by them. Depending on the ease with which donors may go to one district or another, the distribution of such projects becomes skewed, particularly since there is little co-ordination of donor activities in districts. While some donors prefer to deal directly with District Assemblies and communities on their small grants projects, they find it impossible to deal with 110 District Assemblies and therefore become selective. The way of selecting districts is unco-ordinated, thereby leaving some districts with a large number of donor projects and others with nothing. Hence, the current trend in donor involvement at the community level, in the absence of a coherent national policy on rural development, leads to significantly uneven development. First, the projects a district can attract are tied to its advocacy ability, an ability that is correlated with wealth (especially at the extremes). Secondly, a path dependency evolves, where project begets project and some districts benefit across a range of areas, while others benefit from none. As a result, while it would appear that the broad conditions to facilitate and sustain poverty reduction programmes at the grassroots level are being put in place, the inadequacy of the delivery is borne out in the large numbers of young people that migrate to Accra daily.

Programme of Actions to Mitigate the Social Costs of Adjustment (PAMSCAD)

One of the major inter-sectoral initiatives undertaken in the reform period was the Programme of Actions to Mitigate the Social Costs of Adjustment (PAMSCAD). PAMSCAD arose as a response to the ERP and its related social costs. In February 1988, donors pledged a total of $85.7 m. to fund 23 projects under the umbrella of PAMSCAD. The projects ranged from community initiative projects to education, employment generation, basic needs and special projects to help retrenched civil servants.

PAMSCAD was plagued by problems from the start, however. A mid-term review (CIDA, 1990) made the point that donors were slow in releasing funds and this held up the initial phases of implementation. There were also a number of logistical problems including transport. One of the other major problems highlighted by the mid-term review was that PAMSCAD planned to piggy-back on existing institutions, and in many cases, their capacity was inadequate to meet its demands.

In addition to these general problems, the mid-term review (CIDA, 1990) highlighted some specific problems relevant to Ghanaian social policy in general. First, in discussing the decentralized community initiative projects, the review noted that 'some of the projects presented to the Secretariat [did] not address the most vulnerable groups in the districts. This was mainly due to the fact that communities were expected to initiate projects before assistance was given. Since the very vulnerable groups did not have the financial ability to initiate the projects they were not considered' (CIDA, 1990, part 3: 2). This emphasizes the trade-off between ownership and proactive targeting by the government, as well as the need for capacity-building. Capacity-building, of a more infrastructural nature, was also a problem highlighted with the school feeding project. In this case, efforts to feed students were crippled by the fact that schools lacked adequate kitchen facilities and the regional food depots were dilapidated. A project to improve local building materials also highlighted the problem of assuming that a market would form: it spoke of 'the absence of an effective market in the vulnerable areas due to the subsistence level of existence of the people', and proposed that 'special consideration of those segments of the population living below subsistence level to benefit from the programmes through some form of subsidy is necessary'. (CIDA, 1990, part 3: 35–36). How such targeting was to be accomplished was not discussed.

At the end of PAMSCAD, a number of reviews were commissioned. One of these reviews (Kwadzo and Kumekpor, 1994) highlighted new issues in addition to expanding on some that appeared in the mid-term review. The main problem seemed to be inadequate preparation and design. As they explain: 'there was a clear mismatch between expected project outputs and the ability of implementing agencies in terms of manpower available (both skills and number) and other inputs' (Kwadzo and Kumekpor, 1994: 4). The agricultural rehabilitation credit scheme was particularly instructive. First, the repayment rate of 14% highlights the need for sustainable programmes. The review attributes this low repayment rate to the association (at least in the minds of recipients) of the agricultural credit programme with the grant-based community initiative programme. Secondly, the agricultural credit programme illustrates the need for clear monitoring and evaluation mechanisms. The programme consisted of loans to some 17,000 farmers to rehabilitate their farms — an outcome that is fairly easy to monitor and quantify (e.g. a random sample of farms before and after the credit) yet the review gives no evidence of such monitoring.

The PAMSCAD review (Kwadzo and Kumekpor, 1994) also suggests major targeting problems. In discussing the supplementary feeding programme, for example, the review found that in some cases, charges to the parents to supplement the feeding of their children led to their withdrawal from the programme. This critique also extends to other contributions from beneficiaries, a policy that tended to characterize what might be seen as Ghana's social policy reform.

These assessments do not suggest that all the components of PAMSCAD were failures. There were some positive lessons to be learned as well. The Enhancing Opportunities for Women in Development (ENOWID) component was one such case. It was well-prepared and then effectively implemented by an adequately remunerated staff, leading the review to call for its extension. ENOWID was also a favorite among donors and enjoyed substantial donor support. The water and sanitation component of PAMSCAD was also reasonably successful, delivering a significant number of facilities as well as education and awareness. However, all in all, PAMSCAD illustrates well many of the targeting problems that continue to plague social policy in Ghana.

Ownership of Economic Reforms and Social Development
There has been considerable discussion about whether the Ghana Government owned the reform programme or not, and how such ownership or the lack of it affected social development programmes (Aryeetey, 1995). While the government has always maintained that the reform programme was a 'home-grown' response to the calamitous situation it faced, others have contended that there was a dearth of local technical capacity at the time for preparing the appropriate response (Toye, 1991). The reliance on the Bretton Woods Institutions was dictated by a number of factors, including the fact that the government had failed to secure aid from most bilateral

sources. Thus, in negotiating support for the ERP, the government negotiators were fully aware of the need to adjust to a 'Washington consensus' of first seeking macroeconomic stability.

The debate at the time centred around the fear that, under the stabilization programme, the shares of social expenditures would fall. This, of course, led to difficulties with left-wing members of the PNDC government. Since it could be easily shown that adjustment burdens were bound to fall disproportionately on the poor, opponents of the reforms had argued for exemptions and other forms of targeting. Their positions, often only politically argued, were seen, however, as unrealistic under the prevailing circumstances (Aryeetey, 1995).

The lack of ownership was partly derived from the relationship the government had with Western donors at the time. The World Bank's assessment of reform ownership places particular emphasis on the commitment of the leadership and less on the locus of initiative (Johnson and Wasty, 1993). So long as the top echelon of the government was believed to be committed to the reforms, the World Bank was satisfied. Legitimacy was of a lesser concern if the government had a way of achieving results. This probably explains why the Bretton Woods institutions, particularly in the early reforms, barely encouraged the government to consult other institutions, including the universities, the private sector and trade unions.

The result of the non-participatory approach to policy design was reflected in the resistance to the education and health sector reforms, even if limited. The government carried out the massive educational sector reform programme discussed earlier at such great speed (and with little debate), using the timing of World Bank disbursements and conditionalities as the major reason why extensive debate could not be tolerated. The rapid reforms, without broad participation, effectively silenced the 'demand' for a social policy to accompany the economic reforms. As seen, the consequence has been the development of a dual school system that ensures that only the children of the poor attend poorly equipped state schools. Similarly the 'reformed' public health system is used largely by those who cannot afford expensive private care.

4.   The Institutional Dimensions of Social Policy

The most recent policy documents suggest that the state wishes to reduce its role considerably in the provision of social services, and instead promote a greater role for local government, the private sector, NGOs and other donors. In this section, we shall first introduce recent attempts to develop clear programmes for poverty alleviation, looking at their social policy content, and then discuss the institutional arrangements put in place for their realization.

Recent Social Policy Reform Initiatives

The participatory poverty studies mentioned earlier (Norton et al., 1995) found that the expressed needs of communities varied significantly by region. In the rural North, the emphasis was on such basic needs as food security and water supply. These two were often linked, as a steady supply of water could be perceived to ensure dry season food crops. The rural South had a more varied set of needs. Most communities expressed a need for access to safe water. Food security figured less predominantly, with more intra-community variation in this need. A fair number of communities expressed a need for transport infrastructure. In the urban areas, the major concerns of communities were inadequate employment opportunities and a lack of credit for small enterprises. Potable water was also an issue for urban communities; three of the five communities surveyed expressed a need for better water supplies. There were also a number of needs that were expressed in all regions — mainly education and health service accessibility. There was, of course, some variation in the expression of these needs, but such variation usually tended to be correlated with the existing facilities.

The 1992 Constitution of Ghana enjoined the government to put in place a long-term programme to address various issues of social and economic development such as the ones outlined above. The National Co-ordinated Programme for Social and Economic Development (*Ghana*

Vision 2020) is generally seen to be an attempt at responding to this constitutional requirement and is therefore the authoritative government document to guide development across all the major sectors. Donors interested in poverty reduction are expected to tailor interventions to fit into this programme, even though they seldom do (Aryeetey, 1995). The objectives of *Ghana Vision 2020* have been broken down into two main time periods, i.e. the medium term (1996-2000) and the long term (1996–2020). In the medium term, the development objective is to consolidate the gains achieved under the ERP and strengthen the foundations for accelerated growth. 'The aim is to improve the social and economic status of all individuals and to eliminate extremes of deprivation by encouraging the creativity, enterprise and productivity of all citizens' (GoG, 1995: 3).

The development objectives contained in *Vision 2020* have been used to prepare an Action Plan for Poverty Reduction that is currently co-ordinated by the Planning Commission. In this plan, the development objectives are classified under human development, economic growth, rural development, urban development and an enabling environment. Social policy is assumed to flow naturally out of the policies on human development, rural development and urban development. Thus, the long-term human development objective of the action plan remains improvement in the quality of life and the expansion of opportunities for the entire society, which is expected to be achieved through the following medium-term objectives: a) poverty alleviation through an improvement of the access of the poor to basic social and technical infrastructure, economic services, as well as improved participation in decision-making; and b) enhancement of human resources through the implementation of programmes on population, women in development, health and nutrition, etc; increasing employment and leisure opportunities through the promotion of labour-intensive programmes, support for the informal sector, and safe-guarding the rights of rural women.

The attainment of a supportive urban settlement system is one major development theme under the action plan. The broad aim here is to ensure that small and medium-sized towns support their catchment rural hinterlands as a way of ensuring a more equitable spatial distribution of population, services, and opportunities. This is expected to be achieved through two main medium-term objectives, namely, giving priority to the progressive provision of services and infrastructure in small and medium-sized towns in support of economic and social improvements to the rural areas; and also to promoting non-agricultural and non-traditional (agricultural) jobs in selected small and medium-sized towns. It is expected that the achievement of these objectives will assist in the easing of urban population pressures.

In support of our contention that there is no explicit social policy, this action plan is not regarded as an official document by many government agencies, and donors generally disregard it. Very few public agencies know of its existence. The more 'authoritative' *Vision 2020* is generally perceived to be a 'list of ideas' that has not yet been translated into realistic implementable sets of activities. Many see it as a hasty attempt to meet a constitutional demand, thus affecting the credibility of the overall agenda.

A major reason for the current passive attitudes towards *Vision 2020* is the absence of significant procedures for targeting distinct social groups. Once again, the way in which particular social groups will be reached is taken for granted and this might largely be related to the ideological position taken on the economic reforms. The issue of 'small central government' overrides all other ideological considerations, even though small government does not manifest itself in aggregate public spending, as will be seen later. The state, in attempting to pull back from the provision of social services, would like to see more done by local government, the private sector and NGOs but lacks credible tools for providing the needed incentive for their participation.

Decentralization, Local Government and Social Policy

In addition to the ownership of the policy ideas, some social policy reform has aimed to increase the fiscal responsibility of local communities in maintaining social programmes. Beginning in

1988, government opted for a decentralized local government system that would be responsible for ensuring that local communities were better provided with social services. Both the new local government and the planning laws that were put in place emphasized the administrative district as the focal point of planning activity. Responsibility for the preparation of a national development plan was placed with the National Development Planning Commission (NDPC), while responsibility for sub-national development planning became vested in district assemblies operating through their Executive Committees and the District Planning Co-ordinating Unit (DPCU). District Assemblies are now responsible for the overall development of the district and to ensure the preparation and submission to the government for approval of the development plan and budget for the District.

The current interest in the relationship between the 'centre' and those that depend on it for socio-economic development follows a trend that was observable in many developing countries throughout the 1980s. Many countries have attempted, one way or the other, to decentralize their social service-delivery systems with varying degrees of success (Conyers, 1988). Increasingly, decentralization has been regarded as a tool for development. This relationship is often founded on the notion that development must involve popular participation. The need to establish a positive correlation between development and decentralization has been dictated by the increasing difficulty (both logistically and conceptually) the state has had in tackling local-level development problems. Hence, the new planning law sets out in detail the planning functions of District Assemblies and their Development Planning Co-ordinating Units (DPCU).

A major constraint on the provision of social services by local government bodies, however, remains the problem of inadequate financial resources for operation. Central government believes it is the responsibility of District Assemblies to harness a large part of the essential resources for achieving their developmental objectives and also putting in place the necessary institutions at the local level. The only major contribution that the state would like to make to the process of providing social services is made obligatory under the current Constitution which requires that a minimum of 5% of the development budget be paid to all the 110 District Assemblies. Kwapong et al. (1996) report that accounting for these funds has been difficult, and there are obvious cases of misapplication, leading to relatively little going to social service provision. The improper use of the funds is partly attributed to poor management systems in local government. The lack of proper budgeting and accounting systems is reflected in the absence of audited accounts for a number of districts for several years. They simply lack adequately trained people to manage their finances.

There is a tendency to assume that a decentralized provision of community services automatically makes projects sustainable. This is definitely not to be taken for granted. While the PAMSCAD review discussed above shows that it is possible for inadequate decentralization to backfire and lead to community disengagement and policy failure, the PPA study of poverty finds that 'there was a complete recognition that action by the state and NGOs should be matched by an equivalent effort from poor communities and households' (Norton et al., 1995: 15). However, the mechanism by which responsibility is shifted to the community is critical. Part of the PAMSCAD problem was that communities had to make some of the initial outlays; those without the necessary resources were summarily excluded. The amount of contributions required is very important. Even in-kind contributions can be draining, especially if there are recurrent labour demands. Finally, project demands for communal labour can run foul of public goods issues. Indeed, the PAMSCAD review (Kwadzo and Kumekpor, 1994: 7) notes that 'the collective activity approach to providing community facilities, though commendable, did not prove fruitful under PAMSCAD. Rather individualistic tendencies of human nature gave full expression in various projects under PAMSCAD.'

5. Public Spending and Social Development

One of the arguments raised by the opponents of the neo-liberal economic reforms undertaken by Ghana in the 1980s was the expected fall in budgetary allocations to social sectors (Herbst, 1992). Resistance was expected to come mainly from urban workers who have often been perceived to be the beneficiaries of a system of subsidies on social services and deliberate controls on agricultural pricing in order to keep them quiet. For organized labour, reducing the fiscal deficit through the removal of subsidies and cost-effectiveness in the delivery of social services was a major fear right from the beginning of the reforms. The reformers retorted that proper targeting of whatever expenditures were made on those social services would still benefit the genuinely poor (World Bank, 1987). In this section, we argue that while the fears of reduced expenditures were partially realized after 1990, there is hardly any evidence that this was offset by any significant improvement in targeting. Government social spending in Ghana is dominated by the health and education sectors, with much less spent on social security and welfare. Historically, the trends show a sustained upward move in the social sector's share of government spending between 1960 and 1965. Social sector spending fell during the first reform period 1966–8. The decline in the sector's share was reversed between 1972 and 1975 with shares rising to approximately 46% in 1975/76. This effort was not sustained and by 1981 social spending constituted only 33% of the total, which was still above the African average. The proportion of central government spending going to the social sectors rose between 1983 and 1990, as did social sector spending as a percentage of GDP. The share of social sector spending in total spending was, however, not maintained beyond 1990. We can see this in Figure 15.1.

Figure 15.1: Community and Social Service Spending 1983–96

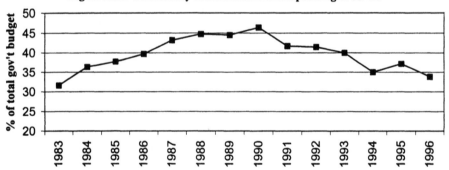

By 1995, social sector spending was 36% of the total, compared with 48% in 1990 (ISSER, 1996). In 1996, the expenditure pattern continued to show a decline for social services. Expenditure for community and social services fell by more than 3.4% to 33.8% in 1996 after the slight upturn in 1995. The decline here was due to decreases in spending for education, health, social security and welfare. The share of total spending allocated to education fell from 19.45% in 1995 to 18.66% in 1996. The share of the government spending on the health sector also fell by 1.43% in 1996 compared with 1995. The main reason for the declining shares of the social sectors in public spending in the 1990s is the crowding out of social spending by public sector interest payments. The share of interest payments doubled between 1990 and 1994 from 10% to 20% of the total budget. Social sector spending in the last few years in particular has been affected by the rise in interest payments as the share of spending on economic services has been maintained in this period (ISSER, 1996). Indeed, the fall in the share of education spending began shortly after the start of the education and health reform programmes. The cost-recovery aspect of these sectoral reforms required that various subsidies were either systematically removed or significantly reduced. The current trends suggest that as private contributions to the funding of public education have increased, the government has perceived some of these resources as substitutes for government spending. We now turn to a direct examination of these two sectors.

Health Sector Spending and Health Sector Reforms

We indicated earlier that the health sector reforms are generally perceived to have had little positive impact on the beneficiaries. This is not surprising considering that government spending on health remains relatively low. Figure 15.2 shows government spending on health, including the steady decline during the 1990s.

Figure 15.2: Health Spending 1982–95

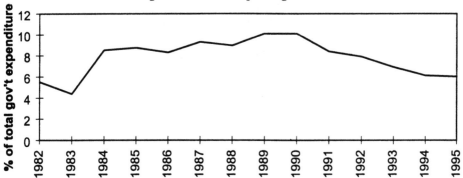

Indeed, government is not the biggest spender on health as private spending comprises some 51% of the total. The government provides only 37% and NGOs 12% (Demery *et al.*, 1995). Over the period 1990–94 Ghana's spending on health averaged 1.2% of GDP, compared with an average of 2% for all developing countries (World Bank, 1995: 36). We note that as far back as 1971, the government introduced user fees as a means to increase cost recovery and improve health expenditures. The fees were kept low until 1985, when they were sharply increased and patients were expected to pay for everything except vaccinations and treatment for some diseases (although, as we discuss below, even these exceptions seem not to hold). After the increases, however, fees were not regularly adjusted and thus their contribution to the Ministry's budget steadily declined.

Aggregate figures yield little insight into who actually benefits from government health spending. Using a technique that matches usage by different groups as well as distribution of spending, Demery *et al.* (1995) approximate the average incidence of public spending. Before discussing their results, however, there are a number of caveats. First, since the Ministry of Health does not provide sufficient disaggregation the figures are for Greater Accra, Eastern, Volta, Ashanti, and Western Regions only. Secondly, given the structure of the Ghana Living Standards Survey, data on in-patient care are severely underestimated, leading the results to underestimate the regressive nature of spending. Finally, one should bear in mind that the poor are less likely to report an illness and to seek treatment in general. We should note that they also found low utilization as a whole; about half of the people who reported sick in 1992 did not seek treatment.

The caveats aside, the results of Demery *et al.* show a significantly regressive spending regime. Their results are shown in Figure 15.3. In 1989, the poorest quintile received 12.2% of total government health spending, while the top quintile received 30.4% of the total health budget. In 1992 the distribution had worsened somewhat as the bottom quintile captured 11.6% of spending and the top quintile 33%. Disaggregating this distribution by gender for the 1992 data also yields some disturbing patterns. While women as a whole have command of a larger share of health expenditure (56.2% to men's 43.8%), this pattern is not found at all among the poorest quintile. Indeed, in that quintile, women garner only 44.3% of health spending. In contrast, women in the top quintile get 65%. All in all, these results are worrying, for when we bring our caveats back into the picture, they (the exclusion of poorer areas, the underestimation of in-patient visits) suggest that the actual picture is worse.

Figure 15.3: Incidence of Health Spending by Quintile

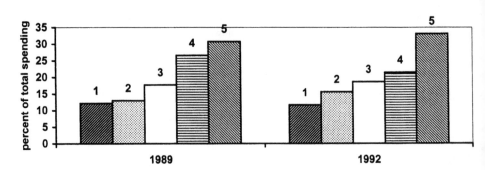

The above trends notwithstanding, there has been some recent progress in health care in Ghana. Infant mortality in 1994 was 66.4 and under-five mortality 119.4 (per 1000 live births), both of which are better than the average for sub-Saharan Africa. Within Ghana, however, there is large variation in these figures by region. For example, the under-five mortality rates in 1992 ranged from 82 in Greater Accra to 217 in the Northern Region (ISSER, 1994). Similar patterns can be found for facilities. For example, all of the Northern Regions (Northern, Upper East, and Upper West) combined accounted for 13% of the maternal and child health/family planning facilities in 1993. Greater Accra, alone, accounted for 16% (ISSER, 1996). Thus, there are sharp regional disparities that persist and suggest that government should better target its policy.

Education Sector Spending and Reform Outcomes

As discussed earlier during the economic decline of the 1970s and early 1980s, education provision suffered drastically. Spending per primary school pupil fell from US$41 in 1975 to US$16 in 1983 (Demery *et al.*, 1995). In gauging the incidence of education spending, the data are of a better quality than those for health. The only caveats are as follows. First, the absence of data on cost recovery leaves us with estimates of gross distribution only. Secondly, the absence of regional data precludes differentiating costs by region and hence results in some loss of variation. As is evident from Figure 15.4, the distribution of education expenditures is far more equitable than for health.

Figure 15.4: Education Spending 1982–95

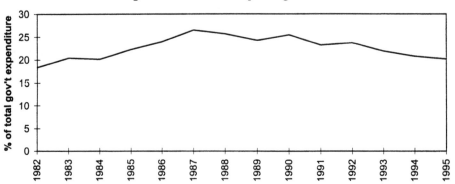

On the attainment of poverty and equity objectives, Demery *et al.* (1995) have analyzed the incidence of education spending in Ghana using the Ghana Living Standards Survey (GLSS).

According to the third round of the GLSS (1992), 49% of the population aged 15 and over was literate in English or a local language. The proportion of the population that could read and write was 61% in non-poor households versus 38% in poor households. The urban population also had a higher literacy rate than the rural population. A significant gender bias also existed. Increases in primary enrolment rates are evident across all groups except for the bottom quintile in urban areas other than Accra.

In terms of the evidence on expenditure incidence, Demery *et al.* (1995) found that developments have been mixed. There has been an improvement in the targeting of primary subsidies, but a deterioration in the targeting of secondary subsidies. Overall the share of the poorest in education spending has not changed much. In 1989 the bottom quintile received 17.1% and the top quintile 23.7%. By 1992, both quintiles had lost part of their shares to the middle quintiles. If these data are broken down by type of education, different patterns emerge. The distribution of spending on primary education is quite equitable, with the bottom three quintiles capturing more than 20% of expenditures. Furthermore, the share of the lowest quintile improved marginally in the 1989–92 period. Tertiary education (with only 12% of the education sector budget) shows the opposite effect. Here the bottom two quintiles, 40% of the population, account for only 16% of total spending. The top quintile alone, on the other hand, accounted for only 45% in 1992. There is also evidence of a persistent gender bias in education spending. Girls in the bottom quintile got only 40.6% of that quintile's education spending. Girls in the top quintile did not fare much better, capturing 44.5% of that quintile's share. In sum, the net effect has been a fairly flat education spending distribution across income quintiles (see Figure 15.5). However, when the demographic composition of the group is taken into account, it appears that whatever trends have occurred in total spending, most of this hardly reaches the poor. There is also evidence of regional inequalities in the provision of education services.

Figure 15.5: Incidence of Education Spending by Expenditure Quintile

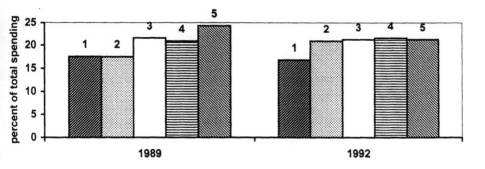

While the current proportion of public expenditures going to education is recognized to be relatively large, the absolute amounts are certainly inadequate for achieving the various goals set for the transformation of the educational system and educating the growing numbers involved. Restructuring the educational system to deliver planned outputs will require significant new investments and recurrent outlays.

Declining Shares of Social Spending and Aid

We now turn to an examination of aid and how aid inflows seem to be affecting social spending. There are indications that overseas development assistance (ODA) to various sectors has begun to substitute for some government expenditures, particularly for social sector spending. Even though development assistance is a relatively small proportion of GDP, aid to a number of key social sectors is becoming increasingly important in relation to the government's commitments to those sectors. Social sector assistance has grown steadily in the past decade and has become crucial to total spending in the sector. Indeed the growth of ODA social sector allocation was faster than government social sector expenditures between 1988 and 1993, as can be seen in Figure 15.6. There has been increased assistance going to education, health, humanitarian aid and relief. Compared with government spending on social services, social spending averaged 18% of total ODA in the period. This might suggest an overall flagging commitment by government to the social sectors, as well as a fungibility of aid. As donors pick up part of the tab, the government can divert part of its expenditures, as seen in Chapter 6.

Figure 15.6: Social Sector Aid as a Percent of Government Social Sector Spending

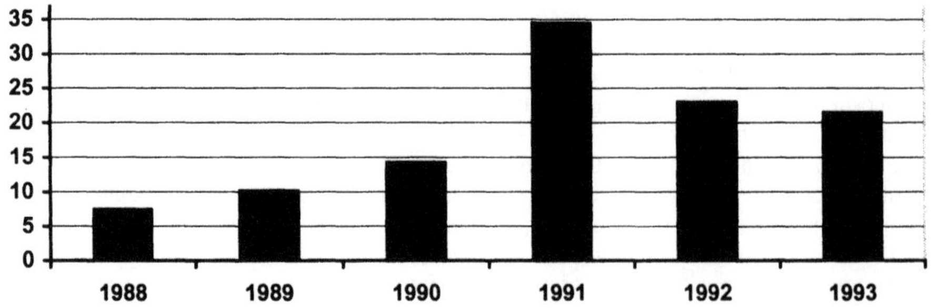

This is a simple, yet powerful phenomenon. Aside from the need to improve on the use of resources in social service delivery, it is reasonable to assume that the flow of additional resources from donors supporting the sectoral reforms has made it easier for the government to pull back some of its support for the social services. The danger with such substitution, however, is that the required level of services is unlikely to be met since the total available resources will not change - prohibiting the needed expansion expressed in the PPA and elsewhere. Indeed, with donor support, total resources available to the social sector have not changed significantly in real terms. For the time being this is discouraging, especially in the health sector where it is most pronounced. If aid were to decrease, which is very possible, given increasing 'donor fatigue', then the burden will shift back to government. The government will be faced with either cutting the social sectors or reallocating its budget.

There is the temptation to view the replacement of support for the social services with increasing aid as meaning that whatever social policy reforms are taking place have been foisted on the government from outside, an issue related to our earlier discussion of ownership. Cobbe (1991) suggests that the reform of the education sector when it began was to meet conditionalities for donor support. While this may be true to some extent, it is important to note that the reform had been discussed as far back as 1974.[5] It had been delayed only because of the lack of resources and the absence of a political will to take harsh decisions whose outcomes were quite unpredictable. Aid made earlier planned reforms easier to undertake. If the government is pulling back resources, it is because its priorities changed substantially after the reforms began, and it was unable to package the entire array of social policy issues that were beginning to emerge into one comprehensive and credible set of policies. There is the temptation to believe that, with the re-introduction of a democratic system of governance, the government has become interested

---

[5] Proposals for the reform of the school system were first made under the Acheampong regime in 1974. These sought to abolish middle schools and break secondary education into a two-stage process of junior and senior secondary schools. After approval by the government implementation was only half-heartedly carried out with a small number of pilot projects.

in providing more visible services, such as roads and electricity, hoping for a political windfall.

Considering the current political trends, it is also possible to conceive the declining share of expenditures on health, education and other welfare services as an indication of a lack of dependence on those who are most likely to be affected by them. Ironically, the most affected are rural communities and the urban poor who have generally been seen as the main backers of the government. We are inclined to believe that the provision of infrastructure in those areas has accurately been seen by politicians to provide more political capital than the health and education services make possible. Thus, as the government comes under pressure from within and outside to reduce the current fiscal deficit of more than 3% of GDP and to meet macroeconomic targets, it is easier for it to argue for a cut in these social services, and switch the available development resources into roads which donors are not likely to fund. The choice of cuts in education and health as opposed to road construction has therefore been a highly rational one, dictated by the need to meet macroeconomic targets while being seen politically to be caring for rural people.

6. Proper Targeting for Ghanaian Social Policy Reform

What this chapter shows is that over the last three decades, Ghana has followed a disparate set of policies for attaining not always properly defined social goals. While reforms have been attempted from time to time, they have tended to be influenced either during their design or implementation by various developments that do not signify commitment to them. While one cannot simply argue that social policy reforms have been imposed from outside, the importance of the outside involvement cannot be downplayed. The apparent lack of commitment to social policy reform is reflected in the poor articulation of a coherent and credible national social policy as embodied in *Vision 2020* and the action programme on poverty reduction, as well as the lack of commitment in recent overall public spending trends. The outcome has been a persistent failure of the institutions to reach their target recipients. But issues of targeting have received little research attention in Ghana and are very little understood in policy-making circles. We use this section to illustrate some of the problems with targeting and then dwell on some of the research issues raised by considerations of targeting before discussing capacity-building requirements for dealing with these.

It is obvious that while the re-allocation of resources that took place in the latter part of the reform period was more pro-poor than previous allocations, the fact that it has not been sustained reflects both the unsustained growth of the revenue base and a smaller commitment to a progressive allocation structure. In other words, both growth and redistribution matter considerably. While an increase in the resources available to government is necessary, it will be insufficient to bring about the desired improvement in social development. Of critical importance is how the resources available to the government are utilized. Important considerations are the shares of recurrent and development spending, the distribution of government spending between social and other categories, the regional pattern of spending and the urban-rural allocations. Other important considerations are whether the provision of these services benefits the poor and reduces gender imbalances.

The introduction/increase of user fees in the social sectors is an oft-touted mechanism for increasing policy sustainability. In Ghana, as in other developing countries, there is evidence that some of these increased fees have resulted in the poor's exclusion from services. Norton *et al.* (1993: 48) noted that 'while the amounts charged at the MCH consultations (for immunizations, weighing and other basic services) may appear small — of the order of ¢200 [then $0.20] per monthly consultation — the evidence from this study shows that rural women sometimes have difficulty meeting this cost. The poorest mothers are, thus, sometimes compelled to skip immunizations.'

The problems with targeting are many. First, there appears to be evidence of an overall lack of commitment to targeting altogether. For example, the Agricultural Rehabilitation Credit component of PAMSCAD neglected to target the regions in greatest need. An evaluation states: 'from the disbursement figures the most vulnerable areas Upper Region [sic], received the smallest amounts of ¢6,270 per head. The highest receipt per head of ¢140,897 was in the Volta Region' (Kwadzo and Kumekpor, 1994, Annex: 3). Another example, from the health sector, is provided by Norton *et al.* (1995: 43): "In response to a question about how well the exemption provisions were working in his area of jurisdiction, the District Medical Officer at Abura Dunkwa replied: 'The exemptions are cumbersome; how do I determine who is a pauper? Besides, my office is not reimbursed for drugs handed out without charge to paupers . . . so we cannot be generous in applying the concessions.'

A second problem with targeting in Ghana is that there is no option on the screening process; the informational and bureaucratic infrastructure is such that only rudimentary targeting is possible. For example, Norton *et al.* found that the Tamale Department of Social Welfare's quarterly budget for facilitating exemptions was around $10. Thus, there does not even appear to be the funding allocated to begin to build an informational infrastructure for effective targeting. Furthermore, the organization of social sector institutions is often such that the service provider is separated by physical as well as bureaucratic distance from the social work institution that could provide an assessment of a recipient's poverty level. Finally, there may be bureaucratic structures that constrain targeting. As Norton *et al.* recount (1995: 51): 'though the Ministry of Education has issued clear instructions forbidding the expulsion of pupils on grounds of non-payment of fees, headteachers often feel compelled to act to the contrary since they are held directly accountable for the collection of fees.'

A third, and related, problem is that, even with well designed policies, the state of Ghanaian social sector institutions can be so disorganized that a targeted intervention will fail. As Norton *et al.* relate (1995: 43): 'Graft further raises the cost of treatment in government hospitals. At Tamale, the government hospital was described, rather disgracefully as a "gold mine". Informants told how "the seriously ill must tip the attendant just to be transported to the lift" and how "tips were demanded before a child could receive a life-saving blood transfusion".'

Finally, there is an issue of information. The poor in Ghana seem to be inadequately informed about any provisions that may exist for them to receive social services at a discount or for free. Thus, the issues discussed above may be secondary. Until the poor know the concessions that exist (on paper, at least) in order to provide them with access to social services, they may be loath to take advantage of these services, let alone press for their legislated rights.

All of this is not to say that targeting is not possible in Ghana. It will require substantial investments in information and monitoring infrastructure. It will also require innovation. Recent experiences by groups working with community health clinics indicate that they can successfully judge the relative poverty of a service recipient by looking at his or her social networks. In order to identify and develop these innovations, more research needs to be done.

References

Aryeetey, E. (1981) 'Interregional and Intersectoral Investment Allocation Problems in Ghana', Unpublished M.Sc. Thesis, Department of Planning, UST. Kumasi.

Aryeetey, E. (1985) *Decentralizing Regional Planning in Ghana*, Dortmunder Beiträge zur Raumplanung, 42, Institut für Raumplanung, Universität Dortmund, Dortmund.

Aryeetey, E. (1995) *Aid Effectiveness in Ghana*. Report of a Study Sponsored by the Overseas Development Council, Washington, DC.

Bortei-Doku, E. and Aryeetey, E. (1996) 'Urban Poverty in Accra: A Case Study of Accra', Report prepared for the Canadian International Development Agency, Accra.

CIDA (1990) *Mid-term Evaluation Report on PAMSCAD*. Accra: Canadian International Development Agency.

Cobbe, J. (1991) 'The Political Economy of Education Reform in Ghana' in Rothchild.

Conyers, D. (1983) 'Decentralization: The Latest Fashion in Development Administration?'. *Public Administration and Development*, Vol. 3: 97–109.

Demery, L., Chao, S., Bernier, R. and Mehra, K. (1995) *The Incidence of Social Spending in Ghana*. Poverty and Social Policy Discussion Paper No. 82. Washington, DC: World Bank (November).

Ghana Statistical Service (1995) *The Pattern of Poverty in Ghana*. Ghana Extended Poverty Study. Accra: GSS.

Ghana Statistical Service and World Bank (1996). 'CWIQ Bulletin' July–August. Accra: processed.

Glewwe, P. and Jacoby, H. (1992) *Estimating the Determinants of Cognitive Achievement in Low-Income Countries: The Case of Ghana*. Living Standards Measurement Study Working Paper No. 91. Washington, DC: World Bank.

Government of Ghana (GoG) (1964) *Seven-Year Development Plan 1963/64–1969/70*, Accra.

Government of Ghana (GoG) (1977) *Five-Year Development Plan 1975/76–79/80*. Accra: Ghana Publishing Corporation.

Government of Ghana (GoG) (1995) *Ghana-Vision 2020*. Presidential Report to Parliament on Co-ordinated Programme of Economic and Social Development Policies, Accra.

Herbst, J. (1992) *The Politics of Reform in Ghana*. Berkeley, CA: University of California Press.

ISSER (1994) *State of the Ghanaian Economy Report 1993*, University of Ghana, Legon.

ISSER (1995) *State of the Ghanaian Economy Report 1994*, University of Ghana, Legon.

ISSER (1996) *State of the Ghanaian Economy Report 1995*, University of Ghana, Legon.

Johnson, J. H. and Wasty, S. S. (1993) *Borrower Ownership of Adjustment Programs and the Political Economy of Reform*. World Bank Discussion Paper No. 199. Washington, DC: World Bank.

Kanbur, R. and Mink, S. (1994) 'Poverty and Accelerated Growth in Ghana: Policy Issues in the Light of Global Experience', *The Economic Bulletin of Ghana*, New Series 4, Vol. 1, No. 1.

Kwadzo, G. T. M. and Kumekpor, M. L. (1994) *PAMSCAD Evaluation (CIDA Supported Programmes)*. Report prepared for the Canadian International Development Agency, Accra.

Kwapong, A. A. *et al.* (1996) *An Assessment of National Capacity-Building in Ghana*. Report of a Study Prepared by the National Capacity-Building Assessment Group for the World Bank, August, Accra.

Mikell, G. (1991) 'Equity Issues in Ghana's Rural Development', in Rothchild.

Morris, J. C. H. (1980) Report of ODA/IBRD Joint Supervision Division to URADEP, 29 September–17 October. Washington, DC: World Bank, West Africa Department.

Norton, A. *et al.* (1995) *Poverty Assessment in Ghana Using Qualitative and Participatory Research Methods*. PSP Discussion Paper Series, No.83. Washington, DC: World Bank.

Rothchild, D (ed.) (1991) *Ghana: The Political Economy of Recovery*. SAIS African Studies Library. Boulder, CO and London: Lynne Rienner Publishers.

Toye, J. (1991) 'Ghana' in P. Mosley, J. Harrigan and J. Toye, *Aid and Power: The World Bank and Policy-Based Lending*, Vol. 2, London: Routledge.

World Bank (1987) *Ghana: Policies and Issues of Structural Adjustment*. Report No. 6635-GH. Washington, DC: World Bank.

World Bank (1995) *Ghana: Poverty Past, Present and Future*. Report No. 14504-GH. Washington, DC: World Bank, Population and Human Resource Division, West Central Africa Department.

16 Poverty in a Changing Environment

KWEKU APPIAH
LIONEL DEMERY
& S. GEORGE LARYEA-ADJEI

1. Introduction

Poverty reduction is the major development challenge for the twenty-first century, and the sub-ject of a significant policy focus in Ghana today. This focus is occasioned by the fact that after forty years of political independence, about one-third of the country's population continues to live below the poverty line (Ghana Statistical Service, 1995a).[1] Moreover, notwithstanding the positive impact of the Economic Recovery Programme (ERP) initiated in 1983, some projec-tions indicate that in the absence of further improved policies, it will take the average poor Ghanaian no less than ten years to escape poverty (World Bank, 1995a: 33–4). For the poorest of the poor, it will take 40 years.

Poverty is a multidimensional phenomenon and can be measured in various ways, each em-bodying different approaches. Economists conventionally measure poverty in terms of the in-come or expenditure needed to sustain a minimum standard of living in a particular country — known as the poverty line. This convention is largely followed here. Because it is inherently subjective, the poverty line can be set at various levels. Those people whose consumption levels fall below the line are considered poor. The poverty line therefore separates the poor from the non-poor and constitutes a starting point for poverty analysis.[2]

But poverty is not measured by income and consumption alone.[3] Poverty affects virtually all aspects of the quality of life and welfare, including life expectancy, health, nutrition, literacy, access to social and economic services, political participation and so on. Therefore, a compre-hensive definition of poverty should encompass these other important dimensions as

---

[1] The Government of Ghana has yet to officially determine a poverty line for Ghana. However, the poverty line estimated by the World Bank and the Ghana Statistical Service based on the Ghana Living Standards Surveys has become a widely accepted standard (see World Bank, 1995a).

[2] Poverty can be measured in absolute or relative terms, where absolute poverty refers to the position of an individual or household in relation to a poverty line whose real value is fixed over time, and relative poverty refers to the position of an individual or household compared with the average income in the country.

[3] Many analysts consider the measurement of income poverty as the best approach to monitoring poverty. This is primarily because indicators of income poverty are principally based on relatively unambiguous (monetary) measures which can be easily compared over time and between locations.

well.[4] Accordingly, available data on both income-based and social measures of poverty are presented here.

This chapter summarizes current knowledge of the dimensions and trends in poverty in Ghana since independence. On the basis of data availability, we distinguish two time periods: from independence to the mid-1980s, and from 1987 to 1994. Owing to the paucity of comprehensive and detailed data for the former period, the post-1987 period is more illuminating. Data from three rounds of the *Ghana Living Standards Survey* (GLSS), two sets of the *Demographic and Health Survey* (GDHS) and a participatory poverty assessment (PPA) are available for the later period.

The chapter is arranged as follows. The next section briefly reviews the economic and social circumstances that gave rise to the current focus on poverty. This is followed by a brief review of the prevalence and trends in poverty prior to 1987. The characteristics of the poor, as revealed by the GLSS and PPA, are presented in section 4. The fifth section reviews our understanding of poverty trends after 1987. The chapter concludes with some policy perspectives.

2.   Economic and Social Trends Prior to 1987

The decade of the 1980s witnessed notable shifts in economic and social development in Ghana. The steep economic decline which dominated the period up to 1983 actually had its origins in the mid-1960s, with more rapid deterioration setting in from about 1975. Annual inflation, below 10% in 1970, rose to 40% in 1975 and exceeded 100% in 1983. Government revenue dropped from over 16% of GDP in 1975 to just 7% in 1983. Public sector investment plunged from around 6% of GDP in the mid-1970s to less than 1% in 1983, resulting in a severe deterioration in the nation's economic and social infrastructure. Between 1975 and 1983 real GDP fell dramatically and real income per capita fell by 27%. Thus by the early 1980s, the Ghanaian economy was in a very critical condition: drastic and chronic shortages of imported goods had reduced the productive capacity of local industries; and, worse still, the cumulative effect of continued and increasing overvaluation of the cedi had eroded all incentives to produce for export or to market through formal channels.

The effect of the economic decline on social services was especially deleterious. Real per capita expenditure on health fell from 6.4% of total public expenditure in 1974 to 0.6% in 1982/ 83. By 1984 around a half of the medical practitioners had left the country. With shortages of drugs, materials and personnel, hospital attendance dropped substantially. Attendance fell by about 41% in Accra, for example, and by 67% in Cape Coast. The maternal mortality rate was 5– 15/1000 and the crude death rate 19–20/1000. Poverty-related diseases became widespread and included diseases previously eliminated. Food supplies became limited; per capita food availability in 1983 was 30% lower than in 1974. The food price indices for locally produced food in 1970, 1980 and 1983, were 11, 393 and 2,755, respectively.

It was within these desperate social and economic circumstances that the government of the Provisional National Defence Council (PNDC), which had come to power on 31 December 1981, took the decision to formulate and implement policies to stem and then reverse the decline. These policies were articulated within the framework of the Economic Recovery Programme (ERP) that was begun in 1983 and which encompassed a series of structural adjustment programmes.

3.   Poverty prior to 1987

With a few exceptions, little systematic effort was made to measure and monitor poverty among the population prior to 1987. As a consequence, the evidence on poverty that exists for this period is fragmentary. This lack of detailed and comprehensive data on poverty before 1987

---

[4] See for example, Mikkelsen (1995) for a discussion of emerging definitions of poverty.

seriously constrains our analysis of poverty for much of this period. The prevalence of poverty from independence to 1987 must therefore be inferred from various related studies conducted in the 1960s, 1970s and early 1980s. For this reason a precise comparison of poverty trends over succeeding decades in Ghana is not possible.

The late 1950s and 1960s

In the absence of national household sample survey data, minimum wage data are used to 'guess-timate' poverty trends in the early years of independence. An obvious limitation here is that the data only refer to formal sector workers, a relatively small and non-representative sample of the population, thereby precluding generalization to the population as a whole. Nevertheless, the limited evidence relating to general improvements in the standards of living suggests that the incidence of poverty at the very least did not worsen for much of this period. Studies for this period confirm that a number of households experienced increasing real incomes. Ewusi (1971), for example, found that there was an overall drop, from 48% in 1957 to 25% in 1966, in the proportion of workers who earned the minimum wage or less (Figure 16.1). The rate of improvement in incomes varied by sector, however. Workers in manufacturing and commerce recorded the greatest improvements. Not surprisingly, the largest proportions of low-income workers throughout the period were to be found in the agricultural and construction sectors, indicating lower income levels and average standards of living among workers in these sectors.

Figure 16.1: **Proportion of Employed Persons in Selected Sectors Earning Minimum Wage or Below (1957–1966)**

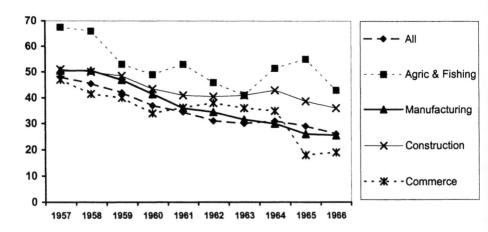

Source: Ewusi (1971).

1970s and early 1980s

The first half of the 1970s have perhaps been the most prosperous years for the average Ghanaian since independence. GDP per capita (1970 prices), for example, increased from ¢226 in 1956 to a peak of ¢272 in 1974, after which it declined, initially very sharply. As the economic malaise deepened, per capita income continued to decline steadily into the 1980s (Brown, 1984). Indices of real average earnings (1970 = 100) registered a substantial drop in the real minimum wage from ¢150 in 1974 to ¢19 in 1984 (Figure 16.2).

Figure 16.2: Trends in Real Earnings 1970–86 (1970 = 100)

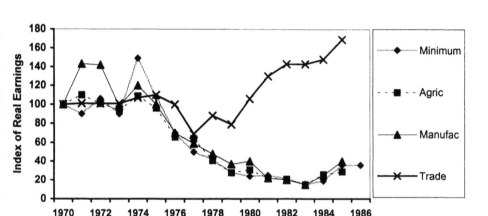

Source: Republic of Ghana and UNICEF (1990).

The deprivation suffered by vulnerable groups in the early 1980s was outlined in a UNICEF study published in 1986.[5] This revealed a picture of unremitting deterioration in key social indicators arising from increasing poverty, inadequate nutrition and ineffective social services between the late 1970s and early 1980s. To illustrate, the study estimated that the proportion of the population below an absolute poverty line determined by UNICEF rose from around 60/65% to 65/75% in rural areas between the late 1970s and early 1980s. In urban areas, the increase was from 30/35% to 45/50%. Another finding was that average calorie availability as a percentage of requirements fell from 97% in 1970 to 88% in the late 1970s, and then to only 68% in the early 1980s. The estimated infant mortality rate rose from 86 per 1000 live births in the late 1970s to 107/120 per 1000 live births in the early 1980s. The study also showed that the deprivation was significantly worse for people who lived in those parts of the country that had historically been substantially below the national average for social indicators. These areas, which are characterized by structural and endemic poverty, difficult environmental conditions, and poor social infrastructure and services, are mainly in the Northern regions which fall within Ghana's savannah zone.

UNICEF's documentation of Ghana's social crisis coincided with a number of significant domestic and global developments. Domestically, Ghanaian policy-makers, having successfully tackled the immediate economic tasks of stabilization and restoration of growth, became increasingly sensitive to the social dimensions of adjustment. As a consequence, and also in response to the problems that had been identified by the UNICEF study, a process was initiated in

---

[5] *Adjustment Policies and Programmes to Protect Children and other Vulnerable Groups,* Accra: UNICEF-Ghana, 1986.

July 1986 to address directly the hardships that were being experienced by the poor and vulnerable. Particularly notable in this process was the formulation in November 1987 of the Programme of Actions to Mitigate the Social Costs of Adjustment (PAMSCAD).[6]

One of the difficulties with the UNICEF study was its failure (explicitly acknowledged in the volume) to distinguish the effects of the shocks (in the case of Ghana, both external, the terms of trade shock, and internal, the 1983 drought) from the adjustment policies which followed. Although the absence of time series household data prevent any precise assessment of poverty trends before and after 1983 (the start of the ERP), Sarris (1993) was able to assess the welfare effects of economic changes before and after the implementation of the ERP. He combined information about the structure of household incomes and expenditures (from the first round of the GLSS in 1987/8) with time series data on prices and wages (which determine real household incomes) in a model of household welfare. He showed that all groups suffered a serious loss in economic welfare between 1977/8 and 1983/4, with the urban poor suffering the largest losses. But between 1983/4 and 1987/8, all groups recovered the previous losses (see Chapter 10). The urban non-poor benefit the most from the post-adjustment price and wage trends, and the urban poor benefit the least. All rural groups are estimated to be better off in 1987/8 than they were in 1977/8.[7]

The reasons for these improvements in economic welfare, especially among rural groups, are well understood. The relative price changes which occurred during 1983–7 had profound effects on the rural economy. They induced a remarkable growth in real exports. Merchandise exports grew in real terms by 22% per annum between 1983 and 1986. Cocoa output expanded during this period. Net payments to cocoa farmers increased from 5 billion cedis in 1983/4 (in constant 1985 prices) to over 13 billion cedis in 1987/8 (Alderman, 1994). This was an immediate and dramatic result of the exchange rate adjustment. And other rural sectors, such as logging and mining, also benefited from the exchange rate policy. Log exports grew in real terms by over 42% per annum between 1983 and 1986. Overall, the share of exports in GDP rose from just 2% in 1983 to 16% in 1986 (World Bank, 1995a). The shift in price incentives brought about by the real exchange rate depreciation prior to 1987, therefore, led to a strong export response from the rural sector, inducing a recovery in rural output and incomes.

4.   Characteristics of Consumption Poverty 1992

There are two reasons why we have distinguished the period 1987–94 from 1983–7. First, there is evidence that the adjustment programme entered a new phase, with the massive depreciation in the real exchange rate having been completed, and a new set of macroeconomic problems being presented by a sharp increase in net transfers from abroad (Younger, 1992). Second, the data from 1987 are significantly better, though, as we shall show, not without their problems. This section first describes the characteristics of poverty based on the results of the 1991/92 GLSS.

What do the data say about the prevalence and incidence of poverty in Ghana in recent years? In this section we focus on an economic measure of wellbeing and poverty. Our measure of wellbeing (or welfare) is the consumption of the household. The GLSS data include detailed measurement of household expenditure, including the consumption of own production (subsistence consumption). Details of how the raw data were combined to obtain meaningful expenditure aggregates are found in Round and McKay (1992). Household expenditure was deflated by a regional price index to take into account geographical price differences (based on the Paasche price index),[8] and was expressed in per capita terms. The welfare measure used here as the basis

---

[6] See Government of Ghana (1987) for details of this programme and World Bank *et al.* (1990) for an evaluation of its results.

[7] However, declines between 1987/8 and 1989/90 take welfare levels back to their 1977/8 levels.

[8] Because of high inflation, price variations within the year are also taken into account. The price index used to deflate household consumption took prices in Accra in May 1992 as the base.

of poverty analysis is therefore *per capita total real household expenditure.*

To identify the poor, two poverty lines are defined and applied to the distribution of real per capita household expenditure. An *upper poverty line* is set at two-thirds of 1988 mean per capita household expenditure, and a *lower line* at one-half of the 1988 mean. Expressed in May 1992 Accra prices, these lines are (respectively) ¢132,230 and ¢107,188 per person per annum. World Bank (1995b) estimated that these lines corresponded to consumption of 2,100 and 1,723 calories of food per person per day.

Having identified who is poor in Ghana based on our welfare measure (real expenditure per capita) and our poverty lines, we use two poverty indices to give an aggregate measure of poverty: the headcount ratio and the poverty-gap ratio.[9] The former, which is simply the proportion of the population that is poor, indicates the *incidence* of poverty. The latter index reflects both the incidence and the *depth* of poverty.[10] Over 31% of Ghanaians were indicated to be below the upper poverty line in 1992, and just under 15% were reported below the lower poverty line (GSS, 1995a). Table 16.1 gives both poverty indices (headcount and poverty-gap) for five geographical localities (two urban and three rural) and seven socio-economic groups based on the upper line.[11] In addition to the poverty index itself, the table gives the contribution of each group

Table 16.1   Poverty Indices by Area and Socioeconomic Group 1992
              (upper poverty line)

	Headcount ratio:		Poverty-gap ratio	
	Index	Contribution	Index	Contribution
Accra	23.0	6.0	5.6	5.7
Other urban	27.7	22.0	7.1	22.0
Rural Coastal	28.6	12.9	6.8	11.2
Rural Forest	33.0	31.0	8.3	30.4
Rural Savannah	38.3	28.1	10.5	30.3
Public employees	21.5	9.3	5.4	9.1
Private formal employee	15.7	2.0	4.9	2.4
Private informal employee	27.7	2.7	6.1	2.3
Export crop farmer	37.4	7.5	10.1	7.9
Food crop farmer	39.0	54.4	10.5	56.7
Non-farm self-employed	25.7	22.7	6.0	20.5
Inactive	19.6	1.3	4.1	1.1
Ghana	**31.4**	**100**	**8.1**	**100**

Source: World Bank, 1995b.

---

[9] These indices can be derived from the P_α class of poverty indices (Foster, Greer and Thorbecke, 1984), which measure different dimensions of poverty depending on the value of α selected. For $\alpha=0$, P_α becomes the headcount index. With $\alpha=1$, the measure becomes the poverty-gap index. Details of these measures are provided in Ravallion (1992).

[10] If there are q poor people in a population of n, the headcount is simply $H=q/n$. The poverty-gap index is given by $H \times I$, where I is the income-gap ratio defined as $(z-\mu_p)/z$, z being the poverty line and μ_p being the mean expenditure of the poor. The poverty-gap ratio therefore measures both the incidence (H) and the depth of poverty (I).

[11] The patterns for the lower poverty line are similar and are not reported here (see GSS, 1995a).

to total poverty. Thus, for example, the first column of the table indicates that 27.7% of the urban population outside Accra was poor in 1992. The second column reports that 22% of poor Ghanaians lived in these urban areas.

All groups in Ghana experience some poverty. But there are noticeable variations. Poverty is greatest in Rural Savannah and Rural Forest. These two areas account for 60% of total poverty (measured either by the headcount or poverty-gap ratios, and taking the upper or lower poverty line — see GSS, 1995a). The poorest area is clearly Rural Savannah, but given the weight of numbers, Rural Forest contributes the most to total poverty. And while 23% of the Accra population is poor, it contributed only 6% to overall poverty.

A similar picture emerges from the socio-economic groupings; all appear to experience poverty, but some more than others. The least affected are formal-sector wage employees (especially those in the private sector). Poverty is clearly a major problem for farmers (both food-crop and export-crop farmers), and for the non-farm self-employed and those employed in the informal sector. Poverty among food-crop farmers represents more than half of total poverty in the country. Because the contribution to total poverty is greater for the poverty-gap index, the data suggest that the depth of poverty is much greater among this group. By the same token, the lower contribution of the non-farm self-employed to the poverty-gap index indicates shallower poverty.

In Rural Savannah, farmers are consistently the poorest group (GSS, 1995a). However, even among the non-farming groups in the area, poverty tends to be greater than for similar groups in other areas. Thus the high levels of poverty in Rural Savannah are not simply a result of the concentration of food-crop farming in the area, but of poor living standards among non-farming groups as well. In a sense, whole communities are poor, in contrast to poverty in urban areas. This characterization was also emphasized by Norton *et al.* (1995) in their qualitative participatory assessment.

Demographic Characteristics of the Poor
Poor households tend to be larger than other households. They comprised, on average, 6.3 members in 1992, compared with a mean of just 3.6 for the non-poor (GSS, 1995a). This finding is a common feature when the underlying welfare measure is *per capita* household expenditure, because the measure does not reflect certain characteristics of households. If, for example, the needs of children are not the same as those of adults, or if there are significant economies of scale in household consumption, a different welfare indicator (for example based on adult equivalence) should be used. This would change the ranking of households, and it is possible that poor households may not be larger than the non-poor (Lanjouw and Ravallion, 1995). If children's consumption needs are lower, using per capita expenditure as the welfare indicator may falsely classify households as poor simply because they contain large numbers of children. Age dependency, resulting particularly from the presence of children in the household, is indeed more marked among the poor than the non-poor (GSS, 1995a). Just under 60% of poor household members were either below the age of 15 or above 65 in 1992. The corresponding share for the non-poor was 44% (GSS, 1995a).

Are the observed patterns of poverty in 1992 sensitive to the choice of *per capita* real expenditure as the welfare measure? Coulombe and McKay (1995) find that using total household real expenditures per adult equivalent as the welfare indicator (based on either Deaton and Muellbauer, 1986, or McClements, 1978) does affect patterns of poverty in Ghana. With the alternative welfare indicator, the incidence and depth of poverty in Rural Coastal are significantly reduced — and with the Deaton and Muellbauer weights, the area emerges with the same poverty indices as Accra (headcounts of 23%). While Rural Savannah retains its ranking as the poorest area in the country (with a headcount of 35%), there is little to choose between other urban areas and Rural Forest (25% and 26% respectively). No changes in geographical rank ordering result from the use of McClements' weights.

The children of poor Ghanaian households are less likely to be currently attending school than their non-poor counterparts, though the area of residence has a more important impact than poverty *per se*. The net primary enrolment rates for the *non-poor* in Savannah — at 59% for boys and 46% for girls — are markedly lower than those of the *poor* in Accra (87% and 78%, respectively). Although poverty clearly reduces the likelihood of school attendance, area of residence appears to be as important, if not more so. Similar considerations apply to secondary enrolments. The net secondary enrolment rate is 56% for the male children of poor Accra residents, but it is only 28% for boys in non-poor Rural Savannah households (corresponding figures for girls are 31% and 22% respectively). GLSS data confirm a marked *gender* bias in school enrolments, especially at the secondary level. This appears to be aggravated by poverty — the gender differentials in enrolment rates being more marked in poor households (GSS, 1995a).

What of the health status of the poor? Despite progress made in health outcomes, the health status of Ghanaians remains a cause for concern. The infant mortality rate is about 66 per thousand and under-5 child mortality is 119 per thousand (World Bank, 1995b). Both are unacceptably high. 26% of children under age three are stunted and 11% are wasted. 45% of one-year-old children are not immunized. According to GLSS3 (which relies on self-reporting) about 22% of the population reported ill during a two-week reference period. As with most surveys relying on self-reporting of illness, the poor are less inclined to report illness in the household (mainly because they perceive many illnesses as a normal condition of life). The proportions reported ill or injured are higher for the richer quintiles. In 1992, 16% of those in the poorest quintile (20% of the population) reported being ill during the two-week reference period, compared with 29% in the richest quintile. Surveys involving the self-reporting of illness tend to underestimate the incidence of illness — especially in lower-income households.

How do the poor in Ghana respond to an injury or illness? The GLSS obtained information on the health care responses of household members (Figure 16.3). Only 42% of the poorest quintile sought care when ill or injured, compared with 57% for the top quintile. Very few were reported to seek care from private traditional practitioners. Poorer households were less inclined to seek modern care, both private and public, compared with the better-off. Richer households have a higher propensity to use *both* privately and publicly funded health facilities. The number of visits to publicly-funded health facilities in the richest quintile far exceeded that in the poorest quintile. This has important implications for the incidence of public spending on health. Demery *et al.,* (1995) estimate that the poorest 20% of the population gains just 12% of government spending on health (see Table 16.4).

Figure 16.3: Reported Illness and Response by Quintile 1992

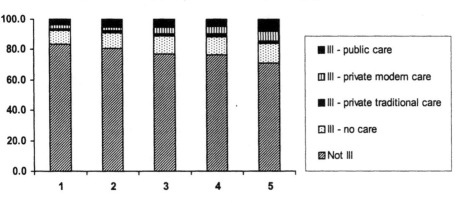

Note: Quintile 1 — poorest   Quintile 5 — richest
Source: GLSS3

An important feature of poverty in Ghana is the *gender* dimension. Unfortunately, with the GLSS data, it is not possible to distinguish between the poverty of men and women, since expenditures are defined only at the household level.[12] World Bank (1995b) found that female-headed households accounted for just over one-third of total poverty in 1992 (using both headcount and poverty-gap indices). Poverty incidence among female-headed households was 28% in 1992 (compared with 33% for male-headed households). Female-headed households do not appear to be as poor as their male counterparts. There are two problems with this conclusion. First, these GLSS data do not distinguish between *de jure* and *de facto* headship. Households reporting a female head but in receipt of significant remittance income are unlikely to be *de jure* female-headed, with the absent spouse providing for the needs of household members. Over 14% of the income gained by female-headed households was remittance receipts in 1992, compared with just 3% in male-headed households (World Bank, 1995b).

Secondly, Bhushan and Chao (1996) have shown that such comparisons are misleading, since they do not take into account household size. Female-headed households tend to be much smaller than male-headed households, and given the use of per capita expenditure as the welfare measure, this results in lower poverty incidence among them. Once household size is controlled for, female headship implies *higher* poverty. Female-headed households tend to exhibit higher poverty than households of similar size headed by males. These conclusions are more consistent with the qualitative evidence of Norton *et al.* (1995) which suggested that female headship was more closely linked to poverty, especially in the North of the country, and when it is combined with widowhood, old-age and the absence of adult children.

Economic Characteristics of the Poor

Using the income aggregates of GLSS3, the sources of income of poor and non-poor households can be identified. These can provide some indication of the main economic activities of the poor. Figure 16.4 contrasts the income patterns of poor and non-poor Ghanaian households in 1992. Typically, poor households derived the bulk of their income (49%) from agricultural activities. Combined with non-farm self-employment, this accounts for over 80% of income. Although these sources were important for the non-poor, they also derived about a fifth of their income from wage labour. Just under 75% of economically active members of poor households are engaged in self-employment — 80% of whom are employed in agriculture (GSS, 1995b). Corresponding figures for the non-poor are 65% and 67% respectively. An important feature of the agricultural sector in Ghana is the contribution of women farmers. In Rural Coastal and Rural Forest women are responsible for about 40% of agricultural activities — operating a farm plot or keeping livestock (GSS, 1995b), and they completely dominate agricultural processing activities.

Evidence from a qualitative assessment

Do the results of this quantitative exercise agree with other approaches, such as the participatory poverty assessment carried out by Norton *et al.* (1995)?[13] The fieldwork for their study was conducted in April/May 1994 — some time after the period covered by the GLSS3 survey (October 1991/September 1992). Nevertheless, the quantitative and qualitative perspectives generally paint a similar picture of poverty in Ghana. Both agree that poverty is greatest in the rural North. While not surprising, this message rings out clearly from both studies. The GLSS results also support the view that poverty in Rural Savannah affects communities as a whole (it was not only food-subsistence farmers who were poor in the area). They show that the non-poor in the Savannah are worse-off than many poor in Accra (for example, in terms of school enrolments

---

[12] Individuals are assigned the per capita expenditure of the household to which they belong.
[13] See also Chapter 15 for detailed discussion of their fieldwork results.

Figure 16.4: Income Sources of Poor and Non-poor Households 1992

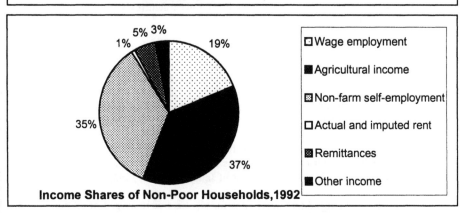

Source: World Bank, 1995.

and water supply). The inadequacy of public services in the rural areas and to poor communities is a major message of both the quantitative and qualitative assessments.

The priority placed by the poor on water supply (especially in the North of Ghana), reported by Norton *et al.* (1995), is very much reflected in survey findings. According to the GLSS3, rural household members spend on average 37 minutes per day fetching water. In Rural Savannah, members devote 48 minutes each day to this task. This contrasts with just 28 minutes in Rural Coastal and 13 minutes in Accra (GSS, 1995b). The GLSS data also confirm the participatory finding that this task is carried out mainly by girls and women. Females in the Savannah spend, on average, 70 minutes per person per day collecting water (compared with just 25 minutes for males). And most of the males assigned to this task are less than 14 years of age. There can be little doubt as to why the poor in the Northern areas considered improved water supply to be a priority for enhancing their quality of life.

5.   Trends in poverty 1987–94

The structural adjustment policies of the 1980s generated considerable interest and debate, in part because of the controversy that surrounded their perceived social impact. The debate revolved around the issue of whether or not structural adjustment policies exacerbated or enhanced the circumstances of the poor and vulnerable in Ghana. The evidence is inconclusive (see also Chapter 10). First, data limitations constrain any robust empirical assessment. Even though three rounds of the GLSS were conducted, the initial impact of the ERP pre-dated the first of these surveys. Secondly, the adjustment itself has been uneven and incomplete. The real exchange rate depreciation tended to level off after 1987, and the recurrence of persistent and high inflation reflects continued macroeconomic instability (manifested also in the continuing nominal depreciation of the cedi). Thirdly, it is difficult to disentangle the effects of macro policies from other events occurring at the same time (for example, the continued deterioration in the terms of trade). For these reasons our assessment of welfare trends during the 1987–95 period is not meant to address the adjustment-poverty debate. Rather, it is intended simply to review the evidence on welfare trends during this period.

A number of recent studies (GSS, 1995a; Coulombe and McKay, 1995; World Bank, 1995a, 1995b) have reported poverty estimates from the three GLSS rounds, which suggest a sharp fall in poverty during 1988–92 (Table 16.2). Although some attention was paid to changes in the questionnaire design between GLSS1 and 2, on the one hand, and GLSS3, on the other, these findings remain open to criticism that the data are not sufficiently consistent to give trends in poverty confidently. Recently, Demery and Mehra (1997) have attempted to correct remaining inconsistencies between the three GLSS rounds, and generated revised estimates of poverty during the period. They adopted the following procedures:

- First, they repeated the previous practice (in Coulombe and McKay, 1995) of correcting estimates of frequently occurring food expenditures from GLSS1 and 2 to compensate for the higher recall errors in these estimates compared with GLSS3.[14]

- Secondly, they applied the same recall correction factor to home-produced food consumption estimates in the GLSS1/2 data.

- Thirdly, the estimate of home-produced food consumption from GLSS1/2 was adjusted upwards to take account of a possible bias in respondent reports of number of months consumed in the year (based on the results of Jones and Xiao, 1995)

- Fourthly, the food expenditure aggregates for all years were purged of all non-common elements.

- Headcount indices in each year were computed on the basis of a 'traditional' poverty line (Z), *estimated separately for each year*, and defined as the food poverty line (z) plus the non-food component. The latter was defined as the non-food expenditure of households whose food consumption was just equal to z. This was derived using a cross-section linear regression of non-food expenditure on food expenditure (see Demery and Mehra, 1997 for details).

The results of this exercise are reported in Table 16.2. The first three columns show for each of five regions the previously reported (in World Bank, 1995b and GSS, 1995a) poverty headcount indices for 1988 (GLSS1), 1989 (GLSS2) and 1992 (GLSS3). These showed an initial increase in poverty (from 36.9% to 41.8% for the country as a whole), followed by a sharp decline (to just 31.4%). The decline is sharp enough to imply a fall in headcount poverty over the whole period (i.e. from 1988 to 1992), compensating for the increase in 1988–9. According to these estimates, poverty fell over 10 percentage points between 1989 and 1992. Thus both the 1988-92 and 1989–92 comparisons suggest a downward trend in consumption poverty in the late 1980s and early 1990s.

---

[14] These corrections were based on the empirical findings of Scott and Amenuvegbe, 1990.

Table 16.2   Poverty Headcount Ratios Under Alternative Data Adjustments

Region	Previous Estimates[a]			Revised Estimates[b]		
	1988	1989	1992	1988	1989	1992
Accra	0.085	0.219	0.230	0.055	0.136	0.202
Other Urban	0.334	0.351	0.277	0.230	0.244	0.210
Rural Coastal	0.377	0.446	0.286	0.268	0.329	0.223
Rural Forest	0.381	0.419	0.330	0.215	0.281	0.233
Rural Savannah	0.494	0.548	0.383	0.429	0.516	0.450
All Ghana	**0.369**	**0.418**	**0.314**	**0.261**	**0.319**	**0.274**

Notes: [a] Previous estimates incorporate adjustments only for recall error in frequent food expenditures, 1988, 1989.
   [b] Estimates based on adjustments for recall error in food expenditures and home-produced food consumption; food aggregate based on common items only; adjustment for number of months home consumption; year-specific non-food component of the traditional poverty line (see text).
Source: World Bank (1995b); Demery and Mehra, 1995.

The second panel of columns reports the revised headcount ratios, based on the above procedures.[15] Although we report both GLSS1 and GLSS2 estimates based on year-specific traditional poverty lines, this procedure was needed to make comparisons of each year's estimate with that of 1992. Comparisons between GLSS1 and GLSS2 could be made without the various adjustments we have made, since these surveys are fully comparable. Time trends between 1988 and 1989 are best judged by the original estimates, which were based on a single poverty line. Two observations are in order. First, the fall in the headcount index between 1989 and 1992 is confirmed in the revised estimates, though the extent of the decline is significantly reduced. The headcount index is estimated to have fallen by 3.5 percentage points compared with the 10.4 percentage points reported previously. This is statistically significant. The pattern of change across the regions in the revised estimates is similar to the pattern originally reported. First, poverty in Accra has risen between 1989 and 1992. In all other regions poverty is shown to decline between 1989 and 1992 (though only marginally in non-Accra urban areas). Interestingly, the revised estimates indicate a much less pronounced fall in poverty in Rural Savannah, where the headcount index is now shown to decline by just 6.6 percentage points (compared with the previously reported 16.5 percentage points).

However, the revised data show no significant change in headcount poverty between 1988 and 1992 — if anything poverty increased marginally, but this is not statistically significant at the 5% level. According to the revised estimates, poverty is indicated to have increased in all areas between 1988 and 1992, except Rural Coastal and urban areas other than Accra.

What has happened to poverty since 1992? There is no hard evidence readily available to answer this question, but the results of the Norton *et al.* (1995) study suggest that there has not been any significant improvement in the quality of the lives of the rural poor. World Bank (1995b: 49) estimated the likely change in the headcount ratio based on the national accounts data on per capita real private consumption and assuming that the distribution of expenditures remain unchanged from 1992 (i.e. all households experience the same growth in per capita consumption).

---

[15] The headcounts using the revised data sets are lower than the previous estimates, because of the downward adjustment in both the welfare indicator (notably the food aggregate) and the poverty line. This has no significance in itself. The purpose of the revised estimates is to yield consistent over-time poverty estimates.

The exercise suggests a reduction in headcount poverty by just one percentage point between 1992 and 1994, and an increase in the absolute numbers in poverty.

Trends in Social Indicators 1988–93

Income and consumption are not the only measures of welfare that we can use to trace poverty trends in Ghana. The nutrition and health status of the population (and other direct measures of wellbeing) are as significant as money metric measures, if not more so. What are the trends in such indicators in the 1980s and early 1990s?

First, as background we note what happened to government spending on health and education during these years of economic reform and adjustment. Unlike many other countries, adjustment re-established the revenue base in Ghana, replenished the available funds for government programmes, and restored key government services on health and education during the first phase of the adjustment programme (Alderman, 1994). The *public expenditure ratio* (defined as government expenditure and lending minus repayments as a percentage of GDP) on key social services, specifically health and education, remained reasonably stable before and during structural adjustment (Table 16.3). The annual average for this ratio in 1975-84 was 15% and 14% from 1985–91.[16] The share of social sector spending in total government spending was not, however, maintained in the 1990s due to crowding out of social spending by public sector interest payments (see Chapters 6 and 10).

Table 16.3   Government Social Spending 1975–91

	Annual Average	
	1975–84	1985–91
Public expenditure ratio (%)	15.0	14.0
Education & Health allocation ratio (%)		
Total	26.2	32.6
Education	19.0	23.5
Health	7.2	9.1
Real per capita spending (constant 1987 US$)		
Education	12.2	11.9
Health	4.7	4.6

Source: World Bank, 1996: 185, 203–6.

However, the extent to which the poor benefited from this spending was limited. Estimates of the benefit incidence of social spending in Ghana (World Bank, 1995a) reveal that the poorest 20% of the population gained only 11% of government health spending and only 16% of education spending in 1992 (Table 16.4). Moreover, there was little evidence of any improvement in the targeting of social spending to the poor — the shares to the bottom quintile in 1992 being very close to those in 1989.

Changes in the public provision of health and education services, while important in themselves, tell us nothing about what happened to social outcomes in Ghana during this period. The health, nutrition and education status of the population depend not only on access to public

---

[16] It should be noted, however, that these ratios were the lowest in Africa and about half the African average during the period (World Bank, 1996: 185).

services, but on the availability of private services, and a range of factors at the household level (household income, food consumption, for example). Two rounds (in 1988 and 1993) of the Demographic and Health Survey (DHS) provide the opportunity to assess whether the improvements in economic welfare (implied in the GLSS data) are confirmed by more direct measures of wellbeing.

Table 16.4   Benefit Incidence of Government Social Spending (%)

	Education		Health	
	1989	1992	1989	1992
Poorest 20% of population	17	16	12	11
Richest 20% of population	24	21	31	34
Urban (35% of population)	41	42	42	49
Rural (65% of the population)	59	58	58	51
Males (48.5% of the population)	59	58	45	44
Females (51.5% of the population)	41	42	55	56

Source: World Bank, 1995a: 36–44.

The data of Table 16.5 generally confirm an improvement in social welfare during 1988–93. All the indicators except one (the prevalence of wasting) appear to have improved. The infant mortality rate, an important indicator not only of health status but also of socio-economic status, fell by 14%, and child mortality by 32%. These are considerable improvements over such a relatively short time-span. There were also improvements in education enrolments. Although the trends are favourable, these gains should not lead to complacency. Some of these indicators compare unfavourably with other countries in the region.

Table 16.5   Selected Social Indicators 1988–93

	1988	1993
Health		
Infant mortality (per 1000 births	77	66
Under-five mortality rate (")	155	119
Child mortality (")	84	57
% children immunized	31	55
Nutritional status:		
Stunted (%)	31	26
Wasted	8	11
Other:		
Total fertility rate	6.4	5.5
Use of modern contraception (%[a]	18.3	18.9
Gross primary enrolment rate (%)[a]	79	88
Gross secondary enrolment rate (%)[a]	37	39

Note: [a] 1989 and 1992
Sources: Demographic and Health Surveys, 1988 and 1993; GLSS1 and GLSS2

6. Conclusion

According to the World Bank's classification, Ghana is ranked among the world's low-income countries: annual GDP per capita is approximately US$450. Real per capita income during the early to mid-1990s remained below the levels achieved in the 1960s and 1970s despite the gains achieved during the ERP period. For much of the past decade poverty reduction has been a major preoccupation of the government as well as its donors. The challenge is considerable and compounded by a high rate of population growth, among other problems. On the one hand, it is evident that for an appreciable proportion of the population the deterioration in the quality of life that was experienced from the latter half of the 1970s to the early 1980s was slowed, if not reversed, during the late 1980s and early 1990s. But with over 30% of the population below the poverty line in 1992, coupled with clear signs of faltering in social and economic progress since 1992, the achievement of an appreciable reduction of poverty remains a challenge of mighty proportions.

The areas in which policy actions are required for poverty reduction in Ghana are broadly defined by the incidence, characteristics and causes of poverty. Current efforts must be intensified and executed within a policy framework that takes the following into account:

- First, a sustainable reduction in poverty in Ghana cannot be achieved without increased economic growth. Consider the number of years it would take to reduce the poverty headcount ratio in Ghana to 10% (at which point it could be assumed that group- and region-specific interventions, as opposed to overall growth, would be needed to reduce poverty further).[17] If per capita incomes grow at 3% per annum, it would take Ghana 12 years to achieve the target. But if per capita growth were to slow to just 1% per annum, it would take over 34 years for poverty to fall to 10%. And an acceleration to 5% would mean that the target could be achieved in just 7 years. The future poverty scenario, therefore, depends critically on the rates of economic growth that are achieved (World Bank, 1995b).

- But growth must also be broad-based. This will require:

  Controlling the macro balances, particularly inflation which is a regressive form of implicit taxation; significantly increasing opportunities for gainful employment; increasing productivity, especially in agriculture and the urban self-employed sectors; and improving access to credit, economic services and markets.

  Reducing the marked regional and rural-urban disparities that currently exist in the distribution of economic and social infrastructure and public investment.

  Improving the circumstances of poor women and children through the eradication of malnutrition and the establishment of household food security; improving the health and educational status of the poor through enhanced access to social services; and reducing the rate of growth of the population.

---

[17] These estimates are based on a mean-income (arc) elasticity of the headcount ratio of −1.78. The elasticity reflects changes in both the mean and distribution of income.

References

Alderman, Harold (1994) 'Ghana: Adjustment's Star Pupil?' in David E. Sahn (ed.) *Adjusting to Policy Failure in African Economies.* Ithaca, NY: Cornell University Press.

Bhushan, Indu and Chao, Shiyan (1996) 'Poverty Reduction Among Female-Headed Households in Ghana: Is it Real?' Washington, DC: World Bank (mimeo).

Brown, C. K. (1984) *Social Structure and Poverty in Selected Rural Communities in Ghana.* ISSER Technical Publications No. 54. ISSER, University of Ghana, Legon.

Coulombe, Harold and McKay, Andrew (1995) *An Assessment of Trends in Poverty in Ghana, 1988-92.* PSP Discussion Paper No. 81. Washington, DC: World Bank, Poverty and Social Policy Department (November).

Deaton, Angus and Muellbauer, John (1980) *Economics of Consumer Behaviour.* Cambridge: Cambridge University Press.

Demery, L., Chao, S., Bernier, R. and Mehra, K. (1995) *The Incidence of Social Spending in Ghana.* Poverty and Social Policy Discussion Paper No. 82. Washington, DC: World Bank (November).

Demery, Lionel and Mehra, Kalpana (1997) 'Measuring Poverty Over Time: Dealing With Uncooperative Data in Ghana'. Washington, DC: World Bank, Poverty, Gender and Public Management Department, mimeo (February).

Ewusi, K. (1971) *The Distribution of Monetary Incomes in Ghana.* ISSER Technical Publications Series No. 14. ISSER, University of Ghana, Legon.

Foster, J. E., Greer, J. and Thorbecke, E. (1984) 'A Class of Decomposable Poverty Measures', *Econometrica,* Vol. 53: 173–7.

Ghana Statistical Service (1995a) *The Pattern of Poverty in Ghana: 1988-92.* Accra: GSS (November).

Ghana Statistical Service (1995b) *Ghana Living Standards Survey: Report on the Third Round (GLSS3).* Accra, (March).

Ghana Statistical Service (1995c) *Analysis of Demographic Data* (Vol. 2). Accra.

Ghana Statistical Service (1995d) *Analysis of Demographic Data* (Vol. 1). Accra.

Ghana Statistical Service (1989) *Ghana Living Standards Survey: First Year Report (September 1987–August 1988).* Accra.

Government of Ghana (1987) *Programme of Actions to Mitigate the Social Costs of Adjustment.* Accra (November).

Jones, Christine and Xiao, Ye (1995) *Accounting for the Reduction in Rural Poverty in Ghana, 1988–92.* PSP Discussion Paper No. 84. Washington, DC: World Bank, Poverty and Social Policy Department, (November).

Lanjouw, Peter and Ravallion, Martin (1994) 'Aggregation Consistent Poverty Comparisons: Theory and Illustrations'. Washington, DC: World Bank, Policy Research Department, (Unprocessed mimeo) 1 June.

McClements, Leslie D. (1978) *The Economics of Social Security.* London: Heinemann.

Mikkelsen, B. (1995) *Methods for Development Work and Research: A Guide for Practitioners.* London: Sage Publications.

Norton, Andy, Korboe, David, Bortei-Doku, Aryeetey, Ellen and Dogbe D. K. Tony (1995) *Poverty Assessment in Ghana using Qualitative and Participatory Research Methods.* PSP Discussion Paper No. 83. Washington, DC: World Bank, Poverty and Social Policy Department (November).

Ravallion, Martin (1992) *Poverty Comparisons: A Guide to Concepts and Methods.* Living Standards Measurement Study Working Paper No. 88. Washington, DC: World Bank.

Republic of Ghana (1996) 'Policy Focus on Poverty Reduction'. Accra: National Development Planning Commission (mimeo).

Republic of Ghana (1995) *Ghana Vision 2020: The First Step (1996-2000).* Accra: National Development Planning Commission.

Republic of Ghana and UNICEF (1990) *Children and Women of Ghana: A Situation Analysis.* Accra.

Round, Jeffrey and McKay, Andrew (1992) 'Income Expenditure Aggregates', Chapter 7 in *The Social Dimensions of Adjustment Integrated Survey.* SDA Working Paper No. 14. Washington, DC: World Bank, Surveys and Statistics (May).

Sarris, Alexander H. (1993) 'Household Welfare During Crisis and Adjustment in Ghana', *Journal of African Economies,* Vol. 2, No. 2: 195–237.

Scott, Christopher and Amenuvegbe, Ben (1990) *Effect of Recall Duration on Reporting of Household Expenditures: An Empirical Study in Ghana.* Social Dimensions of Adjustment Working Paper No. 6. Washington, DC: World Bank.

World Bank (1996) *African Development Indicators 1996.* Washington, DC: World Bank.

World Bank (1995a) *Ghana: Growth, Private Sector, and Poverty Reduction (A Country Economic Memorandum)*. Washington, DC: World Bank.

World Bank (1995b) *Ghana: Poverty Past, Present and Future*. Report No. 14504-GH. Washington, DC: World Bank, West Central Africa Department.

World Bank (1994) *Adjustment in Africa: Reforms, Results and the Road Ahead*, Washington, DC: World Bank.

World Bank (1990) *World Development Report 1990*. Washington, DC: World Bank.

World Bank *et al.* (1990) 'Report of the Donor Review Mission on PAMSCAD'. Accra (August).

Younger, Stephen (1992) 'Aid and the Dutch Disease: Macroeconomic Management when Everybody Loves You', *World Development*, Vol. 20, No. 11: 1587–97.

17 The Participation of Women in the Ghanaian Economy

ELLEN BORTEI-DOKU ARYEETEY

1. Introduction

Apart from equity concerns, the economic empowerment of women has been shown to bring direct welfare benefits for the family and national economic development. At the minimum, women's economic progress shifts labour from the subsistence economy to market production, which promotes growth and incomes (Steel and Campbell, 1982). Expenditure studies in various parts of Ghana have shown that women consistently spend more of their income directly on children and other household supplies, while men tend to concentrate more on capital investments and their own personal needs (see Norton *et al.*, 1995).

Ghanaian women have traditionally occupied a key position alongside men in the production of goods and services for subsistence and for the market, but as happens in most countries the actual contributions that women make to the economy have been underestimated or missing from the national accounts (Steel and Campbell, 1982; Beneria, 1981). A major source of the problem lies in the tendency to subsume home production activities under leisure, as is the convention in neoclassical labour economics (Steel and Campbell, 1982).

One of the main factors that has shaped the direction of women's economic activities in Ghana has been the male-biased allocation of traditional entitlements and modern assets, a relic of neo-patriarchal ideologies of gender relations found in both patrilineal and matrilineal kinship systems in all parts of the country. The same cultural norms, however, embody windows of opportunity for women to acquire wealth, by granting them the right to own their self-acquired property.

In many respects the pattern of men's and women's roles and statuses in Ghanaian society has continued very much as it was in the past, retaining varying degrees of rigidity in a gender-segregated division of labour in non-market production for the home, as well as in market-based production and public office.

While they are subject to the same matrilineal and patrilineal prescriptions on gender roles and statuses, Ghanaian women are not a homogeneous group, not simply because of differences in ethnicity but also in educational background and occupational status. The educational level of parents appears to play a marked positive role in the advancement of women. Consistently women from backgrounds where both parents are educated have achieved higher educational and occupational status than those from less educated backgrounds. But despite these differences they share common constraints, namely, limited decision-making roles and authority, imposed by a traditional gender division of labour in the home, and the general tendency to promote men rather than women into decision-making and leadership positions.

Over the years local and international pressure for the increased participation of women in the economy and other affairs of the nation has led to greater efforts on the part of the state and non-governmental organizations to create more opportunities for girls and women. Nevertheless, despite at least twenty years of such attempts and the evidence of some progress, the gap between women and men in terms of their participation in both the traditional and the modern economy remains wide.

The main objective of this chapter is to examine the nature of women's participation in the economy since 1960, and the contributory factors in this process. It starts with a brief look at the effects of the colonial regime on women's production activities, followed by analysis of their role in the unpaid or non-market production within the household. The chapter generally focuses on women's labour force participation characteristics in the different sectors of the economy both formal and informal, and also discusses the attempts that have been made through policy instruments and the actions of various institutions and agencies to channel resources to, and promote more choices for, women in the economy. Attention is further given to the effects of the structural adjustment programme on women's production and to some extent their consumption behaviour. Questions are raised about the assumption that under the SAP so-called gender-neutral policies act to free the market for women to participate alongside men, in response to market incentives. It is suggested that there are strong structural constraints hampering women's freedom to respond to the economic signals. If the economic reforms are to have any remarkable outcomes for women, direct efforts will have to be made to initiate gender-sensitive institutional changes in both customary institutions and modern organizations.

Women's work is addressed here at three levels: domestic work, informal sector work and formal sector work. The analysis is biased towards agricultural and other informal sector women workers and tends to focus on agricultural households, though mention is made of the progress that has been made by urban and professional women, and the pitfalls they have encountered.

The data and other information have been assembled from various secondary sources, as well as the author's own fieldwork at different times on the participation of women in Ghanaian society. The various censuses taken in Ghana in 1960, 1970 and 1984, as well as reports from the Ghana Living Standard Survey and the *Quarterly Digest of Statistics* are some of the official sources that have been used.

Past literature on women's roles in the economy in Ghana has concentrated on agriculture and food processing and their trading activities (North *et al.*, 1975; Roncoli, 1985; Panuccio, 1989). More recently others have started to pay attention to the situation of women in modern formal sector occupations (Akuffo, 1996; Oppong, 1987; BRIDGE, 1994; *Greenhill Journal of Administration*, 1996).

It is useful to note that quite a few social scientists have tried to study patterns of female labour force participation in Ghana. In his (1981) study of Ghana, Steel sets out to counter the hypothesis that, in the early stages of development, industrialization tends to force a shrinkage of female employment in agriculture and non-farm production, as these areas become modernized through capital-intensive large-scale production. This hypothesis is proposed by Sinha (1967), and described as the U-shaped pattern of female labour force participation, the assumption being that industrialization invariably destroys small-scale artisan(al) industries which are usually in the hands of women. However, the trend shifts upwards as the modern sector grows and excess labour is absorbed, thus creating a demand for female labour. The model has been criticized as oversimplifield (Steel, 1981). In the case of Ghana Steel found that female participation rates improved rather than diminished as the industrial sector grew in the 1960s. Among his insightful observations was the fact that stagnant real incomes rather than expanded demand for labour acted as the big push for female labour force participation. Consequently, women continued to be drawn into informal sector cottage industries because many of them are based at home, and these industries were convenient to manage together with their domestic work.

The Colonial Period

As the Ghanaian economy became increasingly monetized under the colonial regime women followed men into market production, though their main focus was on subsistence production. To some extent the colonial regime opened the way for women to enter into the public arena of work outside the home. Yet it can also be argued that women's roles, with the concomitant resources and power base, may actually have been eroded to some extent by colonialism, through the superimposition of Victorian patriarchal values reinforcing women's subordination, on an already male-biased gender framework. An important outcome of this was the official indifference to women's contribution to the economy.

The outcome for women of the colonial political economy and the accompanying male wage labour market that developed in Ghana was to provide the impetus for the commoditization and expansion of their products and services. The increased production and other activities were absorbed by the emerging urban settlements and burgeoning export enclaves in cocoa, mining, and timber. Men had left the traditional farms to work for wages in these enclaves, and even where they had remained in farming, those who could do so shifted from food crop and other subsistence production to the cultivation of export crops. In either case a shortfall in food production resulted which was invariably picked up by women, who extended their workloads, with or without additional resources.

The Household and Women's Work

The household is the locus of work and production for the majority of women, whether they are engaged solely in non-market (social reproduction) work or involved in market-based production activities. Because of their multiple roles many women carry simultaneous workloads often described as the double workload. The official conception of the household in Ghana is moulded on Western nuclear family models typified by husband, wife and dependants. The main assumption in this pattern is that the husband is the head of household. In traditional contexts this gives him direct control over the labour and other resources of women, children and younger men. Implied in this model are unitary and egalitarian principles that supposedly unite the household, and emphasize the pooling of resources and their fair allocation by the head.

The available evidence, however, shows that the Ghanaian household can take a multiplicity of forms depending on ethnic patterns and socio-economic status. The sharpest contrasts are found in the Northern part of the country where co-residence of multiple male siblings and their conjugal units is common, compared with the coastal Ga of Greater Accra Region, where (separate) duo-local residence of spouses in the same sex kin compounds is the norm.

Female household headship (fhh) is generally high in Ghana, and one-third of Ghanaian households have either *de facto* or jural female heads due to migration, separation/divorce and widowhood or single parenting. The variations amount to 30% in rural areas and 36% in urban areas and 42% in Accra as reported in the Ghana Living Standards Survey (GSS, 1995a).

To put the significance of the household in women's economic activity into focus, two main aspects of household dynamics need to be mentioned: first, an understanding of the gender dynamics, and, second, a method for measuring and recording the value of unpaid work and production for reproduction purposes. In general, household organization has multiple implications for women. The character of the household defines the gender-based division of labour, as well as men's and women's differential access to productive assets. Household heads usually tend to control the major entitlements coming to the household, especially land and labour resources. Customary rules and norms exist to regulate the manner in which the head allocates these to other household members. In nearly all parts of Ghana the division of labour in the home has remained quite segregated, displaying a heavy reliance on female labour.

Oppong and Abu (1987) identified several roles played actively and often simultaneously by women in the household, including those of wives, mothers, workers, and housekeepers. Men also occupy multiple roles but within a much narrower band of activities. Invariably they confine themselves to periodic maintenance and repair work and general security, leaving the daily maintenance and caring tasks to women and children. Because of the low technology absorption, and because the distribution of utility services and infrastructure is below 50% coverage for safe water, electricity and gas, roads, health and communication facilities etc., women are under constant pressure for time leading to chronic time poverty. This is now recognized as one of the factors impacting on their opportunities for self-improvement, among other things.

To appreciate the contribution women's unpaid work makes to the nurturing of household members, women's lobbyists are putting pressure on governments to revise national accounting procedures to incorporate the value of unpaid services and production in the home. A few countries in the West (e.g. Canada) have already started to revise their data gathering strategies to respond to this challenge. The Ghana Statistical Service has taken preliminary steps to record domestic work as a means of estimating women's unsung contribution to production, by collecting time-use information on housekeeping work in GLSS 3. The exercise was biased, however, towards rural living conditions. Table 17.1 presents the findings on the collection of water, firewood and other housekeeping activities.

Table 17.1   Average Time Spent Per Day on Various
Housekeeping Activities, By Sex and Locality
(population aged 7+ years)
(minutes per day)

Activity	Urban		Rural		Country	
	M	F	M	F	M	F
Fetching wood	4	9	11	29	9	22
Fetching water	15	26	25	48	21	40
Other Housekeeping*	59	137	39	114	45	122
All Housekeeping	79	173	74	191	76	185

Note: *)Other housekeeping refers to cooking, cleaning, laundry, shopping
and child care.
Source: GSS, 1995: 41.

Regional data revealed consistently that women spent twice (or more) as much time on domestic work as men everywhere in the country. Even more serious, women in the Upper East and other parts of the North spend more time collecting firewood and fetching water than in other parts of the country, not surprisingly because of the drier conditions and the savannah ecology.

Contrary to the projected image of the unified household, the reality is more accurately one of co-operation and negotiation over resources which are controlled by different members of the household, apart from land and labour. In this arrangement men, women and working children are able to exercise some independence over their own resources. One of the powerful demonstrations of the semi-autonomous co-existence between men and women in the Ghanaian household is the separation of male and female income and expenditure streams, and the evidence of contractual relationships between men and women with respect to the transfer of resources from one party to the other. Being able to break out of the hold of the traditional household, however, requires that women are prepared to compete in the outside world. But socio-cultural inhibitions on their part or that of their parents can reduce the prospects for joining the competition.

2.   Social Antecedents to Women's Labour Force Participation

Education

Education is widely recognized as the gateway to modernity. But socio-cultural biases against women's occupational choices can limit their educational attainment. In several field studies parents suggested that they did not discriminate against girls' education, citing the benefits of a secure future as a reason to promote education for both boys and girls. Yet the evidence indicates quite strongly that boys are favoured compared with girls. A widely accepted possible explanation is that, given the general subordination of women's interests in favour of those of men, girls' needs for education and training are compromised under financial stress in favour of boys. Though the enrolment of girls has risen since 1960 the gender gap in enrolment is still wide.[1]

Over the years constraints which either hold females back from enrolment or prevent them from higher attainment, have been identified as financial stress and social-cultural constraints.[2] In this respect the educational reforms introduced in 1987, far from expanding enrolment for girls, may have exacerbated the gender gap by some of their cost-recovery measures. Socio-cultural handicaps would include factors such as early marriage, teenage pregnancy, and the high opportunity costs of girls' labour. However, school environmental factors have also been cited. The absence of female role models, teacher prejudices and sheer lack of infrastructure in boarding facilities tend to disadvantage girls, particularly after the primary school level.

The norms guiding subject selection in many educational institutions encourage segregation of the sexes, and launch boys and girls on more or less separate paths for their future careers. In the end girls tend to concentrate on the arts and female vocations such as catering, needlework, secretarial work and nursing, with very few going into the physical sciences and technology. Akuffo found, among the 1986 sixth form group of girls, that 26% had opted for arts subjects, 12% selected business while 11% chose science. In the technical schools and polytechnics girls stayed away from the auto-mechanic, electrical and building and construction subjects (Akuffo, 1996).

Parents have consistently said they did not disapprove of girls' education, yet their actions usually created that impression. Though both young boys and girls are subjected to early labour assignments in the home, expectations of girls are significantly higher than for boys. Not only do they have to help with the housework, but they also give valuable assistance in baby sitting and market-oriented production activities and trading. It is not uncommon to find older female siblings having to sacrifice their education to help look after the younger ones in the family. Over the years these strains have encouraged girls to drop out of school. Drop-out rates for girls aged between 6 and 11 years was observed to be about 11% compared with 13% for boys, but for girls aged between 12 and 17 it was about 32% as against 22% for boys (Lloyd and Gage-Brandon, 1993). Once girls drop out of school they are destined for the informal sector in semi-skilled vocational apprenticeships and eventual self-employment or in commerce.

Female literacy rates have consistently been about half male rates, especially in the rural areas. The Ghana Living Standards Survey 3 found the proportions of men and women over the age of 15 who were literate in both English and Ghanaian languages was 52% for males, 29% for females and 39% overall (Ghana Statistical Service, 1995).

The mass education adult literacy programmes introduced in the early 1950s have continued to play an important role in teaching women literacy in Ghanaian languages and numeracy; they have largely attracted adult rural or urban women (63% of the total). However, the high drop-out

---

[1] By the 1994/5 academic year female enrolment at the universities of Ghana and Cape Coast had risen to 25%.

[2] It has been suggested that the mean parental expense on girls is higher than for boys; the mean costs for primary school boys was estimated at ¢3413, compared to ¢4233 for girls using 1988 GLSS data (BRIDGE, 1994).

rate is turning attention to the needs of the illiterate youth. Non-formal education, as it is now known, has received substantial assistance under the educational reforms, and combines literacy with skills upgrading. Some women have complained, however, that they would prefer to learn English, or that the resources should be spent on improving primary school education for their children to reduce the incidence of drop-out.

Fertility Behaviour and Women's Work

There are several indications that to some extent women's work patterns are more often than not a reflection of their life-cycle stages, which for all practical purposes revolve around their marital situation and childbearing and nurturing as well as remunerative work. For this reason, as has been found also in the developed world, women with young children tend to have more restricted choices in occupational selection. Nevertheless the option of self-employment in the informal sector, especially in home-based cottage industries, gives those who are forced to take time off to raise their children the flexibility to continue earning an income.

Early marriage and early childbearing, together with a high fertility rate of 5.5 (TFR), combine to limit women's options early in their working lives. By the age of 22 the majority of girls are married and already have their first child. Wide disparities have been observed between urban and rural areas, where rural women have total fertility rates of 6.4, compared with a TFR of 4 for urban women (GSS, 1994).

The impact of family life on women's work is most pronounced in formal sector work. They regularly have to interrupt their work to look after children or older relatives, and also for maternity leave. Since 1967 women have enjoyed three months' paid maternity leave in the formal sector, though outside the public service there have been some lapses in its enforcement. A recent survey revealed that workers were equally divided over whether or not the leave should be extended or regulated in terms of the number of times and intervals for going on maternity leave. While half the group suggested that regulating the leave would force women to plan their families better in order to advance in their careers, the others rejected absolutely any interference in what they believed to be God's gift to men and women, child birth (ISSER/DPPC, 1998). In contrast, self-employed women, especially those working from home, have better opportunities to schedule their domestic and economic work in ways that reduce the strain (Oppong and Abu, 1987).

3.   General Trends in Labour Force Participation

The most recent household survey (GLSS) conducted by the Ghana Statistical Service in 1991/ 92 (Ghana Statistical Service, 1995) reported an almost even balance of participation in the economy. This section discusses labour force participation rates of men and women, occupational status, and employment status, and comments briefly on some of the factors that have contributed to these patterns.

Labour Force Participation Rates

Overall the labour force participation rates for people aged 15 years and over, showed a rise in women's rates between 1960 and 1984. By 1992, however, the trend revealed a decline over the earlier figures. From the census data women's participation rose from 56.6% in 1960 to 81.6% in 1984. By 1992 the GLSS findings estimated a drop to 78.0%. There have been suggestions that the 1960 data were flawed by possible under-reporting rather than a true reflection of the situation, due to inappropriate classification of economically active groups (Bortei-Doku, 1990). Oduro (1992), commenting on this, noted that in Ghana the poor construction of household survey questionnaires, interviewer prejudice and general male-biased social norms in the conceptions of work and occupation contribute to the underestimation of women's production activities. Table 17.2 shows the steady trend in women's participation rates based on 1960 to 1984 census data. Estimates from 1992 are shown together with the earlier census data.

Table 17.2 Labour Force Participation Rate by
Sex 1960–1984 (%)

Year	Male	Female	Total
1960	89	57	73
1970	84	64	73
1984	84	82	83
1992	74	78	76

Source: Dordunoo, 1996: 66 (derived from 1960–1984 census
data; GSS, 1995, data from GLSS 3, sample survey, 1991/
92). The calculation is based on the Refined Activity Rate
(RAR).

Steel and Campbell noted that the labour force participation rate grew much faster among women at 4% per annum compared with the declining growth for men between 1960 and 1970 as Table 17.2 shows. Much of this growth was found to be in the non-agricultural sector with generally low participation of women in the modern wage sector. For men, however, the relatively slower expansion that had taken place was predominantly in the formal sector. Historically, occupational segregation among the sexes seemed to explain this trend better than employer bias or labour market discrimination. They were unable to find any strong evidence that the increase was due to demand-induced employment, but rather suggested that this was a supply side response to declining real family incomes (Steel and Campbell, 1982). The employment status of men and women shown in Table 17.3 once again illustrates the even balance between men's and women's economic participation.

Table 17.3   Current Employment Status of Men and Women, Aged 15+ Years, 1991/92 (%)

Employment Status	Men (N = 4997)	Women (5835)	All (10832)
Employed	76.8	74.8	75.7
Unemployed			
(seeking)	2.6	2.5	2.6
(available)	0.7	1.4	1.1
Ill/on vacation	0.3	0.3	0.3
Student	9.0	4.9	6.8
Retired	2.1	4.0	3.1
Home-maker	6.1	10.9	8.7
Other	2.2	1.2	1.7

Source: Ghana Statistical Service, 1995: 32.

However, the historical differences in the structure of men's and women's economic activities have not changed significantly, and betray a pattern of gender stereotyping in occupational choices. Table 17.4 describes the occupational profile of men and women in 1992. Noticeable is the occupation of women in agricultural and trading activities.

Table 17.4   Type of Industry by Sex for the Active Population, Aged 15 Years and above, 1992 (%)

Industry	Men (N = 3561)	Women (N = 4337)	All (N = 7898)
Agriculture	66.2	58.9	62.2
Minerals and Mining	1.0	0.1	0.5
Manufacturing	6.7	9.4	8.2
Utilities	0.2	0.1	0.1
Construction	2.5	0.1	1.2
Trading	4.7	25.0	15.8
Transport and Communication	4.5	0.2	2.2
Financial Services	0.9	0.2	0.5
Community and Other Services	13.3	6.0	9.3

Source: Ghana Statistical Service, 1995: 35.

The structure of occupations continues to be predominantly agricultural. This share is bound to be even higher if one takes into consideration the fact that many of the manufacturing and trading activities are directly (agro-processing) or indirectly (trading) linked to agricultural products. The services category hides some of the most lucrative as well as the most precarious jobs for women in the informal sector. Here hairdressers and dressmakers with vocational training and bakers/caterers are to be found, together with vulnerable unskilled groups such as market porters or *kaya* as they are popularly known, and street walkers engaged in prostitution (commercial sex workers). In both cases there is a high concentration of young adult women who have migrated recently from desperate situations in rural areas to work in the big cities, just like their male relatives and friends. They often join the homeless, and become victims of sex and drug abuse in their search for protection in the streets (see Apt *et al.*, n.d.). Many come of their own accord, while others are sent by their parents to work to supplement the household income in view of the increasing economic hardships in the rural areas. Table 17.5 shows that the occupational field of women is predominantly in unskilled or semi-skilled fields. While very few Ghanaians overall occupy professional/technical status jobs, only half as many women as men can be found at this level. Similarly, the whole sample did not capture a single female in the managerial/administrative grade, a reminder of their very low representation in decision-making and leadership positions at work.

Table 17.5   Gender and Occupational Types, Aged 15+ Years, 1991/2 (%)

Occupation	Men (3561)	Women (4337)	All (N = 7898)
Professional/Technical	5.5	3.2	4.2
Administrative/Managerial	0.5	—	0.2
Clerical	3.6	1.6	2.5
Sales	4.4	23.9	15.1
Services	3.4	2.2	2.8
Agricultural	64.3	58.6	61.1
Production	18.4	10.4	14.0

Source: GSS, 1995: 33.

Like their male counterparts, most women describe themselves as self-employed working in informal sector occupations. Both census data and the GLSS findings confirm that only a fraction of the economically active are in wage and salaried employment, presumably in the formal sector. GLSS 3 estimated the number of workers employed by others to be about 12% of the economically active population. The gender differences are quite remarkable. Only about 6% of women worked for an employer, compared with 18% of men. More than twice as many men work for the government and state-owned companies as do women. Table 17.6 indicates the differences in the employer profiles.

Table 17.6   **Main Employer by Sex for the Economically Active Population, Aged 15+ Years, 1991/2 (%)**

Main Employer	Male (N = 4997)	Female (N = 5835)	All (10832)
Government	8.8	3.4	5.9
State-Owned Company	1.7	0.2	0.9
Private Company	7.4	1.9	4.5
Other Employer	0.6	0.2	0.4
Self-Employed	62.3	74.9	69.1
No Main Job	19.2	19.4	19.3

Source: Ibid.

As a significant proportion of Ghanaians hold temporary jobs, and sometimes have more than one job, it is reasonable to assume that the 19% who reported that they had no main job in the previous 12 months may nevertheless have worked during this period. Roughly 20% of both men and women reported that they had held two jobs in the year preceding the study.

Another point of interest in the lower proportions of women in wage and salaried employment in the public sector, is that this is where regular incomes and maternity provisions are available.

Age and Locational Characteristics of Women in the Labour Force

The age structure of the economically active reveals that women enter the labour force at earlier ages than men, and, contrary to ILO Conventions on child labour, many children between the ages 7 and 14 work in part-time jobs for pocket money, on their own or with their parents/ guardians. The GLSS for 1992 revealed that the activity rates for rural and urban children differed quite significantly, at 3% for urban children compared with 10% for rural children. The issue of economically engaged street children in the urban centres is now more significant than when the GLSS 3 was done. From what used to be a male child adventure, the proportion of girls is believed to have increased tremendously, mainly as porters in the markets, but also as labourers and cleaners, and petty traders. There are several indications that young girls are more likely to be committed to child labour compared with boys, for the simple fact that female children are assigned more tasks pertaining to unpaid and paid work in the home, in their apprenticeship with their mothers or as foster children or homehelps. In some rural schools it is common to find high levels of absenteeism on market days, especially among girls (Akuffo, 1987). Both girls and boys start their agricultural duties early, and for many of them it is where they will end up.

4. Women in Agriculture

Women farmers, like their male counterparts, predominantly have no formal education, and farm by traditional methods handed down through the generations. Since independence women's involvement in food production seems to have increased substantially, as men have continued to migrate to the towns, cities and locations abroad, or have shifted into tree crop cultivation and agricultural wage labour.

But it is only in the last 20 years that women have been recognized in official circles as farmers in their own right, and not just as farmers' wives. Time budget studies, for example, have revealed that in some parts of the country women spend more hours in performing farming-related tasks than men (North *et al.*, 1975). Though many of them continue to assist their husbands on their farms, they are increasingly establishing their own farms, over which they have maximum control. Though less than one-third of women were officially classified as independent farmers in the 1984 census, adding in women who maintain private farms as well as assisting their husbands raises this figure substantially (Bortei-Doku, 1990; Whitehead, 1993; BRIDGE, 1994). In addition, a number of rural women who are classified by other occupations (e.g. trader) invariably cultivate subsistence farms (Roncoli, 1985). The transition from farm assistants to their own farms has not always endeared wives to their husbands. In the Ada village of Matsekope in Greater Accra Region, the women who broke away completely to establish their own farms were negatively labelled 'myself women' by their menfolk (Bortei-Doku Aryeetey, 1997). It has been observed that Akan women are the most involved in agriculture, followed by Ewe, Ga and women of the Northern ethnic groups (Roncoli, 1985).

Women have concentrated on cultivating vegetables, roots and tubers and legumes. On the other hand, their involvement in export and other cash crop cultivation has remained limited; 27% of cocoa producers and managers, for example, are said to be women (BRIDGE, 1994). Though they supply a good share of the foodstuffs on the market, women's agricultural production is generally associated with subsistence, the production of 'soup ingredients' as it is popularly described in the Northern regions of Ghana.

The proportion of women farmers involved in staples and vegetable production was estimated to be 70% in 1970, compared with 50% of male farmers.[3] Table 17.7 gives a summary of the types of production activities of farmers.

Table 17.7   Types of Production Activities of Men and Women in Agriculture 1970 (%)

Occupation	Male	Female	Total
Staples and vegetable producers	50.1	70.2	58.7
Cocoa farmers and farm managers	35.8	26.6	31.8
Other farmers	7.5	2.6	5.4
Forestry workers	0.7	0.2	0.5
Fishermen and fishprocessers	5.7	0.1	3.3
Hunters	0.1	0.2	

Source: BRIDGE, 1994: 11 extracted from Ewusi, 1987.

Farm holdings among small-scale farmers range from half a hectare to 3 hectares. In spite of their active record in farming, women's holdings are almost invariably half or less of the total

---

[3] The Ministry of Agriculture has suggested that women produce about 70% of locally grown foodstuffs.

land holdings cultivated by men, in all farming areas (MOFA, 1991). The size of holding may be a reflection not only of lack of access to land but also to low labour resources, which compel some female farmers to restrict themselves to plots they can manage on their own. Migration further reduces women's access to land as they have less recourse to family land (Roncoli, 1985).

Women's farms are also perceived to be less productive, compared with cultivation by men. Productivity, however, has been linked to the level of access to productive assets and extension, which historically have been less accessible to women (Sackey and Dogbey, 1996). Studies that have estimated the production function that controls for input levels have shown that male and female farmers are equally efficient as farm managers (Gladwin, 1996; Alderman *et al.*, 1995). By all indications women farmers have a more difficult task mobilizing land, labour, credit and other inputs to improve their production activities.

There are other economic implications of the concentration of women in food production. This invariably places them at the lower level of socio-economic well-being, given that a significant proportion of what they produce is consumed at home, and indeed a significant proportion of the poor are engaged in food production (Ghana Statistical Service, 1995).

Women's involvement in agriculture extends beyond cultivation. They are extensively and sometimes exclusively involved in the processing, preservation and marketing of foodstuffs all over the country. This requires headloading of crops and finished products over long distances to rural markets. In the urban markets women still control wholesale and retailing operations. This can give them appreciable control over the proceeds of marketing, especially in the South where labour relations often take on the appearance of contractual arrangements, and has often been the source of much tension between spouses. In addition, women also virtually control the small/micro-scale agro-processing industry. Whether or not women are going to be able to extend their agricultural activities in the future will depend to a large extent on their access to key inputs such as land, labour and credit.

Land

Land is traditionally allocated under customary law by male kin, whether in patrilineal or matrilineal kin groups. It appears, however, that in matrilineal groups women can rely more on their own family for their land requirements, whereas in patrilineal groups husbands' families play a larger role in women's access to land. In both cases, however, though both married and unmarried women have extensive use rights they have no jural or disposal rights over land. In spite of the customary rules protecting women's access to land, in reality secure access depends largely on the nature of relationships with male relatives and their goodwill (Bortei-Doku Aryeetey, 1996). The traditional patterns have been showing signs of increased flexibility. Kilson (1974) noted, for example, the growing tendency for Ga women to inherit land directly from their fathers and male relatives.

Women's access to fertile land has shrunk over the years not just because of population pressure, but also because of increased competition for land for commercial use. A clear example is the changing crop mixes among male farmers, in particular the expansion of export tree crop production. Putting more land under permanent production in this way has undermined women's access to land for food production. Increasingly female food crop farmers have been pushed on to marginal lands. To make matters worse their own expanding commitment to market production has forced women food farmers to shorten fallow periods, thus reducing the effectiveness of traditional long fallow periods for the rejuvenation of the soil and its productivity under shifting cultivation. Given the relative lack of security in land tenure for women, they are less inclined to adopt long-term soil improvements or other protective husbandry practices. There have been instances in the past when women have lost their farms together with their crops following a divorce or childless widowhood. It is worth mentioning that hiring of agricultural land is becoming common among women as the pressure on family land increases, making it difficult for them to meet their needs from traditional entitlements.

Labour

The ability to expand farming operations not only has to do with land, but also with labour resources, particularly in the light of the low use of technology in small-scale farming in Ghana. In the majority of cases women tend to rely more on hired labour than men because they have less access to family labour. This appears to be a more acute problem in cocoa-growing areas than elsewhere, and among migrants (Roncoli, 1985). The GLSS showed that 75% of women hired labour for agriculture compared with 62% of men. In many cases assisting their husbands on their farms, as they are obliged to do, delays women's attention to their own farms, especially during the critical planting period at the beginning of the season.

The negative effects of labour constraints and low technology use are also reflected in the substitution of less labour-intensive crops such as cassava to replace more intensive crops such as maize, with important nutritional ramifications for the household. In the past women would have been able to call on traditional reciprocal labour groups (*nnoboa*), but the increased commoditization of labour has made this community arrangement no longer attractive. In addition, the traditional requirement that labour gangs work in exchange for food and refreshment means that this is not necessarily an affordable option for poorer farmers.

Credit

Women farmers often cite lack of credit as one of their biggest handicaps. Continuing past traditions the majority of women still rely on their own resources and informal sources of credit to finance their farming operations. It is common to find that women generate cash from non-farm economic activities to plough back into farming operations. In many rural communities people borrow extensively from their relatives and friends at no interest, but there are also established moneylenders operating at commercial interest rates of 50% or more, depending on the duration of the loan period. In addition, a savings club popularly known as *susu* is practised by some, though it is not as popular among farmers as among those in non-agricultural enterprises. Most of the money that is borrowed will go into hiring male labour to clear land at the beginning of the farming season. Beyond this women tend to invest very little money in chemicals or improved seed varieties. Perhaps one of the most important sources of credit for women engaged in market-oriented production is the advance (including inventory credit) that farmers often obtain from the women marketing intermediaries. Through this type of arrangement, the wholesaler may advance money to purchase inputs and to pay for labour.

Over the years it has been very difficult for farmers to obtain credit from the formal banking institutions. Many of the banks have actually reduced their lending to the farming sector in recent years. Failure of the banks to disaggregate records by gender makes it difficult to know what proportion of women farmers ever received credit at the national level. From past experience, however, it can be concluded that, as women are mostly food producers, they are likely to be among the group of farmers least supported by the banks. Farming is generally considered to be a high risk sector for lending, and the transaction costs of lending to micro and small-scale producers to be too high. Worse still, food farming is seen as too risky because of the influence of the weather, and also because of product perishability and price instabilities. Whatever agricultural lending takes place, therefore, tends to focus on the export tree crop enterprises and the non-traditional fruit export plantations. Evidence from some rural banks reveals that cocoa and other tree crop farmers have received the most agricultural loans over the years. Based on the GLSS Third Round (1991/2) fewer female-headed households have had access to formal credit compared with their male counterparts, and they also tend to attract lower amounts of credit.

Attempts to assist women to gain better access to credit led to the establishment of a number of credit groups by non-governmental organizations and donor-sponsored agricultural projects in the 1980s and early 1990s. The popularity of this strategy has been attributed to the evidence that loan recovery was relatively high among women. The general principle involved is the use of group collateral and peer group pressure, which has not worked so well with men's groups in

Ghana. Admittedly, the most successful credit groups have been in the food processing rather than food cultivation business; the uncertainties and dangers of crop failure that rainfed agriculture presents are believed to be a major contributory factor.

Extension and Technology Transfer

Nationwide extension services have fallen far short of expectations for both officials of the Ministry of Agriculture and the farmers. Women farmers had until recently been quite neglected, owing to prejudice and ignorance about their contributions to production as farmers. The other side of the problem is that the extension service has traditionally had a heavy bias towards export crops, where the majority of producers are men. In the past, extension services for women were perceived more in terms of home extension to disseminate information about improved home management rather than farming. With the agricultural sector reforms under the Economic Recovery Programme the recognition that women deserve more attention as part of the strategy for food security led to the establishment of the Women in Agricultural Development Department (WIAD), to advise the Ministry on strategies for enhancing women's production and processing activities. These reforms notwithstanding, the extension services continue to by-pass women.

The GLSS 3 revealed that out of 135 contacts between farmers and extension agents only 11 (8%) were with women farmers, and in the Ashanti Eastern and Brong Ahafo Regions where women make the most contribution in food production, less than 5% of them were contacted in the previous year (see also Panuccio, 1989). Socio-cultural limitations on contacts between male extension agents and women, as well as the low ratio of female staff to female farmers, inadequate logistics and low morale among staff, have been cited as some of the contributory factors constraining women's access to extension services. The ratio of women extension officers to female farmers is estimated at about 1:11,000 (BRIDGE, 1994).

Access to chemical inputs and improved seed varieties is relatively difficult for all Ghanaian farmers, primarily because of lack of information and costs. Given their relatively more limited access to extension information and cash resources, women are worse placed than men to take advantage of improved technologies in agriculture. In addition, distribution networks have tended to discriminate against small-scale poor producers. Bates (1981), for example, reported that three-quarters of all fertilizers and the bulk of improved seeds imported into Ghana in 1974 went to the large mechanized commercial farms which produced less than 20% of the total agricultural output. In many cases women have relied on more informal networks for information and access to improved seeds and other inputs (Bortei-Doku Aryeetey, 1996). The GLSS 3 revealed that invariably only about half as many women as men used tractors and bought seeds, insecticides and fertilizers (see also Amanor, 1993). Women's use of modern inputs increases where there is a direct focus on market production for high value crops such as vegetables (tomatoes and peppers).

Agricultural mechanization has remained very low in small-scale farming. Hand tools are the most common forms of technology used by farmers all over Ghana, but when new machinery has been introduced it has usually gone to male farmers. Sometimes socio-cultural inhibitions have limited the probability of women adopting improved technologies, as is the case with bullock ploughing in Northern Ghana. Taboos restricting women's ownership and handling of cattle reduced their involvement in the various projects aimed at promoting bullock ploughing in the North.[4] A study in Wenchi in the Brong Ahafo Region showed that 23% of women farmers used tractors compared with 33% of men (Amanor, 1993).

Improvements in technology have not paid much attention to domestic technologies, however, though it is widely agreed that reducing drudgery and the time taken in the performance of

---

[4] These projects included the Binaba Agricultural Station Project (Canadian Government), the Garu Agricultural Station Project (Christian Services Committee) and the Ghana/German Agricultural Project in the Northern and Upper Regions (Roncoli, 1985).

domestic work would greatly improve women's productivity in income-related activities. Improved stoves, more efficient energy sources and better access to utilities such as water would greatly enhance this process. Water and sanitation projects currently in progress all over Ghana are seen to have the additional benefit of reducing domestic burdens for women.

5. Women and the Informal Sector

The informal sector, like agriculture, is a major employer for all Ghanaians, though a higher proportion of women than men are to be found here. Sometimes referred to as the non-agricultural sector, it is relatively easy to enter because there are no entry qualifications in terms of skills and capital base. In 1992 roughly 63% of economically active Ghanaians were employed in non-farm activities (GLSS 3). Overall about 75% of Ghanaian women are self-employed, invariably in agriculture and trading/commerce. Self-employment becomes the only option available for many women because, as noted above, they never acquire the education and training needed to enter the formal sector.

Women's non-agricultural businesses in general tend to be smaller than those of men, for very much the same reasons, lack of credit and skills, as noted earlier. Steel and Webster (1990) found that only 13% of women's businesses had 10 or more workers compared with 31% of men's. They mention, as an additional constraint on women's ability to expand, the substantial demands on their time from domestic responsibilities.

There are numerous rungs of operations in the informal sector, from hawking and table-top petty trading activities to large-scale shopkeeping and services. Many women find themselves at the lowest levels in tray-top or table-top operations that depend on daily credit purchases and sales, or they work as porters and domestic workers.

The main constraints facing women in this sector include uncertainty in the markets reflected in sharp fluctuations in sales, lack of quality assurance, low creditworthiness, and low employment capacity. In addition, there are no legal guarantees in wages, hours and social security, thus creating considerable vulnerability among the self-employed and wage-earners alike. Vulnerability has increased in the informal sector over the years with more people turning to the sector, especially with increased urbanization.

Food Processing

The bulk of locally processed foods found on the Ghanaian market, ranging from dried vegetables, milled grains or legumes to vegetable oils as well as fish, are processed by women, using rudimentary technologies and outmoded tedious labour-intensive methods. Their limited access to production inputs often means that women cannot expand their processing activities. The supply of raw produce for these activities often comes from own farm produce, or, where this is not possible, they purchase the inputs or gather them from the wild in the forest. A considerable amount of processing activities in vegetable oil extraction and gari processing takes place in the forest and transitional ecological zones of Ashanti, Brong Ahafo, Western, middle Volta, Eastern and Central Regions. In the North, in addition to shea butter oil processing and pito brewing from sorghum, a lot of vegetable drying for domestic use and the local market also takes place. Along the coast fish processing is critical to many women's livelihoods. Though the potential exists for women to supplement their incomes significantly from agro-processing activities, many of these take place in the dry season when water shortage and dwindled cash flows prevent women from purchasing adequate inputs to undertake these income-generating activities (BRIDGE, 1994).

A close look at female manufacturing employment by Steel (1981) showed that between 1960 and 1970 women controlled close on 100% of food-related small-scale industries such as local food preparation, vegetable oil extraction and malt brewing, as shown in Table 17.8.

Table 17.8   Sources of Female Manufacturing Employment Increases 1960–70 (%)

Industry	Female Share of Industry Employment		Share of Total Female Employment	
	1960	1970	1960	1970
Local Food Preparation	n.a.	99	5.6	31
Wearing Apparel	62	65	47	28
Local Vegetable Oils	96	91	5	8
Malt Brewing	92	93	6	8
Wooden & Cane wares	35	66	0	2
Clay products	93	97	8	5
Textiles	10	15	1	2
Meat & Fish Products	2	37	0	1
Wine & Spirits	11	13	0	1

Source: Steel, 1981:165.

Essentially the structure of women's small-scale manufacturing has not changed, and the general impression is that women continue to make the same types of contribution in this area as they have done in the past. This is either because women are unable to prepare themselves to shift into other areas, or because the incentives that have been put in place to encourage them to do so have been ineffective.

By the middle of the 1980s when the crises in food production turned attention to women's contribution to food security, attempts were made to boost their production activities by introducing improved ways of prolonging the shelf life of locally produced food. Technology programmes aimed at improving local processing methods were therefore introduced all over the country to address the needs of vegetable oil processing, gari processing and fish processing (Date-Bah, 1985).

Artisans and Services

Another important category of informal sector operators are women artisans and service providers. Typically their work is urban-based, though they may also be found in big villages. The main recruit into vocational jobs is the school drop-out, no longer interested in farming but unable to enter the formal sector. Artisans include dressmakers and hairdressers working as sole proprietors with the help of their apprentices. These were previously considered to be lucrative avenues, but the proliferation of such artisans and the ever growing patronage of the used clothing market have severely cut into the volume of work received by dressmakers. There have been reports of customers never returning to collect their dresses, costing the dressmaker time and effort as well as sewing fees (Norton *et al.*, 1995).

Small numbers of women have also been found in traditionally male-dominated artisanal occupations such as small-scale mining, where they were directly involved as concession holders, members of gangs or licensed buying agents. In addition, women provide support services to the industry by hiring out equipment, and providing food.

Commerce

In the area of commerce once again women had become firmly established as active players by the time of independence. Prior to this period they had gained experience along the coast through conducting business in urban markets and trading with European merchants. Apart from trading in local products, they increasingly took over the retail of imported small merchandise, locally described as petty goods. Women had an advantage over their male colleagues in this business because they were prepared to hawk their goods from house to house and along the busy streets. But the size of their operations was often very small, resulting in low productivity and profit. It has been noted that only a handful of women are involved in trading in high value crops such as cocoa, timber or petroleum (BRIDGE, 1994).

Early entry into trading alongside their mothers, other female relatives or foster-mothers/ mistresses as apprentices, partly explains the younger age at which women enter the labour force compared with men. By all indications it is in trading that one finds the largest informal sector operations belonging to women. They are usually shop owners or wholesale distributors handling clothing and textiles, alcoholic beverages, manufactured foods and cosmetics, to name a few.

The Chit Traders During the economic crisis of the mid-1970s up to the time of the Rawlings coup in 1981, Ghanaian women struggling to maintain their livelihoods and to provide minimum requirements for their families developed all manner of intriguing operations to protect their trading activities. The severe erosion of real incomes during the period increased the propensity to hold multiple jobs, and most men and women turned to trading (BRIDGE, 1994). In the face of the severe shortages and extensive price controls associated with the period, wholesalers evolved a chit system which enabled them and retailers acting through chains of supply channels to obtain consignments of essential goods. A chit enabled a wholesaler or retailer to obtain eventual access to goods after following a chain of chits to the final wholesaler. The attraction of the chit system was its multiple revenue-yield capacity in percentage cuts for every operator along the chain of distribution. An intricate network of contacts developed through which traders of essential goods kept goods on the market, and as a result of which they came to be associated with profiteering, hoarding and smuggling and the parallel economy (*ibid.*). Manuh describes how women were severely harassed and made scapegoats during this period, often resulting in assault by the official security machinery (Manuh, 1993). Building and sustaining contacts was a key aspect of the chit system, and it brought politicians and supply managers and the big-time female traders together in what was almost a business partnership, but which carried little political leverage for women.

Informal Finance

In agriculture, but especially in non-farm occupations, there is evidence of widespread patronage of various organized forms of informal savings mobilization and credit. Though estimates are hard to project, there is a strong impression that this constitutes the next most important source of financing for informal sector business, after own savings. In a study of about 1000 market traders 77% reported that they saved with a *susu* collector, though most of them worked within one kilometre of a formal bank (Aryeetey and Gockel, 1991). Other related studies confirmed that for informal sector operators such types of cash mobilization were seen as more reliable than formal sources.

Two of the most common forms of organized informal sector credit are the urban market-based *susu* collector system, and the more rural-based rotating *susu* savings (*rosca*) group (Aryeetey and Gockel, 1991; Bortei-Doku Aryeetey and Aryeetey, 1996; 1995). Through these local mechanisms low-income women whose operations may be too small to meet formal banking regulations are able to save — individually or within a group — to support their economic ventures. Though *susu* rotating groups and collector networks are described as organized, they nevertheless remain informal in approach and practice. There are no proper records of their numbers, apart from speculations that *susu* collector networks are found in most large urban markets and rotating groups in most large rural periodic markets, as well as in public institutions in urban areas. There are some indications, however, that *susu* savings may be more popular among women than men.

For women in processing, artisanal and services activities the major constraints, as in other cases, have been the lack of resources, including credit, to expand. Current problems with marketing, however, suggest that expansion may not be the answer to low profits. Others regard quality assurance to achieve uniform standards in output, packaging and pricing as important areas to address in order to advance the competitiveness of the products and services of this sector.

6.   Women and the Formal Sector

In general, women's participation in the formal sector has been on an upward trend, though at a slow pace. From about 8% of the public service in 1939, women's participation today is reported to be about 25% of the formal sector.

In the formal sector women are placed mostly in lower grade jobs, and in a narrower spread of jobs compared with men. They work mostly as support staff, often considered as contributing, but not central, to the main goals of the institutions to which they are attached. This appears to be most directly linked to their lower qualifications and concentration in less attractive jobs than men. A closer look at the employment situation also reveals that a combination of women's own lack of confidence and ambition, and scepticism and prejudice on the part of employers, tends to hold women down at the workplace. Where women have been found in senior positions they are more often than not launched on tracks that may lead to high technical posts but not managerial or administrative openings.

That men constitute the overwhelming majority in the formal sector is not surprising. They are better educated, more mobile and less encumbered with domestic responsibilities. In many ways the rigid cultural division of labour protects the unsubstitutability of women's labour in the home, giving them little time to devote to work outside. Date-Bah (1986) found that, whereas 68% of male factory workers named their wives as the main child care providers, only 2% of women mentioned that their husbands assisted with child care.

The main constraints facing women in the formal sector undoubtedly have to do with problems of child care and shouldering a double workload, as well as the handicap of low qualifications. Those with young children face a deep crisis of time poverty, and may not be able to concentrate on their work. Besides these social and organizational constraints, others have suggested that women also lack professional competitiveness. Problems such as lack of confidence and assertiveness, and an often non-committal work culture, work against them.

Recruitment policies over the years have both favoured and penalized women in the public service. On the one hand, small groups of well educated young women have been able to enter various ministries and departments in the public service, at fairly senior starting grades. They have been helped by an overall improvement in women's education and an increased policy focus on women's involvement in public affairs, spurred on by the United Nations Women's Decade Forward-Looking Strategies. At the same time, the relatively large pools of semi-skilled female clerical staff who constitute a significant proportion of the female labour force are being retrenched from the service. In the limited recruitment exercise that has followed this downsizing, women's chances of gaining employment in the service are growing increasingly slimmer, as the focus is now on better qualified people.

7.   Policy and Programme Initiatives to Promote Women's Empowerment

State Responses to the International Lobby.
Ghana has responded positively to various United Nations conventions on the rights of women,

starting from the official abolition of wage discrimination and the introduction of maternity provisions for female workers. The 1965 Industrial Relations Act entitled women to equal pay, and by 1971 they were entitled to three months paid maternity leave. More recently Ghana has ratified the Convention on the Elimination of All Forms of Discrimination Against Women (CEDAW) (1986). As shown in Table 17.9, however, concrete efforts to improve women's representation in public office have not matched the national rhetoric on women's empowerment.

Table 17.9   The Representation of Women in Selected Public Offices
              September 1996 (%)

Office in Public Life	% Women
Members of Parliament	8
Ministers	13
Deputy Ministers	10
Council of State	16
Assembly Members	8
Government Administration	12
Trades Union Executive Council	9
Journalists	19
Industrial Managers	25
Ministers of Religion	2
Legislative Bodies	5

Source: Harlley, 1996: 157.

Following the launch of the United Nations Women's Decade in 1975 Ghana was one of the first countries to create a bureau, the National Council on Women and Development (NCWD), for women's affairs to advise the government on promoting women's equality. The NCWD has taken a number of important initiatives to create awareness and improve understanding of the problems facing women in Ghanaian society through workshops and field research. It has also been involved in technology transfer to women in family planning and income-generating activities. The NCWD has regional offices, and in the past few years has been establishing district-level offices to monitor the needs of women around the country. Operationally the organization has appeared weak and under-resourced both financially and in terms of staff. Some donor agencies have come to its aid with capacity-building assistance, but the high turnover of staff reduces the effectiveness of these efforts.

There is close collaboration between the NCWD and some active women's organizations for the purposes of information dissemination and collaboration on women's projects. It has been closely linked with the 31st December Women's Movement, for example, which is the most visible women's organization in Ghana and was formed in the wake of the 1981 Rawlings coup. The president of the Movement is Nana Konadu Agyeman Rawlings, wife of the President, which many believe gives it political and material advantage compared with other women's groups. It has a wide branch network, and is estimated to be present in most communities in rural Ghana. The Movement has been very active in championing issues affecting women in Ghana.

Non-government Organizations and Women's Groups

Over the past twenty years several women's groups have been formed in communities, districts and at the national level to directly address the handicaps of women in access to productive assets, as well as their exclusion from decision-making. It is not known how many women's groups there are at present, though the indications are that they are quite widespread, especially within religious organizations. On the other hand, there are also a number of traditional loosely organized networks in rural and urban communities which for all practical purposes perform the functions of groups. The most organized women's groups, with some kind of political leverage, have been found in the urban areas, however. They have usually been sponsored by the leading political parties (Tsikata, 1989).

Many of the large NGOs such as Technoserve, ADRA, World Vision, International Freedom From Hunger, Catholic Relief Services and other church development wings, have played an important role in improving women's access to some of the key productive assets. There are several others which are confined to one or two Regions and have limited objectives. Their effectiveness is often hampered by poor organization and lack of co-ordination between various organizations, which sometimes leads to duplication of efforts and waste of scarce resources. But the NGOs have perhaps worked harder than any other agencies in Ghana to include women in decision-making and direct planning of projects that affect their lives. They have taken the lead in working with participatory methods among women.

Donor Agencies

Donor agencies have made serious attempts to address the needs of poor women (CIDA, 1987). Showing a distinct shift from the original women-in-development welfare concerns of the 1960s and 1970s, in the 1980s they turned their attention to the improvement of women's income-earning capacity. To this end the United Nations agencies, and bilateral donors such as GTZ, CIDA, DANIDA, have in collaboration and individually undertaken projects in technology transfer, functional literacy and credit disbursement (Panuccio, 1989). Increasingly these have been conducted in collaboration with government departments such as the NCWD, the National Board for Small-Scale Industries, the Department of Social Welfare and some of the banks, such as Ghana Commercial Bank and the Agricultural Development Bank. Recently some have also taken up issues relating to women's human rights violations, working with local NGOs to improve legislation to protect the rights of Ghanaian women.

8.   Analyzing the Effects of Structural Adjustment on Women

One of the assumptions underlying the structural adjustment programme in Ghana was that under free market-driven reforms women stood to benefit from the new incentives, provided they were able to respond with adjustments in their economic behaviour. But this premise appears to suffer from several limitations where women are concerned, as indicated below:

> The design of economic adjustment measures and the assessment of their impact on the behavior of economic agents, be they individuals, households or firms tend not to consider gender as a distinguishing factor. While both men and women participate in and are affected by economic adjustment, what is often not recognized by policy-makers, and certainly not explicitly, is that this occurs in different ways for men and for women, because men and women play different roles, have different needs and face different constraints in responding to economic policy changes and to shifts in relative prices and incentives (Blackden and Morris-Hughes, 1993).

It has been observed, however, that adjustment has resulted in two gender-based effects. In the first place women, as an especially vulnerable group, suffered disproportionately from the impact of adjustment. Secondly, adjustment exacerbated women's constraints in accessing productive assets by shifting resources in favour of tradeables rather than non-tradeables where the majority of women are concentrated.

In relation to production, structural adjustment did not appear to make it any easier for women producers to improve their production, in spite of the removal of price controls and increased infrastructure development. The general impression is that the gender-neutral investment climate promoted by adjustment nevertheless overlooked structural and systematic bottlenecks that constrained women from venturing outside certain confines in the economy. Credit continued to be scarce and expensive for small producers, making it difficult for them to expand (Steel and Webster, 1990). Structural constraints such as customary male control of land, with its characteristic restrictions on women's access to land, remained intact. Indeed, under the cocoa rehabilitation programme there was an increased impetus for such constraints to deepen as men found it more profitable to reallocate land from food production to export crop production. In addition, opportunities for expanding into tradeables were not available to the majority of women farmers, because of customary land tenure arrangements which prevented people with usufruct rights, as is the case for most women, from establishing permanent crops (trees). It has also been observed that the terms of trade for food fell over the decade of adjustment, with more serious implications for women farmers than for male farmers (Sarris and Shams, 1991). In the mining and energy sector where a lot of expansion took place under adjustment women had neither the training nor the tradition of engagement as wage labour.

Oduro (1992) notes that to benefit fully from the adjustment process women need to shift their work efforts from the present low input low profit areas to the more competitive sectors, as the SAP is re-orienting the economy away from those areas in which female labour is concentrated. Partly in recognition of the peculiar difficulties facing poor women under the SAP, a significant portion of the credit facilities under the Programme of Actions to Mitigate the Social Costs of Adjustment (PAMSCAD) was allocated to a women's credit scheme — Enhancing Opportunities for Women in Development (ENOWID). But ENOWID suffered several delays in implementation, and in the end could only reach about half the targeted 7,200 women with credit (BRIDGE, 1994).

Women in the urban informal sector have experienced similar obstacles as those of farming women in trying to break through the competition under structural adjustment. Clark and Manuh (1991) showed that female traders in Accra and Kumasi reported suffering declining demand for their goods, lack of credit and overcrowding in the sector.

On the consumption side, looking at the evidence from the Ghana Living Standards Survey, it is clear that food producers, 70% of whom are women, have experienced the smallest improvements in their living conditions, especially in the Northern parts of the country.

9.   Conclusion

In agriculture and the informal sector women have continued to make direct contributions to food security and the production of local goods and services. Much of this effort is taken for granted and unaccounted for, however, under the cover of home production. This is partly the fault of unsuitable economic paradigms being used for analyzing women's production.

Women's involvement in the formal sector concentrated in urban areas has improved albeit modestly, but until fundamental constraints on access to education and training are removed they are not likely to make much progress. Currently it has been observed that not only lack of training but also domestic workloads cause strains for women working outside the home. Any further improvements in this area will require policy interventions in the provision of child-care facilities and the availability of labour- and time-saving technologies for average households.

Women's productivity generally is seriously compromised by the constraints on their access to productive assets. In the labour market they are handicapped by lower educational attainment, occupational stereotyping and male-biased socio-cultural norms concerning work and employment. Because most of the new incentives under the SAP were focused on areas in which women are not competitive, namely export crop production, the extraction industries (mining and forestry) and capital-intensive industry structural adjustment has tended to discriminate against women by by-passing their economic interests. A lack of targeting in SAP instruments has thus had a direct gender impact on economic behaviour in Ghana.

References

Akuffo, A. D. (1996) 'Access of Women to Employment in Ghana', *Greenhill Journal of Administration*, Vol. 10: 25–39.

Akuffo, F. O. (1987) 'Teenage Pregnancies and School Drop-Outs, the Relevance of Family Life Education and Vocational Training To Girls' Employment Opportunities', in Oppong.

Alderman, H., Hoddinott, J., Haddah, L. and Udry, C. (1995) *Gender Differentials in Farm Productivity: Implications for Household Efficiency and Agricultural Policy*. Food Consumption and Nutrition Division, Discussion Paper No. 6. Washington, DC: IFPRI.

Amanor, K. (1993) *Wenchi Farmer Training Project: Social/Environmental Baseline Study*. Report Prepared for the Overseas Development Administration, UK, August.

Aryeetey E. and Gockel, F. (1991) *Mobilizing Domestic Resources for Capital Formation in Ghana: The Role of Informal Financial Sectors*. Research Paper No. 3. Accra: African Economic Research Consortium (AERC).

Apt, N., Blavo, E. Q. and Opoku, S. K. (n.d.) *Street Children in Accra*. Department of Sociology, University of Ghana, for Department of Social Welfare, and Save the Children Fund (UK). Accra.

Bates, R. (1981) *Markets and States in Tropical Africa: The Political Bias of Agricultural Policies*. Berkeley, CA: University of California Press.

Beneria L. (1981) 'Conceptualising the Labour Force: The Underestimation of Women's Economic Activities', *Journal of Development Studies*, Vol. 17, No. 3: 10–28.

Blackden, C. M. and Morris-Hughes, E. (1993) *Paradigm Postponed: Gender and Economic Adjustment in Sub-Saharan Africa*. Washington, DC: World Bank, Gender Team. Human Resources and Poverty Division, Africa Region.

Bortei-Doku Aryeetey, E. (1997) 'The Significance of Gender in Seed Transfer Patterns Among Farmers in South-East Ghana', in T. Bezuneh, A. M. Emechebe, J. Sedgo, M. Ouedraogo (eds), *Technology Options for Sustainable Agriculture in Sub-Saharan Africa*. Ouagadougou: OAU/STRC/SAFGRAD,

Bortei-Doku Aryeetey, E. (1996) 'Behind the Norms, Women's Access to Agricultural Resources in Ghana', in *Managing Land Tenure and Resource Access in West Africa*. Proceedings of a Regional Workshop held at Goree, Senegal. 18 to 22 November.

Bortei-Doku, E. and Aryeetey, E. (1995) 'Mobilizing Cash for Business: Women in Rotating Susu Clubs in Ghana', in S. Ardener and S. Burman (eds) *Money-Go-Rounds*. Washington, DC: Berg.

Bortei-Doku Aryeetey, E. and Aryeetey, E. (1996) *Operation, Utilization and Change in Rotating Susu Savings in Ghana*. Technical Publication No. 59. ISSER, University of Ghana. Legon.

Bortei-Doku, E. (1990) *Profile of Women in Ghana*. Accra, CIDA.

BRIDGE (1994) 'Background Paper on Gender Issues in Ghana', Report prepared for the West and North Africa Department, Overseas Development Administration, UK.

Canadian International Development Agency (1987) 'Ghana Women in Development Project, Shiriyan Aiyukan Maata-N-Tud, Plan of Operation', Accra: CIDA.

Clark, G. and Manuh, T. (1991) 'Women Traders in Ghana and the Structural Adjustment Program', in C. H. Gladwin (ed.), *Structural Adjustment and African Women Farmers*. Centre for African Studies, Gainesville, FL: University of Florida Press.

Date-Bah, E. (1985) 'Technologies for Rural Women of Ghana: Role of Socio Cultural Factors', in I. Ahmed (ed.) *Technology and Rural Women: Conceptual and Empirical Issues*. London: George Allen and Unwin; Geneva: ILO.

Date-Bah, E. (1986) 'Sex-segregation and Discrimination in Accra-Tema: Causes and Consequences', in R. Anker *et al.* (eds) *Sex Inequalities in Urban Employment in the Third World*. ILO Studies Series. Basingstoke: Macmillan.

Dordunoo, C. K. (1996) 'Gender Analysis of Labour Force Participation, Employment and Status of Work in Ghana', *Greenhill Journal of Administration*, Vol. 10: 61–81.

Ghana Statistical Service (1994) *Ghana Demograhic and Health Survey (GDHS), 1993*. Accra: GSS.

Ghana Statistical Service (1995) *Ghana Living Standards Survey, Report on the Third Round (GLSS 3), September 1991–September, 1992*. Accra: GSS.

Gladwin, C. H. (1996) 'Women and Sustainable Food Production in Africa'. Paper prepared for Sasakawa Global 2000 International Workshop on Women Agricultural Intensification and Household Food Security: Developing Gender Sensitizing Training Programmes for Policy Makers, Researchers and Extension Workers in Africa. University of Cape Coast, Cape Coast, 25–28 June.

Greenhill Journal of Administration (1996) Vol. 10. Special Issue on Genders at Work.

Haddad, L., Brown, L. R., Richter, A., Smith, L. (1994) 'The Gender Dimensions of Economic Adjustment Policies: Potential Interactions and Evidence to Date', *World Development*, Vol. 23, No. 6: 881–96.

Harlley, E. (1996) 'The Situation of Women in Public Life in Ghana, Some Thoughts', *Greenhill Journal of Administration*, Vol. 10: 156–64.

ISSER/DPCC (1998) *Women in Public Life*. ISSER Research Report. Accra: ISSER.

Kilson, M. (1974) *African Urban Kinsmen: The Ga of Central Accra*. London: G. Hurst & Co.

Lloyd, C. B. and Gage-Brandon, A. J. (1993) 'Women's Role in Maintaining Households: Family Welfare and Sexual Inequality in Ghana', *Population Studies*, Vol. 47, No. 1, March.

Manuh, T., (1993) 'Women, the State and Society under the PNDC', in E. Gyimah-Boadi (ed.) *Ghana Under PNDC Rule*. Dakar: CODESRIA Book Series.

Ministry of Food and Agriculture (MOFA) (1991) *Agriculture in Ghana, Facts and Figures*. Accra: PPME, MOFA.

North, J., Fuchs-Carsch, M., Bryson, J. and Blumenfeld, S. (1975) *Women in National Development in Ghana*. Accra: USAID/Ghana.

Norton, A., Bortei-Doku Aryeetey, E., Korboe, D. and Dogbe, D. T. (1995) *Poverty Assessment in Ghana Using Qualitative and Participatory Research Methods*. PSP Discussion Paper Series No. 83. Washington, DC: World Bank, Poverty and Social Policy Department (November).

Oduro, A. (1992) *Women's Economic Roles*. Gender Analysis Workshop Report, Institute of African Studies, DAWS, University of Ghana, Legon. 14–16 July.

Oppong, C. (1987) *Sex Roles, Population and Development in West Africa*. London: James Currey; Portsmouth, NH: Heinemann.

Oppong, C. and Abu, K. (1987) *Seven Roles of Women: Impact of Education Migration and Employment on Ghanaian Mothers*. Women, Work and Development, 13. Geneva: ILO.

Panuccio, T. (1989) 'Rural Women in Ghana: Their Workloads, Access and Organisations', in W. P. Lineberry (ed.) *Assessing Participatory Development, Rhetoric Versus Reality*. London: Westview Press/IFAD.

Roncoli, M. C. (1985) *Women and Small-Scale Farming in Ghana*, State University of New York, Working Paper No. 89, July.

Sackey, H. A. and Dogbey, G. Y. (1996) 'Women, Inequality and Productivity: Some Reflections and Policy Implications for Ghana', *Greenhill Journal of Administration*, Vol. 10: 133–55.

Sarris, A., and Shams, H. (1991) *Ghana under Structural Adjustment: The Impact on Agriculture and the Rural Poor*. IFAD Studies in Rural Poverty, No. 2. New York: IFAD.

Sinha, J. N. (1967) 'Dynamics of Female Participation in Economic Activity in a Developing Economy', in *Proceedings of the World Population Conference, 1965*. New York: United Nations. Vol. 4.

Steel, W. F. (1981) 'Female and Small-Scale Employment Under Modernisation in Ghana'. *Economic Development and Cultural Change*, Vol. 30, No. 1: 154–67.

Steel, W. F. and Campbell, C. (1982) 'Women's Employment and Development: A Conceptual Framework Applied to Ghana', in E. G. Bay (ed.) *Women and Work in Africa*. Boulder, CO: Westview Press.

Steel, W. F. and Webster, L. M. (1990) *Small Enterprises in Ghana: Responses to Adjustment*. Washington, DC: World Bank, Industry Development Division.

Tsikata, D. (1989) 'Women's Organisations in Ghana, 1951–1987', in E. Hansen and K. Ninsin (eds) *The State, Development and Politics in Ghana*. Dakar: CODESRIA Book Series.

Whitehead, A. (1993) 'Poverty in North East Ghana', Draft Report to ESCOR, West Africa Department, October.

VII The Way Forward

18 Structural Adjustment & After: Which Way Forward?

ERNEST ARYEETEY
& FINN TARP

1. Introduction

Ghana has been described as a front-runner in the economic reform process that has dominated the African policy-making scene since the early 1980s (Leechor, 1994). Accordingly, Ghana was among the first African countries to embark on stabilization and structural adjustment programmes in the formulation and implementation of which the two Bretton Woods agencies, the International Monetary Fund and the World Bank, played — and continue to play — a prominent role. The Economic Recovery Programme was initiated by the military government headed by J. J. Rawlings in April 1983, and over the past 15 years has been pursued with great zeal by the government. In fact, Ghana has regularly been put forward by the Bretton Woods agencies and others as a showcase of success in Africa.

It has been argued by the World Bank (1993a) that 'Ghana's adjustment programme is *by any yardstick* one of the more successful ones in Sub-Saharan Africa' (emphasis added), and Corbo and Fisher (1995) assert that 'Ghana . . . has been the most successful of the African adjusters'. In the donors' praise of Ghana's reform efforts reference has often been made to a range of characteristics such as: (i) the comprehensive nature of the reforms and the stabilization and structural adjustment policies, (ii) the adherence to the prevailing orthodoxy, (iii) the initial growth, (iv) the ability to hit benchmark conditionalities on many occasions, and (v) the improvements in the negotiating machinery on the side of the Ghanaian government.

The last point has been interpreted by some observers to be an indication of Ghana's relatively high degree of ownership of the ERP programme as described in detail by Aryeetey (1995). However, the favourable assessment of local Ghanaian capacity and its ability to formulate a 'home-grown' set of economic policies to deal with the crisis is at variance with the judgement of other analysts such as Green (1987). Green argues that Ghanaian influence on the outline and content of the ERP-programme was highly constrained in 1983, and it is in any case evident that relatively little consultation took place between the government, on the one side, and the larger civil society, on the other. It can, finally, be noted that Ghana was also an early example of trying to give adjustment a 'human face' as suggested by UNICEF (Cornia *et al.*, 1987) through the so-called 'Programme of Actions to Mitigate the Social Costs of Adjustment' (PAMSCAD).

One is nevertheless reminded by Singer (1989), in his review of the lessons of post-1945 development experience, that 'seldom is any splendid story wholly true', and after 15 years of adjustment it is certainly justifiable to contend that there appears to be a 'worm in the apple' in the Ghanaian case. Despite the spurts of growth in the 1980s, progress has not been as quick or as strong as expected. This has been especially so since 1992 when the performance of the economy began slackening considerably as pointed out in Chapter 1, but doubts about the credibility and sustainability of the progress actually began mounting from 1989. Such questions as the following abound today in Ghana: (i) Why is progress so much slower than, for example, that of East Asia, which has followed a less orthodox set of development policies?; (ii) Which are the critical constraints on Ghanaian growth?; and (iii) What needs to be done to put Ghana on a steady long-term development path? These queries are understandable. Ghana has done most of what the foreign actors have demanded, foreign capital inflows have been high, and the country is indeed well endowed with natural resources such as arable land, forests, extensive mineral deposits (including gold and diamonds), and hydro-electric power is also available.

This chapter is meant to contribute to the discussion of these questions, and to provide some insight into them. More specifically, the aim here is to try to synthesize some of the major themes that have emerged from the earlier chapters of this volume, as well as other relevant points that have been discussed elsewhere. Thus, in section 2 we briefly review the path to economic reform and then discuss in more detail the underlying premises and goals of the ERP in section 3. In section 4 we introduce some of the specific policy measures taken and the economic outcomes they led to, and in section 5 we make suggestions for the way forward in the light of policy lessons learnt in Ghana and more recent thinking on development theory and practice. Conclusions are drawn in section 6.

2.   The Path to Economic Reforms

Most of the preceding chapters of this book have pointed to the path that Ghana followed on the way to self-destruction, beginning from the 1960s. It moved from being a country that at independence in 1957 could be classified by international standards as a middle-income country with a relatively well educated population, into a low-income country that could barely feed itself by 1982. An economy that appeared buoyant in the early 1960s, with growing output, hardly any inflation, large international reserves and a position as world leader in cocoa production and export, gave way to one characterized by severe macroeconomic instability and major distortions that incapacitated production and wiped away incomes (ODI, 1996). Thus, a country that previously compared well, as Killick points out in this volume in Chapter 3, with many of the other nations that started out at the time on the road to economic modernization and development, found itself way behind them after two decades. In fact, the per capita income level of the early 1960s was similar to that of countries like Mexico and South Korea, and it was twice that of Thailand.

The path to reforms was generally quite rugged. The distinct political instability that was aggravated by poor economic conditions throughout the 1960s and 1970s was reflected in high levels of corruption, policy reversals and a general lack of direction. As seen in Chapter 1, the growth in the role of the state became pervasive as it branched into many spheres of economic activity that yielded relatively little economic return and contributed significantly to the macroeconomic instability. At the same time, as all attempts at sound economic analysis suffered paralysis, the relative affluence of the army caused demonstrations, and brutal repression became the order of the day.

In the midst of the political turmoil, the downward slide of the economy was most acute during the late 1970s and early 1980s, directly reflecting the corruption and poor economic management installed under previous regimes. However, in addition to domestic disorder, a number of disastrous exogenous shocks began to strike. They included (i) the 1983 drought, which was the worst in decades, with the consequent need to import large quantities of food on commercial terms and the negative impact on the production of hydroelectric power; (ii) the return in 1983 of more than a million Ghanaians, who had been working in Nigeria during the oil boom; and (iii) a drastic fall in the international terms of trade in the early 1980s due to the drop in cocoa prices and rises in oil prices. Exogenous shocks of this magnitude would, as pointed out by Leechor (1994), have been difficult to absorb in any event, but the timing could hardly have been worse given the already weakened state of the Ghanaian economy. And as if this were not enough, capital flight intensified, and large numbers of the educated labour force, who found working and living conditions insecure and unacceptable, started leaving the country, deepening even further the evolving crisis.

As illustration of the gravity of the vicious circle or state of collapse in which Ghana found itself in the late 1970s and early 1980s, the statistical evidence provided in previous chapters is shockingly clear. Thus, it is sufficient here to reiterate that, while income per capita certainly reached its lowest point in 1983, at a level much below that of 1970, following the severe exogenous shocks, income was already low in 1980, and both agricultural and industrial production were, at the time, in conspicuous decline. Moreover, gross domestic savings and investment levels averaged no more than approximately 5% and 4.3% of GDP, respectively, during the early 1980s, and government revenue had fallen from about 20% in 1970 to less than 5%. Ghana had also lost its leading role in cocoa exports, and production of this commodity dropped from 560,000 tonnes in 1965 to only 160,000 tonnes in 1983. The inflation rate, which averaged 40% on an annual basis in the 1970s, jumped to 130% (as shown in Chapter 1), the overvaluation of the cedi reached 816%, and foreign debt and international arrears were piling up in an increasingly unfavourable trade climate. Imports as well as exports had, in fact, fallen by 1981 to no more than 3.5% of GDP as compared with around 20% in 1970, and social conditions were generally deteriorating, illustrated by increasing unemployment and widespread food insecurity.

In sum, the basic macro-balances of the Ghanaian economy were by mid-1982 so perturbed that the necessity for stabilization measures was — in the formulation of Toye (1991) - 'crystal clear'. In addition, that such measures would require large financial inflows to be sustained in a gradualistic manner was taken by most analysts as evident. In spite of previous populist/Marxist leanings, the Rawlings government therefore soon recognized that 'fighting corruption in the context of extreme scarcities and distortions was essentially a lost cause' (Leechor, 1994) and proceeded to reactivate negotiations with the IMF and the World Bank. Subsequently, the first stage of the ERP stabilization and structural adjustment programme was quickly agreed in April 1983.

3. The Goals and Underlying Premises of the Economic Reforms

The Economic Recovery Programme, that was put in place with support from the IMF, the World Bank and other multi- and bilateral donors, has over the past 15 years predominantly revolved around issues of stabilization and structural adjustment in line with mainstream development philosophy and policy approaches on how to deal with macroeconomic imbalances. Moreover, while occasional rhetorical references were made to the importance of exogenous shocks, the earlier poor performance of the Ghanaian economy was largely conceptualized by the architects of the ERP as a consequence of inappropriate state actions and misguided macroeconomic policy. In other words, reform measures were designed on the basis of the then prevailing neo-liberal orthodoxy. This included both a particularly optimistic view about the efficacy of the market mechanism as a vehicle for the promotion of efficiency and development, including misconceptions about the prevalence of institutional pre-conditions for market efficiency, and a set of macroeconomic policy recommendations which were later to be named the 'Washington consensus' (Williamson, 1990, 1993).

Accordingly, while policy concerns have definitely been enlarged gradually in Ghana from their almost exclusive short-to medium-term nature in 1983 to include, more recently, longer-term adjustment and development topics as well, the stated policy goals have focused throughout on (i) changing the balance between the role of the state and market forces in the allocation of resources, (ii) macroeconomic policy changes geared at improving the balance of payments and laying the foundations for sustained output growth, and (iii) improving the capacity of the economy to adjust to both external and internal shocks.

In a similar vein, more specific targets and areas of policy attention have concentrated on (i) introducing a market-based flexible exchange rate policy, (ii) reducing domestic financial imbalances, including monetary and fiscal policies to reduce the inflation rate and government deficit financing, (iii) improving resource allocation and eliminating price distortions in various sectors of the economy through the removal of administrative controls coupled with widespread liberalization of prices, privatization and other institutional changes, (iv) promoting domestic savings and investment, including financial liberalization and measures to increase government revenue and investment efficiency, (v) increasing external trade liberalization and promoting an outward-oriented trade strategy with less reliance on the protection of domestic producers, (vi) reviving orderly relationships with external trading partners and creditors, and (vii) mobilizing additional external resources. Other dimensions which have more recently acquired greater attention relate to the need for basic health and education as well as infrastructure as fundamental conditions for growth.

In line with their conventional character, the complex packages of macroeconomic and institutional policy initiatives pursued in Ghana since 1983 have not relied on a single unified framework of economic theory. In fact, the chief theoretical underpinnings of the ERP are, as elsewhere in sub-Saharan Africa, best described as a rather bewildering array of what is in reality a set of simple mainstream macroeconomic, trade and microeconomic models. These are, in addition, combined in a characteristically selective manner with a variety of arguments picked up from (i) the 'new political economy' summarized by Colander (1984), Meier (1995) and Srinivasan (1985), (ii) traditional trade theory and general empirical studies of the relationship between trade and development by, for example, Bhagwati (1978) and Krueger (1978), as well as (iii) more recent studies of the East Asian miracle (World Bank, 1993b).

More specifically, to the extent that adjustment in Ghana has been about macro-stabilization and changing the composition of output, the underlying theoretical macroeconomic models have included (i) the IMF's financial programming (FP) framework and the World Bank's Revised Minimum Standard Model (RMSM) examined by Tarp (1993), and (ii) the so-called Salter-Swan Australian model of macroeconomic adjustment in a small and open economy, which is characterized as dependent (Salter, 1959; Swan, 1956). In the Salter-Swan model, a distinction is made between traded and non-traded goods in contrast with the one-good nature of the FP and RMSM models. Accordingly, a combination of public expenditure control and devaluations of the cedi has been relied on in order to adjust and regain balance between national absorption, on the one side, and exports and imports, on the other, and — on the opposite side of the coin — balance between domestic savings and investment and foreign capital inflows. Financial programming has been used in this context to calculate non-inflationary limits for the expansion of domestic credit based on prior projections of the rate of growth and the availability of external financing. In other words, the ERP approach has concentrated on trying to switch producer incentives and production towards tradeables (i.e. exports and import substitutes) through changes in relative prices, coupled with attempts at limiting inflationary pressures, especially from government deficit financing, by constraining monetary expansion through the use of credit ceilings.

It follows that there is really little difference between the macroeconomic approach of the ERP and the thinking that is at the core of common stabilization and adjustment policies known also from developed country experiences. Yet, whether the extremely weak initial conditions of the Ghanaian economy (internally as well as externally) were such that this approach would indeed work as predicted does not appear to have been a major preoccupation on the side of the ERP's designers in the earlier years of the adjustment process. Instead, this was taken for granted in much the same way as what happened when import-substituting policies were adopted in the 1960s and 1970s. More recently, greater attention has been given to a range of structural bottlenecks and institutional characteristics as well as an intricate set of social issues, which all imply that output responses and distributional consequences may be neither automatic nor easy to predict. Yet, it would appear that there is need to move much further down this path, as discussed in more detail in section 5.

In parallel, when it comes to the widespread domestic market liberalization inherent in the ERP, the main inspiration originated from a mixture of (i) standard textbook 'laissez-faire' microeconomic theory, and (ii) the set of pessimistic views on the role and nature of the state and public choice that formed part of the core of the neo-liberal 'counter-revolution' of the 1980s (Toye, 1987). This 'counter-revolution' is associated with, for example, Lal (1983). Government failure rather than market failure was 'in' in Washington in 1983, and the state was certainly perceived more as a part of the problem than as a part of the solution by the designers of the ERP. As such, both the concept of the state and the assessment of its room for manoeuvre to promote development in a positive direction were in distinct contrast with the rational actor concept that formed the basis for the development planning efforts undertaken in the 1960s and 1970s. In sum, it was taken for granted that the government had better refrain from intervening in the economy, except for taking care of macroeconomic management and a few other minimalist functions.

Hence, the principles of trade liberalization and 'getting prices right' were relied on to ensure that agriculture, industry and the other sectors could produce in an assumed efficient manner in order to pave the way for an almost self-operating or automated process of development. Nevertheless, not much attention was given to the second-best consideration that trade and market liberalization may not increase efficiency when some markets (such as insurance and credit markets) cannot be made to function perfectly - and in practice this is never possible due either to more conventional types of market failure or for reasons related to the cost of transactions and lack of perfect information. In addition, no weight was given to the problem that even if static efficiency gains were realized by moving the economy on to the production possibility frontier, this in no way implied that this frontier would subsequently shift outwards in a dynamic way.

It can be added, that when it came to financial sector reform, the 'financial repression' theories of McKinnon (1973) and Shaw (1973) were counted on as guidelines for how to promote an efficient allocation of investment resources as well as to help close the savings-investment gap and the imbalance between national output and absorption. In this context, there was, however, little by way of recognition of a potential role for directed allocation of credit, and no attention was paid to the many possibilities for market failure identified in the literature to which Joseph E. Stiglitz has contributed in such a prominent way in the past decade (Weiss, 1995).

Adjustment can in principle be attempted in the form of a 'big bang' in which all reform measures are implemented simultaneously. But the ERP reform process in Ghana was, as already noted, a gradual one from the very beginning in 1983. This choice of design does not appear to have been based on extensive theoretical reflections in which the pros and cons of alternative approaches were weighed against each other. Rather, it was taken for granted that a 'big bang' approach would cause too much damage, given the fragile and highly distorted nature of the economy, coupled with the general impression that such a strategy would in any case have been difficult to implement in practice, given the severely constrained institutional and technical administrative capacity available on the side of the Ghanaian government.

It also appears that major external players soon got the impression that the Ghanaian reforms were indeed credible, successful and sustainable. Consequently, the often heard assertion that a 'big bang' may be necessary in order to ensure that the reform process stays irreversibly on course without being intercepted by opposing forces who would reorganize with time, did not appear as pressing as it would otherwise have. However, whether the credibility problem was in fact adequately addressed is an issue which will be further discussed in section 5.

With regard to the sequencing of the reform measures, the underlying premise was that the ERP should impact on the economy in a series of — partially — overlapping phases, with stabilization up-front leading into the rehabilitation of the economy, which was in turn to give way to a phase of economic liberalization and development (Toye, 1991). Hence, it was implicitly assumed that short-term stabilization was not only feasible but a necessary precondition for moving decisively into the subsequent stage of structural adjustment in which, it was assumed, the private sector would respond quickly and smoothly to revised incentive structures. It was 'crowding out' of the private by the public sector that was seen as the critical impediment responsible for the lack of dynamics in Ghana, and — by implication — little attention went into exploring what was required to make sure that the private sector would indeed respond. The same goes for the rather limited attention to the need for effective regulatory systems to ensure that the potential and much needed welfare gains from liberalization and privatization would in fact materialize.

In sum, the interrelated nature of stabilization and adjustment was largely ignored and the same goes for the fact that sustained stability may well be an illusion unless basic adjustment and development problems are addressed as well. The fallacy that stabilization can be perceived as a short-term measure — and be achieved on a sustainable basis before adjustment is addressed — can, of course, be upheld for some time if foreign resource inflows increase as they did in Ghana. Yet, it is relevant to recall here that Rodrik (1990) has aptly pointed out that in practice stabilization policies focusing on fiscal and external financial imbalances as well as the rate of monetary expansion and inflation have proved not to be short-term in nature.

In the first phase of the ERP (i.e. from 1983 to 1987) little attention was given to distributional issues. It was implicitly assumed that improved stability and less inflation in combination with better prices to farmers would lead to economic growth that would benefit those most in need and help lift them out of poverty. Hence, automatic 'trickle down' was relied on to ensure that poverty and inequality were dealt with. This approach came in for a lot of criticism in Ghana and elsewhere during the 1980s. By 1987 the UNICEF call for 'adjustment with a human face' was sounded as an important reminder both of the importance of distributional issues to growth and of the fact that, if adjustment is not people-centred, it is wrongly conceived. The human implications for the most vulnerable parts of society must — it was argued — be made an integral part of the overall strategy, rather than being ignored or treated as an additional welfare component to be tagged on eventually to the reforms.

In Ghana the recognition of the costs which adjustment may inflict on vulnerable groups led in 1988 to the initiation of a 'Programme of Actions to Mitigate the Social Costs of Adjustment' (PAMSCAD). By then it was evident that producer prices, for example, had not in some cases developed as expected. Moreover, the removal of fertilizer and pesticide subsidies no doubt played a role in affecting poor farmers negatively, and concern with retrenched workers was also expressed. It should be noted, however, as discussed in Chapter 10, that after an initial decline there was a mixed recovery of social welfare indicators and that both meso and macro policies during the 1980s period of the ERP had positive effects on the poor, although not all of the poor benefited. Nevertheless, it would appear that while the idea of the need for a 'human face' was generally accepted, little systematic thinking and action went into ensuring that the PAMSCAD was actually integrated into the ERP (ODI, 1996). As such, it seems fair to affirm that the main conceptual basis for the ERP remained unaltered in spite of the somewhat modified rhetoric.

4.   Specific Targets, Policy Measures and Economic Outcomes

As already indicated, Ghana's reforms were intended first to achieve the goals of economic stabilization, focusing on the financial disequilibrium in the fiscal and external sectors and the rate of inflation, and second, to restructure the productive capacities with a view to increasing efficiency and restoring growth in the medium term. These were followed by sectoral reforms intended to ensure improved linkages among the various sectors. As seen in Chapter 1, they were pursued sequentially. Thus, in addition to the stabilization objectives of the 1983–6 period, the government set itself the following targets for the structural adjustment phase of 1987–9:

- to sustain economic growth at around 5–5.5% per annum;

• to increase the level of investment from about 10% of GDP in 1986 to 23% by 1989;
• to raise national savings from 7% of GDP to 15% by 1989; and
• to improve the management of resources within the public sector.

This section shows the largely inconsistent outcomes from Ghana's structural adjustment efforts. An early stabilization period that yielded relatively positive achievements with various macroeconomic aggregates was followed by less consistent outcomes in the medium term, despite more comprehensive policy reforms and institutional restructuring.

Fiscal Targets and Policies for Stabilization and their Outcomes

In the first few years of reform, fiscal policy was directed at restoring the fiscal balance and subsequently controlling the rate of inflation. The strategy was to reduce government expenditure while raising government revenues significantly. On the revenue side, in early April 1983 tariff schedules were simplified to make the maximum import tariff 30%. New taxes were introduced on wealth (property and non-commercial vehicles), while taxes on rental income were increased. Tax rates on beer, cigarettes and gasoline were raised consistently until 1987. At the same time, the tax collection machinery was considerably restructured and strengthened.

One of the most obvious outcomes of the revenue mobilization effort in the stabilization period was the significant increases in government revenue, reflected in its share of a growing GDP (Table 18.1). This conclusion is valid for all sources of government revenue as the proportion of revenue to GDP rose from 5.6% in 1983 to 14.4% in 1986. The structure of government revenues did not change, however, as they continued to be dominated by indirect taxes.

Table 18.1   Share of Government Revenue in GDP 1983–86

Year	Total Revenue as % of GDP	Tax Revenue as % of GDP	Non-Tax Revenue as % of GDP
1983	5.6	4.6	0.1
1984	8.4	6.6	0.2
1985	11.8	9.3	0.2
1986	14.4	12.0	0.2

Source: ISSER, 1992.

On expenditure, the goal was to restrain the nominal growth of wages, while improving the funding for other goods and services. The initial approach was across-the-board expenditure controls. For 1983, it was planned to reduce government expenditures from 10.2% of 1982 GDP to 9.5%. Actual spending ended up being 8%, following a shortfall in government revenue. From 1984, the targeted expenditure was always exceeded by more than 4% of GDP. It had been planned to restrict expenditures more by restraining the growth in the incomes of upper ranks of the public sector. The differentials were, however, widened again after 1986, when the low morale of public servants had more or less collapsed the public sector. There was very little of a systematic approach to expenditure rationalization. While capital expenditure remained a priority, there was relatively little growth in absolute terms for this item, as capital expenditures only rose from 3.6% of 1984 GDP to 5.9% in 1986.

The consequence of the small progress in expenditures was that the increasing revenues grew at about the same rate as expenditures. Government was thus unable to wholly reverse the negative trend in the fiscal balance, leaving aside grants. It was not surprising that, even though the rate of inflation came down, it remained high at the same time as the share of the fiscal deficit in nominal GDP was declining. Indeed, the small progress on the fiscal balance was achieved not through expenditure reductions but through revenue expansion as the reform of the tax system was helped by the expansionary effect that other policies, including the effect of exchange rate depreciation on the tax base, had on the economy. A good impact of the increasing revenues was reflected in the reduction of government borrowing from domestic sources.

Monetary Targets and Policies for Stabilization and their Outcomes

The government set itself an inflation target of 22% for the stabilization period. The variable generally acknowledged as influencing movements in the general price level was the money supply. It was believed that, for growth, the volume and composition of credit provided by the financial institutions to both the private and public sectors would dictate the magnitude and direction of investment. Hence, the monetary policy stance, supported by a set of financial policies, was to achieve both stabilization and resource allocation objectives. The policy sought to control the money supply by limiting credit expansion, while improved management of the financial sector, as discussed in Chapters 7 and 11, was expected to yield enhanced mobilization of domestic resources. The initial policy package consisted of the raising of interest rates to match inflation, selective credit controls, retirement of government debt to the banks, financial sector restructuring and the establishment of a stock exchange.

The interest rate policy was largely one of allowing the Bank of Ghana to use the discount rate to dictate administratively the direction in which rates should go. Interest rates first went up from 3% to 5% in October 1983. They were again raised by 2% in August 1984 and then continued to rise steadily through 1986. At the same time, banks were informed at the beginning of each quarter of the amount of their portfolios which could go to particular sectors, with agriculture and the export sectors counted as the most important. In this period, however, open market operations were rather limited, thus leaving the selective credit controls, the preferential interest rate policies and the reserve requirements as the major tools for managing money supply.

As seen in Chapter 11, the policy of using preferential interest rates to allocate funds to specific sectors, aided by a policy of quantitative sectoral credit ceilings, had very little impact on the actual allocation of financial resources. In addition, the reserve requirements became inconsequential as actual reserve holdings exceeded the required reserves. The limited impact these had on monetary growth is quite well documented (Kapur *et al.*, 1991). Real broad money continued to grow in the stabilization period, even though this growth was considerably slowed down after 1985. Broad money growth peaked at 72% in 1984, with the rate of growth falling to 35% in 1985. In all these years money supply growth exceeded the annual targets of 20%. The consequences of monetary growth for inflation were discussed in Chapter 1. Even though inflation dropped to under 25% in 1986 from nearly 130% in 1983, it was always obvious that the underlying factors were unstable, in view of the huge importance of such factors as rainfall and food production and the volatility of money supply.

Trade and Payments Targets and Policies for Stabilization and their Outcomes

The reform programme had as its centrepiece trade and exchange rate liberalization, seeking to free the exchange rate and trade from excessive controls. Exchange rate liberalization was achieved by permitting the cedi to depreciate in terms of its dollar/market value and by removing exchange controls. Specific trade liberalization instruments included abolition of import licensing and reduction of tariffs on imports. In addition, export promotion measures were introduced to enable the export sector to take full advantage of the improved incentives created by the trade and payments liberalization measures.

There was a series of devaluations until September 1986, when a foreign exchange auction was introduced. This probably marked the earliest indication of an attempt to let the market determine exchange rates. As noted earlier, the downward revision of import tariffs beginning from 1983 ensured that the most punitive tariff of 100% on certain consumer items was reduced to 30%. Luxury goods continued to attract a sales tax of 50%. There were no further adjustments in these until 1986 when the 30% tariff on consumption goods went down to 25%. Import licensing was continued, however, in the years of stabilization.

A number of assessments of the trade and payments policies in the period of stabilization have tended to be positive (Kapur *et al.*, 1991). As seen in Chapter 8, the divergence between the official and unofficial cedi rates narrowed considerably, with the black market premium falling from 8.7 in 1983 to 2.1 in 1986. The exchange and trade policies were also credited with the growth in the volume of exports and imports. However, balance of payments deficits emerged and the increases in imports are acknowledged to have been made possible essentially through massive external financing. Given the uncertainties in the international markets for Ghana's major traditional exports (cocoa and gold), the issue of how the country could continue to develop through deficits in its current account balance remained pertinent after the initial stabilization.

Sector-specific assessments of the impact of trade and exchange rate policies have concentrated on analysis of output and export trends for agriculture and manufacturing (see Chapters 13 and 14) and other sectors as part of the analysis of the impact of macroeconomic policies. In this connection it should be noted that, though there was not much export diversification in the 1980s, the significant growth in the exports of non-traditional agricultural and industrial products in the mid-1990s has been mentioned.

Fiscal Targets and Policies for Structural Adjustment and their Outcomes

The main thrust of fiscal policy after 1987 was to broaden the scope of the tax system, improving on efficiency and equity. While revenue and expenditure remained stable as proportions of GDP up to 1991, greater attention was also paid to improving the incentive structure for the private sector in order to facilitate production. The development of the economic infrastructure, which had begun earlier, was accelerated. The administration of the tax system was significantly strengthened in order to ensure greater tax compliance among self-employed persons, while also monitoring corporate accounts. Special efforts were also made to monitor the public accounts.

In line with the above objectives, the government reduced corporate tax rates for the manufacturing, agriculture and export sectors from 55% to 45% in 1988. Later in 1989, the corporate tax rate was reduced for all other sectors (except banking, insurance and commercial activities) from 55% to 50%. Again, in 1991, the general rate for corporate taxes was reduced to 35% for agriculture, manufacturing, real estate, construction and services. In addition to this, the manufacturing sector was granted capital allowances provided under the investment code. The capital gains tax was brought down to 5%, while the withholding tax on dividends went down from 30% to 15%. In the post-1987 period, personal income taxes were also reduced considerably, so that, by 1991, the top marginal rate of tax fell from 55% to 25%.

The significance of all these tax changes was that tax revenue as a proportion of GDP rose more significantly after 1987 and the structure of government revenues changed. Even though by 1990 taxes remained the main source of government revenue, grants had replaced non-tax sources as the second major source of government revenue, by 1990 constituting over 10% of total government revenue. This structure changed again after 1992 to give non-tax revenues a more significant share, as discussed below. Despite the improvements, the revenue/GDP ratio hit a plateau after 1986 at about 16% following the impressive rise in the stabilization years. This has been lower than the SSA average of 19%. Indeed, no revenue targets have been met since 1986.

After revenue growth levelled off, government spending also stabilized in the period 1987–90, but at a higher level of about 18% of GDP in broad terms, indicating a continuing broad fiscal deficit, although the narrow budget registered a surplus. The difficulty in containing public expenditures below revenues has been generally attributed to the expenditures on economic and social infrastructure. It was possible, however, for the government to retire domestic debt and service foreign debt through the infusion of foreign aid. Despite the fact that two-thirds of bilateral aid was in grants, compared with 20% of multilateral aid, and that the total debt-service ratio for 1990 was down to 36% from a peak of 57% in 1988, the question of the sustainability of the fiscal programme became critical, in view of the fragility of such assistance.

As observed in Chapter 1, these trends have altered significantly since 1991, and expenditures, carried by a recurrent component fuelled by interest payments, have climbed very fast even as revenues have continued to rise. In 1992, the broad deficit reached 10% of GDP. After that year, the government made attempts to reduce the size of the deficit by increasing receipts dramatically through divestiture of state enterprises in addition to new growth in tax revenue. Aside from the divestiture receipts which were often planned solely for the purpose of 'balancing the budget', the deficit averaged over 7% of GDP in 1992–5. It is important to note that the growth in tax revenues has usually been less than expected in the budget statements, while expenditures have often exceeded those planned.

From the point of view of the impact of the fiscal policies on production, it is noteworthy that the response of the private sector to the incentives created by the corporate tax rate reduction and tax rebates has not been encouraging. The least addressed aspect of the fiscal adjustment policy is its impact on employment, either directly through retrenchment of government workers or indirectly through deflationary fiscal policy measures. Also, the implications of reductions in import duties and restructuring of the sales tax which permitted an equal rate of taxation for imported and locally produced goods, aimed at the development of local industries, especially capacity utilization and hence employment absorption, are not positive. It was assumed that the country had the capacity to absorb displaced workers, as it attempted to do following the expulsion of Ghanaians from Nigeria in 1984. But the informal sector, where most of the retrenched workers were expected to find new livelihoods, constitutes only a 'dumping ground' to the extent that the inflow of displaced labour tends to depress the low productivity which characterizes the sector. Since unemployment has implications for the standard of living, and in particular for poverty alleviation, the extent of the impact of the fiscal balance on employment remained crucial, even if not addressed. Also, the capacity of the private sector to absorb the redundant labour from the public sector became questionable.

Monetary/Financial Targets and Policies for Structural Adjustment and their Outcomes

After the initial stabilization period, the focus of monetary polices was broadened during the structural adjustment period, focusing on the liberalization of controls on interest rates and bank credit, as well as a gradual shift to indirect monetary management. These were accompanied by a major financial sector reform programme (see Chapter 11) that aimed at improving the soundness of the banking system. The financial sector reform programme (FINSAP) was intended to improve the regulatory framework for banking and to improve banking supervision, efficiency and the profitability of banks. This last included attempts to save the non-performing assets of the banks. In a later phase of FINSAP, interest was focused on structural change, including ownership and management structures. Attempts have been made to enhance domestic resource mobilization by restoring positive real interest rates, while improving the range of financial instruments by developing the non-bank financial sector.

Specifically, the limits on maximum bank lending rates and minimum bank deposit rates were removed in September 1987. In February 1988, the controls on sectoral credit allocation were abolished, except for agriculture, which also went in 1990. While all commercial banks were free to determine all their borrowing and lending rates, in order to discourage their recourse to central bank facilities and to promote interbank lending as well as to encourage them to make maximum use of the facilities at the new discount house, the Bank of Ghana raised its lending rate (bank rate) from 23.5% to 26% in 1988. Monetary policy has been tightened substantially as the financial sector reforms have been accelerated. The monetary authorities rationalized minimum reserve requirements and introduced an auction of bills and bonds to absorb excess liquidity. Thus cash reserve requirements against demand deposits were revised to 22% in 1990. At the same time cash reserves against savings and time deposits rose from 15% in 1989 to 20% in 1990. Following the limited responsiveness of interest rates after the tightening of the liquidity position, policy measures were broadened to encompass phased increases in the Bank of Ghana's rediscount rate, rising to 26% in September 1990 and then to 35% in January 1991. Treasury Bills were made more available to the non-bank sector. These trends of tight monetary policy continued well into the 1990s.

The impact of the monetary and financial policies on the performance of the relevant indicators has been mixed. The growth rate of net domestic credit fell in the early adjustment years, dropping to 13% in 1988 from 61% in 1985. This was largely a result of the improvement in government finances which enabled some repayments to the banking system. Despite this situation, money supply continued to grow rapidly, mainly as a consequence of very significant inflows of foreign concessional assistance and the improvements in the balance of payments. The money supply growth of 43% in 1988 exceeded by far the 20% target of the government's monetary programme.

Since 1992, monetary policy has been used to accommodate the excesses of government, which themselves have been highly unpredictable. This is reflected in the significant disparity between actuals and targets for various monetary development indicators. For 1995, government aimed at primarily 'bringing down inflation and stabilising the value of the cedi' (Budget Statement, 1995). For the real GDP growth of 5%, an end-of-period inflation rate of 18% and a balance of payments surplus of $210 m. were targeted. In support of these policy objectives and targets, a tight monetary policy was to be pursued. A target of 14% was set for the growth of money supply in the year, which contrasted sharply with the actual increases experienced in 1992, 1993 and 1994 of 52%, 27% and 46% respectively. In furtherance of the objectives of tight monetary policy, the Bank Rate was raised by 6 points from 33% to 39% in January, and again by another 6 percentage points to 45% in September. The commercial banks were urged to intensify their savings mobilization efforts by raising their deposit rates. The Bank of Ghana increased its Open Market Operations (OMO) efforts to take out excess liquidity emanating from successive years of large monetary increases.

Despite the policy intentions and subsequent efforts to contain monetary growth, broad money supply (M2) rose by as much as 38% (¢362 bn) in 1995, far exceeding the 14% (¢136 bn) increase programmed for the year. This was a reflection of the generally poor targeting outcomes that have become characteristic of economic management in the years of reform as discussed in Chapter 1. Together with the excessively high growth rates experienced in the preceding three years, the average growth rate of money supply during 1992–5 was as high as 41%. The increasing use of net domestic credit to finance the public sector deficit was the main cause of this trend, with the private sector effectively crowded out.

Trade and Payments Targets and Policies for Structural Adjustment and their Outcomes

Essentially the trade and payments policies only saw changes with the greater liberalization of the exchange rate determination process beginning from 1986. Indeed, by the middle of that year, the cedi was still considered to be overvalued in view of the disparity between the official and parallel market rates and the deterioration in the net external position of the Bank of Ghana. Restrictive practices were being employed to support the official exchange rate in order to maintain international payments. Also, by that time, the difficulty of managing large discrete devaluations under the pegged exchange rate arrangement had become apparent.

As seen in Chapter 8, the government continued the reform of the exchange rate management system by first introducing an auction alongside the introduction of two windows for the purchase of foreign exchange. Aside from the major economic reasons for adopting a floating exchange rate system with the auction, it was also a move intended to depoliticize the rate determination process. The auction is acknowledged to have provided the institutional support for the gradual liberalization of the exchange rate (Kapur *et al.*, 1991). An objective of the auction system was to bring about a further depreciation of the cedi regarded as essential for enhancing the balance of payments position, and reduce the spread between the parallel market and official rates. Between December 1985 and December 1986 the cedi depreciated by 43%.

The auction system saw a number of modifications up until 1990. While maintaining the retail nature of the system, the first change was to make bidders pay the bid price instead of the marginal price. Also, the two auction windows were unified early in 1987. Between then and 1990, all foreign-exchange transactions were carried out under the rate determined in the weekly auction. By widening participation in the auction to include consumer goods which were previously excluded, the restrictions on various imports through access to foreign exchange were lifted. By February 1988, all consumer goods were eligible for financing through the auction. This literally lifted all import restrictions, leaving the administrative arrangements for licensing imports unnecessary.

The auctioning of foreign exchange effectively saw a narrowing of the spread between parallel and official rates and between the nominal and real effective exchange rates between 1987 and 1990. The real effective exchange rate depreciated by 23% in 1987 as against 42% in 1986, and by 5% in 1988 and 6% in 1989. Forex bureaux were licensed to operate in 1988. Starting with a monthly sale of US$1.8 m. in early 1988, they sold US$20.9 m. by the end of 1990. Existing alongside the auction system, the rates quoted by the bureaux were much closer to the parallel market rates and quickly overshadowed transactions on the auction floors with lower rates. The growing use of the bureaux rate for more transactions (as bidders were rationed out of the auction floor) provided the basis for the eventual unification of the two systems and the development of one exchange rate for all transactions. This came about with the development of a composite exchange rate arrangement by which the Bank of Ghana auctioned foreign exchange only on a wholesale basis to authorized dealers in April 1990. Since then, an interbank market has developed leading to a closure of the gap between auction and forex bureaux rates.

As Harrigan and Oduro suggest in Chapter 8, it is still unclear how the liberalization of the exchange rate has impacted on macroeconomic developments. The period 1987–90 saw a build-up of reserves at the same time as the exchange rate depreciated and the country was experiencing growing deficits in the balance of trade and the current accounts. The deficits in the current account balance were financed by a combination of sources including grants, official long-term and short-term loans, direct foreign investment and IMF financing arrangements (see Table 8.3).

Export growth rates provide some basis for a closer look at the response of the economy to the exchange rate adjustments. They show, as for the fiscal and monetary outcomes, an inconsistent pattern. During 1986–8, total exports grew by 7.8%, and by 8.9% per annum in the next three years. High growth rates were recorded in the first period for timber, non-traditional exports, bauxite, gold, electricity and non-factor services. Cocoa export earnings grew by only 2.4%, but had a good recovery in 1988–90, when they grew by 12.5%. Unfortunately, for most of the export sectors, actual growth fell far short of targeted growth up to 1990.

In 1991, with the decline in oil import prices and the strong growth in the volume of gold and timber exports, the external accounts saw an improvement. The overall balance of payments recorded a surplus of US$137 m. following an increase in official transfers and net capital inflows. However, as discussed in earlier chapters, the deficits in the balance of trade and in the current account have worsened since 1992. The real effective exchange rate began to appreciate and the value of exports continued to decline faster. With the faster growth in import values against export values, the trade balance deteriorated rapidly in the 1990s with a record deficit of as much as US$664 m. in 1993. The current account deficit rose from US$253 m. in 1991 to a record US$559 m. in 1993 (see Chapter 8). While both the trade deficit and current account deficit were reduced in 1995, it is not clear how the liberalized exchange rate regime has stabilized the economy in the medium term.

5.   Lessons Learnt and Looking Forward

Despite the evident adjustment fatigue one encounters in Ghana, there is by now general agreement locally and in the donor community that continuous adjustment and well thought out macromanagement are necessary conditions for development to proceed. Similarly, it is no longer seriously being questioned that inward-looking, import-substituting policies and state interventionism — or 'dirigisme' as Lal put it in 1983 — can be carried too far. The economic history of Ghana during the Nkrumah decade remains too vivid an illustration for such doubt to remain credible. Thus, Easterly (1993) and Fischer (1993) certainly make points of direct relevance to Ghana when in cross-country context they draw attention to the negative growth effects of macroeconomic imbalances and economic distortions and argue that economic policy matters for development outcomes. Nevertheless, it is equally correct that there are — as highlighted by Helleiner (1993) — no quick economic fixes to the development problems of sub-Saharan Africa, and Ghana is no exception in this respect.

So-called responsible stabilization and structural adjustment policies have by now been pursued consistently under the guidance of the IMF and the World Bank for around 15 years, i.e. a period which is much longer than the Nkrumah years. Some slippage took place in connection with the 1992 elections, but generally all the 'right things' have been done more or less in accordance with the theoretical underpinnings of the ERP as outlined in this book. Yet, critical development constraints remain in place and macroeconomic stability has been difficult to maintain. In other words, the shift to a higher and sustainable growth and development path would appear to require more concerted efforts and a broader development vision than originally perceived in Ghana and elsewhere. An attempt will therefore be made in this section briefly to outline some of the major lessons learnt. The focus will, in addition, be on remaining problems and key elements of an effective forward-looking development strategy.

As pointed out by Aryeetey and Harrigan in Chapter 1, and in section 4 of this chapter, it is true that the Ghanaian reform produced periods of much needed economic growth since 1983, though starting from the crisis condition; and at least up to 1992 a measure of macroeconomic stability was restored following the introduction of the ERP. In parallel, substantial liberalization and privatization were undertaken in the various markets and sectors of the economy, dealing with factor markets as well as the external, industrial and agricultural sectors. Hence, 'policy-induced distortions' have been practically removed and prices are generally established by (imperfect) market forces, although some intervention takes places in the foreign-exchange market to influence the exchange rate of the cedi.

On the other hand, since 1992 growth has slackened considerably, and Killick correctly notes in Chapter 3 that the fact that incomes may still not have reached even their 1960 level places the growth achievements of the ERP in what he pointedly calls sobering context. This is so, in particular, since it is far from obvious that the achievements made are sustainable. Progress was in large measure based on (i) the very considerable increases in the foreign aid influx, which relieved the foreign-exchange and savings constraints, and (ii) static efficiency gains involving a more rational utilization of capacity. Yet, such welcome static gains do not by themselves guarantee that dynamic improvements will follow suit. Moreover, many of the original predictions of the ERP have not in actual fact come true.

It seems, first of all, that very little structural transformation of the economy took place in the period under consideration. Hence, Ghana does not appear to have progressed along the 'typical' development path where an economy moves away from being a backward primary sector-dependent economy to one in which a dynamic industrial sector has taken root (see Chapter 3 and also Chenery and Syrquin, 1975; and Chenery, Robinson and Syrquin, 1986). The sector which has grown in relative importance in Ghana during the ERP is the services sector, including the informal sector as highlighted by Fine and Boateng in Chapter 12. This characteristic is worrisome since the domestic services sector cannot by itself provide the basis for sustained growth. Services produced are non-tradeables, whilst the stated and relevant aim of the ERP is to promote the production of tradeables. This observation suggests that Dutch disease effects related to the ERP capital inflows may have been operating, pushing up the relative price of nontradeables and encouraging their production. Along similar lines, it can be noted that ERP finance has predominantly flowed into the public sector, which tends to produce non-tradeables.

Most contributors to this volume have also drawn attention to a range of complex structural issues, which have gone largely unaddressed in Ghana, as the main focus of the ERP policies has been on macro policy, liberalizing markets and 'getting prices right'. An example is Bortei-Doku Aryeetey, who suggests, in Chapter 17, that there has been little change in the structure of women's economic activities due to structural constraints; but also Harrigan and Aryeetey argue in Chapter 1 that there has not been enough attention to structural constraints and the supply side of the economy. More generally, it can be observed that while agricultural prices and markets were liberalized, the supply response has been poor with the exception of cocoa in the 1980s. This would appear to be so for food as well as most export crops, which implies that food insecurity prevails as a result of the vagaries of weather and the low-level technology used. Nyanteng and Seini point in Chapter 14 to an average annual rate of growth of agriculture of only 2% from 1990 to 1995. In addition, they argue convincingly that the low and wide fluctuations in the per capita growth rate of the economy, around a declining trend since 1990, are due largely to this disappointing performance of the agricultural sector. Thus, Ghana is in this regard quite typical of sub-Saharan Africa.

For the industrial sector, Asante, Tsikata and Nixson stress in Chapter 13 that real manufacturing output experienced positive growth rates after 1984, but at a decelerating rate after 1988. In fact, the slow-down in manufacturing growth was reflected in the annual growth rate of the whole industrial sector, which declined from 6.9% between 1983 and 1987 to 4.4% between 1988 and 1995. This suggests, on the one hand, that trade liberalization is having an impact involving the closing down of some industries in the more competitive environment. It would seem, on the other hand, that while appropriate trade and macroeconomic policies are necessary to bring about manufacturing growth, they are not sufficient to ensure quick, positive and substantial responses that can be sustained. In other words, the disappointingly low degree of structural transformation is in all likelihood linked with the de-industrialization, which has taken place in at least part of the industrial sector following trade liberalization, while newer activities take more time and effort to get established. Relevant here is also the suggestion in Chapter 11 by Aryeetey, Nissanke, and Steel that lack of access to credit explains why private people have not moved from the informal to the formal sector.

Similarly, Oduro in Chapter 9 as well as Asante, Tsikata and Nixson in Chapter 13 show that there has not been significant export diversification, in dire contrast with the stated aims of the ERP. Hence, while the relative shares of the big three exports (cocoa, gold and timber) have changed, with mining gaining in importance, the total share is much the same, and non-traditional exports constituted less than 10% of the total in 1995, although their growth rates are well above average as discussed in Chapters 13 and 14. Finally, linkages between sectors remain weak as evident from Round's and Powell's innovative analysis in Chapter 4, in particular as regards the mining sector. This evidently raises doubts as to the ability of this sector to provide the much needed impetus to the remainder of the economy and puts into question the existing investment strategy, where mining has absorbed considerable finance.

The above lack of structural transformation underlines that, while growth may increase in the short run as import constraints are relieved by donor-mobilized foreign resource inflows, this is far from enough to be confident that development is on track. As such, this serves as an illuminating lesson both to Ghanaian policy-makers and to the donor community. This point is underpinned by the fact that private sector investment, including direct foreign investment, has been very disappointing at a level of no more than 5% of GDP during the ERP period, as shown in Chapters 11 and 7. The only exception is the mining sector, which has attracted some attention, but the sector suffers, as just noted, from low linkages to the rest of the economy.

Thus, gross domestic investment in Ghana has remained at around a clearly inadequate level of no more than 15% of GDP during the ERP, which is low even by African standards. It is not uncommon that investment is sluggish during adjustment as evidenced in general studies by Faini *et al.* (1991), Mosley, Harrigan and Toye (1991) and Mosley and Weeks (1993). Nevertheless, while low investment performance is often related to faltering public investment, this was not so in Ghana during the ERP. In fact, the growth recorded up to 1991 was, as discussed by Harrigan and Younger in Chapter 10, largely driven by aid-funded public sector investment reaching 10% of GDP. This puts the lack of private investment, which has evidently fuelled unemployment, into even starker perspective.

Various explanations for the poor private sector investment performance were put forward in this volume, ranging from lack of credit due to tight monetary policy and public sector crowding out to political uncertainty. Perhaps one policy conclusion is that the government should run a tighter fiscal policy and a looser monetary policy as suggested by Aryeetey and Harrigan in Chapter 1. However, it would appear more generally that the underlying constraints to investment recovery are embedded in the broad Ghanaian environment for investment decision-making, which is influenced by uncertainty and lack of credibility. In such an environment investors shy away from crucial long-term investments and focus their attention on short-term speculative behaviour in sectors such as that of trading where the turnover time of capital is short and profitability is high. An illustration of this is that the business community suffered considerably as a result of the PNDC revolution in the early 1980s and may still resent the Rawlings government (ODI, 1996). Moreover, it is evident that government attitudes towards private sector success still vary. Qualitative evidence suggests that private success breeds suspicion, which is not unusual, but in the case of Ghana there seems to be the added problem that there is ample room for such suspicion to trigger off acts of threat and outright expropriation.

On the side of savings, performance has been equally poor as set out in, for example, Chapter 7 by Brownbridge, Gockel and Harrington. In spite of almost complete financial liberalization, domestic savings mobilization did not increase. Gross domestic savings remained at around 7%; thus, even if investment remained sluggish, the savings-investment gap remained considerable. This gap has, as already noted, been bridged by foreign inflows, including aid, investment in mining and remittances from Ghanaians abroad, for consumption and housing as pointed out in Chapter 8. Yet it is noteworthy that, except for mining, these inflows are not in response to commercial considerations, raising issues already touched upon above, including the perceived risks attached to investment in Ghana.

Moreover, becoming dependent on foreign inflows to close the savings-investment gap is worrisome for several reasons. First, it undermines sovereignty over economic policy. Secondly, it can lead to debt-servicing problems, although the terms of the debt have been improving as shown by Harrigan and Younger in Chapter 10. Thirdly, the economy is becoming more aid-dependent. It is clear, for example, that the foreign-exchange auction and the import liberalization initiatives would not have been undertaken without substantial capital inflows, as discussed by Aryeetey and Harrigan in Chapter 1 and Harrigan and Oduro in Chapter 8. This raises problematic questions about the sustainability of the process in a global context characterized by dwindling aid flows; and this is so even if Ghana may have a measure of special leverage, as donors have to some extent become locked into providing still more aid to a recipient that has indeed 'behaved' well without, however, harvesting all the benefits promised.

When it comes to the role of the state during the ERP, it is evident that it has been changing considerably since 1983. As noted by Gyimah-Boadi and Jeffries in Chapter 2, Ghana has made significant strides from statism towards neo-liberalism, and its traditionally large parastatal and public sector has been pruned down. Yet questions remain as to the efficiency of the public sector when it comes to the implementation of investments as discussed by Wetzel in Chapter 6 and its role in mobilizing the externalities identified in the new endogenous growth literature as being important (see, for example, the contributions by Lucas, 1988, and Roemer, 1986). The public sector investment programme did recover during the ERP as explained in several chapters in this volume, but the general impression is that investment was not used wisely in high impact areas. An example is mining, which has already been touched upon. Yet, evidence as to the efficiency of public sector investment, including estimates of incremental capital-output ratios, is mixed and differs depending on the sub-periods in focus.

When it comes to the social impact of adjustment it is — as elsewhere in Africa — difficult to reach robust conclusions in Ghana. It is clear from Chapter 16 by Appiah, Demery and Laryea-Adjei that poverty in Ghana is predominantly a rural phenomenon, although with distinct regional differences; but, despite ambitious claims by, for example Leechor (1994), little is known empirically about how adjustment has affected poor and vulnerable groups in practice. Chapter 15 on social policies by Aryeetey and Goldstein actually suggests that there has been little focus in dealing with the poor, despite growing public expenditures on rural development. These would explain why, despite the growth in public expenditure, its efficiency remains questionable. Thus, the widely reported increases in spending (including donor spending) on health and education in more recent years have had uncertain poverty effects, although Harrigan and Younger speculate in Chapter 10 that growth in the second half of the 1980s improved social welfare. However, it is difficult, if not impossible, to say whether the growth realized actually helped the very poorest members of Ghanaian society, and certainly more could have been done. In spite of major donor-supported initiatives in the area of household surveying, one is left with rather vague observations. For example, the conclusion to be drawn about poverty trends critically depends, as discussed by Appiah, Demery and Laryea-Adjei, on the choice of base year.

In sum, while continuous adjustment is certainly a necessary condition for development as already asserted above, the Ghanaian case demonstrates that it is by no means a sufficient condition, and this is so in spite of the very substantial foreign resources made available in the form of aid to support the reform efforts. Ghana remains, as correctly pointed out by Killick in Chapter 3, a fragile, poor and open African (mainly rural) economy with low savings and investment, constrained by weak institutions, small domestic markets, rudimentary technology and limited human capital. Moreover, the economy is inflexible, susceptible to market failure and fragmentation as well as exogenous shocks, and exports are heavily dependent on a few primary products. The implication is that domestic policy, the importance of which should not be underestimated, is only one among many causal factors that drive economic performance. In addition, a sound basis for future development is yet to be established.

In speculating about the critical development issues that need to be addressed on a priority basis in Ghana to improve macroeconomic performance and speed up development, it is useful to note as a point of reference that the rate of growth in any economy is influenced by external and internal policies and events that shape (i) the accumulation of physical and human capital, (ii) the efficiency of resource allocation, and (iii) the ability to acquire and apply modern technology (Bigsten, 1996). Furthermore, Bigsten goes on to affirm that this proposition is consistent with all growth theories, including more traditional two-gap models such as the World Bank RMSM mentioned in section 3, the neoclassical growth models of Solow (1956) or modern endogenous growth models although they differ in many other respects. It follows that the present low savings and investment rates in Ghana are extremely critical.

The endogenous models include the formulations proposed by Lucas (1988) and Roemer (1986) as well as the early contribution by Arrow (1985), in which he tries to capture increasing returns through 'learning by doing' effects and as such make technological progress endogenous rather than exogenous. It is consistent with this different focus that the new growth theory puts particular emphasis on human capital investments and the influence of technological innovations, which are less costly in the presence of large capital stocks. Yet, the only difference in terms of outcomes between the Solow model and the endogenous frameworks is that, while higher investment can only lead to higher growth in a transition phase in the Solow model, the better performance may be more permanent in the endogenous growth frameworks. Hence, savings and investment must — without a doubt — increase in Ghana for development to proceed, in particular since the economy is so small and therefore at a disadvantage in acquiring knowledge, which is more readily acquired in economies operating on a larger scale.

Another partly overlapping strand of modern theory includes the proposed 'counter-counterrevolution in development theory' by Krugman (1993). He argues that the counterrevolution of the early 1980s went too far. Hence, he puts renewed focus on the importance of strategic complementarities in production and demand, which aggregate to positive external economies at the level of society as a whole, by drawing on insights from new developments in industrial organization. Accordingly, in the Krugman model, in which there are increasing returns to scale and imperfect competition in the modern sector, the externalities are external to the individual plant and can - under certain specified conditions — be realized only if new technology is introduced across the board rather than in a piecemeal manner. As such, Krugman's analysis brings to mind the considerations behind the balanced 'big push' strategy of Rosenstein-Rodan (1943), needed to bring the economy out of a low-level poverty trap (Nelson, 1956). Yet, at the same time Krugman makes an attempt to interpret the 'linkage concept' inherent in the unbalanced development strategy of Hirschman (1958); and he concludes by noting that, while development economics has been used to justify some highly destructive economic policies, there is a useful set of core ideas, including the need for planning, that should be resurrected. This does not, however, appear to have been done in policy-making in Ghana during the ERP period in contrast to what happened in East Asia.

When it comes to the alternative kinds of theoretical insights that can be gained from more traditional development theory along structuralist and dependency lines of thinking (briefly summarized in Tarp, 1993), they evidently provide a justified and highly relevant warning that it is by no means easy to promote development in a small unbalanced economy such as that of Ghana. Ghana, together with other low-income countries, depends in critical ways on the structure and characteristics of the international economy, a detailed discussion of which is beyond the scope of this chapter. Nevertheless, Ghana will from time to time and in various intricate ways be hurt because of its vulnerability in the global economy where it is on an unequal footing with more developed countries, an example being the declining international price of cocoa which afflicted Ghana throughout much of the ERP period. This dimension does not, however, appear to have preoccupied proponents of export-oriented development strategies to the extent necessary.

Sound and consistent policies should obviously be pursued and may, as already pointed out, matter a great deal to economic outcomes in the short as well as longer term. Yet, the present difficulties with which Ghana has to deal, do indicate very clearly that it is by no means fully settled how 'good economic policies' actually look, even if a good deal of consensus has emerged among academics as well as policy-makers. An eminent overview, which provides further background on the issues raised in this as well as previous chapters of this volume, is provided by Helleiner (1993). He carefully outlines areas of consensus as well as continuing conflict in relation to the role of the state, the import regime and industrial protection,[1] financial sector liberalization and reform, instruments and objectives for agricultural development, aid requirements and the exchange rate.

Hence, what will be done in the remainder of this section is not to review and assess these individual economic policy areas of debate in any detailed way. Instead the focus will be on the argument that there is something fundamental, which has generally been missing from the kinds of economic analyses referred to so far. Furthermore it will be argued that this 'missing' cross-cutting agent — or dimension — can actually help to explain, for example, why it is that savings and investment are so low and ineffective, and why the policies used so far have not produced

---

[1] The theoretical contributions under the heading of new trade theory also merit attention here (see for example the review by Greenaway, 1991).

the desired results. In addition, some suggestions will be made about future development strategy and priorities at the overall level.

What is referred to above is the thinking inherent in what can broadly be referred to as new institutional economics. Bhardan (1989) provides a clear review, and Bigsten (1996) aptly points out that institutional analysis is intermingled with issues from the political arena. Thus, entering this area of enquiry is difficult because of the complex interplay of economic and political variables, about which so little is actually known. The risk of making tautological statements is also permanently looming in the background, as hinted at by Stiglitz (1989). Nevertheless, the approach does point to issues which are particularly pertinent in the Ghanaian case. This is so because it is apparent to even the most casual observer of the Ghanaian economy (i) that transactions costs are significant, and (ii) information is highly imperfect. A few examples may be useful.

It is widely reported that it takes considerable effort to strike economic deals in Ghana, and this is so not only in the local markets where bargaining can certainly be a lengthy process. In addition, even if an agreement is reached, it appears to be common knowledge that it is uncertain whether it will actually be honoured in practice. Even corruption often seems to be unable to deal with this problem. More generally it is relevant to refer to North (1990), as he has stressed that the inability of societies to develop cheap ways of ensuring compliance with contracts is the most important source of stagnation in history and of underdevelopment in the Third World today (Bigsten, 1996). Hence, given the difficulty of making reliable predictions about the future, contracts will tend to be short-term, trade-focused, often involving speculative exchanges rather than longer-term investments with productive impact.

Accordingly, transactions costs are very high indeed in Ghana. Along similar lines one can point to the generalized uncertainty as to whether property rights will actually be respected, so that the returns to investment can be appropriated by investors (Aryeetey, 1994). Hence, investors are for good reasons more careful and spend resources gathering information and insuring themselves, which would not be required in other contexts. In addition, even if firms do consider investing, there are great uncertainties about the possibility of their being able to market new goods, as consumers tend to be conservative and suspicious about product quality. Yet another example relates to women's access to and control over land, where it could certainly be argued that existing institutions governing land rights are largely dysfunctional (Bortei-Doku Aryeetey, 1996), and capital markets are, as elsewhere, characterized by problems of adverse selection and moral hazard. This gives rise to a limited supply of loanable funds, credit rationing, etc. and therefore a less efficient allocation of capital (Aryeetey et al., 1997).

It follows from the above list of examples that Ghana faces a massive problem of collective action. Potential gainers need to act together and take the necessary steps to promote the establishment of efficiency-enhancing institutions (including effective private markets), that would bring transactions costs to a more manageable level and help put the economy on a dynamic growth path. The question is how this can be brought about. This is a wide-ranging question with political economy dimensions, but it certainly points to a potentially crucial role for the government in taking bold social and economic initiatives, including legal measures, that can help remove existing risks and uncertainty and further the effective functioning of private markets and non-market institutions. The need for a strong state in this respect is increasingly being acknowledged in the emerging new orthodoxy, including that held by Ghana's principal donors (World Bank 1997). In this context the issue of corruption, the importance of which is difficult to assess in quantitative terms, needs particular attention. People must also become convinced that the predatory state is a thing of the past. For this to happen, however, the government needs, as argued in general terms by Stiglitz (1997), to be strengthened to enable it to put appropriate regulatory structures in place. Development is impossible without the active participation of the government, and Stiglitz aptly goes on to argue that what is required is not deregulation, but regulatory redesign to promote competition where it is viable and to ensure that monopoly power is not too heavily exploited when competition is absent.

In line with the process outlined above, it would appear particularly important that a well-defined and widely understood development vision is articulated in Ghana that can serve both as a rallying point and as a broad guideline for government action in ensuring that critically needed public goods are supplied. The present rather narrow focus on the need to promote exports in the short run is wanting in several ways. It overlooks the fact that 'breaking into' the world markets presupposes a prior learning process, that the necessary linkage effects may not be present and that external economic relations are better perceived as additional to internal domestic efforts that treat agricultural development as fundamental.

This observation can be further detailed along the lines discussed by, for example, Irma Adelman (1992), who hypothesized that what she termed agricultural development-led industrialization (ADLI) deserves greater attention. The primary mechanism through which ADLI is intended to work is the generation of income for rural people and induced demand for industrial output through increased demand for industrial inputs and increased consumption of manufactures by farmers. Thus, linkages with the industrial sector are seen as important. Successful implementation clearly presumes high inter-sectoral linkages, supply responsiveness in both agriculture and industry and the existence of appropriate technology. Yet, if empirical investigation shows that these preconditions are not in place, the appropriate reaction is not necessarily to drop ADLI, but to initiate action to overcome these constraints.

In other words, ADLI is a strategy that takes as its point of departure the overwhelming importance of the agriculture sector. Moreover, it consists of a strategic focus on improving the productivity of food agriculture on small and medium-sized farms, and argues that agricultural expansion induces concomitant growth in consumer goods and agricultural input industries. For this to work, farmers must obviously be made capable of responding to incentives through the dissemination of appropriate technology and through agricultural research focused on their needs. Yet, it is hard to avoid the impression in Ghana that ADLI should be pursued in a much more concerted manner than has been observed so far.

Debates are evidently ongoing with various degrees of optimism, regarding (i) potential sources of sustained rural income growth to provide the initial purchasing power in rural areas, (ii) whether demand will really be directed towards locally produced goods, and (iii) the price responsiveness of farmers. Yet, the SAM-based analyses referred to earlier (Chapter 4) do provide a useful reminder that agriculture sector multipliers may well be higher than those of industry, so the agriculture sector-focused approach suggested here does deserve to be fully analyzed and tested both from a growth and from a poverty alleviation perspective.

In addition, it may be relevant to point out that, while ADLI is not an export-oriented strategy as such, since it puts emphasis on the dynamic effects of domestic demand, the potential contribution of foreign trade to growth is not in question. ADLI and outward orientation are, in other words, complementary dimensions. Yet, it can certainly be argued that ADLI does seem to have an advantage as the best analytical focal point and overall vision in that it focuses attention on how a well functioning and integrated economy can be developed. It does not assume that countries can start exporting without going through the necessary learning process, which is, as noted, sometimes reflected in more optimistic export-oriented arguments.

6.   Conclusion

Important strides have been made in Ghana during the past 15 years to overcome the economic crisis, which worsened so harshly in the early 1980s. Ghana today is not the Ghana of the 1970s, and some growth was certainly experienced during the period up to 1992 together with the restoration of a degree of macroeconomic stability. This is in itself quite an achievement compared with the state of the economy in the 1970s. Nevertheless, while stabilization and adjustment are necessary conditions for development to succeed, this is not a sufficient condition to break out of the 'vicious circle of poverty', and in Ghana the macroeconomic question remains as to whether the progress made up to 1992 is sustainable. It was argued in this and other chapters of this book that there is justified doubt as to whether this is indeed the case. Growth is stagnating now, and previous progress was due in large measure to external capital inflows.

Moreover, adjustment as practised in Ghana has not so far addressed effectively the complex set of institutional constraints, which can limit or frustrate the country's development process. Liberalization and privatization have been pursued, but the economic and social environment is yet to be modified with a view to promoting the accumulation of factors of production, their efficient use and the introduction of better technologies. Muddling through along the lines of 'orthodoxy' as Ghana has done will not be enough. A clear vision of the direction in which the country is supposed to move is conspicuously absent in spite of the laudable desires expressed in the *Ghana-Vision 2020* document (Government of Ghana, 1995). Accordingly, it is suggested that attention in policy-making should be broadened to include the wide array of factors that need to be in place for private markets and non-market institutions to work effectively and with low transactions costs in support of medium- and long-term growth and development. This will not, however, come about all by itself through liberalization and without a government able to help establish credible regulatory and institutional structures in which the population of Ghana can trust. In other words, good governance, a strong state and the process of debating and implementing broadly accepted policies need more attention. More consultation, information and debate are clearly needed in this field.

Finally, with reference to the strategic balance between agriculture and other sectors of the Ghanaian economy, Ghana has, like other African countries, come a long way as far as the formulation of appropriate development strategy is concerned. More recently also the need to address environmental and population issues and their interrelationship with agriculture have become recognized. Nevertheless, unless agriculture is assigned a priority role in the vision for the future growth process in Ghana, poverty will not be addressed effectively. The implication is that more needs to be done to overcome existing bottlenecks such as that of infrastructure, to strengthen linkages with the rest of the economy, and to minimize informational costs and the risks to which peasant agriculture is subjected.

References

Adelman, I. and Vogel, S. J. (1992) 'The Relevance of ADLI for Sub-Saharan Africa', in Kurt Wohlmuth and Dirk Hansohm (eds) *African Development Perspectives Yearbook 1990/1, Vol. II: Industrialization Based on Agricultural Development.* Münster: Lit Verlag.

Arrow, K. (1985) 'The Economic Implications of Learning by Doing', in *Collected Papers of Kenneth J. Arrow. Vol. 5 — Production and Capital.* Cambridge, MA and London: Harvard University Press, Belknap Press (previously published 1962).

Aryeetey, E. (1994) 'Private Investment Under Uncertainty in Ghana', *World Development,* Vol. 22, No. 8: 1211–21.

Aryeetey, E. (1995) *Aid Effectiveness in Ghana.* Report of a Study Sponsored by the Overseas Development Council, Washington, DC and administered by the Overseas Development Institute (ODI), London. Accra, November, mimeo.

Aryeetey, E., Hettige, H, Nissanke, M. and Steel, W. F. (1997) 'Financial Market Fragmentation and Reforms in Ghana, Malawi, Nigeria and Tanzania', *The World Bank Economic Review,* Vol. 11, No. 2: 195–218.

Bhagwati, J. (1978) *Foreign Trade Regimes and Economic Development: Anatomy and Consequences of Exchange Control Regimes.* Cambridge, MA: Ballinger Publishing Co.

Bhardan, P. (1969) 'The New Institutional Economics and Development Theory', *World Development,* Vol. 17, No. 9: 1390–94.

Bigsten, A. (1996) 'Constraints on African Growth', in M. Lundahl and B.J. Ndulo (eds) *New Directions in Development Economics.* London and New York: Routledge.

Bortei-Doku Aryeetey, E. (1996) 'Behind the Norms: Women's Access to Agricultural Resources in Ghana'. Paper presented at the International Workshop on the Management of Land Tenure and Resource Access in West Africa, 18–22 November, Goree, Senegal.

Centre for Policy Analysis (CEPA) (1997) *Macroeconomic Review and Outlook.* Accra: CEPA.

Chenery, H. and Syrquin, M. (1975) *Patterns of Development 1950-1970.* New York: Oxford University Press.

Chenery, H., Robinson, R. and Syrquin, M. (1986) *Industrialization and Growth.* New York: Oxford University Press.

Colander, D. (ed.) (1984) *Neo-classical Political Economy.* Cambridge, MA: Ballinger Publishing Co.

Corbo, V. and Fisher, S. (1995) 'Structural Adjustment: Stabilization and Policy Reform — Domestic and International Finance', in J. Behrman and T. N. Srinivasan (eds) *Handbook of Development Economics,* Vol. 3B. Amsterdam: North Holland.

Cornia, G. A., Jolly, R. and Stewart, F. (1987) *Adjustment with a Human Face.* Oxford: Clarendon Press.

Easterly, W. (1993) 'How Much Do Distortions Affect Growth', *Journal of Monetary Economics,* Vol. 32, No. 2: 187–212.

Faini, R. *et al.* (1991) 'Growth Oriented Adjustment Programs: A Statistical Analysis', *World Development,* Vol. 19, No. 8: 957–67.

Fischer, S. (1993) 'The Role of Macroeconomic Factors in Growth', *Journal of Monetary Economics,* Vol. 32, No. 3: 485–512.

Government of Ghana (1995) *Ghana-Vision 2020,* Presidential Report to Parliament on Co-ordinated Programme of Economic and Social Development Policies. Accra.

Green, R. H. (1987) *Stabilization and Adjustment Policies and Programmes: Country Study 1, Ghana.* Helsinki: World Institute for Development Economics Research of the United Nations University.

Greenaway, D. (1991) 'New Trade Theories and Developing Countries', in V. N. Balasubramanyam and S. Lall (eds) *Current Issues in Development Economics.* Houndsmills: Macmillan.

Helleiner, G. K. (1993) 'Consensus and Conflict in the Debate', in G. A. Cornia and G. K. Helleiner (eds) *From Adjustment to Development in Africa: Conflict, Controversy, Convergence, Consensus?* New York: St. Martin's Press.

Hirschman, A. O. (1958) *The Strategy of Economic Development.* New Haven, CT: Yale University Press.

ISSER (1992) *State of the Ghanaian Economy 1991.* University of Ghana, Legon.

Kapur, I., Hadjimichael, M. T., Hilbert, P., Schiff, J. and Szymczak, P. (1991) *Ghana: Adjustment and Growth 1983–91.* IMF Occasional Paper No. 84. Washington, DC: IMF, September.

Krueger, A. (1978) *Foreign Trade Regimes and Economic Development: Liberalization Attempts and Consequences.* Cambridge, MA: Ballinger Publishing Co.

Krugman, P. (1993) 'Toward a Counter-Counterrevolution in Development Theory', *Proceedings of the World Bank Annual Conference on Development Economics 1992.* Washington, DC: World Bank.

Lal, D. (1983) *The Poverty of Development Economics.* Hobart Paperbacks 16. London: Institute of Economic Affairs.

Leechor, C. (1994) 'Ghana: frontrunner in adjustment', in Ishrat Husain and Rashid Faruque (eds) *Adjustment in Africa: Lessons from Case Studies.* Washington, DC: World Bank.

Lucas, R. (1988) 'On the Mechanics of Economic Development', *Journal of Monetary Economics*, Vol. 22, No. 1: 3–42.

McKinnon, R. I. (1973) *Money and Capital in Economic Development.* Washington, DC: The Brookings Institution.

Meier, G. M. (1995) *Leading Issues in Economic Development* (6th edn.). New York: Oxford University Press.

Mosley, P., Harrigan, J. and Toye, J. (1995) *Aid and Power: The World Bank and Policy Based Lending*, Vol. 1. London: Routledge.

Mosley, P. and Weeks, J. (1993) 'Has Recovery Begun? Africa's Adjustment in the 1980s Revisited', *World Development*, Vol. 21, No. 10: 1583–1606.

Nelson, R. R. (1956) 'A Theory of the Low-Level Equilibrium Trap in Underdeveloped Countries', *American Economic Review*, Vol. 46, No. 5: 894–902.

North, D. C. (1990) *Institutions, Institutional Change and Economic Performance.* Cambridge: Cambridge University Press.

Overseas Development Institute (ODI) (1996) 'Adjustment in Africa: Lessons from Ghana', *Briefing Paper, No. 3.* London: ODI, July.

Rodrik, D. (1990) 'How Should Adjustment Programs be Designed?', *World Development*, Vol. 18, No. 7: 933–47.

Roemer, P. M. (1986) 'Increasing Returns and Long-run Growth', *Journal of Political Economy*, Vol. 94, No. 5: 1002–37.

Rosenstein-Rodan, P. N. (1943) 'Problems of Industrialization of Eastern and Southeastern Europe', *Economic Journal*, Vol. 53, June–September: 202–11.

Salter, W. E. G. (1959) 'Internal Balance and External Balance: The Role of Price and Expenditure Effects', *Economic Record*, August: 226–8.

Shaw, E. S. (1973) *Financial Deepening in Economic Development.* New York: Oxford University Press.

Singer, H. (1989) *Lessons of Post-War Development Experience: 1945–1988.* IDS Discussion Paper 260. Bringhton: Institute of Development Studies at the University of Sussex, April.

Solow, R. (1956) 'Contribution to the Theory of Economic Growth', *Quarterly Journal of Economics*, Vol. 70: 65–94.

Srinivasan, T. N. (1985) 'Neoclassical Political Economy, the State, and Economic Development', *Asian Development Review*, Vol. 3, No. 2: 40–45.

Stiglitz, J. E. (1989) 'Markets, Market Failures, and Development', *American Economic Association Papers and Proceedings*, Vol. 79, No. 2.

Swan, T. W. (1956) 'Economic Control in a Dependent Economy', *Economic Record*, November: 339–56.

Tarp, F. (1993) *Stabilization and Structural Adjustment: Macroeconomic frameworks for analysing the crisis in sub-Saharan Africa.* London and New York: Routledge.

Toye, J. (1987) *Dilemmas of Development.* Oxford: Basil Blackwell.

Toye, J. (1991) 'Ghana', in Mosley, P., Harrigan, J. and Toye, J. *Aid and Power: The World Bank and Policy-based Lending, Vol. 2: Case Studies.* London: Routledge.

Weiss, J. (1995) *Economic Policy in Developing Countries: The Reform Agenda.* London: Prentice Hall and Harvester Wheatsheaf.

Williamson, J. (1990) *Latin American Adjustment: How Much Has Happened?* Washington, DC: Institute for International Economics.

Williamson, J. (1993) 'Democracy and the Washington Consensus', *World Development*, Vol. 21, No. 8: 1329–36.

World Bank (1993a) *Ghana 2000 and Beyond: Setting the Stage for Accelerated Growth and Poverty Reduction.* Washington, DC: World Bank. Africa Regional Office, Western Africa Department.

World Bank (1993b) *The East Asian Miracle.* Oxford and New York: Oxford University Press for the World Bank.

World Bank (1997) *World Development Report 1997.* New York: Oxford University Press for the World Bank.

Index

Lightning Source UK Ltd.
Milton Keynes UK
UKHW020100230221
379202UK00004B/336